Charles Seale-Hayne Library
University of Plymouth
(01752) 588 588

LibraryandITenquiries@plymouth.ac.uk

PARALLEL COMPUTERS: THEORY AND PRACTICE

PARALLEL COMPUTERS: THEORY AND PRACTICE

Edited by

Thomas L. Casavant
University of Iowa
Iowa City, Iowa, USA

Pavel Tvrdík
František Plášil
Czech Technical University
Prague, Czech Republic

IEEE Computer Society Press
Los Alamitos, California

Washington • Brussels • Tokyo

Library of Congress Cataloging-in-Publication Data

Parallel computers: theory and practice / [edited by] Thomas L. Casavant,
    Pavel Tvrdík, František Plášil.
        p.   cm.
    Includes bibliographical references.
    ISBN 0-8186-5162-8
    1. Parallel computers.   I. Casavant, Thomas L.   II. Tvrdík,
Pavel.   III. Plášil, František.
QA76.58.P37553   1996
004' .35—dc20
                                                        95-10090
                                                          CIP

IEEE Computer Society Press
10662 Los Vaqueros Circle
P.O. Box 3014
Los Alamitos, CA 90720-1264

IEEE Computer Society Press Order Number BP05162
Library of Congress Number 95-10090
IEEE Catalog Number EH0386-3
ISBN 0-8186-5162-8

Additional copies may be ordered from:

IEEE Computer Society Press	IEEE Service Center	IEEE Computer Society	IEEE Computer Society
Customer Service Center	445 Hoes Lane	13, Avenue de l'Aquilon	Ooshima Building
10662 Los Vaqueros Circle	P.O. Box 1331	B-1200 Brussels	2-19-1 Minami-Aoyama
P.O. Box 3014	Piscataway, NJ 08855-1331	BELGIUM	Minato-ku, Tokyo 107
Los Alamitos, CA 90720-1264	Tel: +1-908-981-1393	Tel: +32-2-770-2198	JAPAN
Tel: +1-714-821-8380	Fax: +1-908-981-9667	Fax: +32-2-770-8505	Tel: +81-3-3408-3118
Fax: +1-714-821-4641	mis.custserv@computer.org	euro.ofc@computer.org	Fax: +81-3-3408-3553
Email: cs.books@computer.org			tokyo.ofc@computer.org

Technical Editor: Dharma P. Agrawal
Production Editors: Edna Straub and Lisa O'Conner
Cover Design: Joe Daigle
Printed in the United States of America by Braun-Brumfield, Inc.

The Institute of Electrical and Electronics Engineers, Inc

TABLE OF CONTENTS

II   PROGRAMMING CONCEPTS AND LANGUAGES

4   Parallel Algorithm Fundamentals and Analysis   151
B. McMillin and J.-L. Liu

5   Directions in Parallel Programming: HPF, Shared Virtual Memory, and Object Parallelism in pC++*   183
F. Bodin, T. Priol, D. Gannon, and P. Mehrotra

6   Concurrent Object-oriented Languages and the Inheritance Anomaly   221
D.G. Kafura and R.G. Lavender

III   SYSTEM SOFTWARE FOR PARALLEL COMPUTERS

7   ScaLAPACK: Linear Algebra Software for Distributed Memory Architectures   267
J. Demmel, J. Dongarra, R. van de Geijn, and D. Walker

IV   FORMAL METHODS

PREFACE

This book is based almost entirely on tutorial texts for lectures given at ISIPCALA'93 – *The International Summer Institute on Parallel Computer Architectures, Languages, and Algorithms.* It was held in Prague, Czech Republic, July 5–9, 1993, and was jointly organized by the University of Iowa, Iowa City, USA; the Czech Technical University, Prague; and the Czech ACM Chapter, Prague. This pioneering event in Eastern Europe attracted 90 participants from 15 countries and 3 continents.

The editors would like to acknowledge the hard work of all the authors of the chapters. Also, a number of people supported or contributed to the organization and program of ISIPCALA and the editors sincerely appreciate this. These people include Jan Hlavička, Bořivoj Melichar, Gul Agha, Michel Cosnard, François Meunier, Wolfgang Schröder-Preikschat, Petr Brňák, Richard Fanta, Michal Grof, Radek Hampl, Věra Košvancová, Božena Mannová, Tomáš Smolík, Jan Trdlička, Stanislava Pavelková, Terry Braun, Richard Dietz, and Todd Scheetz.

The editors are also grateful to the reviewers for very useful suggestions, which improved the quality of the text, and to Jon Butler and Dharma Agrawal from the IEEE Computer Society Press for their support of this project.

Thomas L. Casavant, Pavel Tvrdík, and František Plášil
May 1995

INTRODUCTION

PARALLEL COMPUTING: WHERE ARE WE?

An important field in computer science has developed from the need for high-performance computing machines comprising a large number of processors, interconnected by high-speed networks, having fast access to a large memory, and able to work together on large-scale computationally intensive applications. Researchers in many fields of science and engineering seem to have reached a general agreement that parallel machines are the only way to satisfy the ever-increasing need for more computing power. Whatever achievements may be made in new technologies for building faster processors and memory modules, a good understanding of how to group these resources so that they can work in parallel on large tasks is necessary to address the scale problem. The inevitability of this direction is shown by the existence of many important computer applications exhibiting great potential for being split into parts and being solved in parallel.

Rapid developments in VLSI and communication technologies have created a situation in which the hardware designers are able to construct machines with thousands of powerful computing nodes for relatively low cost. The complexity of these machines is naturally at least an order of magnitude higher than the complexity of machines with a single-processor or with a few processors sharing a global address space (bus). It is small wonder then, that so many aspects of design and effective utilization of these machines are still poorly understood and that we are still short of realizing the possibilities provided by this technology.

ABOUT THIS BOOK

The scope of parallel computing is very broad; it spans all levels of the architecture from hardware design to programming interfaces and numerous SW tools, intending to help programmers understand the complexity and grasp the performance of these machines. Undoubtedly, no single book can cover these issues exhaustively. This book tries to cover a broad set of issues inherent to the design of effectively programmable parallel computing machines and to display the difficult trade-offs in the design of their hardware and software components. A collaboration of leading experts in parallel computing resulted in a collection of chapters that provide here an overview of the current state-of-the-art, trace the important historical steps leading to the current state, and explain the latest developments with an eye toward future trends. These unique overview studies cover architecture and network technology, operating systems and programming languages, user interfaces and programming environments, and techniques to analyze and formally describe the complexity of parallel computing machines. Throughout the chapters, stress is placed upon explaining fundamental problems and inherent limits, and on discussing various approaches to overcoming these problems.

This effort produced texts that blend overview with tutorial aspects. The book can serve as a useful guide to state-of-the-art parallel computing for computer scientists and engineers interested in the subject, as well as university students and professors. It can also be useful for a wide range of scientists and engineers working in other fields of science and engineering, who need to learn about available technologies and current methods for speeding up their computationally intensive applications.

STRUCTURE OF THE BOOK

The book consists of four parts, each addressing a major area of interest to parallel computing researchers, designers, and users.

Part I   Architecture and Networks

This part deals with architecture of parallel computers and processing-element interconnection networks. The three chapters cover a broad range of approaches and methods for designing massively parallel machines, discussing the contributions of various projects, and providing a useful cut through the ever-growing set of commercially available and research prototype parallel machine efforts.

Chapter 1   Massively Parallel Architectures (Thomas L. Casavant, Samuel A. Fineberg, Michelle L. Roderick, and Brent H. Pease)   This chapter addresses massively parallel computer architecture. The area is a vast one that combines many aspects of computer science and engineering. The focus of this chapter is to review the main contributions to making parallel computer systems a reality—the prototyping and development of real parallel computer systems, both commercial and experimental. We begin with a brief discussion of the relationship between evolutionary developments and revolutionary ones, and note that while high-performance systems have gone through many *evolutionary* stages, seldom have *revolutionary* changes in architecture had an immediate impact on the commercial market. We describe the underlying reasons for this and then discuss the current state-of-the-art in memory structures and technologies, data path alternatives, and control structures. An attempt at balance between survey and depth is provided via a mixture of brief summary descriptions of many architectures, and then somewhat more in-depth studies of several machines. Furthermore, both commercial systems and research prototypes are covered. The broad survey is presented in the context of a generational taxonomy. As will be seen through the numerous case studies of this chapter, designing a parallel machine that is also efficiently programmed is far from an achieved goal. While they are not directly addressed here, the issues of language, compiler, and operating system design are not separable from hardware design. However, the scope of this chapter is primarily that of hardware design alternatives—past, present, and future.

Chapter 2   Data-driven and Multithreaded Architectures for High-performance Computing (Jean-Luc Gaudiot and Chinhyun Kim)   Although there seems to be general agreement among researchers that parallel computing is the most practical means to satisfy the ever-increasing desire for higher computing power, the question of *how* to design and program large parallel machines remains. One actively pursued approach is the data-driven computation model. This is a radical departure from the traditional approach based on the von Neumann or control-driven computation model. The justification for this new technique is the inherently parallel nature of the model, which makes it a good paradigm for parallel computation. However, it has been learned over the years that implementing a machine based on the data-driven model is not an easy task. In order to succeed, many issues need to be investigated at every level, including algorithm, language, compiler, and machine architecture. This paper discusses past and present research efforts of the dataflow community, all aimed at implementing high-performance computing systems.

Chapter 3   Properties of a Variety of Interconnection Networks for Large-scale Parallelism (Wayne G. Nation, Gene Saghi, and Howard Jay Siegel)   Properties of a variety of interconnection networks for large-scale parallel processing systems (that is, 64 to 64K processors) are discussed. Models of SIMD (synchronous) and MIMD (asynchronous) parallelism are described. A collection of different types of networks are explored, examining properties such as topology, routing control, and partitionability. The mesh and hypercube single-stage (or point-to-point) networks are first overviewed. Then multistage networks are studied, beginning with the multistage cube, which represents an important family of networks including the omega, indirect binary n-cube, multistage shuffle-exchange, delta, baseline, SW-banyan, and generalized cube. The extra stage cube (ESC), a fault-tolerant variation of the multistage cube, is described; the structure of the augmented data manipulator (ADM) multistage network is summarized; the dynamic redundancy network, a fault-tolerant variation of the multistage cube, which supports spare processors, and whose structure is based on the ADM, is presented; the structure and use of a tree-based network is considered; and the difficulty in evaluating and comparing different interconnection networks is examined.

Part II   Programming Concepts and Languages

This part addresses fundamental concepts in the context of various examples of mapping parallel applications onto parallel machines. The basic notions are explained at several levels of abstraction, from direct partitioning and mapping at a low-level view of the machine, to parallel-extended sequential languages such as HPF, up through recent studies of the use of the object-oriented paradigm as in pC++. This part concludes with a comprehensive survey of object-oriented concurrent languages, providing their models, taxonomy, and insights into issues of semantics.

Chapter 4   Parallel Algorithm Fundamentals and Analysis (Bruce McMillin and Jun-Lin Liu)   This chapter explores the "intuition" used in creating a parallel algorithm design and realizing this design on distributed memory hardware. The algorithm class NC and the LSTM machine are used to show why some algorithms realize their promise of speedup better than others and the algorithm class NP is used to show why other algorithms will never be good for parallelization. The realities of algorithm design are presented through partitioning and mapping issues and models.

Chapter 5   Directions in Parallel Programming: HPF, Shared Virtual Memory, and Object Parallelism in pC++ (François Bodin, Thierry Priol, Dennis Gannon, and Piyush Mehrotra)   Fortran and C++ are the dominant programming languages used in scientific computation. Consequently, extensions to these languages are the most popular for programming massively parallel computers. We discuss two such approaches to parallel Fortran and one approach to C++. The High Performance Fortran Forum has designed HPF with the intent of supporting data parallelism on Fortran 90 applications. HPF works by asking the user to help the compiler distribute and align the data structures with the distributed memory modules in the system. Fortran-S takes a different approach in which the data distribution is managed by the operating system and the user provides annotations to indicate parallel control regions. In the case of C++, we look at pC++, which is based on a concurrent aggregate parallel model.

Chapter 6   Concurrent Object-oriented Languages and the Inheritance Anomaly (Dennis G. Kafura and R. Greg Lavender)   A survey of concurrent object-oriented languages is presented. The survey is organized around three models: an *Animation Model* that describes a variety of relationships between threads and objects, an *Interaction Model* that classifies the possible semantics of invocations and returns between a client object and a server object, and a *Synchronization Model* that shows different ways in which concurrent invocations can be managed by a server. A number of representative languages are briefly presented. The problem of synchronization in concurrent object-oriented languages is considered in detail including a discussion of the *inheritance anomaly*. A synchronization mechanism, called a *behavior set*, is shown to avoid this anomaly in certain cases. The implementation of behavior sets in ACT++, an actor-based concurrent programming framework implemented in C++, is also described.

Part III   System Software for Parallel Computers

Programming interfaces present one of the greatest challenges to yielding effective application of parallelism. Compared to the engineering challenges of building parallel hardware, the domain of SW specification, analysis, and performance tuning are easily an order of magnitude more difficult. This section of the text covers three of the most important aspects of programming interfaces. The first approach is the use of special libraries to overcome the difficulties of mapping applications to parallel machines. In the domain of scientific computing and numerical analysis, problems exhibiting highly regular structure can be supported effectively through libraries of commonly used high-level functions such as the simultaneous solution of systems of equations. The second chapter discusses the problem of measuring performance of parallel programming and using this information to do performance tuning. The third chapter provides an excellent comprehensive survey and tutorial on parallel operating systems. It explains key issues in the design of parallel and distributed operating systems and illustrates them through numerous case studies.

Chapter 7   ScaLAPACK: Linear Algebra Software for Distributed Memory Architectures (James Demmel, Jack Dongarra, Robert van de Geijn, and David Walker)

We report the progress of an ongoing project that investigates the reusability of LAPACK code for distributed memory MIMD architectures. This paper discusses the scalability of Cholesky, LU, and QR factorization routines on MIMD distributed memory concurrent computers. These routines form part of the ScaLAPACK mathematical software library that extends the widely-used LAPACK library to run efficiently on scalable concurrent computers. To ensure good scalability and performance, the ScaLAPACK routines are based on block-partitioned algorithms that reduce the frequency of data movement between different levels of the memory hierarchy, and particularly between processors. The block cyclic data distribution used in all three factorization algorithms is described; an outline of the sequential and parallel block-partitioned algorithms is given; and approximate models of algorithms' performance are presented to indicate which factors in the design of the algorithm have an impact upon scalability. These models are compared with timing results on a 128-node Intel iPSC/860 hypercube. It is shown that the routines are highly scalable on this machine for problems that occupy more than about 25 percent of the memory on each processor, and that the measured timings are consistent with the performance model.

Chapter 8   Techniques for Performance Measurement of Parallel Programs (Jeffrey K. Hollingsworth, Barton P. Miller, and James E. Lumpp, Jr.)

Programmers of parallel systems require high-level tools to aid in analyzing the performance of applications. Performance tuning of parallel programs differs substantially from the analogous processes on sequential architectures for two main reasons: the inherent complexity of concurrent systems is greater, and the observability of concurrent systems is complicated by the effects instrumentation can have on the behavior of the system. The complexity of parallel architectures combined with nondeterminism can make performance difficult to predict and analyze. Many approaches have been proposed to help users understand parallel programs. This paper summarizes the problems associated with creating parallel performance measurement tools and describes some of the systems that have been built to solve these problems.

Chapter 9   Operating Systems for Parallel Machines (Bodhisattwa Mukherjee and Karsten Schwan)   The complexity of parallel hardware and the performance requirements of user programs introduce new challenges to the design and implementation of parallel operating systems. This chapter surveys the research and commercial contributions to parallel operating systems to date. We first briefly present the characteristics of various multiprocessor architectures and identify some of the key issues in parallel operating systems. Then we review the interfaces of a few sample threads libraries. Finally, issues and solution approaches are illustrated by case studies of a variety of research and commercial parallel operating system kernels.

Part IV   Formal Methods

Every field of computer science and engineering has an historical component, a state-of-the-art component, and a forward-looking component. While it is straightforward to look at the past with some sense of perspective and context, and the present with factual objectivity, the future is less obvious. The greatest needs at the present in parallel computing are in the areas of efficient programming, analysis, debugging, and performance tuning. This final section of the text consists of three chapters that show possible future approaches to solving these problems via more formal and theoretical aspects of program modeling, abstraction, specification, and analysis.

Chapter 10   Formal Methods to Generate and Understand Distributed Computing Systems (Bruce McMillin, Grace Tsai, and Hanan Lutfiyya)   This session explores correctness through cooperative axiomatic reasoning, provides an additional basis for understanding parallel algorithm design and specification, and is used for run-time assurance of distributed computing systems through operational evaluation. This mathematical model allows for the generation of executable assertions that detect faults in the presence of arbitrary failures. The mathematical model of choice consists of two components: CSP and an associated axiomatic verification system. A method is developed that translates a concurrent verification proof outline into an error-detecting concurrent program.

Chapter 11   Process Calculus and Parallel Object-oriented Programming Languages (David Walker)   Techniques for giving simple accounts of the semantics of parallel object-oriented programming languages are illustrated through a study of the language $\pi o \beta \lambda$ (parallel object-based language). A two-level operational semantics is given in which the global transitions of a configuration are derived in a simple way from labeled transitions describing the possible actions of its constituent objects; a second semantics by translation to a fragment of the Higher-Order π-calculus is presented; and a close correspondence between the semantics is described.

Chapter 12   Formal Design of Parallel Programs Using UNITY (Beverly A. Sanders)
A formal method for program design allows one to construct a proof that a program satisfies

its specification. UNITY is a formal method invented by Chandy and Misra. Its hallmark is its simplicity. Since its introduction in 1988, UNITY has been successfully used for a variety of problems and, based on this experience, modifications have been suggested that make it easier to use. This paper gives a brief tutorial on UNITY, emphasizing recent developments.

PART I
ARCHITECTURE AND NETWORKS

CHAPTER 1

MASSIVELY PARALLEL ARCHITECTURES

Thomas L. Casavant,* Samuel A. Fineberg,** Michelle L. Roderick,*** and Brent H. Pease[†]
ECE Dept, University of Iowa
Iowa City, IA 52242, USA

Abstract. *This chapter addresses the area of massively parallel computer architecture. The area is a vast one, which combines many aspects of computer science and engineering. The focus of this chapter is to review the main contributions to making parallel computer systems a reality, that is, the prototyping and development of real parallel computer systems, both commercial and experimental. We begin with a brief discussion of the relationship between evolutionary developments and revolutionary ones, and note that while high-performance systems have gone through many evolutionary stages, seldom have revolutionary changes in architecture had an immediate impact on the commercial market. We discuss the underlying reasons for this and then discuss the current state-of-the-art in memory structures and technologies, data path alternatives, and control structures. An attempt at balance between survey and depth is provided via a mixture of brief summary descriptions of many architectures, and then somewhat more in-depth studies of several machines. Furthermore, both commercial systems and research prototypes are covered. The broad survey is presented in the context of a generational taxonomy. As will be seen through the numerous case studies in this chapter, designing a parallel machine that is also efficiently programmed is far from an achieved goal. While they are not directly addressed here, the issues of language, compiler, and operating system design are not separable from hardware design. However, the scope of this chapter is primarily that of hardware design alternatives—past, present, and future.*

Keywords: Memory, Data Path, Control Structures and Technologies, Granularity, Pipelining, Shared Memory, Synchronization, Coherency, Distributed Memory, Interconnection Networks, Topology, Protocols, Technology, Latency Tolerance, Prefetching, Multithreading, Communication Coprocessors, Scalability

---

*This work was conducted primarily while on leave at the Dept. of Informatik, ETH Zentrum, CH-8092 Zürich, Switzerland, `tomc@eng.uiowa.edu`

**Computer Sciences Corporation, Numerical Aerodynamic Simulation, NASA Ames Research Center, M/S 258-6, Moffett Field, CA 94035-1000, `fineberg@nas.nasa.gov`

***Adaptec Inc., Boulder Technology Center, 2845 Wilderness Pl., Suite 200, Boulder, CO 80301, `Michelle@btc.adaptech.com`

[†]Apple Computer, Advanced Technology Group/Interactive Media, One Infinite Loop, M/S 301-3k, Cupertino, CA 95014, `brent@taurus.apple.com`

1.1

HIGH-PERFORMANCE SYSTEMS: EVOLUTION AND PERSPECTIVE

High-performance computer systems have gone through many *evolutionary* stages. In fact, seldom have *revolutionary* changes in architecture had an immediate impact on the commercial market. This has clearly been the case with parallel computers. Custom parallel computer systems have been a reality since before the Illiac [7]. Since then, a series of technological advancements have continued to feed this area of architecture exploration, but none has provided the last piece of the puzzle. For example, the microprocessor had the effect of driving parallel architectures in the direction of massively parallel numbers (that is, thousands) of distributed memory processors. This nonshared memory MIMD style of system is most appealing from the point of view of the hardware designer because most of the components of the system are off-the-shelf commodity parts that are cheap and available in large quantities.

While these positive attributes should not be overlooked, the architecture space that can be explored while restricting designs to those that can be constructed with off-the-shelf components is clearly limited. The other extreme, a fully custom-designed system, is also unlikely to succeed, because these machines, while often making large steps forward, defy further *evolution* because the cost of developing each successive generation is prohibitively high. This single example is typical of the sort of difficult design space choices necessary to build real parallel computing *systems*.

As will be seen through the numerous case studies of this chapter, designing a parallel machine that is also efficiently programmable is far from an achieved goal. While they are not directly addressed here, the issues of language, compiler, and operating system design are not separable from hardware design. However, the scope of this chapter is primarily that of hardware design alternatives—past, present, and future.

1.1.1 Memory Structures and Technologies

The classic von Neumann architecture characteristic of fetch-and-execute is deeply entrenched in the field of architecture. It could be said that bypassing this mind-set is the largest hurdle to architectural revolution. The most obvious problem is the latency incurred when data needed to perform a computation are not available at the same time, or in the same place, as the functional unit needed to perform the computation. When one considers the wealth of optimization techniques used to tune the performance of serial programs that try to avoid memory latency by exploiting inherent locality in data and instruction reference patterns, it is clear that serial computer systems today have relatively high levels of performance *despite* the memory bottleneck—clearly not *because* of it. Hierarchies of memories with a range of speeds and costs are half of the solution to the memory latency problem. The other half is the compilation of programs to fully exploit this feature. The marriage of the ideas of memory hierarchies and instruction pipelining to advanced compilation techniques is the essence of the RISC era.

For parallel architectures this problem is much worse, and it is not even clear what direction should be taken for hardware design because so little intuition exists regarding the "normal" behavior of parallel programs. For example, the concept of data locality (and to some extent instruction locality) that is exploited for serial machines may not be of much use in a parallel environment. Indeed, in many current parallel machines, the memory hierarchies of high-performance serial systems prove quite problematic. The problem is partially due to the potential lack of coherency between upper levels of the hierarchy and the DMA accesses of network interfaces, but may manifest itself in a variety of ways. Indeed, even the basic logical issue of shared (global) address space versus non-shared (distributed) address spaces has not been resolved. This one issue, for example, is equally driven by hardware implementation, programming preference, and scalability issues, to name only a few. Rarely are all of these critical issues equally represented in the individuals of an architecture design team.

1.1.2   Data Path Structures

Equally important to the design of high-performance architectures is the issue of data path design. The main point here is how, and to what extent, to replicate the functional units of the data path. In this discussion, we address not only the *internal* issues of manipulation of data *within* the traditional processor, but also *among* processors. For example, in a Cray-like vector processor, there may be a multiplicity of floating point multiply units all within the same internal processor that manipulate various parts of large vector registers. Alternately, a large SIMD machine such as the TMC CM-2 would contain many simple processors, but there also exists a rich interconnection structure between them, thus providing a very complex logical data path in the overall architecture. This latter example illustrates the very rich architecture dimension of interconnection networks—their topology and routing protocols. These are addressed elsewhere in this book, and thus are only mentioned here in passing.

An important point to be addressed in this chapter though, is that of the appropriate overall functional role of the interconnection network. For example, "should the network perform simple arithmetic, or combining of results as is the case for the RP3 or the NYU Ultracomputer?" Or, "should the network provide for tight coupling with data-flow processors to route intermediate results from one functional unit to another without modifying any data in transit as is the case for Monsoon?"

There is also the issue of the degree of control over routing exercised by the processing nodes of a machine. For example, in first-generation machines such as the NCUBE-1, the processor played an active role in the storing and forwarding of data from processor to processor. In the second generation of machines such as the Intel iPSC/2, this function was largely taken over by an independent router that handles (at a minimum) through-routing of messages from source to destination without involving the intermediate CPUs along the path. These routing processors could also exercise DMA control for accessing data in the local processor memories, and also utilize circuit switched, or worm-hole routed mechanisms, as these have proven superior (empirically) in reducing end-to-end latency over store-and-forward, packet-switched mechanisms. In the third commercial generation of machines such as the Intel Paragon, there is even more responsibility assigned to communication coprocessors to allow the CPU to be almost completely relieved of managing interprocessor communications. These machines are still not well understood, but several studies have begun to examine some very sophisticated implications of separating the communication functions from the computation functions. It is not clear, for example, to what degree making communications implicit will impact the need for additional synchronization mechanisms, which may then add unwanted communication latency. Also, the role of operating system overhead is an issue gaining more attention. For example, as lower overhead message passing becomes available, the problem of application mapping is regaining importance. That is, the latency of the hardware communication mechanisms is becoming a longer fraction of end-to-end latency in applications.

1.1.3 Control Structures

The basic choices here still hinge on the issues of symmetry and granularity. Highly symmetrical machines such as the MPP, CM-2, and the MasPar represent massively parallel machines whose runtime behavior is highly synchronized via hardware. Generally, all processors perform the same functions in the same amount of time, and at the same time. If there is any variation in duration of operations, the hardware explicitly enforces synchrony across processors at the end of each atomic operation. While some processors may be idle during some operation cycles, and all processors are normally operating on different data values, the control mechanism is highly regular. The primary implications of this design choice are much simpler programming and debugging, but less versatility in the range of applications supported.

Pipelined-parallel and vector machines constitute a very important portion of *delivered* parallelism to date. From the point of view of the hardware architecture this control mechanism is rather complex, but its main advantage is that in most programs the parallelism that can be exploited statically for these machines is mostly apparent at compile time. Optimizing compilers can therefore readily exploit most of the pipelined parallelism available in these machines, greatly simplifying programming. In fact, serial programs can usually be ported directly onto these machines with little or no modification. Also, programmers of such machines are often only minimally aware of the degree of parallelism present, nor do they care. Unfortunately, the degree of parallelism that may be obtained on actual applications using this approach is quite limited.

MIMD machines represent a more general model, but bring with them more difficulty in program debugging and performance tuning. Also, to be effectively used as massively parallel machines, they have usually been used in the SPMD mode of operation in which each processor executes fundamentally the same object image, but may have very different contexts (that is, different program counter values) at any given point in time. These machines have evolved over time, mainly in the areas of processor power and interconnection technology. More recently, however, several efforts have started to depart from these three dominant varieties of control flow.

These variants have grown, to some degree, out of the operating system area in which lightweight processes, or threads, were initially conceived in an attempt to allow more effective concurrency in workstation environments. These ideas have recently appeared in several machines as lightweight processes and multithreading (in fact they appeared in

HEP [71] long ago). The idea here is to support irregular (or asymmetrical) parallelism, but at a very fine granularity, and without having to exploit vectors. It remains to be seen whether these architectures will achieve a much higher degree of programmability than the alternatives. They clearly represent a region of the architecture space that will require a large effort in the design of custom elements, as has been the case with Tera [2]. The primary appeal of the conventional MIMD (especially with distributed memory) machines is the ability to use already-designed (off-the-shelf) components. This issue, the use of off-the-shelf versus custom designs, will continue to be a critical point determining the *practical* future of parallel computing.

1.1.4 Summary

The subject of parallel architecture is a rapidly evolving one. The space of potential architectures is very large. While the number of actual parallel machines built to date may seem large and far-flung, in fact each parallel machine built usually represents a radical departure from extant machines. Therefore, the machines surveyed here represent "data points," built and used in an attempt to gain an understanding through experimentation. Unfortunately, few of these machines experienced wide use, thereby rendering it very difficult to report comprehensively about their performance, or even the relative merit of specific details of systems. In the descriptions to follow, we have attempted to provide a comprehensive survey of machines but not tried to report experimental results. However, these results are very important, and the reader should pursue the literature to gain a proper understanding of the *delivered* performance and behavior of these systems.

1.2

BRIEF CASE STUDIES

Many parallel systems have been designed and built. This section attempts to conduct a broad survey of historically important parallel machines—both commercial systems and research prototypes. To do so would be difficult and confusing without some logical organization of machines into classes or generations. For the purposes of organizing this survey only, we have provided a *generational* system for classifying, or grouping, machine architectures. This taxonomy is neither unique, nor perfect, nor an attempt to be definitive. It is simply a somewhat less than arbitrary framework upon which we "hang" our machine case studies. The taxonomy itself consists of four generations, as shown in Table 1.1. In some cases, a machine could fit more than one generation equally well. For such machines, we have found a unique "home" simply to facilitate inclusion into our inherently imperfect classification scheme.

The beginning generation consists mainly of pioneering research or very early commercial attempts to construct parallel machines. In most cases, these machines were designed to be studied in and of themselves. In no sense, were any of these machines "commercial successes," however, they provided valuable first insights into the next generation of machines and answered some basic questions about implementation. These machines, mostly built

TABLE 1.1   Generational taxonomy.

Machine Class or Generation	Characteristics	Examples (Incomplete Set)
Early Research Prototype	Pioneering efforts into large subsets of the Arch Space	Illiac, PASM, MPP, NYU Ultra, HEP, TRAC, Cosmic Cube, RP3,
1st Generation	Simple packet-switched, store-and-forward networks; simple shared buses; usually little I/O support	Sequent Balance, iPSC/1, NCU BE-1, CM-2, MP-1, BBN GP1000, Alliant FX/8, IBM GF11, GMD SUPRENUM
2nd Generation	Refinement of 1st-generation designs, HW routing support, coarser data path, better CPU designs	Sequent Symmetry, iPSC/2, NCU BE-2, MP-2, BBN TC2000, Alliant FX/2800, Cedar
Emerging 3rd generation	Tighter coupling of language to hardware, System integration	Paragon, T3D, CS-2, MIT J/M-machines, Tera

prior to the 1980s, constitute the *Early Research Prototype* class. The early to mid-1980s then saw the birth of numerous companies whose primary business was to make and sell parallel computers. Several of these companies where spin-offs from bigger ones such as Intel, DEC, and BBN, but many more were venture-capitalized start-ups such as NCUBE. Due to various end-user problems, such as programming difficulty and upward compatibility of user applications through successive generations of machines from particular vendors, the late 1980s and early 1990s saw many of these start-ups fail commercially. These commercial ventures constitute the majority of the *First-* and *Second-Generation* machines. The *Emerging Third-Generation* machines are still in their initial discovery stages and may still emerge as viable commercial machines or lasting architecture contributions. However, at the time of this writing, there is no clear consensus on their likely general acceptance.

The following list of machines is not meant to be complete but is intended to demonstrate how parallel machines have evolved and how the thinking of the designers of parallel machines has evolved. As with many of the other topics in this volume, the subjects covered are vast, and the space available for describing them is small. In this chapter, an attempt at balance between survey and depth is provided through a mixture of brief to moderate length summary descriptions of many architectures.

1.2.1   Early Research Prototypes

The early research prototype machines are summarized in Table 1.2, and each machine is individually addressed in the following sections. The architecture space investigated in these machines was wide, from SIMD with bit-serial (MPP) or complicated (Illiac) CPUs to SIMD/MIMD (PASM) to full MIMD (Ultra and Cosmic Cube) to data flow (Manchester) and even multithreaded (HEP). While these machines were primarily research tools and had little commercial viability, they significantly influenced later designs.

TABLE 1.2   Early research prototype characteristics.

Machine	Control	Topology	Memory	CPU	# PEs	Date
Illiac IV	(M)SIMD	2D grid (Torus)	Distributed	Custom 64-bit	256 (64)	Univ. of Ill., 1968
MPP	SIMD	2D grid reconfigurable	Distributed	10-MHz bit-serial	16384	Goodyear Aero., 1980
HEP	MIMD	Pipelined Switch	Shared	Multithreaded Custom	4	Late 1970s
PASM	SIMD/MIMD	Extra-Stage Cube	Distributed	MC68010	1024 (16)	Purdue Univ., 1980
TRAC	SIMD/MIMD	SW-Banyan	Shared/Distr.	Custom 8-bit byte-slice	16	U.T. Austin 1977
Manchester	Data-Flow (not Control)	Ring network	Shared	Custom	12	Univ. Manch., 1981
NYU Ultra	MIMD	Omega network	Shared	MC68010	4096 (8)	NYU, 1983
RP3	MIMD	Omega network	Shared/Distr.	Off-the-Shelf	512	IBM, 1983
Cosmic Cube	MIMD	6D hypercube	Distributed	8086	64	Caltech, 1980

Illiac IV   The Illiac IV [7, 21] was a multiple SIMD array-based system developed at the University of Illinois in the late 1960s. A block diagram of the system is shown in Figure 1.1. It consisted of 256 64-bit data path, ECL-based, processing elements (PEs). These were divided into 4 arrays of 64 processors each and were controlled by 4 control units (CUs). The CUs broadcast both shared data and instructions and performed loop control instructions. Each PE directly accessed up to 2048 words of 250ns 64-bit RAM. Processing elements were connected in a 2D-grid topology with a selectable end-around (torus) connection. I/O was controlled through a Burroughs B6500 system attached to the PEs through the Illiac's I/O subsystem. The prototype that was actually constructed consisted of a single 64-processor quadrant.

MPP   The Massively Parallel Processor (MPP) [8] was developed by Goodyear Aerospace for NASA Goddard Space Flight Center. Its primary mission was to process millions of picture elements (pixels) comprising satellite image data. The MPP exploited this characteristic by simultaneously processing each element. Therefore the MPP consisted of a large SIMD Array Unit (ARU) with 16,384 PEs interconnected in a 128×128 mesh. A block diagram of the system is shown in Figure 1.2. Each PE was a 10-MHz bit-serial processor with a small amount (4 Kbits) of local memory. PEs were connected in a 2D-grid topology with I/O connected to the edges. Further, the edges could be reconfigured in software to establish different edge connection topologies. The ARU was controlled by the Array Control Unit (ACU), which broadcasted instructions to the ARU and performed loop control and scalar operations. I/O was controlled through the Program and Data Management Unit

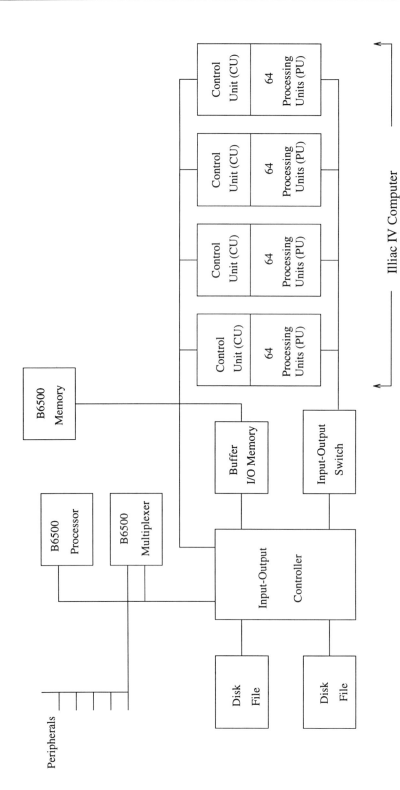

FIGURE 1.1   Illiac architecture.

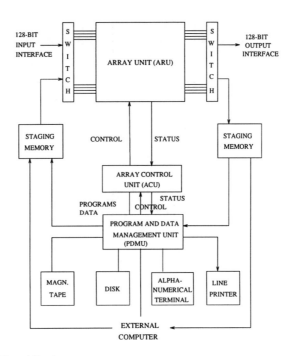

FIGURE 1.2   MPP architecture.

(PDMU). I/O also passed through a Staging Memory in which it could be buffered and/or reformatted before it was loaded to, or after it was stored from, the ARU.

HEP   The HEP computer was a commercially available machine of the late 1970s. It was based on a heavily pipelined MIMD architecture [71]. The first HEP had four processors and 128-K words of memory. A block diagram is shown in Figure 1.3. In each HEP processor, two queues were used to time-multiplex the process states. The first queue fed the instruction pipeline, and the second queue fed the data access pipeline. The instruction pipeline fetched a three-address instruction, decoded the instruction, fetched the operands, and then sent the information to another pipeline to complete the operation. The data memory access pipeline interconnected the data memory modules with the processors. When the access had completed, the result was returned to the first queue.

The HEP architecture incorporated two unique (at the time) features, multiple processes and read/write synchronization, to enhance performance. Each HEP processor could support up to 128 processes. If each processor supported 8 nonconflicting processes and the pipeline could produce a result every 100ns, the processor could achieve about 10 MIPS. This method of using multiple process states running concurrently to avoid data access delays was known as *multithreading*. In addition, HEP had a special form of synchronization called a *full/empty bit*. Full/empty bits were bits associated with words in memory that could be used for data synchronization. When a processor wanted to read a word from memory, it first checked whether the word's associated full/empty bit was full (that is, if

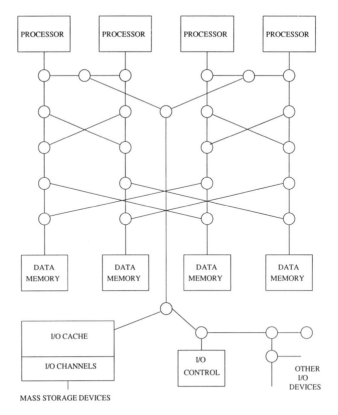

FIGURE 1.3   HEP architecture.

it was available). If the full/empty bit was not full, the current thread (process) blocked and another thread would be dispatched. When the value that the first thread wanted was written into memory, the full/empty bit was set to full, the blocked thread was released, and then the bit was set to empty. These actions on full/empty bits were implicit; thus, a read would implicitly check the full/empty bit and not complete until it was full. Then, when the read succeeded, the bit was automatically reset. Further, a write automatically set the full/empty bit to full. HEP also allowed threads to read and write nonsynchronous data ignoring these full/empty bits.

PASM   The PASM (*PA*rtitionable *S*IMD/*M*IMD) system [68, 69] was a dynamically reconfigurable architecture in which the processors could be partitioned to form independent SIMD and/or MIMD submachines of various sizes [70]. A 30-processor prototype was constructed and is still in operation at Purdue University. The Parallel Computation Unit of PASM contained P PEs (numbered from 0 to $P - 1$) where P is a power of 2, and an interconnection network. Each PE was a processor/memory pair. The PE processors were off-the-shelf CISC microprocessors that performed the actual SIMD and MIMD operations. The PE memory modules were used by the processors for data storage in SIMD mode and

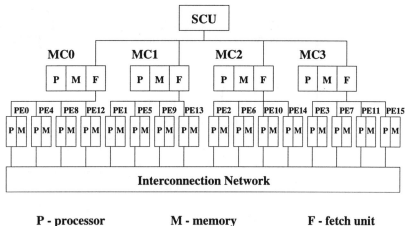

P - processor   M - memory   F - fetch unit

SCU - System Control Unit

FIGURE 1.4   PASM parallel computation unit.

both data and instruction storage in MIMD mode. The Micro Controllers (MCs) were a set of $Q = 2^q$ processors, numbered from 0 to $Q - 1$, which acted as the control units for the PEs in SIMD mode and orchestrated the activities of the PEs in MIMD mode. Each MC controls P/Q PEs. PASM was designed for $P = 1024$ and $Q = 32$ ($P = 16$ and $Q = 4$ in the prototype). A set of MCs and their associated PEs form a submachine. In SIMD mode, each MC fetched instructions and common data from its associated memory module, executed the control flow instructions (for example, branches), and broadcasted the data processing instructions to its PEs. In MIMD mode, each MC fetched instructions and common data for coordinating its PEs from its own local memory.

The PASM prototype system was built for $P = 16$ and $Q = 4$. This system employed Motorola MC68010 processors as PE and MC CPUs, with a clock speed of 8 MHz. The structure of the prototype's Parallel Computation Unit is shown in Figure 1.4. The interconnection network was a circuit-switched Extra-Stage Cube network, a fault-tolerant version of the multistage cube network [67]. One of the unique aspects of PASM was how SIMD operation was implemented with off-the-shelf MC68010 CPUs. The SIMD instruction broadcast mechanism is overviewed below.

Consider the simplified MC structure shown in Figure 1.5. The MC contained a memory module from which the MC CPU read instructions and data. Whenever the MC needed to broadcast SIMD instructions to its associated PEs, it first set the Mask Register in the Fetch Unit, thus specifying which PEs would participate in the following instructions. It then wrote a control word to the Fetch Unit Controller that specified the location and size of a block of SIMD instructions in the Fetch Unit RAM. The Fetch Unit Controller automatically moved this block, word by word, into the Fetch Unit Queue. Whenever an instruction word was enqueued, the current value of the Mask Register was enqueued as well. Because the Fetch Unit enqueued blocks of SIMD instructions automatically, the MC CPU could proceed with other operations without waiting for all instructions to be enqueued.

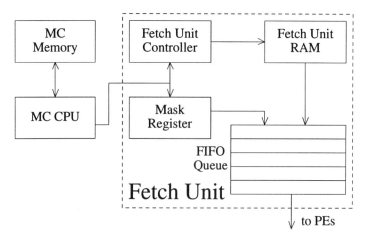

FIGURE 1.5   PASM microcontroller.

PEs executed SIMD instructions by performing an instruction fetch from a reserved memory area called the *SIMD instruction space*. Whenever logic in the PEs detected an access to this area, a request for an SIMD instruction was sent to the Fetch Unit. After all PEs (that were enabled for the current instruction) had issued a request, the instruction was released by the Fetch Unit. Only then were the enabled PEs allowed to receive and execute the instruction. Disabled PEs did not participate in the instruction and waited until an instruction was broadcast that enabled them. This way, switching from MIMD to SIMD mode was reduced to executing a jump instruction to the reserved memory space. Further, a switch from SIMD to MIMD mode was performed by the MC sending its PEs a jump to the appropriate PE MIMD instruction address located in the PE main memory space [62].

The SIMD instruction broadcast mechanism also could be utilized for barrier synchronization [22, 52] of MIMD programs. Assume a program used a single MC group, and required the PEs to synchronize R times. First, the MC enabled all its PEs by writing an appropriate mask to the Fetch Unit Mask Register. Then it instructed the Fetch Unit Controller to enqueue R arbitrary data words, and started its PEs upon the execution of their MIMD programs. If the PEs needed to synchronize (for example, before a network transfer), they issued a read instruction to access a location in the SIMD instruction space. Because the hardware in the PEs treated SIMD instruction fetches and data reads the same way, the PEs would be allowed to proceed only after all PEs had read from SIMD space. The PEs were thus synchronized. The R synchronizations required R data fetches from the SIMD space. Thus, the Fetch Unit Queue was empty when the MIMD program completed, and subsequent SIMD programs were not affected by this use of the SIMD instruction broadcast mechanism.

TRAC   The Texas Reconfigurable Array Computer (TRAC) [64] was another hybrid SIMD/MIMD system. TRAC used custom, microcoded, 8-bit processor technology, and a clever technique for "byte-slicing" the processors to handle vector computations of arbitrary length. It employed an SW-banyan type network and was prototyped and operated with 16 processors. It introduced the concept of *space sharing* in its reconfigurable hardware

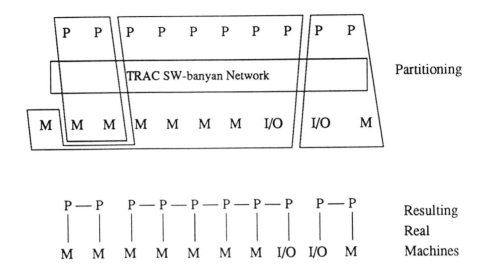

FIGURE 1.6 Overall structure of TRAC and example machine partitioning.

environment to support a variety of differently structured applications, such as iterative linear system solvers, Monte Carlo techniques, and databases.

The byte-slicing was implemented via a special GPC (generate-propagate-carry) bus that interconnected the processors cooperating on the same multiprecision data element. Physically, the machine was of the "dance-hall" variety as was the NYU Ultra, and RP3, but there were two principle differences. First, the TRAC network was not a combining network, and second, the nonprocessor side of the banyan included some secondary memory devices that were "Self Managing" (SMSM). Figure 1.6 illustrates the basic nature of the system, and also illustrates the partitioning of processors, network, memory, and I/O devices.

Manchester The Manchester [81] consumed a different corner of the early research architecture space—*data flow*. A data-flow machine executes operations in an order determined by dynamic data interdependencies and availability of resources. These machines are distinctly different from control-flow parallel machines in the sense that control-flow machines use a centralized control of scheduling (that is, program counter). Data-flow machines are highly decentralized because the processing elements work asynchronously; they are *data-driven*. The parallelism in a data-flow machine comes from a pipeline of logical units in each processing element in which the instructions are executed concurrently. The compiler is responsible for distributing the data and groups of instructions to the processing elements. Following the executing of an instruction, the resulting data is packaged into a *token*, which contains a label of the process for which the data is next intended. The processors receive the tokens, perform the required operations on the data, and pass the result in the form of a new token to the other processors.

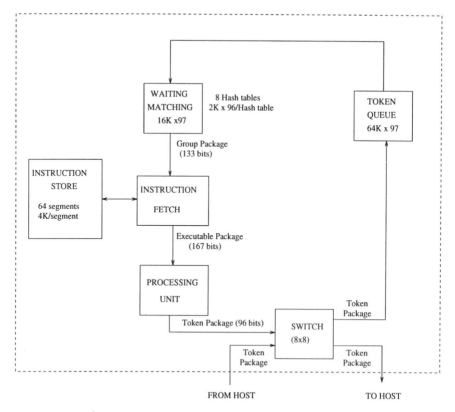

FIGURE 1.7   Manchester data-flow architecture.

The Manchester data-flow machine was a dynamic tagged token architecture that incorporated a ring of processing elements. Each ring contained 12 processors and the rings could be interconnected through a switching network. Upon the receipt of a token in a processing element (see Figure 1.7), the token first went into a token queue, then to the waiting matching unit, then the matched token went to the node store to pick up instructions for the processing unit. The resulting token generated by one of the microprogrammed ALUs was driven back out onto the network. The Manchester prototype was a one-ring design which used 96-bit tokens containing 32 bits of data, a 36-bit label, 18 bits for destination, and 10 bits for control. The rings operated at 5 MHz and were connected to a DEC LSI-11 host computer, which handled the I/O of the ring processors.

NYU Ultracomputer and IBM RP3   The NYU Ultracomputer was a research machine designed to study how to implement a large-scale shared memory MIMD computer. The design of the machine was actually based on the paracomputer model, which was an idealized parallel processor consisting of independent processing elements connected to a central memory [26]. The NYU group extended the paracomputer model with the "fetch-and-add" combining network operation to handle synchronization. The designers of the

NYU Ultra proposed a 4096 processor machine, with "slightly" customized PEs to handle the fetch-and-add operation. The actual implementation design consisted of processing elements connected to memory elements via an Omega-network, as seen in Figure 1.8. A prototype was built and contained eight 10-MHz Motorola MC68010 processors and 8 MB of memory. The processors were equiped with Weitek 1164/65 floating point units, 32-KB caches, and hardware support for the fetch-and-add operation.

The Research Parallel Processor Prototype (RP3) was built by IBM to test hardware and software in MIMD computers. The Ultracomputer and RP3 were very similar in that the RP3 was based on early versions of the Ultracomputer [6]. Later designs of the Ultracomputer evolved some features not in the RP3. The NYU Ultracomputer and the RP3 could interleave consecutive addresses across memory modules; both supported caches in the processing nodes; and both systems used an Omega-network interconnect between processing elements and memory elements. Also, the Ultracomputer and RP3 had queues to handle messages that collided at the switch nodes. The switch nodes could also combine messages bound for the same address. Unlike the Ultracomputer, the RP3 could alter most of these shared-memory features, which facilitated a wide range of experiments.

The RP3 used 512 ROMP microprocessors, had 32-KB cache per node, included up to 8 MB of memory per node, and had a total memory of 2–4 GB. The memory was implemented in such a way that it could be variably configured as entirely global memory, local memory, or a hybrid mix. An application could have been done with the RP3 configured with only global memory for algorithmic simplicity at the cost of network traffic and memory latencies. Ideally, the computationally intensive parts could be moved to reconfigured local memories to increase performance. I/O was supported by 64 data channels with an I/O support processor for each channel, yielding a 192-MB/second peak system bandwidth.

CalTech Cosmic Cube and Intel iPSC/1   The Cosmic Cube [63] was a 64-processor MIMD system developed at Caltech. Each node of this machine consisted of a 5-MHz 8086 CPU, an 8087 math co-processor, and 128 Kbytes of RAM. Processors were attached in a 6-dimensional hypercube, where each connection was bidirectional and operated at about 2 Mbits/sec. Data was routed in 64-bit packets that were stored and forwarded at each node along a path between processors. Routing and process control were managed by a small kernel on each node. The kernel processed messages intended for the node on which it resided and those messages that had to be forwarded to other nodes. This provided a flexible system upon which message-passing libraries were built. Then, programs on each node were normal sequential programs with inserted message passing calls.

The iPSC/1 was an evolution of the Cosmic Cube. For this machine, 128 nodes—each consisting of an Intel i80286 processor and 512 Kbytes of RAM—were connected in a 7-dimensional hypercube. Because the neglect of I/O in the Cosmic Cube architecture caused its performance to be rather poor, an Ethernet I/O channel was introduced at each PE on the iPSC/1. This solution still did not provide adequate I/O bandwidth and was one of the more important lessons learned in this generation of machines.

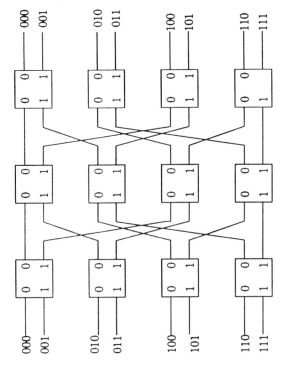

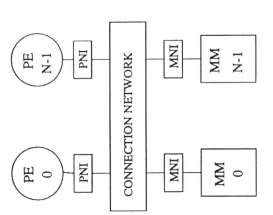

FIGURE 1.8   NYU Ultracomputer architecture.

TABLE 1.3   First-generation system characteristics.

Machine	Control	Topology	Memory	CPU	Max # PEs	Where/When
NCUBE-1	MIMD	Hypercube	Distributed	Custom	1024	NCUBE, 1988
GP1000	MIMD	Multistage Cube Switch	Shared/Dist.	MC68020	64	BBN, 1985
Balance	MIMD	Shared Bus	Shared	NS32032	24	Sequent, 1985
Monsoon	Data-Flow (not Control)	Multistage Packet Switch	Shared	Custom Pipelines	8	MIT, 1991
TRACE	VLIW	Bus	Shared	Custom VLIW Funct. Unit	4 Integer/ FP Pairs	Multiflow, 1987
FX/8	Custom	Shared Bus	Shared	Custom	8	Alliant, 1985
iPSC/1	MIMD	7D hypercube	Distributed	i286	128	Intel, 1985
SUPRENUM	MIMD	Toroidal Grid Clustered	Distibuted		256	GMD FIRST 1985
MP-1	SIMD	Xnet Mesh 3-Stage Routing	Distributed	Custom 4-bit	16 K	MasPar, 1985
CM-2	SIMD	12D Hcube of 4 × 4 meshes	Distributed	Custom 1-bit	64 K	TMC, 1985
GF11	SIMD	Benes Switch	Distributed	Off-the-Shelf	566	IBM, 1986

1.2.2   First Generation

This section provides a description of the *first-generation* parallel machines. These machines were primarily commercial ventures and met with mixed success. The architecture space investigated in this generation is less varied than the previous generations, but is still quite vast, from VLIW (Multiflow) to uniform shared memory (Alliant and Sequent) to nonuniform shared memory (Butterfly) to message passing (NCUBE/1). A summary of the organization and machines is provided in Table 1.3.

Note that although the Intel iPSC/1 is included in this generation, its description appears in the previous section with the Cosmic Cube. This sort of grouping also occurs out of presentational convenience in a number of other cases as well, including the MasPar, Alliant, Sequent, and BBN systems. In these cases, the machines are described in a single section

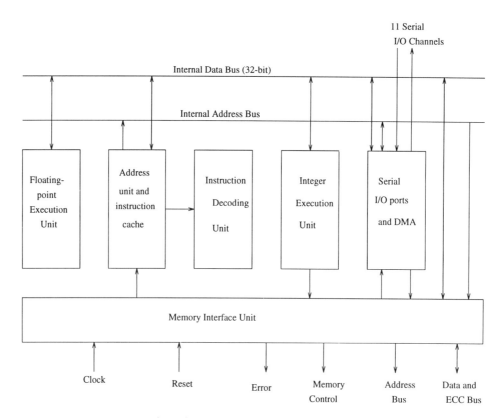

FIGURE 1.9   NCUBE-1 node architecture.

with either the first or second generation, but they actually belong in different generations, and are thus included in different tables.

NCUBE-1   The NCUBE-1 [61] family of computers was based on a custom VAX-like processor with floating point capability and was interconnected via a hypercube network topology. Several configurations were offered ranging from a 4-processor PC card to a fully configured 1024-node system. One of the more prominent features of this system was attention to system packaging and I/O support. The system was packaged in a single cabinet roughly one meter in volume. It was incrementally expandable to 16 processor boards in this one cabinet—each board carrying 64 CPUs and 512 Kbytes of local memory per processor. The I/O system, called the *NChannel,* provided I/O channels directly to the nodes of the machine. The NChannel system comprised 1 to 7 NCUBE I/O nodes, where each node contained an NCUBE processor and 16 serial I/O channels. The I/O nodes were connected to a peripheral controller located next to the main machine. A block diagram of the NCUBE-1 processor is shown in g 1.9.

BBN Butterfly GP1000 and TC2000   The BBN Butterfly family of systems [18] was developed as part of a DARPA-sponsored project. The Butterfly was BBNs second parallel

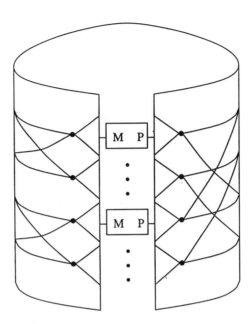

FIGURE 1.10   BBN Butterfly architecture.

machine, the first being the Pluribus (developed in the 1970s), which consisted of several interconnected Lockheed SUE minicomputers. The Pluribus was originally developed for use as an ARPAnet switching node and about 50 machines were sold for this purpose. The original Butterfly was based on the M68000 microprocessor and each node had 512 Kbytes of memory. Later versions of the Butterfly were developed based on the 68020 (the Butterfly Plus and Butterfly GP1000) and the Motorola 88000 (the Butterfly TC2000). The main difference between the Butterfly/Butterfly Plus and the GP1000 was that the original Butterflies were attached systems and had a "front-end" on which code was developed. The GP1000 and TC2000 both ran a version of Mach and supported user development directly on the system. The Butterfly took its name from the switch that the machine's interconnection network was based upon. The Butterfly's network was a multistage implementation and was built from 4×4 crossbar switches in the earlier Butterflies and 8×8 switches in the later TC2000. Memory, while physically attached to each processor, was directly accessible to all nodes, that is, it was a logically shared-memory architecture. This logical organization is depicted in Figure 1.10. Therefore, memory access was quite fast to local memory because no network access was required, however, when data was not local, the request would have to travel through the network to another processor's local memory. This NonUniform Memory Access (NUMA) model made performance quite sensitive to data locality, that is, an application ran slow if most of a processor's accesses were not to the directly attached memory. Unfortunately, the Butterfly did not have any cache or support for data migration so applications that did not explicitly manage data locality suffered poor performance.

Sequent Balance and Symmetry   Sequent Computer Corp. used a straight-forward shared-memory approach for interprocessor communication (see Figure 1.11). The first two

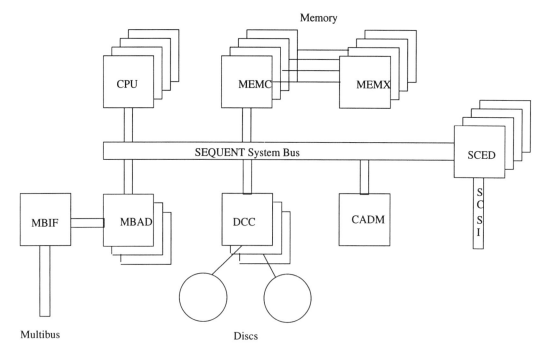

FIGURE 1.11   Sequent architecture.

Sequent machines were the Balance [65] and the Symmetry [66]. The Balance was based on the NS32032 processor. The Symmetry, on the other hand, was based on the i386 CPU. The Symmetry was specially designed to let the i386s operate at their peak performance. This was accomplished by adding extra circuitry to each processor that handled most communication tasks. Each of the nodes consists of an Intel i386 or a NS32032 microprocessor, a floating point coprocessor, and local memory which included an 8-Kbyte cache. Each node was connected to the shared memory via a high-speed 64-bit bus. Due to the shared-bus memory design the maximum number of processors supported was 24 for the Balance and 30 in the Symmetry.

One of the reasons these machines were so popular was that Sequent extended UNIX to "transparently" use all available processors. In particular, the parallel version of the make utility was very attractive as it frequently reduced large compile times almost linearly with the number of processors.

Monsoon   Unlike the other machines of the first generation, Monsoon was a research prototype machine based on the data-flow paradigm. In a data-flow model, data is fed to operators that process the data as soon as it is available, thus *data availability* drives execution. This is unlike a traditional von Neumann model where operations are performed on data in a predetermined order.

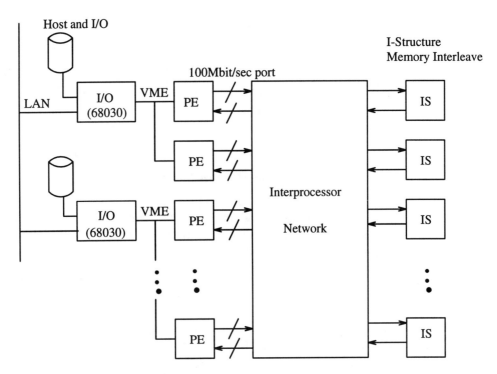

FIGURE 1.12   Monsoon architecture.

A general data-flow model had been generally thought to be much too complicated to be efficiently built in custom hardware. Therefore, Monsoon used a simplified method called an *explicit token store* (ETS) architecture [60]. The generality of the data-flow model was sacrificed by letting the compiler handle low-level storage management and statically assigning nodes to slots in an activation frame. This made the machine implementation much more efficient since this task was not done dynamically at run time.

The machine itself was a collection of PEs connected to each other as well as a set of interleaved I-structure memory modules (ISs), as shown in Figure 1.12. The interconnection network was a multistage packet-switched network and each PE was an eight-stage pipeline that produced up to two tokens. The total memory size of Monsoon was 128-K words of frame-store and 128-K words of instruction memory. The machine was hosted on a NuBus card that operated in a Texas Instruments Explorer Lisp machine.

Multiflow TRACE   The Multiflow TRACE series of machines focused on instruction-level parallelism. They used a custom VLIW (very long instruction word) CPU whose design was driven primarily by advanced compiler technology. The machine had three configurations, which corresponded to 7, 14, or 28 operations per cycle [13]. Although it had long been believed that there was only limited instruction-level parallelism [28, 45, 75] in many serial applications, the architects of Multiflow believed that high levels of instruction parallelism could be extracted via advanced compiler technology.

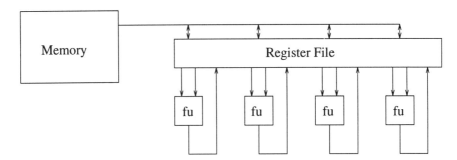

FIGURE 1.13   Multiflow architecture (idealized VLIW).

An ideal VLIW architecture is shown in Figure 1.13. Here the register file fed multiple independent functional units that executed the instructions—which were scheduled statically at compile-time—in parallel. Unfortunately, as the number of functional units increases, so does the number of ports on the register file, which leads to severe implementation difficulties. In order to create a feasible machine, the Multiflow architects split the processor into integer and floating point sections. The integer section consisted of two ALUs while the floating point part consisted of one multiply ALU and one addition ALU. In this way four instructions could be executed simultaneously on each processor board. Contemporary superscalar processors, such as the IBM PowerPC 601 [56], exhibit a strong similiarity in their hardware structure.

Alliant FX/8 and FX/2800   Alliant Computer Systems Corporation was a start-up company whose only business was to design and manufacture parallel computers. The basic structure of all their machines was the same—individual processing elements connected via a bus to shared memory, with each processing element having its own CPU, local memory, and cache. Alliant announced its first machine, the FX/4, in 1985, later introducing the FX/8. These two machines were binary compatible and featured a custom, MC68000-compatible processor.

Unlike its predecessors, the FX/2800 [14] was based on the i860 processor, and was the company's mainstream platform from early 1990 until Alliant's demise in mid-1992. This machine could support up to 28 CPUs, resulting in a peak performance of 1.1 Gflops. As shown in Figure 1.14, the FX/2800 consisted of processor modules, each supporting 4 i860s. Two of these processors were referred to as Super Computational Elements (SCEs) and the other two were called Super Interactive Processors (SIPs). The former were responsible for carrying the computational burden of the machine, while the latter handled most operating system tasks.

GMD FIRST SUPRENUM   The SUPRENUM (SUPer-REchenr fuer NUMerik) [32] was the entry machine of GMD FIRST (supported by the German Federal Government) into the massively parallel computing arena. It was the most powerful MPP built in Europe, eventually supporting up to 5 Gflops peak performance. The goal of the project was to make the Federal Republic of Germany a leading player in the relatively new field of

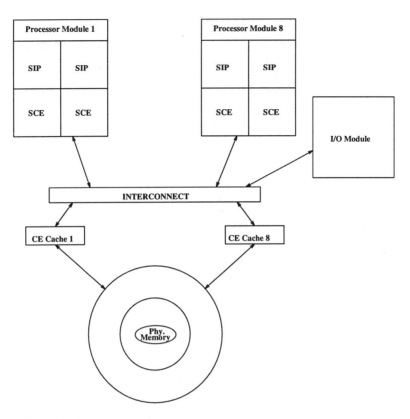

FIGURE 1.14 Alliant FX/2800 architecture.

supercomputing. Specifically, it was to have the highest possible performance for numerical applications, such as solving partial differential equations.

The SUPRENUM architecture consisted of a clustered ring topology. Each cluster was made up of 20 nodes–16 application nodes, 2 communication nodes, 1 I/O node, and 1 diagnostic node. These nodes were interconnected within a cluster by two parallel high-bandwidth (160 MB/sec) buses. Each node consisted of a CPU with 8 + 1 MB of EDC-DRAM, an integrated floating point processor, and elaborate communications hardware. The communications hardware executed the communication protocols and also allowed for DMA transfers between node memories. The floating point processor used was the most powerful available at the time, the Weitek WTL2264/2265, capable of 10 Mflops (double-precision) peak, for single operations and 20 Mflops for chained operations. The clusters were in turn connected together through a matrix of bit-serial ring buses (a toroidal grid) with each row or column ring consisting of two buses, each supporting 10 MB/sec.

MasPar MP-1 and MP-2   MasPar Computer Corporation successfully specialized in large-scale SIMD systems. Both the MP-1 and MP-2 were based on the same principles, the processing element being the most notable difference between them. The MP-1

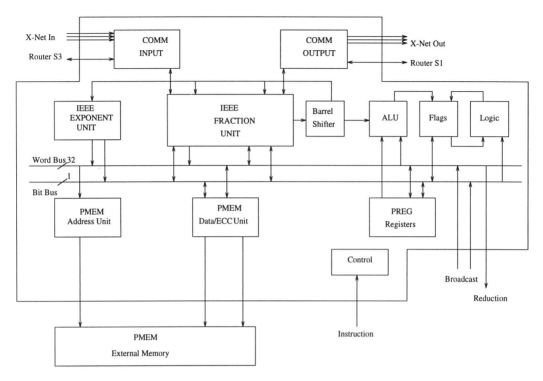

FIGURE 1.15   MasPar MP-2 node architecture.

contained up to 16-K 4-bit custom CPUs connected with the Xnet network. The MP-2 [53] was its second-generation product, consisting of an array of up to 16-K 32-bit PEs.

A full MP-2 system delivered 68,000 MIPS peak performance and up to 2400 peak double precision Mflops. Each PE, as shown in Figure 1.15, was essentially a 32-bit ALU with 40 general-purpose registers and an attached memory. PE memory consisted of 64 Kbytes of ECC memory, giving a full 16-K system 1 GB of RAM. PEs were implemented in fully custom one-micron CMOS and were clocked at 80n sec. The MP-2's PEs were controlled by its Array Control Unit (ACU). The ACU was a 12.5-MIPS scalar processor with custom microcode to handle the PE array. The ACU broadcasted microcode to the entire PE array. PEs all received the same instructions, but individual PEs could be enabled and disabled locally. The PE array was interconnected using the X-net nearest-neighbor mesh network as well as a global multistage router-based network. The X-net was a bit-serial network connecting each PE to its eight nearest neighbors on a 2D mesh. The multistage network was for global communication and each port into the network was shared among 16 PEs.

The MP-2 supported I/O through its IORAM, a large memory attached directly to the multistage network. The memory was used to buffer I/O operations. I/O devices were then attached to an I/O channel and data was transferred directly from the IORAM. Thus, the IORAM appeared as a global shared memory to the PE array and I/O transfers occured by first copying data to the IORAM, then directly transferring the data from the IORAM to the device. Because the IORAM was independent from the CPUs, rearrangement of data

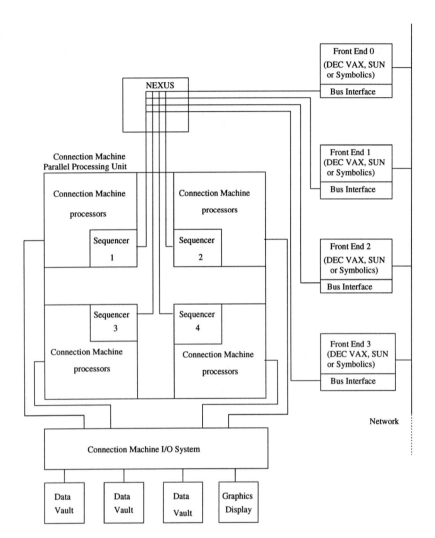

FIGURE 1.16   TMC CM-2 architecture.

could occur in the IORAM before being sent to a disk (or other device) and transfers from the IORAM could be overlapped with computation in the PE array.

Thinking Machines CM-1 and CM-2   Unlike many other parallel computing start-ups, Thinking Machines Corporation (TMC) was one company that was founded before it even had an initial design. Eventually, Danny Hillis of MIT became the originator of the first TMC machine, first called the Connection Memory and later renamed the Connection Machine (CM). The CM-1 [82] was built in 1983–1984. After a year of initial use it became apparent that several improvements were needed, and the CM-2 [77] was introduced in 1987.

The CM-2 can be characterized as an SIMD computer with 1-bit processors. Obviously a 1-bit processor can not accomplish a great deal in small numbers like most other SIMD

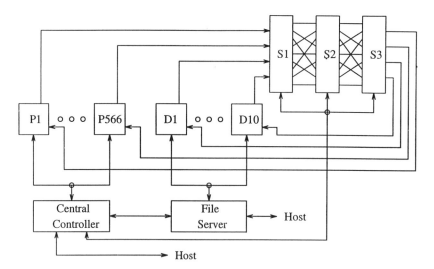

FIGURE 1.17   BBN Butterfly architecture.

machines with more powerful processing elements. Therefore, the CM-2 contained between 16,384 and 65,536 processors. Each processor was directly connected to its own local memory which was between 64 Kbits and 1 Mbit. Groups of 32 1-bit processors were put onto a single chip and two of these chips could be optionally accompanied by a floating point coprocessor—a feature that was driven by customer demand. This formed the basic building block of the machine. A fully configured CM-2 (65,536 processing elements) consisted of eight octants, where an octant consists of 16 boards, and each board contained 16 basic building blocks.

Two different topologies were supported on the CM-2. The first was a hypercube and the second was a 2D mesh called the NEWS grid. The NEWS grid was actually implemented on top of the hypercube network thus saving hardware. A router node was connected to each processor chip to handle communication.

IBM GF11   The GF11 was built by IBM at the Yorktown Research Center and had the distinction of being built for the sole application of calculations originating from quantum chromodynamics. The design incorporated 566 floating point processors [23], with memory distributed among each processor for a total memory of 1.14 GB. Locally each processor had 64 KB static RAM and 2 MB of slower dynamic RAM [3]. Each processor contained essentially 4 32-bit IEEE floating point units (2 multipliers and 2 ALUs), for 2,264 chips in all. The designers used all off-the-shelf components except for one gate array chip in the Benes network. The floating point units were Weitek WTL 1032s and WTL 1033s, placing the GF11 peak performance at 11.4 Gflops. Interestingly, the GF11, which had been built for quantum chromodynamics, did not have hardware specific to quantum chromodynamics calculations, and the designers were confident that the architecture would support a wider range of scientific and engineering applications (at more than 1 Gflops).

TABLE 1.4 Second-generation system characteristics.

Machine	Control	Topology	Memory	CPU	Max PEs	Date
AP1000	MIMD	3 Nets Torus, Bus, Tree	Distributed	SPARC	1024	Fujitsu, 1991
Cedar	MIMD	Omega network	Shared	Vector	32	Univ. of Ill., 1985
iPSC/2 iPSC/860	MIMD	Hypercube	Distributed	i386/i860	128	Intel, 1988/9
NCUBE-2	MIMD	Hypercube	Distributed	Custom 64-bit	8192	NCUBE, 1992
CM-5	MIMD	FatTree	Distributed	Sparc 2	16382	TMC 1992
TC2000	MIMD	Multistage Cube Switch	Shared/Dist.	MC88000	512	BBN, 1989
Symmetry	MIMD	Shared Bus	Shared	i386	30	Sequent, 1990
FX/2800	MIMD	Shared Bus	Shared	i860	28	Alliant, 1990
MP-2	SIMD	Xnet Mesh 3-Stage Routing	Distributed	Custom 32-bit	16 K	MasPar, 1992
KSR1	MIMD	Ring	Shared All Cache	Custom 64-bit	1088	Kendall-Square 1989

The whole system consisted of the 566 processors, a central controller, a three-stage non-blocking Benes switch, 10 disks, and a fileserver (see Figure 1.17). The central controller was an IBM PC/RT that would broadcast 180-bit microcode to the processors every 50 nanoseconds (clearly this places the GF11 in with the SIMD architectures). The Benes network was capable of implementing any processor interconnection topology and could reconfigure into 1 of 1,024 preselected configurations in one processor cycle. Bandwidth of the global data channels was 80 MBs in either direction. Two 32-bit ports on the processor allowed data traffic between RAM and the switching network at 9 bits/50 nanoseconds, and another pair communicated at 32 bits/50 nanoseconds. The central controller controlled the switch settings. An IBM PC/AT performed the role of file server controlling 10 disks of 450 MB each. These were accessed through the switch in the same way as the processors. All together the GF11 used 29 19″ and 24″ standard equipment racks and occupied around 400 square feet.

1.2.3 Second Generation

This section provides a description of the *second-generation* parallel machines. The characteristics and some examples of this generation appear in Table 1.4. In this generation, the architecture space became less diverse, primarily due to the use of microprocessor-based nodes (as in the AP1000 and NCUBE-2). Few of these machines supported shared memory, and most were scalable to over 1000 nodes. There were, however, still significant differences in control structure (the MP-2 was SIMD, the rest were MIMD) and in network topology. Note that several second-generation machines are included in Section 3 as in-depth case studies.

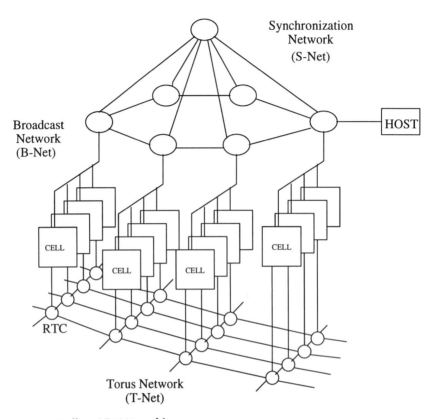

FIGURE 1.18   Fujitsu AP1000 architecture.

Fujitsu AP1000   In the Fujitsu AP1000 [44], three independent networks were employed to route messages, as seen in Figure 1.18. The Torus network (T-net) was used for point-to-point communication between cells, the Broadcast network (B-net) was used for 1-to-N communication, and the Synchronization network (S-net) was used for barrier synchronization. These different networks were used to optimize the use of barrier synchronization and broadcasts. An automatic routing scheme was used for the T-net, which combined worm-hole routing with a structured buffer pool algorithm to reduce communication latency. Each cell incorporated a message controller (MSG) for fast message handling, a SPARC processor and a routing controller (RTC). The MSG supported buffer receiving, index receiving, stride DMA, list/list vector transferring, and out-of-cache line sending. The RTC provided the automatic routing function for the T-net. To provide efficient data distribution and collection of data to and from the host processor, each cell had special hardware for scatter and gather functions. These functions were provided so that the time for data transfer set-up and message assembling/disassembling at the host computer did not increase significantly as the number of cells increased.

Cedar   The Cedar multiprocessor [48] was developed at the Center for Supercomputing Research and Development at the University of Illinois. Its system was made up of 4

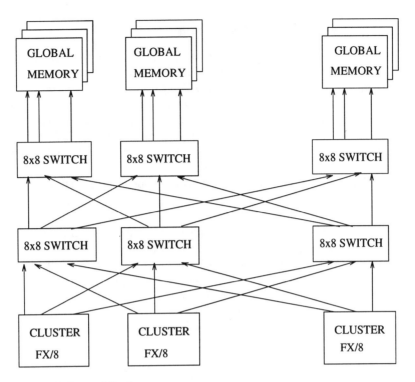

FIGURE 1.19 Cedar architecture.

clusters of the Alliant FX/8 systems along with a switching network that provided access to an additional level of memory hierarchy of globally shared memory space (see Figure 1.19). The FX/8 cluster was itself an 8-processor shared-memory multiprocessor where each vector processor was fully pipelined and rated at 11.8-Mflops peak vector performance. Cedar is a classic example of a NUMA (NonUniform Memory Access) architecture in which the memory access times vary with the location of the memory word. The 4-clusters were interconnected through a two-stage packet-switched Omega network to the shared-memory modules. The Cedar shared memory was comprised of 32 independent modules with a word size of 8 bytes. The Cedar address space was partitioned into 4-cluster memory spaces and a shared-memory space. Cedar also allowed for prefetching so that the number of outstanding read requests was not repeatedly saturated.

NCUBE-2 The NCUBE-2 [57] shared the same basic network topology as the NCUBE-1, and was also an MIMD machine. However, a new fully custom VLSI microprocessor was used in each processing and I/O node. It featured a 64-bit implementation, 64-bit IEEE standard floating point unit, message-routing unit, and 14 bidirectional DMA channels. Like the NCUBE-1 this processor is used in both the compute nodes and the I/O nodes of the machine. However, unlike the NCUBE-1, the NCUBE-2 had a router chip to handle message traffic and used worm-hole routing rather than store-and-forward packet switching. Additionally, the capability of the machine was enhanced by increasing the maximum number of nodes from 1,024 to 8,192.

1.2.4   Emerging Third Generation

This section provides a description of the *emerging third-generation* parallel machines. The characteristics and some examples of this generation appear in Table 1.5. In this generation, hardware architectures once again diverge due to the fact that technology improvements have made it possible to build more complex architectures and still remain commercially viable. To date, there are still shared- and nonshared-memory machines, though uniform shared memory has all but disappeared due to scalability concerns (Tera is a notable exception). MIMD is the primary control architecture, but at least one SIMD system is still available. Finally, software issues (such as OS and compilers) as well as I/O have become more important than with previous generations of architectures.

Cray T3D   Historically, Cray Research has specialized in high-end vector supercomputers. The T3D [14, 15, 58] represents their first entry in the massively parallel processing market. This system incorporates off-the-shelf microprocessors with a custom network developed with technology from Cray's Y-MP line of supercomputers. The T3D is liquid (Flourinert) cooled and currently utilizes DEC Alpha microprocessors which are clocked at 150 MHz, although designed to accomodate up to a 200-MHz processor. The processors are packaged with two processors per node, 4 processors per board with the nodes attached in a three-dimensional torus.

The T3D is a NUMA architecture with support for shared memory supported in hardware, although its cache coherence is maintained in software. The torus network is packet-switched and uses dimension-order routing, that is, messages first traverse the X, then Y, and then Z directions. The network can also be reconfigured to switch in spare nodes in the event of a node failure. The T3D also supports a fast barrier synchronization mechanism, atomic memory synchronization, and lightweight messages using a message-passing library based on PVM 3.0. Currently, the T3D requires a Y-MP model E or a C-90 for I/O and interactive use (see Figure 1.20), although Cray plans to discontinue this requirement in future systems. In succeeding generations, I/O will be directly attached to the T3D through dedicated I/O processors. The nodes in the T3D run a microkernel-based operating system, currently based on Mach 3.0, although this will transition to Chorus in later releases of the operating system.

Fujitsu VPP500   The Fujitsu VPP500 [55] is in many ways closer to a Cray architecture than a massively parallel architecture. It consists of very fast custom VLIW PEs constructed from a combination of GaAs and BiCMOS silicon. The machine is water cooled and can have from 4 to 222 PEs. Each PE has 6 vector pipelines and 128 KB in vector registers, along with a scalar execution unit with 32 32-bit general-purpose registers, 32 64-bit floating point registers, and a 64-KB cache. The PEs can have from 128 to 256 MB of static RAM which is globally addressable (that is, it is a NUMA shared-memory system). Remote memory accesses take place through a data transfer unit attached to a conflict-free crossbar network that can operate at up to 400 MB/sec in each direction. Along with the normal PEs, the VPP500 also supports Control Processors (CPs) which coordinate the inter-PE traffic on the crossbar network. These CPs are essentially the same as the other PEs, but lack the vector

TABLE 1.5   Emerging third-generation system characteristics.

Machine	Processor	Topology	Company	MHz	MFLOPS	Memory	# PEs
T3D	Dec Alpha	3D Torus	Cray Research	150	150	16–64 MB	128–2048
VPP500	Custom GAs, vector	Crossbar	Fujitsu	100	1600	128 MB–256 MB	4–222
SP1 (SP2)	RS/6000	Multi-stage Switch	IBM	62.5 (66)	125 (132)	64–256 MB (64 MB–2 GB)	8–64 (4–128)
Paragon XP/S	i860XP	2D-Mesh	Intel	50	75	64–128 MB	4–2048
KSR2	Custom VLSI	Ring	Kendall Square	40	80	32 MB	2–5120
Cenju-3	NEC/MIPS VR4400SC	Crossbar Multistage	NEC	75	50	32–64 MB	8–256
GC	Motorola Pwr PC 601	2D-Mesh Clusters	Parsytec	50	25	2–32 MB	16–128
CS-2	Sparc scalar + 2 Vector	Multistage Switch	Meiko Limited	40	200	32–128 MB	4–1024
Alewife	SPARCLE	2D Mesh	MIT	33	13.2	8 MB	512
DASH	MIPS R3000	2D Mesh Clustered	Stanford	33	10	256 MB	64 (prototype)
Tera	Custom GAs	3D Torus	Tera	333	1200	256 GB	256
DDM	Motorolla MC88100	Clustered Tree	Swedish Inst. of CS	20	10	8–32 MB	256
SPP	PA-RISC	Multiple SCI Ring	Convex	200	200	32 MB–256 MB	8–128
J-Machine	Custom	3D Torus	MIT, Intel	20	–	1 MB	65536 (4096)

portion of the CPU. The entire system runs UNIX System V Release 4, and is attached to a VP2000 or VPX500 system to which secondary storage devices may be connected (see Figure 1.21).

The VPP500 may therefore be used as a Cray-like system with 7 to 32 processors taking part in vectorization gains, or as an MPP with over 100 very fast processors. Unfortunately, the technology used for the VPP500 makes it quite expensive, and the $O(n^2)$ complexity inherent on crossbar networks limits its scalability. To date, most VPP500 systems sold have been much smaller then 100 processors in size.

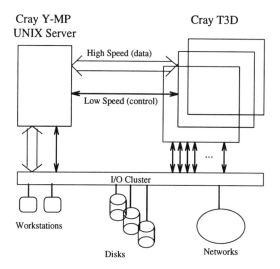

FIGURE 1.20   Cray T3D.

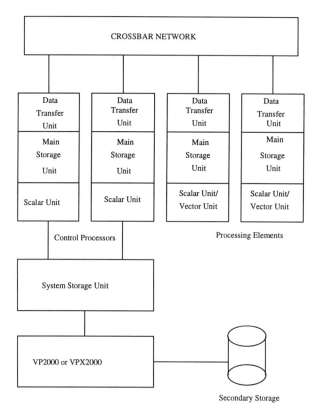

FIGURE 1.21   Fujitsu VPP500 architecture.

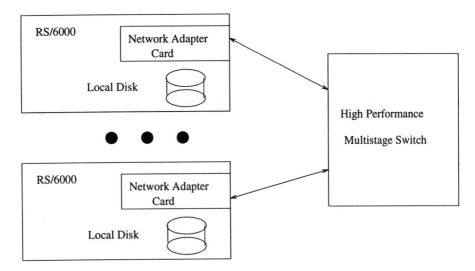

FIGURE 1.22   IBM SP1 architecture.

IBM SP1 and SP2   The IBM SP1 was the first integrated system built around a cluster of truly off-the-shelf workstations. The SP1 essentially consists of a rack of IBM RS/6000 workstations interconnected with a custom multistage switch. Each node runs at 62.5 MHz, has a 32-KB instruction/32-KB data cache, can have up to 256-MB RAM, up to 2-GB disk, and is capable of computing at up to 125 Mflops (32-bit) peak. A system can consist of up to 64 nodes (although one 128-node system was constructed for Argonne National Laboratory). The network is packet switched and is capable of 40-MB/sec bidirectional throughput. The nodes interface to the network through normal microchannel cards, thus eliminating any need to modify the standard RS/6000 systems (see Figure 1.22).

The major differences between the SP1 and the SP2 [29], are that the SP2 uses an "intelligent" switch adapter to interface with the *Vulcan high-performance switch* developed by IBM, and that the SP2 is not based on the AIX diskless workstation management. The SP2 is avaliable with several different processor/memory configurations: 62.5 MHz with 256-MB mem/2-GB disk max, 66 MHz with 512-MB mem/4-GB disk max, and 66 MHz with 2-GB mem/8-GB disk max. The 66 MHz nodes also include 4- and 8-micro-channel expansion slots respectively. The SP2 supports between 4 and 128 nodes, which are interconnected with an "intelligent" switch adapter powered by an i860 microprocessor, which allows computation to be overlapped with communication. In the IBM SP2, each node has its own copy of a boot image, the root directory, and the var and tmp directories. Both the SP1 and the SP2 nodes run a stand-alone copy of IBM's AIX operating system, but in the SP1 the system is tied together using user-level scripts for starting programs and a message-passing library. Currently the SP1 and SP2 support IBM's proprietary message-passing library, EUI, as well as a vendor-supplied implementation of MPI. Finally, because the SP1/SP2 is a collection of workstations, it can use portable message-passing libraries such as Chameleon, MPI-R (a portable implementation of MPI built on Chameleon), PVM, and so on.

Meiko CS-2   The Meiko Computing Surface 2 (CS-2) [54] is a distributed memory MIMD architecture, consisting of two types of nodes: scalar and vector. The scalar nodes use a superscalar implementation of the SPARC CPU, a custom communication processor, and 32 to 512 MB of RAM. The vector nodes are identical to the scalar nodes, except that they have been augmented with two Fujitsu microVP vector units, capable of delivering 100 double-precision Mflops each. Each vector unit is a register-register architecture with 8 KB of configurable vector register memory, 32 scalar registers, and a vector mask register. The chip has separate pipes for floating point multiply, add, divide, and integer operations. The superscalar SPARC CPUs have 20 KB of instruction cache and 16 KB of data cache, and are capable of up to 40 Mflops. The network is a fat tree design with constant bandwidth per stage, built up of 4×4 crossbar switches.

Interprocessor communication is controlled by a Meiko designed custom network interface, which contains two data links into the multistage network with 50-MB/sec bandwidth per link. The network interfaces minimize latency by using remote read and write operations to implement communication without any data buffering. In addition, Meiko's hardware communications allow message-passing libraries to be implemented without requiring them to be layered on top of the Meiko primitives. Support for global memory, broadcast, barrier synchronization, and global reduction is provided through software (CS Tools). Each node has three S-bus connections, as shown in Figure 1.23, through which I/O is performed. Support is provided for striping files over multiple disks attached to different nodes in the system.

Parsytec GC/PowerPlus   The Parsytec GC/PowerPlus is the first parallel computer to use the Motorola PowerPC 601 processor. Although originally intending to use INMOS's transputer CPUs (specifically the T9000), Parsytec decided instead to use the new PowerPC processor. The GC/PowerPlus uses a nano-kernel implementation of PARIX 1.2, derived from the GC systems operating environment, which allows communication to take place entirely in user space. The processors are grouped together two per node with 16 to 80 MB of two-way interleaved shared-memory per node, as seen in Figure 1.24. The system is designed as a two-dimensional fat grid, with each node working as a shared-memory multiprocessor. This topology integrates the high bandwidth and low diameter of a hypercube or fat tree with the scalability of a grid [31]. A cluster is made up of $4 + 1$ nodes interconnected to form a 4×4 fault-tolerant grid of nodes, where each node contains two PPC 601 processors running at 80 MHz along with 4 T805 transputers which are used as virtual channel processors (VCPs). The purpose of the VCPs is to autonomously communicate over virtual channels, and to synchronize with the computing threads executed by the CPUs. They allow for fast context switches in the multithreaded environment thereby masking most of the latency associated with network communication. They also supply 16 bidirectional links to the other nodes. With a peak performance of 80 Mflops (double precision) per processor, a 40-Gflops system peak is attained with a full 512 processors (16 clusters).

Alewife   The MIT Alewife [1] implements a 2D-mesh network, with each node containing a single processor. The processor used is a modified SPARC processor, called

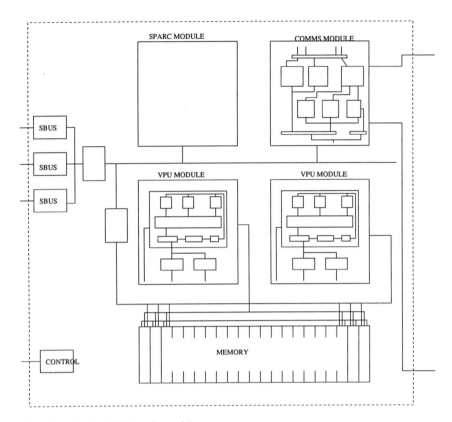

FIGURE 1.23   Meiko CS-2 Node architecture.

SPARCLE [30], designed and produced specifically for large-scale multiprocessing, supporting multithreading and fast context switching. The rapid context switching is meant to hide communication and synchronization delays and achieve higher processor utilization. The SPARCLE processor clocks at around 33 MHz, and has 64 KB of direct-mapped cache and 4 MB of globally shared main memory, along with an additional 4 MB of local memory, which is partially taken up by the coherence directory. The Alewife is limited to 512 nodes due to SPARC's 32-bit addressing scheme, wherein the top few bits of the address determine the node number, and the rest is the index within a specific node. Alewife uses the LimitLESS directory-based cache coherence protocol, which maintains a small set of pointers in the memory modules, but allows for software emulation of a full-map directory. Alewife has a fixed home for each address, and therefore a cache miss must be resolved by referencing the home memory module.

NEC Cenju-3   The Cenju [9] project at NEC is aimed at developing parallel processing technologies for commercial computer systems. The Cenju and Cenju-2 were the first two systems to come from this project, and were kept, almost exclusively, for internal use by NEC. The entire Cenju line is based upon distributed-memory systems that support global

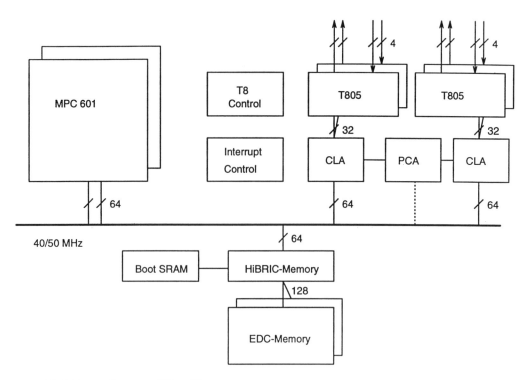

FIGURE 1.24   Parsytec GC architecture.

addressing of memory. This allowed processors to write into other processors' memory without the need for processor synchronization or system buffers. The Cenju and Cenju-2 used a MC68020 and a VR3000/3010 respectively as their CPU, and could be configured up to 64 nodes in the Cenju and 256 nodes on the Cenju-2.

The Cenju-3 consists of 8 to 256 NEC VR4400SC microprocessors running at a clock rate of 75 MHz, and capable of 50 Mflops. This processor is an implementation of the MIPS R4400 fabricated by NEC, which offers a 32-KB on-chip cache and a 1-MB secondary cache, and supports from 32 to 64 MB of local memory. The interconnect is a multistage crossbar network, built up of 4 × 4 crossbar switching units. The Cenju-3 runs an enhanced version of UNIX System V Release 4.0 which allows system management, processor assignment, and initialization, most of which runs on the workstation front end. Also being developed concurrently at NEC is the PCASE software project which assists users in parallelizing their software by providing hierarchical and distributed views of memory. The hierarchical view of memory allows users to parallelize their applications without worrying about the physical distribution of the memory. PCASE also supports explicit parallelization, allowing users to select the best optimization based upon dependency analysis and performance prediction.

Stanford DASH   The Stanford DASH (Directory Architecture for SHared memory) architecture [51], like the Alewife architecture, depends on caching to achieve scalability.

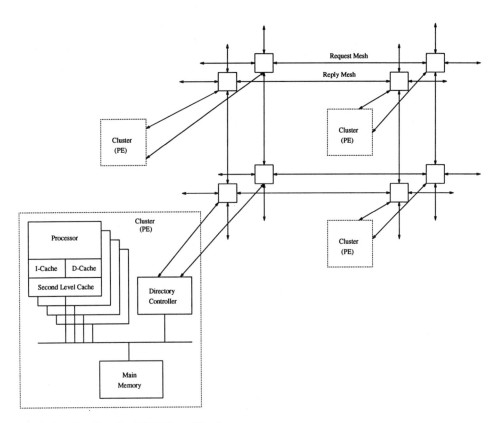

FIGURE 1.25   Stanford DASH architecture.

DASH uses a 2D-mesh topology of nodes (see Figure 1.25). Each node in the system architecture corresponds to a Silicon Graphics 4D/340, which has a cluster of four processors each with a two-level cache implementation accessing locally shared main memory. The first-level write-through data cache, inherent on each processor, is interfaced with a larger second-level write-back data cache. The main purpose of the second-level cache is to convert the write-through policy of the first level to a write-back policy, and to provide extra cache tags for bus snooping. The snooping policy is implemented only within cluster of processors of a node.

The distributed directory-based cache coherence protocol is a function of the memory consistency model adopted by the architecture. The sequential consistency model, inherent in Alewife, essentially represents program execution on a uniprocessor where multi-tasking is available. In DASH, a weaker consistency model called *release consistency* is used. This approach requires the programmer to specify which memory accesses require sequential consistency, but can hide much of the synchronization overhead of write operations. The distributed directory-based cache coherence protocol is implemented entirely in hardware. Additional latency-tolerance features include a forwarding control strategy and special-purpose operations such as prefetching and update writes. Work in progress on this architecture includes expanding the clusters to 16 processors.

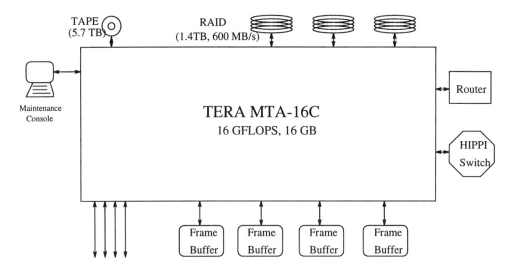

FIGURE 1.26   Tera architecture.

Tera   Tera is an ambitious project funded by ARPA and its own start-up company, Tera Computers. The Tera approach is to build a massively parallel computer using fully custom state-of-the-art VLSI technology, with a targeted clock rate of 333 MHz. The first implementation is planned to have 256 processors, 512 memory units, 256 I/O cache units, 256 I/O processors, and 4,096 interconnection network nodes [2] (see Figure 1.26). The Tera system's primary designer, Burton Smith, was also the architect of the HEP, and Tera incorporates many of the same ideas, and has evolved from the Horizon experimental system [49]. Each processor is multithreaded and can support up to 128 different threads called *streams* [73]. Each stream has its own PC counter and registers, and can issue up to eight different memory references without waiting for earlier ones to finish (see Figure 1.27). Context switching is very rapid since there is hardware for each of the 128 stream states. Thread creation is also handled in hardware so that it is possible to efficiently utilize very fine-grained threads. The processors support a horizontal or VLIW-type of instruction set.

The interconnection network is a sparse three-dimensional network. It is sparse in the sense that some nodes are not fully connected in order to decrease complexity and increase bisection bandwidth. Each data memory unit contains 128 megabytes of byte-addressable memory with a word size of 64 bits. The memory also supports full/empty bit synchronization as in HEP. In addition, the memory system of Tera is interleaved and is capable of delivering a word of data to each processor every machine cycle, though the actual latency of a single-memory reference may still be high.

Multithreading allows Tera to hide memory latency and its hardware process management allows it to take advantage of very fine-grained parallelism. This is significantly different than in vector processors where latency is tolerated by using vector register chaining. Instead, Tera can take advantage of less structured fine-grain parallelism and consequently should perform well for a larger variety of applications.

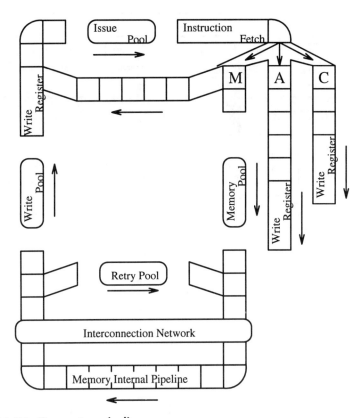

FIGURE 1.27   Tera system pipeline.

DDM   The Data Diffusion Machine (DDM) [34] is a shared-memory MIMD system with a cache only memory architecture (COMA). In a COMA architecture, the entire memory address space resides in cache, that is, there is no "home" location for variables. Therefore, data will naturally migrate to the caches of the processors most frequently accessing that data. This mechanism eliminates the need to explicitly distribute data and works well as long as data is not written to by multiple processors simultaneously. The DDM's cache architecture is implemented as a hierarchy of buses. At the bottom of the hierarchy are processors, with each processor connected to its own *attraction memory*. The processors used in the initial prototype are Motorola MC88100 microprocessors running at 20 MHz, each with 8 to 32 MB of RAM. The attraction memories act as local data and state caches for the processors and deal with requests from other processors. Above the attraction memories are the *directories*. These are similar to the attraction memories, but only contain state information (not data) for the attraction memories located below them in the hierarchy. Processor memory accesses that cannot be satisfied by the connected attraction memory are then forwarded up the tree until one of the directories indicates that the requested cache line is located in an attraction memory below it in the hierarchy. Then, the request propagates back down the tree to the proper attraction memory and the requested cache line is returned.

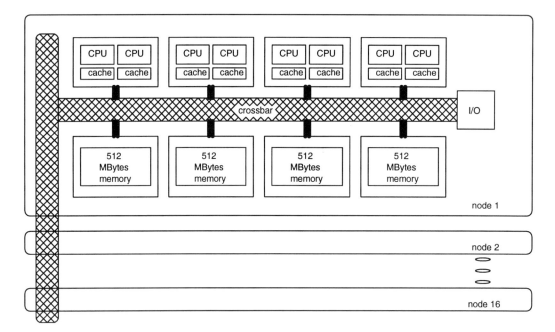

FIGURE 1.28   Convex SPP system overview.

DDM also maintains coherence information for each cache line and supports sequential consistency. A prototype DDM has been built at the Swedish Institute of Computer Science. This prototype consists of a single level (that is, one bus) with 32 processors and 8 two-way set-associative attraction memories (that is, 4 processors are attached to each attraction memory).

Convex SPP   The Convex SPP [6, 78, 79, 80] is the first massively parallel system from Convex. In the past, Convex has concentrated on the vector super-mini computer market. The SPP is an air-cooled, stand-alone system, which is based on off-the-shelf microprocessor and networking technology. The processors in the SPP are Hewlett Packard's PA-RISC 7100 processors running at 100 MHz. Each processor has its own 1-MB data cache and 1-MB instruction cache, and provides a peak performance of 200 Mflops or 200 MIPS. The SPP supports a NUMA memory model called *globally distributed virtual shared memory*. Thus, a node accesses all of the memory in the system by its virtual address regardless of whether it is contained on the local node, on another node, or on disk. The machine consists of up to 16 nodes with 8 processors per node, as shown in Figure 1.28. Each node acts as a tightly coupled shared-memory system, with up to 2 GB of main memory per node. Nodes are interconnected with 4 unidirectional rings and the rings are controlled by chips based on the scalable coherent interface (SCI) standard. SCI is an IEEE standard for an interconnect to be used in NUMA shared memory architectures. I/O and main memory on a node are accessed through a 4-GB/sec distributed crossbar. The system also provides a hardware performance monitor for measuring such characteristics as cache misses and

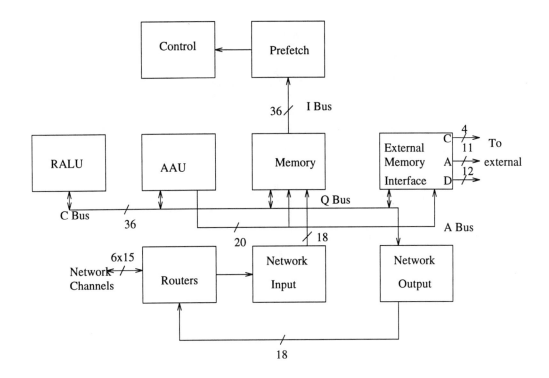

MDP Block Diagram

FIGURE 1.29 J-Machine architecture.

memory latency. The system runs an operating system based on OSF/1 AD. However, unlike standard OSF/1 AD (as used in the Paragon described in Section 3), the Convex does not have to support the no remote memory access (NORMA) model. Instead, it runs a modified version of the system designed for the NUMA model of the Convex SPP.

MIT J-Machine The MIT J-Machine [18, 20] attempts to be able to tolerate communication latency by implementing message-driven processors (MDPs) to handle fine-grained tasks (see Figure 1.29). The J-Machine supports up to 64 K nodes, each with a 36-bit MDP, router, and 6 bidirectional channels. These processors are message-driven in the sense that they begin execution in response to messages, via the *dispatch* mechanism. No *receive* instruction is needed, and this eliminates some of the communication software overhead. The MDPs create tasks to handle each arriving message. Messages carrying these tasks advance, or drive, each computation. To support the fine-grain concurrent programming, the tasks are small, typically about 20 instructions. The two-priority router and the six two-way network ports integrated into each processing node couple the three-dimensional network topology to provide efficient transmission of messages. The sending of messages consumes no processing resources on intermediate nodes and buffer memory is automatically allocated on

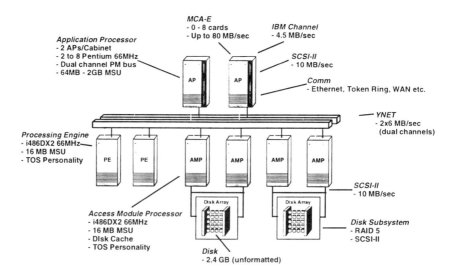

FIGURE 1.30   NCR 3600 architecture.

the receiving nodes. The MDP provides concurrency through fast context switching and also uses prefetching to improve locality. The MDPs provide synchronization by using message *dispatch* and *presence* tags on all states. In response to an arriving message, the MDP may set the presence tags so that access to a value may not be preempted. Where the J-Machine uses task on the order of 20 instructions, its successor, the M-Machine, attempts to push the task size down to one operation through intranode mechanisms.

NCR 3600   Unlike the other systems mentioned in this chapter, the NCR 3600 was not designed for general-purpose parallel computing. Instead, it is a database-oriented system designed for use as a database transaction/index database unit. The 3600 can be broken down into four basic building blocks: application processors (APs), access module processors (AMPs), parsing/processing engines (PEs), and the YNET, which interconnects them.

The APs are located in AP cabinets, shown in Figure 1.30, which contain up to two AP subsytems. AP subsystems are tightly coupled shared-memory multiprocessors, utilizing from two to eight 66-MHz Intel Pentium processors. Each AP has a microchannel architecture (MCA) bus through which networking takes place. Each subsystem consists of up to seven boards:

- 1–4 dyadic processor boards
- 1–2 memory boards (64/128/256/512 MB each)
- 1 processor subsystem interface board

In addition, each board has an MCA bus with eight slots; two for connecting to the YNET, one for internal SCSI peripherals, and the rest to connect external I/O, communication, or the Administration workstation. The AMPs are packaged along with the PEs in shared cabinets. The AMP subsystem consists of a 66-MHz i486DX2 with up to 16 MB of associate RAM. This subsystem consists of four boards: the processor/memory board, the personality board, SCSI connector, and the disk cache RAM. The PEs differ in that they only have the processor/memory board and the personality board. The personality board supports the Teradata Operating System (TOS) as well as the YNET interface logic. The YNET is two independent 6-MB/sec channels in a tree structure that retains the broadcast abilities of a bus while permitting high levels of utilization. The YNET's effective throughput is approximately 10 MB/sec.

The APs are the primary interface that the users deal with. Requests are delivered (given) to the APs, which pass them on to the PEs. The PEs parse the requests breaking them down into subrequests, which they then hand off to the AMPs. At this point the AMPs fill each of the subrequests and send the finished subrequests back to the PEs. The PEs manage the subrequests, merging them to finish the request originally delivered by the APs. Once all subrequests of a given request are finished, the PE forwards that information back to the AP. The interface into the application processors is supported for many major platforms, including DOS, Windows, OS/2, Macintosh, and DEC VAX, as well as UNIX.

1.3

EXTENDED CASE STUDIES

1.3.1   The iPSC/2 and iPSC/860

The iPSC/2 and iPSC/860 [5, 12, 40, 43] family of systems is, to date, one of the most commercially successful lines of parallel systems. These systems were based on off-the-shelf microprocessors and are interconnected in a hypercube topology. Both of these systems supported up to 128 nodes connected in a seven-dimensional hypercube and had an i386 based front-end system from which programs were initiated. A block diagram of the iPSC/2 node architecture is shown in Figure 1.31. The primary difference between the iPSC/2 and the iPSC/860 was the CPU used at each node—the former used an i386 processor with an i387 math coprocessor, while the latter used the Intel i860 processor. In addition, the iPSC/860 connected the routing logic to the CPU through a hardware FIFO rather than through the DMA channel shown in the figure. Finally, the iPSC/2 could use an optional vector accelerator board and had an external CPU cache, both unavailable on the iPSC/860.

The largest difference between these systems (as well as other second-generation message passing systems such as the NCUBE-2) and the first generation of message-passing systems (such as the iPSC/1 and the NCUBE-1) was the addition of hardware support for message routing. The direct-connect routing module (DCM) [59] supported the routing of messages through intermediate nodes without increasing the per-byte latency or involving the node's CPU for messages not destined for that node. In the original message-passing systems, messages were sent in a store-and-forward fashion. Thus, each byte contained in a message had to be stored at each hop along a route and forwarded to the next hop. Consider a message consisting of N bytes that must travel a distance D through the network. The total time required before the message can be received in a store-and-forward network will be of the form,

$$T = D * (C1 + C2 * N)$$

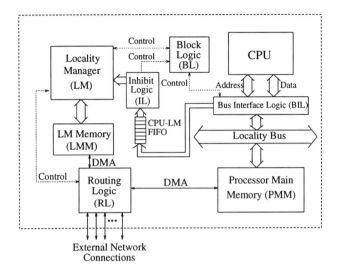

FIGURE 1.31   iPSC/2 PE architecture block diagram.

where $C1$ is a fixed set-up latency required to send a message between two nodes and $C2$ is the internode transfer time per byte. Instead, the DCM created a circuit between message sender and receiver before any data was sent. Then the message was sent directly along the circuit. Thus, while there was still a substantial penalty for additional hops in the start-up overhead, the per-byte latency was mostly unaffected by the distance between communicating nodes. Therefore, the total time required before the message could be received in a DCM network was of the form,

$$T = D * C1 + C2 * N$$

where $C1$ is a per-hop set-up latency for opening a circuit and $C2$ is the internode bandwidth. This greatly reduced the need for considering topology when designing algorithms because the added overhead related to processor distance was negligible in most cases. However, because circuits were maintained throughout message transmission, there was the potential for a substantial delay due to blocked messages [11, 16].

I/O on the iPSC/2 and iPSC/860 was performed through the concurrent file system (CFS). This consisted of a set of i386 nodes attached to individual nodes processing through an extra channel on the DCM. Each of these nodes was connected to a SCSI-based disk with a maximum transfer rate of 1 MB/sec and supported file striping across multiple I/O nodes.

1.3.2   The Thinking Machines CM-5

Thinking Machines Corporation was originally associated with the "data parallel" style of parallel programming. In this style, programs are the same on all processors, but different data is distributed across processors. Further, there is a single thread of control, though each operation within that thread may be replicated among a large number of data elements located at different processors. In the CM-1 and CM-2 [37, 38, 82] this meant using an

SIMD model with many (up to 64 K) small (1-bit) processors to perform the actual computations. These processors were attached by a general-purpose interconnection network (a hypercube and mesh in the CM-1, and only hypercube in the CM-2) with a dynamic router to facilitate communications. While this works well for logical and simple integer data manipulation computations, the 1-bit processor approach provided poor floating point performance. Therefore, to increase the CM-2's appeal to the supercomputing market, up to 2-K optional floating point units were added. The CM-2 was relatively successful. However, its SIMD model, and the way that the floating point units and I/O were attached as an afterthought, limited the scope of computations that could be performed well and made optimization difficult.

Like its predecessors, the CM-5 [74] is tailored to meet the demands of data parallel programs. However, it also implements the more general SPMD model. For this reason, it should be applicable to a broader class of applications that can utilize it as a true MIMD machine for control-parallel tasks. A block diagram of the CM-5 system is shown in Figure 1.32.

The CM-5's computational resources consist of a set of processor nodes (PNs) and a set of control processors (CPs). Each CP can control a partition, the size of these partitions and their assignments to the CPs are set at boot time. A CP controlling a partition is called a *partition manager* (PM). Each PM controls a set of PNs running one or more jobs. Jobs are gang-scheduled and context-switched with an adjustable time quantum. The PNs each consist of a SPARC CPU and four vector units (VUs). Node memory is attached to the VUs so that each VU will have an independent path to its RAM. Each VU has a peak speed of 32 Mflops, giving the PNs a peak speed of over 128 Mflops. A CM-5 can have up to 16-K PNs, though the largest configuration sold as of this writing has only 1024 PNs. The PNs are interconnected via two networks, the *data network* and the *control network.*

The Data Network is a fat-tree topology. In a fat tree [50], nodes are placed at the tree's leaves. Then, as subsequent levels are traversed in the tree, the bandwidth at each level of the tree is increased. Ideally, this should provide a fixed bandwidth regardless of node distance or other network traffic. This is not quite the case on the CM-5, however, because the bandwidth only doubles for the first two levels (though the fan-out is 4). For higher levels, the bandwidth does scale by a factor of 4. Thus, groups of 4 nodes are guaranteed at least 20 MB/sec of bandwidth, groups of 16, 10 MB/sec, and larger groups get at least 5 MB/sec. Further, the bandwidth is increased by increasing the number of wires at each level in the tree, thus, a single message packet cannot use bandwidth greater than that of a single wire. Congestion is reduced by using a random routing strategy which better balances the load among links. The fat tree also has hardware support for context switching. This is performed through a mechanism that allows the tree to be flushed during a context switch and then reloaded when the same job is again activated. The fat tree was chosen because it can support data parallel communication well. Data parallel programs generally communicate through synchronous data permutations involving a large number of one-to-one communication operations between arbitrary nodes. The fat tree performs these well because all of the communication operations will take approximately the same amount of time and the full bandwidth of the network is used. The drawback of the fat tree is that for true MIMD programs, all nodes will almost never use the network simultaneously.

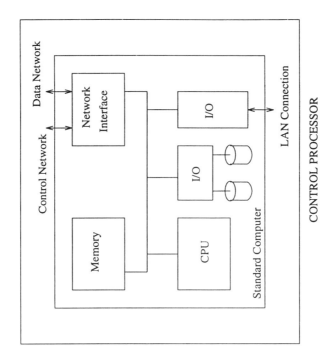

CONTROL PROCESSOR

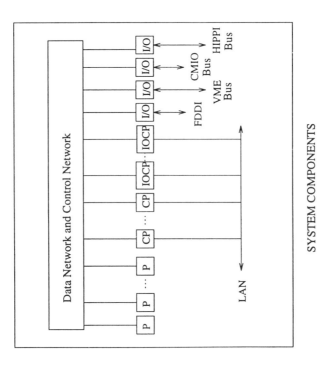

SYSTEM COMPONENTS

FIGURE 1.32   CM-5 architecture block diagram.

Therefore, congestion will be less of a problem, but the bandwidth of the network is limited to that of the slowest link along its path. Thus, the CM-5's network will not perform as well for asynchronous MIMD programs.

As previously described, the CM-5 performs best for tightly synchronous programs. However, being a MIMD machine, its programs will naturally be asynchronous. Therefore, the CM-5 provides a second network for synchronization. The control network attaches the PNs and CPs and is used for operations that require synchronization. It can be used for the barrier synchronization and communication synchronization needed to emulate a SIMD programming model. Further, it can be used for one-to-all, all-to-one, reduction, and combination collective communication operations. It can also be used to trigger and control context switches. When operating in data parallel mode, the control network is used by the PM to maintain the single thread of control model among the PNs as well as for collective communication. In MIMD mode, the control network is used for collective communication and synchronization.

The CM-5's OS is a modified version of SUNOS called CMOST. Most system functionality on the PNs is provided through libraries and works through the PN's PM. The PMs (that is, CPs) are in fact Sun Sparcstation 2s running CMOST. I/O is performed through devices attached directly to the data network or through the PM. The direct network devices include a HiPPI network connection and a Scalable Disk Array (SDA), a set of RAID disks, and controllers. Network I/O devices can be used in synchronous or asynchronous fashion, though synchronous I/O is much faster. I/O operations are still controlled by the CPs, though the actual transfer can be either through the CPs or through the data network. I/O through the CPs is performed using the control network and is much slower than data network I/O.

1.3.3   The KSR1 and KSR2

Examples of NUMA machines are Alewife [1], BBN's Butterfly [17], DASH [51], KSR1 [46], and Tera [2]. In Alewife and DASH, all data is stored at a fixed address in a fixed processor and any migration of data must involve changing a data item's address. Memory latency is reduced by providing a cache at each processor to store copies of frequently used data contained in distant memory modules. In the KSR1 and KSR2 (and in the previously mentioned DDM system), this concept is extended further such that all memory is treated as cache (see Figure 1.33). Thus, data can be bound to a single address and still not be tied to a particular processor's memory. This enables data to be migrated automatically (or manually to take advantage of prefetching) to the local memory of the processor using the data. In addition, multiple processors reading a single data item can obtain individual copies of that data item in their local memory. Programs that exhibit good locality will then be able to have most of their data in local memory. This mechanism also provides a shared-memory model to the programmer and is relatively scalable (to 1088 processors for the KSR1 and 5120 processors for the KSR2). The KSR's memory system is referred to as ALLCACHE memory. Each node consists of a custom processor, an on-chip 256-KB data and 256-KB instruction cache, and 32 MB of local cache memory. The custom CPU includes four cache control units and four cell interconnect units for communicating with other processors. The CPU runs at

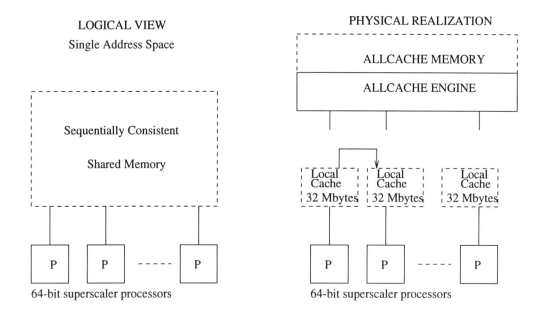

ALLCACHE: Data Moves To The Point Of Reference On Demand. There Is No Fixed Physical Location For An "Address" Within ALLCACHE Memory.

FIGURE 1.33   KSR1 ALLCACHE memory architecture.

a clock speed of 20 MHz for the KSR1 and 40 MHz for the KSR2 and is capable of up to 40 Mflops for the KSR1 or 80 Mflops for the KSR2. Nodes are interconnected in a ring topology of up to 32 nodes making up ALLCACHE Engine:0 (see Figure 1.34). Then, all of the ALLCACHE Engine:0s may be interconnected in a second-level ring to make up an ALLCACHE Engine:1, and in the KSR2 the ALLCACHE Engine:1s can be interconnected to form an ALLCACHE Engine:2. When a cache line is requested, the processor first searches its on-chip and local caches. Then, if it is unavailable locally, a request is sent through the ALLCACHE Engine:0 and if it is not found there, through the ALLCACHE Engine:1, and so on. Normally, when a cache line is read, a copy will be made in the reading processor's cache. In addition, cache lines may be made either *exclusive*, where only a single copy is valid, or *nonexclusive owner*, where only a single processor "owns" a line but multiple copies may be valid. Finally, a cache line may be invalid, where the data contained in the line on a particular processor no longer reflects the current state of that data in the global memory hierarchy. This cache line state is stored in a distributed global directory structure. To enable better program locality, language extensions are available to provide both prefetch and poststore capability.

I/O is handled through a channel located at each node capable of up to 30 MB/sec for the KSR1 and 60 MB/sec for the KSR2. Multiple processors can be used for striped I/O

CACHE ENGINE:0
  Slotted, packetized rotating pipeline
  Packet: 128 Bytes data, 16 Bytes header
  Data Transfer: 8 Megapackets/sec, 1 Gbyte/sec
  Each Cell Interconnect or ARD contributes stages to pipeline
  Multiple packets in flight
  Pipelined directory and data transfer

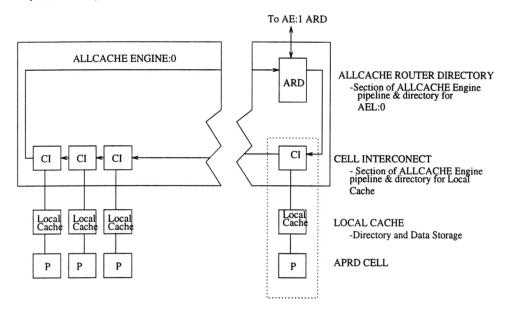

FIGURE 1.34   KSR1 ALLCACHE Engine:0 architecture.

(though this is not currently implemented). There is also a hardware event monitoring unit at each node to facilitate performance monitoring and debugging.

1.3.4   The Intel Paragon

The Intel Paragon is the third-generation product from Intel's Supercomputer Systems Division. A block diagram of a Paragon node is shown in Figure 1.35. It is based on the i860XP processor, an enhanced version of the i860 processor used in the iPSC/860. The system is interconnected in a two-dimensional mesh. Unlike the iPSC/2 and iPSC/860, there is no front-end system. Instead, a portion of the machine (defined dynamically) is set aside as a *service partition*. Nodes in the service partitions act as front-ends and handle compiling, editing, and initiation of programs. Programs are run in the *compute partition*, which can be divided into subpartitions for use by one or more parallel applications. Jobs may also be time-shared within a partition using gang scheduling. I/O is performed through nodes in the *I/O partition*, each of which will have an attached I/O device. Note that there is no physical difference between the nodes in the compute and service partition, and I/O partition nodes only differ in that they have an attached I/O device. Striped disk I/O is

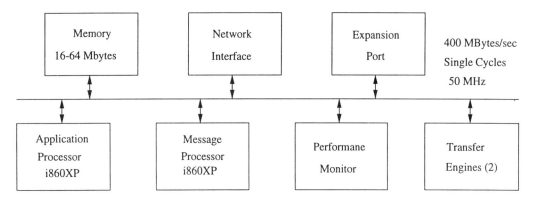

FIGURE 1.35   Paragon node block diagram.

provided through the parallel file systsm (PFS) and files are stored on RAID disk arrays connected to the I/O nodes.

The most striking feature of the Paragon is its communication technology. It uses two approaches to enhance communication performance. First, the Paragon uses a commercialized version of the Caltech mesh routing chip, called the iMRC. This chip is designed to maximize the machines bisection bandwidth by using a small number of connections (four) and driving them at a high bandwidth (175 MB/sec bidirectional). Research has shown that such a system can perform better than higher connectivity networks [19]. These router chips are all connected in an *active backplane* into which node boards are attached. This active backplane makes up a two-dimensional mesh as shown in Figure 1.36. The backplane eliminates wires between adjacent nodes except at cabinet and board boundaries. This increases network reliability and allows for higher bandwidth performance. Backplane slots without nodes simply through-route messages, facilitating the addition or removal of boards (though some software reconfiguration of the operating system, not the network, is generally needed). Unlike the iPSC/860's DCMs, the iMRCs do not create a circuit between sender and receiver. Instead, an initial control message at the start of the message establishes a path through the network and all subsequent data for that message are forwarded along that path. Unlike store-and-forward networks, the message is broken into very small pieces (called *flits*) and the network is pipelined. This is referred to as worm-hole routing due to the way that a message *worms* its way through the system. While there is a start-up overhead related to distance, the entire message is not penalized due to the pipelining. Thus, message transmission time for a worm-hole routed network is of the form:

$$T = C2 * (D - 1) * P + C2 * N$$

where P is the packet size, N is the message length, D is the source to destination distance, and $C2$ is a constant representing the data rate of the network. If P is small relative to N, T will be similar to that for the DCM in that T is not very dependent on D. The primary advantage of such a network is that links need not be blocked for the entire message duration, and it is possible to multiplex messages along individual links.

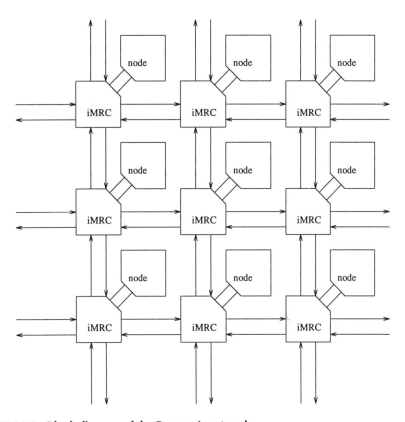

FIGURE 1.36   Block diagram of the Paragon's network.

The second major improvement in communication technology is the addition of a second i860XP at each node to handle communication. This new processor shares memory with the compute processor and handles all communication-related tasks normally handled by the nodes primary CPU except for the actual calls to the send and receive functions. It can handle strided (noncontiguous) data and might also be used to perform communication necessary to provide shared virtual memory. The message processor can alleviate much of the system overhead in the compute CPU and helps it to better utilize its cache. The actual transfer of data from memory to the iMRCs is performed by two DMA transfer engines and does not involve the CPU.

Other than the improvements in communication technology, the Paragon also employs a new operating system technology. Paragon OS builds on top of a new version of the OSF/1 operating system (OSF/1 AD) which is based on the Mach 3.0 microkernel. This allows for full multitasking and virtual memory at all nodes (including those in the compute partition). Further, all system services are available everywhere. OSF/1 is implemented as a swapable server that interfaces with the Mach microkernel. Further, message passing is supported directly in the kernel to enhance performance. This technology greatly increases the capability of the compute nodes, however, its cost in terms of performance and wasted memory is significant.

1.3.5 The Seamless Latency-Tolerant System

This section covers in the greatest level of detail an experimental system being developed by the authors. Its inclusion is provided as a unique example of an architecture designed with the goal of using off-the-shelf components, while still attempting to address the latency tolerance issue being addressed by many other processors in this generation. The presentation aims to be instructive regarding some of the unavoidable problems encountered when trying to balance the above-mentioned goals.

Seamless [26, 27] is a latency-tolerant distributed memory multiprocessor architecture that incorporates an off-the-shelf high-performance RISC processor (for example, Intel's i860) [42]) to form part of each locality (processing element.) The processor is assumed to have an internal instruction cache and data cache with the data cache allowing software flushing and software/hardware invalidation of cache lines. To support communication between processors, each locality utilizes a coprocessor, to independently control communication between localities. Data movement occurs through the routing logic (RL) which is another off-the-shelf component, such as the Intel Direct Connect Module (DCM) [59], the Intel Mesh Routing Chip (iMRC) [41], or the TMC CM5's Network Interface [47], which can control the sending and receiving of data to other localities. The RL also loads data from, or stores data to, the processor main memory (PMM) via DMA.

The Seamless architecture is based on the *data-movement* programming model [24]. In Seamless, the concept of a multicomputer (for example, the iPSC/860 [42, 35], CM5 [74], and NCUBE/2 [61, 76]) is extended by adding a second processor, the locality manager (LM), to each locality.

While the idea of adding a second processor to handle communications is not unique (for example, the Intel Paragon [41]), Seamless interconnects the main CPU to the LM so that communication can be performed transparently to computation. The LM communicates with the CPU by passively detecting events on the address bus. These events indicate to the LM *when* communication operations can occur. The LM can also transparently provide the CPU with data synchronization through a blocking mechanism. Thus the CPU, an unmodified off-the-shelf RISC processor, does not incur the overheads associated with calls to send/receive routines, context switching, or kernel calls that may be needed in other multicomputers. These operations not only consume computational resources, but also impact the cache and pipeline performance of the CPU. Finally, the LM can use event information to prefetch data. If data can be moved prior to its need within the processor, communication latency can be optimally tolerated.

The basic thesis of Seamless is one of leveraging existing components into a multiprocessor architecture. While there are certainly penalties associated with trying to use completely standard, off-the-shelf components for constructing a multiprocessor, *the advantages* cannot be overlooked. The greatest advantage of these is *scalability*. This scalability comes from three sources.

1. As component densities (both processors and memories) become greater, an increasing number of these components can be employed to construct a single computer system.
2. As the workstation market continues to drive the improvement of RISC CPUs, the multiprocessor design that can most rapidly incorporate these improvements into a next-

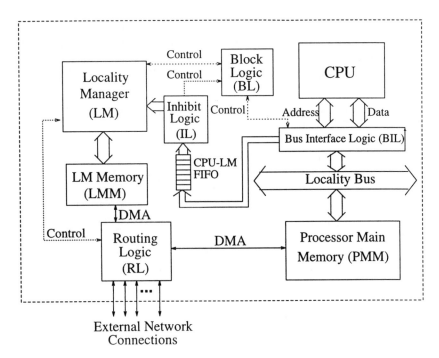

FIGURE 1.37   Seamless locality architecture block diagram.

generation design will benefit most. These improvements cover the areas of the CPU architecture and technology, as well as compiler technology.

3. Finally, as a second market (for example, workstations) is driving the development of CPUs, the cost of these components will comprise a smaller part of overall cost of parallel systems.

Basic Architecture Components   The Seamless locality architecture [27] can viewed as a derivative of machines such as Intel's second-generation multiprocessor, the iPSC/2 [12], which is shown in Figure 1.30. The Seamless architecture, in Figure 1.37, differs from the iPSC/2 generally by the addition of the locality manager and some other associated logic. The major elements of a Seamless locality include the CPU, the processor main memory (PMM), the routing logic (RL), and the locality manager (LM). The CPU is an unmodified, off-the-shelf, high-performance RISC processor that fetches all instructions and data from the processor main memory (PMM). The CPU is also assumed to have an internal cache, which may be divided into separate instruction and data portions, where the data-cache allows software flushing of individual cache lines.

Data movement occurs through the routing logic (RL). The RL is an off-the-shelf component such as the Intel Direct Connect Module (DCM) [59], or the Intel Mesh Routing Chip (iMRC) [41]. The RL controls the sending or receiving of data through the network, and can load data from, or store data to the PMM through a DMA channel. The RL can also act as a router for data to the other localities. The topology connecting the RLs in

Seamless may be any single or multistage network, but is not considered a crucial issue to the Seamless architecture. The basic RL operations are sending a request message to another RL, receiving an item from an RL and placing it either in the PMM or the LM memory (LMM), and sending an item from the PMM to another RL.

The Locality Manager and CPU Events   The LM is an event-driven device. It is controlled by CPU events arriving in the CPU-LM FIFO and by RL events. The main task of the LM is to manage communication among localities, that is, giving directions to the RL regarding the sending and receiving of messages. The basic idea is that the LM executes the communication operations that the CPU would have had to perform in a more conventional implementation such as the iPSC/2. In a sense, the LM knows *what* to do, but it needs to be told *when* to do it. The CPU events arriving via the CPU-LM FIFO perform this duty.

A user-specified task to be performed by the LM is completely described by the ordered triple (V, T, C). V is a variable reference, T is a tag, and C is the code to be executed by the LM when a tagged reference has occurred. With the notion of a tag, multiple-LM actions can be mapped to a single variable and multiple variables can be mapped to the same LM action. To specify an LM task, the programmer must tag a particular variable reference in the source code. This tagged reference will generate a CPU event consisting of the ordered pair (V, T). The LM is responsible for mapping this event to the proper LM task (C). Variables that may be tagged must be declared to be of storage class *taggable*.

Memory Reference Model   Events are generated when references to taggable variables are "tagged." Two major classes of variable references exist. These are:

1. *Asynchronous References*, which represent references to ordinary program variables; and
2. *Synchronous References*, which are references to those variables declared as taggable. Further, synchronous references are divided into two subclasses. These subclasses are:

   a. *Untagged* synchronous references, which are references that are not tagged; and

   b. *Tagged* synchronous references, which are those references that are tagged.

Note that a taggable variable may be referenced in untagged as well as tagged fashion. However, both are synchronous references. Synchronous references are distinct from asynchronous references because they have different cache management and synchronization constraints than that of the asynchronous references.

To identify a reference as tagged-synchronous, untagged-synchronous, or asynchronous, the CPU's address lines are divided logically into two fields, the *physical address* and the *tag*, as illustrated in Figure 1.38.The physical address is the actual address of the variable in the PMM and the tag specifies the class of the variable reference. The tag field can also identify, for the LM, which event is to be processed and whether or not the event is a *data event*. (A data event is an event type that not only passes V and T to the LM, but also the data being written to or read from the PMM.) The number of bits in these two fields is an implementation-dependent parameter. Therefore, the address used for an untagged-synchronous reference, and each of the possible addresses for a tagged-

CPU Address

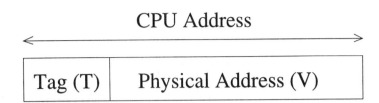

Tag (T)	Physical Address (V)

FIGURE 1.38   Logical mapping of CPU address lines.

synchronous reference, to a taggable variable appear different to the CPU, but they in fact represent the same physical address in the PMM.

Inter-Locality Communication Support   Seamless is able to overlap communication with computation among its localities by distinguishing transient variables from purely local variables. Transient variables are referred to as synchronous; purely local variables are referred to as asynchronous.

The two communication operations the LM can perform are the *request* and the *release* of Synchronous variables. The *request/release* mechanism can be thought of as being similar to prefetching in shared-memory machines such as the KSR1 [46]. The added constraints to this are that all data must be prefetched (that is, there is no hardware/software mechanism for automatically loading remote data into local memory) and management of local data must be done in software. *Request* specifies the remote locality along with the remote and local addresses of the synchronous variable. *Release* specifies the local address of the synchronous variable. The LM is driven by tagged synchronous references that the BIL detects, but the BIL can only interpret these references as *tagged load* or *tagged store* references. Therefore it is the responsibility of the LM to decipher the tag associated with the synchronous address so that it can perform the required communication operation on the variable. The LM also manages the setting and clearing of *blocking bits* in the BL.

The classification of references into synchronous and asynchronous is also needed to maintain a coherent memory hierarchy. The PMM must be partitioned into synchronous and asynchronous memory regions (also referred to as *taggable* and *nontaggable*). Since tagged synchronous references must be observable to the BIL and the LM, they may not be cached. Untagged synchronous references may be cached, but since an untagged synchronous reference and a tagged synchronous reference to the same physical location have different CPU addresses, a potential coherency problem exists.

CPU-LM Interface Details   The *bus interface logic* (BIL) is a passive device located between the CPU and the locality bus. The BIL monitors the tag field of the CPU's address lines and performs one of three functions. First, if an asynchronous reference is detected, the BIL passes that variable to the locality bus with the tag field cleared. Second, if a tagged-synchronous reference is detected, the address and tag are placed in the CPU-LM FIFO. If the event is a data event, then the data is also placed in the FIFO. Third, the BIL communicates with the blocking logic.

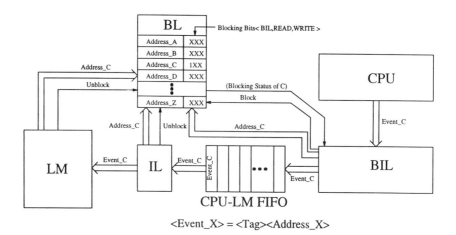

$$\text{<Event\_X> = <Tag><Address\_X>}$$

FIGURE 1.39   CPU Event Execution Path.

The *blocking logic* (BL) is a content addressable memory that *logically* contains synchronization bits for every taggable word in the PMM, similar to the full/empty bits in HEP, Horizon, and Tera [2, 49, 72]. These bits are used to implement the synchronization semantics of references to variables involved in communication. When the BIL detects a synchronous reference, it checks the BL for the blocking status of that reference. If the reference is not blocked, then the CPU may proceed. If the reference is blocked, then the CPU has to wait until the blocking is resolved. Note that this hardware blocking is possible only because a single process is permitted on each CPU. The BL maintains three blocking bits associated with each taggable variable. These bits are the `read`, `write`, and BIL bits. The BIL bit is set when an event is forwarded, by the BIL, to the CPU-LM FIFO and reset when the LM, or IL (described below) finishes processing the event. The other two bits are synchronization bits used to block loads or stores due to pending communication operations.

Between the CPU-LM FIFO and the LM is the *inhibit logic* (IL). The motivation for this component comes from the perceived need to filter events being sent to the LM. The IL filters events based on their tag and address fields so the LM need not be overburdened with events not actually requiring an action on the part of the LM. The IL can only filter events at the head of the event queue because the IL may be set or reset by LM tasks performed in response to events currently in the CPU-LM FIFO. After filtering an event, the IL must clear the BIL bit in the BL that was set by the BIL when the event entered the CPU-LM FIFO. The IL's filters are set by the *inhibit* command in the LM code.

To illustrate the path of CPU events, consider the generation of a tagged synchronous reference by the CPU, for example, Event_C in Figure 1.39. The BIL passes the physical address of Event_C, for example, Address_C, to the BL to determine its blocking status. If Address_C is blocked, the BIL will suspend the current CPU memory access operation until Address_C is unblocked. After the BL indicates to the BIL that Address_C is unblocked, Event_C is sent to the CPU-LM FIFO and the BIL's block bit for Address_C will be asserted in the BL. Once the event reaches the head of the CPU-LM FIFO, it is surveyed by the IL. If Event_C is resident in the IL, then the IL will send Address_C, and an unblock signal, to the

BL. If Event_C is not resident in the IL, the event is removed from the CPU-LM FIFO by the IL, and passed on to the LM which then proceeds with the processing of the event. The LM code segment must then set either the `read` or `write` bit in the BL (to block reading or writing, depending on what operation is to be performed on the data being referenced) and clear the BIL bit. Following the processing of Event_C, the LM resets the `read` or `write` bit in the BL and the BIL resumes examination of the CPU bus.

1.4

CONCLUSION

This chapter overviewed many conributions to parallel computer architecture to date. As with many of the other topics in this volume, the subjects covered are vast, and the space available for describing them was small. In this chapter, an attempt to balance survey and depth was attempted via a mixture of brief summary descriptions of many architectures, and then a more in-depth study of some critical design issues in a contemporary research architecture—Seamless.

Designing a parallel machine that is also efficiently programmed is far from an achieved goal. In fact, while they were not directly addressed here, the issues of language, compiler, and operating system design are not separable from hardware design. However, the scope of this chapter has been primarily that of hardware design alternatives—past, present, and future.

ACKNOWLEDGEMENTS

The authors wish to gratefully thank Terry A. Braun, Richard D. Dietz, and Todd A. Scheetz for their valuable contributions in proofreading and editing the final version of this chapter.

Bibliography

1. A. Agarwal et al., "The MIT Alewife Machine: A Large Scale Distributed Memory Multi-processor," Tech. Report MIT/LCS TM-454, Massachusetts Institute of Technology, 1991.
2. R. Alverson et al., "The Tera Computer System," *Proc. 1990 Int'l Conf. Supercomputing*, IEEE CS Press, Los Alamitos, Calif., 1990, pp. 1–6.
3. G. Almasi and A. Gottlieb, *Highly Parallel Computing*, Benjamin/Cummings Publishing, Redwood City, Calif., 1989.
4. Alliant, *FX/2800 Series System Description*, Alliant Computer Systems Corporation, Littleton, Mass., Aug. 1991.
5. R. Arlauskas, "iPSC/2 System: A Second Generation Hypercube," *3rd Conf. Hypercube Concurrent Computers and Applications*, 1988, pp. 38–42.
6. G. Astfalk, "Convex's View of TFLOPS computing," *Proc. Int'l Conf. Parallel Computing and Transputer Applications '92*, 1992.

7. G.H. Barnes et al., "The Illiac IV Computer," *IEEE Trans. Computers*, Vol. C-17, Aug. 1968, pp. 746–757.

8. K.E. Batcher, "Design of a Massively Parallel Processor," *IEEE Trans. Computers*, Vol. C-29, Sept. 1980, pp. 836–844.

9. W. Bez, "Cenju-3: A Parallel Computer for Research from NEC Corporation," *Proc. Supercomputer '93*, Springer-Verlag, Heidelberg, Germany, 1993.

10. D.L. Bright et al., "Critical Performance Path Analysis, and Efficient Code Generation Issues, for the Seamless Architecture," *Proc. 7th Int'l Parallel Processing Symp.*, 1993, pp. 590–596.

11. D.M. Clarka and T.L. Casavant, "Effects of Contention on Cut-through/Wormhole Routed Multicomputers," University of Iowa, Dept. of ECE Tech. Report, Aug. 1991.

12. P. Close, "The iPSC/2 Node Architecture," *Proc. 3rd Conf. Hypercube Concurrent Computers and Applications*, 1988, pp. 43–50.

13. R.P. Colwell et al., "A VLIW Architecture for a Trace Scheduling Compiler," *IEEE Trans. Computers*, Aug. 1988, pp. 967–979.

14. Cray Research, "Cray T3D Software Overview," Tech. Note SN-2505 1.0, Cray Research, Inc., 1992.

15. Cray Research, "Cray T3D Software Overview," Tech. Note SN-2505 1.1, Cray Research, Inc., 1993.

16. S. Chittor and R. Enbody, "Predicting the Effect of Mapping on the Communication Performance of Large Multicomputers," *Proc. 1991 Int'l Conf. Parallel Processing*, The Pennsylvania State Univ., University Park, Penn., 1991, pp. II–1–4.

17. W. Crowther et al., "Performance Measurements on a 128-node Butterfly Parallel Processor," *Proc. 1985 Int'l Conf. Parallel Processing*, IEEE CS Press, Los Alamitos, Calif., 1985, pp. 531–540.

18. W.J. Dally et al., "The J-machine: A Fine-Grained Concurrent Computer," *Proc. Information Processing'89*, Elsevier Science Publishers, Amsterdam, the Netherlands, 1989, pp. 1147–1153.

19. W.J. Dally, "Performance Analysis of k-ary n-cube Interconnection Networks," *IEEE Trans. Computers*, Vol. C-39, June 1990, pp. 775–785.

20. W.J. Dally et al., "The Message-Driven Processor: A Multicomputer Processing Node with Efficient Mechanisms," *IEEE Micro*, Vol. 12, No. 2, April 1992, pp. 23–38.

21. R.L. Davis, "The ILLIAC IV Processing Element," *IEEE Trans. Computers*, Vol. C-18, Sept. 1969, pp. 800–816.

22. H.G. Dietz and T. Schwederski, "Extending Static Synchronization Beyond SIMD and VLIW," Tech. Report TR-EE 88-25, Purdue University School of Electrical Engineering, June 1988.

23. J. Dongarra, *Experimental Parallel Computing Architectures*, Elsevier Science Publishing Company, Inc., New York, N.Y., 1987.

24. S.A. Fineberg and T.L. Casavant, "The Seamless Approach to Reconciling Communication and Locality in Distributed Memory Parallel Systems," *Proc. 6th Int'l Parallel Processing Symp.* IEEE CS Press, Los Alamitos, Calif., 1992, pp. 51–56.

25. S.A. Fineberg, T.L. Casavant, and B.H. Pease, "A Preliminary Performance Evaluation of the Seamless Parallel Processing System Architecture," *Proc. 1992 Int'l Conf. Parallel Processing*, CRC Press, Boca Raton, Fl., 1992, pp. 280–284.

26. S.A. Fineberg and T.L. Casavant, "Seamless—A Latency-Tolerant, RISC-based, Multiprocessor Architecture," *Proc. 19th Int'l Symp. Computer Architecture*, ACM Press, New York, N.Y., 1992, p. 432.

27. S.A. Fineberg, T.L. Casavant, and B.H. Pease, "Hardware Support for the Seamless Programming Model," *Proc. 4th Symp. Frontiers of Massively Parallel Computation*, IEEE CS Press, Los Alamitos, Calif., 1992, pp. 353–360.

28. C.C. Foster and E.M. Riseman, "Percolation of Code to Enhance Parallel Dispatching and Execution," *IEEE Trans. Computers*, Vol. C-21, 1972, pp. 1411–1415.

29. A. Fredericks, IBM PPS Marketing Support, personal correspondence, Aug. 3, 1994.

30. R. Garner et al., "Scaleable Processor Architecture (SPARC)," *Proc. COMPCON*, IEEE CS Press, Los Alamitos, Calif., 1988, pp. 278–283.

31. R. Geisen and F. Langhammer, "The Parsytec GC/PowerPlus Massively Parallel Computer (mpp)," *Proc. Supercomputer '94*, Springer Verlag, Heidelberg, Germany, 1994.

32. W.K. Giloi, "From SUPRENUM to MANNA and META—Parallel Computer Development at GMD FIRST," *Proc. Supercomputer '94*, Springer Verlag, Heidelberg, Germany, 1994.

33. A. Gottlieb et al., "The NYU Ultracomputer—Designing an MIMD Shared Memory Parallel Computer," *IEEE Trans. Computers*, Feb. 1983, pp. 175–189.

34. E. Hagersten, A. Landin, and S. Haridi, "DDM—A Cache-only Memory Architecture," *Computer*, Vol. 25, Sept. 1992, pp. 44–54.

35. M.T. Heath, G.A. Geist, and J.B. Drake, "Early Experiences with the Intel iPSC/860 at Oak Ridge National Laboratory," Tech. Report ORNL/TM-11655, ORNL, 1990.

36. S. Hiranandani, K. Kennedy, and C. Tseng, "Compiler Optimizations for Fortran D on MIMD Distributed-Memory Machines," *Proc. Int'l Conf. Supercomputing*, IEEE CS Press, Los Alamitos, Calif., 1991, pp. 86–100.

37. W.D. Hillis, *The Connection Machine*, MIT Press, Cambridge, Mass., 1985.

38. W.D. Hillis, "The Connection Machine," *Scientific American*, Vol. 256, June 1987, pp. 108–115.

39. K. Hwang, *Advanced Computer Architecture: Parallelism, Scalability, Programmability*, McGraw-Hill, Inc., New York, N.Y., 1993.

40. Intel Scientific Computers, "The Intel iPSC/2 System," *Proc. 3rd Conf. Hypercube Concurrent Computers and Applications*, 1988, pp. 843–846.

41. Intel, *Paragon XP/S Product Overview*, Intel Corporation, Supercomputer Systems Division, Beaverton, Ore., 1991.

42. Intel, *i860 XP Microprocessor Data Book*, Intel Corporation, Santa Clara, Calif., 1991.

43. Intel Supercomputer Systems Division, *iPSC/2 and iPSC/860 User's Guide*, Intel Corporation, Beaverton, Ore., 1991.

44. Ïshihata et al., "CAP-II Architecture," Tech. report, Fujitsu Laboratories LTD., 1991.

45. M. Katevenis, "Reduced Instruction Set Computer Architectures for VLSI," MIT Press, Cambridge, Mass., 1985.

46. Kendall Square Research, *Tech. Summary*, Kendall Square Research Corporation, 1992.

47. A. Klietz, "The Hitchhiker's Guide to the CM-5," Minnesota Supercomputing Center, Apr. 1992.

48. J. Konicek et al., "The Organization of the Cedar System," *Proc. 1991 Int'l Conf. Parallel Processing*, CRC Press, Boca Raton, Fl., 1991, pp. I-49–56.

49. J.T. Kuehn and B.J. Smith, "The Horizon Supercomputer System: Architecture and Software," *Proc. Supercomputing' 88*, IEEE CS Press, Los Alamitos, Calif., 1988, pp. 28–34.

50. C.E. Leiserson, "Fat-trees, Universal Networks for Hardware-Efficient Supercomputing," *IEEE Trans. Computers*, Vol. C-34, No. 10, Oct. 1985, pp. 892–901.

51. D. Lenoski et al., "The Stanford Dash Multiprocessor," *Computer*, Mar. 1992, pp. 63–79.

52. S.F. Lundstrom and G.H. Barnes, "A Controllable MIMD Architecture," *Proc. 1980 Int'l Conf. Parallel Processing*, IEEE CS Press, Los Alamitos, Calif., 1980, pp. 165–173.

53. MasPar Computer Corporation, "The Design of the MasPar MP-2: A Cost Effective Massively Parallel Computer," MasPar Computer Corporation, Report Number MP/P-11.92, 1992.

54. Meiko, "Computing Surface: CS-2 Product Description," Meiko, 1993.

55. K. Miura, "VPP500 Supercomputing System," *Proc. Supercomputer '93*, Springer Verlag, Heidelberg, Germany, 1993.

56. C.R. Moore, "The PowerPC 601 Microprocessor," *Proc. COMPCON 1993*, IEEE CS Press, Los Alamitos, Calif., 1993, pp. 109–116.

57. NCUBE, *NCUBE 2 Systems: Tech. Overview*, NCUBE Corporation, 1992.

58. S. Nelson, *Notes from the NAS Distinguished Speakers Colloquium*, July 1993.

59. S.F. Nugent, "The iPSC/2 Direct-Connect Communications Technology," *Proc. 3rd Conf. Hypercube Concurrent Computers and Applications*, 1988, pp. 51–60.

60. G.M. Papadopoulus and D.E. Culler, "Monsoon: An Explicit Token-Store Architecture," *Proc. Int'l Symp. Computer Architecture*, IEEE CS Press, Los Alamitos, Calif., 1990, pp. 82–91.

61. J.F. Palmer, "The NCUBE Family of High-performance Parallel Computer Systems," *Proc. 3rd Conf. Hypercube Concurrent Computers and Applications*, 1988, pp. 847–851.

62. T. Schwederski et al., "Design and Implementation of the PASM Prototype Control Hierarchy," *Proc. 2nd Int'l Supercomputing Conf.*, IEEE CS Press, Los Alamitos, Calif., 1987, pp. 418–427.

63. C.L. Seitz, "The Cosmic Cube," *Comm. ACM*, Jan. 1985, pp. 22–23.

64. M.C. Sejnowski et al., "An Overview of the Texas Reconfigurable Array Computer," *AFIPS Nat'l Computer Conference*, AFIPS Press, Reston, Va., 1980, pp. 631–641.

65. Sequent, *Balance 21000 System Description*, Sequent Computer Systems Corporation, Littleton, Mass., July 1988.

66. Sequent, *Symmetry System Description*, Sequent Computer Systems Corporation, Littleton, Mass., Aug. 1990.

67. H.J. Siegel, *Interconnection Networks for Large-Scale Parallel Processing: Theory and Case Studies., Second Edition.* McGraw-Hill, New York, N.Y., 1990.

68. H.J. Siegel, J.B. Armstrong, and D.W. Watson, "Mapping Computer-Vision-Related Tasks onto Reconfigurable Parallel-Processing Systems," *Computer*, Special Issue on Parallel Processing for Computer Vision and Image Understanding, Vol. 25, No. 2, Feb. 1992, pp. 54–63.

69. H.J. Siegel, W.G. Nation, and M.D. Allemang, "The Organization of the PASM Reconfigurable Parallel Processing System," *Proc. 1990 Parallel Computing Workshop*, 1990, pp. 1–12.

70. H.J. Siegel et al., "PASM: A Partitionable SIMD/MIMD System for Image Processing and Pattern Recognition," *IEEE Trans. Computers*, Vol. C-30, Dec. 1981, pp. 934–947.

71. B.J. Smith, "A Pipelined, Shared Resource MIMD Computer," *Proc. Int'l Conf. Parallel Processing*, IEEE CS Press, Los Alamitos, Calif., 1978, pp. 6–8.

72. B.J. Smith, "Architecture and Applications of the HEP Multiprocessor System," SPIE, Vol. 298, *Real-Time Signal Processing IV*, 1981, pp. 241–248.

73. B. Smith, "The Tera MTA Computer System," *Proc. Supercomputer '94*, Springer Verlag, Heidelberg, Germany, 1994.

74. Thinking Machines, *CM5 Technical Summary*, Thinking Machines Corporation, Cambridge, Mass., Oct. 1991.

75. G.S. Tjaden and M.J. Flynn, "Detection and Parallel Execution of Independent Instructions," *IEEE Trans. Computers*, Oct. 1970, pp. 889–895.

76. P.C. Trott, *NCUBE 6400 Processor Manual*, NCUBE Corporation, Beaverton, Ore., 1989.

77. L.W. Tucker and G.G. Robertson, "Architecture and Applications of the Connection Machine," *Computer*, Vol. 21, No. 8, Aug. 1988, pp. 26–38.

78. S. Wallach, *Notes from the Parallel Processing Connection Meeting*, Aug. 1993.

79. S. Wallach, "SPP-1," *Proc. Supercomputer '93*, Springer Verlag, Heidelberg, Germany, 1993.

80. S. Wallach, "The Exemplar Series," *Proc. Supercomputer '94*, Springer Verlag, Heidelberg, Germany, 1994.

81. I. Watson and J. Gurd, "A Practical Data Flow Computer," *Computer*, Vol. 15, No. 2, Feb. 1982, pp. 51–57.

82. S.A. Zenios and R.A. Lasken, "The Connection Machines CM-1 and CM-2: Solving Nonlinear Network Problems," *Proc. 1988 Int'l Conf. Supercomputing*, IEEE CS Press, Los Alamitos, Calif., 1988, pp. 648–658.

CHAPTER 2

DATA-DRIVEN AND MULTITHREADED ARCHITECTURES FOR HIGH-PERFORMANCE COMPUTING

Jean-Luc Gaudiot and Chinhyun Kim
Electrical Engineering-Systems
University of Southern California
Los Angeles, California 90089

Abstract. *Although there seems to be a general agreement among researchers that parallel computing is the most practical means to satisfy the ever-increasing desire for higher computing power, the question of how to design and program large parallel machines remains. One actively pursued approach is the data-driven computation model. This is a radical departure from the traditional approach based on the von Neumann or control-driven computation model. The justification for this new technique is the inherently parallel nature of the model which makes it a good paradigm for parallel computation. However, it has been learned over the years that implementing a machine based on the data-driven model is not an easy task. In order to succeed, many issues need to be investigated at every level, in other words, algorithm, language, compiler, and machine architecture. This paper discusses past and present research efforts of the dataflow community all aimed at implementing high-performance computing systems.*

2.1

INTRODUCTION

Problems of programmability and design of parallel processors can be found to have their root in the model of execution both in its implementation and in its reflection in high-level languages. We will now contrast the features of the conventional model with that of the functional model.

2.1.1 The von Neumann Model

Despite the fact that a large number of parallel computers are available today, parallel computing is still a reality for only a very small group of people. One of the main reasons for this is the difficulty of efficient parallel programming. Indeed, writing a parallel program, at least in the current programming style, is an arduous job even for an expert programmer. The cause of this difficulty is the von Neumann execution model [7] which lies at the heart of most programming languages.

The simplicity of the von Neumann execution model makes it a good paradigm for modeling processors. Indeed, most existing processors are based on this computation model with various hardware optimization techniques built-in for faster execution. Incidentally, the most common techniques are the pipelining and the multiple instruction issue techniques used in many RISC processors. The justification for adopting the von Neumann model by many programming languages is most often efficiency. In other words, a compiler is likely to generate a more efficient code from such languages than it would from a language based on some other computation model. Unfortunately, a language based on the von Neumann model does not migrate well to a multiprocessor environment.

The problem is the mismatch between the computation model reflected in the programming language and the changed computing environment which is no longer sequential. Automatic parallelization of programs written in such languages is very difficult because much of the parallelism existing in the original algorithm is lost during the programming phase. Attempts to automatically parallelize existing programs are still encountering some serious challenges [9, 35]. A common approach practiced currently by most parallel computer vendors is to provide existing languages, such as C and Fortran, with various directives and extensions to specify parallel computations [48].

In many respects, current parallel programming practice is in some cases analogous to the early days of sequential computing when most programs were written in assembly languages. To write a program in an assembly language, a programmer must first understand the architecture and the execution mechanism of the target machine. Indeed, an understanding of the assembly language exactly implies the understanding of these points. Likewise, programming a parallel computer requires the understanding of various aspects of the machine architecture. For example, programming a computer whose architecture is based on the SIMD model is quite different from programming a machine based on the MIMD model. Even among MIMD computers, programming styles are much different in shared-memory machines and in distributed-memory machines that use message passing.

This kind of programming style is not desirable for the same reason that assembly language programming is not desirable. First, software development is difficult because in addition to understanding the algorithm that needs to be implemented, a programmer must be concerned with the low-level machine specifics. Second, once it is written, porting a program to a machine with a different architecture virtually means rewriting the whole program. In the same manner, parallel computing will not succeed until an application programmer is unburdened from the low-level machine specifics.

2.1.2   The Data-driven Model

In the data-driven model, there is no concept of memory as used in the von Neumann model. The concept of memory in the von Neumann model introduces states in which every update of a memory location implies a state transition. This *state-driven* nature of the von Neumann model makes it a sequential model. In the data-driven model, a piece of data is not represented as a static entity (memory) whose value can be updated time after time. Instead, it is a dynamic entity which is produced once and consumed once by instructions. A value produced by an instruction is valid only until it is consumed by another instruction.

In the data-driven model, a program is represented as a directed acyclic graph in which nodes represent instructions and the edges represent the data dependency relationship between the connected nodes. A data element produced by a node flows on the outgoing edge(s) to the connected node(s) for consumption. Node executability is determined by the *firing rule*, which says that a node can be scheduled for execution if and only if its input data become valid for consumption. In this computing abstraction, every node is purely functional in that it causes no side-effect. Also, computation is inherently parallel and asynchronous since any number of nodes can be executed as long as their input data become valid (see Figure 2.1).

There are two different modes of data-driven execution. The first is the *static* model pioneered by Dennis [17]. The name *static* corresponds to the fact that at any given moment, there can only be a single active instance of a node. In terms of a dataflow graph as shown in Figure 2.1, it means that only a single data token can exist on an edge. Although this simple model synthesizes quite nicely into a machine architecture, it is not flexible enough to handle execution mechanisms like recursions modern languages support.

The other execution mechanism is the *dynamic* model pioneered independently by [4] and [57]. This is a more flexible execution mechanism, which allows multiple tokens

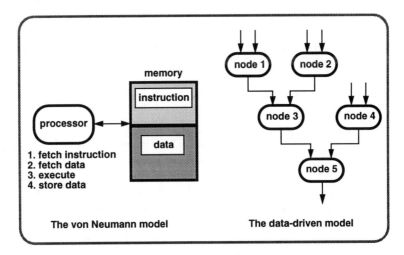

FIGURE 2.1 In the von Neumann model, a piece of processor sequentially fetches instructions and data from memory for execution. In the data-driven execution model, a program is represented as a graph in which nodes can be viewed as virtual processors. They execute as soon as the input operands become available on the input edges.

to exist concurrently on an edge. In order to distinguish tokens that belong to different instances of a node, a tag field containing some unique identifier is added to a token. Thus a set of input tokens belonging to the same instance of a node can be identified through tag matching. While this model is more powerful than the static model, it is also more difficult to implement. For instance, in order to schedule executable nodes as fast as possible, the token matching must be very fast. As will be discussed later, token matching is one of the most important functions of the dynamic dataflow architectures.

At this point, we can envision the following general strategy for parallel computing:

1. Adopt a new high-level programming language based on the data-driven model, which enables a compiler to extract all existing parallelism from a program and represent them in a data dependency graph. This overcomes the first barrier of parallel computing, the extraction of parallelism at compile-time.

2. Develop a new architecture that can efficiently exploit at runtime the parallelism extracted by the compiler. Indeed, conventional von Neumann processors are highly optimized for executing a sequential stream of instructions and are not suitable for executing the data dependency graph according to the firing rule.

Using this strategy, computation and communication can be successfully overlapped to hide high latencies, which is the bane of multiprocessor machines [5]. In conventional parallel machines based on von Neumann processors, a processor idles when read operations are initiated. This can reduce processor utilization, which in turn reduces the overall performance when the data is not in the register or cache memory. Indeed, latency reduction via caching is the conventional approach. However, this is a very difficult problem since dynamic program behavior in a multiprocessor environment is not well understood.

The alternate approach is to provide an execution model that is fundamentally robust against high latencies. The data-driven approach chooses the latter solution by providing an asynchronous execution model that can change context quickly. Thus, whenever a remote read that may incur high latency is executed, the processor switches context and executes other ready instructions instead of waiting for the read operation to complete. Although the data-driven execution model is asynchronous, it has also been successfully adapted to signal processing applications that execute in a synchronous fashion [39].

In this section, the motivations and the basic mechanisms of the data-driven approach have been discussed. In section two, we discuss the development of functional languages for the data-driven execution model. In sections three and four, we describe the past and present work towards achieving high-performance parallel computing based on the data-driven strategy. We will see that although the basic principle of the computation model has not changed, the machine architecture has gone through major changes. Starting from an architecture that is radically different from the conventional von Neumann architecture, it has gradually evolved to include many features of the von Neumann processor. Also, we will see that the compiler has gradually come to play a key role in the overall solution. In the beginning, its role was shadowed by the emphasis given to the architecture mechanisms. In section five, we discuss two implementations of functional languages on conventional parallel machines. Finally, we discuss issues that require further investigation.

2.2

HIGH-LEVEL LANGUAGES FOR IMPLICIT PARALLELISM

It would be best if the programs written in existing imperative languages could be directly transformed into fine-grain data dependency graphs. As of now, such efforts have not been successful. There are two notable languages developed mainly for the data-driven execution model. They are Id (Irvine Dataflow language) [42] and SISAL (Streams and Iterations in a Single Assignment Language) [41]. The Id language development originally started at the University of California at Irvine and was subsequently moved to MIT. The SISAL language development was a collaboration of a number of organizations which included Colorado State University, Digital Equipment Corporation, Lawrence Livermore National Laboratory, and University of Manchester.

Id was designed as a general purpose functional language, suitable for both scientific and symbolic applications. It has characteristics also found in other modern functional languages such as higher-order functions, polymorphism, nonstrict semantics, user-defined abstract data types, and so on [19, 44]. One unique feature of Id, however, is I-Structures. The main usage for I-Structures is to handle structured data such as arrays. Functionality of the structure is guaranteed by the write-once-read-multiple semantics. I-Structures provide nonstrictness which can increase parallelism by overlapping the operations of the producer and the consumer [6].

The SISAL language is developed mainly for scientific applications [21, 22, 47, 51]. It does not allow higher order functions or polymorphism. Unlike some other functional languages that only provide recursion, SISAL provides loop constructs, which are more appropriate when the number of iterations is known. Two types of loop constructs are provided. One is a sequential loop construct (nonproduct form) used when the loop-carried dependencies exist. The other is a parallel loop construct (product form), which is used when the iterations are totally independent from each other. Unlike Id, SISAL does not take a position on the strictness of the language. Instead, this is left as an implementation-level issue.

We now introduce some SISAL program structures for comparison. Unlike imperative languages, SISAL program structures are expressions with inputs and outputs. Because program structures are treated as expressions, the whole program structure can be bound to a name. An example is given in Figure 2.2, which shows equivalent C and SISAL program statements. In C, the `if-else` statement is a control-flow statement in which any variable binding is possible within each clause. In SISAL, on the other hand, because the whole `if-else` expression is bound to a set of one or more values, the data types and the arity of the value(s) produced within each clause must be same. In the first example, the `if` program structure returns values of arity two. The second example shows the case in which the `if` structure is treated as an expression.

In SISAL, variables cannot be arbitrarily introduced with assignment statements as in imperative languages. When new values need to be introduced, the `let` program structure is used as shown in Figure 2.3. The first part of the `let` structure is used to declare and define one or more value names. The actual computations using the declared values (and other values that are already defined in the outer scope) are specified in the second part of

```
if (i >= j) {                    Large, Small := if (i >= j) then
    Large = i;                                      i, j
    Small = j;                                    else
}                                                   j, i
else {                =>                          end if;
    Large = j;
    Small = i;
}

if (add)                         Fval := if (add) then a + b
    Val = a + b;                          else
else                  =>                   a - b
    Val = a - b;                          end if * C;

Fval = Val * C;

C program statements             SISAL program statements
```

FIGURE 2.2   Examples of the SISAL `if` program structure.

```
X = P + 3.7;                     XtimesY := let
Y = Q + 2.4;                              X := P + 3.7;
                                          Y := Q + 2.4
XtimesY = X * Y;      =>          in
                                          X * Y
                                 end let;

C program statements             SISAL program statements
```

FIGURE 2.3   In SISAL, `let` program structure is used for declaring new values.

the `let` structure. In the example, value names X and Y are declared in the `let` structure. The value returned by the structure is the product of X and Y, and the values P and Q are assumed to be already defined in the outer scope.

As previously mentioned, SISAL provides two types of loop structures. The nonproduct form is used when the loop carried dependencies exist. The example given in Figure 2.4 is that of histogramming, which counts the frequency of some events. Because the content of the array subscript `digit[i]` is not known, the loop must be assumed to contain loop carried dependencies. In the SISAL version, a value name `Histo` is bound to the nonproduct form loop structure. The structure consists of the value initialization part, which is similar to the value declaration part of the `let` structure. In the main loop body, the array `Temp` is updated at every iteration. The key word `old` is used to specify the value produced by the previous iteration. This keyword is used to enforce the single-assignment semantics of SISAL.

Figure 2.5 shows two examples of the product form loop structure. The first (upper) example shows the case in which the returned value of the loop structure is an array. The second (lower) example is a matrix multiplication. SISAL provides a keyword `cross`,

```
for (i = 1; i <= N; i++)                    Histo := for initial
    Histo[digit[i]] = Histo[digit[i]] + 1;      Temp := array_fill (1,N,0);
                                                i := 0
                              =>            while i <= N repeat
                                                i := old i + 1;
                                                Temp := old Temp [digit[i] :
                                                    old Temp [digit [i]] + 1]
                                            returns value of Temp
                                            end for;

        C program statements                    SISAL program statements
```

FIGURE 2.4   Nonproduct form of the loop structure is used in the presence of loop carried dependencies.

```
for (i = 1; i <= N; i++)                    Ans := for i in 1,N
    Ans[i] = Q + (Y[i] * (R * Z[i+10]           returns array of
        + T * Z[i+11]));       =>                   Q + (Y[i] * (R * Z[i+10]
                                                    + T * Z[i+11))
                                            end for;


for (i = 1; i <= x; i++)                    C := for i in 1,x cross j in 1,z
    for (j = 1; j <= z; j++)                Elem := for k in 1,y
        for (k = 1; k <= y; k++)                    returns value of sum A[i,k] * B[k,j]
            C[i,j] = C[i,j] + A[i,k] * B[k,j]; =>   end for
                                            returns array of Elem
                                            end for;

        C program statements                    SISAL program statements
```

FIGURE 2.5   Product form of the loop structure is used when loop iterations are independent of each other.

which specifies the cross product of two vectors. The inner loop of the SISAL version of the matrix multiplication produces the inner product of two vectors A[i, *] and B[*, j]. The keyword sum specifies that the results of the following expression from all iterations are to be added to produce a scalar value. Besides the sum keyword, SISAL provides other reduction operations such as max and min which return the maximum and the minimum element of an array.

2.3

MICRO DATAFLOW: THE FIRST GENERATION

The first-generation architectures were characterized by an enthusiastic direct implementation of dataflow principle at the architecture level. This means that synchronization and partitioning were all done at the architecture level.

2.3.1 Some Micro Dataflow Architectures

This section discusses some of the first-generation dataflow machines, which include the Manchester Machine [29, 53, 57] and SIGMA-1 [31, 32]. The discussion of the MIT Monsoon dataflow machine [13, 30] is also included although its architecture is quite different from the others in terms of token-matching mechanism. In a sense, Monsoon is the last, in chronological terms, of the pure dataflow architectures. Note that due to space limitations, static dataflow architectures have not been included in this survey. Interested readers are referred to [53]. More recently, an interesting work on a static dataflow architecture has been reported [54]. Dennis' seminal work [16, 17] in the development of a static dataflow architecture, which stimulated the development of the dynamic dataflow architectures, should be further noted.

The common objective was to efficiently exploit a large amount of fine-grain parallelism extracted by the compiler. Although actual implementation differs from one machine to another, they had the following common characteristics:

- Data elements are physically transported in the form of scalar tokens within a processing element or across different processing elements.
- The firing rule as defined in Section 1 is implemented as one of the basic functions provided by the hardware.
- An instruction is scheduled dynamically when its input data tokens arriving at a processing node are properly synchronized (matched).

Manchester Dataflow Computer   The Manchester dataflow computer was one of the first machines to be actually built. It was developed at the University of Manchester in the United Kingdom. The processor consists of four hardware modules connected by a pipelined ring (Figure 2.6). The modules operate asynchronously from each other and the data tokens are transported in packets around the ring structure. Although the packets are transferred at a maximum rate of 4.37 million packets per second on the machine, the ring is rated for up to 10-million packets per second. An I/O Switch is provided for the interface between the host and the machine and also for multicomputer implementations.

The *token queue unit* consists of a 32-K word circular FIFO store with three buffer registers. The main function of the token queue is to store initial data tokens as well as to smooth out any unevenness in the rate of token generation and consumption between different modules. A word is 96 bits long, which is the length of a token. The format of a token is shown below. The length of each field, in number of bits, is indicated in parenthesis. The `marker` field indicates whether the token belongs to a user or a system operation. Other fields are self-explanatory:

```
Token ≡ [data (37).tag (36).destination (22).marker (1)].
```

The tokens that are temporarily stored in the token queue unit eventually arrive at the *matching unit*, which is responsible for instruction scheduling. An instruction is deemed executable when the matching unit finds all of its input operands available. The input operands of an instruction are found by associatively matching the arriving token with the waiting tokens. The matching is achieved by using the subfields of the token, which are 54

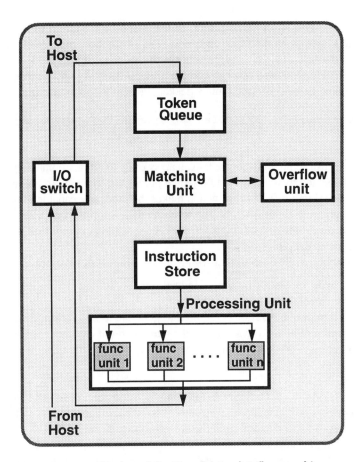

FIGURE 2.6   Processor organization of the Manchester dataflow machine.

bits long. They are the `tag` field (36 bits) and the `instruction address` field (18 bits) of the `destination` field. A 16-bit hashing function is applied and the resulting value is used to address the eight hash tables in parallel. If a match occurs, one would produce the matching token. The matching token and the incoming token are then formed into a single token and are sent to the *instruction store unit*. If a matching operand is not found, the arriving token is stored in the matching unit or in the *overflow unit* if all table entries are full. Incidentally, all instructions are either monadic or dyadic operations. The resulting token is 133 bits long and consists of:

`Token ≡ [data(37).data(37).tag(36).destination(22).marker(1)].`

The instruction unit uses the `instruction address` field of the incoming token to access the instruction. The `instruction address` field is divided into the `segment` field (6 bits) and the `offset` field (12 bits). As in conventional processors, the `segment` field is used to access a location in the segment table to retrieve a 20-bit segment base address. The offset value is then added to the base address to fetch the instruction that would operate on the input operands. The instruction consists of two fields. One is the `opcode` field (10 bits) and the other is the `destination` field. There can be up to two destination fields and one can contain a literal data. Again, the instruction and the rest of the token fields are formed into a packet and sent to the *processing unit* for execution:

```
Token ≡ [data(37).data(37).opcode(10).tag(36).destination(22).
         destination(optional).marker(1)].
```

The instruction unit can contain an array of up to 20 functional units in which each unit is implemented by a microcoded bit-slice processor. The maximum instruction rate for each functional unit is 0.27 MIPS which makes the processor capable of reaching the maximum throughput of about 5 MIPS. The resulting data is formed into a 96-bit token which is then either sent to the host or circulated back to the token queue unit for further processing. This completes the pipeline cycle.

Several conclusions were drawn from the Manchester Project:

1. A wide variety of programs indeed contain sufficient parallelism to fully utilize the functional units.
2. Compiler optimization is required to generate more efficient code.
3. Storing of all data structures in the matching unit can create a high overhead.
4. Even without data structures, the token queue and the matching unit utilization is still high.

ETL SIGMA-1   ETL SIGMA-1 is a dataflow computer developed by the Electro Technical Laboratory (ETL) in Japan. Currently, it is the largest operating dataflow computer based on the tagged token dataflow architecture. The system consists of 128 processing elements and 128 structure store elements connected in a two-level network. A two-stage global network connects 32 group nodes in which each group node consists of four PEs and four SEs connected in a local network. In addition, there are 16 maintenance and a host processor to handle operations such as I/O, system monitoring, performance measurements, and so on.

A processing element consists of five hardware units that are divided into two pipeline stages (Figure 2.7). The first pipeline stage (firing stage) consists of the buffer unit, the matching unit, and the instruction fetch unit. The buffer unit is a FIFO queue that can store up to 8-K tokens where a token is 89 bits in length. The function of this unit is similar to that of the token queue unit of the Manchester machine. When an input operand token of a dyadic operation arrives at the matching unit, a search is initiated to find the matching token from the waiting pool of tokens. An associative search is done using the `tag` field of the token. The token format is as follows :

```
Token ≡ [pe (8).itag (8).tag (32).c (1).type (8).data (32)].
```

The `pe` field indicates the processing element which the token is to be executed. The `itag` indicates the type of a token, for example, a token may be a user data token or a maintenance token. The `c` field is used to indicate the validity of the token, for example, a token is invalid when the field is set. The `type` field indicates the data type. The current

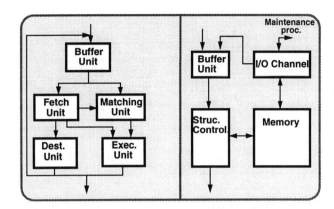

FIGURE 2.7   Sigma-1 has dedicated hardware structure handlers in addition to the process-ing elements. The organization of the processing element is shown at left while that of the structure controller is shown at right.

implementation only allows for a single precision floating point representation of 32 bits. The tag field is further divided into the following fields:

$$\text{Tag} \equiv [\text{i} \ (10).\text{base} \ (8).\text{offset} \ (10).\text{flg} \ (4)].$$

The i field indicates the loop iteration to which the token belongs. The base and the offset fields are used to fetch instructions. The flg field indicates the type of matching functions. For example, the SIGMA-1 machine provides a "sticky" token matching function for loop invariants. While regular tokens are deleted from the matching unit once a match occurs, a sticky token is not deleted. This function enhances performance since a token does not need to be recirculated.

An instruction format is shown below. The length of an instruction can vary from a word to three words in length in which a word is 40 bits long. The fan-out of an instruction is three at the maximum, in other words, there can be at most three destinations. Also, a literal value can be included in an instruction. The ndest field indicates the number of destinations:

$$\text{Instruction} \equiv [\text{literal} \ (40).\text{opcode} \ (8).\text{ndest} \ (2).\text{dest0} \ (20).$$
$$\text{dest1} \ (20).\text{dest2} \ (20)].$$

The execution unit and the distribution unit belong to the second stage (execution stage) of the processor pipeline. The execution unit consists of an integer ALU, a floating point ALU, a multiplier, and a structure address generator. The distribution unit is responsible of forming a result into a token and distributing it to its destinations as specified in the instruction. The two-stage processor is clocked at 10 MHz. and is estimated to provide 1.7 Mflops. The programming language chosen for the SIGMA-1 project is a single assignment language called DFC (Dataflow C) which is a derivative of C.

MIT Monsoon   The common drawback of the aforementioned dataflow machines is the overly complex and expensive hardware needed to implement the matching function. The

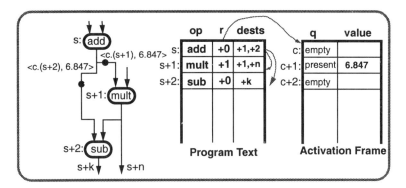

FIGURE 2.8 In the ETS mechanism, tokens are matched directly by using the offset generated at compile-time.

key architectural breakthrough of the Monsoon dataflow machine which evolved from the tagged token dataflow architecture (TTDA) [6] is the explicit token store (ETS) mechanism. Using this mechanism, a matching function becomes a simple read-write operation on a conventional memory device instead of an associative search. The net result is simpler processor hardware and faster token matching.

The ETS mechanism relies on a compile-time analysis which assigns to each token a synchronization point. This information is encoded into the instruction to be used at runtime to directly access the synchronization location. The assigned synchronization point is really an offset from the base of a memory block, which is dynamically allocated to a group of instructions called a *code block*. A code block can be a function body or a loop body in the source program. The allocated memory block is called a *frame* memory and it provides the synchronization space to the tokens that belong to the same code block (see Figure 2.8).

In Monsoon, two values FP and IP constitute a tag. The FP is the base address of the frame memory and the IP is the instruction pointer. The FP uniquely identifies the instance of a code block because every code block activation gets its own unique frame memory block. When a token arrives, a processor can compute the exact synchronization location within the frame memory using these two values:

1. The IP is used to fetch the instruction.
2. The offset stored as part of the instruction is fetched and added to the FP.
3. The computed frame memory location is accessed and the presence bit is checked.
4. If the presence bit is set, a matching token exists. The matching token is read from the frame memory and the two data values are sent to the execution unit. If the presence bit is not set, the incoming token is stored.

The Monsoon processor architecture is shown in Figure 2.9. Unlike the previous dataflow machines, the first unit in the pipeline is the instruction fetch unit. This of course is due to the ETS mechanism which requires the offset value to compute the synchronization location. Because of the simpler token matching hardware, the processing time of the match unit is comparable to the other units in the pipeline, which results in a more balanced and efficiently executing pipe. For most other dataflow machines that use associative matching, the match

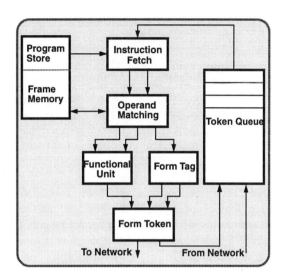

FIGURE 2.9   Organization of the Monsoon processor.

unit is the bottleneck that hampers the pipeline throughput. The current implementation of the Monsoon processor has eight pipeline stages and is based on a 10-MHz clock.

Other Architectures   Other projects are being pursued elsewhere. They include, but are not limited to, the following list:

- The RMIT/CSIRO dataflow architecture
- The Datarol
- The Epsilon project
- The Rapid

The RMIT/CSIRO dataflow machine was studied at the Royal Melbourne Institute of Technology and the Commonwealth Scientific Industrial Research Organization in Australia. The architecture of the machine evolved from the Manchester dataflow machine. The design objective is to provide an efficient execution environment for both static and dynamic execution styles. Thus, the architecture provides two modes of token matching. In addition to token matching by tag (dynamic model), tokens can be queued and executed in the arriving order (static model). The motivation for such a hybrid architecture is that applications such as DSP are more suited for static execution while other applications may benefit from a dynamic execution style [1].

A dataflow architecture called Datarol is under study at Kyushu University in Japan. The Datarol architecture has some features characteristic of recent hybrid architectures. For example, instead of dispatching data tokens to the destination instructions, Datarol provides a *by-reference mechanism* which allows the destination instructions to fetch input operands. This mechanism makes token copying unnecessary when there are multiple destination instructions. In addition, compile-time optimization can be performed to have an internal register as the operand store for improved performance [3].

TABLE 2.1   The list of benchmark programs used in the performance measurements of Monsoon.

Program	Source Lines	Application
MMT	130	Matrix multiplication
GAMTEB	750	Neutron transport
SIMPLE	1000	Hydrodynamics
PARAFFINS	300	Isomer enumeration

The Epsilon-2 architecture is being developed at the Sandia National Laboratories. It is an outgrowth of the Epsilon-1 project. However, unlike Epsilon-1, Epsilon-2 implements a dynamic dataflow execution model. The architecture uses direct token matching similar to that of Monsoon. Its salient feature is the *repeat token* mechanism which is also available on the Epsilon-1 architecture. The purpose of this feature is to reduce the overhead associated with data fanout [27, 28].

A dataflow processor chip set is designed and implemented by a collaboration of Osaka University, the Mitsubishi Electric Corporation, and the Sharp Corporation [38, 46]. The processor called Q-v1 is based on the dynamic data-driven execution model and consists of five chips. The Rapid processor is implemented on a single board using the chip set, which can provide up to 20 Mflops of computing power. A unique feature of the Qv-1 processor is its asynchronous pipelining scheme. In the Qv-1 chips, data transfer between two pipeline stages is achieved by the exchange of send and acknowledge signals between the self-timed data-transfer control circuits. In the future version, the five-chip set will be integrated into a single chip.

2.3.2 The Id Compiler

This section discusses the Id compiler for the Monsoon dataflow machine. The objective of the Id compiler is to efficiently exploit fine-grain parallelism with minimum overhead. Its main function is the controlling of asynchronous parallel execution and the managing of resources (such as frame memory and heap memory). Scheduling is done by the hardware which dynamically schedules instructions by way of token matching. The current Id compiler for Monsoon relies on user annotations which tell the compiler how to control parallelism and manage resources [30]. Two user annotations are currently in use. The first is the *loop bound* value, which is used to control the maximum number of loop iterations that are allowed to be active concurrently. The loop bound value k has a direct relationship to the amount of frame memory needed because k parallel iterations require k frame memory blocks. The second type of annotation is used to reclaim heap storage when it is no longer used.

The results reported in [30] (Table 2.2) show the effect of the compiler improvements on the performance of the benchmark programs (Table 2.1). One compiler improvement is the reduction of heap allocation. In the previous version of the compiler, a called function used the heap memory to return the resulting values to the calling function. Changing the compiler

TABLE 2.2 Performance improvements of the benchmark programs due to the compiler improvements.

Program	Feb. '91	Aug. '91 (hr:min:sec)	Mar. '92	June '92
MMT(500 x 500)	4:04	3:58	3:55	2:57
4 x 4 Blocked MMT	—	—	—	1:46
GAMTEB(40,000 particle)	17:13	10:42	5:36	—
(1,000,000 particles)	7:13:20	4:17:14	2:36:00	2:22:00
SIMPLE(100 x 100, 1 iter.)	0:19	0:15	0:10	0:06
(100 x 100, 100 iter.)	4:48:00	—	—	1:19:49
PARAFFINS (n=19)	0:50	0:31	—	0:02.04
PARAFFINS (n=22)	—	—	—	0:32.02

strategy to avoid expensive heap allocation/deallocation operations by directly sending the return values to the calling function made significant contributions to benchmarks such as Simple and Gamteb. Another compiler improvement is the lifting of the loop initialization code. This optimization is used to move the initialization code (such as frame memory allocation and storing of loop constants) of inner loops as far up as possible to the outer loop. This reduces the initialization cost of the inner loop by overlapping the operations with that of the outer loop operations.

Performance measurements using benchmark programs have shown that the compiler can expose enough parallelism to keep the Monsoon's processor pipeline busy. The experiment has also verified that latency can be effectively hidden by overlapping computations and communications. On the other hand, execution of sequential code was not competitive with that of C on a conventional processor (MIPS R3000). However, this may be due to the Monsoon architecture rather than the compiler [30].

2.3.3 Summary

So far, we have discussed the first research efforts aimed at attaining high-performance computing based on the data-driven execution model. The strategy was to extract as much parallelism as possible, of every granularity, at compile-time and efficiently exploit them at runtime. As part of this strategy, functional languages such as Id and SISAL were developed to allow a compiler to easily extract all the static parallelism as expressed in the program.

The conventional von Neumann processor architectures are highly optimized for executing a sequential stream of instructions and are not capable of efficiently exploiting a large number of parallel tasks. Thus a new architecture was developed to efficiently exploit a large amount of fine-grain parallelism. Actually, it can be said that most emphasis was given to the development of the dataflow architecture during this research era.

As far as the performance (in terms of execution time) is concerned, the first research efforts did not really produce overwhelming results in favor of the dataflow approach. On the other hand, they yielded some valuable insights. First, compiler optimization is an important (perhaps major) area also in the data-driven execution. In addition to extracting parallelism, conventional optimization techniques such as invariant code removal, common subexpression elimination, constant folding, and so on, are still needed for improving performance. Second, pure dataflow architectures may not be the ultimate answer. Although the dataflow architectures satisfactorily exploited parallelism, their performance in executing sequential code was below standards. This was to be expected since dataflow architectures have no mechanism to exploit locality, which is the key to efficient sequential code execution. Thus, the objective for the second stage of the research is set.

2.4

HYBRIDS: THE SECOND GENERATION

Several points became clear as a result of experimenting with the dataflow architectures discussed in the previous section.

First, too many functionalities have been given to the architecture, resulting in overly complex hardware making them economically infeasible. The match unit became a bottleneck in the circular pipeline of the dataflow architectures. The ETS mechanism used in Monsoon is one solution in the right direction. By relying more on a compile-time analysis, a simpler synchronization mechanism was developed to reduce the hardware costs and matching time.

Second, dynamic scheduling of every instruction is expensive and in many cases unnecessary. By analyzing the data dependency graphs at compile-time, dependent instructions can be statically scheduled without losing parallelism. By doing so, many von Neumann processor optimization techniques may be applied. Figure 2.10 shows a portion of a scientific application represented by an IF1 graph [52]. Assuming that the availability of the data tokens representing values i and h cannot be determined at compile-time, the only instructions that require dynamic scheduling are instructions 1 and 4. The instructions 2, 3, and 5 can be scheduled statically according to the data dependency relationship.

This section discusses the recent research activities aimed at addressing these points. The common approach taken by many researchers is a more balanced distribution of functionalities between the compiler and the hardware. It is driven by the fact that, at least in today's technology, pure dataflow architectures are not economically feasible. The resulting solution is also known as *multithreading*.

2.4.1 Architectures

After extensive experimentations with the pure dataflow architectures, the second-generation dataflow architectures have gradually become hybrids in an attempt to combine the best features of the conventional von Neumann architectures and the pure dataflow architectures. With such architectures, a sequential stream of instructions can be efficiently executed according to the von Neumann model while the fine-grain parallelism is exploited according to the data-driven model.

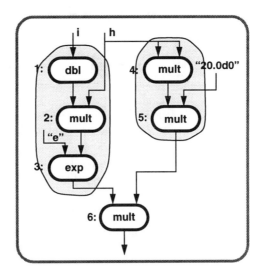

FIGURE 2.10   A portion of a scientific application is shown in the IF1 graph.

P-RISC   The objective of the P-RISC (Parallel-RISC) was to propose an architecture suitable for multiprocessing by starting out with a von Neumann architecture and extending it to provide necessary features to exploit fine-grain parallelism by borrowing from the dataflow architecture [43]. The resulting architecture has four new instructions in addition to its conventional RISC instruction set. They are:

1. `fork IPt`
2. `join x`
3. `start v c d`
4. `loadc a x IPr`

In a pure dataflow architecture, token matching is an implicit operation which is transparent to the compiler. Transmission of the output tokens to their respective destinations is also implicit to the compiler. In P-RISC, however, these functions are under the explicit control of the compiler and the first two instructions `fork` and `join` are the direct consequences of this change. The `fork IPt` instruction creates two active threads by queueing two *continuations* `<FP.IP+1>` and `<FP.IPt>` in the token queue. The `join x` instruction toggles the value at frame location `FP+x` which is the storage location of the presence bits. If the result is one, nothing happens. If the result is zero, a continuation `<FP.IP+1>` is inserted in the token queue. Figure 2.11 shows an example in which these two instructions are used to effect data-driven execution style.

The `start v c d` instruction is used to activate a thread belonging to a different activation which may or may not be executing on the same processor. This is accomplished by sending a message of the form `<START, [FP+v], [FP+c], [FP+d]>` (see Figure 2.12). The second message operand `[FP+c]` is the descriptor of the thread to be activated. Upon arriving at the destination, the value at the first message operand is stored at the frame memory location whose offset is indicated by the third message operand and the thread

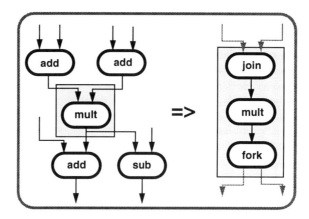

FIGURE 2.11   In P-RISC, token matching and forwarding is explicit under the control of a compiler.

descriptor is inserted into the token queue. This instruction can be used for a procedure call linkage mechanism, in other words, a return value can be sent as the first operand while the second operand indicates the thread that is activated upon receiving a return value.

The start v c d instruction is also used to implement *split-phase* remote read operations. This operation is used in data-driven execution to efficiently utilize a processor when a long latency inducing operation is activated. Instead of idling, a P-RISC processor executes an active thread from the token queue after dispatching a read request message of the form <READ,a,FP.IP+1,x>. In the message, a is the address of the requested memory location, x is the offset of the frame memory location in which the returning value is to be stored. The FP.IP+1 is the thread descriptor that is to be activated upon arrival of the requested data. When a READ message is received, the memory handler saves the thread descriptor and the offset. After reading the value from address a, it executes a start instruction which sends the value along with the thread descriptor and the offset value.

To sustain concurrency, a load instruction is usually surrounded by instructions such as jmp and fork. The loadc a x IPr is an extension of the load instruction that can make coding simpler in many cases. The loadc a x IPr instruction generates a READ message with IPr as the return address and continues execution from IP+1. Thus, loadc instruction performs an implicit fork after generating a READ message [43].

Work is in progress to implement a processor based on the P-RISC concept. The processor is designated *T (pronounced "start") and is to be extended from the existing Motorola 88110 superscalar RISC processor [8, 18, 45]. The *T processor has a functional unit called the message and synchronization unit (MSU) in addition to the existing functional units. The two main functions of the MSU are the handling of messages and scheduling of threads. The MSU provides a close-coupled register-set model of network messaging by providing a set of transmit and receive registers. User level instructions are available to send and receive messages without the operating system support. In *T, the maximum message length is fixed at 24 words.

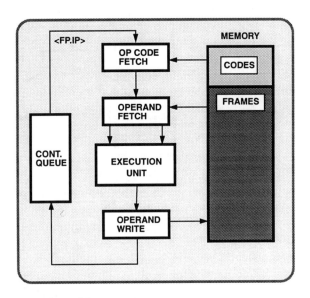

FIGURE 2.12   Organization of the P-RISC processor.

In addition to network support, the *T processor provides mechanisms for multithreading. In the MSU, a 64-entry microthread stack is provided to store thread descriptors. Scheduled threads are stored in the eight scheduled microthread descriptor registers. The threads are scheduled via fixed priority scheme of the scheduled microthread descriptor registers, the network receiver, and the microthread stack.

USC Decoupled Architecture Model   Two factors have influenced the development of the USC Decoupled Architecture Model. First is the need to develop an efficient architecture model for data dependency graphs with variable resolution actors [20]. It has been shown that appropriate fusing of simple nodes into larger macro nodes can improve overall performance without significant loss of parallelism [25]. In such an execution model, however, there can be a great difference in the execution time according to the granularity of the node. As a result, a large buffer is required between the graph stages (match and token formating/routing) and the computation stages (fetch and execute) of the processor [20] (see Figure 2.13). Second, it would be beneficial to borrow advanced pipeline techniques from von Neumann processors to execute sequential streams of instructions belonging to macro nodes.

Figure 2.14 shows the decoupled architecture model, which consists of two processing units. They are the *computation engine* (CE) and the *dataflow graph engine* (DFGE). The CE is responsible for executing the instructions belonging to a node once the node is scheduled for execution. A high-performance conventional von Neumann processor is appropriate for the CE since the instructions within the node are executed in sequence. The role of the DFGE is that of the scheduler. It performs token matching and, once all input tokens of a node are available, the node is scheduled for execution by the CE. The two processing units are connected by two queues. The *ready queue* (RQ) holds the descriptor

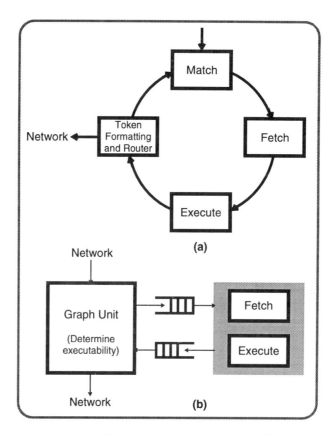

FIGURE 2.13 Basic dataflow architecture organized as (a) a cyclic pipeline and (b) a De-coupled Graph/Computation configuration. (Courtesy of Prentice-Hall, *Advanced Topics in Dataflow Computing*, J-L. Gaudiot and L. Bic, eds., 1991.)

of the ready nodes inserted by the DFGE. The *acknowledge queue* (AQ) holds the descriptor of the node that has been executed by the CE. Upon receiving the descriptor of the executed node, the DFGE can schedule other nodes which depend on the results of the node.

EM-4   The EM-4 multiprocessor machine is developed at the ETL of Japan. Currently, a machine containing 80 processing elements is in operation. Similar to other recent dataflow architectures, the EM-4 architecture is based on a multithreading model called the *strongly connected arc model*. In this model, a thread is called a *strongly connected block* (SCB). Once an SCB is initiated, execution continues without preemption until the SCB terminates. Instructions within the SCB are executed sequentially in a control-driven fashion [49].

As in Monsoon, a direct token matching scheme is used in EM-4 [50]. However, the actual mechanism is different from that of the ETS used in Monsoon. There are two main differences from the ETS scheme. First, in EM-4, the offset value, which specifies the storage/synchronization location of an instruction's operand, is carried in a data token. In

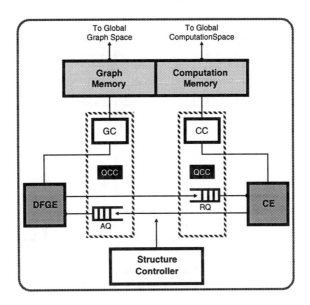

FIGURE 2.14   Dataflow processor with decoupled graph and computation units. (Courtesy of Prentice-Hall, *Advanced Topics in Dataflow Computing*, J-L. Gaudiot and L. Bic, eds., 1991.)

the ETS mechanism, the offset value is stored as part of the instruction. Second, the offset not only indicates the synchronization point of tokens, but also acts as the offset for the instruction that operates on the tokens. In ETS, the offset value is only valid for accessing operands within the frame memory. Figure 2.15 describes the direct matching scheme of EM-4.

The heart of the EM-4 machine is the EMC-R single chip processor. The EMC-R processor architecture provides both the dataflow and the von Neumann execution mechanism within the same processor. The processor contains four pipeline stages in which the first two stages are used for token matching functions while the latter two stages are used for the fetching and the execution of the instructions. For the instructions that belong to a thread (or SCB), only the latter two pipeline stages are used once the thread is activated. The operand match unit, the instruction fetch unit, the destination unit and the execution unit shown in Figure 2.16 correspond to the four stages.

The EMC-R processor chip also contains the switching unit (SU) which performs a three-by-three packet switching function. The tokens that are destined for the local processor are first stored in the input buffer unit (IBU) which is a 32-word FIFO buffer. An 8-K word secondary buffer is located in an off-chip memory in case of an overflow. Although the EMC-R processor does not provide an on-chip floating point execution unit, it is possible to interface a commercially available floating point coprocessor chip.

Other Architectures   The McGill Dataflow Architecture (MDFA) model is yet another hybrid architecture model developed at McGill University in Canada.   MDFA has a

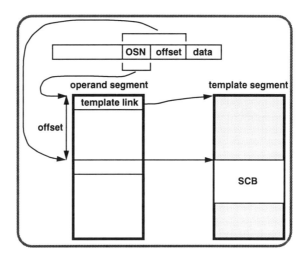

FIGURE 2.15   The direct matching scheme of EM-4.   The operand segment refers to the frame memory and the template segment refers to the code block.   The operand segment number OPN and the offset are carried in the data token packet.

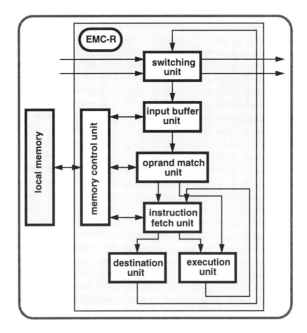

FIGURE 2.16   The organization of the EMC-R single-chip processor.

decoupled architecture similar to the USC Decoupled Architecture. In MDFA, a processor is divided into the instruction processing unit (IPU) and the instruction scheduling unit (ISU). The two units interact with each other by exchanging *fire* and *done* signals. A fire signal, which consists of the instruction pointer and the base address of the frame memory (continuation), is sent from the ISU to the IPU. A done signal, which consists of the continuation of the executed instruction [23], is sent from the IPU to the ISU.

So far, we have discussed hybrid architectures that evolved from the pure dataflow architectures. There are other hybrid architectures that started from the von Neumann architectures. They will not be discussed in this paper, but they include the Hybrid Architecture [33, 34], the Message-Driven Processor (MDP) [15], and the Tera machine [2].

2.4.2 Summary

The driving forces behind the second-generation architectures were efficient sequential execution and simpler and faster synchronization mechanism. The result is a hybrid architecture that provides the von Neumann execution model in addition to the data-driven execution model. With the exception of EM-4, these architectures decouple computing tasks from the synchronization tasks. In *T, this is handled by the message and synchronization unit while in the USC Decoupled Architecture model, the dataflow graph engine is responsible for the job.

Compilers play an important role since the hybrid architectures depend on compilation strategies much more than the first generation dataflow architectures. Performance can vary greatly depending on the criteria used for thread partitioning. Due to relatively recent introduction of the hybrid architectures, however, not much work is reported for compilation strategy.

2.5

COMPILING FOR CONVENTIONAL PARALLEL MACHINES

As it turns out, the principles of functional programs do not necessarily require hardware support. Implicit parallelism through functional programs can indeed be exploited on conventional architectures. Two projects are discussed.

2.5.1 SISAL Compiler

This section discusses the compilation strategy and the performance of the Optimizing SISAL Compiler (OSC) [10]. Currently, OSC is available on many shared-memory parallel machines from companies such as Sequent, Silicon Graphics, and CRAY. Incidentally, OSC can also be used in uniprocessor workstations running Unix operating system. With this compiler, a SISAL program originally written to run on a small workstation can be recompiled to run on a parallel supercomputer such as CRAY C-90 without any program modification.

TABLE 2.3 The list of benchmark programs used to compare the performance of OSC to Fortran on a CRAY Y-MP supercomputer.

Program	Source Lines	Time Steps	Problem Size	Application
KIN16	225	42,000	2×14285	Gel Electrophoresis
RICARD	297	40,000	5×1315	Gel Chromatography
CFFT	517	1	524288	Fourier Transform
BMK11A	1003	200	2560	Particle Transport
LOOPS	1116	4,000	100–1000	Scientific Kernel
SIMPLE	1527	62	100 x 100	Hydrodynamics
UNSPLIT	1937	40	160 x 80	Hydrodynamics
WEATHER	2712	20	420 km	Weather Model

TABLE 2.4 Performance comparison of SISAL and Fortran benchmark programs on a CRAY Y-MP supercomputer.

CRAY Y-MP/864	Concurrent-Vector				Seconds	
	One CPU		Four CPUs		Eight CPUs	
Program	SISAL	Fortran	SISAL	Fortran	SISAL	Fortran
KIN16	74.8	79.9	19.7	20.7	11.6	11.2
RICARD	39.8	38.9	13.8	12.5	8.7	7.4
CFFT	0.33	0.42	0.10	0.15	0.07	0.13
BMK11A	4.8	4.2	3.4	3.0	3.3	2.9
LOOPS	16.1	12.9	12.3	11.4	11.3	11.0
SIMPLE	9.4	9.0	3.1	8.8	2.2	8.8
UNSPLIT	10.1	8.0	2.8	5.0	1.7	4.9
WEATHER	7.3	7.0	2.0	6.7	1.2	6.8
Total	162.6	160.3	57.2	68.3	40.1	53.1

Traditionally, the main drawback of functional languages (such as SISAL) has been the performance. Although these languages gave programmers a high level of abstraction, the lack of performance made them unattractive [40]. However, OSC has shown that high-performance parallel computing is possible with functional programming. Experimenting with a number of numerical application benchmark programs showed that programs compiled by OSC perform competitively to that of a Fortran code on a single-head CRAY Y-MP supercomputer [11]. However, the real advantage is that programs can be run on multi-head CRAY computers without modification with correspondingly improved performance. Table 2.3 describes the type of benchmark programs used in the experiment. Performance results of the benchmarks on a CRAY Y-MP/864 is reported in [11] (Table 2.4). It demonstrates that the programs written in Fortran perform slightly better when one processor is used. However, the programs written in SISAL perform better when multiple processors are used.

The main villain in SISAL has been handling of the aggregate data types such as arrays. Because of the language semantics, which require *referential transparency*, arrays often have to be copied. For example, a simple replacement operation of an array element causes array copying which makes the execution time a function of the array size instead of a constant. The problem becomes much worse if the array replacement operation happens to occur inside a loop. It was observed that a SISAL program that initialized an array of 50,000 elements took approximately one hour on a Sequent Balance while a Fortran version took less than one second to complete [9].

The main strategy of the OSC is to minimize array copying via an automatic static analysis of the program graphs. Specifically, the objective is to transform array operations that cause copying to either *build-in-place* or *update-in-place* operations. Array operations that result in dynamically growing arrays may be optimized into build-in-place operations if the final array size does not depend on the runtime behavior. Array replacement operations can be optimized into update-in-place operations at the cost of losing some parallelism. The optimizers IF2MEM and IF2UP, as shown in Figure 2.17, are responsible for these transformations. The final output of the array optimizers are program graphs in IF2 [58] format with explicit memory management operations.

Although the actual graph analysis aimed at optimizing various array operations is nontrivial, the basic concept is easy to understand. Two simple examples are used to demonstrate the basic intuition. The example of Figure 2.18 shows a loop that initializes an array using the array_addh operation. This operation causes the array to grow dynamically. Initially the array contains only one element and grows by one element at each iteration until N elements are produced. A naive implementation would initially allocate one memory cell for the first element. In each subsequent iteration, a memory allocation is performed followed by a copy operation in which the amount of memory allocated and copied is larger by one element from the previous iteration. This process would repeat until all array elements are initialized. This inefficiency can be reduced to one memory allocation and zero copying by preallocating memory for N array elements all at once before entering the loop once the value of N becomes known. Unfortunately, this optimization is not always possible as shown in Figure 2.19, where the build-in-place optimization is not possible because the size of the array A cannot be determined prior to entering the loop.

According to SISAL semantics, the execution of the two array operations, as illustrated in Figure 2.20, are implicitly parallel. One is an array replacement operation and the other is an array read operation. Since the relationship between the array subscripts of the two operations is not known, array copying results. In this example, if it can be determined that the array read operation shown is the only array read, the array replacement operation can be transformed into an update-in-place operation by forcing the array read operation to occur first. The IF2UP optimizer looks for such cases during its graph analysis.

In addition to the array optimization analysis performed by the IF2MEM and the IF2UP optimizers, IF1OPT performs well-known conventional optimization techniques such as:

- Function inline expansion
- Loop invariant removal
- Record fission
- Common subexpression elimination
- Loop fusion
- Constant folding
- Dead code elimination

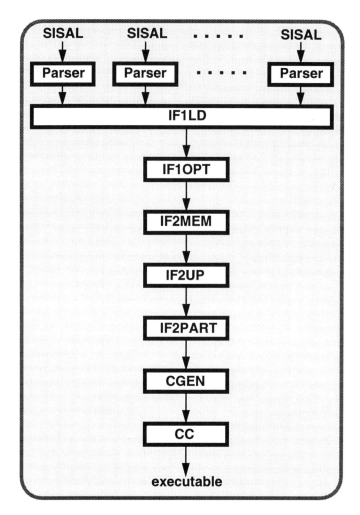

FIGURE 2.17 The current Optimizing SISAL Compiler goes through a number of optimization phases. IF1OPT performs conventional optimization transformations on the IF1 graphs. The resulting graphs are input to the IF2MEM and IF2UP for efficient array usage. After partitioning by IF2PART, C code is generated for final compilation.

2.5.2 Threaded Abstract Machine

In the first-generation pure dataflow architectures, fine-grain parallel execution is provided by special mechanisms that are built into the hardware. For example, matching hardware is provided to dynamically schedule instructions through token matching. Also, a router hardware is provided to automatically route a result data token to its destination. The Threaded Abstract Machine (TAM) [12, 14] takes the opposing approach in that it tries to provide fine-grain parallel computations on conventional parallel machines, which provide none of these hardware mechanisms.

```
type OneDim = array [integer];

function Main (N : integer returns OneDim)
    for initial
        I := 1;
        A := array [1:0]
    while (I < N) repeat
        I := old I + 1;
        A := array_addh (old A, 0)
    returns value of A
    end for
end function
```

FIGURE 2.18   A SISAL program that initializes an array to value zero.

```
for initial
    I := 1
while (I <= 1000) repeat
    I := old I + A[I]
returns array of I
end for
```

FIGURE 2.19   IF2MEM optimizer is not able to transform this program segment to preallocate memory.

```
type TwoDim = array [array [real]];

function Main (I,J:integer; A:TwoDim returns TwoDim, real)
    A[I,J : 0.0], A[J,I]
end function
```

FIGURE 2.20   Without optimization, the two array operations in function Main causes array copying.

To minimize the overhead of frequent transfer of control among a potentially large pool of ready tasks, a fast context switching capability is a prerequisite to providing fine-grain parallel execution. Otherwise, the benefit of parallel execution can easily be wasted by the context switching overhead. Due to large states of modern processors, however, a fast context switching is difficult to attain. TAM overcomes this problem by addressing two key issues, namely, the scheduling strategy and the communication mechanisms.

The key point of the TAM scheduling strategy is to exploit *spatial locality* as much as possible by taking into account the memory hierarchy of the machine. By so doing, the

TABLE 2.5   The list of benchmark programs used in the benchmarking of TAM on a 64-node CM-5 machine.

Program	Source Lines	Problem Size	Application
QS	—	—	Quicksort
GAMTEB	750	8192	Neutron Transport
PARAFFINS	300	—	Isomer Enumeration
SIMPLE	1000	128 x 128	Hydrodynamics
SPEECH	—	—	Speech Processing
MMT	130	60 x 60	Matrix Multiplication

frequency of the expensive context switching may be reduced. To explain this idea, let us first assume that there are a number of active code blocks in a processor. A code block is said to be active when a frame has been allocated to it and is ready to execute, in other words, at least one of its threads is ready for execution. An active code block is called an *activation*. Although there can be many activations in a processor, only one thread belonging to an activation is executed at a time.

Now, assume that a thread has just terminated and a new thread needs to be scheduled. There are a number of possible scheduling strategies. For example, a round-robin scheduling can be used in which threads belonging to different activations are scheduled one after another. In this scheme, the current processor state needs to be saved each time a new thread is scheduled, causing a large overhead. In TAM, ready threads that belong to the current activation have higher priority than other threads. A new activation is scheduled only when no other thread from the current activation can be scheduled. This strategy incurs much less overhead because it takes advantage of the locality as long as possible. In other words, by scheduling threads from current activation, values stored in processor registers and cache need not be saved at every thread context switch. A large overhead is incurred only when a thread from a different activation is scheduled.

Communication is another important element of the TAM model. Without efficient communicating mechanisms, fine-grain parallel execution is not possible due to processor idling caused by long latency. In TAM, the communication is tightly coupled to the computation. Thus, the communication chores are handled by the compiler-generated *message handler* instead of relying on the operating system services. A message handler is called an *inlet* and its objective is to quickly inject the received data into the currently executing activation threads. By doing so, activation that is already resident on the processor can continue executing instead of being switched out and brought back again later at a high cost [56].

To verify the TAM concept, an intermediate language representation called TL0 has been developed. The backend of the Id compiler has been modified to produce the multithreaded code in the TL0 format instead of the dataflow instructions. The resulting TL0 is then translated to a C code and compiled by the native C compiler for execution. Seven benchmark programs, as shown in Table 2.5, are used in the performance measurements. Dynamic scheduling characteristics of the benchmark programs are reported in [12] (Table 2.6). The

TABLE 2.6   Dynamic scheduling characteristics of the benchmark programs on a 64-node CM-5 machine.

	QS	GAMTEB	PARAFFINS	SIMPLE	SPEECH	MMT
Avg. Thread Length	2.6	3.2	3.1	5.3	6.3	17.6
Threads per Quantum	11.5	13.5	215.5	7.5	16.7	530.0
Quanta per Invocation	4.1	3.4	2.7	4.8	21.7	3.4

64-node CM-5 was used as a target machine. Preliminary results are encouraging in that the performance on the 64-node CM-5 is comparable to a 16-node Monsoon. Recall that Monsoon is specially designed and built to support fine-grain parallel execution [12].

The average number of the TL0 instructions per thread on the compiled benchmark programs is approximately six, which is comparable to the run-length of a basic block in conventional programs [12]. With such short threads, it is easy to incur a large context switching overhead. However, the third row of Table 6 shows that many threads are indeed scheduled (depending on the applications) during a single *quantum* where a quantum is defined as a single residency of an activation on a processor. Through the scheduling strategy and the communication mechanism described above, the TAM model keeps the context switching cost to a minimum by restricting the thread switching to those within the current activation as much as possible.

2.6

CONCLUSIONS

Research in the data-driven model has gone through two distinct evolutionary phases. The first-generation dataflow architecture was motivated by the efforts to directly execute dataflow graphs on a hardware with minimum compile-time analysis. Consequently, the resulting hardware became quite complex in order to provide various mechanisms for dynamic dataflow execution.

The second-generation architecture is characterized by its hybrid nature. Driven by the need to provide cheaper and more efficient execution mechanisms for both sequential and parallel code segments, hybrid architectures possess features from the von Neumann as well as the dataflow architectures. While the hardware has become simpler, the compile-time analysis has become very important.

Although many improvements have been made, further investigation is required to determine what can be handled in software without significant performance degradation and what the necessary architectural features are for fine, medium-grain asynchronous data-driven execution model. The works of [11] and [12] discussed in the previous section are a good basis for future research to address this question.

The Optimizing SISAL Compiler work concentrated on the efficient handling of structured data (mainly arrays) by performing optimizations such as build-in-place and update-in-place. However, OSC is aimed at conventional parallel machines that use a shared-memory model and utilize a relatively small number of processors. In addition, only coarse-grain parallelism is exploited by OSC. On the other hand, the emphasis of TAM is in efficient scheduling of fine-grain parallelism. The ideas embodied in OSC and TAM can be combined to develop a testbed system for an efficient fine, medium-grain asynchronous data-driven execution model for massively parallel systems.

In such an environment, a strict array-handling scheme used in the current OSC is not sufficient. To effectively overlap computation and communication, nonstrict array operations may be necessary. I-Structures currently supported in the TAM implementation provide nonstrict operations. This technique, however, has some drawbacks. First, I-Structures must be dynamically allocated and initialized before using and must be deallocated after use. Frequent memory alloc/deallocation operations translate to overheads. Second, due to a split-phase read operation, accessing an I-Structure can result in three remote messages per read/write of an array element.

An alternative array-handling scheme is available that can complement I-Structures. A technique called the *direct array injection technique* (DAIT) is developed for use in multithreading framework [37]. This technique is based on the *token relabeling scheme* that is used in a tagged token dataflow architecture [24, 26, 36]. Unlike I-Structures, DAIT does not use the heap memory. Instead, the activation frame memory is used for the array storage. Thus, the overhead of heap memory alloc/deallocation can be avoided. In addition, since an array element is sent *directly* from a source to a destination, the number of remote messages is reduced. By analyzing program graphs at compile-time, an optimizer can decide the most appropriate array-handling techniques to use for improved performance.

There exist many scientific applications which conventional parallel machines do not perform well. This is due to the inherently dynamic runtime behavior of these applications. For example, the adaptive methods for solving partial differential equations dynamically migrate around the simulation space depending on intermediate results [55]. By providing efficient mechanisms for sequential execution, while still retaining its ability to dynamically exploit fine-grain parallelism, the data-driven execution model may be the natural solution for such applications.

Bibliography

1. D. Abramson and G. Egan, "Design of a High-performance Dataflow Multiprocessor," in *Advanced Topics in Dataflow Computing*, J-L. Gaudiot and L. Bic, eds., Ch. 4, Prentice Hall, Englewood Cliffs, N.J., 1991, pp. 121–141.

2. R. Alverson et al., "The Tera Computer System," *Proc. 1990 Int'l Conf. Supercomputing*, ACM Press, New York, N.Y., 1990, pp. 1–6.

3. M. Amamiya, "An Ultra-multiprocessing Architecture for Functional Languages," in *Advanced Topics in Dataflow Computing*, J-L. Gaudiot and L. Bic, eds., Englewood Cliffs, N.J., Prentice Hall, Ch. 3, 1991, pp. 95–119.

4. Arvind and K. Gostelow, "The U-interpreter," *Computer*, Vol. 15, No. 2, Feb. 1982, pp. 42–49.

5. Arvind and R. Iannucci, "Two Fundamental Issues in Multiprocessing," *Proc. Conf. Parallel Processing in Science and Engineering*, 1987.

6. Arvind and R. Nikhil, "Executing a Program on the MIT Tagged-token Dataflow Architecture," in *Parallel Architectures and Languages Europe*, Springer-Verlag, Heidelberg, Germany, Aug. 1987.

7. J. Backus, "Can Programming Be Liberated from the von Neumann Style? A Functional Style and Its Algebra of Programs," *Comm. ACM*, Vol. 21, No. 8, Aug. 1978, pp. 613–641.

8. M. Beckerle, "An Overview of the START(*T) Computer System," Tech. Report MCRC-TR-28, Motorola Inc., Cambridge Research Center, Cambridge, Mass., July 1992.

9. D. Cann, *Compilation Techniques for High Performance Applicative Computation*, PhD thesis, Colorado State University, Fort Collins, Colo., 1989.

10. D. Cann, *The Optimizing SISAL Compiler: Version 12.0*, Lawrence Livermore National Laboratory, Livermore, Calif., 1992.

11. D. Cann, "Retire Fortran: A Debate Rekindled," *Comm. ACM*, Vol. 35, No. 8, Aug. 1992, pp. 81–89.

12. D. Culler et al., "TAM-a Compiler-controlled Threaded Abstract Machine," *J. Parallel and Distributed Computing*, July 1993.

13. D. Culler and G. Papadopoulos, "The Explicit Token Store," *J. Parallel and Distributed Computing, Special Issue: Dataflow Processing*, Dec. 1990, pp. 289–308.

14. D. Culler et al., "Fine-grain Parallelism with Minimal Hardware Support: A Compiler-controlled Threaded Abstract Machine," *Proc. ASPLOS-IV*, ACM Press, New York, N.Y., 1991, pp. 164–175.

15. W. Dally et al., "The Message-driven Processor: A Multicomputer Processing Node with Efficient Mechanisms," *IEEE Micro*, Vol. 12, No. 2, Apr. 1992, pp. 23–38.

16. J. Dennis, "Dataflow Supercomputers," *Computer*, Vol. 13, No. 11, Nov. 1980, pp. 48–56.

17. J. Dennis, "The Evolution of Static Dataflow Architecture," in *Advanced Topics in Dataflow Computing*, J-L. Gaudiot and L. Bic, eds., Ch. 2, Prentice-Hall, Englewood Cliffs, N.J., 1991, pp. 35–91.

18. K. Diefendorff and M. Allen, "Organization of the Motorola 88110 Superscalar RISC Microprocessor," *IEEE Micro*, Vol. 12, No. 2, Apr. 1992, pp. 40–63.

19. K. Ekanadham, "A Perspective on Id," in *Parallel Functional Languages and Compilers*, B. Szymanski, ed., Ch. 6, ACM Press, New York, N.Y., 1991, pp. 197–253.

20. P. Evripidou and J-L. Gaudiot, "A Decoupled Graph/Computation Data-driven Architecture with Variable-resolution Actors," *Proc. 1990 Int'l Conf. Parallel Processing: Vol. 1 Architecture*, The Pennsylvania State University Press, University Park, Penn., 1990, pp. 405–414.

21. J. Feo, "SISAL," in *A Comparative Study of Parallel Programming Languages: The Salishan Problems*, J. Feo, ed., Vol. 6 of *Special Topics in Supercomputing*, Ch. 9, North-Holland, Amsterdam, The Netherlands, 1992, pp. 337–386.

22. J. Feo, D. Cann, and R. Oldehoeft, "A Report on the SISAL Language Project," *J. Parallel and Distributed Computing*, Vol. 10, No. 4, Dec. 1990, pp. 349–366.

23. G. Gao, H. Hum, and J-M. Monti, "Towards an Efficient Hybrid Dataflow Architecture Model," *Proc. PARLE'91 Parallel Architectures and Languages Europe*, Springer-Verlag, Heidelberg, Germany, 1991, pp. 355–371.

24. J-L. Gaudiot, "Structure Handling in Dataflow Systems," *IEEE Trans. Computers*, Vol. C-35, No. 6, June 1986, pp. 489–502.

25. J-L. Gaudiot and M. Ercegovac, "Performance Evaluation of a Simulated Dataflow Computer with Low-resolution Actors," *J. Parallel and Distributed Computing*, Vol. 2, 1985, pp. 321–351.

26. J-L. Gaudiot and Y. Wei, "Token Relabeling in a Tagged-token Dataflow Architecture," *IEEE Trans. Computers*, Vol. 38, No. 9, Sept. 1989, pp. 1225–1239.

27. V. Grafe and J. Hoch, "The Epsilon-2 Multiprocessor System," *J. Parallel and Distributed Computing*, Vol. 10, No. 4, Dec. 1990, pp. 309–318.

28. V. Grafe et al., "The Epsilon Project," in *Advanced Topics in Dataflow Computing*, J-L. Gaudiot and L. Bic, eds., Ch. 6, Prentice-Hall, Englewood Cliffs, N.J., 1991, pp. 175–205.

29. J. Gurd, C. Kirkham, and I. Watson, "The Manchester Prototype Dataflow Computer," *Comm. ACM*, Vol. 28, No. 1, Jan. 1985, pp. 34–52.

30. J. Hicks et al., "Performance Studies of the Monsoon Dataflow Processor," *J. Parallel and Distributed Computing*, July 1993.

31. K. Hiraki, S. Sekiguchi, and T. Shimada, "Status Report of SIGMA-1: A Dataflow Super-computer," in *Advanced Topics in Dataflow Computing*, J-L. Gaudiot and L. Bic, eds., Ch. 7, Prentice-Hall, Englewood Cliffs, N.J., 1991, pp. 207–223.

32. K. Hiraki, T. Shimada, and K. Nishida, "A Hardware Design of the SIGMA-1: A Dataflow Computer for Scientific Computations," *Proc. 1984 Int'l Conf. Parallel Processing*, IEEE CS Press, Los Alamitos, Calif., 1984, pp. 524–531.

33. R. Iannucci, "Toward a Dataflow/von Neumann Hybrid Architecture," *Proc. 15th Ann. Int'l Symp. Computer Architecture*, IEEE CS Press, Los Alamitos, Calif.,1988, pp. 131–139.

34. R. Iannucci, *Parallel Machines: Parallel Machine Languages, The Emergence of Hybrid Dataflow Computer Architecture*, Engineering and Computer Science, Kluwer Academic Publishers, Norwell, Mass., 1990.

35. M. Kallstrom and S. Thakkar, "Programming Three Parallel Computers," *IEEE Software*, Vol. 5, No. 1, Jan. 1988, pp. 11–22.

36. C. Kim and J-L. Gaudiot, "A Scheme to Extract Run-time Parallelism from Sequential Loops," *Proc. 5th ACM Int'l Conf. Supercomputing*, ACM Press, New York, N.Y., 1991.

37. C. Kim and J-L. Gaudiot, "A Direct Array Injection Technique in a Fine-grain Multithreading Execution Model," *Proc. 8th Int'l Parallel Processing Symp.*, IEEE CS Press, Los Alamitos, Calif., 1994, pp. 187–199.

38. S. Komori et al., "The Data-driven Microprocessor," *IEEE Micro*, Vol. 9, No. 3, June 1989, pp. 45–59.

39. E. Lee, "Static Scheduling of Dataflow Programs for Dsp," in *Advanced Topics in Dataflow Computing*, J-L. Gaudiot and L. Bic, eds., Ch. 19, Prentice-Hall, Englewood Cliffs, N.J., 1991, pp. 501–526.

40. J. McGraw, D. Kuck, and M. Wolfe, "A Debate: Retire Fortran?," *Physics Today*, Vol. 37, No. 5, May 1984, pp. 66–75.

41. J. McGraw et al., *SISAL Language Reference Manual Version 1.2*, Mar. 1985.

42. R. Nikhil, "Id (version 90.1) Reference Manual," Tech. Report CSG Memo 284-2, MIT, July 1991.

43. R. Nikhil and Arvind, "Can Dataflow Subsume von Neumann Computing?," *Proc. 16th Ann. Int'l Symp. Computer Architecture*, IEEE CS Press, Los Alamitos, Calif., 1989, pp. 262–272.

44. R. Nikhil and Arvind, "Id: A Language with Implicit Parallelism," in *A Comparative Study of Parallel Programming Languages: The Salishan Problems*, J. Feo, ed., Vol. 6 of *Special Topics in Supercomputing*, Ch. 5, North-Holland, Amsterdam, The Netherlands, 1992, pp. 169–215.

45. R. Nikhil, G. Papadopoulos, and Arvind, "*T: A Multithreaded Massively Parallel Architecture," in *Proc. 19th Ann. Int'l Symp. Computer Architecture*, ACM Press, New York, N.Y., 1992, pp. 156–167.

46. H. Nishikawa et al., "Architecture of a VLSI-oriented Data-driven Processor: The Q-v1," in *Advanced Topics in Dataflow Computing*, J-L. Gaudiot and L. Bic, eds., Ch. 9, Prentice-Hall, Englewood Cliffs, N.J., 1991, pp. 247–264.

47. R. Oldehoeft and D. Cann, "Applicative Parallelism on a Shared-memory Multiprocessor," *IEEE Software*, Vol. 5, No. 1, Jan. 1988, pp. 62–70.

48. A. Osterhaug, *Guide to Parallel Programming on Sequent Computer Systems*, Sequent Computer Systems, Inc., 2nd ed., 1987.

49. S. Sakai et al., "Design of the Dataflow Single-chip Processor EMC-R," *J. Information Processing*, Vol. 13, No. 2, 1990, pp. 165–173.

50. M. Sato et al., "Thread-based Programming for the EM-4 Hybrid Dataflow Machine," *Proc. 19th Ann. Int'l Symp. Computer Architecture*, ACM Press, New York, N.Y., 1992, pp. 146–155.

51. S. Skedzielewski, "SISAL," in *Parallel Functional Languages and Compilers*, B. Szymanski, ed., Ch. 4, ACM Press, New York, N.Y., 1991, pp. 105–157.

52. S. Skedzielewski and J. Glauert, *IF1 An Intermediate Form for Applicative Languages*, Computing Research Group, Lawrence Livermore National Laboratory, Livermore, Calif., 1985.

53. V. Srini, "An Architectural Comparison of Dataflow Systems," *Computer*, Vol. 19, No. 3, Mar. 1986, pp. 68–88.

54. T. Sterling and J. Arnold, "Fine Grain Dataflow Computation without Tokens for Balanced Execution," *J. Parallel and Distributed Computing*, Vol. 18, No. 3, July 1993, pp. 327–339.

55. T. Sterling and M. MacDonald, "The Realities of High-performance Computing and Dataflow's Role in It: Lessons from the NASA HPCC Program," in *IFIP Transactions: Architectures and Compilation Techniques for Fine and Medium Grain Parallelism*, M. Cosnard, K. Ebcioğlu, and J-L. Gaudiot, eds., IFIP, North-Holland, Amsterdam, The Netherlands, Jan. 1993, pp. 165–176.

56. T. von Eicken et al., "Active Messages: A Mechanism for Integrated Communication and Computation," *Proc. 19th Ann. Int'l Symp. Computer Architecture*, ACM Press, New York, N.Y., 1992, pp. 256–266.

57. I. Watson and J. Gurd, "A Practical Dataflow Computer," *Computer*, Vol. 15, No. 2, Feb. 1982, pp. 51–57.

58. M. Welcome et al., *IF2: An Applicative Language Intermediate Form with Explicit Memory Management*, University of California, Lawrence Livermore National Laboratory, Livermore, Calif., Dec. 1986.

CHAPTER 3

PROPERTIES OF A VARIETY OF INTERCONNECTION NETWORKS FOR LARGE-SCALE PARALLELISM*

Wayne G. Nation
IBM Corporation, AS/400 Division
3605 Highway 52 NW, Rochester, MN 55904, USA

Gene Saghi
Electrical Engineering Department
University of Idaho, Moscow, ID 83844

Howard Jay Siegel
Parallel Processing Laboratory, School of Electrical Engineering
Purdue University, West Lafayette, IN 47907-1285, USA

Abstract.   *Properties of a variety of interconnection networks for large-scale parallel processing systems (in other words, 64 to 64 K processors) are discussed. Models of SIMD (synchronous) and MIMD (asynchronous) parallelism are described. A collection of different types of networks are explored, examining properties such as topology, routing control, and partitionability. The mesh and hypercube single-stage (or point-to-point) networks are first overviewed. Then multistage networks are studied, beginning with the multistage cube, which represents an important family of networks that includes the omega, indirect binary n-cube, multistage shuffle-exchange, delta, baseline, SW-banyan, and generalized cube. The extra-stage cube (ESC), a fault-tolerant variation of the multistage cube, is described. The structure of the augmented data manipulator (ADM) multistage network is summarized. The dynamic redundancy network, a fault-tolerant variation of the multistage cube that supports spare processors and whose structure is based on the ADM, is also presented. The structure and use of a tree-based network is considered. The difficulty in evaluating and comparing different interconnection networks is examined.*

*This work was supported in part by NRaD under contract number N68786-91-D-1799.

3.1

INTRODUCTION

3.1.1 Motivation

Large-scale parallel processing systems that incorporate 2^6 to 2^{16} processors working together to solve a problem represent one important approach to the design of supercomputers. These systems can provide the computational performance for tasks that require real-time response, that involve extremely complex calculations, and/or that need to process immense data sets. Examples of such tasks include weather forecasting, air traffic control, biomedical signal processing, robot vision, satellite-collected image analysis, chemical reaction simulation, and speech understanding. A critical component of any large-scale parallel processing system is the network that interconnects the processors and memories, allowing them to communicate with one another. This is an overview of properties of a number of types of interconnection network schemes that have been built or proposed for use in parallel machines.

3.1.2 Models of Parallel Machines

Parallel systems can be implemented using a PE-to-PE configuration or a processor-to-memory configuration. In the *PE-to-PE* configuration, processing elements (*PEs*) consist of a processor paired with local memory, and each PE is connected to both an input port and an output port of an interconnection network. This type of system is also referred to as a *distributed memory* machine. In the *processor-to-memory* configuration, processors are attached to one side of an interconnection network and memories are attached to the other side. This type of system is also referred to as a *physically shared memory* machine. Although the PE-to-PE configuration is assumed in this chapter, the material presented is applicable to the processor-to-memory configuration. It is also assumed the network is supporting the interconnection of $N = 2^n$ PEs.

One model of parallelism is known as *SIMD* (single-instruction, stream—multiple-data stream) [24]. A machine based on the SIMD model consists of a control unit, N PEs, and an interconnection network, as shown in Figure 3.1. The control unit broadcasts instructions to all the PEs in lock-step fashion (in other words, no PE can proceed to the next instruction until the current instruction has been completed by all active PEs). Each PE operates on data contained in its local memory. Thus, every enabled PE executes the same instruction at the same time, but each operates on its own data. Examples of SIMD machines that have been built include: the Thinking Machine Corporation (TMC) Connection Machine model CM-2 [80], DAP [29], Illiac IV [10], MasPar MP-1 [53], and MPP [14].

A *multiple-SIMD machine* [55] is a parallel processing system that can be dynamically reconfigured to operate as one or more independent SIMD submachines of various sizes. A multiple-SIMD machine consists of N PEs, an interconnection network, and Q control units, where $Q < N$. The CM-2 [80] is an example of a multiple-SIMD machine that has been built. In addition, the Illiac IV was originally designed as a multiple-SIMD architecture [10].

MIMD (multiple instruction stream—multiple data stream) [24] is another model of parallelism. In the MIMD model, each of N PEs functions independently using its own program counter and executing its own instructions on its own data. Any synchronization

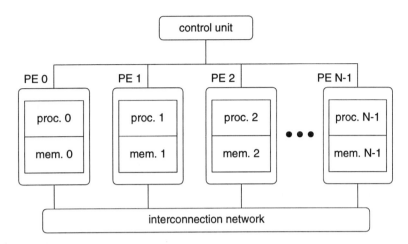

FIGURE 3.1   Block diagram of a SIMD machine with N PEs.

between the PEs must be specified explicitly. Figure 3.2 depicts a machine based on the MIMD model of parallelism. Examples of MIMD systems (or systems capable of MIMD operation) that have been constructed include: BBN Butterfly [18], Connection Machine model CM-5 [79], Intel iPSC [54], nCUBE [27], and IBM RP3 [60].

A *partitionable system* is able to dynamically partition and repartition itself into multiple submachines. The partitioning capabilities supported within partitionable systems are typically realized via their interconnection networks [66, 67]. Such partitioning capabilities include: (1) the ability to partition a network into subnetworks that each maintain complete network functionality, and (2) submachine independence, that is, no submachine can interfere with the proper operation of any other submachine. In a *partitionable mixed-mode machine*, all submachines can independently and dynamically switch between the SIMD and MIMD modes of parallelism. PASM [7, 73, 74] and TRAC [47] are examples of partitionable mixed-mode systems that have been constructed.

The ability to partition a machine into independent submachines implies that the machine's network can support the partitioning. Partitioning is necessary to have multiple-SIMD and partitionable mixed-mode systems. The advantages of partitionable systems include [75]: fault tolerance (if a processor fails, only those partitions that include the failed processor are affected), fault detection (for situations where high reliability is needed, more than one partition can run the same program on the same data and compare results), multiple simultaneous users (because there can be multiple independent partitions, there can be multiple simultaneous users of the system, each executing a different parallel program), easier program development (rather than trying to debug a parallel program on, for example, 1024 PEs, a user can debug the program on a smaller size partition of 32 PEs and then expand it to 1024 PEs), increased utilization (if a task requires only $N/2$ of N available processors, the other $N/2$ can be used for another task/user), optimization of number of PEs used (selecting a submachine size that minimizes task execution time; more PEs are not always better) [69], and subtask parallelism ([50], [67, page 111]) (two or more independent parallel subtasks that are part of the same job can be executed in parallel, sharing results if necessary). In

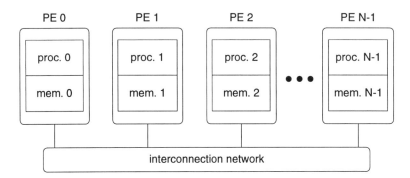

FIGURE 3.2   Block diagram of a MIMD machine with N PEs.

addition, the rules for partitioning a network can be employed in an MIMD machine to group together PEs that communicate frequently to reduce network *conflicts* (two or more messages wanting to use the same network link simultaneously).

All of the networks described in Sections 3.2 and 3.3 can be used to support all of these modes of parallelism. In all cases, there are limitations on the partitionability, and these are discussed.

3.1.3   Extreme Approaches to Network Design

When designing an interconnection network for any of the machine models described above, a trade-off between performance and cost of implementation must be considered. One extreme approach to this trade-off is represented by the single shared bus. This interconnection network has the advantage of being among the least costly, in terms of number of links required (only N links [bus interfaces] needed for N devices). However, such a network is not practical for use in a large-scale parallel processor, where it is often desirable to allow each processor to send data to another processor simultaneously (for example, processor i sends data to processor $i + 1$, where $0 \leq i < N - 1$). Consider the use of a single shared bus to connect N processors, as shown in Figure 3.3. If all N processors wished to communicate simultaneously, all N communications would have to be serialized, and one processor would experience a delay equal to the time required by the other $N - 1$ processors to complete their communications.

The other extreme is illustrated by the *fully connected network* shown in Figure 3.4. In a parallel machine consisting of N processors that are fully connected, every processor is connected to every other processor using $N \times (N - 1)$ unidirectional links. The advantage of this network is that all N processors can communicate simultaneously, that is, with no more delay than that of traversing one link of the network. However, the cost to implement a fully connected network is $O(N^2)$ (or, $N \times (N - 1)$ links are required). When N is large, as is the case for large-scale parallel processors, the cost is prohibitive. For example, if $N = 1024$, then 1,147,552 links are needed.

The *crossbar switch* shown in Figure 3.5 allows the simultaneous direct connection of every processor to a unique memory. One way to implement this is to use one link for each

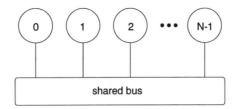

FIGURE 3.3   A single shared bus connecting N devices.

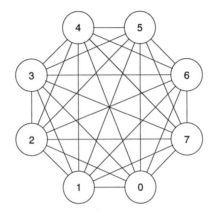

FIGURE 3.4   A fully connected system of eight processors.

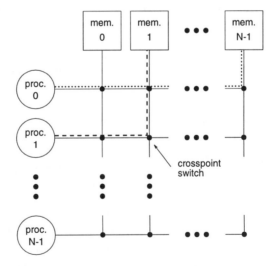

FIGURE 3.5   A crossbar switch used to connect N processors to N memories. The simultaneous paths from processor 0 to memory $N-1$ and processor 1 to memory 1 are shown.

of N processors, one link for each of N memories, and N^2 crosspoint switches. Processors communicate through the memories. A crosspoint switch is capable of providing any connection between each of its two inputs and each of its two outputs. For example, the simultaneous paths from processor 0 to memory $N - 1$, and processor 1 to memory 1 are shown. Similar to the fully connected network, the cost for the crossbar switch increases as N^2 (the number of crosspoint switches required). Thus, the crossbar switch is not suitable for large-scale parallel processors.

3.1.4 Chapter Overview

This chapter presents an important collection of network designs that fall between the extremes discussed above, and that can be used in large-scale parallel systems (for example, 2^6 to 2^{16} processors). That is, these networks can support the communication required by a collection of tightly coupled processors that cooperate to perform a single overall task. Many of these networks can be used in machines that can dynamically reconfigure themselves to form multiple independent submachines, where the submachines can be used to solve different tasks or subtasks concurrently. A variety of networks are explored, considering properties such as topology, routing control, and partitionability.

In this chapter, the networks discussed are divided into two classes: single stage and multistage [67]. Single-stage networks have also been called "point-to-point" networks [71] or "direct" networks (versus "indirect" for multistage networks) [59]. With a *single-stage* network, each network switch is directly connected to a processor; hence, a message goes through a single stage of switching before reaching the next processor (or processor/switch node combination). When a *multistage* network is used, a message must pass through multiple stages (often $n = \log_2 N$) of switches after leaving one processor before reaching another.

A great variety of networks have been proposed and studied in the literature. The goal of this chapter is to introduce a subset of the types of networks that have been proposed and acquaint the reader with some of their properties. After having the background provided here, the interested reader can refer to other books and to the papers listed in the references for information about other types of networks as well as more information about the types presented here. Relevant books include [5, 6, 30, 31, 47, 67, 81, 84, 87].

Section 3.2 examines the mesh and hypercube single-stage networks. Multistage networks are studied in Section 3.3. This begins with the multistage cube, which represents an important family of networks that includes the omega, indirect binary n-cube, multistage shuffle-exchange, delta, baseline, SW-banyan, and generalized cube. The extra stage cube (ESC), a fault-tolerant variation of the multistage cube, is then presented. This is followed by a discussion of the augmented data manipulator (ADM) multistage network. Then there is a description of the dynamic redundancy network, a fault-tolerant variation of the multistage cube that supports spare PEs and whose structure is based on the ADM. Section 3.3 ends with an examination of tree-based networks. In Section 3.4, some reasons why it is difficult to evaluate and compare different interconnection networks are considered.

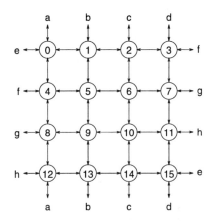

FIGURE 3.6 A four nearest-neighbor mesh network connecting $N = 16$ PEs. Lower case letters represent wraparound edge connections, such as from 3 ($= i$) to 4 ($= i + 1$).

3.2

SINGLE-STAGE NETWORKS

3.2.1 Introduction

In this section, three types of single-stage networks are overviewed: four nearest-neighbor mesh, eight nearest-neighbor mesh, and hypercube. All three types have been implemented in existing systems.

3.2.2 Four Nearest-neighbor Two-dimensional Mesh Networks

Topology In a mesh network, PEs are connected only to "neighbor" PEs. Figure 3.6 shows a *four nearest-neighbor mesh* network connecting $N = 16$ PEs arranged in a $\sqrt{N}$-by-$\sqrt{N}$ array. For a given PE i, PE i connects to PE $i + 1$, PE $i - 1$, PE $i + \sqrt{N}$, and PE $i - \sqrt{N}$, where all of the calculations are performed modulo N. The handling of the edge connections can vary from machine to machine. The Illiac IV [10] and MPP [14] are examples of parallel machines that implemented four nearest-neighbor mesh networks. It is possible to build rectangular meshes also; however, here a square mesh will be assumed.

Routing Control Consider a four nearest-neighbor mesh with no edge connections. One way to find a route for a message from a source PE S to a destination PE D is to precompute the number of row moves and column moves that the message must make. The number of rows R that the message must move is given by $R = \lfloor D/\sqrt{N} \rfloor - \lfloor S/\sqrt{N} \rfloor$. The number of columns C that the message must move is $C = (D \text{ modulo } \sqrt{N}) - (S \text{ modulo } \sqrt{N})$. These row and column counts can be prepended to the message to be sent. Then, a PE receiving the message moves it and updates the row or column count, depending on the link on which the message was sent. Both counts will equal zero on PE D.

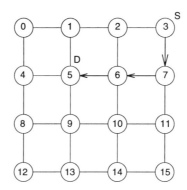

FIGURE 3.7 Example of routing from $S = 3$ to $D = 5$ in a four nearest-neighbor mesh network connecting $N = 16$ PEs.

An example is given in Figure 3.7. In this example, there are 16 PEs in the system and $\sqrt{N} = \sqrt{16} = 4$. The source PE number is $S = 3$, and the destination PE number is $D = 5$. Thus, $R = \lfloor 5/4 \rfloor - \lfloor 3/4 \rfloor = 1$, and $C = (5 \bmod 4) - (3 \bmod 4) = 1 - 3 = -2$. One of the possible routes resulting from this example is shown in Figure 3.7.

Partitioning A four nearest-neighbor mesh with no edge connections can be partitioned to form four size $N/4$ subnetworks, each with the properties of a mesh designed to be of size $N/4$, if $N/4$ is a perfect square. This can be done in a straightforward manner by partitioning the mesh into quadrants and disallowing communications between PEs that are in different quadrants. For the example in Figure 3.6. the four subnetworks would contain the PEs whose physical numbers are: (1) 0, 1, 4, 5; (2) 2, 3, 6, 7; (3) 8, 9, 12, 13; and (4) 10, 11, 14, 15. Within each subnetwork the PEs would be logically labeled from 0 to 3.

Four nearest-neighbor mesh networks with wraparound edge connections (as indicated by the lower-case letters in Figure 3.6) cannot be partitioned into four $N/4$ size networks with the same properties. For the example in the previous paragraph, for the first quadrant there would not be the wraparound edge connection from logical PE 3 (physical PE 5) to logical PE 0 (= 3 + 1) (physical PE 0).

Example of a System Using the Four Nearest-neighbor Network The Supercomputer Systems Division of Intel Corp. has developed the Intel Paragon XP-S, a four nearest-neighbor mesh-connected system of up to 1000 computational nodes [90]. The Paragon system is a direct descendant of the 528-processor Touchstone DELTA [46]. There are three types of nodes in the mesh: *compute nodes*, *I/O nodes*, and *service nodes*. Each compute node can be configured as either a *general-purpose* compute node with two Intel i860 XP microprocessors, or as a *multiprocessor node* containing three microprocessors. One microprocessor in each compute node is dedicated to transmitting and receiving messages on behalf of the other processor(s) of the node. A router chip is responsible for accepting messages from the routing chips of neighboring nodes, checking their addresses, and then either routing the messages to neighboring nodes or passing the messages to the processors of its own nodes. The routing chip in the mesh is based on a chip design originating at the California Institute of Technology [64].

3.2.3   Eight Nearest-neighbor Two-dimensional Mesh Networks

Figure 3.8 illustrates an *eight nearest-neighbor mesh* network connecting $N = 16$ PEs arranged in a $\sqrt{N}$-by-$\sqrt{N}$ array. Assuming modulo N arithmetic, an eight nearest-neighbor mesh connects PE i to PE $i + 1$, PE $i - 1$, PE $i + \sqrt{N}$, PE $i - \sqrt{N}$, PE $i + \sqrt{N} + 1$, PE $i + \sqrt{N} - 1$, PE $i - \sqrt{N} + 1$, and PE $i - \sqrt{N} - 1$. Once again, the way in which edge connections are handled may vary. Routing control and partitioning are similar to that for the four nearest-neighbor mesh.

The MasPar model MP-1 [53] incorporates a network with the connectivity of an eight nearest-neighbor mesh network. This is shown in Figure 3.9. A tri-state switching node at each "X" intersection allows communications with any of eight nearest-neighbors using only four input/output ports per PE. Recall MP-1 is an SIMD machine. To send a message from PE i to PE $i + 1$, each PE transmits out its northeast corner and each PE reads from its northwest corner. To send a message from PE i to PE $i + \sqrt{N} + 1$, each PE can transmit out its southeast corner, and read from its northwest corner. Communication between the other neighbors can be accomplished in a similar manner.

3.2.4   Hypercube Networks

Topology   The *hypercube* interconnection network provides direct links between PEs whose numbers differ by exactly one bit in their binary representations. A hypercube network that connects 2^3 PEs can be represented as an ordinary cube in three dimensions, as shown in Figure 3.10. Thus, the hypercube network of Figure 3.10 is also referred to as a three-cube or a 3-dimensional hypercube. Similarly, a hypercube network that connects $N = 2^n$ PEs is referred to as an n-cube, or alternately as an n-dimensional hypercube. Each dimension corresponds to a bit position in the PE numbers. For example, in Figure 3.10, the link connecting PE number 000 to PE number 001 is a 0-th dimension link because it connects two PEs whose numbers differ only in the 0-th bit position.

An n-cube can be constructed recursively from two $(n - 1)$-cubes by adding connecting links between PEs that have the same number. Then, a 0 is appended as the most significant bit to the PE numbers in the first $(n - 1)$-cube, and a 1 is appended as the most significant bit to the PE numbers in the second $(n - 1)$-cube. The minimum distance between any two PEs, in terms of number of links, is equal to the number of bits that differ in their PE numbers. This distance is known as the *Hamming distance*. The maximum distance between any two PEs connected by an n-cube interconnection network is n and occurs when the numbers of the two PEs differ in every bit position.

Routing Control   One way of routing messages in a hypercube network is described as follows. The sending PE (source PE) prepends a routing tag to the front of the message. This routing tag is formed as the bitwise exclusive-OR of the source and destination PE numbers. Thus, the i-th bit of the routing tag will be 1 if the i-th bits of the source and

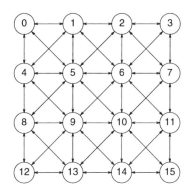

FIGURE 3.8   An eight nearest-neighbor mesh network connecting $N = 16$ PEs without any wraparound connections.

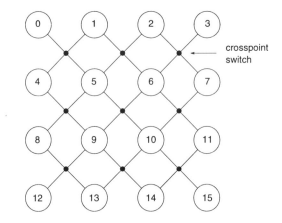

FIGURE 3.9   The X-Net used in the MasPar MP-1 SIMD machine, shown for $N = 16$.

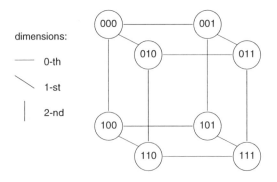

FIGURE 3.10   A three-dimensional hypercube.

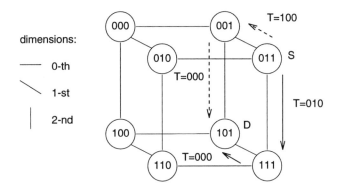

FIGURE 3.11   Routing control in a three-dimensional hypercube.

destination PEs differ, and 0 if the i-th bits of the source and destination PEs are the same. Any PE that receives a message that has a 1 in the i-th bit position, sets that bit to 0 and sends the message on its i-th dimension link. A PE that receives a message with a routing tag equal to all 0s is the destination PE.

Consider the example in Figure 3.11. In this example, the source PE, S, is PE number $3 = 011$, and the destination PE, D, is PE number $5 = 101$. The routing tag is initially $S \oplus D = 110$, where "$\oplus$" means bitwise exclusive-OR. If S sends the message on its first dimension, it resets the first bit of the routing tag and sends the message to PE $1 = 001$. PE 1 then resets the second bit of the routing tag and sends the message to PE $5 = 101$, which is D, and the routing tag is equal to zero. In similar fashion, the message could have arrived at its destination by traveling from S to PE $7 = 111$ to D. Thus, for this example, there exist two independent minimum length paths from PE 3 to PE 5.

Partitioning   An n-dimensional hypercube network connecting N PEs can be partitioned into two hypercube networks that each connect $N/2$ PEs, and that each have all of the properties of an $(n-1)$-dimensional hypercube. For example, the 3-dimensional hypercube of Figure 3.12 is partitioned into two 2-dimensional subcubes by disallowing the use of all of the second-dimension links in the original hypercube. In this example, PEs 0, 1, 2, and 3 reside in one subcube, while PEs 4, 5, 6, and 7 reside in the other. In general, there are n ways to partition an n-dimensional hypercube into two $(n-1)$-dimensional subcubes, because there are n different dimensions along which communication can be disallowed. Each $(n-1)$-dimensional subcube can be further independently partitioned into two $(n-2)$-dimensional subcubes, and so on.

Embedding a Four Nearest-neighbor Mesh in a Hypercube   One of the attractive properties of a hypercube network is that it is possible to embed a four nearest-neighbor mesh network within it. Here, *embedding* refers to the logical assignment of the nodes of a mesh (logical PE numbers) into the physical nodes of a hypercube (physical PE numbers) in such a way as to preserve the connectivity of the mesh network among the logical PE numbers in the hypercube network. That is, for any logical PE number i in the hypercube network, there are direct links to logical PE numbers $i + 1$, $i - 1$, $i + \sqrt{N}$, and $i - \sqrt{N}$.

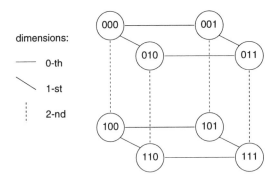

FIGURE 3.12   Partitioning a three-dimensional hypercube along the second dimension.

The logical to physical assignment of PE numbers in the hypercube network is performed using *Gray codes*. One way of generating Gray codes leads to the binary-reflected Gray code. Let G_i^k be the binary-reflected Gray code of the k-bit integer i, and $G(k) = (G_0^k, G_1^k, \ldots, G_{2^k-1}^k)$ be the k-bit code for all 2^k such integers. Then, a binary-reflected Gray code is recursively defined as follows.

$$G(1) = (0, 1) \tag{3.1}$$

$$G(k + 1) = (0G_0^k, 0G_1^k, \ldots, 0G_{2^k-1}^k, 1G_{2^k-1}^k, \ldots, 1G_1^k, 1G_0^k) \tag{3.2}$$

For example, the binary-reflected three-bit Gray code is $G(3) = (000, 001, 011, 010, 110, 111, 101, 100)$.

The example in Figure 3.13 shows how a mesh network is embedded into a hypercube network. In this example, the $N = 16$ PEs connected by a four nearest-neighbor mesh are arranged in a four-by-four array. The mesh logical numbering of the PEs is given by the decimal numbers. To determine the corresponding physical PE numbers, beginning in the upper left-hand corner, the columns of the array are numbered in binary-reflected two-bit Gray code order. The rows of the array are numbered in the same way. The binary code for each of the physical hypercube PE numbers is generated by concatenating the row bits as the two most significant bits and the column bits as the two least significant bits. Thus, in Figure 3.13, the decimal numbers are the logical mesh PE numbers and the binary numbers are the physical hypercube PE numbers. It can be seen from the figure that no two connected physical PE numbers differ by more than one bit (as must be the case for a hypercube network).

Different size and dimension meshes can be embedded in a hypercube. This is discussed in [28].

Example of a System Using a Hypercube Network   The nCUBE Corporation has developed the nCUBE/3 [21], a PE-to-PE MIMD system connected with a hypercube topology. The nCUBE/3 is a direct descendant of the nCUBE/1 and nCUBE/2 systems [27]. Each PE has 16 separate DMA channels devoted to inter-PE communication. Thus, the node design will support up to a 16-dimensional hypercube (that is, up to 2^{16} or 65,536

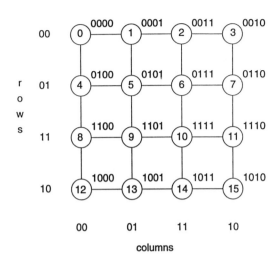

FIGURE 3.13   Embedding a four nearest-neighbor mesh network into a hypercube network.

PEs). Similar to the Intel Paragon, the nCUBE/3 routes messages through a node with no processor intervention, greatly reducing latency. Additionally, there are two more DMA channels per node that are dedicated to I/O.

3.3

MULTISTAGE NETWORKS

3.3.1 Introduction

In this section, five types of multistage networks are overviewed. The five are the multistage cube, the extra stage cube, the data manipulator, the dynamic redundancy, and trees.

3.3.2 Multistage Cube Networks

Topology   Networks topologically equivalent to the multistage cube have been called different names [65, 67, 76, 86], including baseline [86], bidelta [36], butterfly [18], delta $(a = b = 2)$ [58], flip [11], generalized cube [70, 76], indirect binary n-cube [59], multistage shuffle-exchange [78], omega [39], and SW-banyan $(S = F = 2)$ [25, 47] networks. Figure 3.14 shows the *generalized cube* network topology for N inputs and N outputs, which was introduced as a standard for comparing different types of multistage cube networks [76]. There are $n = \log_2 N$ stages, numbered from 0 to $n - 1$, where each stage consists of a set of N links, numbered from 0 to $N - 1$, connected to $N/2$ interchange boxes. Each *interchange box* is a two-input, two-output switch that can be set independently to one of the four states indicated in Figure 3.14. The numbers of the links entering the upper and lower inputs of an interchange box are used as the labels for the upper and lower outputs, respectively. At stage i interchange boxes, links whose numbers differ only in the i-th bit

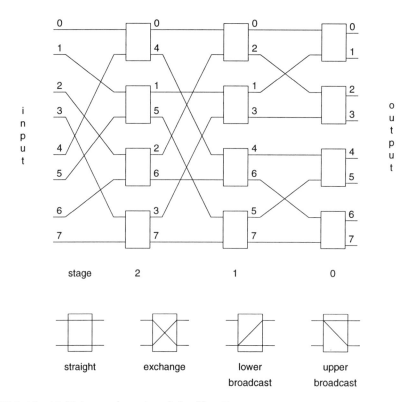

FIGURE 3.14   **Multistage cube network for** $N = 8$.

position are paired. PE j is attached to both network input port j and network output port j. The name *multistage cube* refers to the network consisting of the generalized cube topology and interchange boxes with the capabilities shown in Figure 3.14 [67].

Throughout this subsection, 2×2 interchange boxes are used for discussing new properties. Consider using $b \times b$ crossbars as the interchange boxes, for N a power of b. All of the properties described in this subsection for the 2×2 case can be adapted for the $b \times b$ case by using base b arithmetic as the basis instead of base 2. For example, the b links that differ only in the i-th digit of their base b representation will enter the same interchange box at stage i, $0 \le i < \log_b N$.

Establishing Paths   To establish a path from a source $S = s_{n-1} \ldots s_1 s_0$ to a destination $D = d_{n-1} \ldots d_1 d_0$, the stage i interchange box in the path from S to D should be set as follows: if $d_i = s_i$ then the interchange box is set to straight, and if $d_i = \bar{s}_i$ then the interchange box is set to exchange. For example, if $s_2 s_1 s_0 = 110$ and $d_2 d_1 d_0 = 011$, then the interchange boxes are set as shown in Figure 3.15. The links that a message from S to D traverses are $s_{n-1} \ldots s_1 s_0$ before stage $n-1$, $d_{n-1} s_{n-2} \ldots s_1 s_0$ after stage $n-1$, $d_{n-1} d_{n-2} s_{n-3} \ldots s_1 s_0$ after stage $n-2$, $\ldots$, and $d_{n-1} \ldots d_1 d_0$ after stage 0. In general, the link that a message from S to D traverses after stage i is $d_{n-1} \ldots d_{i+1} d_i s_{i-1} \ldots s_1 s_0$. For

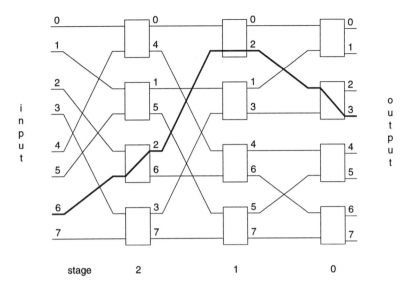

FIGURE 3.15 The path from input 6 to output 3 in the multistage cube network for $N = 8$.

the example in Figure 3.15, the links used are $s_2 s_1 s_0 = 110$ at the input, $d_2 s_1 s_0 = 010$ after stage 2, $d_2 d_1 s_0 = 010$ after stage 1, and $d_2 d_1 d_0 = 011$ after stage 0.

There is only one path for a given source/destination pair because the stage i output link used in the path from S to D must be $d_{n-1} \ldots d_{i+1} d_i s_{i-1} \ldots s_1 s_0$. This unique path property limits the fault tolerance of the multistage cube topology. A single network fault (that is, a faulty interchange box or faulty network link) will prevent some source/destination pairs from being able to communicate. Two fault-tolerant variations of the multistage cube, the extra stage cube and dynamic redundancy interconnection networks, will be described later.

A *conflict* occurs in a multistage cube network when the messages on the two input links of an interchange box require the same output link. Typically, when a situation like this arises, one message is blocked and must wait until the other has completed its transmission. Both requests cannot be accommodated simultaneously.

Networks may be constructed as either circuit-switched or packet-switched structures. In *circuit-switched* networks, once a path is established by the routing tag, the interchange boxes in the path remain in their specified state until the path is released. A complete circuit is set up between the source and destination and data is sent directly over this circuit. In *packet-switched* networks, the routing tag and data to be transmitted are collected together into a *packet*. Packet switching uses data buffers in each interchange box to store packets (or portions of packets) as they move through the network. Unlike circuit-switched networks, which use n interchange boxes to establish a path, packet-switched networks may use as few as one interchange box at a time or may stream a packet through several successive interchange boxes. Techniques that allow the head of a packet to exit an interchange box before the tail of the packet has arrived include worm-hole routing [19] and virtual cut-through routing [34].

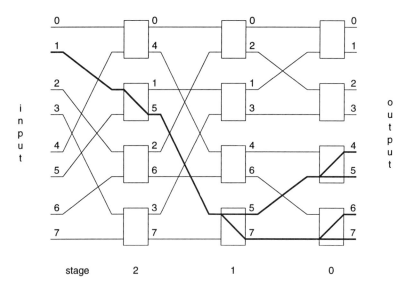

FIGURE 3.16 The multicast path from input 1 to outputs 4, 5, 6, and 7 in the multistage cube network for $N = 8$.

Networks that combine messages are another method of constructing multistage cube interconnection networks. In processor-to-memory configurations, depending on an application's memory access patterns, one memory module may be the target of increased load/store traffic. This creates a *hot spot* at the memory module, possibly causing some of that memory module's requests to be delayed. In a packet-switched network, if the memory module can no longer accept more packets, the network buffers in the interchange boxes leading to the "hot" memory module may begin to fill up and cause traffic destined for other memory modules to be delayed. This phenomenon has been termed *hot-spot contention* [61].

One technique to avoid hot spots is called *combining* [38, 41]. Assume a processor-to-memory configuration and a bidirectional network. When two load requests to the same memory module meet at an interchange box, they can be combined and forwarded to the next stage as a single request. When the response returns through the same interchange box it is de-combined into two responses. This can significantly reduce the traffic at the "hot" memory modules and reduce overall network delay for other traffic. Requests other than loads and stores can be combined. For example test-and-set and fetch-and-add synchronization primitives may be combined [77]. The NYU Ultracomputer and IBM RP3 are two examples of systems that incorporate combining in a multistage cube topology (see case studies later in this subsection).

When the lower and/or upper broadcast states of interchange boxes are used in a path, a *multicast* (one-to-many) connection is established. For example, in Figure 3.16 input 1 connects to outputs 4, 5, 6, and 7.

Routing Control   As with the mesh and hypercube networks, routing control for the multistage cube is distributed among the PEs by using a routing tag as the header (first item) of each message to be transmitted through the network. For one-to-one connections, an n-bit routing tag can be computed by the source PE from its number $S = s_{n-1} \ldots s_1 s_0$ and the desired destination PE number $D = d_{n-1} \ldots d_1 d_0$ in a way similar to that described for the hypercube. The *exclusive-OR routing tag* $T = t_{n-1} \ldots t_1 t_0 = S \oplus D$ [70]. When an interchange box at stage i receives a message, it examines bit t_i of the tag. If $t_i = 0$, the straight connection is used, because $t_i = 0$ implies $d_i = s_i$. If $t_i = 1$, an exchange is performed, because $t_i = 1$ implies $d_i = \bar{s}_i$. For the example in Figure 3.15, when $N = 8$, $S = 6 = 110$, and $D = 3 = 011$, the tag $T = 101$, and the corresponding interchange box settings from input to output are exchange ($t_2 = 1$), straight ($t_1 = 0$), and exchange ($t_0 = 1$).

The same tag used to route data from S to D can be used to route data from D to S because the exclusive-OR operation is commutative (i.e., $S \oplus D = D \oplus S$). This can be used to confirm receipt of the data. Given each PE knows its own address (output port number), it can use the tag to compute the source address S (input port number) that sent the data: $S = T \oplus D$.

The *destination tag* scheme, where the destination $D = d_{n-1} \ldots d_1 d_0$ is the tag sent as the header [39], is another approach to routing tags. This scheme is based on the assumption that the upper output link of a stage i interchange box always has a 0 in the i-th bit position of its label, while the lower output link always has a 1. Thus, using the upper output link of the box leads to a destination where $d_i = 0$, while using the lower output link leads to a destination where $d_i = 1$. When a stage i interchange box receives a message, it examines d_i: if $d_i = 0$ the upper box output is taken, if $d_i = 1$ the lower box output is taken. For the example in Figure 3.15, to go from source 6 to destination 3 the upper output of the stage 2 interchange box ($d_2 = 0$), the lower output of the stage 1 interchange box ($d_1 = 1$), and the lower output of the stage 0 interchange box ($d_0 = 1$) are chosen. This same destination tag ($D = 011$) can be used to route data from any input to output 3.

The destination tag is easier to compute than an exclusive-OR tag, and a destination PE can compare the destination tag that arrives against its own PE number to determine if the message arrived at the correct network output (if it did not, the network must be faulty). The destination tag scheme cannot determine the source, as the XOR scheme can. Either method can have the capability to determine if the data arrived at the proper destination and to identify its source by sending the source address along with the destination tag or sending the destination address along with the exclusive-OR tag.

A multicast routing tag scheme that consists of an n-bit multicast mask along with either type of n-bit routing tag can be used to specify a variety of multicast connections (but not all those physically possible) [67, 70, 85].

Partitioning Partitioning a multistage cube network is conceptually the same as partitioning a single-stage hypercube network. There are n ways to partition a multistage cube of size N into two independent subnetworks of size $N/2$, each one based on a different bit position of the input/output port addresses [66, 67]. One way is to force all of the interchange boxes in stage $n - 1$ to the straight state. This forms two subnetworks: one consisting of input/output ports 0 to $(N/2) - 1$ (those with a 0 in the high-order bit position of their addresses) and the other consisting of ports $N/2$ to $N - 1$ (those with a 1 in the

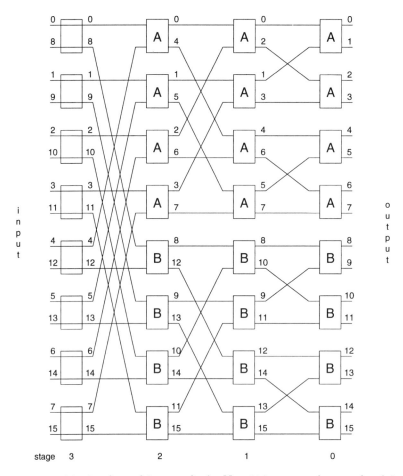

FIGURE 3.17   Partitioning the multistage cube for $N = 16$ into two subnetworks of size eight based on the high-order bit position. Subnetwork A consists of PEs 0 to 7 and subnetwork B consists of PEs 8 to 15.

high-order bit position). These two disjoint sets of input/output ports can communicate with each other only by using the exchange or broadcast settings in stage $n - 1$. By forcing this stage to straight, the subnetworks are independent and have full use of the rest of the network (stages $n - 2$ to 0). This is illustrated in Figure 3.17.

Because each subnetwork has the properties of a multistage cube, each can be further subdivided, as was the case with the hypercube network. Assume the size $N/2$ subnetworks were formed by setting stage j interchange boxes to straight, $0 \le j < n$. Either size $N/2$ subnetwork can then be divided into two size $N/4$ subnetworks by setting all the stage k interchange boxes in the size $N/2$ subnetwork to straight, for any k, $0 \le k < n$, $k \ne j$. Partitioning the B subnetwork of Figure 3.17 into halves based on bit position $n - 2$ is shown in Figure 3.18. The process of dividing subnetworks into independent halves can

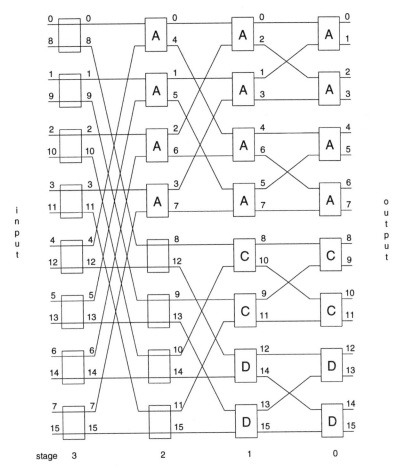

FIGURE 3.18 Partitioning the multistage cube for $N = 16$ into one subnetwork of size eight (A, PEs 0 to 7) and two subnetworks of size four (C, PEs 8 to 11, and D, PEs 12 to 15).

be repeated on any existing subnetworks (independently) to form subnetworks of different sizes. The only constraints are that the size of each subnetwork must be a power of two, each input/output port can belong to at most one subnetwork, the physical addresses of the input/output ports of a subnetwork of size 2^s must all agree in any fixed set of $n - s$ bit positions, and the interchange boxes used by this subnetwork are set to straight in the $n - s$ stages corresponding to these $n - s$ bit positions (the other s stages are used by the subnetwork to form a multistage cube network. of size 2^s).

The routing tag schemes described previously can be used within partitions. In fact, these routing tag schemes can be used to enforce the partitioning, assuming there exist some privileged instructions with which the operating system can set a mask each time a partition is initially created [72]. This is also true for the hypercube network.

Examples of Systems Using a Multistage Cube Network   Existing systems that use some form of the multistage cube network topology include: ASPRO, Cedar, GP1000 (and TC2000), RP3, Allnode, Vulcan/SP1, and Ultracomputer. The following case studies demonstrate some of the ways the multistage cube network topology is being employed.

The Loral ASPRO   The Loral ASPRO, or ASsociative PROcessor [14], is a next-generation evolution of the STARAN series of parallel processors of the 1970s [13]. An ASPRO array unit is composed of up to 16 array modules, where each array module consists of four SIMD machines. Each SIMD machine uses a processor-to-memory organization with 32-bit serial processors and their associated 32×4096 bit array (plane) of multidimensional access (MDA) memory [12] with a flip network similar to the STARAN parallel processors. MDA memory permits horizontal and vertical (row and column) accesses to the bit plane of memory.

The flip network, located between the processors and the memory, is needed to implement MDA memory. In the ASPRO, 32 processors along with a 32-input, 32-output flip network are packaged on a VLSI chip. The flip network is a multistage cube network with individual stage control, that is, interchange boxes in a given stage are all set to exchange or all set to straight. Control of the flip network is centralized; routing tags are not used. Instead, for a flip network with $2^n = 32$ inputs, $n = 5$ control lines from the central controller (one control line for each stage) set the network to any of 2^n permutations. Processor connectivity in the ASPRO is limited to communicating through the MDA memory.

The Cedar System   Cedar [37] is a hybrid processor-to-memory configuration multiprocessor system constructed at the University of Illinois. In Cedar, multiple computing clusters are connected through a multistage cube network to a global shared memory. Each Cedar cluster is a slightly modified Alliant FX/8 minisupercomputer with eight microprocessors. The global shared memory is intended to hold data that must be shared among clusters. The prototype has 32 processors [35], while the architecture is designed to support 1024 processors.

Cedar's prototype multistage cube interconnection network is based on a unidirectional 8×8 interchange box (implemented as an 8×8 crossbar). Thus, two unidirectional networks are required to establish a path from the processors to the global shared memory and a path back from the global shared memory to the processors. Each unidirectional network has two stages of 8×8 interchange boxes. An interchange box consists of an 8×8 crossbar implemented by ECL gate arrays and interface/control logic constructed from off-the-shelf components. Two stages of 8×8 interchange boxes form a network with 64 inputs and 64 outputs. For the 32-processor prototype, a subset of the links and/or interchange boxes that compose a full 64×64 network is used.

The GP1000 and TC2000 Systems   The GP1000 multiprocessor [8] is a commercial PE-to-PE parallel processor manufactured by BBN Advanced Computers, Inc. It is a logically shared memory space MIMD machine with up to 128 PEs that uses a multistage cube type of interconnection network called the "Butterfly Switch" for communication.

The GP1000 Butterfly Switch is unidirectional and uses 4×4 interchange boxes. Each interchange box is implemented on a single VLSI chip. Larger systems ($N > 16$) use an extra stage of 4×4 interchange boxes that allow multiple paths for any given source/destination pair. The alternate paths can be used to route around failed interchange boxes (in most cases) and to route around busy portions of the network. This concept is discussed further in subsection 3.3.

BBN also developed the TC2000 system [9], which is similar to the GP1000. Some of the differences germane to this discussion are: the design can support over 500 PEs, the network is bidirectional, 8×8 interchange boxes are used, and each interchange box is implemented by gate array chips.

IBM RP3   IBM has built an experimental PE-to-PE logically shared memory parallel machine called RP3 (Research Parallel Processor Prototype) [60]. In the RP3 architectural design concept, which has 512 PEs, there are two buffered, packet-switched, multistage cube networks: one combining and one noncombining. The noncombining network consists of four stages of 4×4 interchange boxes. In principle, this would provide 256 ports, but the number of ports is reduced to 128, in exchange for providing dual paths between ports. Furthermore, each port is connected to four PEs through a multiplexer and a demultiplexer. The network is actually composed of two unidirectional networks—one for requests and one for replies.

In the architectural design, the combining network uses 2×2 interchange boxes and can combine the following operations: load, store, fetch-and-store, fetch-and-store-if-zero, fetch-and-add, fetch-and-min, fetch-and-max, fetch-and-OR, and fetch-and-AND. Only like operations can be combined, but loads are treated as fetch-and-adds of zero allowing loads and fetch-and-adds to combine with each other.

In the prototype, the network has 128 ports as described above, but there are only 64 PEs; each PE has its own port and half the ports are unused. There is no combining network in the prototype, but the fetch-and-OP operations (listed above) are still handled indivisibly at the memory modules.

IBM Allnode   IBM has developed the Allnode interconnection network [17] that can be used to connect workstations (PEs) that accept Micro Channel 3 adapters (specifically RISC System/6000 and some PS/2 systems). Using the terminology developed in this chapter, each workstation is a PE and is attached to the Allnode interconnection network via an adapter card. Allnode is a multistage cube, circuit-switched network where PEs communicate via message passing.

The Allnode is based on an 8×8 switching element. The current Allnode has two stages of switches with two switches per stage forming a 16-input/output interconnection network. Larger implementations are also possible. Because the network is circuit switched, there are no buffers for storing messages in the switching elements. Instead, 128 Kbyte buffers in the Micro Channel adapters hold substantial numbers of large messages (up to 4 Kbytes) and assist in speed matching between the Allnode and the workstation. The Allnode offers some degree of fault tolerance because four paths exist for any source/destination pair (within the network).

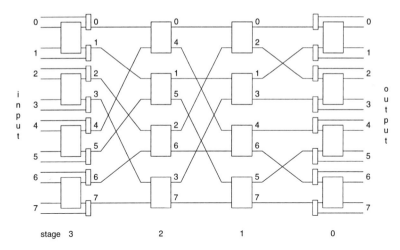

FIGURE 3.19   The extra-stage cube for $N = 8$.

IBM Vulcan/SP1   IBM has developed the Scalable POWERparallel 1 (SP1) workstation cluster [32]. The SP1 supports from 8 to 64 RISC System/6000 (engineering workstation) processing nodes. The processing nodes communicate with other nodes via message passing. Available as an option on the SP1 is the High Performance Switch, which is a multistage, packet-switched, interconnection network. The High Performance Switch is a derivative of the interconnection network used in the IBM Vulcan research prototype [16].

The interconnection network is based on an 8×8 switching element that *can* be used to form a multistage network. In the SP1, the eight unidirectional input links and eight unidirectional output links of the switching elements are arranged such that a 4×4 bidirectional switching element is formed. That is, four of the input/output (bidirectional) links are connected to the previous stage and the other four are connected to the succeeding stage. The switching elements are capable of *turnaround routing* [16] , which allows a packet to enter on one port of a switching element and exit the switching element on any of the eight ports connected to either the previous or succeeding stages. With turnaround routing the topology of the SP1 is more like a fat-tree topology (described in subsection 3.6) than a multistage cube topology. Like the fat-tree topology, messages are routed up and then down a subtree that contains both source and destination PEs. Unlike the fat-tree topology, the number of switching nodes in upper levels does not decrease, in other words, the number of switching elements per level (or stage) remains constant.

NYU Ultracomputer   New York University is developing a processor-to-memory configuration parallel computer called the NYU Ultracomputer [26]. One novel feature of this machine is that it supports the combining of concurrent memory operations, including concurrent fetch-and-adds. This is done using a buffered, packet-switched, combining, multistage cube network.

The Ultra III prototype is under construction [15]. It is composed of 16 processors and memory modules connected by a 16-input/output combining multistage cube network. The

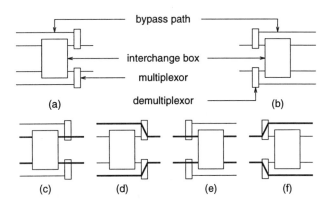

FIGURE 3.20   (a) Details of a stage n interchange box; (b) details of a stage 0 interchange box; (c) stage n enabled; (d) stage n disabled; (e) stage 0 enabled; (f) stage 0 disabled.

Ultra III network uses 2×2 interchange boxes with bidirectional links. This increases the complexity of the single network, but is necessary to support combining (and subsequent de-combining) of messages. Each 2×2 combining interchange box is composed of two types of custom VLSI chips: a *forward path component* and a *return path component*. The forward path component routes messages from processors to memory modules, combines messages, and relays information about combined messages to the return path component. The return path component routes messages from memory modules to processors, using the information obtained from the forward path component to de-combine messages as appropriate.

3.3.3   The Extra-stage Cube Network

Topology   As mentioned in subsection 3.2, there is only one path between any given source and given destination in a multistage cube network. Thus, any network fault (such as, a broken link) will prevent some source-destination pairs from communicating. This subsection describes the *extra-stage cube* (ESC) network, a single-fault-tolerant network derived from the multistage cube [2, 3, 4, 67]. The ESC network is formed from the multistage cube by adding one extra stage at the input, and hardware to allow the bypass, when desired, of the extra stage (stage n) or the output stage (stage 0). Stage n pairs links that differ in the 0-th bit position just as stage 0 does. This results in an additional path being available from each source to each destination. An ESC network for $N = 8$ PEs is shown in Figure 3.19.

   To bypass stage n or 0, logic consisting of dual input/output ports and a set of multiplexors or demultiplexors is incorporated around each interchange box in the stage. Refer to Figure 3.20 for a depiction of this logic. Stage n can be bypassed (disabled) by setting the multiplexors to select data from the network input port that does not route data through the interchange boxes. Stage 0 is disabled by setting the demultiplexors to route data around the interchange box on the alternate set of network output port links. If a stage is not

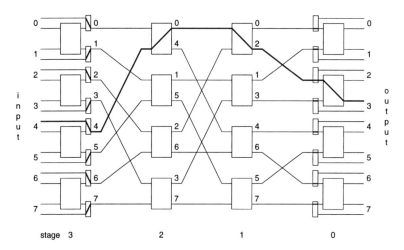

FIGURE 3.21   **The path from input 4 to output 3 in an $N = 8$ ESC network, when stage 3 is disabled and stage 0 is enabled.**

bypassed, it is enabled and messages pass through its interchange boxes. A system control unit or designated PE is responsible for enabling/disabling stages n and 0. Dual input/output ports allow the network to tolerate a fault in the network input/output port links. In normal operation with no fault detected in the network, stage n is disabled and stage 0 is enabled. This yields the multistage cube topology.

Fault Tolerance   The fault model for the ESC network allows a single fault in any of the interchange boxes, links, or interconnection network input/output lines to be tolerated. A failure in a stage n multiplexor or stage 0 demultiplexor is considered to be a link failure and can also be tolerated. When a fault occurs it must be detected and located. A variety of techniques for detecting and locating failed components in the multistage cube topology have been described, including test patterns [20, 23], dynamic parity checking [70], and handshaking signals. Once located, the failed component is assumed to remain unusable until some repair action can be taken.

An interchange box fault in either stage n or 0 can be tolerated by disabling the stage containing the fault. When either the input or output stage is disabled there are still n stages available, one corresponding to each bit position in a link number. Thus, a path is available between any source and destination. This is demonstrated in Figures 3.21 and 3.22.

Consider a fault in a link or stage i interchange box, $0 < i < n$. In this case, both stages n and 0 are enabled. When stage n is enabled, it provides two entry points into stage $n - 1$. The two entry points are links that differ only in the 0-th bit position. This means that the two paths cannot meet at an interchange box until stage 0 (which pairs links that differ in the 0-th bit position). Stages $n - 1$ through 0 of the ESC network form a multistage cube network that provides exactly one path from a given stage $n - 1$ input link to a given stage 0 output link. Thus, the two entry points provided by stage n will meet only in stage 0 and

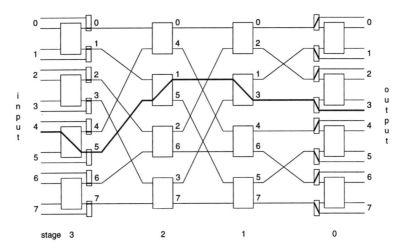

FIGURE 3.22   The path from input 4 to output 3 in an $N = 8$ ESC network, when stage 3 is enabled and stage 0 is disabled.

any single link fault or stage i box fault, $0 < i < n$, can be tolerated. An example is shown in Figure 3.23.

A fault in a network input line from a processor to a stage n multiplexor is tolerated by enabling stage n and using the stage n box input/output links. If a fault occurs on a stage n box input line, that fault is ignored because the line is unused unless there is a second fault elsewhere. (Recall only a single fault is considered.) If a fault in a stage 0 box output line is detected, then stage 0 is bypassed as if there was a stage 0 box fault. If the fault were in a stage 0 multiplexor output line, then the fault is ignored because the line is unused elsewhere.

Routing Control   Routing tags for the ESC can be generated in the same way as for the multistage cube, with the addition of an n-th high-order bit to control stage n (the extra stage) [3, 67]. Consider exclusive-OR tags (destination tags are analogous). If there is no fault or a stage n box fault, enable stage 0, disable stage n, use the regular tag bits for stages 0 to $n - 1$, and set the n-th bit of the tag to X ("don't care" because stage n is bypassed and never examines the tag). Similarly, if there is a stage 0 box fault, disable stage 0, enable stage n, use the regular tag bits for stages 1 to $n - 1$, use the stage 0 tag as the n-th bit of the tag so stage n will do whatever stage 0 was supposed to do, and set the 0-th bit of the tag to X. If there is a link fault or stage i box fault, $0 < i < n$, then enable both stage n and stage 0, use the regular tag bits for stages 1 to $n - 1$, and two cases must be examined for the other tag bits. If the fault is not on the path from the source to the destination when stage n is bypassed, then stage n for this path is set to straight by making the n-th bit 0. If the fault is on that path, then the alternate path is used by setting the stage n box the source enters to exchange by making the n-th bit of the tag a 1 and the 0-th bit of the tag the complement of $t_0 = s_0 \oplus d_0$ to compensate for this exchange in the extra stage.

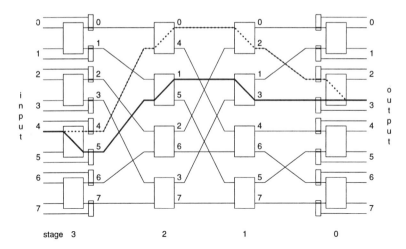

FIGURE 3.23   The two paths from input 4 to output 3 in an $N = 8$ ESC network, when both stages 3 and 0 are enabled.

Partitioning   Partitioning the ESC network is similar to partitioning the multistage cube network with one additional constraint. The partitioning cannot be based on the 0-th bit position of the input/output port addresses (that is, partitions of even and odd numbered PEs are not allowed). This constraint is necessary because in the ESC network both stages n and 0 must be available for use to supply the alternate paths needed for fault tolerance. By controlling the bypass of each stage n and 0 box individually, each partition can be an independent ESC network.

Example of a System Using the Extra-Stage Cube   PASM is a partitionable SIMD/MIMD parallel processing system design intended to support as many as 1024 PEs [7, 69, 73, 74, 75]. PASM can be partitioned dynamically to work as one or more independent or cooperating submachines of various sizes. Each submachine can independently switch between SIMD and MIMD modes of operation at instruction-level granularity with negligible overhead; that is, it is a partitionable mixed-mode machine as defined in Section 3.1. These features, in conjunction with the multistage cube type of interconnection network used, make PASM a highly reconfigurable architecture. A 30-processor prototype, with 16 PEs in the computation unit, has been constructed at Purdue University [73, 74].

The PASM prototype uses a five-stage, $N = 16$ ESC network. The network uses the destination tag routing scheme. Each interchange box is a 2×2 crossbar implemented with standard TTL components.

3.3.4   Data Manipulator Networks

Topology   The data manipulator network family [67] is a class of multistage that includes the data manipulator [22], the augmented data manipulator (ADM) [76], the inverse augmented data manipulator (IADM) [48], and the gamma [57] multistage interconnection

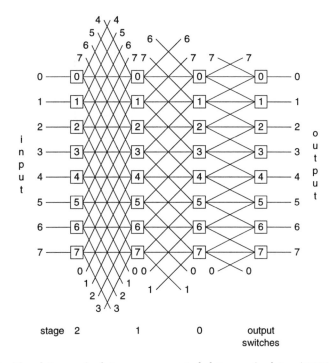

FIGURE 3.24   The data manipulator or augmented data manipulator (ADM) network for $N = 8$.

networks. The *data manipulator* (Figure 3.24) consists of n stages ($N = 2^n$). Each stage is a column of N switches. There is also an $(n + 1)$-st column of network output ports. The stages are ordered from $n - 1$ to 0. At stage i, switch j can pass data to switch $j + 2^i$ modulo N of stage $i - 1$, switch j of stage $i - 1$, or $j - 2^i$ modulo N of stage $i - 1$. A *switch* has three input links and three output links. Each switch can pass data from one of its input links to any one of its output links for a "one-to-one" setting. Data can also be passed from one of a switch's input links to more than one of its output links for a "broadcast" setting.

The *augmented data manipulator* (*ADM*) is a data manipulator network constructed so that each switch can be set independently. The *inverse augmented data manipulator* (*IADM*) (Figure 3.25) is similar to the ADM except the stage ordering is reversed (stage 0 is the input stage). It is called the "Inverse" ADM because for any data permutation the ADM can do in one pass through the network, the IADM can do the inverse of that permutation [67]. The *gamma* network is a data manipulator network that has reverse stage ordering and individual switch control. The gamma network uses a 3×3 crossbar in each switch. This allows a gamma switch to perform several one-to-one settings at once; that is, all of the switch inputs can each be connected to a unique switch output concurrently.

In some cases, data manipulator networks have a single path from a source S to a destination D while in other cases multiple paths exist; in other words, the number of paths between a given S and D may vary from one S/D pair to the next [51]. Having a variable number of paths impacts the network throughput, permuting ability, and routing tag control.

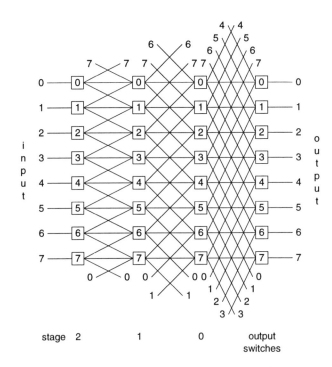

FIGURE 3.25   The inverse augmented data manipulator (IADM) or gamma network for $N = 8$.

There are no implementations of the data manipulator network mentioned in the literature to our knowledge. However, this family of networks is being studied by a large number of researchers, for example, [22, 40, 42, 45, 48, 56, 62, 63, 67, 82, 83, 88, 89].

Routing Control   To route data from a source S to an output D, the data must traverse links whose sum is $(D - S)$ modulo N ($-x = (N - x)$ modulo N). As an example, for an ADM network with $N = 8$, the links traversed for $S = 1$ and $D = 6$ are: $+2^2$ ($+2^2$ link in stage 2), $+0$ (straight link in stage 1), $+2^0$ ($+2^0$ link in stage 0). The sum of the traversed links is $+2^2 + 0 + 2^0 = 5$. Two other paths that route data from 1 to 6 are: $+2^2$, $+2^1$, -2^0; and straight, -2^1, -2^0. Assuming that the network is implemented with both $+2^{n-1}$ and -2^{n-1} links at stage $n - 1$ (even though $(+2^{n-1} = -2^{n-1})$ modulo N), then two more paths between 1 and 6 are: -2^2, straight, $+2^0$; and -2^2, $+2^1$, -2^0. In general, if $S \neq D$, there are multiple paths from S to D.

To specify an arbitrary path in an ADM network, a *full routing tag*, $F = f_{2n-1} \ldots f_0$, can be used [48]. A stage i switch examines bits f_i and f_{n+i}. If f_i is 0, that stage i switch uses the straight link (the value of f_{n+i} is ignored). If f_i is a 1 then the switch will use the $+2^i$ link if f_{n+i} is a 0 and the -2^i link if f_{n+i} is a 1. For example, for an $N = 16$ ADM network, the tag $F = 00111011$ will route from 1 to 6 on the path $+2^3$, straight, -2^1, -2^0. The tag scheme using a full routing tag requires a $2n$-bit tag, but can be used to specify any arbitrary path through the network.

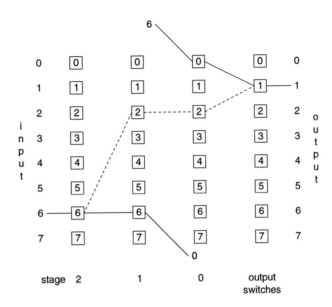

FIGURE 3.26 An $N = 8$ ADM network showing the two disjoint paths from $S = 1$ to $D = 6$. The solid line shows the path specified by $T = 0101$. The dashed line shows the path specified by $T' = 1011$.

A *natural routing tag* uses only one bit to specify the sign of the nonstraight links used in the path. Thus, all the nonstraight links traversed are of the same sign [48]. An $n + 1$ bit routing tag T is formed by computing the signed magnitude difference between the destination and the source: $T = t_n \ldots t_1 t_0 = D - S$. The *sign bit* is t_n, where $t_n = 0$ indicates positive or zero (that is, $D \geq S$), and $t_n = 1$ indicates negative (that is, $D < S$). Bits $t_{n-1} \ldots t_0$ equal the absolute value of $D - S$, the *magnitude* of the difference. The natural routing tag is interpreted in the same way as the full routing tag, except t_n is used as the sign bit at every stage. For any natural tag T for S to D ($S \neq D$), an alternative routing tag from S to D can be computed that uses links of the opposite sign by taking the two's complement of T [48]. For example, for $N = 8$, $S = 1$, and $D = 6$, $T = 0101$, and the two's complement of $T = T' = 1011$. This is shown in Figure 3.26. A *positive dominant* routing tag is a natural tag with $t_n = 0$, while a *negative dominant* routing tag has $t_n = 1$. The positive dominant path is the path specified by the positive dominant tag and the negative dominant path is the path specified by the negative dominant tag. The two's complement of one sign dominant tag from S to D produces the sign dominant tag from S to D of opposite dominance.

Partitioning   The data manipulator topology can be partitioned into independent subnetworks in a manner similar to that used for the multistage cube. The only difference is that the lowest order stage of a (sub)network must be set to straight to divide it into two equal data manipulator subnetworks, where in the multistage cube any stage could be forced to straight [66, 67]. For example, to subdivide an $N = 16$ network into two subnetworks, the only way is to force the stage 0 switches to straight, creating one subnetwork of even-numbered ports and one subnetwork of odd-numbered ports.

3.3.5 Dynamic Redundancy Network

Motivation   One weakness in the fault-tolerance properties of many large-scale PE/network combinations is that PE faults are neglected in the fault model. For larger systems the possibility of PE failures is increased. A system can tolerate faulty PEs if the design incorporates spare PEs that can be used to replace faulty PEs when detected. This approach to system design takes advantage of *dynamic redundancy*. For example, the ESC network discussed above does not have extra input/output ports for spare PEs and, thus, cannot be used directly in a system that incorporates dynamic redundancy.

This section describes the *dynamic redundancy* (*DR*) network [33, 67] which uses dynamic redundancy in the network topology to tolerate any single switch or link failure (including input and output stage switches and input/output ports of the network) and provides the necessary capabilities for the system to recover from any single PE failure. Like the ESC network, the DR network provides all the functionality of the multistage cube network. In addition, when configured to tolerate a fault, the DR network can continue to route permutations in a single pass, unlike the ESC network, which requires two passes for permutations when a fault exists. It will also be seen that the DR network, when partitioned, can provide single fault tolerance (to the extent described above) for each subsystem.

Topology   The structure of the DR network is based on the graph topology of the multistage cube network. Figure 3.27a shows an equivalent SW-banyan graph of the multistage cube topology for $N = 8$ [47, 67]. It can be seen that this is an equivalent graph representation by considering each node as a link and each edge as part of a switch (Figure 3.27b). With this representation of the multistage cube network, each stage has $N = 2^n$ switches and $2N$ links. Recall that the underlying property of the multistage cube topology is that, at stage i, PEs whose network input port labels differ in the i-th bit position can exchange data. An analog of this property holds in Figure 3.27a because a node in stage i can exchange data with the node whose number differs only in the i-th bit position.

The DR network is used in systems with N *functioning* PEs and σ *spare* PEs. A spare PE can become a functioning PE when a faulty PE is detected and isolated. Thus, the DR network must have $N + \sigma$ input/output ports. The DR network contains n stages (where $N = 2^n$), like the multistage cube network, as shown in Figure 3.28 for $N = 8$. Stages are ordered from $n - 1$ down to 0 from the input side of the network to the output side. Each stage has $N + \sigma$ switches followed by $3(N + \sigma)$ links. Following stage 0 is a stage of output switches. Let the PEs of the system be numbered from 0 to $N + \sigma - 1$. PE j is connected to the input of switch j in stage $n - 1$ and to network output switch j, where $0 \leq j < (N + \sigma)$. Each switch j in stage i has three output links to stage $i - 1$. The first output link is connected to the input of switch $(j - 2^i)$ modulo $(N + \sigma)$ in stage $i - 1$, the second output link is connected to the input of switch j in stage $i - 1$, and the third to the input of switch $(j + 2^i)$ modulo $(N + \sigma)$ in stage $i - 1$. The stage of output switches serves as the output ports of the network.

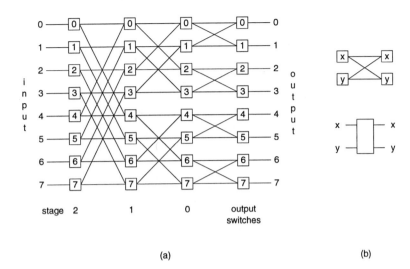

FIGURE 3.27 (a) Graphical interpretation of the multistage cube network for $N = 8$; (b) relationship between graphical interpretation and interchange box representation.

The graph representation of the DR network is similar to that of an ADM network described in subsection 3.4. The difference is that the ADM has N input/output ports and uses modulo N instead of modulo $(N + \sigma)$ in the connection functions. Because the ADM does not incorporate spare input/output ports, the ADM network's interconnection and fault-tolerance capabilities [49, 51] are quite different from those of the DR network.

Fault Tolerance   Because only N of the PEs are functioning at any given time, only N of the $N + \sigma$ are needed at any time to provide inter-PE communication. Thus, at any time, only a subgraph (subset) of the DR network is of interest here rather than the entire network.

Consider the graphical representation of the multistage cube network in Figure 3.27 and the DR network in Figure 3.28. It should be apparent that the multistage cube network is a subgraph of the DR network. In fact, there are $N + \sigma$ ways in which the multistage cube network graph can be "placed" into the DR network graph. When there are no faults, PEs 0 to $N - 1$ are used as the functioning PEs, and switches numbered 0 to $N - 1$ and their associated links emulate the multistage cube network. At stage i, DR network switches j and j' (where j' differs from j only in the i-th bit position) emulate the stage i interchange box with inputs j and j'. Assuming $j < j'$, setting stage i switch j to $+2^i$ and switch j' to -2^i emulates "exchange," and setting switches j and j' to straight emulates "straight." Upper and lower broadcasts are defined similarly.

If a fault is detected in PE j or switch j (any stage) or a link attached to switch j, the system is reconfigured such that the PE and switches physically numbered P are logically renumbered

$$P - (j + \sigma) \quad \text{modulo} \quad (N + \sigma).   \qquad (3.3)$$

Then PEs logically number 0 to $N - 1$ are used as the functioning PEs, and switches logically numbered 0 to $N - 1$ and their associated links emulate the multistage cube network in the

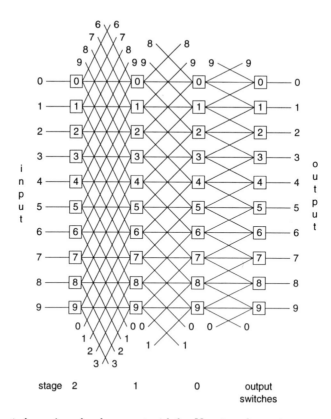

FIGURE 3.28   **A dynamic redundancy network for $N = 8$ and $\sigma = 2$.**

same manner as described for the fault-free case above (but based on the logical numbering). An example of reconfiguration is shown in Figure 3.29, where each logical number can be obtained by subtracting 5 from the corresponding physical number given (using subtraction modulo 10).

Routing Control   Routing tags for the DR network are based on the logical numbers for the PEs and switches (as defined above). In the fault-free case, physical PE and switch i are logically numbered $i, 0 \le i < N$. The exclusive-OR routing tag T, as described for the multistage cube network, can be used with logical PE addresses for the source PE S and destination PE D. When a switch in stage i receives a message, it examines t_i. If $t_i = 0$, then the straight link is used. If $t_i = 1$, then the switch must decide to use the $+2^i$ link or the -2^i link. Let $W = w_{n-1} \ldots w_1 w_0$ represent the logical address of the switch. If $w_i = 0$, switch W will use the $+2^i$ link; otherwise it will use the -2^i link. This emulates a stage i exchange setting.

This approach requires that each switch have knowledge of, at most, the i-th bit of its logical address W. This one-bit flag in each switch can be set by special messages sent from PEs during system initialization and after each reconfiguration due to a fault. This allows

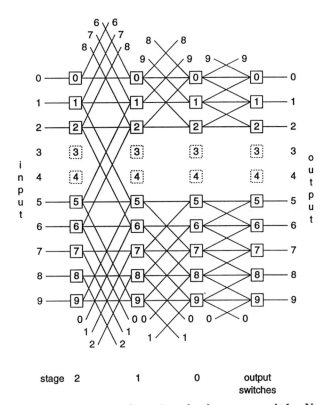

FIGURE 3.29 **Reconfiguration of a dynamic redundancy network for** $N = 8$ **and** $\sigma = 2$ **where PE 3 is faulty. The solid lines show the multistage cube subgraph of the dynamic redundancy network.**

the same routing tags used in the multistage cube network to be used directly to control the DR network.

There are alternative methods of controlling the DR network with routing tags including a method based on the destination tag scheme [33]. Multicasting is also supported in the DR network [33].

Partitioning The partitionability of the DR network depends on the value of σ and has the characteristic that up to σ single-fault-tolerant partitions are supported [33]. However, the ways in which the DR network can be partitioned are constrained such that the lower order stages are set to straight (similar to the ADM network).

3.3.6 Tree Networks

Topology In a tree network, all PEs are "leaves" of a tree structure (for example, binary tree). Messages are routed through one or more dedicated switch devices at the nodes of the tree.

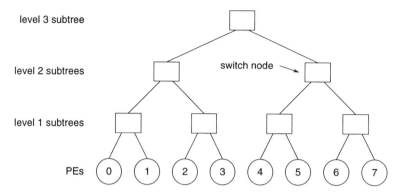

FIGURE 3.30   **A tree network for $N = 8$.**

An example of a tree network for $N = 8$ is shown in Figure 3.30. Each switch node has three input/output ports; one connected to a parent switch node and two connected to child nodes (or PEs, at level 1). It can be seen that an $N = 2^n$ tree network can be formed from two 2^{n-1} tree networks by connecting their root nodes to a new switch node. This new switch node becomes the root node of the $N = 2^n$ tree network. For example, the 8-PE tree network of Figure 3.30 is formed by connecting two 4-PE trees to a new switch node. These two 4-PE trees are *subtrees* within the 8-PE tree. Likewise, each 4-PE subtree contains two 2-PE subtrees. Thus, a given PE is a member of a 2-PE, 4-PE, ... , and an N-PE subtree (the N-PE subtree is the entire tree).

For an $N = 2^n$ tree network, PEs in the same level i subtree (with 2^i PEs) agree in the most significant $n - i$ bits of their PE addresses. The level of a node within the network is given by the value of i for the smallest (2^i)-PE subtree that contains the node. All PEs in a tree network are on level 0.

Routing Control   When routing a message from a source PE S to a destination PE D in the tree network, the message is first routed to the root node of the smallest subtree that contains PE addresses S and D. Then the message is routed from the root node to PE D. This distributed routing control technique guarantees that the shortest route is taken.

Consider the routing algorithm that each switch node at level i follows to accomplish routing in a tree network. The destination PE address D is used as the routing tag. A switch node may receive a message from either a parent switch node or a child node. A message received from a parent node is destined for some PE in the subtree for which this node is the root. In this case, the level i switch node examines bit $i - 1$ of the routing tag (the destination PE address D). If $d_{i-1} = 0$, the node routes the message to the left child node, and if $d_{i-1} = 1$, the message is routed to the right child node. When a node receives a message from one of its child nodes the message should be routed to this node's parent if the message is destined for some other subtree, else routed to the other child node (because the destination is in the same subtree for which this node is the root). This is accomplished by comparing the most significant $n - i$ bits of D, to the most significant $n - i$ bits of the PE addresses of this subtree. (These bits can either be stored in the switch node or obtained from the source PE address S, which can be included in the message header.) If these bit patterns agree, then the message is routed to the other child node, else the message is routed to the parent node (because the message has not yet reached its destination subtree).

Partitioning   An N-PE tree network can be partitioned into two $N/2$-PE subnetworks such that each $N/2$ subnetwork has all the properties of an $N/2$ tree network. This is accomplished by disallowing communication through the level n root node. (Recall that the N-PE network was formed by connecting two $N/2$-PE networks to this new root node.)

Examples of Systems Using a Tree Network   Two commercial systems that use variants of the tree network are the Teradata DBC-1012 database engine [52] and the Thinking Machines Corp. Connection Machine Model CM-5 [44]. The Teradata system exploits an advantage offered by tree networks for merging and broadcasting messages, while the CM-5 implements a variation of the tree network designed to overcome the bandwidth bottleneck disadvantage encountered at upper levels of tree networks. The use of the tree network in the CM-5 is briefly summarized below.

Connection Machine CM-5   The Thinking Machine Corp. Connection Machine Model CM-5 is a MIMD system in a PE-to-PE configuration. The CM-5 uses two networks based on the tree topology, a *control network* and a *data network*. The control network is a binary tree with PEs as the leaves. The switch nodes have the ability to broadcast messages from one PE to all other PEs in the same partition. The switch nodes of the control network can also operate on and combine data from certain messages. For example, the combining hardware can be used to produce a global maximum operation, addition, or bitwise OR or exclusive-OR of data from all PEs in a partition.

The data network of the CM-5 uses a variant of the tree network to overcome the bandwidth limitations for the volume of messages that must traverse upper-level switch nodes. The data network uses a *fat-tree* topology [43]. In the fat-tree topology, switch nodes do not necessarily have only one link to a parent node. Instead, a switch node may use two or more links to connect to a parent node (or multiple parent nodes). A message to be routed to a parent node may use any of the links available, thus reducing the potential for conflict when multiple messages are to be routed to a parent node.

The data network of the CM-5 is not based on a binary tree, but is instead based on a 4-ary tree (each node has four child nodes rather than two). The routing algorithm for the binary tree described above can be extended to a k-ary tree by using base k representations of PE addresses and base k variations of the routing algorithms. In the CM-5 4-ary fat-tree, each PE has two connections to the data network (to two distinct switch nodes). In the first two levels of the data network, each switch node has two parent node connections (to distinct parent nodes). Switch nodes higher than the first two levels connect to four (distinct) parent nodes.

3.4

THE DIFFICULTY OF COMPARING NETWORKS

As stated in subsection 3.1.4, the interconnection networks introduced in the previous sections are only a subset of the many possibilities that exist. Given this wide variety of approaches, there is much interest in a methodology for the direct comparison of networks with the goal of determining the "best" approach. The problem is one of determining which metric or weighted set of metrics should be used, and how the metrics should be applied to yield meaningful information [68].

There exists a plethora of performance measures that can be used to evaluate networks. These include message delay, traffic throughput, fault tolerance, average distance between nodes, maximum distance between nodes, ease of use, cost effectiveness, and others. In general, it is difficult to select the "important" metrics, because they may vary with the intended application and operating assumptions. For example, in [1] the binary hypercube and twisted cube topologies are examined. The twisted cube has a maximum distance between nodes that is approximately one-half of that for the hypercube. However, the paper shows that in some cases the hypercube will have a smaller message delay. One must be careful in considering the meaning and implications of the various performance metrics that have been proposed in the literature.

Given a set of performance measures, the next step is to collect data on systems employing the communication networks under consideration. Two sources of data that can be used are theoretical models and actual systems. In the case of theoretical models, the problem of the practicality of the model becomes a factor. For example, it is common to assume an infinite-length message queue for packets within a network switch. It remains to be seen if current or future theoretical models can demonstrate sufficiently realistic behavior for use in comparing networks.

To compare actual systems, one standard approach is to assemble a set of benchmark programs to run on the systems to determine the "best" machine. The difficulty with this approach is that it is not clear what benchmarks actually measure. The implementation of a task on a machine depends on the translation of the task to an algorithm, the encoding of the algorithm into a programming language, the compilation of the program into machine code, the operating system routines of the machine used at execution time, and the machine design (architecture, hardware design, technology used). The difference in execution time of a benchmark from one machine to another could be due to any one or more of the above. Therefore, a benchmark program is not a reliable indicator of the performance of a communication network.

Another issue that must be addressed when trying to compare networks is determining the effect of various network parameters on the performance of the network. The classical experimental approach to study the impact of a parameter is to hold all other parameters fixed except the parameter of interest. Then, the parameter of interest is varied and measurements are taken for each different setting to determine how the parameter affects the system. In the case of networks, possible parameters include frequency of communications, message sizes, routing control, conflict resolution scheme, number and width of communication links per node, implementation technology, packaging constraints, and many more. Given a set of parameters, which of these should be held constant and which should be varied to do fair and accurate experiments to compare network features? How does one determine that two different networks are of comparable implementation "costs" in order to perform a fair comparison? Dollar costs that are a function of marketing policies that can change instantly seem a poor standard for scientifically quantifying and equating the values of components used in different networks. Furthermore, how are the constant values selected for those parameters that do not vary? The answers to such questions are still being sought.

The following questions (from [68]) summarize some of the issues that must be considered in studying the comparison of networks. Which metrics or weighted collection of metrics should be used to evaluate network performance? Can current or future analytically tractable theoretical models demonstrate sufficiently realistic behavior? How can benchmarks across different machines be devised to evaluate different network features? How can the "experimental method" be applied fairly to evaluate networks? What parameters should be held constant when comparing and evaluating networks?

3.5

SUMMARY

This chapter has overviewed some properties of various types of interconnection networks. Both single-stage (point-to-point) and multistage networks were considered. The single-stage networks included four and eight nearest-neighbor (mesh) networks and hypercube networks. Included in the multistage networks were the multistage cube, extra-stage cube, data manipulator network family, dynamic redundancy, and tree networks. Properties such as topology, routing control, and partitionability for each network type were described. The background provided here should aid the reader in understanding how the different networks can be used in parallel systems. The references listed provide more details of the structure of these and other networks that appear in the literature.

Acknowledgments   The authors gratefully acknowledge the following people for providing information for the case studies: Ken Batcher, William Brantley, Jim Feeney, John Goodhue, Allan Gottlieb, Richard Kenner, Wally Kleinfelder, Duncan Lawrie, Kevin McAuliffe, Pierre Pero, Craig Stunkel, Alex Viedenbaum, and Pam Waterman.

Bibliography

1. S. Abraham, and K. Padmanabhan, "The Twisted Cube Topology for Multiprocessors: A Study in Network Asymmetry," *J. Parallel and Distributed Computing*, Vol. 13, No. 1, Sept. 1991, pp. 104–110.

2. G.B. Adams III, D.P. Agrawal, and H.J. Siegel, "A Survey and Comparison of Fault-tolerant Multistage Interconnection Networks," *Computer*, Vol. 20, No. 6, June 1987, pp. 14–27.

3. G.B. Adams III, and H.J. Siegel, "The Extra Stage Cube: A Fault-tolerant Interconnection Network for Supersystems," *IEEE Trans. Computers*, Vol. C-31, No. 5, May 1982, pp. 443–454.

4. G.B. Adams III, and H.J. Siegel, "Modifications to Improve the Fault Tolerance of the Extra Stage Cube Interconnection Network," *Proc. 1984 Int'l Conf. Parallel Processing*, IEEE CS Press, Los Alamitos, Calif., 1984, pp. 169–173.

5. D.P. Agrawal, ed., *Tutorial: Advanced Computer Architecture*, IEEE CS Press, Los Alamitos, Calif., 1986.

6. G.S. Almasi, and A. Gottlieb, *Highly Parallel Computing*, Benjamin/Cummings, Redwood City, Calif., 1989.

7. J.B. Armstrong, D.W. Watson, and H.J. Siegel, "Software Issues for the PASM Parallel Processing System," in *Software for Parallel Computation*, J.S. Kowalik, and L. Grandinetti, eds., Springer-Verlag, Berlin, Germany, 1993, pp. 134–148.

8. *BBN Advanced Computers, Inc.: Inside the GP1000*, BBN Advanced Computers, Inc., Cambridge, Mass., 1988.

9. *BBN Advanced Computers, Inc.: Inside the TC2000*, BBN Advanced Computers, Inc., Cambridge, Mass., 1989.

10. G.H. Barnes et al., "The Illiac IV Computer," *IEEE Trans. Computers*, Vol. C-17, No. 8, Aug. 1968, pp. 746–757.

11. K.E. Batcher, "The Flip Network in STARAN," *Proc. 1976 Int'l Conf. Parallel Processing*, IEEE CS Press, Los Alamitos, Calif., 1976, pp. 65–71.

12. K.E. Batcher, "The Multidimensional Access Memory in STARAN," *IEEE Trans. Computers*, Vol. C-26, No. 2, Feb. 1977, pp. 174–177.

13. K.E. Batcher, "STARAN Series E," *Proc. 1977 Int'l Conf. Parallel Processing*, IEEE CS Press, Los Alamitos, Calif., 1977, pp. 140–143.

14. K.E. Batcher, "Bit Serial Parallel Processing Systems," *IEEE Trans. Computers*, Vol. C-31, No. 5, May 1982, pp. 377–384.

15. R. Bianchini et al., "The Ultra III Prototype," *Proc. 1993 Int'l Parallel Processing Symp., Proc. Parallel Systems Fair*, 1993, pp. 2–9.

16. J. Bruck et al., *Survey of Routing Issues for the Vulcan Parallel Computer*, Research Report RJ 8839, IBM Corporation, Research Division, Yorktown Heights, N.Y., 1992.

17. T. Chen et al., "A Low-latency Programming Interface and a Prototype Switch for Scalable High-performance Distributed Computing," *Proc. Int'l Symp. High-performance Distributed Computing*, IEEE CS Press, Los Alamitos, Calif., 1993, pp. 160–168.

18. W. Crowther et al., "Performance Measurements on a 128-node Butterfly Parallel Processor," *Proc. 1985 Int'l Conf. Parallel Processing*, IEEE CS Press, Los Alamitos, Calif., 1985, pp. 531–540.

19. W.J. Dally, and C.L. Sietz, "Deadlock-free Message Routing in Multiprocessor Interconnection Networks," *IEEE Trans. Computers*, Vol. C-36, No. 5, May 1987, pp. 547–553.

20. N.J. Davis IV, W.T.-Y. Hsu, and H.J. Siegel, "Fault Location Techniques for Distributed Control Interconnection Networks," *IEEE Trans. Computers*, Vol. C-34, Oct. 1985, pp. 902–910.

21. B. Duzett, and R. Buck, "An Overview of the nCUBE/3 Supercomputer," *Proc. 4th Symp. Frontiers of Massively Parallel Computation*, IEEE CS Press, Los Alamitos, Calif., 1992, pp. 458–464.

22. T.Y. Feng, "Data Manipulating Functions in Parallel Processors and Their Implementations," *IEEE Trans. Computers*, Vol. C-23, Mar. 1974, pp. 309–318.

23. T.Y. Feng and C.-L. Wu, "Fault-diagnosis for a Class of Multistage Interconnection Networks," *IEEE Trans. Computers*, Vol. C-30, Oct. 1981, pp. 743–758.

24. M.J. Flynn, "Very High-speed Computing Systems," *Proc. IEEE*, Vol. 54, No. 12, Dec. 1966, pp. 1901–1909.

25. G.R. Goke and G.J. Lipovski, "Banyan Networks for Partitioning Multiprocessor Systems," *Proc. 1st Ann. Symp. Computer Architecture*, 1973, pp. 21–28.

26. A. Gottlieb et al., "The NYU Ultracomputer—Designing an MIMD Shared-memory Parallel Computer," *IEEE Trans. Computers*, Vol. C-32, No. 2, Feb. 1983, pp. 175–189.

27. J.P. Hayes and T.N. Mudge, "Hypercube Supercomputers," *Proc. IEEE*, Vol. 77, No. 12, Dec. 1989, pp. 1829–1841.

28. C.T. Ho and S.L. Johnsson, "Embedding Meshes in Boolean Cubes by Graph Decomposition," *J. Parallel and Distributed Computing*, Vol. 8, No. 4, Apr. 1990, pp. 325–339.

29. D.J. Hunt, "AMT DAP—A Processor Array in a Workstation Environment," *Computer Systems Science and Engineering*, Vol. 4, No. 2, Apr. 1989, pp. 107–114.

30. K. Hwang, *Advanced Computer Architecture, Parallelism, Scalability, Programmability*, McGraw-Hill, New York, N.Y., 1993.

31. K. Hwang and F.A. Briggs, *Computer Architecture and Parallel Processing*, McGraw-Hill, New York, N.Y., 1984.

32. *IBM Corporation: IBM 9076 Scalable POWER parallel 1*, GH26-7219-0, IBM Corporation, 1993.

33. M. Jeng and H.J. Siegel, "Design and Analysis of Dynamic Redundancy Networks," *IEEE Trans. Computers*, Vol. C-37, No. 9, Sept. 1988, pp. 1019–1029.

34. P. Kermani and L. Kleinrock, "Virtual Cut-through: A New Computer Communication Switching Technique," *Computer Networks*, Vol. 3, 1979, p. 267.

35. J. Konicek et al., "The Organization of the Cedar System," *Proc. 1991 Int'l Conf. Parallel Processing*, Vol. I, CRC Press, Boca Raton, 1991, pp. 49–56.

36. C.P. Kruskal and M. Snir, "A Unified Theory of Interconnection Network Structure," *Theoretical Computer Science*, 1986, pp. 75–94.

37. D.J. Kuck et al., "Parallel Supercomputing Today and the Cedar Approach," *Science*, Vol. 231, Feb. 1986, pp. 967–974.

38. M. Kumar and G.F. Pfister, "The Onset of Hot Spot Contention," *Proc. 1986 Int'l Conf. Parallel Processing*, IEEE CS Press, Los Alamitos, Calif., 1986, pp. 28–34.

39. D.H. Lawrie, "Access and Alignment of Data in an Array Processor," *IEEE Trans. Computers*, Vol. C-24, No. 12, Dec. 1975, pp. 1145–1155.

40. D. Lee and K.Y. Lee, "Control Algorithms for the Augmented Data Manipulator Network," *Proc. 1986 Int'l Conf. Parallel Processing*, IEEE CS Press, Los Alamitos, Calif., 1986, pp. 123–130.

41. G. Lee, C.P. Kruskal, and D.J. Kuck, "The Effectiveness of Combining in Multistage Interconnection Networks in the Presence of 'Hot Spots'," *Proc. 1986 Int'l Conf. Parallel Processing*, IEEE CS Press, Los Alamitos, Calif., 1986, pp. 35–41.

42. K.Y. Lee and W. Hegazy, "The Extra Stage Gamma Network," *Proc. 13th Ann. Symp. Computer Architecture*, IEEE CS Press, Los Alamitos, Calif., 1986, pp. 175–182.

43. C.E. Leiserson, "Fat-trees, Universal Networks for Hardware-efficient Supercomputing," *IEEE Trans. Computers*, Vol. C-34, No. 10, Oct. 1985, pp. 892–901.

44. C.E. Leiserson et al., "The Network Architecture of the Connection Machine CM-5," *Proc. 4th Ann. ACM Symp. Parallel Algorithms and Architectures*, ACM Press, New York, N.Y., 1992, pp. 272–285.

45. M.D.P. Leland, "On the Power of the Augmented Data Manipulator Network," *Proc. 1985 Int'l Conf. Parallel Processing*, IEEE CS Press, Los Alamitos, Calif., 1985, pp. 74–78.

46. S.L. Lillevik, "DELTA, A 30 Gigaflop Parallel Supercomputer for Touchstone," *Northcon Conf. Record*, 1990, pp. 294–304.

47. G.J. Lipovski and M. Malek, *Parallel Computing: Theory and Comparisons*, John Wiley and Sons, New York, N.Y., 1987.

48. R.J. McMillen and H.J. Siegel, "Routing Schemes for the Augmented Data Manipulator Network in an MIMD System," *IEEE Trans. Computers*, Vol. C-31, Dec. 1982, pp. 1202–1214.

49. R.J. McMillen and H.J. Siegel, "Evaluation of Cube and Data Manipulator Networks," *J. Parallel and Distributed Computing*, Vol. 2, Feb. 1985, pp. 79–107.

50. W.G. Nation, A.A. Maciejewski, and H.J. Siegel, "A Methodology for Exploiting Concurrency among Independent Tasks in Partitionable Parallel Processing Systems," *J. Parallel and Distributed Computing, Special Issue on Performance of Supercomputers*, Vol. 19, No. 3, Oct. 1993, pp. 271–278.

51. W.G. Nation and H.J. Siegel, "Disjoint Path Properties of the Data Manipulator Network Family," *J. Parallel and Distributed Computing*, Vol. 9, No. 4, Aug. 1990, pp. 419–423.

52. P.M. Neches, "The Ynet, An Interconnect Structure for a Highly Concurrent Data Base Computer System," *Proc. Frontiers '88, 2nd Symp. Frontiers of Massively Parallel Computation*, IEEE CS Press, Los Alamitos, Calif., 1988, pp. 429–435.

53. J.R. Nickolls, "The Design of the MasPar MP-1, A Cost Effective Massively Parallel Computer," *Proc. Compcon*, IEEE CS Press, Los Alamitos, Calif., 1990, pp. 25–28.

54. S.F. Nugent, "The iPSC/2 Direct-connect Communications Technology," *Proc. 3rd Conf. Hypercube Computers and Applications*, 1988, pp. 51–60.

55. G.J. Nutt, "Microprocessor Implementation of a Parallel Processor," *Proc. 4th Ann. Symp. Computer Architecture*, IEEE CS Press, Los Alamitos, Calif., 1977, pp. 147–152.

56. D.S. Parker and C.S. Raghavendra, "The Gamma Network: A Multiprocessor Interconnection Network with Redundant Paths," *Proc. 9th Ann. Symp. Computer Architecture*, IEEE CS Press, Los Alamitos, Calif., 1982, pp. 73–80.

57. D.S. Parker and C.S. Raghavendra, "The Gamma Network," *IEEE Trans. Computers*, Vol. C-33, No. 4, Apr. 1984, pp. 367–373.

58. J.H. Patel, "Performance of Processor-memory Interconnections for Multiprocessors," *IEEE Trans. Computers*, Vol. C-30, No. 10, Oct. 1981, pp. 771–780.

59. M.C. Pease III, "The Indirect Binary n-cube Microprocessor Array," *IEEE Trans. Computers*, Vol. C-26, No. 5, May 1977, pp. 458–473.

60. G.F. Pfister et al., "The IBM Research Parallel Processor Prototype (RP3) Introduction and Architecture," *Proc. 1985 Int'l Conf. Parallel Processing*, IEEE CS Press, Los Alamitos, Calif., 1985, pp. 764–771.

61. G.F. Pfister and V.A. Norton, "'Hot Spot' Contention and Combining in Multistage Interconnection Networks," *IEEE Trans. Computers*, Vol. C-34, No. 10, Oct. 1985, pp. 933–938.

62. D. Rau, J.A.B. Fortes, and H.J. Siegel, "Destination Tag Routing Techniques Based on a State Model for The IADM Network," *IEEE Trans. Computers*, Vol. C-41, No. 3, Mar. 1992, pp. 274–285.

63. S.M. Reddy and V.P. Kumar, "On Multipath Multistage Interconnection Networks," *Proc. 1985 Int'l Conf. Distributed Computing Systems*, IEEE CS Press, Los Alamitos, Calif., 1985, pp. 210–217.

64. C. Seitz, and C. Flaig, *VLSI Mesh Routing Systems*, CS-TR-87-5241, California Institute of Technology, 1987.

65. H.J. Siegel, "Interconnection Networks for SIMD Machines," *Computer*, Vol. 12, No. 6, June 1979, pp. 57–65.

66. H.J. Siegel, "The Theory Underlying the Partitioning of Permutation Networks," *IEEE Trans. Computers*, Vol. C-29, No. 9, Sept. 1980, pp. 791–801.

67. H.J. Siegel, *Interconnection Networks for Large-scale Parallel Processing, Theory and Case Studies*, 2nd Ed., McGraw-Hill, New York, N.Y., 1990.

68. H.J. Siegel, J.K. Antonio, and K.J. Liszka, "Metrics for Metrics: Why Is It Difficult to Compare Interconnection Networks OR How Would You Compare an Alligator to an Armidillo?" *Proc. The New Frontiers, A Workshop on Future Directions of Massively Parallel Processing*, 1992, pp. 97–106.

69. H.J. Siegel, J.B. Armstrong, and D.W. Watson, "Mapping Computer Vision Related Tasks onto Reconfigurable Parallel Processing Systems," *Computer, Special Issue on Parallel Processing for Computer Vision and Image Understanding*, Vol. 25, No. 2, Feb. 1992, pp. 54–63.

70. H.J. Siegel and R.J. McMillen, "The Multistage Cube, A Versatile Interconnection Network," *Computer*, Vol. 14, No. 12, Dec. 1981, pp. 65–76.

71. H.J. Siegel, R.J. McMillen, and P.T. Mueller Jr., "A Survey of Interconnection Methods for Reconfigurable Parallel Processing Systems," *Proc. AFIPS 1979 Nat'l Computer Conf.*, AFIPS Press, Reston, Va., 1979, pp. 529–542.

72. H.J. Siegel et al., "Using the Multistage Cube Network Topology in Parallel Supercomputers," *Proc. IEEE*, Vol. 77, No. 12, Dec. 1989, pp. 1932–1953.

73. H.J. Siegel et al., "An Overview of the PASM Parallel Processing System," in *Computer Architecture*, D.D. Gajski, V.M. Milutinovic, H.J. Siegel, and B.P. Furht, (eds.), IEEE CS Press, Los Alamitos, Calif., 1987, pp. 387–407.

74. H.J. Siegel et al., "The Design and Prototyping of the PASM Reconfigurable Parallel Processing System," in *Parallel Computing: Paradigms and Applications*, A.Y. Zomaya, ed., Chapman and Hall, London, U.K., 1995, in press.

75. H.J. Siegel et al., "PASM, A Partitionable SIMD/MIMD System for Image Processing and Pattern Recognition," *IEEE Trans. Computers*, Vol. C-30, No. 12, Dec. 1981, pp. 934–947.

76. H.J. Siegel and S.D. Smith, "Study of Multistage SIMD Interconnection Networks," *Proc. 5th Ann. Symp. Computer Architecture*, IEEE CS Press, Los Alamitos, Calif., 1978, pp. 223–229.

77. H.S. Stone, *High Performance Computer Architecture*, Addison-Wesley, Reading, Mass., 1987.

78. S. Thanawastien and V.P. Nelson, "Interference Analysis of Shuffle/Exchange Networks," *IEEE Trans. Computers*, Vol. C-30, No. 8, Aug. 1981, pp. 545–556.

79. *Thinking Machines Corporation: CM5: Technical Summary*, Thinking Machines Corporation, 1992.

80. L.W. Tucker and G.G. Robertson, "Architecture and Applications of the Connection Machine," *Computer*, Vol. 21, No. 8, Aug. 1988, pp. 26–38.

81. L. Uhr, *Algorithm-Structured Computer Arrays and Networks: Architectures and Processes for Images, Percepts, Models, Information*, Academic Press, Orlando, Fla., 1984.

82. A. Varma and C.S. Raghavendra, "Performance Analysis of a Redundant-path Interconnection Network," *Proc. 1985 Int'l Conf. on Parallel Processing*, IEEE CS Press, Los Alamitos, Calif., 1985, pp. 474–479.

83. A. Varma and C.S. Raghavendra, "On Permutations Passable by the Gamma Network," *J. Parallel and Distributed Computing*, Vol. 3, No. 3, Mar. 1986, pp. 72–91.

84. A. Varma and C.S. Raghavendra, eds., *Interconnection Networks for Multiprocessors and Multicomputers, Theory and Practice*, IEEE CS Press, Los Alamitos, Calif., 1994.

85. K.Y. Wen, *Interprocessor Connections—Capabilities, Exploitation, and Effectiveness, Ph.D. thesis*, Report UIUCDCS-R-76-830, University of Illinois at Urbana-Champaign, 1976.

86. C.L. Wu and T.Y. Feng, "On a Class of Multistage Interconnection Networks," *IEEE Trans. Computers*, Vol. C-29, No. 8, Aug. 1980, pp. 694–702.

87. C.L. Wu, and T.Y. Feng, *Tutorial: Interconnection Networks for Parallel and Distributed Computing*, IEEE CS Press, Los Alamitos, Calif., 1984.

88. H. Yoon, K.Y. Lee, and M.T. Liu, "Performance Analysis and Comparison of Packet Switching Interconnection Networks," *Proc. 1987 Int'l Conf. Parallel Processing*, IEEE CS Press, Los Alamitos, Calif., 1987, pp. 542–545.

89. H. Yoon, K.Y. Lee, and M.T. Liu, "A New Approach to Internetworking of Integrated Services Local Networks," *Proc. 1987 Int'l Conf. Distributed Computing Systems*, IEEE CS Press, Los Alamitos, Calif., 1987, pp. 390–397.

90. G. Zorpette, "The Power of Parallelism," *Spectrum*, Vol. 29, No. 9, Sept. 1992, pp. 28–33.

PART II
PROGRAMMING CONCEPTS AND LANGUAGES

PARALLEL ALGORITHM FUNDAMENTALS AND ANALYSIS

Bruce McMillin* and Jun-Lin Liu

Department of Computer Science
University of Missouri-Rolla
Rolla, MO 65401 USA

Abstract. *This session explores the "intuition" used in creating a parallel algorithm design and realizing this design on distributed memory hardware. The algorithm class NC and the LSTM machine are used to show why some algorithms realize their promise of speedup better than others and the algorithm class NP is used to show why other algorithms will never be good for parallelization. The realities of algorithm design are presented through partitioning and mapping issues and models.*

4.1

PARALLEL ALGORITHMS AND PARALLELIZATION OF ALGORITHMS—INTUITIVE DESIGN

Parallel processing can really only make sense if we understand how to program the parallel hardware that the technology is capable of producing. For example, 10,000 personal computers, each capable of 1 Mflops, have an enormous aggregate processing power of 10 Gflops, however, there is really no way to exploit this processing power for a realistic single job. Organizing these 10,000 PCs together, using a high-speed interconnection, such as in a *multicomputer*, helps, but the task remains to make the job run well. This is the study of parallel programming and parallel algorithms.

The goal of parallel programming and parallel algorithm study is to find a way to break a job into N units that can execute concurrently on N or fewer processors. Given the complexity of programming, in general, trying to program in parallel seems an insurmountable task. Indeed, a parallelizing compiler which transforms a sequential program into a parallel

---

*Supported in part by the National Science Foundation under Grants MSS-9216479 and CDA-9222827, and in part by the Air Force Office of Scientific Research under contract number F49620-92-J-0546.

program would be very attractive. This idea, also coined the "Dusty Deck Syndrome" has received much research attention.

Parallelizing compilers work, for the most part, on identifying certain constructs within the sequential language. Execution profiles of computationally intensive programs can show that often, only a few percent of code (by volume) accounts for 50 percent of the runtime of the program. It's not hard to see where this lies. **DO** loops and computational kernels account for a great deal of a program's runtime. Loops typically appear in program code as follows.

$$\mathbf{DO}\ i = 1,\ 100$$
$$100 \qquad a(i) = b(i){+}c(i)$$

This loop parallelizes easily, and it is easy for the compiler to detect and produce the following parallel (vector) code which executes all 100 assignments independently, in parallel.

$$a(1) = b(1) + c(1)$$
$$a(2) = b(2) + c(2)$$
$$\vdots$$
$$a(100) = b(100) + c(100)$$

or $a(1{:}100) = b(1{:}100) + c(1{:}100)$ Now, of course, not all loops are easily decomposed. Sometimes there are loop dependencies. These can be solved by the introduction of temporary storage. Other times, there are dependencies that cannot be removed, such as in the case of linear recurrences of the form $a_i = a_{i-1}b_i + c_i, i > 1$. FORTRAN code appears as follows:

$$\mathbf{DO}\ 100\ i = 2,\ N$$
$$100 \qquad a(i) = a(i{-}1){*}b(i) + c(i)$$

Notice that the data dependency between $a(i)$ and $a(i-1)$ cannot be parallelized completely. The (rather complex) solution

$$a(1{:}N) = c(1{:}N)$$
$$\mathbf{DO}\ i = 1,\ \log_2 N$$
$$\qquad \mathbf{DO}\ \text{in parallel for all}\ P_j\ \text{where}\ 2^i \le j \le N$$
$$\qquad\qquad a(j) = a(j) + b(j){*}a(j{-}2^{i-1})$$
$$\qquad\qquad b(j) = b(j){*}(j{-}2^{i-1})$$
$$200 \qquad\qquad \text{continue}$$

builds up partial results in parallel, that is, at $i = 2$, at the end of the parallel statement, we have (for $j \ge 4$):

$$a(j) = b(j){*}b(j{-}1){*}[b(j{-}2){*}c(j{-}3){+}c(j{-}2)]{+}b(j)\ {*}c(j{-}1){+}c(j)$$
$$b(j) = b(j){*}b(j{-}1){*}b(j{-}2)$$

Now, while the above construction is complex, once it is derived, a compiler can identify this looping structure and perform the appropriate parallel code substitution.

The problem with relying too much on compilers to do our work is twofold:

1. A compiler can only detect loop parallelism. Thus, there is still 50 percent of the runtime unaccounted for that a compiler cannot easily detect. In terms of parallel program performance, this will limit the *speedup* or increase in performance obtained by parallelism.
2. The sequential algorithm may actually obscure parallelism inherent in the problem such that even an ideal compiler can't extract it. Indeed, a sequential algorithm may not be the best parallel algorithm, at all.

In the next section we will examine the first issue more closely when we discuss the metrics of speedup. The second issue is really one of language.

4.1.1 Language as an Impediment to Parallelism

The choice of language can inhibit the expression of parallelism that may be inherent in an application. Consider the model of *Imperative Language Programming* which is the basis for FORTRAN, C, PASCAL and such. An imperative language consists of statements which are a sequence of predicate transformations on a program's state. For example, an imperative matrix multiplication $c_{l \times n} = a_{l \times m} b_{m \times n}$ is expressed as follows:

for i **from** 1 **to** l
   for j **from** 1 **to** m
      for k **from** 1 **to** n
         $c_{i,k} = c_{i,k} + a_{i,j} b_{j,k}$

This is the way that matrix multiplication is usually presented. However, it is not clear at all how to perform the operations in parallel. Certainly, since this is loop parallelism, we can create $l \cdot m \cdot n$ processes, as above. However, a better way is to reexamine the *specification* of matrix multiplication rather than its implementation in a particular (here imperative) language.

Matrix multiplication is, fundamentally, a collection of inner products of the elements of the multiplier and multiplicand matrices. This is expressed below, in a version of matrix multiplication expressed in FP [2].

Given a pair of matrices stored as a sequence of rows,
    $< a, b >$, with $a = < a_1, \ldots, a_l >$ and $a_i = < a_{i,1}, \ldots, a_{i,m} >$
$c \leftarrow$ *Inner_Product* $\cdot$ *Distribute_Left* $\cdot$ *Distribute_Right* $\cdot$ $[a, transpose(b)]$
whose evaluation results in:
$c \leftarrow$ *Inner_Product* $\cdot$ *Distribute_Left* $\cdot$ *Distribute_Right* $< a, b' >$
$c \leftarrow$ *Inner_Product* $\cdot$ *Distribute_Left* $<< a_1, b' >, \ldots, < a_l, b' >>$
$c \leftarrow$ *Inner_Product* $< p_1, p_2, \ldots, p_l >$ where $p_i = << a_i, b'_1 >, \ldots, < a_i, b'_m >>$

By the Church-Rosser property, the Inner_Products may be applied in parallel in any order. Thus, we note that the execution order is neither constrained nor specified as in imperative languages. The maximum amount of parallelism is expressed by the functional program.

Now the FP example is rather extreme. No one is suggesting that everyone switch to functional languages simply to use parallel computing. Note, however, that by analyzing the specification of the problem, the observation that matrix multiplication is nothing more than a collection of inner products, yields not only the functional program above, but the imperative program, below:

do in parallel for $P_{ij}, i = 1, \ldots, l, j = 1, \ldots, m$
    for k **from** 1 **to** n
        $c_{i,k} = c_{i,k} + a_{i,j}b_{j,k}$

Thus, rather than express or constrain the computation of these inner products, as in the imperative algorithm, we just write an imperative program, which is expressed in the fundamental parallel units of the problem. We then feed the inner product computations, in any order, to the processors of the system. Thus, rather than a parallel version of a sequential algorithm, this is a parallel algorithm.

Successful parallel programming consists of (1) specifying the problem, (2) identifying the fundamental units and their interaction, and (3) mapping these fundamental units to processes with their interactions specified by communication primitives.

Given that the only control we have in parallel programming at the system level is process creation and send/receive communication, all examples can be constructed using this primitive set of operations. Later we will present a more formal model of this in Hoare's CSP [9].

4.1.2 Parallel Sorting

Consider the problem of sorting an array **a** into ascending order using the (very simple) Sequential Sorting Algorithm (Exchange Sort).

Sort N numbers a(1), a(2), $\ldots$, a(N) into ascending order
for i **from** 1 **to** N
    for j **from** 1 **to** N
        if (a(i) > a(j))
            temp=a(i)
            a(i)=a(j)
            a(j)=temp

This algorithm runs in N^2 comparisons. If we identify the fundamental units and operations in sorting, the compare/exchange is the basic function which operates on the array elements. If we have N processors available we should be able to make it run in N time by using the N processors to do N comparisons in parallel.

If we arrange the N processors in a linear array and let processor P_i hold value a(i), then processors alternately exchange their values based on whether their index is even or odd, as shown in Figure 4.1.

Code for each processor P_i

for j $= 0, N - 1$
    do in parallel **for** all $P_i, i = 0, N - 1$
        if j is even and i is even or j is odd and i is odd
            send a(i) **to** $P_i - 1$
            receive a(i) **from** $P_i - 1$

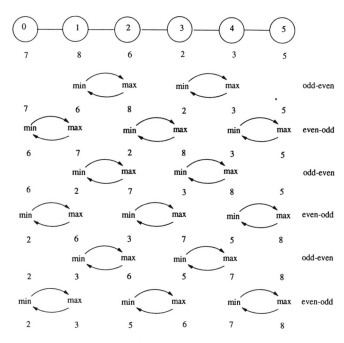

FIGURE 4.1 Odd-even transposition sort.

```
        else
                receive a(i+1) from P_i + 1
                if a(i+1) < a(i)
                    temp = a(i)
                    a(i) = a(i+1)
                    a(i+1) = temp
                send a(i+1) to P_i + 1
end
```

This achieves the desired result, a parallel algorithm which runs in N time on N processors.

4.1.3 Relaxation

Perhaps the most important use of parallel computing is the relaxation methods for solving iteratively, partial differential equations of the form

$$\frac{\partial^2 u}{\partial x^2} + \frac{\partial^2 u}{\partial y^2} = 0$$

A numerical approximation $\mathbf{U}$ to the solution $\mathbf{u}$ yields the matrix form

$$AU = 0$$

where the matrix $\mathbf{A}$ is a sparse, tridiagonal system of linear equations.

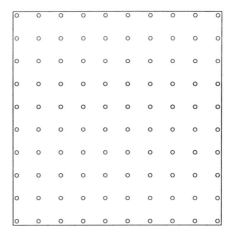

FIGURE 4.2   Discretization of physical domain—domain decomposition.

The problem of parallelizing a solution to this seems insurmountable. However, this problem is amenable to *domain decomposition*, which splits the physical model's domain over the processors as in the point discretization of Figure 4.2.

Let $U = (U_{i,j})$ be the approximation of the solution u

$$U_{i,j}^{(k+1)} = \frac{1}{4}(U_{i,j+1}^{(k)} + U_{i,j-1}^{(k)} + U_{i+1,j}^{(k)} + U_{i-1,j}^{(k)})$$

Each point (element) is iteratively solved as a function of its neighbors as in Figure 4.3.

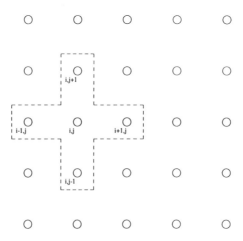

FIGURE 4.3   Localized computational molecule.

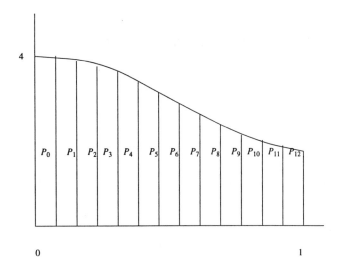

FIGURE 4.4   Domain decomposition.

4.1.4 Numerical Integration

As another example of domain decomposition, consider the problem of an approximation to calculating π using numerical integration.

$$\pi \approx f(x) = 4 \int_0^1 \frac{1}{1+x^2} dx$$

The natural numerical decomposition is to break the problem domain into strips and calculate the numeric function value at each strip to approximate the solution to the problem.

$$P_i :$$
$$\textbf{return } \tfrac{1}{N} f(x_i)$$

In parallel, each P_i gets $1/N$th of the integration to perform, as in Figure 4.4. A tree reduction summation is used to sum up all the slices in logarithmic time.

4.1.5 Summary

In creating a parallel algorithm, one must start with the specification of the problem to be solved. From this specification, identifiable units can be extracted that can be solved in parallel. Attempting to "engineer" a parallel solution from an existing sequential code, written in an imperative language, will not yield the best parallel algorithm since the imperative language imposes a computational order that does not always express the maximal parallelism present in the problem.

4.2

ANALYSIS OF PARALLEL ALGORITHMS

In the previous section, we presented a vague idea of how to measure the effectiveness of a parallel algorithm. In this section, we refine these concepts and present a theoretical basis for parallel algorithm performance.

4.2.1 Speedup

From a hardware standpoint, it's easy to build parallel hardware with enormous speed ratings. What the user desires is a machine to make the job run fast. If we assume that we can decompose the job into N parts, then *speedup* is just how much faster the decomposed job runs on N processors. Speedup measures address both the optimal and expected performance. Figure 4.5 characterizes the best case, pessimistic case, and average case for possible speedups.

Minsky's conjecture [11] forms a lower bound on what we can reasonably expect from a parallel program. The key observation is that as N grows, the performance becomes dominated by system bottlenecks and communication. Thus, perhaps the best speedup S is $O(\log_2 N)$. This is a disappointing result, if true, as it says there is not much benefit from parallelism beyond only a few processors.

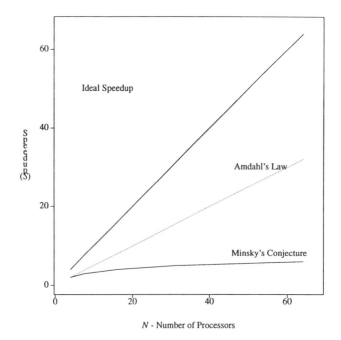

FIGURE 4.5   Speedup models.

In sharp contrast to Minsky's conjecture is the notion of ideal speedup. For ideal speedup to be realized, the problem must be perfectly decomposed in N parts and no communication or system bottlenecks must occur. Then the speedup is linear, as N grows, the speedup $S = N$.

Between these two extremes are two measures of what occurs when system bottlenecks, overhead, and imperfect parallel decomposition occur.

Amdahl's law [1] treats every program as consisting of a sequential component s and a parallel component $p = 1 - s$. The crucial observation is that a program's speedup will be limited severely by the amount of nonparallelizable code. Simply put, if there are N processors, then the speedup S is bounded as follows:

$$S \leq \frac{s + p}{s + \frac{p}{N}}$$

For example, if $N = 1024$ and $s = 0$, then

$$S \leq \frac{1}{0 + \frac{1}{1024}}$$

or $S \leq 1024$, which is, essentially, the ideal speedup case. However, if even a small sequential component is present, such as if $N = 1024$ and $s = 0.01$, then

$$S \leq \frac{1}{0.01 + \frac{0.99}{1024}}$$

or $S \leq 91.18$.

Under the Amdahl's law speedup model, the limitations of parallelizing compilers become apparent. If we believe that 50 percent of the code is recognizable as parallel ($p = 0.5$), then 50 percent is not parallelizable ($s = 1 - p = 0.50$). Thus the maximum speedup is

$$\lim_{N \to \infty} S \leq \lim_{N \to \infty} \frac{1}{0.50 + \frac{0.50}{N}}$$

or $S \leq 2$ no matter how many processors are used!

These results seem disappointing. However, Gustavson, [8] observed in 1988 that programs are made parallel, for the most part, as they have runtimes that grow as the problem scales. This scaling can be a finer grid resolution or an increase in the number of time steps proportional to the number of processors in the system. However, the sequential time, which is the time to load the program, collect the results, and perform overhead calculations remains relatively constant over varying computational problem sizes. This *scaled size* model assumes that, by contrast to Amdahl's law, p is not independent of N. Thus, we can calculate a scaled speedup S_s, as

$$S_s = \frac{s + p \cdot N}{s + p}$$

Experimental results using this speedup measure report scaled speedups of 1020 on a 1024 processor machine [8]. There is still much debate, however, on the usefulness of this model.

4.2.2 Theoretical Basis for Speedup

Given the two speedup models for S and S_s above, it is easy to calculate the speedup for a particular application. If the actual ratios p and s are not known, then experimentation is necessary. However, given that the best tools available are parallelizing compilers, determining p may be difficult since the p obtained is only an estimate of the amount of parallelism inherent in the problem. What is necessary is a way of classifying algorithms by their parallel complexity. The class $\mathcal{NC}$ is one such class. To explore the class $\mathcal{NC}$, we need to first examine the fundamental nature of parallel processes.

4.2.3 CSP

Hoare's model of concurrent programming, Communicating Sequential Processes (CSP) [9], is a model reflecting properties that should be in all concurrent programming languages. It was not intended to be used as a programming language per se, but it does reflect Hoare's concerns of proving the correctness of programs. However, CSP has provided a medium of discussion of synchronous systems and has inspired a great deal of development. One result is the multitasking and rendezvous properties of Ada. Hoare has suggested the following three properties that every concurrent language should have: the ability to express parallelism, communication primitives, and nondeterminism. This section provides an informal brief description of the syntax and meaning of CSP commands. Full details of CSP are contained in [9].

CSP was proposed as a preliminary solution to the problem of defining a synchronous message-based language.

A CSP program consists of a static collection of processes. The basic command of CSP is $[\rho_1 \| \ldots \| \rho_n]$, expressing concurrent execution of sequential processes $\rho_1, \ldots, \rho_n$. Each individual process ρ_i has a distinct address space and consists of statements S_i. We can also express parallelism between program statements as well as between processes.

Coordination between processes is implemented by message exchange between pairs of processes. It involves the synchronized execution of *send* (output) and *receive* (input) operations by both processes. The send and receive operations in processes ρ_j and ρ_i take the following forms: $\rho_i!y$ *and* $\rho_j?x$, respectively.

Input command $\rho_j?x$ expresses a request to ρ_j to assign a value to the (local) variable x of ρ_i. Output command $\rho_i!y$ expresses a request to ρ_i to receive a value from ρ_j. Execution of $\rho_j?x$ and $\rho_i!y$ is synchronized and results in assigning the value of y to x. $\rho_j?x$ and $\rho_i!y$ are said to be a *matching pair* of communication statements. We define a *communication sequence* of process ρ_i as the sequence of all communications that ρ_i has so far participated in.

The alteration command allows for a path to be nondeterministically chosen from a set of paths. The repetition rule allows for repeated nondeterministic choosing of a path from a set of paths.

The alteration and repetition commands are as follows:

$$\textbf{if}\, b_1; c_1 \rightarrow S_1 2 \ldots 2\, b_n; c_n \rightarrow S_n \textbf{fi}$$
$$\textbf{do}\, b_1; c_1 \rightarrow S_1 2 \ldots 2\, b_n; c_n \rightarrow S_n\, \textbf{od}$$

Alteration and repetition are formed from sets of guarded commands. A guarded command $b; c \rightarrow S$ consists of a guard $b; c$ and a command S. In the guard, b is a Boolean expression and c is either skip or one of the communication primitives. The symbol ";" is used as a delimiter for separating different program statements. If b is false, the guard is failed. If b is true and $c = skip$, the guard is ready. If b is true and c is one of the communication primitives, then the guard is prepared to communicate with the process named in the communication primitive. It is ready when the other process is prepared to communicate and blocked at other times.

Execution of an alteration command selects a guarded command with a ready guard and executes the sequence $c; S$. If c is skip, execution is independent of other processes. If c is a communication command, then a matching communication command must be executed simultaneously. When some guards are blocked and none are ready, the process is blocked and must wait. If all guards are failed, the process aborts.

Execution of the repetitive command is the same except that, whereas execution of alternation selects one guarded command and is completed, for repetition the selection is repeated until all guards are failed, at which time execution of the repetition is repeated until all guards are failed, at which time execution of the repetition is completed.

4.2.4 Complexity

The questions of complexity and computability that exist for sequential computer programs, are also interesting questions for concurrent/parallel computer programs. If the Turing Machine is the abstract computational model for a sequential program, what is the corresponding model for a concurrent program and how does this model relate to the sequential Turing Machine model?

From [10], the fundamental measures of complexity are *parallel time*, *space*, and *sequential time*. If we have an abstract model which provides these three measures, then we can succinctly define speedup and characterize classes of algorithms that are amenable to parallelism.

If the model of concurrent computation is represented by CSP, concurrent programs are really expressed by sequential programs that communicate with each other. Since the Turing Machine is the model of sequential programs, it is natural to express a concurrent program as a set of communicating Turing Machines. Specifically, a concurrent program is represented by a multitape Turing Machine, which has a read-only input tape, k work tapes ($k > 1$), and a write-only output tape. Roughly, the input tape and output tape correspond to the message passing that occurs in CSP ?, ! barrier rendezvous and each work tape corresponds to the internal storage of one of the k processes of the CSP program.

Definition 1.   *Formally, a Turing Machine (TM) is described by*

$$M = (Q, I, \Sigma, \delta, \flat, q_0, F)$$

where Q is the finite set of states, Σ is the tape alphabet, $I \subseteq \Sigma$ is the input, δ is the move function, $\flat$ is a special blank symbol, $q_0 \in Q$ is the start state, and $F \subset Q$ is the set of final states.

Definition 2.   *For a TM M and input w, $t(w)$ is the total number of steps taken for input w and*

$$t(n) = \max\{t(w) \mid |w| \le n\}$$

is the time complexity of M.

Definition 3.   *For a TM M and input w, $s(w)$ is the total maximum length of any work tape used for input w and*

$$s(n) = \max\{s(w) \mid |w| \le n\}$$

is the space consumption of of M.

Definition 4.   *Let $I D$ be the instantaneous description of M,*

$$I D \equiv \Sigma^* Q \Sigma^* \equiv xqy$$

where xy are tape contents and the tape head is scanning the leftmost symbol of y in state q and $\vdash$ represents a move of M.

Definition 5.   *Let $I D_0 \vdash I D_1 \vdash I D_2 \vdash \cdots$ be a computation of M for input w. If, in two successive steps, $I D \vdash I D' \vdash I D''$ a work tape moves in different directions, we say a head changes its movement during $I D \vdash I D' \vdash I D''$. Define $(i, j), i < j$ as a phase of this computation if no work tape head changes its movement direction during $I D_i \vdash I D_i + 1 \vdash I D_i + 2 \vdash \cdots \vdash I D_j$ where in $I D \vdash I D'$, every tape head moves $R, L,$ or S where R and L are different directions and S is no movement.*

Next we define a machine that will help relate the phases to the concept of data dependencies between sequential processes through message passing.

Definition 6.   *Let a transform machine be a TM constructed from M adding a special state q'. Upon entering q', it removes all the contents from the input tape, copies the output tape to the input tape, changes the work tape and output tape to blanks, and works normally starting in state q_0.*

Definition 7.   *The width complexity $w(n)$ is the maximum total length of the input and output tape contents during the computation for all input of length $\le n$.*

Remark   What these definitions show is that if we can use n work tapes in a single phase, independently, this implies there are no data dependencies between the work tapes. The end of a phase (entering state q') implies that a communication or synchronization is necessary. Thus, in the Turing Machine formulation, the width complexity corresponds to the total amount of computational space (complexity) and the space complexity corresponds to the longest space complexity of an individual work tape (process).

A special type of transform machine is of interest, since it describes a computation which is amenable to parallelism in logarithmic time.

Definition 8. *If a transform machine satisfies*

$$s(n) = O(\log(w(n))),$$

it is a log-space transform machine (LSTM).

For example, there is an LSTM that satisfies the computation of a tree-reduction summation.

Example 1. An LSTM that satisfies the computation of $\sum x_i$ for $x_1 \# x_2 \# \cdots \# x_k$ where the $X_k's$ are binary numbers input as follows.

In Phase 1, M gets $y_1 \# y_2 \# y_3 \# \cdots$ on its output tape where $y_i = x_{2i} + x_{2i+1}$.

In Phase 2, M $y_1 \# y_2 \# \cdots$ becomes the input and M gets $z_1 \# z_2 \# \cdots$ on its output tape where $z_i = z_{2i} + z_{2i+1}$.

This continues until the output is $\sum x_i$. This clearly takes $\log k$ phases. The width complexity $w(n) = O(n)$, $k \leq n$ and the phase complexity is $\log k$.

The problems that can be solved by an LSTM form a complexity class, $\mathcal{NC}$.

Definition 9. *A problem is in $\mathcal{NC}$ if there exists an LSTM solving it in polynomially related phase $O(\log^* n)$ and width $O(n^*)$ where $g(n) = f^*(n)$ if $g(n) = p(f(n))$ for some polynomial, p.*

Thus, the class $\mathcal{NC}$ represents the class of nicely parallelizable problems with time polynomial in the logarithm of the size of the problem (poly-log) using only a polynomial number of processors. Clearly any problem in $\mathcal{P}$ is in $\mathcal{NC}$, since any problem in $\mathcal{NC}$ when solved serially, is in $\mathcal{P}$. However, the reverse is not necessarily true since, for example, the best-known parallel algorithm for maximum flow is $O(n^2 \log n)$ steps using $O(n)$ processors.

4.2.5 NP-Completeness and Parallel Computing

While the results above show that the class $\mathcal{NC}$ contains problems amenable to parallel computing, there are algorithm classes in which parallel computing is ineffective.

The class of $\mathcal{NP}$-Complete problems, or those solvable in nondeterministic polynomial time, form just such a class. Since it is not known if any $\mathcal{NP}$ problems can be solved in deterministic polynomial time, attempting to solve an $\mathcal{NP}$-complete problem requires exponential time on a sequential computer.

Since, by the above discussion, our notion of a parallel computer is really expressed by a multitape Turing Machine, and, since multitape and single-tape Turing Machine computations are related, then, by the Church-Turing hypothesis, any $\mathcal{NP}$-Complete problem can be expressed as a parallel algorithm on the multitape Turing Machine. However, by our notion of speedup, S, using N processors, the best speedup is N, a linear factor. However, an exponential problem, E, grows in some exponential power of N, $E = O(c^N)$. Thus, since a parallel machine grows in power, only linearly, it cannot effectively reduce the exponential complexity of the problem. Put more succinctly, parallel computers only reduce the complexity of an exponential problem by a polynomial factor S, thus, leaving the complexity exponential since $E/S = C^N/N$ is still exponential.

However, parallel computers are useful in evaluating expensive hueristics for approximation to the solution of $\mathcal{N}P$-Complete problems. Techniques such as simulated annealing [14] provide good results, but are computationally complex. Parallel computing can help speed their evaluation.

4.3

INTERCONNECTION NETWORKS AND EMBEDDINGS

In the presentation so far, we have assumed that all processors are connected to each other (a completely connected network). The crossbar switch [11] attempts to connect each processor to each other processor. However, the number of switch elements grows as the square of the number of processors, making this technology infeasible for large multicomputer networks. The bus interconnection [11], by contrast, is inexpensive but exhibits a performance bottleneck as interprocessor communication grows.

Multistage interconnection networks attempt to minimize the cost of interconnecting processors by providing a subset of possible interconnection patterns between the processors, at any one time. Multistage interconnection networks are the basis for many commercial and research parallel processors such as PASM [16] and the IBM RS/6000-based POWERparallel 1 (SP1) System [12]. However, if we examine the examples of Section 4.1 the communication patterns between processors are all *nearest neighbor*. Indeed, the most natural parallel algorithms result from domain decomposition into spatially local communication patterns such as mesh, ring, or tree. Thus, a fixed architecture that can be a host to these guest graphs is all that is really necessary.

A fixed interconnection topology is the usual choice in constructing multicomputers. The topology is based on a graph theoretical model in which processors are represented by nodes or vertices and links are represented by edges so that all links are bidirectional.

A *path* is a sequence of links from the source node to a destination node. The *path length* (distance) between two nodes is the minimum number of links between these two nodes. The *degree* of a node is the number of links (bidirectional) connecting to a node.

4.3.1 Graph Embedding

The need for the embedding arises from at least two different directions. First, with the widespread availability of distributed-memory architectures based on the hypercube interconnection scheme, there is an ever-growing interest in the portability of algorithms developed for architectures based on other topologies, such as linear arrays, rings, two-dimensional meshes, and complete binary trees, into the hypercube. Clearly, this question of portability reduces to one of embedding the above interconnection schemes into the hypercube. Second, the problem of mapping parallel algorithms onto parallel architectures naturally gives rise to graph embedding problems. Graph embedding problems have applications in a wide variety of computational situations. For example, the flow of information in a parallel algorithm defines a program graph and embedding this into a network tell us how to organize the computation on the network. Other problems that can be formulated as graph embedding problems are laying out circuits on chips, representing data structures in computing memory, and finding efficient program control structures.

The problem of mapping a graph representing the computation and communication needs of the program onto the underlying physical interconnection of a multiprocessor so as to minimize the communication overhead and maximize the parallelism is called the mapping problem. The mapping problem is the assignment of processes to processors so as to maximize the number of pairs of communicating processes that fall on pairs of directly connected processors.

In mapping problems, the *guest graph* G is the network topology that we are interested in simulating using a *host graph* H. Let V_G and V_H denote the vertex sets of the graph G and H, respectively, and E_G and E_H denote the edge sets of the graph G and H, respectively. An *embedding* f of a graph G into a graph H is a mapping of the vertices of G into the vertices of H, together with a mapping of the edges of G into the simple paths of H such that if $e = (u, v) \in E_G$, then $f(e)$ is a simple path of H with endpoints $f(u)$ and $f(v)$. If $f(e)$ has length greater than one, then it has one or more intermediate nodes which are all nodes on the path other than the two endpoints. An embedding f is *isomorphic* if it is injective and for each $(u, v) \in E_G, (f(u), f(v)) \in E_H$. Throughout this paper, unless indicated otherwise the term "embeddings" will always means isomorphic embeddings, and the terms "embedding" and "mapping" will mean the same and be used interchangeably.

It has been known for a long time that the general graph embedding problem (that is, subgraph isomorphism problem) is $\mathcal{N}P$-complete. It was shown that the embedding of general graphs into the binary hypercube is also $\mathcal{N}P$-complete [4]. However, with rich interconnection structure the hypercube contains as a subgraph many the regular structures (that is, rings, two-dimensional meshes, higher-dimensional meshes, and almost complete binary trees). Most of the mapping research in these years has dealt with effectively simulating these regular structures in the hypercubes, (for example, [17]).

Let f be an embedding function which maps a guest graph G into a host graph H. $|V_G|$ denotes the cardinality of the set V_G. Terminology related to the mapping problem is formally defined as follows.

Definition 10. *The expansion of the mapping is the ratio of the size (in number of nodes) of the host graph to that of the guest graph, that is, $E_f = \frac{|V_H|}{|V_G|}$. If the embedding is injective, then the expansion is a measure of processor utilization.*

Definition 11. *The edge dilation of edge $(i, j) \in E_G$ is $dist(f(i), f(j))$. The dilation of the mapping is $D_f = \max(dist(f(i), f(j)), \forall(i, j) \in E_G$. The average edge dilation is $\frac{1}{|E_G|} \sum_{(i,j) \in E_G} dist(f(i), f(j))$. The dilation of a mapping represents the communication delay between the communication nodes.*

Definition 12. *The congestion of an edge $e' \in E_H$ is the cardinality of $e \in E(G)$: e' is in path $f(e)$. That is, $\sum_{e \in E_G} |e' \cap E_{f(e)}|$. The congestion of the mapping is $\max\{\sum_{e \in E_G} |e' \cap E_{f(e)}|\}, \forall e' \in E_H$. The average congestion of the mapping is similarly defined.*

Definition 13. *The max-load is the maximum number of nodes in G that are mapped to a node in H. Max-load $= 1$ if the mapping is one-to-one.*

It should be noted that unit dilation implies unit congestion. Thus the class of dilation-1 embeddable graphs in a hypercube is a proper set of the class of congestion-1 embeddable graphs. If each node of the guest graph is mapping to a distinct node of the host, the slow down due to nearest neighbor communication in the original graph being extended to communication along paths is a function of the length of the path (that is, edge dilation) and the congestion of the edges on the path.

4.3.2   The k-ary n-cube Interconnection Topology

One of the most general types of interconnection network is the k-ary n-cube which has k^n nodes organized as a cube with dimension n and k nodes in each dimension. Each node i is identified by an n-digit radix k number, the b-th digit of the number represents the node's position in the b-th dimension. The nodes are interconnected to their nearest neighbors in a radix k representation as follows.

Definition 14.   *If $i_{n-1} \cdots i_0$ is the radix k representation for node i, then its neighbors in the interconnection are*

$$i_{n-1}i_{n-2} \cdots i_{b+1}i_b^+ i_{b-1} \cdots i_0$$

and

$$i_{n-1}i_{n-2} \cdots i_{b+1}i_b^- i_{b-1} \cdots i_0 \text{ for each } 0 \le b \le n - 1$$

where

$$i_b^+ = (i_b + 1) \bmod k$$

and

$$i_b^- = (i_b - 1) \bmod k$$

An example of a 3-ary 2-cube is shown in Figure 4.6g.

Some special cases of this topology are the $k = 2$ case of the hypercube or Boolean n-cube. For $n = 2$ a superset of a k-dimensional mesh is generated and $n = 1$ specifies a ring.

Boolean n-cube   Various supercomputer architectures interconnecting hundreds or thousands of processors have been proposed for many years. The Hypercube is used on both SIMD and MIMD parallel processors. Some commercial examples are the NCUBE/2, the Intel iPSC/860, and the CM-2.

An n-cube system has $N = 2^n$ nodes (processors) indexed from 0 to $2^n - 1$ and there is a link between any two nodes if and only if the binary representations of their indices differ by exactly one bit. An n-cube can be recursively constructed by combining two $(n - 1)$-cubes. Let $(a_{n-2} \ldots a_0)$ be an index in $(n - 1)$-cube. Then in n-cube, there is a link between two corresponding nodes in $(n - 1)$-cube, $(0a_{n-2} \ldots a_0)$ and $(1a_{n-2} \ldots a_0)$. A 2-ary 3-cube is shown in Figure 4.7.

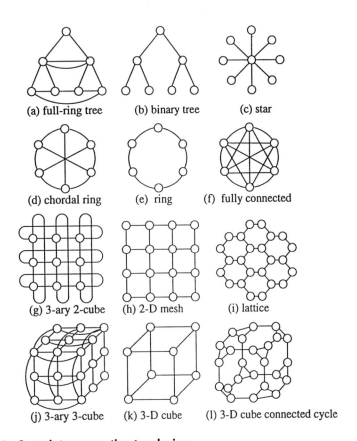

(a) full-ring tree (b) binary tree (c) star

(d) chordal ring (e) ring (f) fully connected

(g) 3-ary 2-cube (h) 2-D mesh (i) lattice

(j) 3-ary 3-cube (k) 3-D cube (l) 3-D cube connected cycle

FIGURE 4.6 Some interconnection topologies.

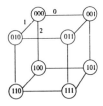

FIGURE 4.7 A 2-ary 3-cube.

4.3.3   Pattern Embedding in a Hypercube

The hypercube is a powerful topology because it is a superset of many other topologies, such as ring, mesh, and tree. Commonly, each of these nodes in these topologies is given a binary representation. However, the binary representation chosen needs to preserve the nearest neighbor adjacencies present in the k-ary n-cube representation. Fortunately, the Gray-code provides just such a representation.

Definition 15.   *A binary reflected Gray code (BRGC) G_k is a code of length k such that $G_{k-1}(i_l)$ is the $k-1$-bit Gray-code representation of digit i_l of the radix $k-1$ number i and $G_{k-1}(i_l)^R$ is its reversal.*

$$G_k = \begin{cases} \{0, 1\} & if\ k = 1 \\ \{0G_{k-1}(0), 0G_{k-1}(1), \ldots, 0G_{k-1}(2^{k-1} - 1), \\ 1G_{k-1}(2^{k-1} - 1), 1G_{k-1}(2^{k-1} - 2), \ldots, 1G_{k-1}(0)\} \\ = \{0G_{k-1}, 1G_{k-1}^R\} & k > 1 \end{cases}$$

Ring Embedding   Rings are of interest, and are of increasing interest, due to the computational problems that arise in genetics. One of the central questions of molecular biology is the discovery of the semantics of DNA. Just knowing the syntax, that is, the sequence, tells the biologist little. The biologist must understand the biochemical functions of the DNA. To understand the semantics, one needs to know the relationship between DNA and proteins. The essence of the problem is that given a set of protein sequences, efficient alignment-matching algorithms are needed that can deal elegantly with insertion, deletion, substitution, and even gaps in the series of sequence elements. One way of measuring the optimality of an alignment is by computing a score based on a matrix of weights reflecting the similarity between pairs of sequences. In some situations a penalty is imposed for each gap introduced. Such a score can be computed by a dynamic programming algorithm in time proportional to the product of the lengths of the sequences.

The subsequence matching problem can be formulated as follows:

Given two sequences A, B, of symbols chosen from a same domain

$$A = (a_1, a_2, \ldots, a_n),\ B = (b_1, b_2, \ldots, b_m),$$

find the subsequences

$$A' = (a_{i_1}, a_{i_2}, \ldots, a_{i_x}),\ B' = (b_{j_1}, b_{j_2}, \ldots, b_{j_x})$$

where $1 \leq i_1 < i_2 < \ldots < i_x \leq n,\ 1 \leq j_1 < j_2 < \ldots < j_x \leq m$

which maximizes the comparison function $C(A', B')$. C can depend on the symbols a_{i_l}, b_{j_k} in A' and B' and on the numbers of symbols in A and B which are omitted between successive symbols in A' and B' (gaps).

For such comparison functions, one can use a dynamic programming algorithm to determine the best subsequence match for a given pair of sequences A, B in serial time $O(nm)$ where n and m are the length of the sequences A and B. This dynamic programming

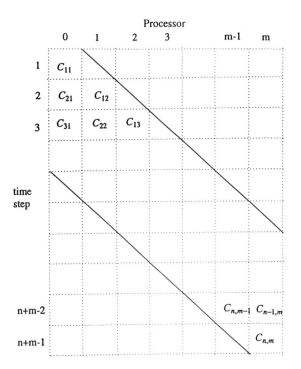

FIGURE 4.8 Diagram indicating activity of processor i at time step t. If $1 \leq t - p \leq n$, then processor i computes $C_{t-p,p+1}$ at step t. Otherwise, the processor is inactive.

algorithm can best be understood by considering the matrix

$$C_{r,s} = \max \begin{cases} 0 \\ C_{r-1,s-1} + D(a_r, b_s) \\ C_{r-1,s} + g \\ C_{r,s-1} + g \end{cases}$$

where the gap constant $g < 0$, and D is a correlation function between single elements [13].

A parallel version of the dynamic programming algorithm is quite straightforward to derive [5]. Since computing the value of $C_{r,s}$ only depends on knowing the values of $C_{r-1,s}$, $C_{r,s-1}$, and $C_{r-1,s-1}$, we see that all of the elements on one antidiagonal of the matrix can be computed simultaneously if the values along the two previous antidiagonals are known. That is, for a fixed value of t, the matrix elements $C_{t-s,s}$ can be computed simultaneously for all s provided that they are known for $t-1$ and $t-2$. Thus, one can parallelize the above algorithm by computing successive antidiagonals of the matrix $C_{r,s}$ on successive time steps. This is represented schematically in Figure 4.8. The algorithm requires $n + m - 1$ time steps and m processors to compare proteins of length m and n.

Since each communication in the above algorithm is nearest neighbor, mapping the ring computational structure to directly connected processors is important.

Theorem 1.   *A k-ary 1-cube is a subgraph of a 2-ary n-cube when $n = \log_2 k$ and $k = 2^j$ for some integer j.*

Proof.   The idea is to number the nodes of the k-ary 1-cube using a BRGC. For each node i of the k-ary 1-cube, renumber that node by $G_k(i) = g_{k-1}g_{k-2}\cdots g_l \cdots g_0$. The predecessor and successor nodes of the k-ary 1-cube are numbered (from Definition 14 with $n = 1$)

$$i^- \text{ and } i^+$$

where

$$i^+ = (i + 1) \bmod k \text{ and } i^- = (i - 1) \bmod k$$

which, using the definition of G_k are the nodes

$$g_{k-1}g_{k-2}\cdots \overline{g_l} \cdots g_0$$

and

$$g_{k-1}g_{k-2}\cdots \overline{g_{l+1}}g_l \cdots g_0$$

Corollary 1.   *A ring of length of 2^m can be mapped into the 2-ary n-cube when $2 \leq m \leq n$.*

Proof.   Since a 2-ary $n - 1$ cube is a subgraph of a 2-ary n-cube, the result is immediate.

If we notice that a ring of length 2^n exists within a G_n because a path of length of 2^{n-1} exists within the first half of $G_n(= 0G_{n-1})$ and is connected to a path of length of 2^{n-1} within the second half of $G_n(= 1G_{n-1}^R)$, then we can also construct rings of any even length by starting with shorter paths.

Corollary 2.   *A ring of length $p = 2q$ can be mapped into the 2-ary n-cube when $4 \leq p \leq 2^n$.*

Proof.   Find a path of length q as follows

$$\{0G_{n-1}(i), 0G_{n-1}(i + 1), \ldots, 0G_{n-1}(i + q - 1),$$

$$1G_{n-1}(i + q - 1), 1G_{n-1}(i + q - 2), \ldots, 1G_{n-1}(i)\}$$

For example, of a ring of length

$$p = 12 : \{0011, 0010, 0110, 0111, 0101, 0100, 1100, 1101, 1111, 1110, 1010, 1011\}$$

Mesh Embedding   Of great interest in computational science and engineering is programs whose structure is the mesh. Consider the mode fluids problem [15] of cavity-driven flow whose physical domain chosen is shown in Figure 4.9. The pair of nonlinear coupled differential equations 4.1, 4.2 that describe this flow are easily solved sequentially using a standard second-order central differencing scheme. Central differencing calculates the new values at a particular point by taking a weighted average of the values of the nearest

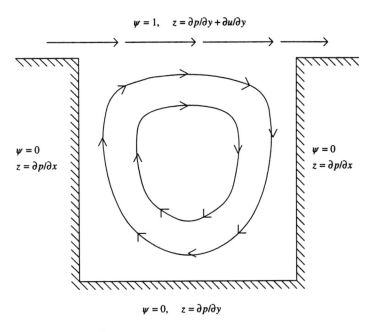

$$\psi = 1, \quad z = \partial p/\partial y + \partial u/\partial y$$

$$\psi = 0 \qquad\qquad\qquad\qquad\qquad\qquad \psi = 0$$
$$z = \partial p/\partial x \qquad\qquad\qquad\qquad\qquad z = \partial p/\partial x$$

$$\psi = 0, \quad z = \partial p/\partial y$$

FIGURE 4.9 Cavity-driven flow.

neighbors, as shown in Figure 4.10, where the weights are dependent on the flow patterns.

$$\zeta = -\nabla^2 \psi \tag{4.1}$$

$$\frac{\partial \zeta}{\partial t} + \frac{\partial}{\partial x}(u\zeta) + \frac{\partial}{\partial y}(v\zeta) = \frac{1}{Re}\nabla^2 \zeta \tag{4.2}$$

where $u = \frac{\partial \psi}{\partial y}$ and $v = -\frac{\partial \psi}{\partial x}$.

These two equations represent the flow conditions in the physical domain. Lines of constant stream function, ψ, value are parallel to the local flow, while the vorticity, ζ, is a measure of the local shearing rate, or swirl, in the flow.

These equations were solved using successive over-relaxation with the resulting discrete equations as follows:

$$\psi_{i,j}^{k+1}$$
$$= \psi_{i,j}^{k} + \frac{\omega}{2(1+\beta^2)}\left[\psi_{i+1,j}^{k} + \psi_{i-1,j}^{k} + \beta^2\left(\psi_{i,j+1}^{k} + \psi_{i,j-1}^{k}\right) - \zeta_{i,j}\Delta x^2\right] \tag{4.3}$$

$$\zeta_{i,j}^{n+1}$$
$$= \zeta_{i,j}^{n} + \Delta t\left[\frac{-u_{i+1,j}^{n}\zeta_{i+1,j}^{n} - u_{i-1,j}^{n}\zeta_{i-1,j}^{n}}{2\Delta x} + \frac{-v_{i,j+1}^{n}\zeta_{i,j+1}^{n} - v_{i,j-1}^{n}\zeta_{i,j-1}^{n}}{2\Delta y}\right.$$
$$\left. + \frac{1}{Re}\left(\frac{\zeta_{i+1,j}^{n} + \zeta_{i-1,j}^{n} - 2\zeta_{i,j}^{n}}{\Delta x^2} + \frac{\zeta_{i,j+1}^{n} + \zeta_{i,j-1}^{n} - 2\zeta_{i,j}^{n}}{\Delta y^2}\right)\right] \tag{4.4}$$

where ω is the over-relaxation factor and $\beta = \frac{\Delta x}{\Delta y}$.

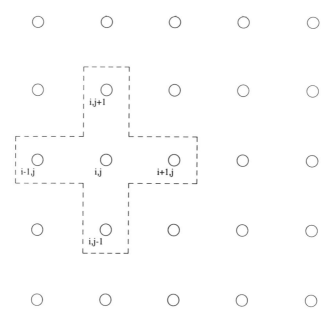

FIGURE 4.10   Localized computational molecule.

Superscript k indicates the current iteration value and n is the value at the current time. The boundary values for ζ are calculated by using first-order accurate, away-from-the-wall equations:

$$\zeta_{i,w} = -\frac{2}{\Delta y^2}\left(\psi_{i,w} - \psi_{i,w+1}\right)\left[+\frac{u_{i,w}}{\Delta y}\right] \tag{4.5}$$

$$\zeta_{w,j} = -\frac{2}{\Delta x^2}\left(\psi_{w,j} - \psi_{w+1,j}\right) \tag{4.6}$$

In equations 4.5 and 4.6, w is the location of the boundary, and the bracketed term is only used at the top of the cavity, where the external flow affects the values.

The standard solution method is to take an initial guess of the values of u, v, and ζ, along with a Δt appropriate for the fineness of the grid, and iterate equation 4.4 once. These values are then used to iterate equation 4.3 to convergence, update the values of u and v, calculate the boundary values for ζ, then repeat the process until the values of ζ and ψ have both met desired convergence criteria.

Optimal Matrix Multiplication (in the abstract sense)   As another mesh problem, consider Gentleman's Algorithm [7] which is an explicit parallel solution using a 2D mesh of processors to multiply two matrices.

Assume we have N^2 processors arranged in an $N \times N$ mesh. Each processor $\rho_{i,j}$ holds $a_{i,j}$ and $b_{i,j}$ and we have a toroidal mesh (an easily implemented subgraph of an n-cube).

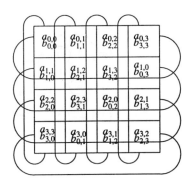

FIGURE 4.11 Toroidal shift.

Optimal OMEGA(n) Algorithm:

foreach $\rho_{i,j}$ SEND and RECEIVE to
    left circular shift all $a'_{i,j}s$ by $i - 1$
    up circular shift all $b'_{i,j}s$ by $j - 1$
foreach $\rho_{i,j}$
    $c_{i,j} \leftarrow a_{i,j}b_{i,j}$
    do $n - 1$ times
        left circular shift $a_{i,j}$; up circular shift $b_{i,j}$
        $c_{i,j} \leftarrow c_{i,j} + a_{i,j}b_{i,j}$

Example 2. Consider the example of matrix multiplication shown in Figure 4.11. The result $c_{2,3}$ is calculated as follows, $c_{2,3} \leftarrow a_{2,1}b_{1,3} + a_{2,2}b_{2,3} + a_{2,3}b_{3,3} + a_{2,0}b_{0,3}$

Embedding Results for Meshes

Theorem 2. *A k-ary 2-cube is a subgraph of a 2-ary n-cube when $n = 2 \log_2 k$ and $k = 2^j$ for some integer j.*

Proof. As in the proof of Theorem 1, we number the digits of the k-ary graph using G_j. Specifically, for each node $i = i_1 i_0$ of the k-ary 2-cube, renumber that node by $G_j(i_1)G_j(i_0)$. Consider the 4 neighbors of i,

$$i_1 i_0^+ \quad i_1 i_0^-$$
$$i_1^+ i_0 \quad i_1^- i_0$$

where

$$i^+ = (i + 1) \ mod \ j$$

and

$$i^- = (i - 1) \ mod \ j$$

and their Gray-code ordering

$$G(i_1)G(i_0^+) \quad G(i_1)G(i_0^-)$$
$$G(i_1^+)G(i_0) \quad G(i_1^-)G(i_0)$$

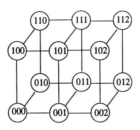

FIGURE 4.12   3D-mesh interconnection.

Since we change only one dimension of i at a time for each neighbor, we can consider each mapping individually, as in the ring case. Using the definition of G_j, a particular i_m, $G(i_m)$'s neighbors are the nodes

$$g_{j-1}g_{j-2}\cdots\overline{g}_l\cdots g_0$$

and

$$g_{j-1}g_{j-2}\cdots\overline{g}_{l+1}g_l\cdots g_0$$

Thus, each $G_j(i_m)$ enumerates a 2-ary j-cube. Taking the cross product of $G_j(i_1) \times G_j(i_0)$ yields a 2-ary n-cube.

A d-dimensional mesh is an $m_0 \times m_2 \times \ldots m_{d-1}$ mesh in the d dimensional space. An example of $d = 3$ is shown in Figure 4.12.

Corollary 3.   *An $m_0 \times m_1 \times \cdots \times m_{d-1}$ mesh in d-dimensional space, where $m_i = 2^{k_i}$ and $\sum_{i=0}^{d-1} k_i = n$ can be mapped into a 2-ary n-cube where the mapping is $G_{k_{d-1}}(i_{d-1}) \times \cdots \times G_{k_1}(i_1) \times G_{k_0}(i_0)$.*

Pyramid Embedding   Tree computations occur more infrequently than either the mesh or ring, however, an extension of the tree, the pyramid, occurs frequently in multigrid algorithms.

The Multigrid Method   The initial idea behind multigrid is that convergence time decreases dramatically with an improved initial guess. From this idea, it seems reasonable to use a coarse grid to get a rough solution, and then interpolate this answer to finer and finer arrays as shown in Figure 4.13. Although this does work, multigrid methods are much more powerful than this simple concept.

Given the system of equations

$$AU = F, \tag{4.7}$$

the usual procedure is to guess a solution, **V**, to **U**, then calculate **AV** and correct the guess by comparison to **F**. The estimate **V** is known to be some amount **E** away from the exact solution, giving

$$U = V + E$$

and by substituting into equation 4.7,

$$A(V + E) = F.$$

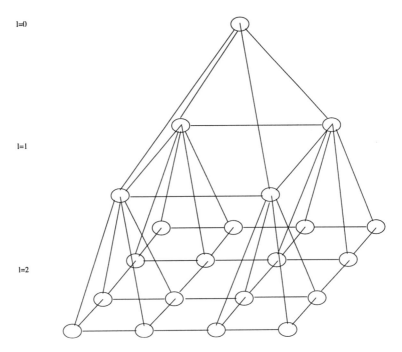

l=0

l=1

l=2

FIGURE 4.13   Multigrid structure for N = 16 processors at the finest level.

Initially, this doesn't help since neither **U** nor **E** is known. However, after rearranging,

$$AE = F - AV$$

and finally,

$$AE = R, \tag{4.8}$$

where **R** denotes the residual, $R = F - AV$. This resulting equation can be solved exactly as the first equation, since all of the variables except **E** are known.

The reason why equation 4.8 is solved instead of equation 4.7 has to do with the size and frequency of the error. If the error in the value is small, but not yet small enough to satisfy convergence criteria, and the absolute value of the result is large, the small error will be hard to distinguish from the result. If, instead, the values are subtracted out, the magnitude of the error will then be centered around zero, so the relative size of the error will be magnified.

The observed frequency of the error is dependent on the coarseness of the array, as shown in Figure 4.14. What may be seen as a relatively smooth change at the finest level appears as rapid changes when restricted to a coarser level. Thus, solving the errors at a coarser level increases the speedup of the solution by damping out the errors faster, along with increasing convergence rate due to better guesses.

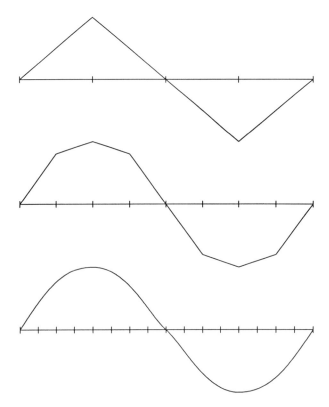

FIGURE 4.14   Error frequency reduction using multigrid.

As illustrated in Figure 4.15 and as described by [3], there are many ways to implement the multigrid idea. In the figure, level 0 represents the finest array of points, while level 3 is the coarsest.

In the V-cycle, level 0 does a set number of iterations of equation 4.7, then passes its residuals to level 1. Level 1 then iterates equation 4.8 and passes its residuals to level 2, where the process is repeated until the coarsest level is reached. When the coarsest level finishes its computations, it passes the error corrections back down through the levels, until level 0 is reached.

The W-cycle takes additional advantage of the speed of the coarser grids by having them also do some improvement of the errors before the errors get passed back down the levels. This helps speed up the damping out of the smooth changes since the coarser levels converge faster.

Finally, the full multigrid (FMV) cycle takes advantage of both the error correction and improved initial guesses. Instead of starting at the finest level, FMV-cycles start at the coarsest arrays and compute an initial guess that is passed down to the next level. That level then does a few iterations and does a single V-cycle to improve its guesses before passing them down. Once the lowest level is reached, the process continues as a regular V-cycle.

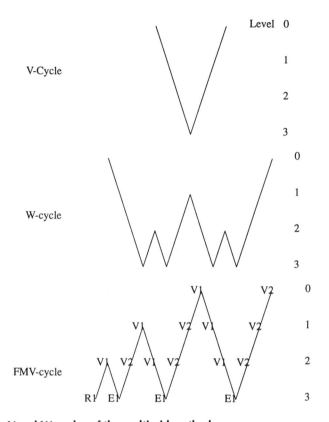

FIGURE 4.15   V and W cycles of the multigrid method.

4.3.4   Embedding of Pyramid into *n*-cube

In observing Figure 4.13, it is clear that embedding the pyramid into the *n*-cube is not going to be possible with $D_f = 1$ since between each pair of levels of the pyramid there are odd length cycles. However, $D_f = 2$ mappings exist. The mapping makes use of the following Gray code.

Definition 16.   *A hierarchical binary reflected Gray code (HBRGC) is a BRGC such that*

$$h(G_n(i), G_n(i + 2^j)) = 2 \text{ when } i + 2^j \leq 2^n - 1, j > 0$$

Definition 17.   *The hierarchical binary reflected Gray code HG_k is a code of length k such that*

$$HG_k = \begin{cases} \{0, 1\} & \text{if } k = 1 \\ \{HG_{k-1}(0)0, HG_{k-1}(0)1, HG_{k-1}(1)1, HG_{k-1}(1)0, \ldots, \\ HG_{k-1}(2^{k-1} - 2)0, HG_{k-1}(2^{k-1} - 2)1, \\ HG_{k-1}(2^{k-1} - 1)1, HG_{k-1}(2^{k-1} - 1)0\} & k > 1 \end{cases}$$

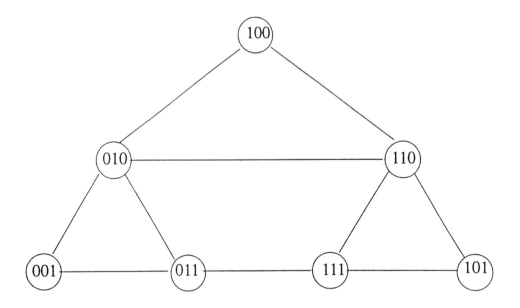

FIGURE 4.16   2D-pyramid generated by HBRGC $H B$.

If we define $R_l(HG_k) = \{HG_{k-1}(0)10^{l-1}, HG_{k-1}(1)10^{l-1}, \ldots, HG_{k-1}(2^{k-1}-2)10^{l-1},$
$HG_{k-1}(2^{k-1}-1)10^{l-1}\}$, which is just HG_k1, then R_kHG_k defines level $k+1$ of a two-dimensional pyramid. Level k of the pyramid is created by $R_k+1(HG_k-R_k(HG_k))$ which yields HG_k0, or the subset of HG_k whose nodes are at least a power of 2 distance away from the nodes of $R_k(HG_k)$. The process recurses until the entire pyramid is constructed. In general, at level $l+1$, of the pyramid, each node at that level is labeled $HG_{k-l}(i)10^l$, thus reflecting that each node at level $l+1$ is, at most, a distance of 2 away from child nodes at level $l+2$.

Example 3. HG_2 generates the following pyramid depicted in Figure 4.16:

- $HG_2 = \{000, 001, 011, 010, 110, 111, 101, 100\}$
- $R_2(HG_2) = \{001, 011, 111, 101\}$
- $R_1(HG_2 - R_2(HG_2)) = \{010, 110\}$
- $R_0(R_1((HG_2 - R_2(HG_2)))) = \{100\}$

4.4

MODELS OF EMBEDDING, PARTITIONING, AND MAPPING

The goal of partioning and mapping of a parallel program onto an architecture is to provide a balanced node utilization by allocating processes to processors maximizing parallelism while simultaneously reducing communication overhead. These two goals are contradictory. The number of processes assigned to each node is application dependent and is dependent on the ratio between computation and communication time.

Optimal load balancing under perfect information is possible. In this case, you are given a set of processes $\rho_0, \rho_1, \ldots, \rho_N - 1$ with execution time requirements of $w(\rho_0)$, $w(\rho_1)$, $\ldots, w(\rho_N - 1)$ and a set of communication costs $C = C(i, j)$, which is the length of a message sent in communicating from process ρ_i to process ρ_j.

Classically [6], the goal of load balancing, given a process/communication digraph $G(P, C)$, where P is the set of processes and C is the set of directed arcs $C(i, j)$, is to find a partition

$$G = G_0 \cup G_1 \cup \cdots \cup G_T - 1$$

of G and a mapping of processes to processors $n(\rho)$ subject to the following constraints,

$$W_n = \sum_{p \in G_n} w(\rho) = constant \tag{4.9}$$

$$C = \frac{1}{2} \sum \sum_{\rho \neq \rho'} C(\rho, \rho') \cdot dist(n(\rho), n(\rho')) \text{ is minimized} \tag{4.10}$$

The problem with this metric is that, in modern multicomputers, such as the NCUBE/2, Intel Paragon, and CM-5, the time to traverse multiple hops in the k-ary n-cube is roughly equivalent to the time to perform nearest-neighbor communication. Thus, we can simply rewrite Equation 4.10 as

$$C = \frac{1}{2} \sum \sum_{\rho \neq \rho'} C(\rho, \rho') \text{ is minimized} \tag{4.11}$$

Intuitively, however, this model is also inadequate for it does not take into account *congestion* from Definition 12. Consider an example of the effects of congestion from a ring embedding of the protein sequence comparison from Section 4.3.

For simplicity, if we model the communication in a hypercube as circuit switching, then a hardware communication circuit between two communicating nodes must be established before communication begins, and a link of the circuit is released at a time after the last bit of the message is transmitted. We, therefore, define the communication time needed for two communicating nodes in a hypercube as follows,

$$t_{comm} = t_{cong} + t_{hops}$$
$$= t_{cong} + [\tau_s + \tau_t C(\rho, \rho')]$$

where t_{comm} is the time needed to send a C-byte message from one node to another. For the circuit switching model, if a circuit cannot be established because a desired link is being used by other packets, the circuit is said to be blocked. Here we assume that when a circuit is blocked, the partial circuit may be torn down, with establishment to be attempted later. t_{cong} here denotes the waiting time for reestablishment. Note that, if the mapping of the linear array in a hypercube is dilation-1, then it will be congestion-1 also, and no edges of a hypercube will be contained in more than one mapping linear array edge. That is, if the mapping is dilation-1, t_{cong}, the communication delay due to congestion will be zero.

t_{hops} is the ideal communication time between two communicating nodes such that the edge congestions of the desired circuit between these two nodes are all one. The value of t_{hops} is determined by the three terms: τ_s, τ_t, and C, where τ_s is the communication latency and τ_t is the time needed to transmit one byte of data. In the parallel protein sequence comparison, each processor in the linear array will send messages to its right neighbor twice, therefore, $T_{comm} = 2 \cdot t_{comm} = 2 \cdot (t_{cong} + t_{hops})$.

Suppose that, during the course of the computation, some processor fails. In the beginning we select one designated spare node and let the rest of nodes all do the computation. If a node becomes faulty during processing, just replace this faulty node with this designated spare node. For this approach, it is *very* possible that the length (or hops) of the desired path from the left or right neighbor of the faulty node to the designated spare node is equal to the dimension of the embedding hypercube, and, moreover, the desired path has congestion-2. These factors (number of hops and congestion) have to be taken into account for calculating the communication time. From the algorithm of parallel protein sequence comparison, we can derive that t_{cong} is equal to $\tau_s + \tau_t C$. For simplicity, we also assume that the path from the faulty node's left neighbor to the designated spare node and the path from the designated spare node to the faulty node's right neighbor are edge-disjoint. The total running time for this approach is about,

$$t_{cong} = \tau_s + \tau_t C$$
$$t_{hops} = \tau_s + \tau_t C$$
$$T_{comm} = 2 \cdot (t_{cong} + t_{hops})$$
$$T_\rho = T_{comm} + w(\rho)$$

which, by comparison with an embedding with no congestion, essentially, doubles the communication time of the entire problem.

4.5

SUMMARY

This session has covered a broad expanse of topics in an effort to provide an informal basis for constructing parallel applications and seeing how they are mapped onto a popular existing architecture.

Bibliography

1. G.M. Amdahl, "Validity of the Single Processor Approach to Achieving Large-Scale Computing Capabilities," *AFIPS Conf. Proc.*, AFIPS Press, Reston, Va., Vol. 30, 1967, pp. 483–485.
2. J. Backus, "Can Programming Be Liberated from the von Neumann style? A Functional Style and Its Algebra of Programs," *Comm. ACM*, Vol. 21, No. 8, 1979, pp. 613–641.

3. W. Briggs, *Multigrid Tutorial*, Society for Industrial and Applied Mathematics, Philadelphia, Penn., 1987.

4. G. Cybenko, D.W. Krumme, and K.N. Venkataraman, "Fixed Hypercube Embedding," *Information Processing Letters*, Vol. 25, 1987, pp. 35–39.

5. E. Edmiston and R.A. Wagner, "Parallelization of the Dynamic Programming Algorithm for Comparison of Sequences," *Proc. Int'l Conf. Parallel Processing*, IEEE CS Press, Los Alamitos, Calif., 1987, pp. 78–80.

6. G.C. Fox and W. Furmaski, "Load Balancing Loosely Synchronous Problems with a Neural Network," tech. report, California Institute of Technology, Pasedena, Calif., Feb. 1988.

7. W.M. Gentleman, "Some Complexity Results for Matrix Computations on Parallel Computers," *J. ACM*, Vol. 25, No. 1, Jan. 1978, pp. 112–115.

8. J. Gustafson, "Reevaluating Amdahl's Law," *Comm. ACM*, Vol. 31, No. 5, pp. 532–533.

9. C. Hoare, "Communicating Sequential Processes," *Comm. ACM*, Vol. 21, No. 8, 1978, pp. 666–677.

10. J. Hong, *Computation, Computability, Similarity, and Duality*, Pittman, London, UK, 1986.

11. K. Hwang and F. Briggs, *Computer Architecture and Parallel Processing*, McGraw-Hill, N.Y., 1984.

12. *IBM Scalable PowerParallel System 9076-SP1*, IBM, 1993.

13. E. Lander and J.P. Mesirov, "Protein Sequence Comparison on a Data Parallel Computer," *Proc. Int'l Conf. Parallel Processing*, IEEE CS Press, Los Alamitos, Calif., 1988, pp. 257–263.

14. H. Lutfiyya et al., "Composite Stock Cutting through Simulated Annealing," *J. Mathematical and Computer Modeling*, Vol. 16, No. 1, 1992, pp. 57–74.

15. D. Riggins et al., "Modeling of Supersonic Combustor Flows Using Parallel Computing," *Computer Systems in Engineering*, Vol. 3, pp. 217–219.

16. H.J. Siegel et al., "PASM: A Partionable SIMD/MIMD System for Image Processing and Pattern Recognition," *IEEE Trans. Computers*, Vol. C-30, Dec. 1981, pp. 934–947.

17. Q.F. Stout, "Hypercubes and Pyramids," in V. Cantoni and S. Levialdi, eds., *Pyramidal Systems for Computer Vision*. Springer-Verlag, New York, N.Y., 1986.

CHAPTER 5

DIRECTIONS IN PARALLEL PROGRAMMING: HPF, SHARED VIRTUAL MEMORY, AND OBJECT PARALLELISM IN PC++*

François Bodin and Thierry Priol
IRISA, University of Rennes, France

Dennis Gannon
Department of Computer Science & CICA, Indiana University, Bloomington, Indiana, USA

Piyush Mehrotra
ICASE, NASA Langley, Hamptom, Virginia, USA

Abstract.   *Fortran and C++ are the dominant programming languages used in scientific computation. Consequently, extensions to these languages are the most popular for programming massively parallel computers. We discuss two such approaches to parallel Fortran and one approach to C++. The High Performance Fortran Forum has designed HPF with the intent of supporting data parallelism on Fortran 90 applications. HPF works by asking the user to help the compiler distribute and align the data structures with the distributed memory modules in the system. Fortran-S takes a different approach in which the data distribution is managed by the operating system and the user provides annotations to indicate parallel control regions. In the case of C++, we look at pC++ which is based on a concurrent aggregate parallel model.*

5.1

INTRODUCTION

Exploiting the full potential of parallel architectures requires a cooperative effort between the user and the language system. There is a clear trade-off between the amount of information the user has to provide and the amount of effort the compiler has to expend to generate

*This research is supported by DARPA under contract AF 30602-92-C-0135 from Rome Labs, National Science Foundation Office of Advanced Scientific Computing under grant ASC-9111616, and Esprit BRA APPARC, and by the National Aeronautics and Space Administration under NASA contract NAS1-19480, while one of the authors was in residence at ICASE, Mail Stop 132C, NASA Langley Research Center, Hampton, VA 23681.

optimal parallel code. At one end of the spectrum are low-level languages where the user has full control and has to provide all the details while the compiler effort is minimal. At the other end of the spectrum are sequential languages where the compiler has the full responsibility for extracting the parallelism. Clearly, there are advantages and disadvantages to both approaches.

5.1.1 Explicit-tasking Languages

Current programming environments for parallel machines follow the first approach providing low-level constructs such as message-passing primitives as their principal language constructs. In such programming environments, an algorithm is specified as a set of sequential processes that execute concurrently, synchronizing and sharing data explicitly via messages. Since such environments directly reflect the underlying hardware, such an explicit-tasking approach allows the user to effectively exploit the full potential of the machine.

However, for data parallel algorithms, as one typically finds in scientific programming, such environments have proven quite awkward to use. The basic issue is that programmers tend to think in terms of synchronous manipulation of distributed data structures, such as grids, matrices, and so forth, while the languages available provide no corresponding language constructs. The hardware support for most current architectures is such that locality of data is critical for good performance. Thus, the programmer must decompose each data structure into a collection of pieces, with each piece "owned" by a single processor. All interactions between different parts of the data structure must then be explicitly specified using the low-level data-sharing constructs such as message-passing statements supported by the language.

Decomposing all data structures in this way, and specifying communication explicitly, leads to programs that can be extraordinarily complicated. Experience has shown that message-passing versions of algorithms can be five to ten times longer than the sequential version. This code expansion hides the original algorithm among the details of low-level communications. Programs written in low-level languages also tend to be highly inflexible, since the partitioning of the data structures across the processors must be incorporated in all parts of the program. Each operation on a distributed data structure turns into a sequence of "send" and "receive" operations intricately embedded in the code. This "hard-wires" all algorithm choices, inhibiting exploration of alternatives, as well as making the parallel program difficult to design and debug.

5.1.2 Direct Compilation of Conventional Languages

The second approach to programming multiprocessors—direct compilation of conventional languages for parallel execution—provides a number of important advantages. First, it allows programmers to continue using familiar languages as they move to newer and more complex machines. Second, there is a large body of existing programs which can be transported to parallel architectures without change. Third, the details of the target architecture are invisible to the programmer, so the complex load-balancing and program design issues, which must be faced with the explicit-tasking languages, are not present.

This approach is, in a real sense, a direct outgrowth of successful research in construction of vectorizing compilers, and is currently being actively explored by several research groups [6, 7, 26, 51, 56, 63, 65]. Since the millions of lines of existing sequential programs cannot be easily replaced, nor are they readily modifiable, there is clear importance to this approach, and it will surely continue.

There are, however, a number of difficulties with this approach. The major one is that the semantics of conventional languages strongly reflects the sequential von Neumann architecture, making the task of automatic restructuring very difficult. Extracting parallelism from such programs requires very aggressive data-flow analysis including array subsection and interprocedural analysis. Moreover, existing languages, especially Fortran, encourage programming styles that make it extremely difficult for compilers to extract much parallelism. Freely "equivalenced" arrays and passing of "pointers" to simulate dynamic allocation, severely limit the compiler's ability to extract parallelism.

Also, once the parallelism has been exposed, it has to be mapped onto the target architect The appropriate mapping, including the distribution of data and work across the processors, is critically dependent on the characteristics of the program and also that of the target machine. Because the general mapping problem has been shown to be NP-complete, the heuristic algorithms used tend to generate suboptimal code. Given all these problems, the end result seems to be that direct compilation of sequential languages can extract only modest amounts of loop-level parallelism.

5.1.3 The Alternative: Modest Language Extensions

As argued above, the state of the art in advanced compiler design is not yet up to the task of parallelizing a sequential application for execution on a massively parallel system with a complex memory hierarchy. Consequently, the programmer must participate in this process. While there is a wide variety of new parallel programming languages that help solve this problem, we will focus attention on three approaches based on modest extensions and annotation systems for Fortran and C++. The goal of each system is to provide high performance and portability across the three prevailing classes of computer architectures, which are distinguished by the memory model they present to the programmer.

True Shared Memory The address space is global to the machine and access to memory is uniform. Examples of this class include the CRAY C90 and the SGI Power Challenge Series.

Shared Memory with Nonuniform Memory Access (NUMA) The address space is global to the machine and access to memory is nonuniform, that is, access time depends on the address and the processor doing the data access. Examples of this class include the BBN TC2000, the CRAY T3D, and the Convex MPP.

Distributed Memory Architecture The address space is local to each processor and access to remote data is done usually via message passing. Examples here include the Intel Paragon, NCUBE, Parsytec, Meiko, and Thinking Machines CM-5.

Because the first two categories provide a global address space for referencing data, they are the closest to the model most familiar to users. Consequently, the most direct way to make all three share this property is to build an operating system layer for the distributed memory machines that provides a "shared virtual memory" model on top of the native message-passing system. Given such a system, any Fortran or C program can execute without modification on the machine. The problem is then reduced to providing a way for the compiler to partition parallel loops and schedule access to shared objects. Fortran-S, designed at IRISA, is one such system. In the paragraphs that follow, we shall describe many of the important ideas that go into the construction of a shared virtual memory operating system and the Fortran-S compiler.

Fortran-S uses program annotations to partition control and the operating system automatically partitions the data. An alternative strategy is to ask the user to specify the way the data should be partitioned and have the compiler decide how to partition the control. High Performance Fortran (HPF) follows this approach. While HPF code could be compiled for a shared virtual memory, most systems will use the compiler to generate explicit message passing on distributed memory machines. In the third section of this paper we describe the HPF model and the language annotations and extensions required to implement it.

A third approach, which combines the features of both HPF and shared virtual memory is pC++, based on a language extension called concurrent aggregates, which allows the programmer to define a set of distributed objects that may be referenced from any processor in this system. As with HPF, the user provides information to the system about how the data objects should be partitioned among the system memory modules. However, communication between objects uses a mechanism based on the SVM paging model, but instead of migrating pages of data, copies of data objects are migrated. In the last section of this paper we describe pC++ and its execution model.

In this paper we have not described other promising approaches. Among these are functional programming languages such as SISAL [43] and ID, and task parallel systems such as CC++ [31], Linda [5], Fortran-M, or that proposed in [9].

5.2

FORTRAN-S AND SHARED VIRTUAL MEMORY

Programming with shared memory or NUMA is usually simpler than programming distributed memory architectures because they offer a global view of the memory where distributed memory architectures let the user deal with data exchanges between processors by means of messages passing. Shared memory architectures are attractive from the programming point of view but they cannot afford scalability. As the number of processors increases, the cost of the switch used to connect memory to processors increases very fast, and may even not be built at the required speed. Fully distributed memory architectures, on the other end, are scalable but do not offer to the programmer a single address space, making programming more complex.

For programming distributed memory architectures, an approach such as HPF proposes a global address space to the programmer and fills the gap between the programmer model and the machine by using sophisticated compiler techniques and getting help from the programmer in charge of specifying (at a high level) the data distribution on the processors.

Another alternative consists in providing the functionalities of a shared memory (it becomes virtual in this case), implemented either using hardware support or using operating system support. This approach makes distributed memory architectures look like NUMA architectures, which makes programming simpler and the compiler much easier to design.

5.2.1 Shared Virtual Memory

A Shared Virtual Memory (SVM) provides to the user an abstraction from an underlying memory architecture of a distributed-memory parallel computer (DMPC). This memory abstraction is also named VSM (Virtual Shared Memory), DSM (Distributed Shared Memory) [48], and so on. We will use SVM to name this memory abstraction. An SVM [39] is somewhat similar to the one that is currently used on classic mainframe computers. However, it differs in the fact that this virtual memory is shared by several processors. It provides a virtual address space that is shared by a number of processes running on different processors of a distributed-memory parallel computer. The virtual address space is made up of pages,[1] which are spread among local processor memories according to a mapping function. Compared to a global address space available on shared-memory parallel computers (SMPCs), SVM relies on page caching and heavily on spatial locality. A global address space, like the one available on the BBN, usually allows access to a single word through the use of a fast interconnection network. In most cases DMPCs are loosely coupled architectures that have a high-latency network. Accessing the data at a page level absorbs this high latency when spatial locality is exposed. Since the granularity of the data accesses is a page, several problems arise. For example, how does one keep pages coherent that are stored in several caches? How do we locate an up-to-date copy of a given page within the architecture? What happens when there is not enough room in a cache?

The first problem is related to *cache coherence*. Since processors may have to read from or to write to the same page, several processors have a copy of a page in their cache . If one processor modifies its copy, other processors run the risk of reading an old copy. A cache coherence protocol is needed to ensure that the shared address space is kept coherent [13]. A memory is considered to be *strongly coherent* if the value returned by a read from a location of the shared address space is the value of the latest store to that location [13]. In most cases, implementation of strong coherence in an SVM for DMPCs is based on an *invalidation* mechanism. It assumes that there is only one copy of a page with write access mode at a given time or, if there are multiple copies of a page, each of them is in read-only access mode. The processor that has written most recently into the page is called the *owner* of the page. When a processor needs to write to a page that is not present in its cache or is present in read-only mode, it sends a message to the owner of the page in order to move it to the requesting processor. It then invalidates all the copies in the system by sending a message to the relevant processors. This *invalidation* strategy seems to be the best approach for DMPCs. The faulting-management mechanism of an MMU is sufficient to implement this approach efficiently.

The second problem is called *page ownership*. When a processor needs to access a page (either in write or read access mode) not located in its cache, it must ask the owner

---

[1] The granularity afforded by hardware virtual memory.

to send it a copy of the page. This problem is related to the cache coherence protocol described previously. With the invalidation protocol, there is always one owner for a page and the ownership changes according to the page requests coming from other processors. Therefore, the problem is how to locate the current owner of a given page considering that ownership of a page changes. A solution is to update a database that keeps track of the movement of pages in the system. This database can be either *centralized* or *distributed* [39]. In the centralized approach, a processor (called the manager) is in charge of updating the database for every page. When a processor needs a page, it sends a request to the manager, which forwards the request to the owner of the page. Consequently, the manager is aware of all the movement of pages in the system. However, it may be a bottleneck since the manager processor receives requests from all other processors. The user's process running on the manager will be interrupted frequently and this approach will also create potential contention in the network. Distributing the database over several processors is a means to avoid these drawbacks.

The last problem is called *page swapping*. The problem arises when a processor is the owner of all the pages located in its cache and there is no more space in the cache. If it requests a new page, it has to find space in its cache. It cannot throw away a page from its cache since it owns all the pages. Therefore, pages have to be moved on to external high-speed storage devices, like disks. Some implementations, such as KOAN [34], use the other local memory for page swapping. However, the size of the virtual address space is bounded by the sum of all local memory.

The implementation of SVM mechanisms is done mostly by software: page requests are processed by the operating system running on each node. This implementation involves a substantial overhead since user's processes have to be stopped by the operating system to resolve page requests. This task could be done by using dedicated VLSI hardware, which is done with the KSR [2] machine and SCI bus-based parallel architectures [1] such as the new Convex MPP.

5.2.2 Why Shared Virtual Memory May Not Work

Shared Virtual Memory has many intrinsic problems. In the following paragraphs, we discuss some of them.

Initial Page Distribution   The initial page distribution may lead to cold-start misses, however this has a marginal effect on performance. After the beginning of the application, pages migrate to processors according to data accesses.

Page Thrashing   Page thrashing can lead to capacity misses. For instance consider the following loop:

```
doall i = 1,n
  do j = 1,n
    A(j,i) = f(..., B(i,j),...)
  enddo
enddo
```

Due to the Fortran column-wise data layout, each access to matrix B will create a page fault if n is large enough. In that case interchanging the loop would not help, but loop blocking would.

False Sharing   False sharing occurs when more than one processor at a time writes to the same page. The strong coherence mechanism ensures that each processor writing into a page sees the last modification of it. For example, consider the following loop:

```
doall i = 1,n
  A(i) = f(.....)
enddo
```

Assuming that A is allocated in a shared address space and is only stored into one page, when increasing the number of processors, the page will exhibit a **ping-pong phenomenon**. That is, the page will move back and forth between processors, each write costing one page fault at worst (each word written will cost a data transfer of the size of the page). The execution of the loop becomes sequential because a page manager will serve only one page request at a time. This phenomenon may severely degrade performance. However, by increasing the size of the vector this phenomenon may become negligible.

Barrier   When programming using message passing, synchronization between processes comes for free; data exchanges synchronize processes. When using shared variables, synchronization must be inserted to ensure data dependences between processes. However synchronization does not have to be implemented using shared variables. Most systems support some sort of barrier operation which can be used as the primary synchronization mechanism. If the barrier is too slow, serious performance problems may result.

Broadcast   A drawback of shared virtual memory on DMPCs is its inability to run efficiently parallel algorithms that contain a producer/consumers scheme. In these cases, a page is modified by a processor and then it is accessed by the other processors. Since all page requests are sequentially processed by a page manager, the accesses to the data are done sequentially. This obviously constitutes a serious bottleneck when the number of processors grows.

5.2.3   Why Shared Virtual Memory May Work

Shared virtual memory may work surprisingly well (see Section 5.3.3) for the following reasons.

Vectorized Page Access to Data (Block Transfer)   Transferring a page makes efficient use of the network, masking most network latencies. There is clearly a trade-off when choosing the page size. A large page size makes efficient use of the network, but increases the amount of unnecessary data transferred, and false sharing becomes a greater problem. A small page size transfers a greater percent of useful data and decreases false sharing, but it makes inefficient usage of the network. To deal with a small transfer size on the KSR,

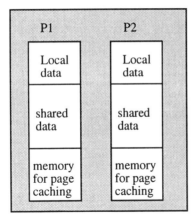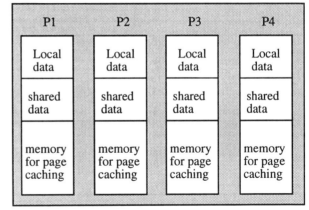

FIGURE 5.1   Allocation of data in memory assuming two processors and assuming four processors; in the case of four processors more memory can be devoted to page caching.

where subpages of 128 bytes are the basic transfer unit, prefetch and poststore facilities are used to hide large access latencies.

Page Caching Allows the Exploitation of Data Locality   Page caching is the only way to compensate for the cost of moving a page between processors. This decreases the size of the effective SVM. Indeed the page-caching memory is the remainder of the memory not used by the local data and the shared data. At some point, if data are too big, the remaining memory may be too small to keep pages necessary for an algorithm to behave efficiently (see Figure 5.1). The main advantage of SVM over other mechanisms is that, even when locality properties of the program cannot be discovered at compile time, the SVM can still exploit it. In this respect shared virtual memory addresses the same problem as the Parti inspector/executor scheme [66].

All Variables Do Not Have to Be Shared   Only variables that are subject to parallel computation should be shared. Sharing all variables leads to very inefficient code.

Not All Parallel Computations Depend on the SVM   For example, exploiting reduction parallelism is usually not done using shared virtual memory. Instead it can be implemented by the compiler by using message passing.

The Compiler Can Help a Lot   Compiler technique can help by optimizing programs so that they make better use of the virtual shared memory and also by decreasing the number of synchronizations in the program (that is, decreasing the number of barriers).

5.2.4   Parallel Loop Scheduling and Shared Virtual Memory

Parallel loops scheduling is a critical issue in a programming environment that relies on shared virtual memory. Data movements are in charge of the system/hardware where loop scheduling is in charge of the compiler/user. Good scheduling has to ensure data locality and load balancing. Bad loop scheduling may result in many unnecessary page migrations, false sharing, or an unbalanced load. It should be noted that techniques such as self-guided scheduling are not very well suited to shared virtual memory, because as the execution of a parallel loop proceeds, the size of blocks of iterations that are assigned to processors decreases. Consequently, false sharing increases. However, when associated with a cache coherence protocol that allows concurrent access to the same page, this technique may become adequate if it can be implemented efficiently on massively parallel distributed-memory architecture.

There are two main scheduling techniques that are well-suited to shared virtual memory because they can be used to reduce data movements. The first technique addresses the problem of false sharing, especially when strong coherence protocols are used, and the second technique is concerned with data reuse across loops. In addition, they can be used together to provide good locality and to decrease the false-sharing.

Page Aligned Scheduling   Page aligned scheduling can be used to reduce false sharing. The principle consists of distributing iteration such that chunks of iterations allocated on processors are aligned with page boundaries. For example, if we use a simple block scheduling strategy of a simple loop:

```
do i = 1, N
   A[i] = A[i] + ...
enddo
```

we get:

```
bf = ceiling(N/P)
doall pid = 1,N,bf
   do i = pid,min(pid+bf-1,N)
     A[i] = A[i] + ...
   enddo
enddo
```

If N/P is not a multiple of the page size there will be false-sharing for each page shared by two processors. A simple solution in that case is to consider a blocking factor bf that takes into account the page size (assuming $A[1]$ is aligned on a page boundary):

```
bf = ceiling(ceiling(N/pagesize)/P) * pagesize
doall pid = 1,N,bf
   do i = pid,min(pid+bf-1,N)
     A[i] = A[i] + ...
   enddo
enddo
```

However this technique does not always balance the workload. In general, this technique works well when the amount of data is large. A more complete description of the method is given in [25].

Affinity Scheduling   The affinity scheduling tries to minimize data movement by allocating iterations to processors according to data location [42]. An affinity scheduling technique is provided on the KSR1 machine.

It should be noted that dynamic scheduling to improve load balancing can be implemented with SVM, but on distributed memory architectures the implementation of such a technique is usually very costly at runtime.

5.2.5   Compiler Optimizations for SVM

Compiler optimization for shared virtual memory consists of increasing data locality, and thus minimizing data transfers. Optimization consists of removing shared variables as much as possible, changing the data layout, and applying loop transformations to improve locality without killing the load balance.

Removing Shared Variables   In some cases, it is possible to localize shared variables. The idea behind this optimization relies on the compiler's ability to detect accesses to data structures that are disjoint between processors. Compiler techniques used in this case are very close to the ones used for compiling Fortran D and HPF programs [30, 62].

Array Padding and Data Layout   The array padding operation consists of extending array dimensions such that dimensions of the array are aligned with page boundaries. This reduces false sharing because different vectors of the array do not share any pages. The main disadvantages of this technique are that it wastes memory (and so decreases the size of the memory that can be allocated to the cache) and also that this may increase the amount of communication (unused data are loaded when accessing useful data). More generally, data layout optimization tries to store data so that it minimizes false sharing [18, 61].

Optimizing Data Locality   Optimizing data locality relies on changing the access order to data structure so that it increases the spatial locality of a loop or it exploits better temporal locality. Loop transformations like loop interchanging, blocking, and unimodular transformation may be used. When temporal locality exists, it may be possible to exploit data locality using localization of a portion of an array section that is subject to reuse. These techniques are common to global address space optimization and cache locality optimization. For example, considering the following loop:

```
doall i = 1,n
  do j = 1,n
    do k = 1,n
      A(k,i) = f(...,A(k,i),...)
    enddo
  enddo
enddo
```

It can be transformed into

```
doall i = 1,n
  do t = 1,n
    temp(t) = A(t,i)
  enddo
  do j = 1,n
   do k = 1,n
     temp(k) = f(...,temp(k),...)
   enddo
  enddo
  do t = 1,n
    A(t,i) = temp(t)
  enddo
enddo
```

where *temp* is allocated locally on processors. This optimization may reduce the number of page faults and the false sharing. It should be noted that the array *temp* is the reference window as defined in [21, 31]. The cost of the copy is amortized by exploiting the temporal locality. However if there was no page thrashing and no false sharing on array *A* in the original loop, there is no gain in using this transformation. When applying this kind of optimization, the size of temporaries must be limited. These techniques [3, 4, 16, 23, 41, 44, 55, 63, 64] are well known but usually targeted for hardware cache or local memory. Most of these techniques should be revisited to take into account the characteristics of shared virtual memory and in particular the false-sharing phenomenon.

Barrier Removal   When programming with a shared-memory model (especially when the execution model is SPMD) synchronization between processes relies on barriers. One optimization the compiler can perform is to decrease the number of synchronizations in the program. More generally, part of the optimization process consists in removing, as much as possible, calls to the runtime system.

5.2.6   Runtime Optimization for SVM

In some cases, support for optimizations may come from system capabilities.

Weak Coherence   Several weak cache coherence protocols have been studied in the past. Each of them has some properties that can be exploited in a specific context [50, 57]. A modified version of the strong-coherence protocol can be considered as a weak cache coherence protocol. If data accesses are made in different memory locations, it allows processors to modify their own copy of a page, without invalidating copies in other processors. When restoring the strong-coherence protocol, all the copies of a page that have been modified are merged into a single page that reflects all the changes. From the programmer's point of view, the memory is always strongly coherent at a word level but is weakly coherent at a page level. However such a weak-coherence scheme does not come for free; its cost depends (usually linearly) on the maximum number of page copies to be merged at the end of the page weak-coherence phase to be performed. Weak-coherence protocol can be used for parallel loops because there is no data dependence between iterations of the loops and so no several writes to the same word of a page are performed by several different iterations.

Page Broadcast   Producer/consumers scheme can be efficiently managed by using the broadcasting facility of the underlying topology of DMPCs (hypercube, 2D-mesh, and so on). All pages that have been modified by the processor in charge of running the producer phase are broadcast to all other processors that will run the consumer phase in parallel. Since the producer has to keep track of all pages that have been modified, two new operating system calls have to be added in the user's code in order to specify both the beginning and the ending of the producer phase.

Page Locking   Page locking allows a processor to lock a page into its cache until it decides to release it. This basic mechanism can be used to implement atomic update in a memory location. The user is responsible for adding two system calls that specify the beginning and the ending of the code section where each remote data access requires a page to be locked into the cache. Page locking is very efficient and minimizes the number of critical sections within a parallel code. On loosely coupled parallel architectures, such as DMPCs, using critical sections are time expensive. To illustrate this, let us take a small example such as a matrix assembly found in finite element applications. A loop is used to scan an irregular mesh and values are accumulated into a matrix. Access to this matrix is made by means of an index scheme and there are often runtime data dependences. Consequently the loop can be parallelized if the accumulation is executed within a critical section to avoid multiple processors writing at the same time to the same matrix element. A page locking mechanism can replace many critical sections. Before updating a matrix element, the page that contains the matrix element is locked into the cache and then released after the update. The cost of such synchronization is simply related to the number of processors that access the same page at the same time.

5.2.7   Mixing Messages and Shared Virtual Memory

Mixing of message passing and shared variables can be used to improve performance in library code. When dealing with shared variables and messages, programming is somewhat simplified since the programmer does not have to worry about the data distribution. The programmer only has to think in terms of parallel processes. One of the main advantages of this approach, is that an efficient algorithm may be implemented independently of the program it is called from. For example, consider the in-place matrix transpose. This algorithm behaves very badly with SVM when data transfer is at the level of pages. But by using message passing to do the transpose, it is possible to get speedup on this operation. The algorithm can be written so it is independent of the data distribution of the matrix. In a pure message passing programming environment, it is not possible to provide such a primitive without forcing the programmer to use a predefined data distribution of the matrix on the processor, this data layout that may be completely inadequate in the remainder of the application.

5.3

FORTRAN-S: A PROTOTYPE ENVIRONMENT FOR SVM

Fortran-S is a Fortran programming environment that relies on the shared virtual memory KOAN. The programming model is based on shared variables and parallel loops. Parallel loops and shared variables are declared to the compiler via directives. The project's main goal is to study the compiler and programming environment for shared virtual memory. Fortran-S differs from the KSR-Fortran mainly in the execution model. KSR-Fortran relies on fork-and-join execution (that is, the main thread is spawed in multiple threads when parallel phases of execution occur) where Fortran-S relies on an SPMD execution model (that is, a thread is created on every processor during the loading phase). To illustrate Fortran-S, we provide the following small example:

```
        real v(n, n)
C$ann[Shared(v)]
        do i = 1, n
          tmp = 0.0
          do k = 1, n
            tmp = tmp +v(k, i)*v(k, i)
          enddo
          xnorm = 1.0 / sqrt(tmp)
          do k = 1, n
            v(k, i) = v(k, i)*xnorm
          enddo
C$ann[DoShared("BLOCK")]
          do j = i + 1, n
            tmp = 0.0
            do k = 1, n
              tmp = tmp +v(k, i)*v(k, j)
            enddo
            do k = 1, n
              v(k, j) = v(k, j) − tmp*v(k, i)
            enddo
          enddo
        enddo
```

This is a parallel version of the Modified Gram-Schmidt algorithm. It is made up of two nested loops. The outer loop normalizes each vector stored in the matrix v. When a vector is normalized, the remaining vectors in the matrix are then corrected by executing the inner loop. These corrections can be done in parallel. By adding two Fortran-S directives, the code generator is able to generate an SPMD code that will be executed in every processor. The first directive (C$ann[Shared(v)]) specifies that matrix *v* has to be stored in the shared virtual memory, since it will be updated within a parallel loop. Other variables are replicated in the local memory of each processor. Every processor executes the outer loop as well as all assignments that modify a local variable. However, for each outer loop iteration, only one processor updates the shared variable *v(k,i)*. (In the previous example, every processor will write into replicated variables *tmp* and *xnorm*.) The second directive (C$ann[DoShared("BLOCK")]) indicates that the following loop is a parallel loop. Each processor is in charge of executing a chunk of the iteration space. A detailed description of Fortran-S can be found in [12].

5.3.1 KOAN Runtime

The KOAN SVM is embedded in the operating system of the iPSC/2. It allows the use of fast and low-level communication primitives as well as a memory management unit (MMU). The KOAN SVM implements the fixed distributed manager algorithm as described in [39] with an invalidation protocol for keeping the shared memory coherent at all times. A detailed description of the KOAN SVM can be found in [34]. Let us now summarize some of the functionalities of the KOAN SVM runtime.

KOAN SVM provides the user with several memory management protocols for efficiently handling special memory access patterns. One of these occurs when several processors have to write into different locations of the same page. This pattern involves many messages since the page has to move from processor to processor (as with the *ping-pong effect* or *false sharing*). At a cost of adding some new subroutine calls in the parallel code, KOAN can let processors concurrently modify their own copy of a page. Another drawback of shared virtual memory on DMPCs is its inability to run efficiently parallel algorithms that contain a producer/consumers scheme: a page is modified by a processor and then accessed by the other processors. KOAN SVM can efficiently manage this memory access pattern by using the broadcasting facility of the underlying topology of DMPCs (hypercube, 2D-mesh, and so on). All pages that have been modified by the processor in charge of running the producer phase are broadcast to all other processors that will run the consumer phase in parallel. KOAN SVM provides barrier synchronization as well as subroutines to manage critical sections. These features are implemented by using messages instead of shared variables. KOAN is compatible with the NX/2 operating system, that is, primitives provided by the system can be used simultaneously with KOAN.

We have performed measurements in order to determine the costs of various basic operations for both read and write page faults (the size of a page is 4 Kbytes) of the KOAN shared virtual memory. For each type of page fault (read or write), we have tested the best and worst possible situation on different numbers of processors. For a 32-processor configuration, the time required to resolve a read page fault is in the range of 3.412 ms to 3.955 ms. For a write page fault, timing results are in the range of 3.447 ms to 10.110 ms depending on the number of copies that have to be invalidated. These results can be compared with the communication times of the iPSC/2: the latency is roughly 0.3 ms and sending a 4-Kbyte message (a page) costs between 2.17 ms and 2.27 ms depending on the number of routing.

5.3.2 Fortran-S Code Generator

Fortran-S[2] relies on parallel loops to achieve parallelism. Parallel execution is achieved using the SPMD (single program multiple data) execution model. At the beginning of the program execution, a thread is created on each processor and each processor starts to execute the program. One of the main functions of the Fortran-S compiler is to make the SPMD execution look like a single-threaded execution by appropriate insertion of synchronization and correct updating of shared variables. The programming model uses directives to specify shared variables and parallel loops. A shared variable is accessible in read or write from all the processors. A nonshared variable is duplicated on all the processors. Since every processor executes the sequential code sections, nonshared variables always have the same value. The iteration space of a parallel loop is distributed over the processor. Each processor executes only a subset of the iteration space. Fortran-S provides several directives to generate efficient parallel code [12].

5.3.3 Performance

In this section we present the first results obtained using Fortran-S on an Intel iPSC/2 with 32 nodes. The goal of these experiments was to port sequential Fortran 77 programs to Fortran-S and to measure the performance obtained. We did not intend, in those early performance measurements, to modify the applications extensively. Rather, we intended to measure performance of Fortran-S in a straightforward translation from Fortran 77. Very few modifications have been done to the original program. The primary modification was to expose parallel loops in the programs. However no modification of the data structure used in the program was made. Also there were no major modifications to the algorithms, so the scalability of an application is not limited by Fortran-S but by the algorithm used in the application. The problem of false sharing that appears in many applications was solved using a weak-coherence protocol.

The first code used is taken from a Jacobi iteration. Table 5.1 gives the speedups and efficiencies for different problem sizes when using either a strong or a weak cache coherence protocol. For a matrix size set to 100×100, we get a "speed-down" when the number of processors is greater than 16. False sharing could be avoided by using weak-coherence protocol. For the same problem size, this cache coherence protocol improves the speedups a little, but the speedup remains flat. For a larger problem size (200×200) we did not observe such phenomena. However when the number of processors is set to 32, the efficiency is bad (20.71 percent). The weak cache coherence protocol increases the efficiency to 32.49 percent. This behavior is observed only for small matrices. For large matrices the efficiency is close to the maximum.

The second parallel algorithm we studied is the matrix multiply. Table 5.2 gives timing results for small matrices (100×100 and 200×200). For larger matrix size, speedups are near the maximum. This can be seen in this table; for a 32-node configuration, speedups increase from 3.58 to 24.57 when the number of matrix elements quadruples. However, for small matrices, the results can be improved by using the weak cache coherence protocol.

---

[2]The prototype compiler has been implemented using the Sigma System [22].

TABLE 5.1   Performance results for the Jacobi loops.

	With strong coherence					
	100×100			200×200		
# proc.	Times (ms)	Speedup	Eff.	Times (ms)	Speedup	Eff.
1	3112	—	—	12933	—	—
2	1927	1.61	80.75	7323	1.77	88.30
4	1280	2.43	60.78	3975	3.25	81.34
8	1322	2.35	29.43	2284	5.66	70.78
16	3882	0.80	5.01	1446	8.94	55.90
32	5339	0.58	1.82	1928	6.71	20.96
	With weak coherence					
1	3112	—	—	12933	—	—
2	1972	1.58	78.90	7323	1.77	88.30
4	1311	2.37	59.34	4016	3.22	80.51
8	923	3.37	42.15	2305	5.61	70.14
16	921	3.38	21.12	1567	8.25	51.58
32	1151	2.70	8.45	1244	10.40	32.49

TABLE 5.2   Performance results for the matrix multiply.

	With strong coherence					
	100×100			200×200		
# proc.	Times (ms)	Speedup	Eff.	Times (ms)	Speedup	Eff.
1	15694	—	—	127657	—	—
2	7920	1.98	99.08	64037	1.99	99.67
4	4056	3.87	96.73	32292	3.95	98.83
8	2206	7.11	88.93	16522	7.73	96.58
16	3393	4.63	28.91	8982	14.21	88.83
32	4379	3.58	11.20	5196	24.57	76.78
	With weak coherence					
1	15694	—	—	127657	—	—
2	7923	1.98	99.04	64036	1.99	99.68
4	4048	3.88	96.92	32276	3.96	98.88
8	2202	7.13	89.09	16521	7.73	96.59
16	1287	12.19	76.21	8972	14.23	88.93
32	884	17.75	55.48	5206	24.52	76.63

TABLE 5.3   Performance results for the MGS algorithm (200 × 200).

	Strong coherence			Weak coherence			Weak + Broadcast		
# proc.	Times (s)	Speedup	Eff.	Times (s)	Speedup	Eff.	Times (s)	Speedup	Eff.
				200 × 200					
1	125.99	—	—	125.99	—	—	125.99	—	—
2	79.34	1.59	79.40	66.34	1.90	66.34	66.69	1.89	94.46
4	64.20	1.96	49.06	37.07	3.40	84.97	37.09	3.40	84.92
8	61.59	2.05	25.57	23.99	5.25	65.65	23.04	5.47	68.35
16	65.49	1.92	12.02	20.61	6.11	38.21	16.85	7.48	46.73
32	78.79	1.60	5.00	23.62	5.33	16.67	14.88	8.47	26.46
				500 × 500					
1	1986.81	—	—	1986.81	—	–	1986.81	—	—
2	1029.11	1.93	96.53	1007.51	1.97	98.60	1013.20	1.96	98.05
4	562.52	3.53	88.30	517.57	3.84	95.97	522.38	3.80	95.08
8	339.23	5.86	73.21	276.17	7.19	89.93	278.72	7.13	89.10
16	233.10	8.52	53.27	163.98	12.12	75.73	158.97	12.50	78.11
32	205.75	9.66	30.18	124.71	15.93	49.79	101.62	19.55	61.10

Indeed, the poor performance is always due to the same effect—false sharing. The same table provides timing results when the parallel loop is executing with weak coherence. For the small matrix, the gain in performances is impressive. When the number of processors is set to 32, speedup augments from 3.58 to 17.75.

The last experiment involved the Modified Gram-Schmidt algorithm described above. This algorithm consists of two nested loops. We added some directives in order to improve the efficiency of the parallel MGS algorithm. The vector, which is modified in the sequential section, is broadcast to every processor, since it will be accessed within the parallel loop. A weak cache coherence protocol is also associated with the inner loop to avoid false sharing. A detailed study of this algorithm can be found in [52, 53]. Table 5.3 summarizes the results we obtained with different strategies.

Several other parallel algorithms and applications have been ported to KOAN. Their performance results are presented in [11, 54].

5.4

HIGH PERFORMANCE FORTRAN

Recently an international group of researchers from academia, industry, and government labs formed the High Performance Fortran Forum aimed at providing an intermediate approach in which the user and the compiler share responsibility for exploiting parallelism. The main goal of the group has been to design a high-level set of standard extensions to Fortran, called High Performance Fortran (HPF), intended to exploit a wide variety of parallel architectures [28, 40].

The HPF extensions allow the user to carefully control the distribution of data across the memories of the target machine. However, the computation code is written using a global name space with no explicit message-passing statements. It is then the compiler's responsibility to analyze the distribution annotations and generate parallel code, inserting communication statements where required by the computation. Thus, using this approach, the programmer can focus on high-level algorithmic and performance-critical issues such as load balance while allowing the compiler system to deal with the complex low-level machine specific details.

Earlier Efforts   The HPF effort is based on research done by several groups, some of which are described below. The language IVTRAN [47], for the SIMD machine ILLIAC IV, was one of the first languages to allow users to control the data layout. The user could indicate the array dimensions to be spread across the processors and those that were to be local in a processor. Combinations resulting in physically skewed data were also allowed.

In the context of MIMD machines, Kali (and its predecessor BLAZE) [45, 46] was the first language to introduce user-specified distribution directives. The language allows the dimensions of an array to be mapped onto an explicitly declared processor array using simple regular distributions such as *block, cyclic,* and *block-cyclic*, and more complex distributions such as *irregular*, in which the address of each element is explicitly specified. Simple forms of user-defined distribution are also permitted. Kali also introduced the idea of dynamic distributions, which allow the user to change the distribution of an array at runtime. The parallel computation is specified using *forall* loops within a global name space. The language also introduced the concept of an *on clause* which allows the users to control the distribution of loop iterations across the processors.

The Fortran D project [19] follows a slightly different approach to specifying distributions. The distribution of data is specified by first aligning data arrays to virtual arrays knows as decompositions. The decompositions are then distributed across an implicit set of processors using relative weights for the different dimensions. The language allows an extensive set of alignments along with simple regular and irregular distributions. All mapping statements are considered executable statements, thus blurring the distinction between static and dynamic distributions.

Vienna Fortran [14, 68] is the first language to provide a complete specification of distribution constructs in the context of Fortran. Based largely on the Kali model, Vienna Fortran allows arrays to be aligned to other arrays, which are then distributed across an explicit processor array. In addition to the simple regular and irregular distributions, Vienna Fortran defines a generalized block distribution, which allows unequal-sized contiguous segments of the data to be mapped the processors. Users can define their own distribution and alignment functions, which can then be used to provide a precise mapping of data to the underlying processors. The language maintains a clear distinction between distributions that remain static during the execution of a procedure and those that can change dynamically, allowing compilers to optimize code for the two different situations. It defines multiple methods of passing distributed data across procedure boundaries including inheriting the distribution of the actual arguments. Distribution inquiry functions facilitate the writing of library functions that are optimal for multiple incoming distributions.

High Performance Fortran effort has been based on the above and other related projects [8, 27, 38, 48, 58, 59, 60]. In the next few subsections we provide a short introduction to HPF, concentrating on the features that are critical to parallel performance.

5.4.1 HPF Overview

High Performance Fortran[3] is a set of extensions for Fortran 90, designed to allow specification of data parallel algorithms. The programmer annotates the program with distribution directives to specify the desired layout of data. The underlying programming model provides a global name space and a single thread of control. Explicitly parallel constructs allow the expression of fairly controlled forms of parallelism, in particular data parallelism. Thus, the code is specified in high-level portable manner with no explicit tasking or communication statements. The goal is to allow architecture-specific compilers to generate efficient code for a wide variety of architectures including SIMD, MIMD shared, and distributed memory machines.

Fortran 90 was used as a base for HPF extensions for two reasons. First, a large percentage of scientific codes are still written in Fortran (Fortran 77, that is), providing programmers using HPF with a familiar base. Second, the array operations as defined for Fortran 90 make it eminently suitable for data parallel algorithms.

Most of the HPF extensions are in the form of directives or structured comments that assert facts about the program or suggest implementation strategies such as data layout. Since these are directives, they do not change the semantics of the program, but may have a profound effect on the efficiency of the generated code. The syntax used for these directives is such that if HPF extensions are at some later date accepted as part of the language, only the prefix, **!HPF$,** needs to be removed to retain a correct HPF program. HPF also introduces some new language syntax in the form of data parallel execution statements and a few new intrinsics.

Features of High Performance Fortran In this subsection we provide a brief overview of the new features defined by HPF. In the next few subsections we will provide a more detailed view of some of these features.

- *Data mapping directives:* HPF provides an extensive set of directives to specify the distribution and alignment of arrays.
- *Data parallel execution features:* The **FORALL** statement and construct and the **INDEP-ENDENT** directive can be used to specify data parallel code. The concept of *pure* procedures callable from parallel constructs has also been defined.
- *New intrinsic and library functions:* HPF provides a set of new intrinsic functions including system functions to inquire about the underlying hardware, mapping inquiry functions to inquire about the distribution of the data structures, and a few computational intrinsic functions. A set of new library routines has also been defined to provide a standard interface for highly useful parallel operations such as reduction functions, combining scatter functions, prefix and suffix functions, and sorting functions.
- *Extrinsic procedures:* HPF is well suited for data parallel programming. However, in order to accommodate other programming paradigms, HPF provides *extrinsic* procedures.

---

[3]This chapter is partially based on the High Performance Fortran Language Specifications draft document, [28] which has been jointly written by several of the participants of the High Performance Fortran Forum. Also, the specifications (as described here) are still under review and may change when the final document is released.

These define an explicit interface and allow codes expressed using a different paradigm, such as an explicit message-passing routine, to be called from an HPF program.

- *Sequence and storage association:* The Fortran concepts of sequence and storage association[4] assume an underlying linearly addressable memory. Such assumptions create a problem in architectures that have a fragmented address space and are not compatible with the data distribution features of HPF. Thus, HPF places restrictions on the use of storage and sequence association for distributed arrays. For example, arrays that have been distributed can not be passed as actual arguments associated with dummy arguments that have a different rank or shape. Similarly, arrays that have been storage associated with other arrays can be distributed only in special situations. The reader is referred to the HPF Language specification document [28] for full details of these restrictions and other HPF features.

5.4.2   Data Mapping Directives

A major part of the HPF extensions are aimed at specifying the alignment and distribution of the data elements. The underlying intuition for such mapping of data is as follows. If the computations on different elements of a data structure are independent, then distributing the data structure will allow the computation to be executed in parallel. Similarly, if elements of two data structures are used in the same computation, then they should be aligned so that they reside in the same processor memory. Obviously, the two factors may be in conflict across computations, giving rise to situations where data needed in a computation resides on some other processor. This data dependence is then satisfied by communicating the data from one processor to another. Thus, the main goal of mapping data onto processor memories is to increase parallelism while minimizing communication such that the workload across the processors is balanced.

HPF uses a two-level mapping of data objects to abstract processors as shown in Figure 5.2. First, data objects are aligned to other objects and then groups of objects are distributed on a rectilinear arrangement of abstract processors.

Each array is created with some mapping of its elements to abstract processors either on entry to a program unit or at the time of allocation for allocatable arrays. This mapping may be specified by the user through the **ALIGN** and **DISTRIBUTE** directives or, in the case where complete specifications are not provided, the mapping may be chosen by the compiler.

Processors Directive   The **PROCESSORS** directive can be used to declare one or more rectilinear arrangements of processors in the specification part of a program unit. If two processor arrangements have the same shape, then corresponding elements of the two arrangements are mapped onto the same physical processor, thus ensuring that objects mapped to these abstract processors will reside on the same physical processor.

The intrinsics **NUMBER_OF_PROCESSORS** and **PROCESSOR_SHAPE** can be used to determine the actual number of physical processors being used to execute the program.

---

[4]Informally, sequence association refers to the Fortran assumption that the elements of an array are in particular order (column-major) and hence allows redimensioning of arrays across procedure boundaries. Storage association allows COMMON and EQUIVALENCE statements to constrain and align data items relative to each other.

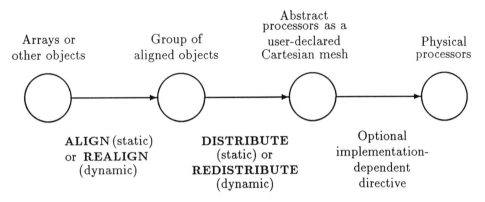

Arrays or other objects   Group of aligned objects   Abstract processors as a user-declared Cartesian mesh   Physical processors

ALIGN (static) or **REALIGN** (dynamic)   **DISTRIBUTE** (static) or **REDISTRIBUTE** (dynamic)   Optional implementation-dependent directive

FIGURE 5.2   **HPF data distribution model.**

This information can then be used in declaring the abstract processor arrangement.

```
!HPF$ PROCESSORS  P(N)
!HPF$ PROCESSORS  Q(NUMBER_OF_PROCESSORS())
!HPF$ PROCESSORS  R(8, NUMBER_OF_PROCESSORS()/8)
!HPF$ PROCESSORS  SCALARPROC
```

Here, P is a processor arrangement of size N. The size of Q (and the shape of R) is dependent upon the number of physical processors executing the program, while *SCALARPROC* is conceptually treated as a scalar processor.

A compiler must accept any processor declaration that is either scalar or whose total number of elements match the number of physical processors. The mapping of the abstract processors to physical processors is compiler-dependent. It is expected that implementors may provide architecture-specific directives to allow users to control this mapping.

Distribution Directives   The **DISTRIBUTE** directive can be used to specify the distribution of the dimensions of an array to dimensions of an abstract processor arrangement. The different types of distribution allowed by HPF are: *BLOCK(expr), CYCLIC(expr)* and ***.

```
      PARAMETER (N = NUMBER_OF_PROCESSORS())

!HPF$ PROCESSORS  Q(NUMBER_OF_PROCESSORS())
!HPF$ PROCESSORS  R(8, NUMBER_OF_PROCESSORS()/8)

      REAL A(100), B(200), C(100, 200), D(100, 200)

!HPF$ DISTRIBUTE  A(BLOCK) ONTO Q
!HPF$ DISTRIBUTE  B(CYCLIC(5))
!HPF$ DISTRIBUTE  C(BLOCK, CYCLIC) ONTO R
!HPF$ DISTRIBUTE  D(BLOCK(10), *) ONTO Q
```

In the above examples, A is divided into N contiguous blocks of elements, which are then mapped onto successive processors of the arrangement Q. The elements of array B are first divided into blocks of 5, which are then mapped in a wrapped manner across the processors of the arrangement Q. The two dimensions of array C are individually mapped to the two dimensions of the processor arrangement R. The rows of C are blocked while the columns are cyclically mapped. The one-dimensional array D is distributed across the one-dimensional processor arrangement Q such that the second axis is not distributed. That is, each row of the array is mapped as a single object. To determine the distribution of the dimension, the rows are first blocked into groups of 10 and these groups are then mapped to successive processors of Q. In this case, N must be at least 10 to accommodate the rows of D. Note, that in the case of array B, the compiler chooses the abstract processor arrangement for the distribution.

The **REDISTRIBUTE** directive is syntactically similar to the **DISTRIBUTE** directive but may appear only in the execution part of a program unit. It is used for dynamically changing the distribution of an array and may only be used for arrays that have been declared as **DYNAMIC**. The only difference between **DISTRIBUTE** and **REDISTRIBUTE** directives is that the former can use only specification expressions while the latter can use any expression including values computed at runtime.

> **REAL** $A(100)$

> !HPF$ **DISTRIBUTE** (**BLOCK**), **DYNAMIC** :: A
> $\ldots$
> $k = \ldots$
> $\ldots$
> !HPF$ **REDISTRIBUTE** $A($ **CYCLIC** $(k))$

Here, A starts with a block distribution and is dynamically remapped to a cyclic distribution whose block size is computed at runtime.

When an array is redistributed, arrays that are *ultimately aligned* to it (see next subsection) are also remapped to maintain the alignment relationship.

Alignment Directives   The **ALIGN** directive is used to indirectly specify the mapping of an array (the alignee) by specifying its relative position with respect to another object (the align-target), which is ultimately distributed. HPF provides a variety of alignments including identity alignment, offsets, axis collapse, axis transposition, and replication using dummy arguments, which range over the entire index range of the alignee. Only linear expressions are allowed in the specification of the align-target, with the restriction that an align dummy can appear in only one expression in an **ALIGN** directive. The alignment function must be such that alignee is not allowed to "wrap around" or "extend past the edges" of the align-target.

> !HPF$ **ALIGN** $A(:,:)$ **WITH** $B(:,:)$ *! identity alignment*
> !HPF$ **ALIGN** $C(I)$ **WITH** $D(I\text{-}5)$ *! offset*
> !HPF$ **ALIGN** $E(I, *)$ **WITH** $F(I)$ *! collapse*

```
!HPF$ ALIGN G(I)    WITH H(I, *)   ! replication
!HPF$ ALIGN R(I, J) WITH S(J, I)   ! transposition
```

If A is aligned to B, which is in turn aligned with C, then A is considered to be *immediately aligned* to B but *ultimately aligned* to C. Note that intermediate alignments are useful only to provide the "ultimate" alignment since only the root of the alignment tree can be distributed.

The **REALIGN** directive is syntactically similar to the **ALIGN** directive, but may appear only in the execution part of a program unit. It is used for dynamically changing the alignment of an array and may only be used for arrays that have been declared as **DYNAMIC**. As in the case of **REDISTRIBUTE**, the **REALIGN** directive can use computed values in its expression. Note that only an object that is not the root of an alignment tree can be explicitly realigned and that such a realignment does not affect the mapping of any other array.

Template Directive   In certain codes, we may want to align arrays to an index space that is larger than any of the data arrays declared in the program. HPF introduces the concept of *template* as an abstract index space. Declaration of templates uses the keyword **TEMPLATE** and a syntax similar to that of regular data arrays. The distinction is that templates do not take any storage.

Consider the situation where two arrays of size $N \times (N + 1)$ and $(N + 1) \times N$ have to be aligned such that bottom right corner elements are mapped to the same processor. This can be done as follows:

```
!HPF$ TEMPLATE T(N + 1, N + 1)

!HPF$ REAL A(N, N + 1), B(N + 1, N)
!HPF$ ALIGN A(I, J) WITH T(I + 1, J)
!HPF$ ALIGN B(I, J) WITH T(I, J + 1)
!HPF$ DISTRIBUTE T(BLOCK, BLOCK)
```

As seen above, templates can be used as align-targets and may be distributed using a **DISTRIBUTE** (or **REDISTRIBUTE**) directive but may not be alignees.

Procedure Boundaries   HPF allows distributed arrays to be passed as actual arguments to procedures. As noted before, HPF places restrictions on sequence association; therefore the rank and shape of the actual arguments must match with those of the corresponding dummy arguments. HPF provides a wide variety of options to specify the distribution of the dummy argument. The user can specify that the distribution of the actual argument be inherited by the dummy argument. In other cases, the user can provide a specific mapping for the dummy, and the actual argument may need to remapped to satisfy this mapping. If the actual is remapped on entry, then the original mapping is restored on exit from the procedure. The user can also demand that the actual argument be already mapped as specified for the dummy argument. In this case, it is incumbent upon the callee to explicitly remap before the call to the procedure. In the presence of interface blocks, such a remap may be implicitly provided by the compiler.

HPF also provides an **INHERIT** directive, which specifies that the template of the actual argument be copied and used as the template for the dummy argument. This makes a difference when only a subsection of an array is passed as an actual argument. Without the **INHERIT** directive, the template of the dummy argument is implicitly assumed to be the same shape as the dummy, and the dummy is aligned to the template using the identity mapping.

5.4.3 Data Parallel Constructs

Fortran 90 has syntax to express data parallel operations on full arrays. For example, the statement $A = B + C$ indicates that the two arrays B and C should be added, element by element (in any order), to produce the array A. The two main reasons for introducing these features are the conciseness of the expressions (note the absence of explicit loops) and the possibility of exploiting the undefined order of elemental operations for vector and parallel machines. HPF extends Fortran 90 with several new features to explicitly specify data parallelism. The **FORALL** statement and construct generalize the Fortran 90 array operations to allow not only more complicated array sections but also the calling of *pure* procedures on the elements of arrays. The **INDEPENDENT** directive can be used to specify parallel iterations.

Forall Statement   The **FORALL** statement extends the Fortran 90 array operations by making the index used to range over the elements explicit. Thus, this statement can be used to make an array assignment to array elements or sections of arrays, possibly masked with a scalar logical expression. The general form of the **FORALL** statement is as follows:

> **FORALL** (*triplet,* ... [, *scalar-mask*])
>   *assignment*

where, a *triplet* has the form:

> *subscript* = *lower*: *upper* [: *stride*]

Here, the **FORALL** header may have multiple triplets and *assignment* is an arithmetic or pointer assignment. First the lower bound, upper bound, and the optional stride of each triplet are evaluated (in any order). The cartesian product of the result provides the valid set of subscript values over which the mask is then evaluated. This gives rise to the active combinations. The right-hand side of the assignment is then evaluated for all the active combinations before any assignment to corresponding elements on the left-hand side.

> **FORALL** $(I = 1, N, J = 2, N)$
> $A(I, J) = A(I, J - 1)*B(I)$

In the above example, the new values of the array A are determined by the old values of A in the columns on the right and the array B.

Forall Construct   The **FORALL** construct is a generalization of the **FORALL** statement, allowing multiple statements to be associated with the same **FORALL** header. The only kind of statements allowed are assignment, the **WHERE** statement, and another **FORALL** statement or construct.

    FORALL (*triplet,* ... [, *scalar-mask*])
       statement
       ...

    END FORALL

Here, the header is evaluated as before and the execution of one statement is completed for all active combinations before proceeding to the next statement. Thus, conceptually, in a **FORALL** construct, there is a synchronization before the assignment to the left-hand side and between any two statements. Obviously, some of these synchronizations may not be needed and can be optimized away.

Pure procedures   HPF has introduced a new attribute for procedures called **PURE,** which allows users to declare that the given procedure has no side effects. That is, the only effects of the procedure are either the value returned by the function or possible changes in the values of **INTENT(OUT)** or **INTENT(INOUT)** arguments. HPF defines a set of syntactic constraints that must be followed in order for a procedure to be pure. This allows the compiler to easily check the validity of the declaration. Note that a procedure can only call other pure procedures to remain pure.

    Only pure functions can be called from a **FORALL** statement or construct. Since pure functions have no side effects other than the value returned, the function can be called for the active set of index combinations in any order.

Independent Directive   The **INDEPENDENT** directive can be used with a **DO** loop or a **FORALL** statement or construct to indicate that there are no cross-iteration data dependences. Thus, for a **DO** loop, the directive asserts that the iterations of the loop can be executed in any order without changing the final result. Similarly, when used with a **FORALL** construct or statement, the directive asserts that there is no synchronization required between the executions of the different values of the active combination set.

    With a **DO** loop, the **INDEPENDENT** directive can be augmented with a list of variables that can be treated as private variables for the purposes of the iterations.

    !HPF\$ **INDEPENDENT , NEW** (X)
        DO $I = 1, N$
         $X = B(I)$
         ...
         $A(f(I)) = X$
        END DO $I = 1, N$

Here, the **INDEPENDENT** directive is asserting that the function $f(I)$ returns a permutation of the index set, that is, no two iterations are going to assign to the same element of A.

Similarly, the *new clause* asserts that the loop carried dependence, due to the variable X, is spurious, and the compiler can execute the loops by (conceptually) allocating a *new* X variable for each iteration.

5.4.4   Examples of HPF Codes

In this section we provide two code fragments using some of the HPF features described above. The first is the Jacobi iterative algorithm and the second is the Modified Gram-Schmidt algorithm discussed earlier.

The HPF version of the Jacobi iterative procedure, which may be used to approximate the solution of a partial differential equation discretized on a grid, is given below.

```
!HPF$ processors  p( number_of_processors ())
        real u(1 : n,1 : n), f(1 : n,1 : n)
!HPF$ align u :: f
!HPF$ distribute u (*, block )
        . . .
        forall (i = 2 : n − 1, j = 2 : n − 1)
          u(i, j) = 0.25*(f(i, j) + u(i − 1, j) + u(i + 1, j) +
                          u(i, j − 1) + u(i, j + 1)
        end forall
```

At each step, it updates the current approximation at a grid point, represented by the array u, by computing a weighted average of the values at the neighboring grid points and the value of the right-hand side function represented by the array f.

The array f is aligned with the array u using the identity alignment. The columns of u (and thus, those of f indirectly) are then distributed across the processors executing the program. The computation is expressed using a **FORALL** statement, where all the right-hand sides are evaluated using the old values of u before assignment to the left-hand side.

To reiterate, the computation is specified using a global index space and does not contain any explicit data motion constructs. Given that the underlying arrays are distributed by columns, the edge columns will have to be communicated to neighboring processors. It is the compiler's responsibility to analyze the code and generate parallel code with appropriate communication statements inserted to satisfy the data requirements.

The HPF version of the Modified Gram-Schmidt algorithm is given below.[5]

```
        real v(n, n)
!HPF$ distribute v (*, block )
        do i = 1, n
          tmp = 0.0
          do k = 1, n
            tmp = tmp + v(k, i)*v(k, i)
```

---

[5] A Fortran 90 version of the code fragment, not shown here, would have used array constructs for the k loops. This would make the parallelism in the inner loops explicit.

```
              enddo
              xnorm = 1.0 / sqrt(tmp)
              do k = 1, n
                v(k, i) = v(k, i) * xnorm
              enddo
!HPF$ independent, new (tmp)
              do j = i + 1, n
                tmp = 0.0
                do k = 1, n
                  tmp = tmp + v(k, i)*v(k, j)
                enddo
                do k = 1, n
                  v(k, j) = v(k, j) − tmp*v(k, i)
                enddo
              enddo
            enddo
```

The first directive declares that the columns of the array v are to be distributed by blocks across the memories of the underlying processor set. The outer loop is sequential and is thus executed by all processors. Given the column distribution, in the ith iteration of the outer loop, the first two k loops would be executed by the processor owning the ith column.

The second directive declares the j loop to be *independent* and *tmp* to be a *new* variable. The iterations of the j loop can be executed in parallel, thus, each processor updates the columns that it owns in parallel. Since the ith column is used for this update, it will have to be broadcast to all processors.

The distribution of the columns by contiguous blocks implies that processors will become idle as the computation progresses. A *cyclic* distribution of the columns would eliminate this problem. This can be achieved by replacing the distribution directive with the following:

!HPF$ **distribute** v (*, **cyclic**)

This declares the columns to be distributed cyclically across the processors, and thus forces the inner j loop to be strip-mined in a cyclic rather than in a block fashion. Thus, all processors are busy until the tail end of the computation.

The above distributions only exploit parallelism in one dimension, whereas the inner k loops can also run in parallel. This can be achieved by distributing both the dimensions of v as follows:

!HPF$ **distribute** v (**block**, **cyclic**)

Here, the processors are presumed to be arranged in a two-dimensional mesh and the array is distributed such that the elements of a column of the array are distributed by block across a column of processors whereas the columns as a whole are distributed cyclically. Thus, the first k loop becomes a parallel reduction of the ith column across the set of processors owning the ith column. Similarly, the second k loop can be turned into a **FORALL** statement executed in parallel by the column of processors that owns the ith column. The second set of k loops, inside the j loop, can be similarly parallelized.

Overall, it is clear that using the approach advocated by HPF allows the user to focus on the performance-critical issues at a very high level. Thus, it is easy for the user to experiment with a different distribution, just by changing the DISTRIBUTE directives. The new code is then recompiled before running on the target machine. In contrast, the effort required to change the program if it was written using low-level communication primitives would be much more.

5.5 OBJECT PARALLELISM WITH PC++

pC++ is an experimental extension to C++ designed to allow programmers to build distributed data structures with parallel execution semantics. These data structures are organized as *concurrent aggregate* collection classes that can be aligned and distributed over the memory hierarchy of a parallel machine in a manner modeled on the High Performance Fortran Forum (HPF) directives for Fortran 90. The first version of the compiler is a preprocessor that generates single program multiple data (SPMD) C++ code, which runs on the Thinking Machines CM-5, the Intel Paragon, the BBN TC2000, and the Sequent series of machines. As HPF becomes available on these systems future versions of the compiler will allow object-level linking between pC++ distributed collections and HPF distributed arrays.

The basic concept of pC++ is the notion of a distributed collection, which is a type of concurrent aggregate *container class* [15, 35]. More specifically, a *collection* is a structured set of objects distributed across the processing elements of the computer. A runtime system uses the memory hierarchy and processor interconnect topology of the target machine to guide the distribution of collection elements. A collection can be an *array*, a *grid*, a *tree*, or any other partitionable data structure.

Collections have the following components:

- A collection class describing the basic topology of the set.
- A size or shape for each instance of the collection class, for example, the dimensions of an array or the height of a tree.
- A base type for collection elements. This can be any C++ type or class. For example, one can define an array of *Floats*, or a grid of *FiniteElements*, or matrix of *Complex*, or a tree of *X*s, where *X* is the class of each node in the tree.
- A *Distribution* object. The distribution describes an abstract coordinate system that will be distributed over the available memory modules of the target by the runtime system.
- A function object called the *Alignment*. This function maps collection elements to the abstract coordinate system of the *Distribution* object.

The pC++ language has a library of standard collection classes that may be used (or subclassed) by the programmer [17, 20, 36, 40]. This includes collection classes such as *DistributedArray*, *DistributedMatrix*, *DistributedVector*, and *DistributedGrid*. To illustrate the points above, consider the problem of creating a distributed 5 by 5 matrix of floating point numbers. We begin by building a *Distribution*. A distribution is defined by its number of dimensions, the size in each dimension, and how the elements are mapped to the processors. In HPF [28] this mapping is called a distribution. Current distributions include BLOCK, CYCLIC, and WHOLE, but more general forms will be added later. Let us assume that the distribution is distributed over the processor's memories by mapping *Whole* rows of the distribution to individual processors using a *Cyclic* pattern where the ith row is mapped to processor memory i mod P, on a P processor machine.

pC++ uses a special implementation dependent library class called *Processors*. In the current implementation, it represents the set of all processors available to the program at run time. To build a distribution of some size, say 7 by 7, one would write

```
Processor P;
Distribution myDist(7, 7, &P, Cyclic, Whole);
```

Next, we create an alignment object called *myAlign* that defines a domain and function for mapping the matrix to the distribution. The matrix A can be defined using the library collection class *DistributedMatrix* with a base type of *Float*.

```
Align myAlign(5, 5, ``[ALIGN( domain[i][j], myDist[i][j])]'');
DistributedMatrix<Float> A(myDist, myAlign);
```

The collection constructor uses the alignment object, *myAlign*, to define the size and dimension of the collection. The mapping function is described by a text string corresponding to the HPF alignment directive. It defines a mapping from a domain structure to a distribution structure using dummy index variables.

The intent of this two-stage mapping, as it was originally designed for HPF, is to allow the distribution to be a frame of reference so that different arrays could be aligned with each other in a manner that promotes memory locality. For example, suppose we wish to perform a matrix vector multiply. Since the *DistributedMatrix* and *DistributedVector* library classes provide many common functions through C++ function overloading, a matrix vector multiply is simply written as

```
Y = A*X;
```

where X and Y are distributed arrays. While the semantic meaning and computed result of the expression is independent of alignment and distribution, performance is best if the alignment of the operands matches the library function for matrix vector multiply. In this case, the algorithm broadcasts the vector operand along the columns of the array and then performs a reduction along rows. Aligning X along with the first row of the matrix A, and Y with the first column yields the best performance. The vectors are declared by

```
Align XAlign(5, ``[ALIGN( X[i], myDist[0][i])]'');
Align YAlign(5, ``[ALIGN( Y[i], myDist[i][0])]'');
DistributedVector<Float>  X(myDist, XAlign);
DistributedVector<Float>  Y(myDist, YAlign);
```

The two-stage mapping process for this example is illustrated in Figure 5.3

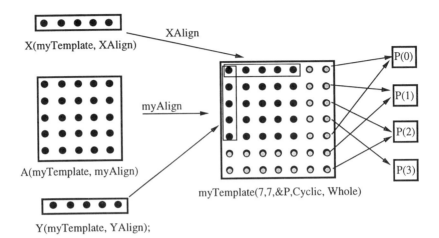

FIGURE 5.3   Alignment and distribution.

5.5.1   Collection Functions and Parallelism

There are two forms of concurrency in pC++. One is based on the concurrent application of a method function, associated with the element class across the entire collection, and the other type is associated with special functions that are invoked as a set of parallel threads, one running on each processor. More precisely, a collection is a set of element objects. A local collection is the subset of elements mapped to one processor by the alignment and distribution functions. Each local collection is realized as a *Processor Object* and there is an associated thread of computation that executes all method functions that modify or access the local elements.

The memory model used by pC++ is not shared. As with HPF Fortran, there is a single main thread of computation, and parallel operations are invoked from that thread. Collection elements are distributed over the processor objects, which each have a private address space. Global data, which can be accessed and modified by the main thread, is visible to the processor objects, but a processor object cannot modify Global data. Each processor object can read and write its local collection of elements, but the only way a processor object or the main thread of execution can access remote collection elements is through special kernel functions, which provide a copy of remote collection elements.

A collection class C is a data type that is parameterized by the class of the element, $C\langle ElementType\rangle$. Collections have two types of methods: the standard *public*, *private*, and *protected* methods of any normal class; and a set of fields and methods that are added to the element class to provide access to the collection structure. These additional fields and methods are called *MethodOfElement* fields.

Syntactically, a collection class takes the form:

```
collection CollectionName: ParentCollection {
    public:
    private:
```

```
protected:
    // Field variables declared here are local to each
    // processor object.
    // Methods declared here are executed in parallel by
    // the associated processor object thread.
MethodOfElement:
    // Field variables declared here are added to each element.
    // Methods declared here are added to the element class.
    // These methods are the ``data parallel'' functions.
}
```

Data fields defined in the public, private, and protected areas are duplicated in each processor object. Methods in these areas are executed by the threads of the processor objects.

5.5.2 An Example: The Gram-Schmidt Algorithm

To illustrate these ideas we will consider the same Gram-Schmidt algorithm discussed earlier. pC++ programmers work by building collections classes derived from the base library. Because Gram-Schmidt works on column vectors of a matrix, we will cast our matrix as a distributed collection of column vectors. Consequently, we shall assume we have a library of double precision vectors which have all the standard vector-vector and vector-scalar operators,

```
class Vector{
    public:
        Vector(int n);   // a constructor.
        Vector & operator *=(double);   // V = V * 3.14
        double dotProduct(Vector *);    // the dot product
        Vector & operator -=(Vector);   // V = V - W
        Vector operator *(double);      // mult. expression
        ...
```

We will define a collection *MyMatrix*, which will be a distributed array of elements of class *Vector*. The matrix object and the Gram-Schmidt operation will be invoked as

```
main(){
    Processor P;
    int n = 100;
    Distribution myDist(n, &P, Cyclic);
    Align myAlign(n, ``[ALIGN( domain[i], myDist[i])]'');
    MyMatrix<Vector>  M(myDist, myAlign, n);
    M.gramSchmidt(n);
}
```

This declares *M* to be a *MyMatrix* collection of size *n* of elements of class *Vector*. The extra parameter *n* on the declaration of *M* is passed to the element constructor so that each vector element has size *n*. The function *gramSchmidt()* will be a processor object parallel function of the collection which is defined as

```
collection MyMatrix: DistributedArray{
    public:
      void GramSchmidt(int n);
    MethodOfElement:
      void update(ElementType *);
      virtual ElementType & operator *=(double);
      virtual double dotProduct(ElementType *);
      virtual ElementType & operator -=(ElementType);
      virtual ElementType operator *(double);
    }
```

The element-level data parallel functions in this collection include a method *update* which will be described below, and four virtual functions provided by the element class which, in our case, is *Vector*. Because the collection is defined separately from the element, if we wish to assume the element has special properties, these are listed as virtual functions. In the case of the Gram-Schmidt algorithm we need to be able to compute the dot product of vectors, multiply vectors by a scalar, and subtract a multiple of one vector from another.

The Gram-Schmidt function is nearly a direct translation of the program in Section 5.3.

```
    void MyMatrix::gramSchmidt(int n){
        ElementType *v;
        int i;
        double temp;
        for(i = 0; i < n; i++){
            v = this->Get Element(i);
            temp = v->dotProduct(v);
            v * = 1.0 / sqrt(temp);
            (*this)[i+1 : n-1].update(v);
            }
        }
```

In this program *gramSchmidt(n)* is a collection public function, which means that it is invoked on each processor object. The main loop first extracts the *i*th column vector element. The pointer *v* obtained by the kernel function *Get_Element(i)* references a copy of the *i*th element if it is not part of the local collection of the invoking processor object. Otherwise, *v* references the actual element. Notice that each processor thread then duplicates the work of computing the dot product and normalizing its copy of *v*.

The element function *update(v)* is invoked in *data parallel* mode on each element in the local collection that has indexes in the given subrange. In pC++ this is accomplished with an expression of the form

```
        collection . elementMethod()
```

which invokes the element method function *in parallel* on each of the elements of the collection. To invoke the method on a subrange we use a Fortran 90 style triplet

```
collection [ lower : upper : stride ] . elementMethod()
```

The parallel operation *update* is identical to the *DoShared* loop in the Fortran-S program.

```
void MyMatrix::update(ElementType *v){
        double temp;
        temp = this->dotProduct(v);
        *this -= v*temp;
};
```

There are two further observations that should be made about this program. First, the use of *Get_Element()* by each processor object can create a serial section. Each processor object other than the owner of the ith element will request a a copy. A more efficient program would use a coordinated element broadcast, *Element_Broadcast()*, to make sure each processor object would get a copy in the smallest amount of time. Second, and more important, is the choice of data distribution. In our case we have selected a cyclic distribution so that as i increases in the expression $[i+1 : n-1].update(v)$, a majority of processors can participate for as long as possible. A block distribution would decrease the parallelism much faster.

5.6

CONCLUSION

In this paper we have examined three different approaches to programming scientific, data parallel applications.

Fortran-S plus SVM provides the user with a familiar model: Fortran 77 plus annotations to distribute loops over processors. Initial experiments with the KOAN SVM system look very promising, but we need much more experience with large applications on large new systems before we can declare success. In the future we expect that more shared virtual memory systems will be implemented on a variety of massively parallel systems. While the details of each system will vary, the Fortran-S project demonstrates that the compiler technology exists to make this model work.

High Performance Fortran provides a high-level approach to data parallel programming for a wide variety of architecture. Initial experience has shown that the directives as currently provided by HPF are adequate for simple scientific codes. However, it is also clear that HPF does not have enough expressive power to specify the distributions required for other types of codes such as multiblock and unstructured computations, adaptive computations and multidisciplinary applications, which require integrating different types of parallel programming paradigms.

Currently there are no existing compilers for HPF; several vendors have promised initial implementations in the near future. However, several research projects have built prototype compilers for HPF-like languages. This includes the Kali compiler [33], the SUPERB project [67] (on which the Vienna Fortran compiler is based), the Fortran D compiler, [29] and several other efforts [8, 24, 27, 32, 38, 48, 58, 59, 60] that have contributed to the overall goal of compiling global name space programs for distributed memory SIMD and MIMD machines.

pC++ is just one example of a number of efforts to add parallelism to C++. While pC++ has been ported to a wide variety of machines including the TMC CM-5, Intel Paragon, BBN TC2000, and the KSR-1, it does have serious drawbacks. First, it relies on an extension to the C++ language. While not a large departure from C++, the collection plus processor object model requires considerable sophistication on the part of the user to use it correctly. Also the common alternative, building class libraries that operate in SPMD parallel execution, is very popular and it does not require extensions to the language. In the future, the success of object parallel extension to C++ will depend on providing more functionality than Fortran S or HPF. The features that will be important are heterogeneous (polymorphic), dynamic collections, and nested data parallelism.

We have not attempted a complete survey of the parallel programming landscape. The three parallel programming language extensions described here represent only a small fraction of the approaches currently being investigated. It is clear that this area will continue to undergo rapid evolution. Different application areas may require different programming paradigms and some multidisciplinary problems will need a combination of programming styles.

Bibliography

1. "Scalable Coherence Interface," tech. report, IEEE Standard P1596, 1991.
2. "Ksr Parallel Programming," tech. report, Kendall Square Research Corporation, Feb. 1992.
3. Porterfield A, "Compiler Management of Program Locality," tech. report, Rice University, Houston, Texas, Jan. 1988.
4. W. Abu-Sufah, D. Kuck, and D. Lawrie, "On the Performance Enhancement of Paging System through Program Analysis and Transformations," *IEEE Trans. Computers*, Vol. C-30, No. 5, May 1981, pp. 341–356.
5. S. Ahuja, N. Carriero, and D. Gelernter, "Linda and Friends," *Computer*, Vol. 19, Aug. 1986, pp. 26–34.
6. F. Allen et al., "An Overview of the PTRAN Analysis System for Multiprocessing," Research Report RC 13115 (#56866), IBM T.J. Watson Research Center, Yorktown Heights, NY, Sept. 1987.
7. J.R. Allen and K. Kennedy, "Automatic Translation of Fortran Programs to Vector Form," *ACM Trans. Programming Languages and Systems*, Vol. 9, No. 4, Oct. 1987.
8. F. André, J.-L. Pazat, and H. Thomas, "PANDORE: A System to Manage Data Distribution," *Proc. Int'l Conf. Supercomputing*, IEEE CS Press, Los Alamitos, Calif., 1990, pp. 380–388.
9. J. Van Rosendale et al., "A Software Architecture for Multidisciplinary Applications: Integrating Task and Data Parallelism," Icase Report, Institute for Computer Applications in Science and Engineering, Hampton, Va., 1994.
10. F. Bodin et al., "A Quantitative Algorithm for Data Locality Optimization," *Code Generation— Concepts, Tools, Techniques*, Springer Verlag, Heidelberg, Germany, 1992.
11. F. Bodin, J. Erhel, and T. Priol, "Parallel Sparse Matrix Vector Multiplication Using a Shared Virtual Memory Environment," *Proc. 6th SIAM Conf. Parallel Processing for Scientific Computing*, 1993.

12. F. Bodin, L. Kervella, and T. Priol, "Fortran-S: A Fortran Interface for Shared Virtual Memory Architectures," *Proc. Supercomputing'93*, IEEE CS Press, Los Alamitos, Calif., 1993, pp. 274–283.

13. L.M. Censier and P. Feautrier, "A New Solution to Coherence Problems in Multicache Systems," *IEEE Trans. Computers*, Vol. C-27, No. 12, Dec. 1978, pp. 1112–1118.

14. B. Chapman, P. Mehrotra, and H. Zima, "Programming in Vienna Fortran," *Scientific Programming*, Vol. 1, No. 1, 1992, pp. 31–50.

15. A. Chien and W. Dally, "Concurrent Aggregates (CA)," *Proc. 2nd ACM SIGPLAN Symp. Principles & Practice of Parallel Programming*, ACM Press, New York, N.Y., 1990.

16. E.D. Granston and A.V. Veidenbaum, "Integrated Hardware/Software Solution for Effective Management of Local Storage in High-Performance Systems," *Proc. 1991 Int'l Conf. Parallel Processing*, CRC Press, Boca Raton, Fla.,1991, Vol. 2, pp. 83–90.

17. J.K. Lee, and D. Gannon, "On Using Object-Oriented Parallel Programming to Build Distributed Algebraic Abstractions," *Conpar-Vap*, Springer Verlag, Heidelberg, Germany, 1992, pp. 769–774.

18. S.J. Eggers and T.E. Jeremiassen, "Eliminating False Sharing," *Proc. Int'l Conf. Parallel Processing*, CRC Press, Boca Raton, Fla., 1991, pp. 377–380.

19. G. Fox et al., "Fortran D Language Specification," Department of Computer Science Rice COMP TR90079, Rice University, Mar. 1991.

20. D. Gannon, "Libraries and Tools for Object Parallel Programming," *Proc. Advances in Parallel Computing: CNRS-NSF Workshop on Environments and Tools For Parallel Scientific Computing, Saint Hilaire du Touvet*, Vol. 6, Elsevier Science Publisher, Amsterdam, The Netherlands, 1993, pp. 231–246.

21. D. Gannon, W. Jalby, and K. Gallivan, "Strategies for Cache and Local Memory Management by Global Programming Transformation," *J. Parallel and Distributed Computing*, Vol. 5, No. 5, Oct. 1988, pp. 587–616, Special issue on languages, compilers, and environments for parallel programming.

22. D. Gannon et al., "Sigma II: A Tool Kit for Building Parallelizing Compilers and Performance Analysis Systems," *Programming Environments for Parallel Computing, IFIP Trans. A-11*, 1993, pp. 17–36.

23. K. Gallivan, D. Gannon, and W. Jalby, "Strategies for Cache and Local Memory Management by Global Program Transformation," *Proc. Int'l Conf. Supercomputing,* Springer Verlag, New York, N.Y., 1987 and *J. Parallel and Distributed Computing*, Oct. 1988.

24. H.M. Gerndt, *Automatic Parallelization for Distributed-Memory Multiprocessing Systems,* PhD Thesis, University of Bonn, Dec. 1989.

25. E.D. Granston and H. Wijshoff, "Managing Pages in Shared Virtual Memory Systems: Getting the Compiler into the Game," *Proc. Int'l Conf. Supercomputing*, ACM Press, New York, N.Y., 1993.

26. M. Gupta and P. Banerjee, "Automatic Data Partitioning on Distributed Memory Multiprocessors," University of Illinois at Urbana-Champaign tech. report CRHC-90-14, Center for Reliable and High-Performance Computing, Coordinated Science Laboratory, Oct. 1990.

27. M. Hatcher et al., "A Production Quality C* Compiler for Hypercube Machines," *Proc. 3rd ACM SIGPLAN Symp. Principles Practice of Parallel Programming*, ACM Press, New York, N.Y., 1991, pp. 73–82.

28. "High Performance FORTRAN Language Specification," tech. report, Rice University, 1993.

29. S. Hiranandani, K. Kennedy, and C. Tseng, "Compiling Fortran D for MIMD Distributed Memory Machines," *Comm. ACM*, Vol. 35, No. 8, Aug. 1992, pp. 66–80.

30. J. Li, and M. Chen, "Generating Explicit Communication from Shared-memory Program References," *Proc. Supercomputing*, IEEE CS Press, Los Alamitos, Calif., 1990, pp. 865–876.

31. C.F. Kesselman and K.M. Chandy, "CC++: A Declarative Concurrent Object-Oriented Programming Notation," In *Research Directions in Object Oriented Programming*, MIT Press, Cambridge, Mass., 1993.

32. K. Knobe, J. Lukas, and G. Steele, Jr, "Data Optimization: Allocation of Arrays to Reduce Communication on SIMD Machines," *J. Parallel and Distributed Computing*, Vol. 8, 1990, pp. 102–118.

33. C. Koelbel and P. Mehrotra, "Compiling Global Name-space Parallel Loops for Distributed Execution," *IEEE Trans. Parallel and Distributed Systems*, Vol. 2, No. 4, Oct. 1991, pp. 440–451.

34. Z. Lahjomri and T. Priol, "Koan: A Shared Virtual Memory for the ipsc/2 Hypercube," *Proc. CONPAR/VAPP92*, 1992.

35. J.K. Lee, "Object-Oriented Parallel Programming Paradigms and Environments for Supercomputers," tech. report, PhD Thesis, DCS, Indiana University, June 1992.

36. J.K. Lee and D. Gannon, "Object-Oriented Parallel Programming: Experiments and Results," *Supercomputing 91*, IEEE CS Press, Los Alamitos, Calif., 1991, pp. 273–282.

37. D. Lenoski et al., "The Directory-based Cache Coherence Protocol for the DASH Multiprocessor," *Proc. 17th Ann. Symp. Computer Architecture*, IEEE CS Press, Los Alamitos, Calif., 1990, pp. 148–160.

38. J. Li and M. Chen, "Index Domain Alignment: Minimizing Cost of Cross-referencing between Distributed Arrays," tech. report YALEU/DCS/TR-725, Yale University, New Haven, Conn., Nov. 1989.

39. Kai Li, *Shared Virtual Memory on Loosely Coupled Multiprocessors*, PhD Thesis, Yale University, Sept. 1986.

40. D. Loveman, "High Performance Fortran," *IEEE Parallel and Distributed Technology*, Vol. 1, Feb. 1993, pp. 25–42.

41. M. O'Boyle, *Program and Data Transformation for Efficient Execution on Distributed Memory Architectures*. PhD thesis, University of Manchester, 1993.

42. E.P. Markatos and T.J. Leblanc, "Using Processor Affinity in Loop Scheduling on Shared Memory Multiprocessors," *Proc. Supercomputing*, IEEE CS Press, Los Alamitos, Calif., 1992, pp. 104–113.

43. J. McGraw et al., "SISAL: Streams and Iteration in a Single Assignment Language: Language Reference Manual," Report M-146, Lawrence Livermore National Laboratory, Livermore, Calif., Mar. 1985.

44. K.S. McKindley, *Automatic and Interactive Parallelization*. PhD Thesis, Rice University, 1992.

45. P. Mehrotra, "Programming Parallel Architectures: The BLAZE Family of Languages," *Proc. 3rd SIAM Conf. Parallel Processing for Scientific Computing*, 1988, pp. 289–299.

46. P. Mehrotra and J. Van Rosendale, "Programming Distributed Memory Architectures Using Kali," A. Nicolau, D. Gelernter, T. Gross, and D. Padua, eds., *Advances in Languages and Compilers for Parallel Processing*, Pitman/MIT-Press, 1991, pp. 364–384.

47. R.E. Millstein, "Control Structures in ILLIAC IV Fortran," *Comm. ACM*, Vol. 16, No. 10, Oct. 1973, pp. 621–627.

48. *MIMDizer User's Guide, Version 7.02*, Pacific Sierra Research Corporation, Placerville, Calif., 1991.

49. F. Bodin et al., "Implementing a Parallel C++ Runtime System for Scalable Parallel Systems," *Proc. Supercomputing'93*, IEEE CS Press, Los Alamitos, Calif., 1993, pp. 588–597.

50. D. Mosberger, "Memory Consistency Models," *ACM Operating Systems Review*, Feb. 1993.

51. D.A. Padua, D.J. Kuck, and D.H. Lawrie, "High-speed Multiprocessors and Compilation Techniques," *IEEE Trans. Computers*, Vol. C-29, No. 9, Sept. 1980, pp. 763–776.

52. T. Priol and Z. Lahjomri, "Experiments with Shared Virtual Memory on a ipsc/2 Hypercube," *Proc. Int'l Conf. Parallel Processing*, CRC Press, Boca Raton, Fla., 1992, pp. 145–148.

53. T. Priol and Z. Lahjomri, "Trade-offs between Shared Virtual Memory and Message-passing on an ipsc/2 Hypercube," Tech. Report 1634, INRIA, 1992.

54. Because Esprit Project, *Because Test Programs: BBS.2.5.1 (Matrix Assembly)*, 1992.

55. G.R. Gao et al., "Collective Loop Fusion for Array Contraction," *Proc. 5th Workshop Languages and Compilers for Parallel Computing*, 1992, pp. 1–31.

56. J. Ramanujam and P. Sadayappan, "Nested Loop Tiling for Distributed Memory Machines," *Proc. 5th Distributed Memory Computing Conference*, IEEE CS Press, Los Alamitos, Calif., 1990, pp. 1088–1096.

57. M. Raynal and M. Mizuno, "How to Find His Way in the Jungle of Consistency Criteria for Distributed Objects Memories (or How to Escape from Minos' Labyrinth)," *Proc. IEEE Conf. Future Trends of DCS*, IEEE CS Press, Los Alamitos, Calif., 1993, pp. 340–353.

58. A.P. Reeves and C.M. Chase, "The Paragon Programming Paradigm and Distributed Memory Multicomputers," *Compilers and Runtime Software for Scalable Multiprocessors*, J. Saltz and P. Mehrotra, eds., Elsevier, Amsterdam, The Netherlands.

59. A. Rogers and K. Pingali, "Process Decomposition through Locality of Reference," *Proc. Conf. Programming Language Design and Implementation*, ACM Press, New York, N.Y., 1989, pp. 1–999.

60. M. Rosing, R.W. Schnabel, and R.P. Weaver, "Expressing Complex Parallel Algorithms in DINO," *Proc. 4th Conf. Hypercubes, Concurrent Computers, and Applications*, 1989, pp. 553–560.

61. J. Torrellas, M.S. Lam, and J.L. Hennessy, "Shared Data Placement Optimizations to Reduce Multiprocessor Cache Miss Rates," *Proc. Int'l Conf. Parallel Processing*, 1990, pp. 266–270.

62. C.-W. Tseng, *An Optimizing Fortran D Compiler for MIMD Distributed-Memory Machines*, PhD thesis, Rice University, 1993.

63. M.E. Wolf and M. Lam, "A Data Locality Optimizing Algorithm," *Proc. ACM SIGPLAN 91*, ACM Press, New York, N.Y., 1991.

64. M. Lam and M. Wolf, "A Data Locality Optimizing Algorithm," *Proc. ACM Conf. Programming Language Design and Implementation*, ACM Press, New York, N.Y., 1991, pp. 26–28.

65. M.J. Wolfe, "More Iteration Space Tiling," *Proc. Supercomputing'89*, 1989.

66. J. Wu, J. Saltz, S. Hiranandanu, and H. Berryman, "Runtime Compilation Methods for Multicomputers," *Proc. 1991 Int'l Conf. Parallel Processing*, The Pennsylvania State Univ. Press, University Park, Penn., Vol. II, 1991, pp. 26–30.

67. H. Zima, H. Bast, and M. Gerndt, "Superb: A Tool for Semi-automatic MIMD/SIMD Parallelization," *Parallel Computing*, Vol. 6, 1986, pp. 1–18.

68. H. Zima et al., "Vienna Fortran—A Language Specification," Internal Report 21, ICASE, Hampton, Va., Mar. 1992.

CHAPTER 6

CONCURRENT OBJECT-ORIENTED LANGUAGES AND THE INHERITANCE ANOMALY

Dennis G. Kafura
Dept. of Computer Science
Virginia Tech
Blacksburg, VA 24061, USA

R. Greg Lavender
MCC
3500 W. Balcones Center Dr.
Austin, TX 78759, USA

Abstract. *A survey of concurrent object-oriented languages is presented. The survey is organized around three models: the* animation model, *which describes a variety of relationships between threads and objects, an* interaction model, *which classifies the possible semantics of invocations and returns between a client object and a server object, and a* synchronization model, *which shows different ways in which concurrent invocations can be managed by a server. A number of representative languages are briefly presented. The problem of synchronization in concurrent object-oriented languages is considered in detail including a discussion of the* inheritance anomaly. *A synchronization mechanism, called a* behavior set, *is shown to avoid this anomaly in certain cases. The implementation of behavior sets in ACT++, an actor-based concurrent programming framework implemented in C++, is described.*

6.1

INTRODUCTION

Programming languages play an important role in parallel processing. A language whose conceptual basis, constructs, and paradigm are coherent with the programmer's problem model can support the effective expression of the programmer's intent. Equally, a language lacking in these qualities impedes the program's development. These effects are no less true in parallel programming than in other programming domains.

Languages have been defined for programming highly parallel computing systems, including both tightly and more loosely coupled multicomputers. The languages considered

221

in this survey are those that combine parallelism (or more generally, concurrency), with an object-orientation.

The relevance of concurrent, object-oriented languages to parallel programming includes:

1. The availability of numerous processors in a parallel or distributed system is a direct realization of the abstract multiprocessor model embodied in a concurrent object-oriented language. Some languages (such as POOL and Cantor) were designed for specific parallel architectures.

2. While applications coded in sequential languages must be subjected to extensive analysis or restructuring to uncover latent parallelism, the inherent parallelism in concurrent object-oriented languages is readily apparent. This property is being exploited in the Mentat system and the Ellie language.

3. The mapping (scheduling or dynamic load balancing) of objects to processors is given a simple and intuitive basis.

4. The existence of numerous, concurrent objects can help to mask the effects of latency; there is always work to be scheduled.

5. The SPMD (single-program, multiple-data) model is cleanly represented in a concurrent, object-oriented language where the data and the code that manipulates that data are clearly identified.

While other language forms are also being explored for parallel programming (such as parallel extensions to imperative languages like Fortran, and tuple-spaced languages like Linda), the family of concurrent object-oriented languages is a relevant and interesting one.

This survey of concurrent object-oriented programming languages is organized along the following lines:

1. A review of historical and technical factors motivating the synthesis of concurrency and object-orientation including a discussion of the relevance of this sythesis to parallel computing.

2. A description of the most significant problems confronted by designers of concurrent object-oriented languages, an overview of the solutions to these problems, and a summary of what appear to be commonly accepted solutions.

3. A brief overview of each of several languages illustrating attempts to integrate the individual design solutions into a coherent language.

4. An in-depth presentation of the inheritance anomaly, and a solution to this problem, called *behavior sets*, which has been developed as part of the ACT++ project.

The remainder of this introductory section considers the first point. Subsequent sections consider each of the other points in order.

This paper relies heavily on a previous survey by Wegner [29] and a taxonomy presented by Papathomas [23]. While differing in terminology and in some conclusions, the thorough work of Papathomas was an especially important information source for the survey undertaken here.

As a final preparatory comment, the terms *language*, *object-oriented*, and *parallel* are given generous interpretations in this survey. The term *language* is taken to encompass:

1. Class hierarchies or frameworks for concurrent object-oriented programming that are not, strictly speaking, new languages.

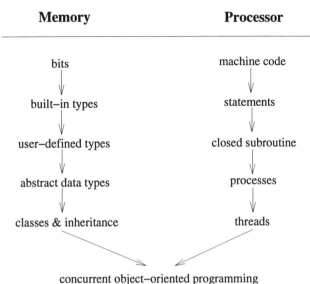

FIGURE 6.1   Evolution of concurrent object-oriented programming.

2. Run-time systems that provide services for concurrency in an object-oriented context.
3. "Real" languages with a uniquely defined syntax and supported by a translator.

Similarly, *object-oriented* is interpreted broadly. A useful distinction is drawn by Wegner between *object-oriented*, which implies the existence of a sharing mechanism (for example, inheritance) and *object-based* languages, which have no such sharing mechanism. This distinction, while important, is not used; the term *object-oriented* includes both. Finally, no discrimination is made on the basis of what architectural form is reflected in a particular language. Languages are included for shared-memory multiprocessors, distributed-memory multiprocessors, and distributed systems of workstations.

Programming languages combining concurrency with object-orientation can be seen as the most evolved form of abstraction for the two essential computing resources: processor and memory. These two resources are essential whether one considers real machines or theoretical models. It is the express purpose of programming languages to provide expressive and safe abstractions by which these primitive essential resources can be manipulated. In Figure 6.1, the major successive abstractions of processor and memory are traced.

The most basic memory abstraction is that of a storage location (machine byte, word, or register). This is the only abstraction in low-level assembly languages. The earliest high-level languages introduced a fixed set of built-in types, providing greater ease in organizing an application's data and greater safety in manipulating this data. The provision of user-defined types extended to the programmer the ability to define application specific types that had the same standing as the previous built-in types. The development of abstract data types recognized the importance of the separation of the type's interface from its (possibly many) differing implementations. Object-oriented programming adds to abstract data types the important ability to incrementally extend an existing type.

Abstractions for a processor also can be traced by considering how programming languages have treated the notion of control. The primitive manipulation of control, by directly and explicitly affecting machine registers, was abstracted in higher level languages through the statement structure, some of which implicitly managed control (expressions) and some of which explicitly managed control (branches, loops). The invention of the closed subroutine introduced a major control abstraction. Each subroutine could be envisioned as an extension of the instruction set of the physical processor. Advances in architecture and operating systems encouraged application developers and language designers to depart from the sequential model resulting in languages with a process concept. Coroutines, parallel tasks, and their associated coordination devices (such as monitors) provided an abstraction of a complete machine. More recent operating system research has reduced the previously high cost of multiprocess applications through the invention of lightweight processes or threads.

As shown in Figure 6.1, concurrent object-oriented languages unify the previously separated abstractions for processor and memory. It is interesting to note that current research is following the pattern of natural evolution. A large number of experimental concurrent object-oriented languages are being developed; the technical and market forces that shape the environment of computing will select only a small number of survivors from among this rich variety.

As opposed to the historical factors just considered, the technical factors motivating concurrent object-oriented languages include at least the following three. First, conceptual economy is achieved by unifying the processor and memory abstractions. It is not necessary for the application developer to consider how to organize the application's control separately from the question of how to organize the application's objects. This is an especially important advantage in that it avoids presenting the developer with two semantic models—one model for control and a different model for data and functions. Second, modeling fidelity is enhanced in those applications where autonomous, real-world entities are pervasive. In this case the attributes of the real-world entity are more completely, overtly, and simply reflected in concurrent objects than would be the case if the autonomy and the functionality of the object were realized disjointly. Third, simplicity is attained for the two reasons already presented but also for two other reasons. An important goal in language design is to focus attention on important abstractions while suppressing from attention aspects that are irrelevant to this purpose. A concurrent object-oriented language suppresses substantial detail about control flow management, specifically the invocation and scheduling of object executions. By contract, sequential languages force the developer to explicitly construct a, perhaps elaborate, invocation and scheduling structure. For example, the last step in Jackson's JSD design method [11] is just to create a scheduler. Not only are these explicit control organizations difficult to construct but they are often fragile, incapable of being extended simply to accommodate simple extensions of functionality. This is the case because each object may contain code not only for its own function but also as part of the invocation and scheduling structure for other objects. In this sense, a design expressed in sequential languages becomes overspecified as it must encompass details not inherent to the problem domain or relevant to the solution method. Simplicity, especially as it applies to the design and implementation of synchronization, is also derived from the incremental extension offered by object-oriented languages. While synchronization is generally a difficult matter, incremental extension offers the hope of building the synchronization structure in smaller, more intelligible, and reusable pieces. As will be seen, this hope is negatively affected by the inheritance anomaly and can only be realized by carefully designed concurrent object-oriented languages.

6.2

SIGNIFICANT DESIGN ISSUES

A survey of numerous languages is best done within a framework that organizes the essential and discriminating features of the languages in a comprehensible way. The survey presented here organizes the language features into the three models shown in Figure 6.2. Each model contains a number of specific but interrelated issues.

The selection of the three models is not intended to imply that this is the only, or even necessarily the best, taxonomy of the features of concurrent object-oriented languages. It is merely an organization to facilitate the current survey. In addition, it should not be thought that the issues pertinent to each model are unrelated—choices made in one model do influence choices made in another model.

6.2.1   The Animation Model

The *animation model* captures those aspects of the object model that relate to the relationship between an object and the active processing entity of the system. The active processing entity is commonly termed a thread. The factors in the animation model are shown in Figure 6.3. In this, as in subsequent figures about the other two models, an independent choice is denoted by a diamond symbol below the name of the factor. Thus, in Figure 6.3, the related forms have two independent (orthogonal) dimensions (uniformity and multiplicity). The absence of a diamond indicates that the dependent factors are strictly exclusive. For example, in Figure 6.3, the animation model presented by a language is either related or unrelated.

The most global decision about animation is the extent to which the threads respect the boundary of an object. The first of two alternatives in the animation model may be termed the unrelated case. In the unrelated case, threads and objects are treated as independent

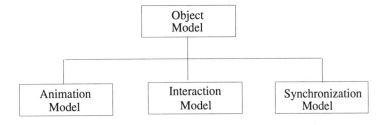

FIGURE 6.2   The three models.

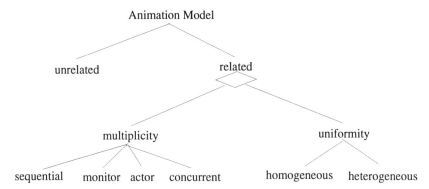

FIGURE 6.3   The animation model.

concepts. An object is defined and created without regard for how any thread may animate that object. Similarly, a thread is free to cross an object's boundary and to have at a single point in time an execution history in which any number of object boundaries have been crossed. The unrelated approach has been used in the earliest concurrent object-oriented languages and in later low-level, general-purpose, runtime frameworks.

The unrelated approach has several advantages. First, it is easy to develop such a language—combining any threads facility with an object-oriented language will suffice. Few requirements are imposed on either the language or the existing threads package. Second, this approach is attractive in application domains that are strongly "activity centered" as opposed to "object centered." The activity, being directly associated with the thread, has an explicit representation that captures the activity's properties and maintains the activity's state.

The disadvantages of the unrelated approach are more fundamental than its advantages. First, the presence of multiple threads within a single object recreates all of the synchronization problems that have been the bane of concurrent programming from its inception. Second, the modeling advantages offered by object-oriented programming are eroded by the unconstrained license given to threads in this approach. Part of the erosion results from the extraneous attributes added to objects to cope with thread synchronization. Additional erosion results if the threads are merely an elaborate control structure superimposed on the object structure. In this case a significant aspect of the application cannot be addressed within an object-oriented framework. Third, and most significant, the unrelated approach fails to advance our understanding of either the object-oriented paradigm or concurrency; each aspect exists unchanged and, as implied by the name, unrelated to the other.

The second alternative in the animation model, the related approach, involves a deeper integration of concurrency and object-orientation. In this approach a thread exists only within an object; the thread's locus of control may not migrate beyond the encapsulating boundary of this object. As a thread's scope of effect is now limited, it is necessary to consider how a client thread in one object interacts with the thread in a server object. The nature of this interaction is significant and is considered in the interaction model presented in Section 6.2.2.

The related approach allows language and system researchers to probe, and application developers to benefit from, the answers to two key questions:

1. Can concurrency be transparently encapsulated within an object?
2. Can inheritance be used to organize and specialize synchronization policies in the same way that inheritance is used to organize and specialize an object's functionality?

The answer to the first question is remarkably straightforward. The second question is remarkably subtle, and a complete answer remains elusive. Further consideration of the second question is deferred until Section 6.4 where a partial answer is presented. Only the first of these questions in considered further at this point.

Mapping threads to objects in the related approach involves two independent dimensions: uniformity and multiplicity. Uniformity refers to whether the object model invests every object with a thread (the homogeneous case) or whether some objects possess threads while others do not (the heterogeneous case). An object possessing a thread is often termed an *active* object while *passive* is used to describe an object without a separate thread. Multiplicity refers to the number of threads that exist within an active object. While all concurrent object-oriented languages provide some form of concurrency among objects (interobject concurrency), allowing more than one thread within an object creates, in addition, a finer level of concurrency (intraobject concurrency). The various forms of multiplicity are considered further below.

The first choice on the uniformity dimension, the homogeneous approach, offers a simple view of the relationship between threads and objects; only a single protocol of interaction among objects needs to be understood, implemented, optimized, and employed. Papathomas [23] argues that homogeneous objects are more easily reused as all objects inherently possess the ability to be used in a concurrent environment without any synchronizing actions being required of the client. In contrast, the clients must themselves provide the synchronization required to access passive objects. Finally, in some languages the syntaxes or mechanisms for accessing active and passive objects are different. Changing an object definition from one form to the other requires not only internal changes to the object itself but also changes to the clients of the object. This is generally viewed as contrary to the philosophy of object-oriented programming where changes in the implementation of the server should not affect the client.

The second choice on the uniformity dimension, the heterogeneous approach, is argued for on the basis of both modeling and implementation. From a modeling perspective, some objects are more usefully viewed as being passive in nature while others are active. For example in designing an application for a library simulation, the librarians, patrons, and the wall clock might be taken to be active entities while the books, tables, and chairs might be considered passive. While such decisions vary with changes in the modeling perspective, each perspective offers some important distinction between entities that can engage in activity and entities that are the subjects of this activity. Preserving this important modeling distinction in the object's implementation assists in traceability and validation. From an implementation viewpoint, having a thread in each object may not be feasible if there are a relatively large number of objects and the runtime environment does not efficiently support lightweight threads. The performance of the application in this case will not be acceptable.

A middle ground on the uniformity dimension is taken by languages that permit passive objects but require that they be encapsulated within the implementation of an active object.

Thus, homogeneity is preserved at the outer (active object) level while heterogeneity is permitted within an active object.

The final factor in the animation model is that of multiplicity. This factor determines the number of concurrent threads that can be executed within an object at the same time. The first of the four alternatives is the sequential case in which an active object always has a single thread of control. Such objects are simple to reason about as there is no concurrency within the object boundary. Languages that take this approach divide the world into the outer, highly concurrent part (where concurrency is achieved by invocations among autonomous, active objects) and the inner, sequential environment within each active object. While programming within a sequential object is simpler, performance gains are jeopardized if the object size is overly large so that opportunities for parallel execution are unavailable. For example, encapsulating a large matrix in a single object makes parallel operations on this matrix impossible. The next choice for multiplicity is a monitor-like (also called quasi-concurrent) form. In this case, an object may have several logical threads executing within its boundaries, but only one of these may be active at a time. Primitive constructs (such as sleep/wakeup in monitors) or automatic mechanisms are used to determine which of the possible several schedulable threads will execute next. Reasoning about the internal operation of monitor-like objects is somewhat more difficult than reasoning about sequential ones, but there is added flexibility as well. For example, a server object that accepts requests from clients, delegates the requests to worker tasks, and monitors the reply to the client is difficult or impossible to implement using a sequential object, while it is straightforward to construct such a server using the monitor-like approach. The third form of multiplicity is called the actor form. In this case, an object may have multiple threads executing within it, subject to the requirement that only the most recently created one of them has the ability to change the "state" of the object. The other threads may interrogate the state of the object and may alter their own local execution state. This notion follows directly from the relationship among the several behaviors of a given actor that operate exactly as described. The fourth, and last, form of multiplicity is concurrent. This form allows multiple threads to execute freely within an object. The weakness of this approach is that additional synchronization needs to be added in order to insure that the state of the object remains consistent in the face of concurrent alterations. The advantage of this approach is the possible performance enhancements that can be achieved by having multiple threads operating concurrently on large amounts of data encapsulation within an object.

6.2.2 The Interaction Model

The *interaction model* is concerned with the semantics of the interaction between a client object and a server object. The two aspects of this relationship are:

1. What are the semantics of the invocation as viewed by the client?
2. How is the result computed by the server returned to the client?

If not evident, the discussion below will show that these two questions are intimately related. It will also be seen that the concurrent object-oriented language perspective contributes little to the first question but provides a novel perspective on the second question. The elements of the interaction model are shown in Figure 6.4.

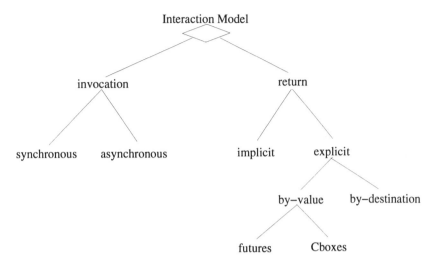

FIGURE 6.4   The interaction model.

An interaction between a client object and a server object is initiated by the client's invocation, which may be either synchronous or asynchronous. These forms of interaction have been extensively studied in the operating system and distributed computing domains; their application in the context of concurrent object-oriented languages is unsurprising.

Synchronous and asynchronous invocations differ in their effect on the client. A synchronous invocation causes the client to block from the time the invocation is made until the time the server's reply is returned. By contrast, an asynchronous invocation allows the client to proceed concurrently with the delivery of the request to the server, the server's computation (which generates the reply), and the delivery of the reply.

Neither form of interaction can claim to be inherently superior. Neither is more "powerful," as each can be used to implement the other and each possesses disadvantages absent in the other. Two disadvantages of a synchronous invocation are:

1. The client is unnecessarily blocked in those cases where the client simply informs the server of some event and expects no reply. This is a particular problem if the server is in the condition described in the second disadvantage.
2. Great care must be taken in designing a server so that, in servicing one request, a synchronous invocation made by the server itself does not cause the server to become blocked for such a period of time that the server cannot expeditiously serve other clients' requests.

The asynchronous form of invocation is free from these problems. Two disadvantages of an asynchronous invocation are:

1. Lacking a clear structural tie to the client, it is more difficult for the server to return the result to the client. Some additional responsibility must be borne by the language or the programmer to return the proper result. The lack of a clear tie to the client also makes

exception handling more difficult. In the worst case, a server experiences an exception in servicing the request of a client that has already terminated because it did not expect a reply.

2. Runtime buffering of requests (such as in mailboxes or ports) is required to support asynchronous invocations. This additional expense is not justified if the application requires only, or at least predominately, synchronous forms of interaction.

These disadvantages do not occur in the synchronous case.

The choice between synchronous and asynchronous invocation semantics is properly based on the needs of the application and for this purpose two kinds of applications can be distinguished: transactive and reactive. A transactive system is one in which the dominant issue is the sequence of actions performed across multiple objects; the key design and implementation decisions depend on this issue. For transactive systems a synchronous invocation is preferred because the progress of each transaction is represented directly by the sequence of synchronous invocations leading to the current locus of control. In reactive systems, however, the dominant issue is how each agent maintains its integrity in the face of requests over which it has little, if any, direct control. Reactive systems prefer asynchronous semantics as they more directly reflect the autonomous nature of the agents in the application.

This discussion of the invocation semantics is concluded by noting two interesting variations. First, a *proxy* object may be interposed between the client and the real server for whom the proxy is only a representative. A proxy object is found in a distributed system when the client and the proxy are located on the same node and the real server is remotely located. In this case the invocation semantics between the client and the proxy may be synchronous while the invocation semantics between the proxy and the real server may be asynchronous. Second, a broadcast style of asynchronous message passing may be used instead of the point-to-point form more commonly associated with method invocation. Broadcasting may also be matched with a form of "coordinated termination" to insure that all messages have been received before the client resumes.

The second major aspect of the interaction model concerns how the server's result is returned to the client. The alternatives are shown in Figure 6.4. The return semantics may be either implicit or explicit, indicating whether the identity of the object to receive the result is implicitly or explicitly known to the server.

The implicit form of return implies that the knowledge of where to deliver the reply is carried by the structure of the invocation and cannot be altered by the application. The most obvious case of an implicit form is the return semantics commonly used for synchronous invocations. The invocation environment (typically a stack of activation records) implicitly contains the identity of the client to whom the result is returned. When the server returns, the environment is adjusted to deliver the result to the invoking client. The implicit form may also be used for asynchronous invocations. A message, for example, may automatically be stamped with the identity of the sender so that an implicit return can be performed by the server.

The explicit form of return allows greater flexibility because the application is permitted to control the destination to which the server's result will be delivered. The value of this flexibility is seen in the common *coordinator-worker model*. In this model a single *coordinator* receives the clients' requests and forwards each request to an available *worker*. Upon receiving the forwarded request, a worker computes the required reply value and transmits this value directly to the originating client. The worker informs the coordinator that it is ready to service another request. Notice that the direct transmission of the result from the worker to the client did not involve the coordinator. This is not possible with implicit returns as the result would have to be passed from the worker to the coordinator and then from the coordinator to the client. The explicit form of return allows for the direct transmission of this value as the worker is aware explicitly of the identity of the originating client.

Explicit returns may take one of two forms. In one case, the by-value case, the mechanism is a conduit through which the returned value is delivered. The server may not know what object is awaiting the value at the receiving end of the conduit. Variations of by-value mechanisms give some means of explicitly manipulating their end of the conduit to either the client alone, the server alone, or possibly both. For example, the server may be able to pass its end of the conduit to another server as would be desired in programming the coordinator in the coordinator-worker problem. Alternatively, the client may have some ability to pass its end of the conduit to another object to whom the client is obligated to deliver a value. The second form of explicit return is by destination. In this case the identity of the client is explicitly visible to the server. It may be possible that a client may provide a return identity other than its own or a server may be programmed to deliver its result to a known destination other than the client.

Two alternative approaches to explicit by-value returns are futures and Cboxes. The essential differences between these approaches are:

1. A single future is directly associated with an invocation whereas any number of Cboxes can be created and passed as arguments of an invocation.
2. The future associated with an invocation is not visible to the server whereas Cboxes are visible to the server.
3. The future can only be given a value by a return in the server whereas the Cbox can be given a value before the server returns or after the server returns (by another object).

The code fragments in Figure 6.5 illustrate the use of futures and Cbox styles of explicit returns.

As shown in Figure 6.5(a), the future variable is created in conjunction with an invocation. The client proceeds with its execution until an evaluation of the future is attempted. The client will block only under the condition that the server has not already returned, thus supplying the value to the future. It should be observed that the future variable is not visible to the server. The case of Cboxes, shown in Figure 6.5(b), differs from futures in two ways. First, the Cbox is visible to the server as an explicit argument and, second, more than one Cbox can be associated with an invocation. Also, part (c) of Figure 6.5 shows that the immediate server (function g) may delegate all or a portion of its Cboxes to other servers. In the example shown in part (c), function g delegates to function h the responsibility for providing a value for the Cbox v2.

Additional factors related to futures are whether the future is first class and whether it is typed. To be first class means that a future variable may be passed as an argument without forcing its evaluation. The undesired evaluation of a future can occur because the formal

(a)

```
    future v = f(arg1,...argn);          //invocation of f
    ...                                  //execute concur-
rently with f
    integer i = v;                       //block until re-
sult available
```

(b)

```
    Cbox v1, v2;                         //client creates Cboxes
    g(args1,...,argsn,v1,v2);            // Cboxes passed as arguments
    ...
    integer i = v1;                      //block until value in v1
    ...
    integer j = v2;                      //block until value in v2
```

(c)

```
    function g(arg1,...,argn,v1, v2);

    {    ...
        v1 = value;                      //give value to Cbox v1
        ...
        h(args, v2);                     //delegate v2 to function h
    }
```

FIGURE 6.5   Future and Cbox usage.

parameter is expecting a realized value (such as an integer) and not a potential value (such as a future integer). The forced evaluation of the future, unfortunately, limits the usability of the future because its scope of effect is limited to the method in which it is created. The other factor related to futures is whether the future is typed, that is whether the type of the potential value is included as part of the type of the future itself. For example, a future that will provide an integer value may be typed as a "future integer" or more weakly as an untyped future.

The discussion of the interaction model is concluded by mentioning two other related issues. The first issue, naming, is straightforward. The question here is how the client and the server are identified to each other for the purpose of an invocation. The three alternatives are:

Symmetric, as in CSP, the client and the server must each name the other.
Asymmetric, the client must name the server but the server need not name the client.
Anonymous, neither the client nor the server name each other explicitly.

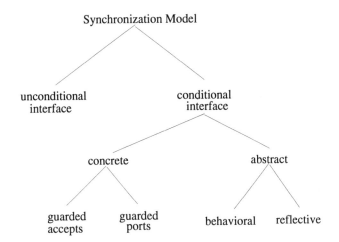

FIGURE 6.6   The synchronization model.

The most common usage is asymmetric. The second issue is whether the language is statically typed. Type conformance in object-oriented languages is a deep issue. As concurrency adds little to this issue, it is simply noted here as a factor without further comment.

6.2.3   The Synchronization Model

The third element of the object model, the *synchronization model*, is the most intricate and the most interesting of the three models considered in this review. The framework of the synchronization model, shown in Figure 6.6, closely parallels that of Papathomas [24], though some terminology and organization has been changed.

The synchronization model considers what, if any, controls are imposed over concurrent invocations impinging on a given object. Invocation control is considered a synchronization issue because it involves the management of concurrent operations so as to preserve some semantic property of the object being acted upon. As with other synchronization problems, those invocations that are attempted at inappropriate times are subject to delay. Typically, the internal "state" of the receiving object dictates which subset of invocations is permitted to occur at a given time. Postponed invocations are those that would invalidate desired properties of the internal state. The need for this form of synchronization should be clear: guarantees of many semantic properties cannot be made in the absence of guarantees about the internal state of the object. Notice that only interobject concurrency is involved; intra-object concurrency, if it is permitted, must be synchronized by some other means that are not discussed further in this paper.

The two basic alternatives in the synchronization model are between an unconditional interface and a conditional interface. An unconditional interface implies that invocations are free to occur without regard for the condition of the receiving object. Notice that the application developer cannot prevent an invocation from occurring, the developer can only attempt to control the progress of the invocation already begun. For this purpose, a locking mechanism or condition variables are usually provided. A monitor is an example of an unconditional interface. The unconditional interface approach inevitably extracts a price by increasing the internal complexity of the object. Furthermore, the code added to achieve the synchronization runs afoul of the inheritance anomaly (discussed in Section 6.4), which limits the use of inheritance to specialize the synchronization control. A conditional interface is one in which an invocation is subject to postponement until its execution is compatible with the state of the object. In this case the object boundary is exploited as a synchronizing barrier. Synchronization is achieved by manipulating the object's boundary. The interesting question, of course, is how such manipulation is carried out.

Two different approaches to creating a conditional interface can be distinguished: concrete and abstract. Each of these approaches creates a connection between a pending invocation and the internal state of the object. These approaches differ in how the state of the object is determined, the variety of information available about the object state and the invocation, and the mechanisms employed to achieve the synchronization.

In the *concrete* case the internal state of the object is determined by direct interrogation of the object's state variables. Tests made on the internal state determine which invocations to permit. The two identifiable forms of concrete state testing are guarded accepts and guarded ports.

In the guarded-accept approach a monolithic, multiway, conditional, nondeterministic, fair selection is used. Examples of this approach are the guarded select in CSP and the select construct in Ada. Such constructs are monolithic because they are an integral whole—all of the alternatives are required to be expressed at the same place in the object. The construct is multiway and conditional meaning that any number of alternatives may be expressed and each alternative may present a condition whose truth value determines whether this alternative is available for selection. The conditions are propositions over the object's state variables. The selection is nondeterministic to deal with the case where more than one alternative is possible at a given time. Finally, the construct is usually defined to be "fair" in its selections so that a pending and selectable invocation is eventually allowed to proceed.

The subtle disadvantage of a guarded accept, implied by its monolithic nature, is that it interferes with the inheritance mechanism in two ways. To illustrate the first form of interference, consider an object definition that is based on a guarded-accept construct. Now consider the problem of creating a new object definition from the existing one by inheritance. Since the guarded accept is monolithic, the subclass must provide its own guarded accept for all methods (its own new or redefined methods in addition to all of the inherited methods). Such necessity is contrary to the intent of inheritance to provide an incremental definition. It is precisely this incremental definition of the concurrency control that is lost by the guarded accept. The second form of interference is a weakening of encapsulation. Since the inheriting definition must completely reestablish the guarded accept, it must have extensive knowledge of the existing definition's state variables in order to properly form the guarded accept's conditions.

In the guarded-port approach an invocation is placed in a port associated with the method being invoked. Each such port may be opened or closed depending on tests made of the object's state variables. The statements to open or close any port may be placed in any method of the object. For example, consider a bounded buffer object with methods named put and get, which are associated with ports of the same name. At creation only the object's put port is opened. If the buffer contains at least one element and is not full, both the put and get ports would be opened. Finally, if the buffer becomes full, the put port is closed.

The guarded-port approach is more flexible than the guarded-accept approach because it is not monolithic. However, this does not completely remove the defects in inheritability and encapsulation cited earlier for guarded accepts. These defects persist because the code to manipulate the ports is intimately interwoven with the code to perform the manipulation of the object's state. There is no clear separation between these two distinct, but related, aspects of the object. As with the example of guarded accepts, an inheriting definition might need to have extensive knowledge of the existing definition's state variables and port names in order to add or redefine a method. Such knowledge would be required because the new or redefined method's action of opening or closing ports has an obvious affect on the other inherited methods.

The second major kind of conditional interface is termed *abstract* to reflect the fact that some abstraction exists to separate the synchronization aspects of the object from its functional aspects. The separation thus achieved overcomes the difficulties seen above with inheritability and encapsulation. In one approach, termed *behavioral*, the abstraction is based on a description of the object's behavior expressed as a subset of currently available methods. In the other approach, termed *reflective*, an abstraction of the object's underlying execution mechanism is exposed to explicit manipulation.

In the behavioral case an object is seen as projecting a time-varying interface to its potential clients. At different times, a client observes different interfaces being projected by the server depending on the server's current condition. The projected interface changes in accordance with changes in the internal state of the object. The internal state of the object and its projected interface are linked through state-testing predicates that are programmed or are available implicitly. Synchronization is achieved by an enforcement mechanism that guarantees that an invocation is suspended until the projected interface contains the method named in the invocation. Thus, no invocation can occur when the server is in a state that is incompatible with the invocation. The term *behavioral* is used because this view of an object is similar to the notion of observable behavior used in CCS [20] and other similar theories of concurrency. Each projected interface is a subset of the maximal statically defined interface of the server. In this way the usual static type-checking rules can be applied.

In the reflective approach, the execution of an object is open to inspection and alteration by a "meta-object." In the general case, the meta-object is itself an object that can be inspected and altered by a meta-meta-object, and so on. This general reflective mechanism can be used for object synchronization by placing the synchronizing aspect of an object in that object's meta-object. For example, whenever the object is the target of an invocation, the meta-object inspects the state of the receiving object and alters the execution of the object as necessary. If the meta-object's inspection indicates that the object is in an inappropriate state for the invocation to occur, the invocation may be preserved for later execution. When the object finishes the execution of a method, the meta-object again intervenes and determines if there are any postponed invocations that are now compatible with the state of the object. Since the meta-object has access to the structure of the object, the meta-object can perform the state testing necessary to determine whether an invocation is compatible with the object's state.

6.3

A SURVEY OF SEVERAL LANGUAGES

In this section a variety of concurrent object-oriented languages are briefly described. The description of each language is related to the element of the object model presented in the previous section. In most cases, example programs are shown to illustrate significant language features. The authors readily admit that this set of example languages is limited in two ways. First, space limitations preclude the inclusion of all concurrent object-oriented languages. Languages have been included that are well known, known by the authors, or possess an interesting set of features or an interesting approach. Second, each language is only briefly described and justice is certainly not done to the language as a whole, particularly for rich or complex languages. This survey should be viewed as only highlighting certain features of each language.

6.3.1   ACT++

While the ACT++ framework for concurrent object-oriented programming and, in particular the concurrency control mechanism used in ACT++ will be presented in the next section, a brief description is given here for comparison purposes.

ACT++ is a class hierarchy developed in C++. This hierarchy provides the programmer with abstractions for concurrent programming based on the *actor model* of computation [1]. An application in the actor model comprises a number of actors—autonomous agents that execute concurrently and reactively in response to the arrival of messages. Message passing is one-way and asynchronous. An actor has a mail queue to hold messages that have been received but not yet processed. An actor has a distinguished current behavior that processes one of the queued mail messages. At some point in its execution the current behavior establishes a *replacement* behavior to processes another message from its queue. The replacement behavior is established by a *become* operation. It is possible to use the become operation so that the current and the replacement behaviors execute concurrently, by executing the become operation before the current behavior finishes. Alternatively, by placing the become operation at the end of the execution of the current behavior, a serial execution is enforced. In addition to the become operation, an actor may send messages and create new actors. The ACT++ framework provides classes for the basic elements of this model: actor, behavior, message, and their associated operations.

In terms of the language taxonomy presented in the previous section, ACT++ uses a related approach in the animation model; threads are only permitted to execute within the boundary of an actor. ACT++ was intended to be used to define homogeneous objects. However, there are two ways in which heterogeneous objects may be used. First, a behavior may internally implement some number of passive objects. Second, since ACT++ is based on

C++ it is possible to define passive objects that are passed among actors or that are operated on concurrently by several actors. It should be noted, however, that this second case falls outside of the scope of the intended model of computation. The multiplicity employed by ACT++ is the actor form of concurrency. In terms of the interaction model, ACT++ uses asynchronous invocations, and results are conveyed explicitly though Cboxes. Finally, in the synchronization model, ACT++ uses a behavioral form of an abstract conditional interface through a mechanism called *behavior sets*.

While a more complete example is given in Section 4, a brief example of bounded buffer behavior is given in Figure 6.7. In this example, only the skeleton of the synchronization code is shown. The *bounded buffer* class contains three behavior sets initialized by the constructor to contain (the address of) the `in` method, the `out` method and both of these methods. Two state testing functions named `empty` and `full` are defined to determine the buffer's condition. The key aspect of the synchronization technique is the `nextBehavior` method. The `nextBehavior` method uses the state testing functions to select among the three defined behavior sets. Using the `become` method (defined in the class `Actor`), the selected behavior set is used to control the selection of the next message accepted by the actor, namely the next accepted message must be invoking a function named (by its address) in the current behavior set. A more complete description of this mechanism is given in Section 6.4.

6.3.2 ABCL

ABCL is the name given to a family of languages. Only the features of *ABCL/1* [30] are described here. Like ACT++, ABCL/1 is an actor-based language. All objects are homogeneous and each object may be described as serialized; its execution is sequential, or unserialized, meaning that it may be executed concurrently without restriction. In this way, ABCL/1 supports two forms of multiplicity both of which may be used in a single program. The underlying interaction model of ABCL/1 is asynchronous message passing with an explicit form of return. However, syntactic structuring allows a variety of other forms to be used. For example, while the basic form of interaction is asynchronous, the syntax of the language allows the programmer to discriminate three variations of invocations: *past type*, which is strictly asynchronous; *now type*, which is a synchronous send; *future type*, in which a future variable is passed as part of the invocation. Two variations of the explicit return are supported in the language. The first form is of the future variety. In this case the sender specifies a future variable as part of the invocation and this is pattern matched in the server as a vehicle for delivering the reply. The second form is of the destination variety. Thus, an invocation message bears a reply point indicating to what object the result should be delivered. The reply point is available to the server object as a pattern-matched variable. The language allows the programmer the flexibility of using an implicit form of return, in which the default reply destination (the reply destination specified by the sender) is used. The synchronization model used in the original ABCL/1 language was a guarded-accept form. A select statement allowed queued messages to be pattern matched against the alternatives of the select. One of the messages satisfying a pattern matching would be selected for execution. It should also be noted that a later variant, named ABCL/R [28], uses a reflective form

```
class BoundedBuffer : Behavior {
...
protected:    // instance variables and methods visi-
ble to subclasses

    BehaviorSet B0, Bn, Bi;

    virtual bool empty(){...}
    virtual bool full() {...}

    virtual BehaviorSet nextBehavior() {
        if (empty())
           return B0;
        else if (full())
          return Bn;
        else
          return Bi;
    }

public:    // methods visible to subclasses and clients

    void in(T x) {
        ...
        become nextBehavior();
    }

    T out() {
        ...
        become nextBehavior();
    }

    BoundedBuffer() {    // construct initial "empty" object
        ...
        B0 = &in; Bn = &out; Bi = B0 + Bn;
    }
};
```

FIGURE 6.7   A bounded buffer in ACT++.

of synchronization control. Two other minor observations about ABCL are the following. First, inheritance is not supported in the base language. Instead a form of task delegation is used. Second, messages may be sent in either normal mode or express mode. *Express-mode* messages provide a means of interrupting the normal processing of a message by a server. This useful facility is lacking in most other concurrent object-oriented languages. An example of ABCL/1 is shown in Figure 6.8. In this example a three-element buffer is created and its use by a producer and consumer are illustrated. Note that an object consists of a *state part* (private data of the object) and a *script part* (the methods or operations defined by

```
[object Buffer3
    (state [ s= (create-storage 3)])
    (script
        (=>[:put aProduct]
            (if (full? s) then
                (select
                    (=>[:get]
                        ! (fetch s))))
            (store aProduct s)
            ! "done" )

        (=> [:get] ...
    )
]

[Buffer3 <==[:put aValue]]        ; use by producer

[x := [Buffer3 <== [:get]]]       ; use by consumer
```

FIGURE 6.8   A three-element buffer in ABCL/1.

the object). In the put method the use of the select construct can be seen. When the buffer is full, an arriving put method cannot be executed. Thus, the select construct is executed to await the arrival of a get method that will create empty space in the buffer. After such a get method has been executed, the put method can be resumed to store the provided value in the buffer. The Hybrid language and runtime system [21] employs homogeneous active objects that use a monitor-style form of multiplicity. Recall that this allows an object to have at most one active thread at a time from among several threads that may execute within the object at different points in time. A mechanism called a domain provides additional structuring of objects and threads. A domain is viewed as a *top-level* object that may encapsulate several lower-level objects. It is the domain that is subject to the monitor-style control of thread execution. By implication, this restriction extends to all of the objects within a domain. Hybrid uses a synchronous form of invocation with implicit return. However, to gain needed flexibility, the language also defines a *delegated* form of invocation. In a delegated invocation, the thread of the client is suspended until the server returns. While the client thread is suspended, another thread within the same domain as the client may be scheduled for execution. When the server returns, the client thread is unblocked and will be scheduled to resume its execution at some time when its domain is idle. The synchronization model used by Hybrid is that of guarded ports, which are termed delay queues. Each operation of an object may be associated with a delay queue. An operation can only be invoked when its delay queue is open. The opening and closing of delay queues is done by code within the object's methods.

The synchronization aspects of Hybrid are illustrated in the example shown in Figure 6.9. This example shows the familiar bounded buffer. The abstract part of the type description declares that invocations of put and get operations are controlled by a delay queue. The name of the delay queue is not relevant in the abstract type description. In the private part of the type definition two specific delay queues, putDelay and getDelay, are created. The

```
type boundedBuffer : abstract {
    init: ->;
    put: string ->; uses delay;
    get: -> string; uses delay
};
private {
    var putDelay, getDelay : delay;
    ...

    init: ->;
    { ...
        putDelay.open();
        getDelay.close();
    }

    get:-> string; uses getDelay;
    { ... get an item
        if buffer is now empty
            putDelay.close();
        getDelay.open();
    ... }

    put: string ->; uses putDelay;
    { ... insert an item
        if buffer is now full
            putDelay.close();
        getDelay.open();
    ... }
};
```

FIGURE 6.9   Use of delay queues in Hybrid.

init method opens the putDelay queue (thus allowing the put method to be invoked) and closes the getDelay queue (thus forbidding a get method to be invoked as the first operation of the bounded buffer). The put method opens the getDelay queue (as a get method is now possible) and possibly closes the putDelay method when the buffer is full (to prevent the buffer from overflowing).

6.3.3   Procol

The *Procol* language [16, 27] incorporates a wide variety of interesting features including constraints and object persistence. The brief survey given here cannot do justice to the full scope of this language.

Objects in Procol are sequential and homogeneous. Two kinds of methods may be specified for an object: *actions* and *intactions*. Actions are normal methods or operations. An intaction has the capability of interrupting the execution of an action. In this case the thread executing the action is suspended, the intaction is executed and the suspended action

```
Obj         STACK(int length)

Declare     int n, element, *array;

Protocol    (n<length-1) : ANY(element) -> Push +
            (n>0)        : ANY           -> Pop

Init        n = 0;
            array = (int*)malloc(length*sizeof(int));

Cleanup     free((char*) array);

Actions     Pop = { n=n-1; send sender.(array[n]);}
            Push= { array[n] = element; n=n+1; }

Endobj      STACK
```

FIGURE 6.10   A protocol declaration in Procol.

thread is then resumed. An intaction itself may not be interrupted by another intaction. Intactions are similar to express messages in ABCL/1.

Objects communicate through two message-passing operations. A one-way asynchronous send operation is provided along with a synchronous request operation. The later operation is used when a return value is expected. To provide flexibility to the server, a form of delegated send is also included in the language. Similar to delegation in Hybrid and other languages, a delegated send allows the server to transfer to another object the responsibility for providing the return value needed by the client. One interesting feature of the send operation is that the target (the object to receive the message) may be indirectly named by specifying only the type of the target, not an instance of this type. In this case the message is delivered to any one instance of the specified type.

Return values are handled by an explicit form in which the server specifies the destination to which the result is to be sent. The common case is expressed as send sender. (result) in which the sender is evaluated by the runtime mechanism to yield the identity of the original requesting/sending client. The identity of the originating client is preserved through delegated calls.

Finally, Procol uses a behavioral form of an abstract conditional interface. The object definition specifies a *protocol* that defines the conditions under which its actions may be invoked. A protocol may use both expressions and guards. An expression, similar to the familiar path expression, is formed by combining actions names with the operators for composition (||), selection (+), sequencing (;), and repetition (*). Preceding an expression may appear a guard (denoted by an action name followed by a colon). A guard may use state variables of the object to form a *guarding predicate*.

An example of a Procol object with a protocol is given in Figure 6.10. The protocol of the object specifies:

1. The Push action can be invoked only if the stack is not full (the guard $n < length - 1$ is true) and a message from ANY client is requesting this operation.

2. The Pop operation can be invoked only if the stack is not empty (the guard $n > 0$ is true) and a message from ANY client is requesting this operation.

The authors of Procol draw special attention to the clear separation between the specification of the protocol and the definition of the actions.

6.3.4 Pool-T

The *Pool* family of languages was developed specifically to support parallel programming. Philosophically the languages in this family are designed to be small, compact, cohesive languages with well-understood interactions among their features.

In *Pool-T* [3] all entities are objects, all objects are sequential, and all objects communicate with each other via synchronous message passing. As is usually the case with synchronous invocations, the receiver of a server's return value is known implicitly by the server. One minor exception to the use of synchronous message passing allows an object to communicate with itself (that is, invoke one of its own methods) through a simple function call. The exception is necessary to avoid self-deadlock when using the selective message acceptance mechanism described later.

Unlike many other concurrent object-oriented languages, Pool-T objects are *active* and not *reactive*. That is, a Pool-T object may execute without the need to be enlivened by an arriving message. Each object has a *body* part that begins executing when the object is created. The body, at its own discretion, may choose to block in order to allow an invocation of one of its methods to occur. Since all objects are sequential, the body of an object and one of the object's methods cannot execute concurrently. When the body wishes to allow an invocation, the body executes an *answer* statement that names a list of methods. A single invocation of a method named in the answer's list is selected for execution. For additional flexibility, an Ada-like select construct also exists. This allows conditions to be associated with the acceptance of an invocation for a method. Thus, the synchronization model used in Pool-T is the guarded-accept form of a concrete, conditional interface.

The following are two minor observations about Pool-T. First, a server may *return*, thereby unblocking the client and yet continue in the same method to complete post-processing actions in parallel with the resumed client. Second, passive objects may be created by declaring an object with no body. In this case a default body is supplied. The default body simply accepts messages in sequential order.

6.3.5 ESP

The extensible system platform (ESP) [17] was develop at the Microelectronics and Computer Technology Corporation (MCC) as the software component of a research effort to develop flexible hardware and software components for building parallel systems. One of the major design goals of ESP was to retain as much as possible the syntax and semantics of C++ programming in ESP. Ideally, the parallelism of ESP would be transparent to the application developer. The ESP system is most appropriately used for distributed-memory machines as it employs a medium-grain concurrency and fairly substantial kernel for object management and messaging.

In ESP all objects are homogeneous. However, as with several other concurrent extensions to C++ (for example, ACT++), an ESP object may define, as part of its local state information, arbitrarily complex passive C++ entities. ESP objects are sequential. Concurrency in ESP, therefore, arises from the concurrent execution of different objects on different machines. By using the *placement syntax* of the C++ new operation, the programmer is given the ability to control or influence the placement of objects on the nodes constituting the execution environment. The programmer is able to specify the exact node on which the created object must run, specify that the object must (or must not) execute on the same node as another object, or specify that the object may execute on any node, thus allowing the system's load balancing strategy to decide on the object's placement.

The interaction model in ESP provides an asynchronous invocation mechanism matched with a future style of return by-value. Both of these promote higher levels of concurrent execution. The futures, however, are not first-class. An attempt to pass a future as an argument results in blocking until the value of the future is available. This form of future is more limited than that available in Eifell// or Mentat (both described later). However, ESP provides flexible ways of manipulating futures through a *future set*. As implied by the name, the programmer may create a set of future variables associated with invocations that are in progress. It is then possible, for example, to await the availability of any one of the futures in the future set or await all of their availability.

The synchronization model in ESP is based on a technique called *method locking* that allows an object to lock or unlock its methods. When locked, a method cannot be invoked. Messages that would cause the invocation of a locked method are held pending in the object's mail queue until the method is unlocked. This form of synchronization falls in the category of a guarded-port style of concrete, conditional interface.

6.3.6 Ellie

A distinguishing aspect of the *Ellie* language [4] is the pervasive use of fine-grain concurrency matched with a strategy for compile-time grain adaptation. The aim of grain size adaptation is to allow the compiler to aggregate several fine-grain concurrent objects into one larger grain object in order to achieve more efficient execution on the target architecture. This approach confronts directly the phenomenon that different machine architectures support different grain sizes with varying efficiencies. For example, a massively parallel shared-memory architecture will work better with fine grain objects than with large-grain objects while the reverse is true for a distributed-memory parallel machine or a distributed collection of workstations. The goal of Ellie is to allow the programmer to describe the solution to the problem while leaving the details of the grain size selection to the compiler. It remains to be seen how completely this goal can be achieved.

In Ellie, as in Pool-T, all entities are objects. Each object has a single associated process. Thus, Ellie is a homogeneous, sequential related object model. The language differentiates between functions (methods that have no side effects), and operations (methods that may have side effects). This distinction allows immutable objects to be recognized and used efficiently in a parallel environment as the immutable object may be freely copied.

Invocations in Ellie are synchronous. The value return mechanism distinguishes between *bounded processes* that act like a synchronous invocation and *unbounded processes* that act like a future. A bounded process is created to execute a method that is a regular function or method. Invocations of methods declared as *future functions* or *future operations* cause the creation of unbounded processes. Thus, the interaction model used in Ellie is synchronous and provides an explicit return mechanism through futures.

Delegation is also provided in Ellie through a mechanism called *interface inclusion*. The following example is provided in [4]:

```
export local1, (local2), (local3).(remote1, remote2)
```

When given as the export interface of object *X*, the above declaration implies that the interface of *X* is taken to be the union of:

1. The locally defined name `local1`.
2. The names that are accessible in the locally defined object `local2`.
3. The two names `remote1` and `remote2` defined in the object bound to the local name `local3`.

Since the binding to the local names may be altered by the program's execution, the interface may be implemented at different times by different objects.

The Ellie synchronization model provides an abstract conditional interface via a form of behavioral specification. An object may have an *accept interface* that is dynamically alterable by the object's operations. Note that this is different than the dynamic aspect of the *export interface*. The export interface is constant over time, only its implementation may vary; the accept interface changes with time, including or removing methods from the interface as determined by the state of the object.

An example of an accept interface is given in Figure 6.11. A semaphore object is defined with an accept interface of `accept wait, signal;`. In each method, the `include` statement defines a new accept interface. (The `include` statment is misleading since it does not add the specified names to the accept interface; but rather its defines a new accept interface). Thus, when the integer `val` reaches zero, the `wait` operation is removed from the accept interface. When a method's name is not in the current accept interface, processes trying to invoke that operation are suspended. Therefore, when `val` is zero, processes trying to execute a `wait` method will be delayed in accordance with the usual understanding of a semaphore. When a `signal` operation is performed, so that `val` has the value one, the `wait` operation is reinserted into the accept interface. A process suspended on the `wait` method would now find the method available in the interface and its invocation could then be initiated.

6.3.7 Sina

The *Sina* language [5, 26] makes straightforward choices in its animation and interaction models. Invocations in Sina are synchronous with an implicit return. In the animation model, all objects are uniformly active. The language, however, is somewhat ambivalent in its position on multiplicity. By default the Sina preprocessor generates only sequential objects. However, the user may override this default, in which case all objects have unrestricted

```
semaphore
  : [function <: value :- integer :> self;
    accept wait, signal;

    wait :: [operation;
        val <- value - 1;
            option [
                if : val = 0;
                then : [ include [ signal :: any]]
            ]
        ]

    signal :: [operation;
        val <- val + 1;
            option [
                if : val = 1;
                then : [include [wait, signal :: any]]
            ]
        ]
  ];
```

FIGURE 6.11   Controlling the accept interface in Ellie objects.

concurrency. The language thus offers both of the two extreme choices in this factor. Note, however, that these two alternatives cannot be combined in a single application.

The most interesting aspect of Sina is its synchronization model that uses a technique called *composition filters*. The basic concept is that a message is subject to screening by any number of filters. The filters are applied in an order determined by the object's definition. An invocation occurs only when a message passes through all of the filters defined for the target object. A filter is created out of conditions and predicates over the state variables of the object. Thus, Sina synchronization falls into the behavioral class of an abstract conditional interface.

The composition-filters mechanism will be explained by reference to the example in Figure 6.12, which shows the definition of a synchronized stack. First, note that the object definition is divided into an interface part and an implementation part as indicated by the keywords. In the interface specification, the keyword internals introduces private data members of the class. An instance of a predefined unsynchronized class named Stack is declared as a private member of the SyncStack class. The keyword conditions introduces named condition variables. The implementation of these conditions is given in the implementation part. In this example the NonEmpty condition is defined in terms of the size of the internal inStack member. The Inputfilters keyword introduces the filters to be applied to incoming messages. In this example there are two input filters. The first input filter is named sync and is of type Wait. This filter declares that the pop method can only be invoked when the NonEmpty condition is true; all other methods except pop can be invoked at any time. The second input filter is named disp and is of type Dispatch. This is a predefined type of filter that indicates that all of the methods of the inStack

```
class SyncStack interface

    internals
        inStack: Stack;

    conditions
        NonEmpty;

    Inputfilters
        sync:Wait={NonEmpty=>pop; True=>*\pop};
        disp:Dispatch={inStack.*};

end;

class SyncStack Implementation
    ...
    conditions
        NonEmpty:
            begin return inStack.size>0; end;
    ...
end;
```

FIGURE 6.12   Example of Sina composition-filters.

member may be invoked. A filter of type `Dispatch` is used to indicate that any message that succeeds in reaching this filter may be invoked.

Sina also allows synchronization counters to be included in the definition of filters. The standard object model defines a number of such counters including dispatched, completed, and received, which indicate how many messages are in each of these states.

6.3.8   Presto

Presto [6] is a C++-based framework for parallel programming of shared-memory multi-processors. The goal of Presto is to provide low-level mechanisms for developers to create specialized, domain-specific abstractions. One kind of *developer* experiments with various concurrent programming models that are more highly structured than is Presto itself. That Presto has had some success in achieving this goal is evidenced by the ACT++ system described earlier, which is implemented using Presto. Thus, Presto is in the unrelated class in the animation model in keeping with its role as a low-level, neutral base.

In terms of the interaction model, both synchronous and asynchronous invocations are possible. The synchronous style of invocation is that of the base C++ language. The asynchronous form of invocation is provided via the threads management facilities. Figure 6.13(a) shows the basic facility of asynchronous invocation. In this example a stack, S, is created. Also created is a thread, t, that will asynchronously execute the push method on object S. The single argument of the push operation is the integer value 43. Notice that the argument list cannot be type-checked against the definition of the push method.

```
(a)

    Stack *S = new Stack(100);
    Thread *t = new Thread("pusher", TID);
    t->start(S, S->push, 43);

(b)

    class Matrix {
    ...
    public:
        ...
        multiply(Matrix* M) {
            Matrix *P = new Matrix(ma`rows, m->numcolums());
            for(int i = 0; i < ma`rows; i++)
                for(int j = 0; j < M->numcolums(); j++) {
                    Thread *t = new Thread("multiplier");
                    t->start(this, this-
>ma`dotproduct, &(P[i][j],M,i,j);
                }
            ... wait for thread to terminat
            return P;
    }
    };
```

FIGURE 6.13   **Presto thread operations.**

Notice also that the implementation of the stack is unaware of the fact that it is being in-voked asynchronously. Figure 6.13(b) illustrates how multiple threads can be created to perform matrix multiplication. In this usage, the `Matrix::multiply` method creates concurrency, which is transparent to the client. Also observe that the multiply method can be invoked either synchronously or asynchronously without any change to the `Matrix` class itself. Finally, return values are handled implicitly. For an asynchronous invocation, a thread `join` operation is provided, by which the return value can be extracted from a thread previously started in some method.

The Presto synchronization model is an unconditional interface. To provide basic mech-anisms for creating more structured interface semantics, Presto provides primitive locks and a monitor-style set of facilities. These basic synchronization tools allow low-level control of the invocation process to be created. This is possible since the threads facility is implemented as a C++ class that can be subclassed to create other forms of asynchronous invocations. Alternatively, a thread may be created only when an invocation has been accepted, rather than when the invocation is initiated. This later strategy is used in the ACT++ system.

6.3.9   Guide

Guide [15] is a language developed for the programming of distributed applications that manipulate permanent data. The language and an operating system (also called Guide) were developed at the University of Grenoble. Aside from the features explicitly considered below, Guide provides a separation between the type hierarchy and the class (implementation) hierarchy, distribution transparency, and automatic persistence.

Like Presto, Guide falls in the unrelated class in the animation model. A distinction is drawn between passive, persistent objects and the execution vehicles, called *jobs* and *activities*. A job represents the execution of an application that consists of several activities. Activities are created by means of a simple cobegin-coend construct.

The interaction model provides synchronous invocations and implicit returns. The Guide programming paradigm is one in which jobs or activities operate directly on passive objects and, if communication or synchronization is desired, coordination is achieved through shared passive objects. The shared passive objects are provided with synchronization mechanisms to safeguard their internal consistency in the face of concurrent invocations.

The synchronization model of Guide is a behavioral form of an abstract conditional interface. A passive object may regulate the sequence of invocation that it accepts through the specification of a control clause. The control clause may name one or more methods defined in the object and, for each method, list an *activation condition*. The activation condition is a predicate that must be true in order for the method with which it is associated to be invoked. The activation condition may refer to instance variables defined in the object, the actual parameters contained in the invocation, and special *activation counters*. The activation counters, similar to those defined in Sina, provide counts of the following for each method: the number of invocations of the method, the number of accepted invocations of the method, and the number of completed executions of the method. Other conditions may be defined in terms of these basic ones.

An example of the use of the Guide mechanisms is shown in Figure 6.14. In this example the implementation of a typical bounded buffer is given. The interesting aspect of this example is the control clause at the end of the class definition. This clause specifies constraints on the invocations of both the Put and Get methods. The activation condition associated with the Put method states that the number of complete Put invocations (each adding an element to the buffer) cannot exceed by more than the size of the buffer the number of complete Get invocations (each removing an element from the buffer). Furthermore, the activation condition also insist that no Put methods are executing concurrently. The activation condition for the Get method requires that the buffer is not empty (i.e., that more Put invocations have completed than Get invocations).

6.3.10   Eiffel//

The primary goal of *Eiffel//* [8], a concurrent extension to the Eiffel language, is to achieve performance improvements with as few changes as possible to an application developed as a nonconcurrent Eiffel system. This goal is similar to that of ESP, which retains the programming model of C++ but allows for transparent distributed execution. In Eiffel//, class inheritance is used extensively to achieve its goals.

In terms of the animation model, Eiffel// uses a related approach that is homogeneous and sequential. The language is classified as homogeneous because, even though both active and passive objects are permitted, passive objects are required to be private objects of a single

```
CLASS FixedSizeBuffer IMPLEMENTS ProducerConsumer IS
    CONST size = <some constant>;
        buffer: ARRAY[0..size-1] OF Element;
        first, last: Integer = 0,0;

    METHOD Put (IN m : Element);
        BEGIN
            ... code for Put method
        END;

    METHOD Get (OUT m: Element);
        BEGIN
            ... code for Get method
        END;

    CONTROL
        Put: (completed(Put)-completed(Get) < size)
            AND current(Put) = 0);

        Get: (completed(Put) > completed(Get)
            AND current(Get) = 0;

END FixedSizeBuffer;
```

FIGURE 6.14   Synchronization of a passive object in Guide.

active object. This restriction is similar to that in ACT++. In Eiffel//, passive objects are passed among active objects only by value (for example, by a deep copy). Each active object is a member of a class derived from the predefined base class PROCESS. A distinguished method, Live, is provided by the PROCESS class, but may be redefined in a subclass. The Live method, automatically invoked when the object is created, defines the script or code for the active object. The default Live method accepts messages in FIFO order.

In terms of the invocation model, the language uses asynchronous invocations and returns values by a mechanism termed *wait by necessity*. This return mechanism is an explicit return by-value in the style of futures. As in other future mechanisms, an invocation immediately yields an *awaited object*. An attempt to access the value of an awaited object causes the accessing process to block. A powerful aspect of Eiffel// is that the awaited object can be passed as an argument or assigned to another object without blocking. Only the explicit attempt to obtain the value of the awaited object causes blocking to occur.

The synchronization model provided by Eiffel// is an interesting one and is similar in many respects to the behavior set concept in ACT++, which is detailed in the next section of this paper. The technique employed in Eiffel// is that of a behavioral form of an abstract, conditional interface. The key concept in Eiffel// is that both *routines* (that is, methods) and *requests* (for example, invocations) are first-class objects amenable to manipulation by the provided base classes in Eiffel// and by the application developer. To support the desired synchronization structure, two base classes are provided, ROUTINE and REQUEST.

```
class ABSTRACT`PROCESS
    inherit
        PROCESS redefine Live
    feature
        Live is ...
        associate is ...
        synchronization is do end;
end

class ABST`BUFFER [T]
    export put, get,
    inherit
        FIXED`LIST [T];
        ABSTRACT`PROCESS
            redefine synchronization;
    feature
        synchronization is
          do
            associate (&put, &full);
            associate (&get, &empty);
          end;
end
```

FIGURE 6.15   Synchronization in Eiffel//.

The operator & applied to a routine yields an object of type ROUTINE. Mechanisms are also available to examine the set of REQUEST objects pending at a given object.

Synchronization in Eiffel// is illustrated with reference to the example in Figure 6.15. This figure shows the skeleton of the ABSTRACTPROCESS class, derived from the PRO-CESS base class, and the ABSTBUFFER class derived from both the FIXEDLIST and ABSTRACTPROCESS classes. The key elements in the ABSTRACTPROCESS class are the routines associate and synchronization. The synchronization routine is empty, providing a default FIFO policy defined in the PROCESS class. The associate routine allows two routines to be associated: one routine is a method whose invocation is to be regulated and the second routine is a function that determines (based on the state variables of the object) whether the first method is invocable. For example, the statement associate(&put, &full); indicates that the put routine is not invocable unless the full routine returns false. Similarly, the get routine cannot be invoked unless the empty routine returns false. These routines (get, put, empty, full) are the usual routines defined in the FIXEDLIST class. The key to making this scheme work is that the invocations can be controlled by the receiving object and the invocation control can be modified via inheritance to yield a control that is specialized for the receiving object.

6.3.11   Mentat

Mentat [10] is both a language and runtime system. The Mentat programming language (MPL) is based on C++. The primary goal of Mentat is to allow the same application to be run across different parallel architectures with no changes in the application itself. This goal is achieved by compile-time analysis of the program written in MPL. In this sense Mentat is similar to Ellie in its use of compiler technology to support parallel programming. However, Ellie uses fine-grain concurrency while Mentat uses a courser grain of concurrency. The Mentat compiler translates from MPL into a macro data-flow representation that is then analyzed to discover inherent parallelism. The C++ code generated by the MPL compiler is executed in the Mentat virtual-machine environment. Portability across different machine architectures is achieved by porting the Mentat runtime system. The authors of Mentat report that they regularly write Mentat programs that run unchanged across shared-memory and distributed-memory machines.

The Mentat language takes a homogeneous and concurrent approach in the animation model. Each Mentat object is active and concurrency is achieved both among Mentat objects (interobject concurrency) and, possibly, within Mentat objects (intraobject concurrency). The Mentat compiler, of course, plays a key role in discovering and exploiting such forms of concurrency although interobject concurrency is fairly apparent in the structure of the Mentat program itself.

The interaction model in Mentat uses asynchronous invocations and a value-based form of explicit returns, which is similar to a future. The difference between the Mentat return mechanism and a future is that the future in Mentat is implicit. The programmer simply declares the invocation and names the variable to receive the return value. Since the invocation is asynchronous, the value of the return variable is initially undefined. However, the Mentat compiler generates code that allows the continued execution of the sender until such time as the sender actually needs the return value. In addition, as in Eiffel//, the variable to receive the result value may be passed as an argument or used in an assignment without causing the execution to block. Mentat carefully records all objects that are dependent on the return value. When the invoked method finally returns, via the *return to future* (rtf) primitive, a result value is delivered to all objects awaiting the value.

An important measure of Mentat's success, and for other similar approaches as well, is the speedup that can be obtained across different machine architectures. In [10] the following performance data is reported for Mentat. Two applications, matrix multiply and Gaussian elimination, were run on two different machine architectures, a network of eight Sun workstations and a 32-processor Intel iPSC/2. For the matrix multiply problem of size 400, a maximum speedup of between 6 and 7 was obtained on the Sun workstations and a maximum speedup of between 18 and 20 was obtained on the iPSC/2 for a matrix size of approximately 300. For the Gaussian elimination problem, a maximum speedup of approximately 4 was obtained on the Sun workstations for a matrix of size 500 and a maximum speedup between 12 and 14 was obtained on the iPSC/2 for a matrix of size 350. The Mentat authors acknowledge that better speedup could probably be obtained in each case by specialized programming for each individual architecture. They argue, however, that the simplicity and portability of the Mentat approachis ultimately of higher value especially given the rapid advances in parallel processing architectures and the need to execute applications on different architectures throughout their lifetimes without the substantial cost of reengineering the application for each new architecture.

TABLE 6.1   Language summary.

Language	Related	Multiplicity	Uniformity	Invocations	Reply	Synchronization
ACT++	yes	actor	homogeneous	asynchronous	Cbox	behavioral
ABCL	yes	sequential + concurrent	homogeneous	synchronous + asynchronous	destination + future	guarded accepts
Hybrid	yes	monitor	homogeneous	synchronous + delegated	implicit	guarded ports
Procol	yes	sequential	homogeneous	synchronous + asynchronous + delegated	destination	behavioral
Pool-T	yes	sequential	homogeneous	synchronous	implicit	guarded accepts
ESP	yes	sequential	homogeneous	asynchronous	future	guarded ports
Ellie	yes	sequential	homogeneous	synchronous	future	behavioral
Sina	yes	sequential	homogeneous	synchronous	implicit	behavioral
Presto	no	—	—	synchronous + asynchronous	implicit	unconditional
Guide	no	—	—	synchronous	implicit	behavioral
Eiffel//	yes	sequential	homogeneous	asynchronous	future	behavioral
Mentat	yes	concurrent	homogeneous	asynchronous	future	unconditional

6.3.12   Summary of Language Characteristics

A sumary of the characteristics of the languages surveyed in this section is given in Table 6.1. While there is a rich diversity among these languages, several general observations can be made. First, most of the languages provide or promote a homogeneous and related model, all objects being viewed as active objects where the activity is directly tied to the objects. These similarities are, perhaps, not surprising given that the intent of the language designers was to explore the utility of active objects. Second, most of the languages choose to allow only one thread of control within an object. The conceptual simplicity offered by a sequential choice appears to have been more important than the possible performance advantages to be gained from the alternative of concurrent processing within a single object. Third, there is an even division between languages with synchronous invocations and those with asynchronous invocations, some languages offering both. Given that each form can be used to implement the other, the choice between synchronous and asynchronus appears to have been made on the basis of application domain considerations or personal preference.

Fourth, the handling of return values and the synchronization mechanisms exhibit the most variation of all of the characteristics studied. This variety is natural for two reasons. First, while the implicit form of return is natural for languages with synchronous invocation, languges that use an asynchronous invocation must devise some mechanism for managing to get the returned value to a useful destination. A variety of mechanisms for handling the return value have been invented. Second, the synchronization mechanisms are often the distinguishing research issue underlying the development of the language. These widely different synchronizing methods are motivated, in part, by a search for a solution to the *inheritance anomaly* that is described in more detail in the following section.

6.4

THE INHERITANCE ANOMALY AND ITS SOLUTION IN ACT++

In a concurrent object-oriented language, one would like to be able to inherit behavior and realize synchronization control without compromising the flexibility of either the inheritance mechanism or the synchronization mechanism. A problem called the inheritance anomaly [19] arises when synchronization constraints are implemented within the methods of a class and an attempt is made to specialize methods through inheritance.

In this section, concurrent object behavior is formalized using the equational notation of the CCS [20]. The formalization facilitates a characterization of the fundamental cause of the inheritance anomaly, and leads to the definition of a set of conditions necessary for inheritance and synchronization constraints to coexist in concurrent object-oriented languages.

For those not familiar with the inheritance anomaly, the problem is reviewed in Section 6.4.1. Those familiar with the problem may wish to continue with Section 6.4.2 where the notation of CCS is used to characterize and reason about the behavior of a concurrent object. The characterization results in the definition of the set of conditions necessary to avoid having to reimplement synchronization constraints when specializing a class. Section 6.4.3 demonstrates that the characterization is applicable to real programming problems. Two examples are given that show that behavior sets can be implemented in C++, extended through inheritance, to support actor-style concurrency.

6.4.1   The Inheritance Anomaly

An object is an encapsulation of state and code in the form of instance variables and methods, respectively. In object-oriented languages, the declaration of the types and names of instance variables and the signatures of the methods are typically declared in an explicit class definition. The class definition serves as a contract between objects of that class and clients or subclasses that intend to use instances of the class. A subclass is a specialization of a particular class. Specialization is achieved through the class inheritance mechanism.

In standard object-oriented models, all the methods declared in a class definition are always available for execution by a client regardless of the internal state of an object of that class. The class implementor typically provides, within the implementation of each method, the code necessary to determine whether or not the object is in a state in which execution of the requested method is appropriate.

For example, a stack object with a pop method must first verify that the stack is nonempty before proceeding. Typically, the pop method will return an error value indicating that an underflow condition has occurred. The traditional mechanism for communicating the underflow condition to the client requires an overloading of the return type of the method; that is, the return value is outside the domain of values returned by a legitimate operation. The client of the stack object must be aware of this value and always verify that either the stack is in a state consistent with the required operation or check the return value of each operation. Alternatively, an exception mechanism might be used.

A nonstandard object-oriented model can be defined in which the collection of methods in a class definition are partitioned into subsets with respect to the values of the state variables of an object. Depending on the object state, only a subset of the methods declared in the class definition is available for execution at any one time. In a sequential object-oriented language, an object interface with these semantics may or may not be useful. In a concurrent object-oriented language, an interface mechanism based on such semantics provides a natural and elegant means for expressing synchronization control.

In this section, only concurrent objects that, by necessity, employ some form of synchronization control are of interest. Of particular interest is the specialization of the synchronization constraints defined as part of the representation for such objects. The concurrent behavior of an object is captured in part by the static class definition of the object and in part by the dynamic mechanism employed by the method interface to guarantee synchronization. The *inheritance anomaly* occurs when an attempt is made to specialize concurrent behavior using an inheritance mechanism. The anomaly occurs when a subclass violates the synchronization constraints assumed by the base class. A subclass should have the flexibility to add methods, add instance variables, and redefine inherited methods. Ideally, all the methods of the base class should be reusable. However, if the synchronization constraints are defined by the superclass in a manner prohibiting incremental modification through inheritance, the methods cannot be reused, they must be reimplemented to reflect the new constraints; hence, inheritance is rendered useless. Recent work on the problem has demonstrated that the anomaly occurs across a spectrum of concurrent object-oriented languages, regardless of the type of mechanism employed for specifying synchronization constraints [2, 7, 12]. A deeper issue is that the concurrent object-oriented research community does not yet have a good semantic model that relates the type features and the concurrency features of concurrent object-oriented languages. In the following, the inheritance-synchronization conflict is addressed in a formal way. A formalism is presented that exposes the essential elements of concurrent object behavior and leads to conditions that must exist if the inheritance anomaly is to be avoided.

6.4.2 Defining Concurrent Object Behavior

The behavior of an object is defined by the set of messages that the object will accept at a given point in time; or alternatively, the set of methods that are visible in the interface of the object upon receipt of a message. From this perspective, the behavior of an object is its observable behavior since all that is relevant is how the object appears to those clients that communicate with the object. This notion of observable behavior is motivated by a similar notion described in [20]; however, the machinery of CCS is used here in a superficial manner to characterize the behavior of individual objects, not systems of objects.

In dealing with concurrent objects, the relationship between the state of an object and the subset of methods that define its observable behavior is critical. In order to understand how to implement and then inherit synchronization constraints without encountering the inheritance anomaly, this relationship must be clearly defined.

6.4.3 Specifying Behavior

The behavior of an object may be defined as a set of behavior equations that capture the states of an object and the subset of methods visible when the object is in a particular state. Informally, the "state of an object" is the set of instance variable-value pairs that define the object at a particular step in a computation. As an example, the behavior of an object that maintains some prescribed linear order over a collection of items, whose size is bounded, is defined. The observable behavior of an object representing a bounded linear order is completely described by the following equations:

$$A_0 \stackrel{\text{def}}{=} in(x_1).A_1(x_1)$$
$$A_1(x_1) \stackrel{\text{def}}{=} in(x_2).A_2(x_1, x_2) + \overline{out}(x_1).A_0$$
$$\vdots$$
$$A_n(x_1, \ldots, x_n) \stackrel{\text{def}}{=} \overline{out}(x_1).A_{n-1}(x_1, \ldots, x_{n-1})$$

This set of behavior equations is similar to an example in [20]. The equations capture precisely the states that an object representing a bounded linear order may occupy during its lifetime. In the equations, only the prefix (.) and summation (+) combinators of CCS are required. In each of the equations the name on the left-hand side denotes an agent whose behavior is defined by the right-hand side. Intuitively, agent $A_i(x_1, \ldots, x_i)$ represents the behavior of the object when the size of the collection is i, where $1 \leq i \leq n$, with A_0 representing the empty collection. One can verify through induction that this set of equations defines all possible behaviors of a bounded linear order.

In the behavior definition of the $A_1(x_1)$ agent, the summation combinator conveys that the agent offers both the in and $\overline{out}$ operations simultaneously to a client. If the in operation is chosen, the prefix combinator requires that an agent accept an input value denoted by x_2 and then become agent $A_2(x_1, x_2)$. Similarly, if the $\overline{out}$ operation is chosen, the agent outputs a value denoted by x_1 and then assumes the behavior defined by agent A_0.

In general, agent $A_i(x_1, \ldots, x_i)$ becomes agent $A_{i+1}(x_1, \ldots, x_{i+1})$ following an in operation and agent $A_{i-1}(x_1, \ldots, x_{i-1})$ following an $\overline{out}$ operation, with the behavior of agents A_0 and $A_n(x_1, \ldots, x_n)$ being special cases. From this perspective, the behavior equations define the operations offered by an agent as well as a replacement behavior. The notion of replacement behavior is a fundamental aspect of the actor model [1]. Hence, it seems appropriate to use behavior equations as a formal means for specifying and reasoning about the behavior of individual objects with actor-like semantics.

Although a generic bounded linear order is specified, the above set of behavior equations is isomorphic to a set of equations representing a bounded buffer accepting put and get operations, a stack accepting push and pop operations, or a queue accepting enq and deq operations. The isomorphism is realized through an application of the CCS relabeling (/) operator to yield the desired name substitution:

$$Buffer \equiv A_0[put/in, get/out], \ldots, A_n(x_1, \ldots, x_n)[put/in, get/out]$$
$$Stack \equiv A_0[push/in, pop/out], \ldots, A_n(x_1, \ldots, x_n)[push/in, pop/out]$$
$$Queue \equiv A_0[enq/in, deq/out], \ldots, A_n(x_1, \ldots, x_n)[enq/in, deq/out]$$

The isomorphism can be achieved because at this level of abstraction there is no concern for the actual semantics of the in and out operations, for example, whether or not the out operation returns values according to FIFO or LIFO semantics. To maintain generality, the equations describing a bounded linear order are used in the remainder of this paper with the understanding that the isomorphism can be applied at any time.

6.4.4   Object States and Behavior Sets

Behavior equations may be viewed as defining independent agents representing the various states of an object. In this section a model is defined that captures the essential elements used in developing a programming abstraction to represent a collection of behavior equations.

   In the model, each agent is associated with an object state σ_i and a set β_i called the observable behavior set. For a given behavior equation, the observable behavior set β_i is constructed from the nonrestricted prefix operations on the right-hand side of behavior equations. Nonrestricted prefix operations are those operation names that do not appear within the scope of the CCS restriction operator, thereby removing those operations from the set of observable behaviors.[1] The collection of all states is given by the state set $S = \{\sigma_0, \sigma_1, \ldots, \sigma_n\}$. The set of all possible observable behavior sets is the powerset $B = \ ^.(M)$, where $M = \bigcup_{i=0}^{n} \beta_i$. To complete the model, a function relating states to behavior sets is required.

6.4.5   Mapping States to Behavior Sets

The function $f_\beta : S \to B$ maps elements of the state set to elements of the powerset of observable behaviors. One can argue that in developing an abstract data type of a bounded linear order in a sequential object model, a programmer implicitly defines a mapping from S to B when defining the operations on the type. More precisely, each σ_i is always mapped to a single element in B, namely M, where $M = \{in, \overline{out}\}$. The map f_β is called the *behavior function* since it defines the observable behavior (the set of available methods) of an object in a given state. In standard object models, all methods are usually visible regardless of the state of the object; hence, f_β is defined in a manner that does not distinguish the internal object states, for example:

$$f_\beta(\sigma_0) = M$$
$$f_\beta(\sigma_1) = M$$
$$\vdots$$
$$f_\beta(\sigma_n) = M$$

---

[1] The restriction operator is a primitive mechanism for defining a scope.

Hence, objects in a standard object model always have the same behavior set regardless of any transitions in the state of the object.

The definition of f_β in the case of σ_0 and σ_n is unnatural. In defining $f_\beta(\sigma_0) = \{in, \overline{out}\}$, a programmer is forced to implement the method implementing the out operation in such a way that an underflow condition is detected. A similar situation occurs for $f_\beta(\sigma_n)$. A more natural mapping from S to B can be given as follows:

$$f_\beta(\sigma_0) = \{in\}$$
$$f_\beta(\sigma_1) = M$$
$$\vdots$$
$$f_\beta(\sigma_n) = \{\overline{out}\}$$

Consider that one wants to realize the semantics of the behavior equations by implementing an object in an appropriate object-oriented language that embodies the abstraction of a linear order. The mapping defined by f_β indicates that a useful abstraction is to partition the above behavior equations into three sets based on the notion of the state of the object. This partitioning appeals to intuition about the behavior of a linear ordering; furthermore, it is only necessary to reason about three behaviors, not $n + 1$; that is, the structure is either empty, full, or partially full. A reasonable implementation of the abstraction just formed is to define a class that exports two public methods, in and out, and that either explicitly or implicitly implements synchronization constraints consistent with the behavior equations previously formulated. That is, the out method is prohibited when the object corresponds to the agent defined by A_0 (state σ_0) and the in method is prohibited when the object corresponds to $A_n(x_1, \ldots, x_n)$ (state σ_n).

To extend the example, suppose that an additional constraint is introduced. For example, the behavior given by the $A_1(x_1)$ equation is distinguished from the other behaviors because a new operation is introduced that augments the other behavior sets. In distinguishing the $A_1(x_1)$ behavior, a new partitioning must be defined that distinguishes the conditions empty, full, singleton, and partial.

If an attempt is made to specialize the previously implemented abstraction through inheritance, it becomes necessary to extend the mapping given by f_β. Extending the mapping means that the domain S, the codomain B, and the mapping of elements in S to elements in B must be redefined. If the linear order abstraction has been implemented such that these components are implicitly imbedded in the class methods, then it is impossible to reuse the methods. Reuse is made impossible because the components of the mapping f_β are implicitly imbedded in the implementation. The only way the mapping can be redefined to permit the new synchronization constraints is to reimplement the methods in which the components representing the mapping f_β are embedded. The solution presented in the next section is to separate the components of the mapping from the method implementations.

6.4.6 Inheriting Concurrent Behavior

The types of concurrent object-oriented systems of interest are composed of objects with concurrency properties consistent with those described in the actor model. Each object possesses its own thread of control and communicates with other objects via message passing. Concurrency in the system is limited to interobject concurrency, which is achieved using message passing and an actor-like become operation. The actor become operation results in a replacement behavior with its own thread of control. Fine-grained intraobject concurrency is not a feature of objects in the systems under consideration here.

Of specific interest is expressing and inheriting concurrent object behavior in ACT++ [13, 14, 18], a prototype object-oriented language based on the actor model and C++ [9]. ACT++ is a collection of classes that implement the abstractions of the actor model and integrates these abstractions with the encapsulation, inheritance, and strong-typing features of C++. The language falls in the nonorthogonal category of concurrent object-oriented languages [23], since there are both active and passive objects. Active objects are instances of any class derived from a special Actor class defined as part of the language runtime. Any instance of a class not derived from the Actor class is a passive object. Concurrency is achieved using the become operation that is implemented in the Actor class.

The notion of *behavior abstraction* was originally proposed in ACT++ as a mechanism for capturing the behavior of an object. Upon initial examination, behavior abstraction seems powerful, since synchronization can be achieved naturally by dynamically modifying the visibility of the object interface using the become operation. The efficacy of this mechanism and its degree of interaction with the C++ inheritance mechanism has been examined by others and has been found to have serious limitations [19, 23]. The most serious limitation occurs because a behavior abstraction is not a first-class entity in the language and is thus subject to the effects of the inheritance anomaly.

A construct called an *enabled set* improves on the notion of behavior abstraction by promoting the control of the visibility of an object's interface to a dynamic mechanism that can be manipulated within the language. Enabled sets were implemented in Rosette, an interpreted actor language with dynamic typing [25].

The flexibility offered by enabled sets is difficult to achieve in a statically typed language like ACT++. Behavior sets represent a compromise between the enabled sets and behavior abstraction. The ACT++ language mechanism that represents the behavior set has the following properties:

1. It is a natural extension of formal methods for specifying concurrent object behavior.
2. It does not interfere with the C++ inheritance mechanism.
3. It is free from known inheritance anomalies.
4. It can be expressed entirely within ACT++ (hence C++).
5. It can be enforced efficiently at runtime.

In the following sections, the syntax of ACT++ is used to illustrate how to express elements of the object state set S, subsets of the observable behavior powerset B, and the behavior function f_β, such that synchronization constraints may be implemented and inherited in a manner that supports method reuse.

6.4.7 Expressing Concurrent Behavior

To represent concurrent object behavior within the ACT++ language, three first-class entities expressible within the language are defined:

1. *State functions* representing some or all of the elements of the state set S.
2. A *next behavior function* representing the function f_β.
3. *Behavior sets* representing elements of the observable behavior powerset B.

In the example shown in Figure 6.16, each of the above entities is expressed and used in a class definition of a bounded linear order. The LinearOrd class defines two Boolean functions (empty and full) to distinguish three states: empty, full, and partial.[2] Although not shown, the functions are computed based on implementation-dependent instance variables representing the actual number of elements in the structure representing the linear order. Both functions are used by the nextBehavior function, which maps the current object state to a behavior set represented by an instance of the BehaviorSet class. There are three behavior sets defined: B_0, B_n, and B_i. The B_0 and B_n behavior sets correspond to the previously expressed behavior equations A_0 and $A_n(x_1, \ldots, x_n)$, respectively. The B_i behavior set is used in this abstraction to collectively represent the observable behaviors of the intermediate behavior equations. Each behavior set is initialized in the class constructor. Instances of the BehaviorSet class are first-class objects and an overloading is given to the binary addition operator denoting set union when applied to two behavior sets; hence, B_i is formed as the union of the behavior sets B_0 and B_n.

6.4.8   Inheriting Concurrent Behavior

To substantiate the claim that the inheritance anomaly is avoided, a new class Hybrid-LinearOrd is derived from the LinearOrd class. The main feature of the HybridLinearOrd class is that a new method is introduced that forces a change in the mapping given by f_β. The new method allows a client of an instance of the HybridLinearOrd class to atomically extract a pair of elements instead of a single element. The method cannot simply invoke the out method twice since the out method executes a become operation after each invocation. Due to the concurrency in the system, another object may have its out *request* executed before the second out request is processed; therefore, a new operation $\overline{outp}$ is required to output a pair. The behavior of this new type of object is specified by the following behavior equations:

$$A_0 \stackrel{\text{def}}{=} in(x_1).A_1(x_1)$$
$$A_1(x_1) \stackrel{\text{def}}{=} in(x_2).A_2(x_1, x_2) + \overline{out}(x_1).A_0$$
$$A_2(x_1, x_2) \stackrel{\text{def}}{=} in(x_3).A_3(x_1, x_2, x_3) + \overline{out}(x_1).A_1(x_1) + \overline{outp}(x_1, x_2).A_0$$
$$\vdots$$
$$A_n(x_1, \ldots, x_n) \stackrel{\text{def}}{=} \overline{out}(x_1).A_{n-1}(x_1, \ldots, x_{n-1}) + \overline{outp}(x_1, x_2).A_{n-2}(x_1, \ldots, x_{n-2})$$

The behavior equations for the hybrid linear order differ from the equations specifying the behavior of a traditional linear order only in the addition of the choice of an $\overline{outp}$ operation in the definitions of the $A_i(x_1, \ldots, A_i)$ equations, where $2 \le i \le n$. There are two effects

---

[2]Technically the LinearOrd class is defined as a C++ *template* that is parameterized by a type T representing the type of the elements in the linear order.

```
template<class T> class LinearOrd : Actor {
...
protected:    // instance variables and methods visi-
ble to subclasses

    BehaviorSet B0, Bn, Bi;

    virtual bool empty(){...}
    virtual bool full() {...}

    virtual BehaviorSet nextBehavior() {
        if (empty())
            return B0;
        else if (full())
            return Bn;
        else
            return Bi;
    }

public:    // methods visible to subclasses and clients

    void in(T x) {
        ...
        become nextBehavior();
    }

    T out() {
        ...
        become nextBehavior();
    }

    LinearOrd() { // construct initial "empty" object
        ...
        B0 = &in; Bn = &out; Bi = B0 + Bn;
        become nextBehavior();
    }
};
```

FIGURE 6.16   ACT++ linear order class definition.

of this refinement. First, the $\overline{outp}$ operation is added to the appropriate observable behavior sets and a new powerset B' is computed. Second, the $A_1(x_1)$ behavior is now a distinguished behavior and $B' \supset B$; hence, a new mapping f'_β is required:

$$f'_\beta(\sigma_0) = f_\beta(\sigma_0)$$
$$f'_\beta(\sigma_1) = f_\beta(\sigma_1)$$
$$f'_\beta(\sigma_2) = \{in, \overline{out}, \overline{outp}\}$$
$$\vdots$$
$$f'_\beta(\sigma_n) = \{\overline{out}, \overline{outp}\}$$

Clearly there is cause to reuse the implementations of the in and out methods defined in the LinearOrd class. In addition, the function representing the new mapping f'_β can reuse the nextBehavior function defined in the LinearOrd class. However, in order to achieve reuse, both the B_i and B_n behavior sets must be redefined to include the method representing the $\overline{outp}$ operation. A new instance of the BehaviorSet class containing the methods representing the in and $\overline{outp}$ operations specified in the $A_1(x_1)$ behavior equation must also be defined in the HybridLinearOrd class.

The definition of the HybridLinearOrd class shown in Figure 6.17 inherits from the LinearOrd class and introduces the following:

1. A new state function singleton.
2. A new behavior set B_1.
3. A redefinition of the behavior function nextBehavior.
4. A new method outPair.

The singleton function corresponds to distinguishing the agent $A_1(x_1)$ from the remaining agents. The new BehaviorSet object B_1 corresponds to the behavior set associated with agent $A_1(x_1)$. The B_i and B_n behavior sets are augmented in the class constructor with the outPair method corresponding to the enlarged codomain B'. Thus, the inherited nextBehavior function can be trivially redefined to correspond to the new mapping f'_β by adding a check for the state corresponding to agent $A_1(x_1)$ and invoking the superclass behavior function LinearOrd::nextBehavior for all other states.

In order to inherit synchronization constraints it must be possible to specialize the mapping given to f_β by the superclass. This implies that the elements of S, the elements of B, and the function f_β must be representable in the language and the representations must be:

1. First-class,
2. Inheritable, and
3. Mutable.

The inheritance anomaly occurs in previous formulations of this problem precisely because the behavior sets and the behavior function, as they occurred in the superclass, were neither first-class nor mutable.

State functions representing elements of S, instances of the BehaviorSet class representing elements of B, and the nextBehavior function representing f_β have these

```
template<class T> class HybridLinearOrd : public LinearOrd<T> {
protected:

    BehaviorSet B1;

    virtual bool singleton() { ... }

    BehaviorSet nextBehavior() {
        if (singleton()
            return B1;
        else
            return LinearOrd::nextBehavior();
    }

public:

    Pair<T> outpair() {
        ...
        become nextBehavior();
    }

    /* Note: base class constructor is executed first */

    HybridLinearOrd() {
        B1 = Bi;
        Bi = Bi + &outPair;
        Bn = Bn + &outPair;
        become nextBehavior();
    }
};
```

FIGURE 6.17   ACT++ Hybrid linear order class definition.

properties. All are first-class language entities inheritable by a subclass. Instances of the BehaviorSet class are mutable by a subclass since they are defined within the scope of a protected clause. The empty and full predicates representing object states and the nextBehavior function representing the behavior function are subject to redefinition since they have the virtual attribute and are within the scope of the protected clause.

6.5

SUMMARY AND STATUS

This paper has presented the beginnings of a formal framework for investigating the relationship between concurrent object behavior and inheritance. The approach emphasizes the relationship between the state of an object and subsets of methods visible in the interface to the object, called behavior sets. This relationship is embodied in the mapping given by the behavior function. If the inheritance anomaly is to be avoided, behavior sets and the behavior function must be first-class, inheritable, and mutable. It was shown that the language mechanisms of ACT++ (and therefore C++) are sufficiently expressive in this regard.

We are exploring the techniques presented here in the context of distributed object-oriented systems with a high degree of both intranode and internode concurrency. In particular, we are developing an object-oriented structure for peer-to-peer protocols and are investigating concurrency issues. We are also addressing the semantic issues in a more rigorous fashion than is presented here. We suspect that type-theoretic semantics currently applied to object-oriented languages are incapable of addressing the temporal nature of a changing object interface as captured by the behavior function. Interesting work in this area is [22], which also uses CCS as a starting point.

We have not discussed the details of the runtime enforcement of behavior sets. ACT++ and behavior sets have been implemented on the Sequent Symmetry, a shared-memory multiprocessor [14]. A subject of our current research is to determine the relationship between our implementation approach and others based on reflection. Our Actor language prototype continues to evolve as we gain an understanding of the semantic issues underlying concurrent object-oriented languages.

6.6

ACKNOWLEDGMENTS

The previous work of Keung Hae Lee on behavior abstraction in ACT++ and the work on enabled sets in Rosette by Chris Tomlinson and Vineet Singh set the stage for the results described here. Satoshi Matsuoka formulated the inheritance anomaly in the context of behavior abstractions in ACT++, which motivated us to pursue the issue more deeply. We thank Mani Mukherji for implementing the behavior set mechanism in ACT++.

Bibliography

1. G. Agha, *ACTORS: A Model of Concurrent Computation in Distributed Systems*, MIT Press, Cambridge, Mass., 1986.
2. P. America, "Inheritance and Subtyping in a Parallel Object-oriented Language," *ECOOP'87 Conf. Proc.*, Springer-Verlag, New York, N.Y., 1987, pp. 234–242.
3. P. America, "Pool-T: A Parallel Object-oriented Language," in *Object-oriented Concurrent Programming*, A. Yonezawa and M. Tokoro, eds., MIT Press, Cambridge, Mass., 1987, pp. 199–220.
4. B. Anderson, "Fine-grained Parallelism in Ellie," *J. Object-oriented Programming*, Vol. 5, No. 3, June 1992, pp. 55–61.
5. L. Bergmans et al., "An Object-oriented Model for Extensible Concurrent Systems: The Composition-filters Approach," in *Trese Papers on OO Software Engineering*, Department of Computer Science, University of Twente, Netherlands.
6. B. Bershad, E. Lazowska, and H. Levy, "PRESTO: A System for Object-oriented Parallel Programming," *Software: Practice and Experience*, Vol. 18, No. 8, Aug. 1988, pp. 713–732.
7. J.-P. Briot and Akinori Yonezawa, "Inheritance and Synchronization in Object-oriented Concurrent Programming," in *ABCL: An Object-oriented Concurrent System*, A. Yonezawa, ed., MIT Press, Cambridge, Mass., 1990.

8. D. Caromel, "Concurrency: An Object-oriented Approach," *TOOLS-2 Conf. Proc.*, 1990, pp. 183–197.

9. M.A. Ellis and B. Stroustrup, *The Annotated C++ Reference Manual*, Addison-Wesley, Reading, Mass., 1990.

10. A. Grimshaw, "Easy-to-Use Object-oriented Parallel Processing with Mentat," *Computer*, Vol. 26, No. 5, May 1993, pp. 39–51.

11. M. Jackson, *System Development*, Prentice-Hall, New York, N.Y., 1983.

12. D. Kafura and K.H. Lee, "Inheritance in Actor-based Concurrent Object-oriented Languages," *ECOOP'89 Conf. Proc.*, Cambridge University Press, Cambridge, Mass., 1989, pp. 131–145.

13. D. Kafura and K.H. Lee, "ACT++: Building a Concurrent C++ with Actors," *J. Object-oriented Programming*, Vol. 3, No. 1, May/June 1990, pp. 25–37.

14. D. Kafura, M. Mukherji, and G. Lavender, "ACT++ 2.0: A Class Library for Concurrent Programming in C++ Using Actors," *J. Object-oriented Programing*, 1993.

15. S. Krakowiak et al., "Design and Implementation of an Object-oriented, Strongly Typed Language for Distributed Applications," *J. Object-oriented Programming*, Sept./Oct., 1990, pp. 11–22.

16. C. Laffra, *Procol: A Concurrent Object Language with Protocols, Delegation, Persistence, and Constraints*, doctoral dissertation, Erasmus University, Rotterdam, 1992.

17. W.J. Leddy and K.S. Smith, "The Design of the Experimental System's Kernel," *Proc. Hypercube and Concurrent Applications Conf.*, 1989.

18. K.H. Lee, "Designing a Statically Typed Actor-based Concurrent Object-oriented Programming Language," doctoral dissertation, Department of Computer Science, Virginia Tech, 1990.

19. S. Matsuoka, K. Wakita, and A. Yonezawa, "Analysis of the Inheritance Anomaly in Concurrent Object-oriented Languages," extended abstract presented at *ECOOP-OOPSLA'90 Workshop on Object-based Concurrency*, 1990.

20. R. Milner, *Communication and Concurrency*, Prentice-Hall, New York, N.Y., 1989.

21. O. Nierstrasz, "Active Objects in Hybrid," *OOPSLA'87 Proc.*, ACM Press, New York, N.Y., 1987, pp. 243–253.

22. O. Nierstrasz and M. Papathomas, "Towards a Type Theory for Active Objects," in *Object Management*, D. Tsichritzis, ed., Centre Universitaire D'Informatique, Université De Geneva, 1990, pp. 295–304.

23. M. Papathomas, "Concurrency Issues in Object-oriented Languages," in *Object Oriented Development*, D. Tsichritzis, ed., Centre Universitaire D'Informatique, Université De Geneva, 1989, pp. 207–245.

24. M. Papathomas, *Language Design Rationale and Semantic Framework for Concurrent Object-oriented Programming*, doctoral dissertation, University of Geneva, 1992.

25. C. Tomlinson and V. Singh, "Inheritance and Synchronization with Enabled-sets," *OOPSLA'89 Conf. Proc.*, ACM Sigplan Notices, ACM Press, New York, N.Y., 1989, pp. 103–112.

26. A. Tripathi and M. Aksit, "Communication, Scheduling, and Resource Management in SINA," *J. Object-oriented Programming*, Vol. 1, No. 4, Nov./Dec. 1988, pp. 24–37.

27. J. Van Den Bos and C. Laffra, "Procol: A Parallel Object Language with Protocols," *ACM Sigplan Notices, Proc. OOPSLA'89*, ACM Press, New York, N.Y., 1989, pp. 95–102.

28. T. Watanabe and A. Yonezawa, "Reflection in an Object-oriented Concurrent Language," *ACM Sigplan Notices*, Vol. 23, No. 11, 1988, pp. 306–315.

29. P. Wegner, "Dimensions of Object-based Language Design," OOPSLA'87 *Conf. Proc., ACM Sigplan Notices*, ACM Press, New York, N.Y., 1987, pp. 168–182.

30. A. Yonezawa et al., "Modeling and Programming in an Object-oriented Concurrent Language ABCL/1," in *Object-oreinted Concurrent Programming*, M. Tokoro, ed., MIT Press, Cambridge, Mass., 1987, pp. 55–89.

PART III

SYSTEM SOFTWARE FOR PARALLEL COMPUTERS

ScaLAPACK: LINEAR ALGEBRA SOFTWARE FOR DISTRIBUTED MEMORY ARCHITECTURES*

James Demmel
Computer Science Division and Mathematics Department,
University of California, Berkeley, CA 94720

Jack Dongarra
Computer Science Department,
The University of Tennessee, Knoxville, TN 37996
Mathematical Sciences Section,
Oak Ridge National Laboratory, Oak Ridge, TN 37831

Robert van de Geijn
Mathematical Sciences Section,
Oak Ridge National Laboratory, Oak Ridge, TN 37831
Department of Computer Sciences,
The University of Texas, Austin, TX 78712

David Walker
Department of Computer Sciences,
The University of Texas, Austin, TX 78712

Abstract. *We report the progress of an ongoing project that investigates the reusability of LAPACK code for distributed-memory MIMD architectures. This chapter discusses the scalability of Cholesky, LU, and QR factorization routines on MIMD distributed-memory concurrent computers. These routines form part of the ScaLAPACK mathematical software library that extends the widely used LAPACK library to run efficiently on*

*This project was supported in part by the National Science Foundation Science and Technology Center Cooperative Agreement No. CCR-8809615, the Applied Mathematical Sciences subprogram of the Office of Energy Research, US Department of Energy, under Contract DE-AC05-84OR21400, and Intel Scientific Supercomputing Division.

scalable concurrent computers. To ensure good scalability and performance, the ScaLAPACK routines are based on block-partitioned algorithms that reduce the frequency of data movement between different levels of the memory hierarchy, and particularly between processors. The block cyclic data distribution, which is used in all three factorization algorithms, is described. An outline of the sequential and parallel block-partitioned algorithms is given. Approximate models of algorithms' performance are presented to indicate which factors in the design of the algorithm have an impact upon scalability. These models are compared with timings results on a 128-node Intel iPSC/860 hypercube. It is shown that the routines are highly scalable on this machine for problems that occupy more than about 25 percent of the memory on each processor, and that the measured timings are consistent with the performance model.

7.1

INTRODUCTION

Massively parallel, distributed-memory, concurrent computers are playing an increasingly important role in large-scale scientific computing and, in particular, are the primary target machines for "Grand Challenge" applications. In addition, massively parallel computers are also beginning to be more widely used in production engineering environments, and to a somewhat lesser extent in the business and finance sectors. A number of key software technologies are helping to accelerate the more widespread use of massively parallel computers in these areas. These include the development of parallelizing compilers, parallel language extensions such as Fortran D [19] and High Performance Fortran [23], the adoption of a standard message-passing interface [15], support for parallel constructs and operations (such as guard layers and object migration), and a variety of tools for debugging and visualizing/analyzing performance on massively parallel computers.

Another important and active research area is the development of reusable software for multicomputers in the form of libraries and "tool-kits" [5, 18, 27]. Linear algebra—in particular, the solution of linear systems of equations—lies at the heart of most calculations in scientific computing. We are currently building a software library for performing linear algebra computations on multicomputers, and this chapter deals primarily with the performance and scalability of the dense LU, Cholesky, and QR factorization routines that form the core of this library. In addition, we shall discuss how the design goals for the library, particularly the performance requirements, influenced the implementation of the core routines.

The scalable library we are developing for multicomputers will be fully compatible with the LAPACK library for vector and shared-memory computers [1, 2, 8, 12], and is therefore called ScaLAPACK. LAPACK was designed to implement the earlier EISPACK and LINPACK linear algebra libraries efficiently on shared-memory vector supercomputers, and to improve the robustness of some of the algorithms. These types of computers have hierarchical memories, and a key concept in the design of LAPACK was to improve performance by minimizing the movement of data between the different layers of the memory. This was done by recasting the algorithms in block-partitioned form, so that the bulk of the computation is performed by matrix-matrix operations using the Level 3 Basic Linear Algebra Subprograms (BLAS) [10, 11]. This approach permits locality of reference to be preserved.

ScaLAPACK also uses block-partitioned algorithms to ensure good performance on MIMD distributed-memory concurrent computers, by minimizing the frequency of data movement between different levels of the memory hierarchy [6, 7]. For such machines the memory hierarchy includes the off-processor memory of other processors, in addition to the hierarchy of registers, cache, and local memory on each processor, so the block partitioned approach is particularly useful in reducing the start-up cost associated with interprocessor communication. This optimization is essential to the scalable performance of the library routines. The fundamental building blocks of the ScaLAPACK library are distributed-memory versions of the Level 2 and Level 3 BLAS and a set of Basic Linear Algebra Communication Subprograms (BLACS) [3, 17] for performing communication tasks that arise frequently in parallel linear algebra computations. In the ScaLAPACK routines, all interprocessor communication takes place within the distributed BLAS and the BLACS, so the source code of the top software layer of ScaLAPACK looks very similar to that of LAPACK.

7.2

REQUIREMENTS OF SCALABLE LIBRARIES

In developing a library of high-quality subroutines for performing dense linear algebra computations, the design goals fall into three broad classes:

- Performance goals
- Ease-of-use goals
- Range-of-use goals

These design goals will be discussed in the following three subsections.

7.2.1 Performance

Two important performance metrics are *concurrent efficiency* and *scalability*. We seek good performance characteristics in our algorithms by eliminating, as much as possible, overhead due to load imbalance, data movement, and algorithm restructuring. The way in which the data are distributed (or decomposed) over the memory hierarchy of a computer is of fundamental importance to these factors. Concurrent efficiency, ϵ, is defined as the concurrent speedup per processor [20], where the concurrent speedup is the execution time, T_{seq}, for the best sequential algorithm running on one processor of the concurrent computer, divided by the execution time, T, of the parallel algorithm running on N_p processors. When direct methods are used, as in LU factorization, the concurrent efficiency depends on the problem size and the number of processors, so on a given parallel computer and for a fixed number of processors the running time should not vary greatly for problems of the same size. Thus, we may write,

$$\epsilon(N, N_p) = \frac{1}{N_p} \frac{T_{\text{seq}}(N)}{T(N, N_p)} \qquad (7.1)$$

where N represents the problem size. In dense linear algebra computations the execution time is usually dominated by the floating point operation count, so the concurrent efficiency is related to the performance, G, measured in floating point operations per second by,

$$G(N, N_p) = \frac{N_p}{t_{calc}} \, \epsilon(N, N_p) \qquad (7.2)$$

where t_{calc} is the time for one floating point operation. For routines that iterate, such as eigensolvers, the number of iterations, and hence the execution time, depends not only on the problem size, but also on other characteristics of the input data, such as condition number. A parallel algorithm is said to be scalable [22] if the concurrent efficiency depends on the problem size and number of processors only through their ratio. This ratio is simply the memory requirement of the problem per processor, often referred to as the granularity. Thus, for a scalable algorithm the concurrent efficiency is constant as the number of processors increases while keeping the granularity fixed. Alternatively, Equation 7.2 shows that this is equivalent to saying that for a scalable algorithm the performance depends linearly on the number of processors for fixed granularity.

The degree of scalability may be gauged by the isoefficiency function, $\rho_\epsilon(N_p)$, which is defined to be the problem size necessary to maintain some fixed efficiency, ϵ, as the number of processors, N_p, varies. Thus, if $\rho_\epsilon(N_p)$ depends linearly on N_p then the concurrent efficiency is a function of the grain size, $g = N/N_p$. Such algorithms are highly scalable. Algorithms for which $\rho_\epsilon(N_p)$ is a rapidly increasing function of N_p are said to scale poorly.

The scalability of a parallel algorithm can be assessed by plotting the isoefficiency function for different values of ϵ, that is, by plotting curves in the (N_p, N) plane on which ϵ is constant. On any particular machine we are usually interested in how an algorithm scales within a "window" in the (N_p, N) plane. This is shown schematically in Figure 7.1, in which the window is bounded to the right by the number of processors in the parallel machine, below by the size of the smallest problem of interest, and to the left and above by either the memory size per processor or runtime considerations. For some algorithms there may also be an upper bound on the problem size imposed by considerations of stability and accuracy. In Figure 7.1 we have assumed that the memory requirements scale linearly with the problem size. The runtime bound turns over as N_p increases as the concurrent efficiency falls off.

In designing an algorithm for a scalable library, we seek one that is scalable within the windows of interest of as large a set of machines as possible. It should be noted that scalability studies conducted on small machines are of little use if the problem sizes considered are below the minimum size of interest. In the absence of an accurate performance model it is not valid to infer that an algorithm that scales well on one machine will also scale well on another machine, or even on the same machine for a larger number of processors. It is also important to note the distinction between good scalability and high efficiency. Suppose we have two algorithms with the same order of computational complexity that perform the same task. Algorithm 1 is efficient and scalable for some number of processors $N_p \leq N_*$, but loses scalability as the number of processors increases further. Algorithm 2 is less efficient than Algorithm 1 for a given problem size in the $N_p \leq N_*$ regime, but maintains good scalability for all N_p. In this case it is unclear which algorithm is "best" overall.

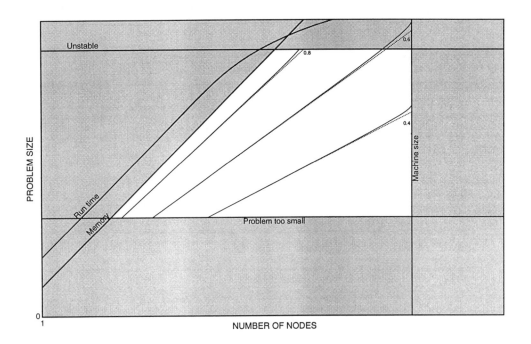

FIGURE 7.1 Schematic representation of isoefficiency curves within the window of interest, shown unshaded. The solid curves represent isoefficiency curves labeled by the efficiency. The dotted lines correspond to high scalability.

For a sufficiently small number of processors Algorithm 1 is preferable, but for a larger machine Algorithm 2 is better. Such dilemmas raise the possibility of using polyalgorithms, that is, applying different algorithms on different machines or for different regions of the (N_p, N) plane.

7.2.2   Ease of Use

Ease of use is concerned with factors such as portability and the user interface to the library. Portability in its most inclusive sense means that the code is written in a standard language, such as Fortran, and that the source-code can be compiled on an arbitrary machine to produce a program that will run correctly and efficiently. In our modular approach to ScaLAPACK it is assumed that the distributed Level 3 BLAS and the BLACS that form the building blocks of the library routines are available in optimized form for each target platform and are linked in during compilation. Thus, only the upper layers of the ScaLAPACK library are fully portable in the source-code sense. Ease of use is also related to the user interface and is enhanced if implementation details are largely hidden from the user, for example, through the use of an object-based interface to the library. In addition to the LAPACK-compatible interface, we are also experimenting with developing interfaces for LAPACK and ScaLAPACK that are compatible with Fortran 90 [6] and C++ [16].

7.2.3 Range of Use

Range of use may be gauged by how numerically stable the algorithms are over a range of input problems and the range of data structures the library will support. For example, LAPACK deals with dense matrices stored in a rectangular array, packed matrices where only the upper or lower half of a symmetric matrix is stored, and banded matrices where only the nonzero bands are stored.

7.3

THE SCALAPACK EFFORT

7.3.1 Algorithms to Be Included

Over the past three years the LAPACK linear algebra library has been designed and implemented for a wide range of shared-memory supercomputers. When complete, ScaLAPACK will extend LAPACK to distributed-memory concurrent computers. This section gives an overview of the functionality provided by LAPACK. LAPACK is based on the successful LINPACK [9] and EISPACK [21, 28] libraries. A functional extension of these libraries has been developed that is portable and more efficient across the range of large-scale, shared-memory, general-purpose computers. To achieve this, LINPACK and EISPACK have been redesigned to use a set of basic linear algebra subroutines (called the Level 1, 2, and 3 BLAS), which perform basic operations such as scalar-vector, matrix-vector, and matrix-matrix multiplication. These subroutines, especially the matrix-matrix operations, can be optimized for each machine while the Fortran code that calls them remains identical and hence portable across all the machines. This approach lets us extract most of the performance that each machine has to offer, while restricting machine-dependent code to the BLAS and a few integer "tuning parameters."

In addition to developing faster code, new functions have been added, some of which solve new problems (such as computing condition numbers of eigenvalues and eigenvectors), and some of which solve old problems more accurately (the bidiagonal singular value decomposition).

A comprehensive test package for the entire library has also been developed. The test package has drivers that test groups of related subroutines for accuracy and stability. In addition, a set of performance-measuring routines to test the efficiency of the LAPACK routines and their variants have been developed.

LAPACK provides approximately the same functionality as LINPACK and EISPACK together, namely, solution of systems of simultaneous linear equation, least-squares solution of over-determined systems of equations, and solution of matrix eigenvalue problems (standard and generalized). The associated matrix factorizations (LU, Cholesky, QR, SVD, Schur, generalized Schur) are also provided, as are related computations such as reordering of the factorizations and condition numbers (or estimates thereof). Dense and band matrices are provided for, but not general sparse matrices. In all areas, similar functionality is provided for real and complex matrices.

Many of the algorithms of LINPACK and EISPACK are carried over with only minor modifications to their numerical behavior, although often with extensive restructuring of the code in order to improve performance. Some algorithms have been deleted, especially where there is duplication or overlap in functionality between the contents of the two packages or if they were thought to be no longer useful. Other algorithms are extended to provide additional functionality. Where the state of the art was sufficiently clear, new algorithms have been added.

For most computations there are matching routines, one for real and one for complex data, but there are a few exceptions. For example, corresponding to the routines for real symmetric indefinite systems of linear equations, there are routines for complex Hermitian and complex symmetric systems, because both types of complex systems occur in practical applications. However, there is no complex analogue of the routine for finding selected eigenvalues of a real symmetric tridiagonal matrix, because a complex Hermitian matrix can always be reduced to a real symmetric tridiagonal matrix.

LAPACK includes routines for solving systems of linear equations for different types of matrices. In addition to general solvers for dense, banded, and tridiagonal matrices, special solve routines exist for symmetric/Hermitian indefinite and positive definite matrices, complex symmetric matrices, and positive definite banded and tridiagonal matrices. For the symmetric and Hermitian cases, versions exist that assume packed storage, thereby halving the memory required to store the matrix.

In addition to the linear system solvers, LAPACK includes routines for solving the linear least squares problem, computing the singular value decomposition, and solving the eigenvalue problem (general, symmetric, and generalized problems).

7.3.2   Target Architectures

The EISPACK and LINPACK software libraries were designed for supercomputers in use in the 1970s and early 1980s, such as the CDC-7600, Cyber 205, and Cray-1 computers [24]. These machines featured multiple functional units that were pipelined to get good performance. The CDC-7600 was basically a high-performance scalar computer, while the Cyber 205 and Cray-1 were early vector computers.

The development of LAPACK in the late 1980s was intended to make the EISPACK and LINPACK libraries run efficiently on shared-memory vector supercomputers. The ScaLAPACK software library extends the use of LAPACK to distributed-memory concurrent supercomputers. The development of ScaLAPACK began in 1991 and was completed by the end of 1994.

The underlying concept of both the LAPACK and ScaLAPACK libraries is the use of block-partitioned algorithms to minimize data movement between different levels in hierarchical memory. Thus, the ideas discussed in this paper for developing a library for performing dense linear algebra computations are applicable to any computer with a hierarchical memory that (1) imposes a sufficiently large start-up cost on the movement of data between different levels in the hierarchy, and for which (2) the cost of a context switch is too great to make fine-grain size multithreading worthwhile. Our target machines are, therefore, medium- and large-grain size advanced-architecture computers. These include "traditional" shared-memory, vector supercomputers, such as the Cray Y-MP and C90, and MIMD distributed-memory concurrent supercomputers, such as the Intel Paragon, and Thinking Machines' CM-5, and the more recently announced IBM SP1 and Cray T3D concurrent systems. Since these machines have only very recently become available, most of the ongoing development of the ScaLAPACK library is being performed on a 128-node Intel iPSC/860 hypercube and on the 520-node Intel Delta system.

The Intel Paragon supercomputer can have up to 2000 nodes, each consisting of an i860/XP processor and a communications coprocessor. The nodes each have at least 16 Mbytes of memory, and are connected by a high-speed network with the topology of a two-dimensional mesh. The CM-5 from Thinking Machines Corporation [29] supports both SIMD and MIMD programming models, and may have up to 16 K processors, though the largest CM-5 currently installed has 1024 processors. Each CM-5 node is a Sparc processor with up to 4 associated vector processors. Point-to-point communication between nodes is supported by a data network with the topology of a "fat tree" [25]. Global communication operations, such as synchronization and reduction, are supported by a separate control network. The IBM SP1 system is based on the same RISC chip used in the IBM RS/6000 workstations, and uses a multistage switch to connect processors. The Cray T3D uses the Alpha chip from Digital Equipment Corporation and connects the processors in a three-dimensional torus.

Future advances in compiler and hardware technologies in the mid- to late-1990s are expected to make the multithreading paradigm a viable approach for masking communication costs. Since the blocks in a block-partitioned algorithm can be regarded as separate threads, our approach will still be applicable on machines that exploit medium- and coarse-grain size multithreading.

7.3.3 Data Distribution Schemes

The fundamental data object used in the ScaLAPACK library is the block-partitioned matrix. In this section, we describe the block-cyclic method for distributing such a matrix over a two-dimensional mesh of processes, or template. In general, each process has an independent thread of control, and with each process is associated some local memory directly accessible only by that process. The assignment of these processes to physical processors is a machine-dependent optimization issue.

An important property of the class of data distribution we shall use is that independent decompositions are applied over rows and columns. We shall, therefore, begin by considering the distribution of a vector of M data objects over P processes. This can be described by a mapping of the global index, m, of a data object to an index pair (p, i), where p specifies the process to which the data object is assigned, and i specifies the location in the local memory of p at which it is stored. We shall assume $0 \leq m < M$ and $0 \leq p < P$.

7.4

PARALLEL COMPUTING MODEL

We assume that our multicomputer consists of p nodes, logically configured as a $P \times Q$ grid and indexed by an ordered pair (I, J), where $0 \leq I < P$ and $0 \leq J < Q$. Each is equipped with CPU and local memory. The nodes are connected by some communication network that allows broadcasting of messages within rows and columns, in addition to point-to-point communication. Messages that arrive over the network are buffered until absorbed by an appropriate call to a receive routine.

In our approach, it is actually not necessary to restrict the model to one process per node. Indeed, whenever we refer to a node, this could just as easily be a process, where many processes could be assigned to a single node.

7.5

MAPPING MATRICES TO NODES

There are many ways that matrices can be distributed among nodes. A general class of such mappings can be obtained by partitioning the matrix A like

$$A = \begin{pmatrix} A_{11} & \cdots & A_{1m} \\ \vdots & & \vdots \\ A_{m1} & \cdots & A_{mm} \end{pmatrix}$$

where each subblock A_{ij} is $n_b \times n_b$. These blocks are mapped to nodes by assigning A_{ij} to node $((i-1) \bmod P, (j-1) \bmod Q)$. We refer to this last mapping as the *block-torus-wrapped* mapping. Another common name for this mapping is the *block scatter decomposition*.

When $P = 1$, this mapping is equivalent to our original column panel-wrapped mapping. In this case, n_b would correspond to the width of the panels.

Our algorithms actually work for much more general layouts. Indeed, if A_{ij} is stored on processor (σ_i, τ_j), where σ and τ are permutations that store equal numbers of rows and columns on each processor, then running the algorithms *unchanged* is equivalent to computing the LU, QR, or Cholesky decompositions of $P_\sigma A P_\tau$, where P_σ and P_τ are permutation matrices. These permuted decompositions are completely adequate for linear equation solving and least squares problems.

7.6

PARALLEL IMPLEMENTATION OF THE ALGORITHMS

In this section, we outline the parallel implementation of the various algorithms. All are based on right-looking variants of the algorithms. In effect, for the two-dimensional mapping, columns of nodes cooperate to perform the computation that was previously performed by a single node, when panel-wrapped storage was used.

7.6.1 LU Factorization

Assume the LU factorization has proceeded so that all but the labeled portions of the matrix have been updated:

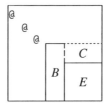

where $B \in \mathbf{R}^{m \times n_b}$, $C \in \mathbf{R}^{n_b \times (m-n_b)}$, and $E \in \mathbf{R}^{(m-n_b) \times (m-n_b)}$. During the next step, the right-looking algorithm factors panel B, pivoting if necessary. Next, the pivots are applied to the remainder of the matrix. Blocks C and E now become blocks $\bar{C}$ and $\bar{E}$, a triangular solve updates submatrix $\bar{C}$, and a rank n_b update updates submatrix $\bar{E}$. This process continues with the updated matrix.

Turning now to the distributed-memory implementation, assume the matrix is block-torus-wrapped onto a grid of nodes of dimension $M \times N$, with block size n_b. The above described process proceeds as follows:

- The nodes held in column B collaborate to factor this panel.
- Pivot information is distributed to all other columns of nodes.
- Columns of nodes collaborate to pivot the remainders of the matrix rows.
- Factored panel B is distributed within rows of nodes.
- The row that holds $\bar{C}$ performs the triangular solve, the results of which are distributed within columns of nodes.
- The update of $\bar{E}$ is performed in parallel.

Several implementation details are important to keep in mind:

- Broadcasting the factored panel can be done by sending the panel around the ring of node columns. This has proved to be efficient for column panel-wrapped algorithms, allowing communication and computation to be pipelined, and is efficient for block-torus-wrapped approaches for similar reasons [4, 14].
- The broadcast of the updated $\bar{C}$ must be done in a manner that requires the least total time. We have implemented this as a minimum spanning tree broadcast.
- During the factoring of panel B, determining the pivot row and the distribution of this row has been combined to avoid excessive start-up overhead.

7.6.2 Cholesky Factorization

This algorithm proceeds similarly, except that, due to symmetry, only the lower triangular portion is stored and updated. Moreover, no pivoting is necessary since the matrix is assumed to be positive definite.

7.6.3   QR Factorization

Again, this algorithm proceeds as the LU factorization, except that it uses Householder transformations to factor the panels. Although no pivoting is necessary, the equivalent of inner products must be accumulated within columns of nodes.

7.7

EXPERIMENTS ON THE INTEL TOUCHSTONE DELTA AND iPSC/860

In this section, we report preliminary performance results from implementations of the above algorithms on the Intel Touchstone Delta and iPSC/860. The former resides at Caltech and consists of up to 512 nodes, configured as a grid. The latter resides at Oak Ridge National Laboratory and consists of 128 nodes connected by a hypercube network. Each node consists of an Intel i860 microprocessor. The Delta has 16 Mbytes of memory per node, the iPSC/860 has 8 Mbytes. All performance results are for the double-precision implementations.

The performances attained by various numbers of nodes for the different algorithms are given by Figures 7.2 through 7.4. Performance is directly related to the ratio between communication and computation. This ratio is most favorable for the QR factorization and least favorable for Cholesky factorization. This is in part due to the fact that the total number of floating point operations for a given matrix dimension, n, equals $2/3n^3$, $4/3n^3$, and $1/3n^3$ for the LU, QR, and Cholesky factorization, respectively.

We report performance per node attained for the largest problem size as a function of machine size in Figure 7.5. In theory, approximately constant efficiency can be maintained

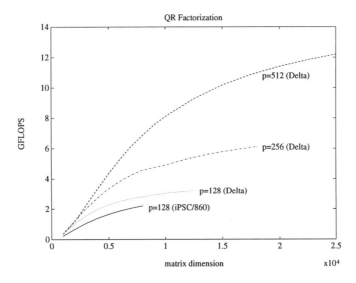

FIGURE 7.2   Performance attained by the QR factorization.

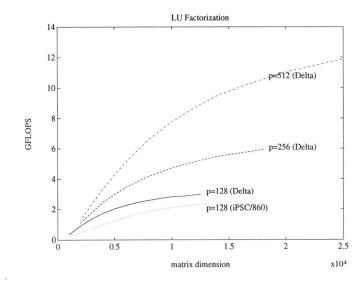

FIGURE 7.3   Performance attained by the LU factorization.

when the problem size is increased with the squareroot of the number of nodes [13]. This criteria is approximately met by the data used for Figure 7.5.

It should be noted that maximum performance per node is around 38 Mflops (DP) for matrix-matrix multiplication. However, the reported experiments used a set of BLAS that attained only 30–32 Mflops for such operations. This report will be updated with data from

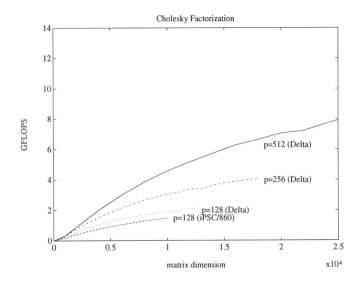

FIGURE 7.4   Performance attained by the Cholesky factorization.

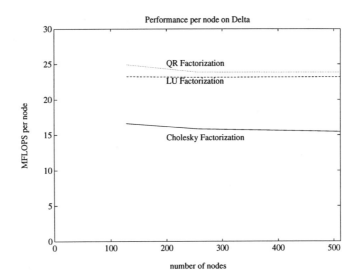

FIGURE 7.5   Performance per node on various machine sizes for the largest matrix dimension ($n^2/p \approx$ constant).

a set of BLAS that approaches the 38 Mflops performance. Results for the LU factorization using these BLAS have been reported in [13], reaching a peak performance of 14 Gflops on the Delta.

The data for the LU factorization reported in this paper were obtained using a faster version of the operating system, allowing slightly faster communication.

7.8

CONCLUSION

Our research shows that good performance can be attained for these algorithms on architectures like the Intel machines. Portability is enhanced through the use of the BLACS. The two-dimensional data distribution allows more flexibility, in addition to better performance and scalability (for details see [13]).

ACKNOWLEDGMENTS

This research was performed in part using the Intel Touchstone Delta System operated by the California Institute of Technology on behalf of the Concurrent Supercomputing Consortium. Access to this facility was provided by the California Institute of Technology and Intel Supercomputer Systems Division. In addition, the Intel iPSC/860 at Oak Ridge National Laboratory was utilized.

APPENDIX: MESSAGE-PASSING INTERFACE FORUM

During 1993 there was quite a bit of activity in the community to develop a standard interface for message-passing [15]. The main advantages of establishing a message-passing standard are portability and ease of use. In a distributed-memory communication environment in which the higher level routines and abstractions are built upon lower level message-passing routines, the benefits of standardization are particularly apparent. Furthermore, the definition of a message-passing standard provides vendors with a clearly defined base set of routines that they can implement efficiently, or in some cases provide hardware support for, thereby enhancing scalability. The standards activity goes by the name Message-Passing Interface (MPI) Forum and is composed of the major hardware and software vendors, as well as researchers from universities and laboratories around the world.

Simply stated, the goal of the MPI is to develop a standard for writing message-passing programs. As such the interface should establishing a practical, portable, efficient, and flexible standard for message passing.

A complete list of goals follows.

- Design an application programming interface (not necessarily for compilers or a system implementation library).
- Allow efficient communication: Avoid memory-to-memory copying and allow overlap of computation and communication and offload to communication coprocessor, where available.
- Allow for implementation that can be used in a heterogeneous environment.
- Allow convenient C and Fortran 77 bindings for interface.
- Assume a reliable communication interface: User need not cope with communication failures; such failures are handled by the underlying communication subsystem.
- Define an interface that is not too different from current practice, such as PVM, Express, and P4, and provide extensions that allow greater flexibility.
- Define an interface that can be implemented on many vendors' platforms, with no significant changes in the underlying communication and system software.
- Semantics of the interface should be language independent.
- The interface should be designed to allow for thread-safety.

This standard is intended for use by all those who want to write portable message-passing programs in Fortran 77 or C. This includes individual application programmers, developers of software designed to run on parallel machines, and creators of higher level programming languages, environments, and tools. In order to be attractive to this wide audience, the standard must provide a simple, easy-to-use interface for the basic user, while not semantically precluding the high-performance message-passing operations available on advanced machines.

The standard includes (this is temporarily as inclusive as possible):

- Point-to-point communication
- Collective operations
- Process groups
- Communication contexts
- Process topology
- Bindings for Fortran 77 and C
- Environmental management and inquiry
- Profiling interface
- Subset specification

An initial definition was completed in 1994. If you are interested in finding out more about the MPI effort, contact David Walker (walker@msr.epm.ornl.gov) at Oak Ridge National Laboratory.

Bibliography

1. E. Anderson et al., "LAPACK: A Portable Linear Algebra Library for High-performance Computers," *Proc. Supercomputing '90*, IEEE CS Press, Los Alamitos, Calif., 1990, pp. 1–10.
2. E. Anderson et al., *LAPACK Users' Guide*, SIAM Press, Philadelphia, Penn., 1992.
3. E. Anderson et al., "Basic Linear Algebra Communication Subprograms," *Proc. Sixth Distributed Memory Computing Conf.*, IEEE CS Press, Los Alamitos, Calif., 1991, pp. 287–290.
4. E. Anderson et al., "LAPACK for Distributed Memory Architectures: Progress Report," *Proc. Parallel Processing for Scientific Computing, 5th SIAM Conference*. SIAM Press, Philadelphia, Penn., 1991.
5. Z. Bai and J. Demmel, "Design of a Parallel Nonsymmetric Eigenroutine Toolbox, Part I," *Proc. 6th SIAM Conf. Parallel Processing for Scientific Computing*, SIAM Press, Philadelphia, Penn., 1993.
6. J. Choi et al., "ScaLAPACK: A Scalable Linear Algebra Library for Distributed Memory Concurrent Computers," *Proc. 4th Symp. Frontiers of Massively Parallel Computation*, IEEE CS Press, Los Alamitos, Calif., 1992, pp. 120–127.
7. J. Choi, J.J. Dongarra, and D.W. Walker, "The Design of Scalable Software Libraries for Distributed Memory Concurrent Computers," *Proc. CNRS-NSF Workshop on Environments and Tools for Parallel Scientific Computing*, Elsevier Science Publishers, Amsterdam, The Netherlands, 1993.
8. J. Demmel et al., "Prospectus for the Development of a Linear Algebra Library for High-performance Computers," Tech. Report 97, Argonne National Laboratory, Mathematics and Computer Science Division, Sept. 1987.
9. J.J. Dongarra et al., *LINPACK User's Guide*, SIAM Press, Philadelphia, Penn., 1979.
10. J.J. Dongarra et al., "A Proposal for a Set of Level 3 Basic Linear Algebra Subprograms," Tech. Report 88, Argonne National Laboratory, Mathematics and Computer Science Division, Apr. 1987.
11. J.J. Dongarra et al., "A Set of Level 3 Basic Linear Algebra Subprograms," *ACM TOMS*, Vol. 16, Mar. 1990, pp. 1–17.

12. J.J. Dongarra et al., *Solving Linear Systems on Vector and Shared Memory Computers*, SIAM Press, Philadelphia, Penn., 1990.

13. J. Dongarra, R. van de Geijn, and D. Walker, "A Look at Scalable Dense Linear Algebra Libraries," *Proc. Scalable High Performance Computing Conf.*, IEEE CS Press, Los Alamitos, Calif., 1992, pp. 372–379.

14. J. Dongarra and S. Ostrouchov, "LAPACK Block Factorization Algorithms on the Intel iPSC/860," LAPACK working note 24, Tech. Report CS-90-115, University of Tennessee, Oct . 1990.

15. J.J. Dongarra et al., "A Proposal for a User-level Message Passing Interface in a Distributed Memory Environment," Tech. Report TM-12231, Oak Ridge National Laboratory, Feb. 1993.

16. J.J. Dongarra, R. Pozo, and D.W. Walker, "An Object-oriented Design for High-performance Linear Algebra on Distributed Memory Architectures," *Proc. Object-oriented Numerics Conference*, 1993.

17. J.J. Dongarra and R.A. van de Geijn, "Two-dimensional Basic Linear Algebra Communication Subprograms," Tech. Report, LAPACK working note 37, Computer Science Department, University of Tennessee, Knoxville, Tenn., Oct. 1991.

18. J.J. Dongarra, R.A. van de Geijn, and D.W. Walker, A Look at Scalable Dense Linear Algebra Libraries, *Proc. Scalable High Performance Computing Conf.*, IEEE CS Press, Los Alamitos, Calif., 1992, pp. 372–379.

19. G.C. Fox et al., "Fortran D Language specification," Tech. Report CRPC-TR90079, Center for Research on Parallel Computation, Rice University, Dec. 1990.

20. G.C. Fox et al., *Solving Problems on Concurrent Processors*, Vol. 1. Prentice-Hall, Englewood Cliffs, N.J., 1988.

21. B.S. Garbow et al., *Matrix Eigensystem Routines—EISPACK Guide Extension*, Vol. 51 of *Lecture Notes in Computer Science*, Springer-Verlag, Berlin, Germany, 1977.

22. A. Gupta and V. Kumar, "On the Scalability of FFT on Parallel Computers," *Proc. Frontiers 90 Conf. on Massively Parallel Computation*, IEEE CS Press, Los Alamitos, Calif., 1990, pp. 69–74. Also available as Tech. Report TR 90-20 from the Computer Science Department, University of Minnesota, Minneapolis, Minn. 55455.

23. High-performance Fortran Forum, *High Performance Fortran Language Specification, Version 0.4*, Nov. 1992.

24. R.W. Hockney and C.R. Jesshope, *Parallel Computers*, Adam Hilger Ltd., Bristol, UK, 1981.

25. C. Leiserson, "Fat Trees: Universal Networks for Hardware-efficient Supercomputing," *IEEE Trans. Computers*, Vol. C-34, No. 10, pp. 892–901, 1985.

26. S.L. Lillevik, "The Touchstone 30 Gigaflop DELTA Prototype," *Proc. 6th Distributed Memory Computing Conf.*, IEEE CS Press, Los Alamitos, Calif., 1991, pp. 671–677.

27. A.J. Skjellum and C. Baldwin, "The Multicomputer Toolbox: Scalable Parallel Libraries for Large-scale Concurrent Applications," Tech. Report, Numerical Mathematics Group, Lawrence Livermore National Laboratory, Livermore, Calif., Dec. 1991.

28. B.T. Smith et al., *Matrix Eigensystem Routines—EISPACK Guide*, Vol. 6 of *Lecture Notes in Computer Science*, Springer-Verlag, Berlin, Germany, 1976.

29. Thinking Machines Corporation, Cambridge, Mass., *CM-5 Tech. Summary*, 1991.

CHAPTER 8

TECHNIQUES FOR PERFORMANCE MEASUREMENT OF PARALLEL PROGRAMS

Jeffrey K. Hollingsworth and Barton P. Miller
Computer Sciences Department, University of Wisconsin, Madison WI 53706, USA

James E. Lumpp, Jr.
Department of Electrical Engineering, University of Kentucky, Lexington, KY 40506-0046, USA

Abstract. *Programmers of parallel systems require high-level tools to aid in analyzing the performance of applications. Performance tuning of parallel programs differs substantially from the analogous processes on sequential architectures for two main reasons: the inherent complexity of concurrent systems is greater, and the observability of concurrent systems is complicated by the effects instrumentation can have on the behavior of the system. The complexity of parallel architectures combined with nondeterminism can make performance difficult to predict and analyze. Many approaches to help users to understand parallel programs have been proposed. This paper summarizes the problems associated with creating parallel performance measurement tools and describes some of the systems that have been built to solve these problems.*

8.1

INTRODUCTION

The primary reason for writing parallel programs is speed. Once a parallel program has been written and the errors have been eliminated, programmers generally turn their attention to the performance of their program. Most application programmers gauge the performance of their program by turnaround time, not throughput. Performance measurement tools exist to provide insight to programmers to help them understand why their programs do not run fast enough. For these tools to be effective, they need to collect data about the application, the operating system, and the hardware, and to synthesize it in a way to let programmers concentrate on getting their work done.

As the number and computational power of processors in parallel computers increase, the volume and complexity of performance data that must be gathered can explode. This wealth of information is a problem for the programmer who is forced to navigate through it, and for the tools that must store, process, and present it. This large volume of the performance data also has a high cost associated with collecting it. We divide the problem of measuring the performance of parallel programs into two parts: performance analysis and instrumentation. Performance analysis tries to sift through the huge volume of statistics available about a parallel program's execution and provide useful information to the programmer. The performance instrumentation problem focuses on how to efficiently collect enough information about a computation. A variety of different approaches have been designed to address these problems. We present an overview of some of these approaches and try to compare and contrast their relative advantages and disadvantages.

8.2

PERFORMANCE ANALYSIS TOOLS

The range of potential bottlenecks possible in parallel programming (compared to programming sequential machines) dramatically increases the need for performance analysis tools. Parallel machines not only have many copies of the resources (CPU, registers, IO systems) that can cause bottlenecks in sequential programs, but they also include unique features such as interconnection networks and coherency protocols that can contribute to performance problems. In this section, we concentrate on techniques designed to help programmers to improve the execution time of their program on a particular machine. We will not address the related problem of system tuning (tuning a parallel machine and operating system for a particular workload), which is also dramatically more complicated on parallel machines. However, it is worth noting that many of the tools described below are also appropriate for this problem.

The complexity and diversity of the hardware being used in today's parallel computers has led to a variety of different approaches in parallel performance tools. We divide these approaches into three categories: performance metrics, search-based tools, and performance visualization. However, in practice, most complete systems incorporate different approaches from several of these categories.

8.2.1 Performance Metrics

We define performance metrics as any statistic about a parallel computation designed to help programmers reduce the running time of their programs. Profile metrics are performance metrics that associate a single value with components of a parallel application (often procedures). Metrics are often presented as sorted tables so that the most important items are at the top of the display. Performance metrics originated in sequential programming as a simple profile of the CPU time consumed by each procedure in a program. The UNIX utility CPU time profiler, Prof [23], is an example of such a tool. A logical extension of this technique to parallel programs is to aggregate the CPU time profiles from each process (or thread) to provide a single profile for a parallel program. The profiling environment on the Connection Machine [68] provides this type of metric.

Simply extending sequential metrics to parallel programs is not sufficient because, in a parallel program, improving the procedure that consumes the largest amount of time may not improve the program's execution time. Interprocess dependencies in a parallel program influence which procedures are important to a program's execution time. The differences in parallel program performance metrics can be seen in the way they account for these interactions. We describe the various metrics in terms of a graph of the application's execution history, which incorporates both these interprocess dependencies as well as the sequential time. This graph is called a program activity graph (or PAG). Nodes in the graph represent significant events in the program's execution (such as lock and unlock operations, procedure calls, and returns). Arcs represent the ordering of events within a process or the synchronization dependencies between processes. Each arc is labeled with the amount of process and elapsed time between events. Figure 8.1 shows a simple PAG for a parallel program with three processes. The solid arcs represent useful CPU time intervals. The dashed lines indicate nonuseful CPU time from activities such as spinning on a lock.

One of the first metrics specifically designed for parallel programs is *Critical Path Analysis* [72]. The goal of this metric is to identify the procedures in a parallel program that are responsible for its execution time. The *critical path* of a parallel program is the longest CPU time weighted path through the PAG . Nonproductive CPU time, such as spinning on a lock, is assigned a weight of zero. The *critical path profile* is a list of the procedures along the *critical path* and the time each procedure contributed to the length of the path. The time assigned to these procedures determines the execution time of the program. Unless one of these procedures is improved, the execution time of the application will not improve.

Although Critical Path provides more accurate information than Prof, it does not consider the effect of subcritical paths (that is, second and third longest paths) in limiting the improvement possible by fixing a component on the critical path. An extension to Critical Path, called Logical Zeroing [51], addresses this problem. This metric sets the weight of all instances of a procedure in the PAG to zero, and computes the length of the new critical path. The difference between the old and new critical paths is an indication of how much the execution time of the program can be improved by fixing the selected procedure. Critical Path provides detailed information about how to improve a parallel program, but building the PAG and calculating the metric requires significant space and time.

The Quartz NPT [1] metric also addresses the interprocess dependencies that limit Prof's usefulness. NPT normalizes CPU time for each procedure based on the effective parallelism while that procedure is executing. No time is accumulated for procedures that are blocked due to synchronization. As a result, a procedure that executes serially is assigned a higher value (indicating it is more important) than a procedure with the same CPU time that executes during a parallel section of the code. This metric provides more accurate information than Prof. Unlike Critical Path, NPT does not use synchronization dependencies directly. This makes it easier to compute NPT while the program is executing. However, because NPT only looks at instantaneous information, it does not consider the effect of procedures prior to a bottleneck on that bottleneck. For example, if a process that is load imbalanced contains several procedures, NPT would give a higher value to the latter ones even though improving any procedure would reduce the load imbalance.

The first three metrics focused on finding CPU time bottlenecks. However, another source of bottlenecks in parallel programs is the memory hierarchy. By necessity, the

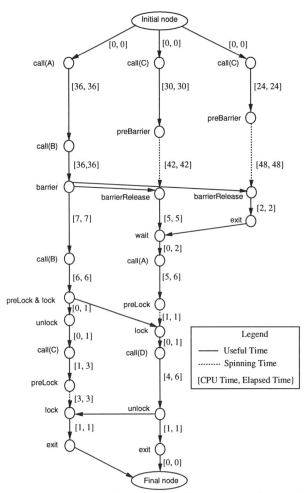

FIGURE 8.1 A sample program activity graph. Nodes represent interesting events in the application (such as procedure calls and message passing). The ordered pair indicates the CPU and elapsed times between events.

memory hierarchy in parallel computers is more complex than in sequential machines. Shared-memory parallel computers typically have several levels of caches and some form of cache coherency protocol. Effective use of this memory hierarchy is essential for high-performance applications. One way to try to understand the impact of the memory system on a parallel program was used in MTOOL [21]. The technique compares the observed execution time for each sequential region of the PAG to the ideal execution time if all memory references were serviced by the fastest part of the memory hierarchy. Differences between the observed and predicted execution times are due to instruction stalls that result from memory contention and extra time to access nonlocal memory. Information for each procedure can be combined to produce a table showing which procedures had the greatest impact on the memory system. An advantage of this approach is that users are able to get information that is not available directly from other systems. Unfortunately, the metric requires an accurate model of instruction costs to compute the predicated performance of each basic block.

Rather than trying to find a single metric to characterize the entire program, many tools provide sorted profiles of the utilization of several different resources. Some commonly profiled resources are: CPU utilization, synchronization time, disk operations, vectorization, and cache performance. INCAS [24], ANALYZER/SX [35], and JEWEL [37] are examples of this approach. An advantage of multiple metric tools is that they can provide information about several types of bottlenecks. In addition, the particular resource that is being overused can be isolated. However, this forces the user to select the appropriate resources to profile. For large programs running on massively parallel systems, there will be thousands (if not millions) of combinations of resources and program components to consider.

Building a tool that includes all possible metrics a user might want is difficult. One approach to this problem is to make a tool extensible and permit users to create their own metrics. An example of a tool that provides this feature is IPS-2 [29] which permits users to create new metrics as algebraic expressions of previously defined metrics. For example, IPS-2 does not have a built-in metric to indicate what share of the actual CPU time used went to each process. However, it is possible to define this metric in terms of a process's useful CPU time plus its spinning time divided by the total user CPU time on the system. This simple expression language provides an easy way to extend a performance tool. However, the types of metrics that can be defined by the user are limited by the base metrics provided by the tool developer.

Another way to make performance tools extensible is to provide a tool kit for building metrics. PPUTT [16] uses this approach by providing a set of analysis modules and a well-defined interface to an event stream. User's create new metrics by combining predefined analysis modules or writing their own. Extensible systems provide a powerful tool for a sophisticated user and a convenient way for tool developers to explore new metrics. However, many users do not know what additional metrics might be useful and are unable to use this functionality.

The major problem with having many metrics is knowing which one to use. Hollingsworth and Miller [31] compared several different metrics (including Critical Path , Logical Zeroing , and NPT) and concluded that there was no single best metric. In fact, the guidance from several of the metrics conflicted. However, they were able to characterize the types of programs where each metric would be useful. This information is valuable to programmers, and could help them select appropriate metrics. In addition, different metrics have different costs of computation. Sometimes a cheaper metric (for example, Prof) is sufficient, and so there is no need to calculate complex metrics. Unfortunately, no current tools incorporate these metametrics.

8.2.2   Search-based Tools

Performance metrics provide useful guidance for some types of bottlenecks; however, since different metrics are required for different types of bottlenecks the user is left to select the one to use. To provide better guidance to the user, rather than providing an abundance of statistics, several tools have been developed that treat the problem of finding a performance bottleneck as a search problem. These systems attempt to both identify the problem (descriptive) and to give advice on how to correct it (prescriptive).

AtExpert [36] from Cray Research uses a set of rules to help users improve Fortran programs written with the Cray auto-tasking library. The auto-tasking library provides automatic parallelism for Fortran programs; however, there are a number of directives that can greatly affect performance. AtExpert measures a program that has been auto-tasked and attempts to suggest directives that would improve the performance of the program. Since the tool works on a very specific programming model—Fortran programs on small-scale shared-memory multiprocessors—it is able to provide precise prescriptive advise to the user.

Crovella and LeBlanc's predicate profiling [15] provides a search system to compare different algorithms for the same problem as well as the scalability of a particular algorithm. They define a set of rules that test for possible losses in performance of a parallel program. They classify losses due to load imbalance, starvation, synchronization, or the memory hierarchy. All values are calibrated in terms of cycle times. The information is displayed as a bar chart showing where the available cycles went (both to useful work and various sources of loss). Information is presented for the entire application, which provides descriptive information about the type of bottleneck. However, it does not include prescriptive information about how to fix the problem or an indication of which procedure contains the bottleneck.

One way to search for performance bottlenecks is to have programmers specify assertions about the expected performance of their program. For example, programmers can express the expected CPU utilization or cache miss tolerances. The PSpec language [56] uses this approach. Using the tool is a three-step process. First, programmers specify their performance assertions. Second, the application is run with monitoring code enabled. Third, after the application has executed, a postmortem tool, called the *checker*, processes the logs and looks for assertion failures. Because performance assertions come from programmers, they can contain precise descriptions of the expected performance. However, writing assertions does create additional work for programmers. Also, they provide no prescriptive information to the users.

Another approach is to provide a search system that is independent of the programming model and machine architecture. The Performance Consultant [30] uses a hierarchical three-axis search model (the "why," "where," and "when" of a performance bottleneck). The "why" axis represents hypotheses about potential bottlenecks in a parallel program (such as message passing, computation, IO). The "where" axis defines a collection of resource hierarchies (CPU, interconnect, disk) that could cause a bottleneck. The "when" axis isolates the bottleneck to a specific phase of the program's execution. A unique feature of the Performance Consultant is that it searches for bottlenecks while the program is executing. This requires an adaptive style of instrumentation, but it can greatly reduce the volume of performance data that needs to be collected. Only the performance data required to test the current hypothesis for the currently selected resources need be collected. In addition to finding bottlenecks, the Performance Consultant includes an explanation system to both textually and graphically relate the performance bottleneck back to the user.

8.2.3 Visualization

A different approach to finding performance problems in parallel programs is to provide pictures to help programmers visualize the problems. We consider parallel program visualization to be any visual or aural tool that tries to provide the users feedback about how a parallel program is running. This definition includes tools to visualize low-level activity on a parallel machine, algorithm animation, and auralization.

A basic visualization is a representation of the physical machine. For example, MAP [11] represents the memory (really Fortran arrays) in a parallel computation as a two-dimensional grid. Whenever a memory location is referenced, its location in the grid is highlighted, and then slowly decays back to its original color (similar to the phosphor in a CRT screen). Frequently accessed memory locations get refreshed frequently and appear as a constant glow, while transient memory references are only flashes of light. This visualization is simple but effective for identifying memory contention.

Another tool that lets users view a parallel computation is PIE [42]. PIE provides a color graph consisting of coded bars representing a timeline. There is one timeline per CPU and the color of the timeline indicates what the CPU was doing at that point in time (such as useful work, blocked, spinning). The tool can also show which procedures are executing by assigning a different color to each procedure in the program. In addition, timelines for other levels of abstraction (for example, individual processes) can also be displayed. These displays are colorful and provide a feel for a program's execution, but it is difficult to interpret the pictures.

Similar to PIE, PF-View [70] illustrates the status of a parallel computation at multiple levels of abstraction. However, rather than presenting information as a timeline, it uses animation and graphical representations of program abstractions. The tool also provides a text window that shows the source code for the program being animated. This approach provides a display that is easier to understand and relate to the original code than PIE. A limitation of this tool is that the users are forced to watch a graphical execution of the program, looking for the bottlenecks, rather than having the tool show them the problem.

Another common visualization is an illustration of the synchronization patterns in a parallel computation. This is essentially drawing the program activity graph shown in Figure 8.1. The MAD debugger [73] provides what the authors call a *causality graph*. This is a graph with each thread indicated by a vertical line and the interthread communication and synchronization shown as diagonal lines. This picture shows a parallel computation in great detail. Unfortunately programmers must scan a complex graph trying to find the relevant events. In addition, scaling this visualization to massively parallel machines would be difficult.

The visualization tools discussed so far use a single visualization. Several tools have been developed that incorporate multiple visualizations. A good example of this type of tool is Paragraph [27] developed by Mike Heath and Jennifer Etheridge. Paragraph supports over 20 different types of displays. Many of these displays can be configured to plot values for different resources (such as messages and CPU time). This approach provides a vast number of different ways to display performance data. Unfortunately, not every visualization is useful for every program, and the users are left with the formidable task of selecting appropriate displays and resources.

One of the most difficult parts of creating visualization tools is selecting what to visualize. A solution to this problem is being explored in two systems, Pablo [58] and JEWEL [37]. Both of these systems contain tool kits for building visualization modules. The tool kits provide drawing primitives, event streams, and filtering modules. The users construct visualizations from these building blocks. This method permits an almost unlimited number of visualization modules to be built. However, these systems provide no assistance to the users in creating appropriate visualizations to find their performance bottlenecks.

Another type of visualization is algorithm animation. Algorithm animation tries to graphically represent a program's execution at a level of abstraction similar to the programmers' mental model of the program. According to Pancake and Utter [55], if the programmers can see the program the way they think about it, rather than how it is represented on the physical machine, it will be easier to find the problem. The difficult part is mapping events on the physical machine back to an abstract model. Two approaches have been tried to solve this problem.

The first approach is to provide a library of graphics primitives and let the programmers make calls to animation routines from the program. IVE [18] and Voyeur [65] use this approach. This provides great flexibility because users are able to create a precise animation that illustrates what the program is doing. However, it places the additional burden on the users of creating and debugging their animation while they are trying to create their program.

A second approach, used in Belvedere [32], is to provide an event stream and let the users define reduction and animation operations over it. Belvedere provides a higher level interface to the programmers since they don't need to identify the events in their program directly. In addition, it is possible to build up a library of standard visualizations to make the process of creating animations easier. However, it still requires that the programmers define their animation and maintain it along with their source program.

A variation on algorithm animation is auralization [17, 63, 66]. Instead of representing a program graphically, auralization animates it using sound, or a combination of sound and pictures. For example, message sends could be mapped to tones on the left channel and receives to the right channel. This permits programmers to get information about the frequency of messages, message flight time, and unmatched send and receive pairs. This technique provides an extra dimension to represent the program, but is still limited by the work required by programmers to select appropriate operations for auralization.

A major problem with visualization systems is that they are constrained by a trade-off between relevance and reusability. To provide information at a sufficiently high level to be useful, many visualization modules are specific to a single programming paradigm or, worse yet, a single application. To be useful for a wide variety of applications, visualization modules need to be based on low-level events (for example, message passing) that are common to a large number of programs. The single-visualization tools try to be useful for a wide variety of applications. The multiple-visualization and tool kit systems try to provide more specific information but are forced to incorporate large numbers of displays.

8.3

INSTRUMENTATION

For parallel computing tools to be useful, they need to collect sufficiently detailed data from a parallel program without perturbing it such that the data collected is not representative of the uninstrumented program. Performance tuning, debugging, and testing all require instrumentation to provide information about the execution. However, for each of these usages the type of information required varies. Performance tuning requires information about utilization of architectural features, while debugging and testing require detailed information concerning the global state of the computation. Many approaches have been tried to solve this problem: software traces, software event filters, and even custom hardware.

8.3.1 Program Instrumentation

One way to collect data about an application is to instrument the application executable so that when it runs it generates the desired information as a side effect. There are many ways to do this type of instrumentation: by inserting it into the application source code directly, by placing it into runtime libraries, or even by modifying the linked executable. Each of these approaches has advantages and disadvantages. Figure 8.2 shows the stages of a compilation and a sample of the places that different tools insert their instrumentation.

Collecting data via the runtime library (such as the C library) provides an easy way to collect data about the interactions between processes. IPS-2 [51] and Cedar tracing [46] use this approach. An advantage of runtime library instrumentation is that it does not require the users to modify their program, just relink ít with special flags. However, application-specific events are not visible at this level. For example, while tuning a database system the user might wish to trace commits and aborts.

Another approach is to directly instrument the user's application. AE [38] and CONVEX [25] use a modified compiler to insert instrumentation at the desired location. This provides access to information that is only available to compilers (such as data and loop dependencies). However, to add instrumentation into a compiler requires access to the source code for the compiler, and each compiler must be separately instrumented.

Alternatively, the instrumentation can be inserted directly into the executable image. QP [4] and MTOOL [21] use this technique. Binary instrumentation permits data to be collected in a language-independent way, and makes it easy to collect information about the runtime libraries in the same way that application data is collected. In addition, since recompilation is not necessary to insert instrumentation, it is easier to instrument large multimodule programs, which are time-consuming to recompile. It is also possible to insert instrumentation into programs and libraries for which the source code is not available. Using direct instrumentation of the application (as compared to kernel or library instrumentation) makes it possible to collect finer grained information. For example, loop-level or basic-block data can only be collected with these techniques.

It is also possible to hand modify an application to insert calls to collect performance data. JEWEL [37] uses this approach. This is the easiest way to implement an instrumentation system, and it provides the user a great degree of selectivity. Only what the user desires

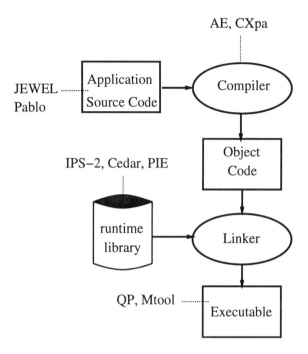

FIGURE 8.2   **Inserting instrumentation into a program. Instrumentation can be inserted at any stage of the compilation and linking process.**

to instrument gets collected. However, for large systems that require large amounts of instrumentation, this is a tedious process.

Finally, it is possible to use source-to-source translation of the program. This provides a means to automatically insert instrumentation before the program is compiled. An advantage of this approach is that instrumentation can be inserted without needing to modify the compiler. However, the data dependencies are not available, and of course, the program must be recompiled to collect the data. Pablo [58] uses this technique.

Most monitoring systems use some degree of software instrumentation. Because of the difficulty of inferring process-level information from the hardware view of the processor state, pure hardware systems are rare. Software solutions are also desirable to avoid the high cost of dedicated hardware. However, the consequence is increased intrusion of the collection activity on the monitored systems.

8.3.2   System Instrumentation

Sometimes collecting data by creating modified application processes is not desirable. Another software-based approach is to collect data via dedicated monitoring processes or via the operating system. This approach decouples the monitored system from the application process at the expense of easy access to application data structures. Figure 8.3 shows some of the ways in which programs can be externally monitored. This section

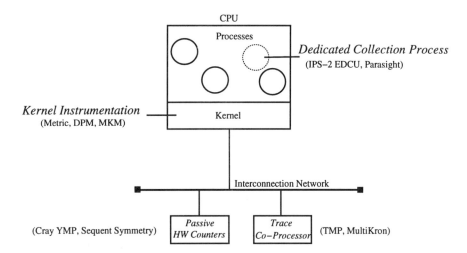

FIGURE 8.3 Inserting instrumentation into a system. External monitoring can be accomplished via software or special-purpose hardware.

describes the software approaches shown in the figure and the next section outlines options for additional hardware to support monitoring.

A common approach to collect performance data is to modify the operating system kernel to collect trace data and send it to a file or data reduction node. Kernel-based instrumentation has two advantages. First, it is easy to instrument programs, all that is required is a single kernel call to turn on the instrumentation. Second, some types of data (such as context switches and page faults) are difficult (if not impossible) to collect from user space or via hardware. However, kernel-based approaches suffer two limitations. First, modifying a kernel is time consuming, error prone, and requires users to run a modified kernel to use the tool. Second, some types of information (such as procedure calls) are not available from kernel-based instrumentation. Several systems have used this style of instrumentation. Smith's Spider debugger [62] used kernel-based instrumentation to track all interprocess communication, but it only worked on a single machine. Miller's Distributed Program Monitor [52] traces interprocess message passing in a multiprocessor distributed environment. The Mach Kernel Monitor [41] instruments context switches to trace the state of processes through time.

If modifying the operating system is not feasible or desirable, monitoring can be accomplished via dedicated data collection processes. The External Data Collection facility of IPS-2 [29] provides this capability. Information from the operating system is gathered by the collector processes and reported to the user. Most operating systems collect many statistics and make this information available via system calls. Hence much of the data that can be collected by directly instrumenting the operating system is available using external data collection.

If information specific to an application is desired, a hybrid approach is possible. For example, Parasight [2] uses monitoring threads (parasights) that run on idle processors to maintain monitoring information. "Light-weight" instrumentation in the target nodes is used to write monitoring information to shared memory while the Parasight threads read the data. Threads can be created dynamically, and instrumentation can be included or removed dynamically during execution of the program.

8.3.3   Hardware Instrumentation

Completely nonintrusive detection requires dedicated, stand-alone hardware instrumentation for the recognition of events. Additionally, a nonintrusive hardware monitor for a CPU with no special support for monitoring must passively monitor the CPU buses. Several CPU bus cycles, each representing state changes of the *processor*, will occur per instruction executed in the monitored system. Therefore, a change of state of the active process or an event in the active process will correspond to several processor state changes. A nonintrusive monitoring system must be capable of inferring process-level events from processor-level events that may be produced by the target processors at high rates. To monitor distributed multiprocessor systems, the monitoring system must itself be physically distributed and capable of cooperation between various monitoring units in order to recognize events that may be defined across a number of nodes. The design of the monitoring system becomes that of a complete distributed system with real-time inputs; however, the specialization of the system allows its implementation in a very efficient way.

Passive hardware monitors observe activity on a parallel computer and record results for later analysis. They are often implemented as a set of programmable counters that count the occurrences of events on the bus, in the memory hierarchy, and on the processor. The performance monitors built into the Sequent Symmetry [67], and the PEM Monitor [13] are examples of this approach. Advantages of this passive approach include no perturbation of the observed system, and relatively straightforward hardware requirements. Since these passive monitors record information for all activity on a system, it is difficult to correlate performance information with its source. The hardware monitor on the Cray Y-MP [14] improves this situation by providing per-process hardware collector information (by saving and restoring the state of the hardware collector as part of a context switch). However, all of these systems have two limitations. First, not all interesting events in a program's execution are visible to the hardware monitor; tracing procedure calls and returns is particularly difficult. Second, since there are more event signals than counters, the user must select appropriate events to monitor.

An example of a passive hardware monitor is the RP3 [10], which includes hardware instrumentation built into almost every subsystem of the computer. Each device recognizes its own events and passes the information through I/O pins to a performance monitor chip (PMC), which counts the events. The PMC also samples memory references in order to provide some statistics on memory usage. The capabilities are limited, however, due to constraints on space and cost imposed on the designs.

A more complex system to allow the nonintrusive monitoring of real-time distributed systems was proposed by Tsai et al, [69]. The processors are mimicked by an additional, identical processor in the monitoring system so that the state of the processor can be known explicitly when monitoring begins. The state of the mirror processor can be saved in response to events occurring within the monitored processor. All interactions of the processors are assumed to be explicit (for example, semaphores for shared data) and all significant events are recorded. The system also allows executions to be replayed.

Passive hardware monitors, however, have the disadvantage of having to infer process-level state changes from processor-level changes, typically processor bus signals. While it is possible for hardware to extract process-level events from bus signals, it is unrealistic to expect cost-effective hardware to do so. The cost for the monitoring system can easily equal the cost of the nodes of the target system. In addition, many popular high-performance architecture features work against hardware monitoring. Pipelines, register files, and on-chip memory management make many of the internal activities of the processor invisible from the external pins. A pipeline may fetch instructions never executed, variables of interest may be mapped to registers, and only the physical addresses output by the memory management unit are visible on the external address lines of the CPU. Also, because standards for monitoring support for microprocessors are not likely to occur in the near future, hardware monitoring systems must contain target specific designs, at least at the lowest levels of physical contact with the processors buses.

An approach to overcome the cost and information visibility limitations of passive hardware monitors is to build a hybrid software and hardware monitor. Reilly did comprehensive work instrumenting the DEC M31 system [59] and compared pure software, hardware, and hybrid monitoring. He noted that passive monitors required significantly more hardware than the hybrid approach. In addition, he reported that his hybrid system reduced the intrusion of the measured system by a factor of 10 to 20 times compared to software approaches. Based on this study, he concluded hybrid approaches were more practical than completely nonintrusive (passive) ones.

One approach to a hybrid monitor, used in the ZAHLMONITOR [28], is to have the program signal an event occurrence to the hardware via writes to special registers. The hardware counts each event occurrence, and either periodically sends the data to a file or reports it to an analysis process.

DISDEB uses nonintrusive hardware to monitor buses of the shared-memory Selenia Mara architecture (a system aimed at real-time process control applications) [39]. Compound event specifications are supported along with predicates for nonlocal events. The system includes monitoring boards with processors of equal power to the target nodes (8086 and 80286). The distributed hardware monitoring boards communicate via a signal bus. Event-action bindings can change dynamically, with interactive commands. Event-action predicates are necessarily limited by the limited hardware capabilities.

Another approach is to have the hardware collector generate trace data and send it to a data reduction station over a separate bus or interconnection network. MultiKron [54], TMP [24], and HYPERMON [48] are examples of this type of monitor. These are hybrid collectors because the user program initiates event recording by making a request to the hardware collector. This approach provides the flexibility and event visibility of direct instrumentation of an application with the low overhead of dedicated hardware collectors.

MultiKron is a custom VLSI coprocessor for performance monitoring. It is designed to look like a memory-mapped device to the main processor. To generate performance data, the main processor writes the event data to the coprocessor, which adds a processor ID and time stamp, and then generates the trace record. Traces are sent via a special-purpose monitoring bus to a central data reduction station. The chip also provides several programmable counters to record event frequency. MultiKron is designed as a general-purpose performance-monitoring coprocessor and can be used with a variety of different processors.

The TMP system uses software probes with hardware support to minimize intrusion. Each test and measurement processor (TMP) consists of a general purpose microprocessor and custom hardware to monitor the bus of the main processor. Application programs signal events to the TMP by generating references to a well-known (and otherwise unused) range of memory addresses. The system uses concepts of user and system events (called optional and standard). The microprocessor at each node filters events locally (to a degree) and then periodically sends updates to the central monitoring facility which handles the user interface. The system provides an option to view the state of programs in execution to aid in the debugging of long-running programs.

HYPERMON is a software instrumentation system assisted with hardware on iPSC/2 [48]. The system is aimed at providing performance monitoring support. The system includes a hardware board that monitors backplane signals, which can be manipulated with special I/O instructions in the processors. Data can be moved from the processes in 4-bit chunks that can prove to be a bottleneck. Unfortunately, the I/O operations are considerably slower than memory accesses.

The monitoring system proposed for PASM is a completely nonintrusive hardware-based system to support both debugging and performance evaluation [44]. The system includes physically distributed event recognition hardware with a central collection facility. It also includes a powerful event specification language based on the Event-Action Paradigm. The system allows intrusive actions to modify the state of the program for debugging and almost all event recognition is done in real-time.

Hardware instrumentation was included from the early stages in the design of Cedar in order to allow evaluation of the architecture and the programs subsequently written [46]. Information is gathered on the interconnection network, memory system, and signals from the backplane of the Alliant clusters. This information includes processor activity, cache requests, and address references. There is some support for "triggers" to support monitoring of software events. In order to use this feature, the processor writes to special memory ranges that enable/disable monitoring. The system supports profiling with actual execution time of code segments and processor utilization. It also permits tracing of some process and program-level activities.

Lumpp and Casavant have also designed a system to exploit the similarities between the monitoring requirements of testing and debugging. They employ a nonintrusive monitor of the target CPU buses [45]. Event specifications are divided into primitive (or runtime) events and compound events. The primitive events are monitored during execution, while compound events are identified in a postexecution analysis phase. The complexity of the primitive events is driven by the complexity of the runtime monitoring hardware and the compound events are defined by temporal or logical predicates involving primitive and compound events. An intrusive host-based prototype has been developed and is being evaluated [53].

All of these hardware monitors can reduce the intrusion of collecting data for parallel tools. However, a potential problem with hardware-based approaches is that they make it possible to cheaply collect so much data that it swamps the file system storing the data or the workstation trying toprocess it. Hardware-based instrumentation alone is not able to solve the data collection problem; tools must also be developed to assist with the intelligent collection of relevant data.

8.3.4 Event Specification

One of the key aspects of any monitoring system is how events are specified. The specification can have profound effects on the monitoring in both the types of information that can be gathered and the volume of data that must be handled. Monitoring cannot be separated from the specification of events. Many systems have included some type of specification language for events and almost all of them have included the ability to make temporal assertions on the events being monitored.

Snodgrass suggests storing monitoring information in a relational database called a *historical database*, which contains a history of objects [64]. The user can also generate all queries before execution and selectively monitor only events useful for identifying the relational queries. The performance penalty and intrusion would be much higher if the historical database approach is taken, because the number of primitive events to be recognized would greatly increase. Then complex events can be identified by queries on the database in TQuel and primitive events are gathered with software instrumentation in the users code or OS.

MPD applies path expressions and predecessor automata to event specification (regular expressions with history and concurrency constraints) [57]. The system uses the GDB debugger developed at CMU for Mach threads programs. Users set breakpoints corresponding to the terms of the path expressions defined previously. As breakpoints are reached the occurrence is recorded and used to evaluate the path predicates. The system assumes reproducibility of executions, which is odd for a debugger.

Many specification languages use temporal logic predicates to specify constraints (or assertions) on the monitored system. Goldszmidt proposed the division of debugging tools into two parts, a language-dependent part and language-independent part [22]. They implemented a prototype for Occam and Nil in which user code is automatically instrumented to communicate information to the debugger process through standard communication channels. In a post-execution phase the traces were traversed to verify assertions made with a temporal specification language. The user could also make database-like queries on the traces. In IDD (Interactive Distributed Debugger) the user specifies a set of temporal logic (interval logic) assertions, which are checked during the execution [26]. The prototype system was aimed at a distributed workstation environment. The system included runtime identification of assertion violations that were flagged for the user. The ECSP debugger (a debugger for ECSP, a CSP-like language) on the muTEAM system includes an event specification language based on assertions on the runtime behavior of the system [3]. The system attempts to compensate for intrusion by delaying for an equal amount of time any threads that synchronize with a thread delayed by instrumentation. They do not suggest how such a system could be implemented. However, it would rely on hardware for tightly coupled systems.

Another specification language is Peter Bates' Event Definition Language (EDL) [7]. EDL is a language permitting the user to create complex predicates for event classes composed of primitive events and logical and temporal operators. This provides the ability to abstract the activities of the system to higher level events and states specified by the user. The specification and identification of primitive events is left open, as are the problems of global time.

Several debugging systems have used EDL for event specification. Belvedere uses EDL to define events to be animated [33]. The system assumes most bugs in parallel programs are communication errors. The system uses postmortem animation of communications only; there is no support for events in sequential segments of code. Garcia and Berman also use EDL in a debugger that maps Path Pascal expressions to petri-net representations for debugging [20]. Path Pascal is based on monitor-like objects for concurrency control. The nets are used to represent a mutual exclusion scheme (objects in path pascal) on a multiprogrammed single CPU machine. Monitoring threads compete for system resources with the monitored program and no effort is made to limit bandwidth loss due to debugging information.

8.3.5   Event Filtering

The instrumentation techniques described above make it possible to track a vast number of metrics and events during an application's execution. However, they are limited by the large amount of performance data they can generate. One approach to reduce the amount of trace data generated is to filter it so that only interesting events are recorded. EDL, Segall's *receptacles* [61], and Jade [34] use predicates and actions to recognize desired events (or sequences of events) and then generate synthetic events based on recognized events. ISSOS [60] and Meta [50] also use predicates to detect interesting states in a program, but rather than use an event stream abstraction, users adds calls to the event recognizer into their program. Filtering greatly reduces the amount of performance data collected. However, all of these tools force users to select the desired events prior to starting their program.

Several tools incorporate dynamic control of the event recognition and filter process. EBBA [5, 6] is based on EDL, but permits dynamic insertion of the predicates. BEE [12] permits the dynamic control of the filtering of events based on event type and by insertion of more complex predicates called *event interpreters*. TOPSYS [8] and JEWEL [37] require that predicates be defined before the program starts execution, but permit dynamic control of which ones are enabled. Dynamic control of the information collected can greatly reduce the volume of performance data generated, but it creates that additional problem of selecting what data to collect. None of these tools directly addresses this problem.

8.3.6   Perturbation Compensation

In all of the instrumentation techniques described above (except purely passive), some perturbation of the application program will occur. While most techniques attempt to minimize the impact of these delays, a different approach is to compensate for this effect.

The concept of intrusion has been studied in several contexts and is also known as the *probe effect* [19]. Intrusion can be defined as any use of target system resources for monitoring activities [49]. For example, a print statement being used for debugging to log the contents of a variable constitutes intrusion through the use of CPU cycles and the I/O data paths. Intrusion includes both direct contention for resources (for example, CPUs, memory, or communication links), and secondary interference with resources (for example, interactions with cache replacement or virtual memory). Both of these effects must be considered for all resources in the system to quantify the intrusion introduced by the instrumentation.

Approaches to addressing the intrusion problem can be divided roughly into four categories. These are (listed in increasing order of difficulty to implement):

1. Realize that intrusion affects measurement and treat the resulting data as an approximation.
2. Leave the added instrumentation in the final implementation.
3. Try to minimize the intrusion.
4. Quantify the intrusion and compensate for it.

Clearly, approach 1 is not generally desirable. It leads to nondeterminism, eliminates the possibility of cyclic debugging, and leaves the user wondering, "What really happened?" Although approach 2 effectively eliminates intrusion, it does so at the expense of the performance of the application. Approach 2 may indeed be feasible for applications that do not depend on performance; however, these problems are in the minority of problems typically targeted for high-performance systems. As a result, approach 3 is by far the most popular approach to date. Even though it does not assure the elimination of intrusion like approach 2, it does not degrade the performance of the final application. This approach is most popular in systems with a sufficient amount of nondeterminism already present in the computation. In this case, the goal is to assure the perturbation does not produce an execution flow that was not "likely." These techniques do not actually remove the intrusion but hide them in the inherent asynchrony and delays of the computation. Unfortunately, there is still the chance the intrusion changed the behavior of the application.

Some systems simply subtract the time required for the intrusion. An example is the PREFACE system [9]. In PREFACE, programs are assumed to be composed of parallel and serial portions; the bulk of the intrusion is done in the serial portions where the time perturbations can be subtracted without the possibility of changing any event orderings. In the parallel regions, the time necessary for execution of the instrumentation is also subtracted. However, no attempt is made to identify when intrusion actually introduces changes in the ordering of events, and the approach is not useful in the general case.

Compensation for intrusion of software instrumentation was studied carefully for the PIE system [40]. The PIE system was designed for tightly coupled shared-memory multiprocessors and was intended as a portable performance-tuning environment. The software intrusion model includes both probes within processes and monitoring processes that can compete with the monitored processes. Intrusion is assumed to be limited to time delays incurred and is assumed to be constant and measurable. Again, no attempt was made to compensate if the ordering of events changed due to delays. However, they did differentiate between the *orders* of intrusion: *order 1* is delays in threads, *order 2* is a change of order of events, and *order 3* is a change that alters the outcome of the computation.

Maloney and Reed studied the intrusion of software instrumentation for performance monitoring on the Intel iPSC/2, Cray X-MP, and Cray-2 [47]. They studied the timing delays introduced by intrusion and attempted to quantify changes in the ordering of events. They modeled intrusion as delays and constructively recovered the compensated timings. Both *time-based* and *event-based* models were developed to compensate for the temporal changes to the application and the order changes possible through differential delays of processes. Because the goal was to approximate the performance of the instrumented applications, precise order information was not necessary. Their approach was to develop approximate models of instrumentation intrusion and then refine them until acceptable predictions of performance were possible.

Lumpp and Casavant, et al. developed techniques for compensation of perturbations in message-passing systems [43]. The approach includes requirements on the parallel system, the instrumentation, and the parallel program in order to assure that recovery is possible. Their work differs from previous work in that the correctness of the ordering of events is paramount. The concurrent program and the target architecture are viewed as a single complex system and modeled. Control theoretic techniques are employed to analyze the traces [71]. Given sufficient trace information, it is possible to recover the timings that would have occurred in the absence of the instrumentation. In addition, the technique determines when the instrumentation causes event order changes that can affect the subsequent behavior of the computation.

Bibliography

1. T.E. Anderson and E.D. Lazowska, "Quartz: A Tool for Tuning Parallel Program Performance," *Proc. 1990 SIGMETRICS Conf. Measurement and Modeling of Computer Systems*, ACM Press, New York, N.Y., 1990, pp. 115–125.

2. Z. Aral and I. Gertner, "A High-level Debugger/Profiler Architecture for Shared-memory Multi-processors," *Proc. 1988 Int'l Conf. Supercomputing*, IEEE CS Press, Los Alamitos, Calif., 1988, pp. 131–139.

3. F. Baiardi, N.D. Francesco, and G. Vaglini, "Development of a Debugger for a Concurrnet Language," *IEEE Trans. Software Eng.*, Vol. SE-12, No. 4, Apr. 1986, pp. 547–553.

4. T. Ball and J.R. Larus, "Optimally Profiling and Tracing Programs," *Proc. Conf. Record 19th ACM Symp. Principles of Programming Languages*, ACM Press, New York, N.Y., 1992, pp. 59–70.

5. P. Bates, "Distributed Debugging Tools for Heterogeneous Distributed Systems," *Proc. 8th Int'l Conf. Distributed Computing Systems*, IEEE CS Press, Los Alamitos, Calif., 1988, pp. 308–315.

6. P. Bates, "Debugging Heterogeneous Distributed Systems Using Event-based Models of Behavior," *Proc. ACM SIGPLAN/SIGOPS Workshop Parallel and Distributed Debugging*, ACM Press, New York, N.Y., 1988, pp. 11–22.

7. P.C. Bates and J.C. Wileden, "EDL: A Basis For Distributed System Debugging Tools," *Proc. 15th Hawaii Int'l Conf. System Sciences*, IEEE CS Press, Los Alamitos, Calif., 1982, pp. 86–93.

8. T. Bemmerl et al., "The Design and Implementation of TOPSYS," Tech. Report TUM-INFO-07-71-440, Technische Universitat Munchen, Germany, July 1991.

9. D. Bernstein, A. Bolmarcich, and K. So, "Performance Visualization of Parallel programs on a Shared-memory Multiprocessor System," *Proc. Int'l Conf. Parallel Processing (ICPP)*, The Pennsylvania State University Press, University Park, Penn., 1989, pp. 1–10.

10. W.C. Brantley, K.P. McAuliffe, and T.A. Ngo, "RP3 Performance Monitoring Hardware," in *Instrumentation for Future Parallel Computer Systems*, R.K. Margaret Simmons and I. Bucker, ed., Addison-Wesley, Reading, Mass., 1989, pp. 35–47.

11. O. Brewer, J. Dongarra, and D. Sorensen, "Tools to Aid in the Analysis of Memory Access Patterns for FORTRAN Programs," *Parallel Computing*, Vol. 9, No. 1, 1988/89, pp. 25–35.

12. B. Bruegge, "A Portable Platform for Distributed Event Environments," *Proc. 1991 ACM/ONR Workshop Parallel and Distributed Debugging*, ACM Press, New York, N.Y., 1991, pp. 184–193.

13. H. Burkhart and R. Millen, "Performance Measurement Tools in a Multiprocessor Environment," *IEEE Trans. Computers*, Vol. 38, No 5, May 1989, pp. 725–737.

14. Cray Research Inc., *UNICOS File Formats and Special Files Reference Manual*, SR-2014, 5.0 edition.

15. M.E. Crovella and T.J. LeBlanc, "Performance Debugging Using Parallel Performance Predicates," *Proc. 1993 ACM/ONR Workshop Parallel and Distributed Debugging*, ACM Press, New York, N.Y., 1993, pp. 140–150.

16. R.J. Fowler, T.J. LeBlanc, and J.M. Mellor-Crummey, "An Integrated Approach to Parallel Program Debugging and Performance Analysis on Large-scale Multiprocessors," *Proc. SIGPLAN/SIGOPS Workshop Parallel and Distributed Debugging*, ACM Press, New York, N.Y., 1988, pp. 163–173.

17. J.M. Francioni, L. Albright, and J.A. Jackson, "Debugging Parallel Programs Using Sound," *Proc. 1991 ACM/ONR Workshop Parallel and Distributed Debugging*, ACM Press, New York, N.Y., 1991, pp. 68–75.

18. M. Friedell et al., "Visualizing the Behavior of Massively Parallel Programs," *Proc. Supercomputing 91*, IEEE CS Press, Los Alamitos, Calif., 1991, pp. 472–480.

19. J. Gait, "A Probe Effect in Concurrent Programs," *Software—Practice and Experience*, Vol. 16, No. 3, Mar. 1986, pp. 225–233.

20. M.E. Garcia and W.J. Berman, "An Approach to Concurrent Systems Debugging," *Proc. 5th Int'l Conf. on Distributed Computing Systems*, IEEE CS Press, Los Alamitos, Calif., 1985, pp. 507–514.

21. A.J. Goldberg and J.L. Hennessy, "Performance Debugging Shared-memory Multiprocessor Programs with MTOOL," *Proc. Supercomputing 91*, IEEE CS Press, Los Alamitos, Calif., 1991, pp. 481–490.

22. G.S. Goldszmidt, S. Katz, and S. Yemini, "Interactive Blackbox Debugging for Concurrent Languages," *Proc. ACM SIGPLAN/SIGOPS Workshop Parallel and Distributed Debugging*, Vol. 24, No. 1, ACM Press, New York, N.Y., Jan. 1989, pp. 271–282.

23. S.L. Graham, P.B. Kessler, and M.K. McKusick, "gprof: A Call Graph Execution Profiler," *Proc. 1982 SIGPLAN Symp. Compiler Construction*, ACM Press, New York, N.Y., 1982, pp. 120–126.

24. D. Haban and D. Wybranietz, "A Hybrid Monitor for Behavior and Performance Analysis of Distributed Systems," *IEEE Trans. Software Eng.*, Vol. 16, No. 2, Feb. 1990, pp. 197–211.

25. G.J. Hansen, C.A. Linthicum, and G. Brooks, "Experience with a Performance Analyzer for Multithreaded Application," *Proc. 1990 Int'l Conf. Supercomputing*, 1990, pp. 124–131.

26. P.K. Harter, Jr., D.M. Heimbigner, and R. King, "IDD: An Interactive Distributed Debugger," *Proc. 5th Int'l Conf. Distributed Computing Systems*, 1985, pp. 498–506.

27. M.T. Heath and J.A. Etheridge, "Visualizing Performance of Parallel Programs," *IEEE Software*, Vol. 8, No. 5, Sept. 1991, pp. 29–39.

28. U. Hecksen et al., "Measuring Simultaneous Events in a Multiprocessor System," *Proc. 1982 SIGMETRICS Conf.*, ACM Press, New York, N.Y., 1982, pp. 77–88.

29. J.K. Hollingsworth, R.B. Irvin, and B.P. Miller, "The Integration of Application and System-based Metrics in a Parallel Program Performance Tool," *Proc. 1991 ACM SIGPLAN Symp. Principals and Practice of Parallel Programming*, ACM Press, New York, N.Y., 1991, pp. 189–200.

30. J.K. Hollingsworth and B.P. Miller, "Dynamic Control of Performance Monitoring on Large-scale Parallel Systems," *Proc. 7th ACM Int'l Conf. Supercomputing*, ACM Press, New York, N.Y., 1993.

31. J.K. Hollingsworth and B.P. Miller, "Parallel Program Performance Metrics: A Comparison and Validation," *Proc. Supercomputing '92*, IEEE CS Press, Los Alamitos, Calif., 1992, pp. 4–13.

32. A.A. Hough and J.E. Cuny, "Perspective Views: A Technique for Enhancing Parallel Program Visualization," *Proc. Int'l Conf. Parallel Processing (ICPP)*, The Pennsylvania State University Press, University Park, Penn., 1990, pp. II.124–132.

33. A.A. Hough and J.E. Cuny, "Initial Experiences with a Pattern-oriented Parallel Debugger," *Proc. SIGPLAN/SIGOPS Workshop on Parallel and Distributed Debugging*, ACM Press, New York, N.Y., 1988, pp. 195–205.

34. J. Joyce et al., "Monitoring Distributed Systems," *ACM Trans. Computer Systems*, Vol. 5, No. 2, May 1987, pp. 121–150.

35. K. Kinoshita, "An Experience with the ANALYZER/SX Performance Tuning Tool," in *Instrumentation for Future Parallel Computer Systems*, R.K. Margaret Simmons and I. Bucker, ed., Addison-Wesley, Reading, Mass., 1989, pp. 223–231.

36. J. Kohn and W. Wiliams, "ATExpert," *J. Parallel and Distributed Computing*, Vol. 18, 1993, pp. 205–222.

37. F. Lange, R. Kroeger, and M. Gergeleit, "JEWEL: Design and Implementation of a Distributed Measurement System," *IEEE Trans. Parallel and Distributed Systems*, Vol. 3, No. 6, Nov. 1992, pp. 657–71.

38. J.R. Larus, "Abstract Execution: A Technique for Efficiently Tracing Programs," *SPE.*, Vol. 20, No. 12, Dec. 1990, pp. 1241–1258.

39. B. Lazzerini and C.A. Prete, "A Programmable Debugging Aid for Real-time Software Development," *IEEE Micro*, Vol. 6, No. 3, June 1986, pp. 34–42.

40. T. Lehr, *Compensating for Perturbation by Software Performance Monitors in Asynchronous Computations*, doctoral thesis, Carnegie Mellon University, 1990.

41. T. Lehr et al., "MKM: Mach Kernel Monitor Description, Examples and Measurements," Tech. Report CMU-CS-89-131, Carnegie Mellon University, Mar. 1989.

42. T. Lehr et al., "Visualizing Performance Debugging," *Computer*, Vol. 21, No. 10, Oct. 1989, pp. 38–51.

43. J.E. Lumpp, Jr., *"Models for Recovery from Software Instrumentation Intrusion,"* doctoral thesis, University of Iowa, 1993.

44. J.E. Lumpp, Jr., et al., "Specification and Identification of Events for Debugging and Performance Monitoring of Distributed Multiprocessor Systems," *Proc. 10th Int'l Conf. Distributed Computing Systems*, IEEE CS Press, Los Alamitos, Calif., 1990, pp. 476–483.

45. J.E. Lumpp, Jr., R.K. Shultz, and T.L. Casavant, "Design of a System for Software Testing and Debugging for Multiprocessor Avionics Systems," *Proc. 15th Ann. Int'l Computer Software and Applications Conf. (COMPSAC91)*, IEEE CS Press, Los Alamitos, Calif., 1991, pp. 261–268.

46. A.D. Malony, "Multiprocessor instrumentation: Approaches for Cedar," in *Instrumentation for Future Parallel Computing Systems*, M. Simmons, R. Koskela, and I. Bucher, ed., Addison-Wesley, Reading, Mass., 1989, pp. 1–34.

47. A.D. Malony, *Performance Observability*, doctoral thesis, University of Illinois, 1990.

48. A.D. Malony and D.A. Reed, "A Hardware-based Performance Monitor for the Intel iPSC/2 Hypercube," *Proc. 1990 Int'l Conf. Supercomputing*, 1990, pp. 213–226.

49. D.C. Marinescu et al., "Models for Monitoring and Debugging Tools for Parallel and Distributed Software," *J. Parallel and Distributed Computing*, Vol. 9, No. 2, June 1990, pp. 171–184.

50. K. Marzullo and M.D. Wood, "Tools for Constructing Distribued Reactive Systems," Tech. Report 91-1187, Cornell University, Jan. 1991.

51. B.P. Miller et al., "IPS-2: The Second Generation of a Parallel Program Measurement System," *IEEE Trans. Parallel and Distributed Systems*, Vol. 1, No. 2, Apr. 1990, pp. 206–217.

52. B.P. Miller, C. Macrander, and S. Sechrest, "A Distributed Programs Monitor for Berkeley UNIX," *Proc. 5th Int'l Conf. Distributed Computing Systems*, IEEE CS Press, Los Alamitos, Calif., 1985, pp. 43–54.

53. S.P. Miller, J.E. Lumpp, Jr., and G.B. Doak. "Modified Decision/Condition Testing," Tech. Report WP91-2005, Rockwell International Corporation, 1991.

54. A. Mink et al., "Multiprocessor Performance Measurement Instrumentation," *Computer*, Vol. 23, No. 9, Sept. 1990, pp. 63–75.

55. C.M. Pancake and S. Utter, "Models for Visualization in Parallel Debuggers," *Proc. Supercomputing '89*, ACM Press, New York, N.Y., 1989, pp. 627–636.

56. S.E. Perl and W.E. Weihl, "Performance Assertion Checking," *Proc. 14th ACM Symp. Operating Systems Principles*, ACM Press, New York, N.Y., 1993, pp. 134–145.

57. M.K. Ponamgi, W. Hseush, and G.E. Kaiser, "Debugging Multithreaded Programs with MPD," *IEEE Software*, Vol. 8, No. 3, May 1991, pp. 37–43.

58. D.A. Reed et al., "The Pablo Performance Analysis Environment," Tech. Report, Dept. of Comp. Sci., University of Illinois, 1992.

59. M. Reilly, "Instrumentation for Application Performance Tuning: The M31 System," in *Instrumentation for Future Parallel Computer Systems*, R.K. Margaret Simmons and I. Bucker, ed., Addison-Wesley, Reading, Mass., 1989, pp. 143–158.

60. K. Schwan et al., "A Language and System for Parallel Programming," *IEEE Trans. Software Eng.*, Apr. 1988, pp. 455–471.

61. Z. Segall et al., "An Integrated Instrumentation Environment for Multiprocessors," *IEEE Trans. Computers*, Vol. C-32, Jan. 1983, pp. 4–14.

62. E.T. Smith, *Debugging Techniques for Communicating, Loosely-Coupled Processes*, doctoral thesis, University of Rochester, Dec. 1981.

63. S. Smith and M.G. Williams, "The Use of Sound in an Exploratory Visualization Environment," Tech. Report R-89-002, University of Lowell, 1989.

64. R. Snodgrass, "A Relational Approach to Monitoring Complex Systems," *ACM Trans. Computer Systems*, Vol. 6, No. 2, May 1988, pp. 157–196.

65. D. Socha, M.L. Baily, and D. Notkin, "Voyeur: Graphical Views of Parallel Programs," *Proc. ACM SIGPLAN/SIGOPS Workshop Parallel and Distributed Debugging*, ACM Press, New York, N.Y., 1988, pp. 206–215.

66. D.H. Sonnenwald et al., "InfoSound: An Audio Aid to Program Comprehension," *Proc. 23rd Hawaii Int'l Conf. System Sciences*, Vol. 11, IEEE CS Press, Los Alamitos, Calif., 1990, pp. 541–546.

67. S.S. Thakkar, "Performance of Parallel Applications on a Shared-memory Multiprocessor System," in *Performance Instrumentation and Visualization*, M. Simmons and R. Koskela, ed., Addison-Wesley, Reading, Mass., 1990, pp. 233–256.

68. R. Title, "Connection Machine Debugging and Performance Analysis: Present and Future," *Proc. ACM/ONR Workshop Parallel and Distributed Debugging*, ACM Press, New York, N.Y., 1991, pp. 272–275.

69. J.J.P. Tsai, K.Y. Fang, and H.Y. Chen, "A Noninvasive Architecture to Monitor Real-time Distributed Systems," *Computer*, Vol. 23, No. 3, Mar. 1990, pp. 11–23.

70. S. Utter-Honig and C.M. Pancake, "Graphical Animation of Parallel Fortran Programs," *Proc. Supercomputing '91*, IEEE CS Press, Los Alamitos, Calif., 1991, pp. 491–500.

71. K.J. Williams et al., "Conditions for Tracking Timing Perturbations in Timed Petri-Nets with Monitors," in *Discrete Event Systems: Modeling and Control*, S. Balemi, P. Kozak, and R. Smedinga, ed., Berkhauser-Verlag, Basel, Switzerland, 1993, pp. 141–151.

72. C.-Q. Yang and B.P. Miller, "Performance Measurement of Parallel and Distributed Programs: A Structured and Automatic Approach," *IEEE Trans. Software Eng.*, Vol. 12, Dec. 1989, pp. 1615–1629.

73. D. Zernik and L. Rudolph, "Animating Work and Time for Debugging Parallel Programs Foundation and Experience," *Proc. 1991 ACM/ONR Workshop Parallel and Distributed Debugging*, ACM Press, New York, N.Y., 1991, pp. 46–56.

CHAPTER 9

OPERATING SYSTEMS FOR PARALLEL MACHINES

Bodhisattwa Mukherjee and Karsten Schwan
College of Computing
Georgia Institute of Technology
Atlanta, Georgia 30332-0280

Abstract. *The complexity of parallel hardware and the performance requirements of user programs introduce new challenges to the design and implementation of parallel operating systems. This chapter surveys the research and commercial contributions to parallel operating systems to date. We first briefly present the characteristics of various multiprocessor architectures and identify some of the key issues in parallel operating systems. Then, we review the interfaces of a few sample threads libraries. Finally, issues and solution approaches are illustrated by case studies of a variety of research and commercial parallel operating system kernels.*

9.1

MULTIPROCESSOR HARDWARE

Depending on the coupling of processors and memory, multiprocessors may be broadly divided into two major categories [3, 67]:

- *Shared-memory multiprocessors*. In a shared-memory multiprocessor, all main memory is accessible to and shared by all processors. Shared-memory multiprocessors are classified on the basis of the cost of accessing shared memory:

  - *Uniform memory access (UMA) multiprocessors*. In a UMA architecture, the access time to shared memory is the same for all processors. A sample UMA architecture is the bus-based architecture of the Sequent multiprocessor, where a common bus links several memory modules to the computing modules.

  - *Nonuniform memory access (NUMA) multiprocessors*. In a NUMA architecture, all physical memory in the system is partitioned into modules, each of which is local to and associated with a specific processor. As a result, access time to local memory is less than that to nonlocal memory. Sample NUMA machines are the BBN Butterfly parallel processor [30] and the Kendall Square Research supercomputer [77].

- *No remote memory access (NORMA) multiprocessors.* In this class of architectures, each processor has its own local memory that is not shared by other processors in the system. Hypercubes like the NCube multiprocessors, past *Intel iPSC* hypercubes and current *Intel iSC* mesh machines [69], the Thinking Machines CM-5 [85], and workstation clusters are examples of nonshared memory multiprocessors. Workstation clusters differ from hypercube or mesh machines in that the latter typically offer specialized hardware for low-latency intermachine communication and also for implementation of selected global operations like global synchronization, addition, or broadcast.

UMA architectures are the most common parallel machines, in part because most such machines are simply used as high-throughput multiprogrammed, multiuser timesharing machines, rather than as execution vehicles for single, large-scale parallel programs. Interestingly, although all memory is accessed via a single shared bus, even UMA machines often have NUMA characteristics because individual processors access shared memory via local caches. Cache misses and cache flushing can result in effectively nonuniform memory access times. Furthermore, bus contention may aggravate variability in memory access times, and scalability is limited in that the shared global bus imposes limits on the maximum number of processors and memory modules it can accommodate.

A NUMA architecture addresses the scalability problem by attaching local memory to each processor. Processors directly access local memory and communicate with each other and with remote memory modules through an interconnection switch. One type of switch is an interconnection network consisting of multiple levels of internal nodes, in which systems are scaled by addition of internal switch nodes, as in the BBN Butterfly multiprocessors [30]. A second type of switch consists of a hierarchical set of buses [47, 77], in which access times to remote memory depend on either the number of internal switch nodes on the access path between the processor and the memory or on the number of traversed system buses. Because a NUMA architecture allows a large number of processors in a single machine, many experimental, large-scale multiprocessors are NUMA machines, an example being the *IBM RP3*, which was designed to contain up to 512 processors [17], and the *KSR* machine, also offering up to 512 processors.

NORMA multiprocessors are the simplest to design and build, and have become the architecture of choice for current supercomputers such as the Intel Paragon [69], the Cray T3D machine, and others. In the simplest case, a collection of workstations on a local area network constitutes a NORMA multiprocessor. A typical NORMA multiprocessor consists of a number of processors interconnected on a high-speed bus or network; the topology of interconnection varies. One major difference between NUMA and NORMA multiprocessors is that there is no hardware support for direct access to remote memory modules. As a result, NORMAs are more loosely coupled than NUMA machines. However, recent advances in supercomputer technologies are leading to tradeoffs in remote to local memory access times for NORMA machines (for example, roughly 1:500 for local versus remote memory access times) that can approximate those achieved for shared-memory machines like the KSR (roughly 1:100). This suggests that future NUMA or NORMA parallel machines will require similar operating system and programming tool support in order to achieve high-performance parallelism.

The variety of different kinds of multiprocessor architectures coupled with diverse application requirements have resulted in many different designs, goals, features, and implementations of multiprocessor operating systems in university research projects and in the commercial domain. The purpose of this chapter is to review some of the major concepts in operating systems for parallel machines, roughly reflecting the state of the art in the early 1990s.

9.2
KEY OPERATING SYSTEM ISSUES

The basic functionality of a multiprocessor operating system must include most of the functions of uniprocessor systems. However, complexities arise due to the additional functional capabilities in multiprocessor hardware and more importantly, due to the high requirements of performance imposed on the operating system. Specific problems to be addressed concerning performance include the efficient representation of asynchronous active entities like processes or threads, the provision of alternative communication schemes and synchronization mechanisms, and resource scheduling like process assignment to different processors and data placement in physically distributed memory [128], and finally, the parallelization of the operating system itself, again in order to provide scalable performance for varying application requirements [47].

9.2.1 Processes

The classic functions of an operating system include creation and management of active entities such as processes. The effectiveness of parallel computing depends on the performance of such primitives offered by the system to express parallelism.

One way to express parallelism is by using *heavyweight* processes/threads sharing portions of their address spaces. Such a process consists of a single address space and a single thread of control. Kernels supporting such processes do not distinguish between the thread and its address space. The parallelism expressed using heavyweight processes is coarse-grained and can be inefficient for parallel programs. First, the creation and deletion of heavyweight threads is expensive because the kernel treats a thread and its address space as a single entity, so that threads and address space are created, scheduled, and destroyed together. Second, context switches for such threads are expensive since there are additional costs due to address space management. Finally, there is a long term cost associated with cache and TLB performance due to the address space change [100].

In many contemporary operating system kernels, address spaces and threads are decoupled resulting in address spaces containing multiple execution threads. Such threads are referred to as *middleweight* threads or *kernel-level* threads. The advantage of middleweight threads is that since they are managed by the operating system kernel, the kernel can directly schedule an application's threads onto the available physical processors. Such kernel-level

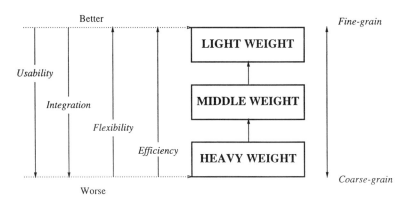

FIGURE 9.1   Evolution of threads.

threads offer a general programming interface to the application. However, kernel-level threads also exhibit some problems that can make them impractical for use in fine-grained parallel programs, including (1) relatively costly protected kernel calls are required to invoke thread management operations, and (2) the single model of parallel computation presented by kernel-level threads is unlikely to be efficient for all parallel programs.

To address the above problems with kernel-level threads, system researchers have turned to *user-level* threads, also known as *lightweight* threads. Since user-level threads are managed by runtime library routines linked into each application, a thread management operation does not require an expensive kernel call. Furthermore, lightweight threads enable an application program to use a thread management system most appropriate to its problem domain. Mach Cthreads [27], the University of Washington threads [5, 6], and Georgia Tech threads [102, 103] are a few popular lightweight threads implementations (Section 9.3 reviews the interfaces of a few sample threads libraries). Lightweight threads are scheduled on top of middleweight or heavyweight threads, which in turn are scheduled by the kernel on the available physical processors. There are a few problems with such a *two-level scheduling* policy: (1) typically, user-level threads do not have any knowledge of kernel events (for example, processor preemption, I/O blocking and resuming, and so on), so that the application library cannot identify and schedule threads on "just idle" processors, and (2) when the number of runnable kernel-level threads in a single address space is greater than the number of available processors, kernel-level threads must be multiplexed on the available processors. This implies that user-level threads built on top of kernel-level threads are actually scheduled by the kernel's thread scheduler, which has little or no knowledge of the application's scheduling requirements or current state [5] (Figure 9.1 summarizes the discussion).

Problems with multilevel scheduling arise from the lack of information flow between different scheduling levels. Therefore, these problems can be solved by (1) implementing mechanisms for efficient communication between the user-level thread scheduler and the kernel-level thread scheduler [96], (2) explicit vectoring of kernel events to the user-level thread scheduler [5, 141], and (3) notifying the kernel of user-level events affecting processor allocation [96].

9.2.2   Process Scheduling

A thread/process scheduler allocates available time and processors to a job or a process statically or dynamically [91] according to a certain scheduling policy. Basic theoretical results on static process scheduling on parallel machines show that the scheduling problem is NP-hard. There is much available literature [86, 98, 147, 148] reviewing and evaluating various scheduling policies. In this section, we briefly describe a few important policies focusing on dynamic scheduling [98], and on scheduling for shared-memory machines, where variations in distances between different processors on the parallel machine [128] are not considered.

Static and Dynamic Scheduling   A static scheduler makes a one-time decision per job regarding the number of processors to be allocated. Once decided, the job is guaranteed to have exactly that number of processors whenever it is active. A static scheduler offers low runtime scheduling overhead [39], but it also assumes a stable parallel application. This is a reasonable assumption for many large-scale scientific applications in which parallelism is derived by decomposition of regular data domains [124]. Recent work, however, is focusing more on dynamic scheduling for two reasons: (1) because most complex large-scale parallel applications exhibit irregular data domains or changes in domain decompositions over time, so that a static processor allocation rapidly becomes inefficient, and (2) because large-scale parallel machines are often used in multiuser mode, so that scheduling must take into account the requirements of multiple parallel applications sharing a single machine [31, 94, 95, 130]. Comparisons of the performance of static and dynamic schedulers for multiuser workloads [148] demonstrate that (1) dynamic scheduling performs best when context-switch overheads are small, (2) the advantage of dynamic scheduling at low context-switch costs increases with larger and more rapid changes in the parallelism exhibited by a workload, and (3) dynamic scheduling performs increasingly well relative to the static counterpart as system load increases.

As with uniprocessors, multiprocessor schedulers can be classified as preemptive or nonpreemptive, according to their scheduling granularity and according to queue ordering policy. A majority of multiprocessor scheduling policies are extensions of the *single queue of tasks* scheduling policy of uniprocessors [86].

Single Shared Ready Queue   Research addressing UMA multiprocessors has typically assumed the use of a single ready queue shared by all processors. With this queue, policies like first come, first served (FCFS), shortest job first (SJF), or round robin (RR) are easily implemented, and have been evaluated in the literature. More interesting to us are schedulers and scheduling policies directly addressing the primary requirement of a parallel program: if performance improvements are to be attained by use of parallelism, then the program's processes must be scheduled to execute in parallel.

Coscheduling   The goal of coscheduling (or gang scheduling) [86, 106] is to achieve a high degree of simultaneous execution of processes belonging to a single job. This is particularly useful for a parallel application with cooperating processes that communicate frequently. A coscheduling policy schedules the runnable processes of a job to run simultaneously on different processors. Job preemption implies the simultaneous preemption of all of its processes. Effectively, the system context switches between jobs.

Hand-off Scheduling   A thread scheduler can accept user hints [15] to chose the next thread from running. A *discouragement hint* is used to discourage the scheduler from running the current thread. A *hand-off hint* is used to suggest to the scheduler to run a specific thread. Using a hand-off hint, the current thread hands off the processor to another thread without intermediate scheduler interference. Hand-off scheduling has been shown to perform better when program synchronization is exploited (for example, the requester thread hands off the processor to the holder of a lock) and when interprocess communication takes place (for example, the sender hands the processor off to a receiver).

The performance of an application has been observed to worsen considerably when the number of processes in the system exceeds the total number of processors. This decreased performance is attributed to several problems [57, 141], including the interaction of spinlocks and scheduling policies—a process may be preempted while inside a spinlock-controlled critical section, while the other processes "busy wait" to enter the critical section. Identical problems arise when programs' processes are engaged in producer/consumer relationships. Furthermore, frequent context switches occur when the number of processes greatly exceeds the number of processors. Last, when a processor is interleaved in multiple-address space, cache misses are a major source of performance degradation [138].

Careful application design and coscheduling [40] may handle the problems associated with spinlock-controlled critical sections and those with producer-consumer processes, but they do not address the problem of cache corruption or frequent context switches.

Affinity Scheduling   The problems of cache corruption and context switch frequency are addressed by the affinity scheduling policy [82, 142]. A process's processor affinity is based on the contents of the processor's cache. The basic policy schedules a process on a processor on which it last executed hoping that a large percentage of its working set is still present in the processor's cache. Since the policy inherently discourages process migration, it may lead to severe load imbalance. A few variations of this policy [82] address this issue. The affinity (for local memory) also plays a vital role in scheduling processes in a NUMA machine; the context of a process resides mostly near the processor on which the process executed last.

Dynamic Partitioning   The dynamic partitioning [109, 141] (also known as *process control with processor partitioning*) policy has the goal of minimizing context switches, so that less time is spent rebuilding a processor's cache. The policy is based on the hypothesis that an application performs best when the number of runnable processes is the same as the number of processors. As a result, each job is dynamically allocated an equal fraction of the total number of processors, but no job is allocated more processors than it has runnable processes. Each application program periodically polls a scheduling server to determine the number of processes it should ideally run. If the ideal number is less than the actual number, a process suspends some of its own processes, if possible. If the ideal number is greater than the actual number, a previously suspended process is woken up. This policy has limited generality since it requires interactions between user processes and the oper-

	FCFS	SJF	RR	Co-sched	Hand-off	Affinity	Dyn-part
spin-lock	Y	Y	Y	N	Y	Y	N
context switch	N	Y	Y	Y	Y	Y	N
cache misses	Y	Y	Y	Y	Y	N	Y
generality	Y	Y	Y	Y	Y	Y	N
load balance	N	N	N	N	Y	Y	N

FIGURE 9.2   Comparison of scheduling policies.

ating system scheduler, and since it requires that user programs are written such that their processes can be suspended and woken up during program execution.

Figure 9.2 compares these scheduling policies by the spinlock problem (does the spinlock problem exist?), the context switch problem (can the policy cause frequent context switch?), the cache problem (does the policy consider the cache affinity factor?), generality (is the policy general enough for all applications?), and the load balancing problem (is there a chance of load imbalance in the system?).

Ongoing research also addresses the development of schedulers for specific application domains or for specific target machines. One such area is real-time systems. In a real-time system, a scheduling policy must satisfy timing constraints such as deadlines, earliest start times, and so on, of an incoming job. Before a job is assigned one or more physical processors, the scheduler checks whether the system can satisfy the job's timing constraints. This analysis is known as *schedulability analysis* [34, 149].

9.2.3   Synchronization

When multiple cooperating processes execute simultaneously, synchronization primitives are needed for concurrency control [54]. Two fundamental properties are enforced by synchronization: (1) mutual exclusion and (2) event ordering. Classical synchronization primitives such as *semaphores*, *monitors*, and so on, are widely discussed in textbooks and are, therefore, not described here. Also not discussed are more complex synchronization mechanisms such as path expressions and serializers [16], in part because such mechanisms are not in widespread use. Instead, this section briefly reviews some common and efficient synchronization constructs supported by recent multiprocessor operating systems.

Locks   A lock is a shared data structure used to enforce mutual exclusion. To enter a critical section, a process first atomically gains ownership of the associated lock (called *locking*). A contender process for the lock waits by either spinning or blocking until the lock is released by its current owner. When a process exits a critical section, it atomically releases the lock ownership (called *unlocking*). Parallel operating systems typically support multiple types of locks. *Spinlocks* are the most primitive lock types in which a contender process spins (*busy-waits*) until the lock is released. On the other hand, when using a *blocking lock*, a waiting process blocks until awakened by the process releasing the lock. Although spin-waiting consumes processor, bus, and memory cycles, early research in multiprocessor operating systems clearly demonstrates the advantages of spinlocks [47, 73, 144] in two situations—when the critical section is small (compared to the cost of thread context switch) or when no other useful work is available for the processor (since spin-waiting results in minimum latency between lock release and reacquisition) [6, 99].

A *read-write lock* allows either multiple readers or a single writer to enter a critical section at the same time. The waiting processes may either spin or block depending on whether the lock is implemented as a *spinning read-write* lock or a *blocking read-write* lock.

A *barrier lock* [99] implements a barrier in a parallel program. Once a process reaches a barrier, it is allowed to proceed if and only if all other cooperating processes reach the barrier. A waiting process may either spin or block depending on the implementation of the lock.

Configurable locks [75, 104, 105] allow applications to dynamically alter the waiting (spin, block, or both) mechanism and the request handling mechanism (how the lock is scheduled) to suit application and hardware characteristics. Hints from lock owners may be used to configure a lock for improving its waiting strategy ("advisory" or "speculative" locks). Such locks together with an adaptation policy, called *adaptive multiprocessor locks* [105], can detect changes in application characteristics and adapt themselves in response to changes in an application's locking pattern. A few object-oriented operating systems such as Choices [19] and Renaissance [122] take an object-oriented approach to lock configuration/customization. These systems define a few basic classes that provide simple and crude locks (implemented using hardware-provided instructions). More sophisticated locks are implemented either on top of these existing classes or by customizing the existing locks.

In distributed-memory machines such as hypercube or mesh multiprocessors, operating system constructs (for example, I/O, exception handling, multicast communications, and so on [72]) are physically distributed in order to offer efficient access to the global operating system functionalities required by application programs. Synchronization is no exception because it is a computation that must be performed globally for many physically distributed processes and processors. As a result, synchronization must be performed using explicit communication structures such as rings or spanning trees, which touch upon all members of the group of processes being synchronized. In essence, a lock in a distributed memory machine is a fragmented and distributed abstraction shared among several independently executable processes, where the importance of this particular abstraction is demonstrated by explicit support in hardware in several parallel machines, including the Intel Paragon and the Thinking Machines CM line of machines. However, in contrast to the OS support for UMA and NUMA multiprocessors, synchronization abstractions for distributed-memory machines can often be optimized substantially if they can be made *programmable* by application programmers or if synchronization can be combined with other communications being performed in application programs [43, 126]. This is reflected in modern hardware. For example, the CM-5 machine's hardware offers a rich set of global operations for use by application programs, also called *idioms* by compiler writers. In contrast, the communication coprocessor of the Intel Paragon offers a computational communication library that implements many of the useful global operations and data manipulations described in [126] or offered by the CM-5's hardware.

Other Synchronization Constructs   *Condition variables* [12] make it possible for a thread to suspend its execution while awaiting an action by some other thread. *Events* are mainly used to control thread orderings. A process may wait on an event; it blocks until the event occurs. Upon event occurrence, a signal wakes up one or all waiting processes. More complicated event structures have been shown useful for several application domains and target machines, most prominently the event-handling facilities for *active messages* [90, 126] or the *synchronization points* for real-time applications [50].

The new generation of parallel machines provides a few powerful atomic operations such as test-and-set and compare-and-swap (or their counterparts for distributed-memory machines), which can simplify the implementation of synchronization primitives and can even allow certain concurrent data structures to be implemented without blocking [62]. Moreover, instructions such as fetch-and-add [52] allow certain common operations to be performed in parallel without critical sections [75].

9.2.4   Interprocess Communication

Cooperating processes or threads in a multiprocessor environment often communicate and synchronize. Such interprocess communication employs one of two schemes: shared variables or message passing. This section focuses on interprocess communication without using explicit shared variables.

In a shared-memory multiprocessor, message-passing primitives between disjoint address spaces may be implemented using global memory. Exchange of messages is a more abstract form of communication than accessing shared-memory locations. Message passing subsumes communication, buffering, and synchronization.

Multiprocessor operating systems have experimented with a large variety of different communication abstractions, including *ports* [42, 146] *mailboxes* [72], *links* [78, 133], and so on. From an implementation point of view, such abstractions are kernel-handled message buffers. They may be either *unidirectional* or *bidirectional* and may have certain *rights* (such as send, receive, or ownership rights) associated with them.

The two basic communication primitives in all such abstractions are *send* and *receive*, which may be *blocking* versus *nonblocking*, or *conditional* versus *unconditional*. Communication between processes using such primitives may be either *synchronous* or *asynchronous*. Many additional issues must be considered for an interprocess communication mechanism [135, 136] including (1) whether the underlying hardware supports reliable or unreliable communication, (2) whether messages are typed or untyped and of variable or fixed length, (3) how to support message priority (it may be necessary that some messages are handled at higher priorities than others), (4) how to transmit names, and (5) how kernel and user programs must interact to result in efficient message transfers. Recent research in communication protocols for high-performance or parallel machines also addresses the association of computational activities with messages [32, 90], the user-driven configuration of communication protocols for improved performance [64], and the parallelization of protocol processing [88].

Many parallel programs use both message mechanisms and shared memory (when available) for interprocess communication. This is demonstrated by implementations of message systems like PVM on the KSR supercomputer, and by implementations of message systems for the BBN Butterfly NUMA machine. Interestingly, comparisons of message passing with direct use of shared memory often result in inconclusive results, in part because such results strongly depend on the sizes, granularities, and frequencies of communications in parallel programs [84].

Most recent shared-memory multiprocessor operating systems support *cross-address space remote procedure calls* [9] (*RPC*) as a means of interprocess communication. RPC is a higher level abstraction than message passing. It hides the message communication layer beneath a procedure call layer. RPC allows efficient and secure communications. Furthermore, cross-address space RPCs can be made to look identical to cross-machine RPCs, except that messages do not go out over the network and in most cases, only one operating system kernel is involved in RPC processing.[1] Otherwise, the same basic paradigm for control and data transfer is used. Messages are sent by way of the kernel between independent threads bound to different address spaces.

A recently developed kernel-based communication facility called *lightweight remote procedure call* (*LRPC*) [9], which is designed and optimized for communication between address spaces on the same machine, combines the control transfer and communication model of capability systems with the programming semantics and large-grained protection model of RPC. Another interprocess communication scheme, called *user-level remote procedure call* (*URPC*) [10], decouples processor allocation from data transfer and thread management by combining fast cross-address space communication protocol using shared memory with lightweight threads managed entirely at the user level.

Research on object-oriented operating systems for parallel machines is concerned with a generalized form of remote procedure calls used for interobject communications, also called *object invocations*. Specific results include the provision of mechanisms for implementation of alternative ways to invoke an object, as offered by the Spring operating system's *subcontract* mechanism [60], the Chaos operating system's building blocks for diverse invocation primitives [127], and the Chaos-arc system's *policy* abstraction [50]. The basic need for such alternatives is again derived from performance or reliability considerations, where applications would like to have the ability to vary the performance or even the semantics of object invocation (for example, reliable versus unreliable invocations) separately from the target objects being invoked or the precise parameters being passed. This is the ability provided by subcontracts in Spring, by attributes and policies in Chaos, and by invocation attributes associated with individual accesses to fragmented objects built for hypercube machines [126] and for multiprocessors [26].

9.2.5 Memory Management

Memory management for UMA multiprocessors is conceptually similar to that for multiprogrammed uniprocessors. However for UMA machines, operating system writers must exploit the available hardware parallelism when implementing efficient memory management. For early research on memory management in parallel machines, including the implementation of physically distributed, internally parallel memory managers, the reader

---

[1]It is possible to have more than one kernel in a NUMA machine.

is referred to [47, 72, 73], which present the innovative designs and structures of memory or object managers for the Cmmp and Cm* multiprocessor systems. Recent research has focused primarily on page management, namely, on memory management in the context of virtual memory systems implemented for parallel machines.

A typical virtual memory system manages a memory hierarchy consisting of a cache, uniformly accessible primary memory, and significantly slower secondary memory. Unlike the traditional approach of a three-level store, the Accent operating system [42], supports *a single-level store*, in which primary memory acts as a cache of secondary storage. File-system data and runtime allocated storage are both implemented as disk-based data objects. Copies of large messages are managed using *shadow paging* techniques.

A central feature of Accent is the integration of virtual memory and communication. Large amounts of data can be transmitted between processes with high performance using memory mapping techniques. As a result, client and server processes can exchange potentially large data objects like files without concern for the traditional data copying cost of message passing. In effect, Accent carries into the domain of message passing systems the notion that I/O can be performed through virtual memory management.

The design of the Mach system's memory management is largely derived from the Accent system [114, 146]. Its single-level store is attractive because it can simplify the construction of an application program by allowing programmers to map a file into the address space of a process, and because it can improve program performance by permitting file data to be read directly into physical memory pages rather than into intermediate buffers managed by the operating system. Furthermore, because physical memory is used to cache secondary storage, repeated references to the same data can often be made without corresponding disk transfers.

Memory management services and implementations are generally dependent on the operating system as well as the underlying machine architecture. Some of the current research has focused on designing memory management functionalities and interfaces that are independent of the machine architecture and the operating system kernel [1, 114] by isolating the machine-dependent portion of the virtual memory subsystem as a separate module. Some operating systems [7, 42] even allow applications to specify the protection level (inaccessible, read-only, read-write) of pages, and allow user programs to handle protection violations.

A NUMA multiprocessor organization leads to memory management design choices that differ markedly from those that are common in systems designed for uniprocessors or UMA multiprocessors. Specifically, NUMA machines like the BBN Butterfly do not support cache or main-memory consistency on different processors' memory modules. Such consistency must be explicitly enforced for shared memory by user- or compiler-generated code performing explicit block or page moves. As a result, NUMA architectures implementing a shared-memory programming model typically expose the existing memory access hierarchy to the application program [140], giving programmers the ability to minimize relatively expensive remote versus less expensive local memory references (that is, maximize program locality [73]), and permitting programmers to customize applications by avoiding several forms of potential contention (switch or memory contention).

Most early NUMA multiprocessor systems did not offer virtual memory support. However, recent NUMA or NORMA parallel machines like the Thinking Machines CM-5, the Kendall Square KSR, and the Intel Paragon offer virtual memory support. For example, the KSR machine offers consistent global virtual memory. However, the performance reasons for exposing programmers to the underlying machine's NUMA properties persist, leading the system designers to include hardware instructions for page prefetches and poststores [68].

Other research in memory management for parallel machines has focused on designing techniques for NUMA multiprocessors that relieve programmers from the responsibility of explicit code and data placement. A few common techniques used (multiprocessor operating systems such as Mach [114], Psyche [83], and Platinum [29] use a variation or a mix of these algorithms) are the migration algorithm, the read-replication algorithm and the full-replication algorithm [134, 150]. The first algorithm migrates data to the site where it is accessed in an attempt to exploit locality in data accesses and decreases the number of remote accesses. The other two algorithms replicate data so that multiple accesses can happen at the same time using local accesses. Realizing that the problem of memory management is similar to the problem of cache management and consistency for UMA multiprocessors, such systems [114, 146] attempt to minimize the amount of data-copying and replication by using lazy techniques like page *copy-on-write*.

Current research is exploring how shared memory may be represented on parallel or distributed machines such that its performance can approximate that of message-passing systems. For example, some memory models exploit the fact that synchronization is used to control access to shared state (for example, properly labeled memory [48] or data race-free memory [2]). This allows the underlying system to weaken memory consistency requirements. The weaker consistency does not guarantee that the execution of memory operations of all processes is equivalent to some sequential execution of these operations as in a sequentially consistent system. To execute applications in such weakly consistent memory systems, either the applications must have data sharing patterns that are not affected by the weaker consistency, or the program must explicitly deal with the lack of strong consistency. The resulting, weakened shared-memory abstraction presented to programmers may be implemented efficiently because strong consistency (and therefore, interprocessor communication) is not required for all memory accesses. Other models of shared memory developed for distributed architectures exploit programmer directives to reduce the cost of coherence maintenance [22], or they provide explicit primitives with which users can maintain application-specific notions of coherence of shared state [4].

Since differences in remote to local access times are significant in NUMA machines and distributed machines such as sets of workstations connected via high-speed networks, notions of distributed objects [26] have been a topic of research for such systems for quite some time, as evidenced by work on weak memory abstractions [22] and fragmented objects [131].

9.2.6 Concurrent I/O

Input/Output in Parallel Machines   Input/output in a parallel machine is performed via two media: (1) to attached medium- or long-term storage devices such as disks, optical disks, or tapes, and (2) to attached network devices connecting the machine to remote storage and/or visualization engines. Unfortunately, improvements in the CPU and main-

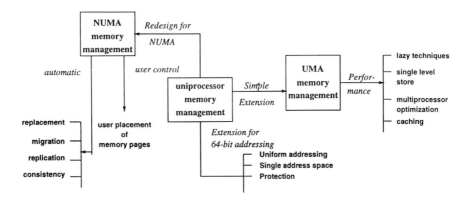

FIGURE 9.3   Trends in memory management research.

memory speeds of parallel machines have outpaced improvements in their I/O performance. The performance of single CPU systems has improved by more than 100 times in the last several years, whereas I/O latencies and bandwidths for disk-based I/O have improved only by factors of two to four [56]. This disparity has caused the I/O systems of parallel architectures such as the storage subsystem (for example, the disk drive hardware) to become a serious bottleneck for many parallel application programs [63]. Therefore, for all but the most compute-intensive applications, overall system throughput of complex applications is typically limited by the speed of the underlying architecture's I/O subsystem.

In response to the problem of limited I/O bandwidth in parallel machines, I/O system designers have resorted to parallelism to increase I/O bandwidth or even to decrease I/O latencies. For example, parallel transfer disks that can access multiple disk heads simultaneously are commercially available [45]. Similarly, there are commercially available storage arrays to manage a collection of disk drives under a single controller, spreading data across all drives so that it can be accessed in parallel [97]. The RAID project at Berkley [110] aims to develop storage arrays to as many as 1000 disks. However, their initial focus was to incorporate internal redundancy to increase reliability instead of performance.

Another approach to improving I/O performance is to use the main memory of idle machines (or processors) on a network as a backing store for the machines (or processors) that are active [41], thereby reducing disk I/O. However, such approaches will be successful only if designers also increase the access latencies and speeds to the underlying network devices used for intermachine communication. Recent research has shown that those speeds depend more on the implementation and performance of network communication protocols than on the speeds of the physical network devices [64]. This is leading to increased attention being paid to alternative implementations of communication protocols, including their configurability and the use of parallelism in protocol execution [64, 89]. Furthermore, it should be apparent that increased performance in network access will require the connection of multiple physical network devices to each single, large-scale parallel machine.

High-performance I/O subsystems have been a key element in a few earlier computer systems. For example, in the early 1960s the CDC6600 used 10 to 20 peripheral processors to control I/O with a powerful central processor to provide computation cycles. Recently, NCUBE and Intel Scientific Computers have introduced I/O subsystems that support parallel access to multiple disks from the computer nodes of a hypercube to provide scalable mass storage and I/O bandwidth.

Current research in I/O systems is targeted toward developing I/O subsystems that provide low latency and high bandwidth as well as high-level abstractions that make it easy for programmers to use such systems [56]. Some of the central issues in the design of such systems include [44]: (1) the architecture of the subsystem (synchronous versus asynchronous disk access, device connection network, distribution, reliability), (2) disk caching, and (3) file storage structure (striped versus declustered). The remainder of this section surveys some of the concurrent file systems developed to date, and briefly outlines current and past research in configurable and parallel communication protocols.

NCUBE's I/O Subsystem   The NCUBE I/O architecture is based on separate *NChannel Boards*, each containing a ring of 16 I/O nodes. Each such node uses the same processor as used for the machine's compute nodes, and it controls a single I/O channel to a disk controller handling from 1 to 4 disks. Parallelism in disk access is achieved at several levels: (1) the single I/O channel can handle up to four concurrent requests to one of its attached disks, (2) each I/O node is directly connected to several (1 to 8) compute nodes, and latency in I/O is small because the paths between the compute and I/O nodes are organized such that every fourth compute node has a direct path to the NChannel node. This implies that each compute node is no more than two hops away from an I/O node. Once a message arrives at the NChannel board, it is routed to the proper I/O board using the board's ring interconnection [112].

File system software (that is, software support for the NChannel board) is simple. Unlike Intel's CFS system described next, files are not automatically spread (or striped) across multiple disks. Instead, each disk implements a separate file system. File pathname prefixes determine the disk on which a file is stored [112]. A comparison of the Intel and NCUBE systems, reported in [112], concludes that the Intel CFS software support allows applications to easily use the parallel I/O capabilities of the hardware without any special application software. It also makes the I/O system easy to evolve without affecting application programs. In comparison, application programs on the NCUBE need system-specific code to use the I/O subsystem.

Intel's Concurrent File System   The Intel iPSC/2 system, and later systems iPSC/3 and iPSC/860 consist of a number of compute nodes, interconnected in a hypercube geometry, and a number of I/O nodes. The Intel iSC Paragon and the Touchstone Delta machine use a mesh node interconnect, but again permit systems to be configured with any number of I/O versus compute nodes, such that typically each I/O node is connected to a different compute node[2]. Each I/O node controls from 1 to 7 I/O devices (disks) via a SCSI bus, and permits the attachment of one of several network devices (for example, Ethernet).

---

[2]One way to visualize a large-scale Paragon machine is as a number of compute nodes at the "bottom" of the mesh, connected to some number of I/O nodes at the "top," each of which is connected to some number of physical I/O devices such as disks or network links.

Since there are no physical connections between all compute and I/O nodes, however, I/O communications are typically performed via the same interconnect as the one used by the compute nodes. This can cause problems as I/O traffic increases [44, 112]. Few parallel machines have addressed these problems as part of their architectural design, instead assuming the use of software solutions. One notable exception is the RP3 machine, which used additional buses for the machine's I/O subsystem and directly connected those buses to the parallel machine's main memory. Similar solutions are now being used in the newly developed Convex MPP machine.

Using the hardware described above, the concurrent file system (CFS) implements a fully parallel file system on the Intel iPSC/2 (and later systems). The CFS hides the I/O system's implementation from the user and provides an extended UNIX user interface [44].

The CFS implementation consists of a single process that maintains all directory information for CFS files (this process services the file-open and directory-service requests) and multiple disk processes (one per I/O node) that each service read and write requests from compute nodes [112]. Each file is split into blocks (4 kbytes) upon creation, and is spread (striped) across multiple disks by default. Blocks are assigned to different I/O nodes for storage. Such CFS files can be accessed in parallel by multiple compute processes. The disk processes receive access requests for individual blocks directly from application programs. Each disk process caches copies of recently used blocks in local memory for improved performance [112].

A performance study [44] concludes that the primary reasons for performance improvements in the CFS are declustering, concurrent access, disk caching, and prefetching on the I/O nodes.

ELFS   ELFS (extensible file system), developed at the University of Virginia, attacks the problem of providing high-bandwidth and low-latency I/O. It attempts to reduce the burden on application programmers to optimize I/O operations for existing file system models, to manage the proliferation of data formats and architectural differences. This is achieved by using language and runtime support that permits the specification of a hierarchy of file classes [55, 56]. Such classes can define domain-specific I/O operations, prefetching and caching strategies, and class-specific optimization information. ELFS file objects may be partitioned and striped across multiple physical devices in a domain sensitive manner, thereby improving I/O bandwidth. Instances of the file classes are accessed asynchronously and in a pipelined manner (if possible) to improve performance. Furthermore, ELFS classes may be constructed to hide data format heterogeneity, automatically translating data as it is accessed.

ELFS file abstractions are structured as a user-extensible class hierarchy with inheritance, thus providing an object-oriented programming model to the application designer. The class hierarchy contains the base class *unix-file* supporting the standard UNIX file operations. There are four subclasses currently defined in the class hierarchy: *pfos* distribute a file across multiple devices for improved bandwidth, *2D_matrix_files* provide matrix I/O operations that are efficient for row and column operations, *binary_tree_files* perform aggressive prefetching for nonsequential data structures based on object structure, and *variable_consistency_files* implement various application-specific consistency policies and can be used to avoid the consistency semantics of NFS files.

Bridge   Bridge [35, 36], developed at the University of Rochester, is an implementation of a parallel interleaved file system on the BBN Butterfly parallel processor. The file system is designed to operate in parallel and maintains the logical structure of files while physically distributing their data. One key feature of Bridge is that it allows user-provided code to be incorporated into the file system dynamically.

Bridge has two main functional layers. The lower layer consists of a self-sufficient local file system (LFS) on each of the processors and disks. The upper layer, called the *Bridge server*, maintains the integrity of the file system as a whole and provides the initial interface to application programs. Except for a few functions that act on the state of the server itself, the Bridge server interprets I/O requests and dispatches them to the appropriate LFSs. LFSs operate independently and are capable of maintaining local files outside the Bridge file system. The LFS implementation is based on the elementary file system developed for the Cronus distributed operating system [58].

To satisfy the needs of different types of users, the Bridge server implements three different system views—two views hide significant amounts of the underlying parallel structure to be used by applications in which a familiar interface is more important than performance, and the third view reveals the interleaved structure of files to applications. The third view is based on "tools," which are application-specific programs connecting the Bridge server and LFSs. Tools communicate with the server as application programs, but they communicate with the LFSs as if they were servers. These tools allow programmers to add high-level operations to the file system dynamically.

Vesta   Vesta [28], under development at the IBM T. J. Watson Research Center, is a parallel file system to be used in the Vulcan parallel computer. The objective of Vesta is to provide the users with the ability to explicitly specify the data distribution of files in parallel I/O subsystems to extract the maximum parallelism available. It also provides checkpointing and recovery mechanisms for files in the event of system failures. It is designed to be scalable to many hundreds of I/O and compute nodes.

Like UNIX, Vesta is a hierarchical file system. However, since file names are hashed to directly point at the file metadata, it is not necessary to read a directory for a file access. Files are distributed across a number of I/O nodes (physical partitions of files). The number of I/O nodes and the granularity of the interleaving is file dependent. One of Vesta's main innovations is the option of dividing the file data into a set of disjoint logical partitions, which may be accessed independently of each other. Since logical decomposition of files divides it into mutually exclusive sets of bytes in the physical storage, there is no need for mechanisms to maintain consistency between tasks accessing different partitions of the file. Additionally, good performance can be achieved by parallel programs whose tasks access different logical partitions in parallel.

Experiments performed on an Intel Touchstone Delta and NCUBE 2 I/O system in [116] demonstrate that the performance of existing parallel I/O systems can vary by several orders of magnitude as a function of the data access pattern of the applications. Therefore a two-phase access strategy, in which the first phase performs parallel data access using a data distribution stripe size conforming with the distribution of data over the disks, and the second phase redistributes the data at runtime to match the application's desired data distribution, improves performance by several orders of magnitude over direct-access-based data distribution methods [116].

9.2.7 Configurable and Parallel Communication Protocols

Researchers have used several approaches to address the needs of future communication networks, including:

- Protocol adjustments,
- Reference model changes, and
- Implementation improvements.

Protocol adjustments include lightweight protocols that streamline the code that is executed when packets arrive correctly (see [38] for a good survey), custom protocols written to support *a specific application*, and *application-level framing*, which gives the application access to misordered data, so that the application can process it immediately and, therefore, avoid falling behind [25].

Reference model changes involve modifications to the framework under which protocols are designed. Typically, this involves violating the layered model. For example, in the x-Kernel, a protocol is decomposed into *miccroprotocols*, which can be combined in order to configure the protocol for each application's needs [66, 111]. Furthermore, Clark and Tennenhouse's "integrated layer processing" suggests that protocols be designed in layers, but then permit protocol programmers to merge such layers during implementation [25]. Haas' HOPS protocol and Zitterbart's Transputers are also functionally decomposed protocols, but their functions can be performed in parallel [59, 151].

Implementation improvements range from improving the operating system support for protocols [37, 65, 143] to using parallelism to pipeline STREAMS layers [46].[3]

All such techniques are important when operating high-performance communication devices with parallel machines. However, when performing I/O via network devices from a parallel machine, additional issues must be addressed. First, it is not useful to limit protocol parallelism to the pipelined parallelism of the STREAMS protocol, or to the functionally decomposed parallelism in the work of Haas or Zitterbart. This would not result in the significant additional protocol processing and I/O speeds required for large-scale parallel machines. Second, protocol designs and implementations must be modified to address parallelism, as demonstrated below with a parallel communication protocol implemented on a KSR supercomputer. Third, since the data to be sent across (or received from) the network is typically decomposed and resides on different compute nodes (or in different memory units) of the parallel machine, this decomposition must be taken into account when moving it to one or several network devices attached to the machine. Otherwise, excessive data movement during communication or after communication (for example, from one receiving process to many processes that actually need the data) will increase communication latencies and reduce I/O throughput. Furthermore, parallelism in protocol

---

[3]Pipelining, in this case, refers to having a processor for each protocol layer and then allowing each layer to process a different packet. Therefore, for the OSI Model, up to seven packets are processed simultaneously, but each of these individual packets still sequentially passes through the same seven layers.

processing (and therefore, protocol processing speeds), may vary across different parallel machines, ranging from higher degrees of parallelism on a parallel supercomputer (in conjunction with the application's parallelism on that machine) to smaller-scale parallelism employed on moderately parallel visualization engines attached to the supercomputer. The resulting asymmetries in protocol processing and parallelism must be considered. These requirements give rise to three attributes of protocols for such heterogeneous supercomputer systems:

- Protocols must be configurable to multiple target machines, so that they can exploit the underlying network architecture, the diverse processor nodes, and the underlying parallel machines, including the simultaneous use of multiple network devices attached to a single parallel machine.
- Protocols should be able to support desired data processing in conjunction with network transmissions, such as data compression and/or encryption.
- Protocols must be able to interact with application programs in order to understand, exploit, or even affect the data decompositions used by sending and receiving sets of communicating processes.

One approach to parallel protocol processing is described in [89], where a prototype protocol is described as a set of protocol *objects*, each of which performs an isolated protocol processing task. Each object contains single or multiple threads of execution that perform processing specific to that protocol object. Objects communicate with each other by asynchronous invocations implemented as messages delivered via shared memory mailboxes, much like the implementation of object invocations in other multiprocessor operating systems [11, 23]. Objects cooperate in the processing of protocol packets, and they may be composed to result in different communication protocol configurations in a manner more flexible than the layers of traditional protocol architectures allow. For instance, an outgoing user packet may be encrypted by an encryption object *while* the sequence numbers for the packet are computed by a reliability object. In addition, individual objects may contain internal parallelism, such as the encryption object implementing DES encryption.

Performance results from such research demonstrate clearly that parallelism in protocol processing can be exploited at the *presentation* level of communication protocols, including tasks like DES encryption processing, compression, and so on. Moderate additional performance improvements due to parallelism may be gained at lower protocol levels. More specifically:

- Substantial parallelism exists in communication protocols, but it must be exploited in conjunction with the parallelism inherent in the application programs using the protocol. Otherwise, needless overhead may arise from data movement required by interactions of protocol components with application code. This implies that one must perform both (1) the mapping of application and protocol code to different processors and (2) the decomposition of message data by the application and in the parallel protocol such that data movement is minimized and such that parallelism among protocol components is maximized.

- The cost of collecting data originating on multiple processors into a single message sent to a single network device can be prohibitive on large-scale parallel machines. This implies that single large-scale machines (such as the Kendall Square Research supercomputers) should use multiple communication devices attached to different processors of the machine (much like manufacturers are now routinely attaching multiple disks to such machines).

Additional research issues identified in [89] are the need for support of connection-specific caching of message fragments, for dynamic protocol configuration in response to application needs or network status, and for the enforcement of real-time constraints in protocol processing. In addition, as with the file systems described above, it is clear that parallelism and performance in protocol processing require that application-level knowledge about initial (at the sender) and final (at the receiver) data decompositions must be made available to the communication protocol in order to reduce data movement during protocol processing.

9.2.8 Operating System Structure

A multiprocessor operating system's performance, maintainability, expandability, adaptability, and portability strongly depend on its internal structure. The various structuring techniques described in this section are not mutually exclusive; several such techniques may be used together in the construction of a single system.

Some operating systems such as UNIX [115] and VMS are implemented with large, *monolithic kernels* insulated from user programs by simple hardware boundaries. No protection boundaries exist within the operating system kernel, and all communication among processes implementing higher level operating system functionality (for example, file system daemons) happens through system-supplied shared memory or through explicit message-based communication constructs. Monolithic systems are difficult to modify, debug, validate, and to adapt for use in a distributed environment. Recent experiences with the implementation of monolithic operating system kernels for parallel machines have been confined mainly to UMA machines. More recent work in multiprocessor operating systems for machines like the RP3, the BBN Butterfly, and the KSR supercomputer have been based on Mach or on OSF UNIX, both of which have smaller structured kernels. This is exacerbated by 64-bit architectures' large address spaces, for which it seems important to offer some inner-kernel and user-level, inner-address space notions of protection, such as what was offered in earlier, capability-based systems [144].

In a *message passing system* (for example, V [24] or Accent [113]), a process always remains within its address space. When a process in one address space requests a service from another address space, it creates a message describing its requirements, and sends it to the target address space. A process in the target address space receives the message, interprets it, and services the request. The primary motivation behind the design of such systems is to decentralize the structure of an operating system running on a single computer and to build an operating system on a structure of distributed computers. A message-passing system enforces modularity and is suitable for distribution. However, programs have to be manually structured in a paradigm that is foreign to the control and data structuring mechanism of traditional "Algol-like" languages.

Some *single-language systems* (Distributed Smalltalk, Emerald [74], and Linda [21]) integrate the underlying message-based communication into the programming environment, either by defining all control structures in terms of messages, or by using messages as the basis for building "Algol-like" or entirely new control structures. The advantages of such language-based systems are transparency and portability. References to local versus remote objects are handled transparently and automatically by the language's runtime system. However, specific language primitives often impose performance penalties of which programmers must be aware in order to write efficient parallel programs. Another inherent problem with language-based systems can be protection, where language-level typing mechanisms must be mapped to the protection mechanisms available in the underlying operating system [8], which is not always easily done. In addition, any language-based system will require all cooperating modules to be written in the same language, which precludes the use of mixed-language environments.

Systems supporting *remote procedure calls (RPC)* [13] occupy a middle ground between message-based and single-language systems. The use of RPC allows isolated components to be transparently integrated into a single logical system. In an RPC system, a procedure call interface hides the underlying communication mechanism that passes typed data objects among address spaces. Subsystems present themselves to one another in terms of interfaces implemented by servers. The absence of a single, uniform address space is compensated for by automatic stub compilers and sophisticated runtime libraries [13, 125] that transfer complex arguments in messages.

Several ongoing projects are using or exploring the *object-oriented* paradigm for building operating systems. Such systems may be broadly classified as object-oriented or object-supporting operating systems, depending on their internal structures and on the interfaces they provide to the user level [118, 131]. In an *object-oriented operating system (OOOS)*, objects encapsulate the system entities [20, 93]. An object-oriented language is primarily used to implement such an operating system [121], therefore, the properties of the language such as data encapsulation, data abstraction, inheritance, polymorphism, and so on, are used to structure the system itself. An OOOS may or may not support objects at the user level.

An *object-supporting operating system (OSOS)* [49, 50], on the other hand, is not necessarily structured in an object-oriented fashion. However, it supports objects at the user level; the objects are typically language independent. OSOSs can further be classified into different groups depending on the kinds of objects they support. In the *active-server* model of computation, objects are active entities containing threads of execution that service requests to the object [49, 50]. An OSOS supporting passive objects offers an *object-thread* model where a single thread of execution traverses all objects within an invocation chain [33, 79].

One use of object orientation in operating systems is to use object-based encapsulation of operating system services in order to represent operating system services internally in different ways, invisibly to services users. Examples of such uses are the internally parallel operating system servers offered in the Eden system [81] and in KTK [50, 127], or the internally fragmented objects [53, 131, 132] for distributed systems, in "topologies" [126] for hypercube machines, and in "distributed shared abstractions" [26] for multiprocessor engines.

Microkernel-based operating systems (Mach [14] and Chorus [117]) are structured as a collection of system servers running on top of a minimal kernel. The microkernel itself only

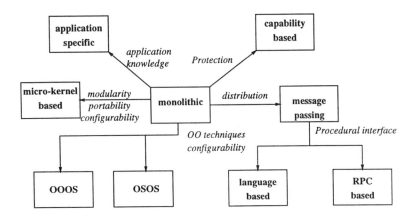

FIGURE 9.4   Evolution of operating system structures.

implements the lowest-level (mostly hardware dependent) functions of an operating system including task and thread management, interprocess communication/synchronization, low-level memory management, and minimal device management (I/O). All higher level operating system services are implemented as user-level programs. Therefore, applications must use cross-address space RPC to interact with most operating system services. This implies that the performance of interprocess communication (IPC) mechanisms play a critical role in the performance of such operating systems. The primary characteristic of microkernel-based operating systems is modularity, thereby attempting to improve system extensibility, portability, reconfigurability, and improved support for distribution [50, 51]. The use of common underlying services provides support for the coexistence and interoperability of multiple operating system environments on a single host as user-level programs [14].

Many application domains impose specific requirements on operating system functionality, performance, and structure resulting in development of *application-specific operating systems*. For example, in the real-time domain, application software and operating system support can be so intertwined that many systems may be better described as consisting of *operating software*—combined application software and operating system support functions—rather than as application software and an underlying operating system. Other examples of application-dependent operating system structures occur for database systems, where an operating system's I/O facilities and networking facilities may be determined or at least strongly affected by the primary application running on this system: a large-scale database performing transaction processing. Figure 9.4 summarizes the discussion by illustrating the evolution of various structuring mechanisms depending on the design motivation.

In current multiprocessors, a copy of the operating system kernel resides on each processor providing various services for user programs. These services are requested using system calls that appear as procedure calls to the caller. Some critical services are often provided using specialized processes that reside on a specific processor (such "master processors" serialize multiple requests for a service from different processors). Multiple copies of the kernel may communicate using either shared memory (*remote references*) or explicit message communication (*remote invocation*).

9.3

A FEW SAMPLE THREADS LIBRARIES

Lightweight threads libraries are commonly used for support of concurrent programming on shared-memory multiprocessors. This section raises a few implementation issues and describes the interfaces of some available packages.

The performance of applications using a threads library depends on the performance of the primitives offered by the library, which in turn depends on the primitives offered by the underlying operating system and the machine architecture. The hardware and the OS primitives that affect the performance of threads libraries are support for fast synchronization operations, efficient context switch mechanisms, and fast access to the *timer* mechanism. Additionally, the type of the *thread of control* provided by the active entities supported by the operating system kernel has a significant impact on application performance using the threads library. For example, processes with partially shared address space are observed to be appropriate for threads implementation [103]. Similarly, a coscheduling policy for the processes significantly improves application parallelism.

Currently available lightweight threads libraries implement and export a similar set of functionalities to the applications. As illustrated in Figure 9.5, such interfaces include library initialization routines, thread management functions, synchronization primitives, support for dynamic shared memory, exception handling capabilities, and a few configuration routines (to change attributes of existing components such as locks or schedulers). The remainder of this section reviews the functionalities of a few sample threads implementations.

Cthreads   The Cthreads package [27], developed at Carnegie Mellon University, is a runtime library to provide a C language interface to manipulate Mach threads. Before using, applications initialize and configure the library using an initialization routine. Thread management support includes routines for creation, termination, join, and detach operations of threads. Additionally, it allows application threads to voluntarily release a processor. Synchronization primitives supported by the library include mutex lock and unlock (blocking locks), conditional locks, condition variables (signal, broadcast, and wait), and allocation/deallocation of locks and condition variables. All threads share all global and static variables of the application and dynamic allocation and freeing of dynamic memory is accomplished using the standard C functions (malloc and free). The library allows users to associate names with different entities (thread, mutex, and condition) that are used for debugging threads applications.

Pthreads   The interface and the functionalities of POSIX Pthreads [108] package are very similar to Cthreads. Like Cthreads, Pthreads support thread management functionalities such as creation, termination, join, detach, and voluntary preemption; synchronization prim-

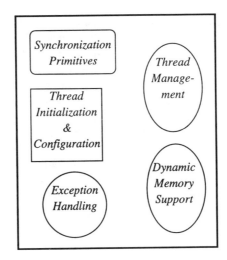

FIGURE 9.5   Components of a threads library.

itives such as mutexes and conditions (Some extensions of Pthreads like KSR OS's Pthreads library offer barrier synchronization too); allocation/deallocation of locks and condition variables; and a library initialization routine. Similar to Cthreads, all threads share the global and static variables of the application. One unique feature of Pthreads is its object attribute manipulation functions. It allows applications to query and/or set attributes for objects such as threads (scheduling policy, priority, stacksize, and so on), mutex, and conditions.

GT threads   The basic set of functionalities of the Georgia Tech threads package [102, 103] is a superset of the Cthreads interface. Since the package was primarily implemented from scratch to run on multiprocessors (especially NUMA machines), it has support for user-specified binding of threads to processors and for allocation of dynamic memory in a user-specified node. Additionally, the library supports a few configuration routines that allow users to configure the package to suit application characteristics. One important goal of the implementation of the library was portability. Currently, the GT threads library runs on diverse platforms, including SUN SPARCstation, Kendall Square Research supercomputer, SGI uniprocessor and multiprocessor, GP1000 BBN Butterfly multiprocessor, and Sequent Symmetry.

9.4

CASE STUDIES OF SAMPLE OPERATING SYSTEMS

9.4.1   Early Research Systems

HYDRA [73, 87, 144, 145] was one of the earliest successful multiprocessor kernels. The major contributions of HYDRA are the concept of separation of mechanism from policy, a generalized notion of *resources*, and its flexible *capability-based protection mechanism* controlling access to resources within a domain with which different types of security (policies) can be implemented. Other significant research results relevant to parallel operating systems include (1) establishing the concept of program locality, the effects of bus and memory contentions on parallel program performance, and the importance of asynchrony in parallel program design and implementation [144], (2) demonstrations that high performance parallel programs require choices in the operating system mechanisms being provided (for example, a variety of different synchronization mechanisms), since programs differ in granularities of parallelism, in frequencies of access to shared data, and so forth, and (3) experiences with the use of specific operating system facilities by parallel programs. One such insight was that parallel programmers seek performance and therefore, will prefer using simple, fast mechanisms over easy-to-use, slower mechanisms. This insight has affected most modern operating system designs for parallel machines in areas ranging from process to thread representations, communication systems designs, and the implementation of synchronization constructs [73, 144].

StarOS [71, 72], a HYDRA follow-up at Carnegie Mellon University, is an experimental operating system for the *Cm** [47] multimicroprocessor. The design of StarOS is influenced by the protection mechanisms of Hydra, the underlying Cm* architecture, and its principal goals of achieving high performance and reliability for parallel machine users. One of the attributes of StarOS of interest to parallel systems is its definition of *modules*, *functions*, and *module invocations*, which are the blueprint for the implementation of similar functionality in modern object-oriented operating systems such as Eden [81], Choices [19], and Chaos [50, 127]. Another important concept that originated with StarOS is that function (or object) invokers will require substantial flexibility in how synchronization is performed in conjunction with object invocation. As a result, StarOS simply offers a low-level mechanism for implementing different synchronization schemes, on which complex primitives can be built. A third concept in parallel operating systems originating with both the StarOS and the Roscoe operating systems [133] is the structuring of operating systems and even operating system kernels as microkernels (called a *nucleus* in StarOS). Specifically, a small subset of the StarOS functions, called *instructions*, is defined to execute sequentially and synchronously with the invoking function. Collectively they are referred to as the nucleus. A copy of the nucleus software runs on each computer module in its own address space, as its microkernel. All other operating system functionality resides at user-level.

A unique feature of StarOS is the support for task forces, collections of cooperating processes that collectively accomplish some joint task. A task force can be programmed to take advantage of parallelism to achieve enhanced reliability (by triplication of selected services) and performance (by use of parallelism to implement services), and to adapt to changes in user requirements or in the underlying hardware by growing or shrinking dynamically. Since the StarOS operating system itself is also represented as a task force, its configuration changes over time, as determined by the system's reconfiguration processes, which periodically examine the environment and adjust the StarOS configuration accordingly, to improve system performance or maintain some desired reliability level.

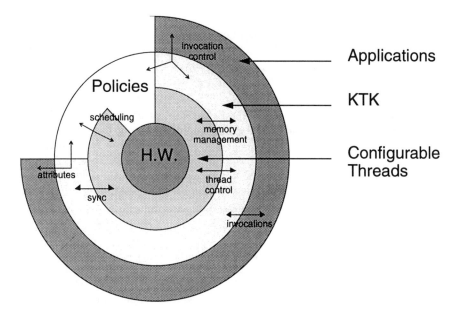

FIGURE 9.6   Structure of the Kernel Tool Kit (KTK).

9.4.2   KTK

The *Kernel Tool Kit* (KTK) [49, 50, 103] under development at the Georgia Institute of Technology is a configurable object-based operating system kernel (designed using microkernel technology). The major design goal of the KTK project is to provide explicit support for on- and off-line program configuration. KTK is layered on a portable and configurable threads-based microkernel [103]. As a result, KTK can be run on diverse platforms, including at user level on SUN SPARCstations, on a Kendall Square Research supercomputer, SGI machines, and as a native operating system kernel on the GP1000 BBN Butterfly multiprocessor.

The Kernel Tool Kit consists of the three major components shown in Figure 9.6: (1) a configurable micro-kernel as the threads layer, (2) the Kernel Tool Kit's built-in object types and its support for attributes and policies, and (3) the various *policies* and *attributes* implemented for the application programs built with KTK.

The configurable microkernel is the partially machine dependent component [103] that implements the basic abstractions used by the remainder of KTK: *execution threads*, *virtual memory regions*, *synchronization primitives*, *monitoring support* for capture of parallel program and KTK state, and a limited number of *basic attributes* for the configuration of threads-level abstractions, such as synchronization primitives and low-level scheduling.

A KTK application program consists of a number of independent objects that interact by invoking each other's operations (methods). Each object maintains its own state, and that state is not directly accessible to other objects. Objects can range from *light-weight* procedure-like entities to multithreaded servers with associated concurrency control and scheduling policies. *Complex* objects can be built by having objects as components of other objects, starting with a few built-in object classes chosen for their usefulness in a wide variety of parallel applications constructed with KTK, including an ADT resembling a procedure object and a TADT offering an execution thread used for object execution (much like the notions of passive and active objects now being offered by systems such as Concurrent C++). In addition to these primitive objects, KTK also provides support for distributed objects (DSA) [26], which permits programmers to define and create encapsulated, fragmented objects, and offers low-level mechanisms for implementing efficient, abstraction-specific communications among object fragments.

Typical KTK programs consist of complex objects constructed from the primitive object classes ("layered extension"). KTK offers dynamic configuration by permitting the definition of new policy classes and their linkage with the kernel, and by offering two distinct views of each object: (1) the *application view* and (2) the *system view*. The application view of objects is presented in terms of their classes characterizing their external interfaces (methods), where a class is an abstraction for a number of similar objects. The system view, on the other hand, is defined by each object's *policy* and *attributes*. Essentially, policies define a parameterized execution environment for objects in terms of attributes, *invocation semantics*, and *kernel interactions*:

- A policy interprets attributes defined at the time of creation for classes, objects, states, and operations.
- A policy can define the invocation semantics to an object by intercepting invocation requests and defining and interpreting invocation time attributes that can be specified as part of the invocation.
- A policy can also extend the KTK interface with special services.

Since policies are executed implicitly as a result of object creation and invocation, typical application programs see only the objects and classes defined in their code and offered by KTK.

In addition to primitive spinlocks and blocking locks, KTK supports configurable lock objects that can be configured to suit application's requirements [104, 105]. Such locks contain a set of implementation-dependent attributes, which can be dynamically altered to result in a continuous spectrum of lock configurations ranging from *busy waiting* to *blocking*. Some useful configurations are combined locks, advisory locks, priority locks, hand-off locks, and adaptive locks. Furthermore, configurable locks implement a *customized monitor* module that can be used to sense the current state of a lock [105].

KTK's support for reconfiguration consists of three mechanisms—attributes, policies, and a monitoring mechanism (to sense current program state). The Kernel Tool Kit offers explicit support for on- and off-line object configuration using the above mechanisms:

- KTK allows the specification of (configuration) attributes for object classes, object instances, state variables, operations, and object invocations.
- Attributes are interpreted by system- or programmer-defined policies, which may be varied separately from the abstractions with which they are associated. For example, policies and attributes may be used to vary objects' internal implementations without changing their functionalities.
- Dynamic configuration may be performed by policies at or below the object level of abstraction, therefore permitting programmers to make dynamic changes of selected

attributes of lower-level runtime libraries and to exploit peculiarities of the underlying multiprocessor hardware. KTK also offers efficient mechanisms for the on-line capture of the program or operating system state required for dynamic configuration.

The mechanisms for configuration in KTK can also be used for kernel customization by specializing and/or modifying existing kernel abstractions. In addition, KTK is *extensible* in that new abstractions and functionality (that is, classes, policies, and attributes) are easily added while potentially maintaining a uniform kernel interface (for example, when not adding any new kernel classes) [50, 88].

9.4.3 Choices

The Choices (class hierarchical open interface for custom embedded systems) [18, 19] operating system, designed to accommodate diverse parallel applications, supports a set of components that can be combined and customized through object-oriented inheritance and specialization to match different application concurrency requirements. Choices uses frameworks to allow the design of layers, to permit the construction of complex structures, and to permit design and code reuse. The components of the system are defined as classes within the framework, and the interactions in the system are defined in terms of classes, instances, constraints, inheritance, inclusion polymorphism, and rules of composition. The subframeworks refine the general operating system framework to specific subsystems. Choices, implemented in C++, is a multitasking operating system and runs stand-alone on the Sun SPARCstation II and Encore Multimax and runs as a virtual operating system on top of SUN-OS and MS/DOS. It supports distributed- and shared-memory multiprocessor applications, virtual memory, and has both conventional file systems and a persistent object store.

The Choices framework consists of three abstract classes—*MemoryObject* for data storage, *Process* (providing a thread of control), and *Domain* (providing an environment that binds names to storage locations—similar to address spaces). Figure 9.7 illustrates the class relationship diagram for process management in Choices (a single bar denotes one-to-one relationship and a three-pronged fork indicates a one-to-many relationship; a mandatory relationship is denoted by an additional bar; and an optional relationship is denoted by a circle), which consists of five components—the Process providing a control path through a group of C++ objects, the *ProcessorContext* that saves and restores the machine dependent state of a Process, the *Processor* encapsulating the processor dependent details of the CPU, the *Gang* that groups Processes as a single unit, which can be gang scheduled to run simultaneously, and the *ProcessContainer* implementing scheduling of Processes. Each Process, which can be either *System-Process*, *ApplicationProcess*, or *InterruptProcess*, is associated with exactly one Domain. Processes can share Domains with other Processes. Subclasses of ProcessContainer perform scheduling, and inherit the uniform interface for scheduling. Choices implements a light-weight context switch between Processes in the same domain and a heavy-weight context switch between Processes in different domains.

Choices provides three abstract classes for synchronization of processes—*Locks*, *Semaphores*, and *Barriers*. Locks can be either *SpinLocks* or *BusyWait* locks. Choices supports six types of semaphores—Semaphores, *GraciousSemaphores* (a V operation directly

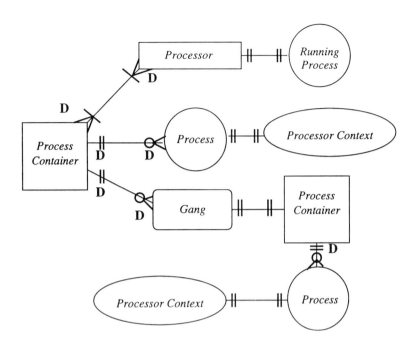

FIGURE 9.7   Abstract class relationship diagram for process management in choices.

puts the resumed Process on the Processor), *LazySemaphores* (allows the V method to be invoked more that the number of times the P is invoked), *BinarySemaphores* (allows alternate sequences of P and V), *MutexSemaphores* (a BinarySemaphore initialized to one), and *MultiVSemaphores* (a V operation puts multiple blocked Processes in the ready queue).

The message-passing system of Choices consists of six components—the *MessageContainer*, like Mach ports, is a named message buffer; the *MessageSystemInterface* provides an adaptation layer encapsulating features to a particular parallel or distributed-programming paradigm; the *Transport* specifies the message communication mechanism (shared memory versus network); the *DataTransfer* specifies the buffering strategies in sending messages; the *Reliability* determines the reliability of message transfer (such as at-most-one and exactly-once semantics); and the *FlowControl*, controls the data-flow between the sender and the receiver. A MessageContainer may have multiple senders and multiple receivers.

The Choices virtual memory system, which supports 32-bit address space, one- and two-level paging, and shared memory, has the following components: the *MemoryObject* representing a data store that might contain a process stack, code, heap, or data area of program; the Domain, which maintains the mapping between virtual addresses and data stores; the *PageFrameAllocator* to allocate and deallocate physical memory; the *AddressTrans-*

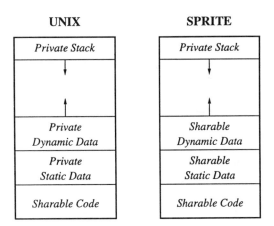

UNIX   SPRITE

Private Stack	Private Stack
Private Dynamic Data	Sharable Dynamic Data
Private Static Data	Sharable Static Data
Sharable Code	Sharable Code

FIGURE 9.8   User process's view of the organization of virtual memory in Unix and Sprite.

lation, which encapsulates the translation hardware; and the *MemoryObjectCache*, which stores the mapping between virtual memory pages and the physical memory pages in a machine-independent form. Choices also supports a persistent storage framework introducing a hierarchy of classes that can be used to support both persistent storage systems and traditional file systems. Similarly, it provides a uniform interface for device management with a set of abstract classes.

9.4.4   Sprite

The motivation behind Sprite [61, 107], developed at the University of California at Berkeley, was to provide an operating system for networks of computers, to efficiently utilize the large physical memory available in the current and the future machines, and to provide support for development of parallel applications on multiprocessor workstations. Sprite's kernel interface is much like that of 4.3 BSD UNIX, however, Sprite has a multithreaded kernel and is developed from scratch to provide a high degree of network integration. Sprite has many useful features (such as network transparency, transparent access to remote I/O devices, transparent process migration, remote procedure call mechanism and others) for networks of workstations. However, in this chapter, we primarily focus on Sprite's support for multiprocessors.

Sprite supports "UNIX-like" heavy-weight processes. However, processes can chose to share their address spaces to facilitate a fast interprocess communication mechanism (see Figure 9.8). Sprite's mechanism provides all-or-nothing sharing. Multiprocessor applications synchronize using hardware mutual exclusion instructions directly on shared memory. However, the kernel provides mechanisms to block and unblock processes.

Being a multithreaded kernel, Sprite uses monitor-style locking and condition variables to provide synchronization and mutual exclusions. There are two basic types of locks within the Sprite kernel—*monitor locks* used to implement monitors with similar semantics to those in Mesa [80], and *master locks* (spinlocks with interrupts disabled) used to provide mutual exclusion between processes and interrupt handlers. Sprite uses condition variables for threads to wait for conditions to occur.

9.4.5   DYNIX and UMAX

The *Dynix* operating system [129], developed to run on the Sequent multiprocessors, and the *UMAX* operating system [101], developed to run on the Encore Multimax multiprocessors, are enhanced versions of the UNIX operating system for bus-based uniform access shared-memory (UMA) machines.

Both Dynix and UMAX are commercial multiuser and multiprogrammed operating systems supporting mostly similar features. They support "UNIX-like" heavy-weight processes as well as middle-weight threads for medium-grained parallelism. In Dynix, a process can restrict itself to a particular processor;[4] the process is placed in the private queue of the processor. Both kernels provide locks and semaphores for mutual exclusion and synchronization.

The virtual memory system of these systems are enhanced versions of UNIX. Unlike Unix, which uses a *global model*, Dynix uses a *local model*, which means that a process has a greater role in its own paging activity.

9.4.6   RP3

The *RP3* [17] is a NUMA shared-memory multiprocessor developed at T. J. Watson Research Center. IBM designed it to be scalable up to 512-way multiprocessing. The RP3 operating system, like most other commercial systems, is an extension of UNIX. Mach is the base implementation of UNIX on the RP3.[5] Like Mach, Mach/RP3 also has a master processor, which is reserved for UNIX system call service.

Mach/RP3 supports a version of coscheduling or gang scheduling known as *family scheduling*. A *family* is a set of cooperating processes working towards a single goal. A *thread family* is the largest schedulable unit on the RP3, and corresponds to the notion of a family. A port is associated with a family. A thread that has rights to a family port can request a processor to be allocated to or deallocated from the family. The threads in a family are allowed to run only on the allocated processors; non-family threads are barred from the allocated processors. The members of a family time-share its processors. A thread in a family can choose to be bound to a particular processor. A notable feature of RP3 family scheduling interface is its flexibility in allowing a thread to issue requests for other threads. For example, a thread can bind another thread and a thread can request processor allocation for another family.

RP3 exports the nonuniform memory model to applications and, therefore, does not deal with issues like data placement and cacheability. Mach/RP3 allows a task to specify *virtual memory attributes* for pages of its virtual address space (like inheritance and protection attributes in Mach). Such attributes include *location attributes* (a thread may specify ranges of virtual pages to be placed in the local memory), *replication attributes* (a thread can request

---

[4]also known as *processor/process affinity*.

[5]A second operating system for the RP3, developed at NYU, was never deployed on the actual machine [3].

to replicate ranges of virtual memory in different memory modules), and *cacheability attributes* (a thread can request ranges of virtual pages to be made cacheable).

9.4.7 IRIX

The IRIX operating system, developed to run on the SGI uniprocessors and multiprocessors, is an enhanced version of the UNIX operating system. It extends UNIX to provide support for multiprocessing.

In addition to "UNIX-like" heavy-weight processes, which do not share their address spaces, IRIX supports lighter threads of control, share group processes. Similar to middle-weight threads, such processes can share virtual address spaces.

IRIX supports the standard UNIX timesharing scheduling techniques. However, applications can control the scheduling characteristics of share processes to independent (UNIX-like) scheduling or gang scheduling. In gang scheduling mode, all the members of the share group are scheduled as a unit if possible.

IRIX allows users to create and initialize *shared arenas* from which shared memory can be allocated dynamically. In addition to semaphores, IRIX provides users with a few synchronization routines to provide test-and-set facility. The locks are based in user address space to avoid system call overheads. Unrelated processes synchronize via shared arenas, implemented using extensive memory mapping techniques to minimize overhead.

9.4.8 KSR OS

KSR OS [76], the operating system for KSR, is an extended multithreaded UNIX operating system based on OSF/1. It is fully compatible with AT&T System V and with Berkeley BSD, and it supports two major standards for system calls—IEEE POSIX and X/OPEN.

KSR OS supports heavy-weight "UNIX-like" processes each running in its own address space. To support finer grain parallelism KSR OS provides threads—Mach threads [137]—inside the operating system. Each thread provides a separate control path and they share a single address space. *Pthreads*, the IEEE POSIX threads library [108], is built on top of Mach threads (one Mach thread normally executes one Pthread) to provide a more usable interface and portability. The KSR OS's hierarchical scheduler supports multiple run queues.

Like Mach, the KSR virtual memory management implements a single-level store model to address all storage, both data and files. The virtual memory supports both shared and nonshared address spaces. The page-based virtual memory allows the operating system to map a memory region into several address spaces simultaneously. KSR's ALLCACHE memory architecture. Like the local memory modules in a NUMA architecture, each processor has a 32-MB local cache. These local caches together comprise all the main memory of the KSR. Such an architecture, also known as COMA (cache only memory architecture), implements a sequentially consistent shared address space programming model by hiding the physical distribution of local caches. In ALLCACHE memory architecture, data moves the point of reference on demand (see Figure 9.9). ALLCACHE allows data replication for parallel access. However, a write operation invalidates the replicated copies in parallel to

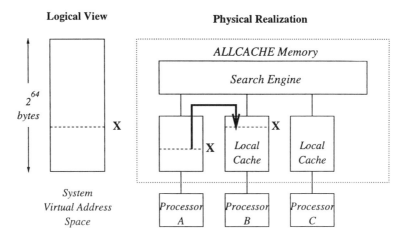

FIGURE 9.9   On-demand data movement in ALLCACHE memory.

maintain consistency. Two additional mechanisms, prefetch and poststore, are available to improve data locality and memory latency. The prefetch instruction moves a subpage into the local cache of the requesting processor, thus allowing a processor to fetch data before it is needed. Similarly, a poststore operation allows a processor to broadcast a new data value to other cells that may need it.

At the lowest level, KSR supports hardware synchronization locks by setting a subpage (128 bytes) to atomic state. Such a lock operation, which can be either blocking or nonblocking, finds the subpage, returns it to the requesting processor in atomic state, and invalidates all other copies of the subpage. The corresponding unlock operation removes atomic state from a subpage. The Mach threads and the Pthreads packages use these locks to implement higher level synchronization primitives.

The KSR I/O system supports parallel file system operations like read and write. The disk striping technique is used to support large files over a large number of physical disks. The single-level store model is used to implement memory-mapped files by caching the most recently accessed files, thus increasing I/O performance. Furthermore, KSR OS overlaps computing and I/O operations by means of asynchronous I/O.

9.4.9   CMost

CM-5 operating system, CMOST [139], is an enhanced version of the UNIX operating system. It provides all the basic UNIX services including timesharing and batch processing, standard UNIX protection, security and user interfaces, support for all standard UNIX-based communication protocols, ability to use NFS protocols as client as well as server, the network queuing system (NQS) and other standard network-oriented programs, and binary compatibility with SUNOS for scalar programs. The enhancements over UNIX optimize computation, communication, and I/O performance within the CM-5 system. Specifically, it provides high-speed file access, fast parallel interprocessor communication capabilities,

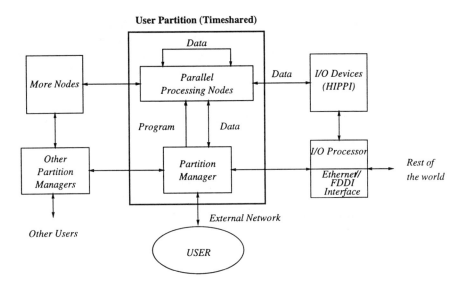

FIGURE 9.10   User's view of CM-5.

parallel operations for optimal utilization of CM-5 hardware, central administration and resource management for computational and I/O facilities, support for extended models for data parallel programming (such as data parallel pipes), support for various programming models, and checkpointing.

The computational nodes on a CM-5 are grouped into partitions, controlled by the system administrator. Each partition operates independently under the control of a processor (see Figure 9.10) called the *partition manager (PM)*. Even though each user process executes on a single partition, it may exchange data with processes on other partitions. A process executing in a partition has full access to the PM; to all the nodes in the partition; and (through the operating system) to all the I/O resources, partitions, and network connections of the CM-5 system. Each partition runs the CMOST operating system, which is responsible for all operating system resource allocations and all swapping decisions for the partition, as well as most system calls for process execution, memory management and I/O. Partitions use UNIX timesharing technique to allow multiple users in a partition. Each member of a partition runs an operating system microkernel supporting the mechanisms required to implement the policy decisions made by the PM. When running a user process, the partition manager initiates loading the program by broadcasting blocks of instructions to the parallel processing nodes. When all nodes are operating on a single thread of control, the processing nodes are kept closely synchronized and blocks are broadcast as needed. When the nodes take different branches, they independently fetch the required instructions and synchronize only as required by the algorithm of the program [139].

Interprocess communication between nodes within an application is entirely handled by user code, without any operating system overhead. However, the operating system is responsible for external communications. Data may be transferred between two processes running timeshared in the same partition or between two concurrent processes on different partitions. Interprocessor communications in CM-5 belong to the following categories: *replication* (for example, a single data value is broadcast to all processors for read access); *reduction* (for example, a set of values is used to perform a global sum to produce a single data value); *permutation* (for example, data values come from one processor and go to another processor); and *parallel prefix* (each result is a reduction of multiple inputs, and each input contributes to multiple results).

The CM-5 message-passing library, CMMD, supports the host/node programming model in which one program runs on the partition manager and independent copies of the node program run asynchronously on the processing nodes. Synchronization among nodes occurs only via message communication. The library supports synchronous communication (blocking send and receive) and a limited amount of asynchronous communication (for short messages). It also supports global functions including broadcasts, reduction, parallel prefix, concatenation, and others. In addition, it supports global synchronization operations such as barriers and global_or.

The CM-5 extends the standard UNIX I/O mechanisms (sockets, pipes, character devices, block devices, and serial files) to support parallel read and write operations and very large files. The CM-5's high-performance file system manages the high-speed disk-based mass storage system, the *data vaults*. Each file system attached to the CM-5 manages service requests for its I/O devices using a single I/O control processor (IOCP) implementing device-independent file behavior (currently, supports standard UNIX file system, NFS, and the high-performance file system). Within CM-5 files, data is stored in canonical ordering, thus allowing its use by serial and parallel systems and processes. CM-5 transparently stripes files on multiple I/O devices for performance.

9.4.10 Paragon

The operating system of Paragon, Paragon OSF/1, extends the standard OSF/1 features to provide a single system image across multiple nodes, to provide message-passing capabilities, to support parallel file system access and to support some machine-specific utilities [70]. The most common programming model used with Paragon OSF/1 is the SPMD (single program, multiple data) model.

The paragon OSF/1 supports processes (with multiple threads of control) and process groups. Processes do not implicitly share address spaces. Explicit virtual memory calls are required for two or more processes to share portions of their memory.

The nodes of Paragon are divided into overlapping partitions that include the root partition, containing all the usable nodes in the system; the service partition, used to execute the user's shells and other commands; and the compute partition, used to run parallel applications. Typically, the service partition and the compute partition are children of the root partition and do not overlap. Every parallel application executes on a partition (see Figure 9.11). However, the configuration of the system determines whether users can create subpartitions in the compute partition or can execute applications in the compute partition itself. Once created, the set of nodes allocated to a partition does not change for the lifetime of the partition. Each partition has a parent partition, an ID, a set of nodes, protection modes, and a set of scheduling characteristics.

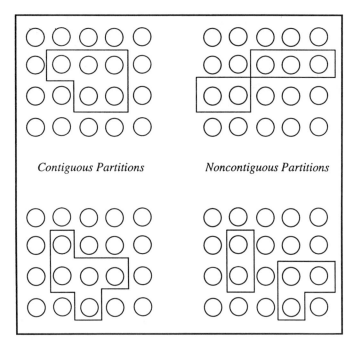

FIGURE 9.11 Contiguous and noncontiguous partitions in paragon.

The scheduling characteristics of a partition can be one of two different forms of scheduling: *standard scheduling*, the standard OSF/1 scheduling mechanism (a node using such technique schedules individual processes with no attempt to coordinate related processes on separate processors), which is good for interactive applications but results in poor performance for parallel applications; and *gang scheduling*, which attempts to schedule the nodes so that all the processes in an application are active simultaneously. Unlike standard scheduling, which swaps processes frequently, gang scheduling swaps between applications on the basis of the partition's *rollin quantum*, a time period that can be very long to improve the performance of parallel applications. Typically, the root partition and the compute partition (and its potentially overlapping subpartitions) use gang scheduling, whereas the service partitions use standard scheduling.

Since the nodes do not share physical memory, message passing is the standard means of communication among processes in Paragon OSF/1. Messages can be of variable length. The operating system guarantees that all messages arrive in the same order as they are sent. In addition to synchronous and asynchronous point-to-point message communication, Paragon OSF/1 supports asynchronous *handler* calls (similar to interrupts, this mechanism permits a user-provided interrupt handler, which is called when the message is received) with associated *interrupt masking mechanisms*, *multicasting* (sending messages to multiple nodes), and mechanisms to wait for multiple messages. The primary primitives supported are *send*, *receive*, *sendrecv* (send a message and receive a reply), and *probe* (probe for a pending message).

Paragon OSF/1 supports a few global operations (synchronizing calls) that perform operations using data from every node in the application. If any node in an application makes one of these calls, it blocks until all the nodes belonging to the application have made the same call. The operation is performed on data formed by collecting a piece of data from each node, and the result is returned to each node. The supported global operations include *concatenation, vector sum, vector multiply, vector max & min, global synchronization,* and others.

The Paragon OSF/1 operating system supports a parallel file system, PFS, optimized for simultaneous access by multiple nodes. It also supports parallel I/O calls to facilitate I/O from multiple nodes to large files in PFS file systems.

9.5

CONCLUSION

Our primary motivation behind this chapter is the realization that current developments in parallel operating systems can be assisted tremendously by judicious reviews of past research because the OS community's research focus on parallel systems in the late 1970s shifted to distributed systems for much of the 1980s, and is only now again addressing parallel machines. Hoping to remind researchers of past results and insights, we have included relatively "old" operating systems like HYDRA, which can be thought of as one of the culminations of research on protection issues as well as a starting point for operating system developments for parallel machines. Similarly, the StarOSStarOS system, along with Roscoe and Medusa, provides early implementations of microkernels, of user-level operating system services, of internally parallel or reliable system services, and of alternative operating system constructs providing similar functionalities at differing costs.

A second motivation for writing this chapter is the convergence of several technologies relevant to parallel computing. First, the convergence of high-performance computing and networking technologies is now resulting in large-scale, physically distributed, and heterogeneous parallel machines. The associated technologies were originally developed for parallel versus distributed systems, by partially divergent technical communities who sometimes used different terminologies. Technological convergence is driven by recent hardware developments, where (1) multiprocessor engines, when scaled to hundreds of processors, can appear much like distributed sets of machines, and (2) distributed machines linked by high-performance networks (especially local area networks or network devices derived from current ATM or even supercomputer routing technologies) are being increasingly used as parallel computing engines. This has become increasingly obvious with the evolution of the Mach operating system from one which addressed single or networks of workstations, to one also running on NUMA and now on NORMA machines. We believe that many of the ideas in those designs and implementations can be fruitfully applied toward the development of future parallel machine operating systems.

Finally, our third motivation is the current excitement in operating systems research in general, where new applications such as interactive distributed systems, and new software technologies such as object-oriented software development and languages, are prompting designers to seek new dimensions of system configurability, not only for large-scale parallel machines addressed by this survey, but also for sequential machines ranging from simple hand-held communication and computation devices to supercomputers. The sample research systems we have reviewed are Kernel Tool Kit and Choices.

The interesting future research questions in parallel operating system include: What are the cutpoints between user-level versus kernel functionality? What are the appropriate interfaces between both? What are the most suitable mechanisms for provision of such externally driven system configurability? A different statement posing the same questions is the admission that there is probably no single parallel programming model that is appropriate for all parallel application programs. As a result, future systems are more likely to offer multiple, diverse programming models rather than focusing on a single powerful parallel programming paradigm.

Bibliography

1. V. Abrossimov, M. Rozier, and M. Shapiro, "Generic Virtual Memory Management for Operating System Kernels," *Proc. 12th ACM Symp. Operating Systems Principles, (SIGOPS Notices Vol. 23, No. 5)*, ACM Press, New York, N.Y., 1989, pp. 123–136.

2. S.V. Adve and M.D. Hill, "Weak Ordering—A New Definition," *Proc. 17th Ann. Int'l Symp. Computer Architecture*, IEEE CS Press, Los Alamitos, Calif., 1990, pp. 2–14.

3. G.S. Almasi and A. Gottlieb, *Highly Parallel Computing*, Benjamin/Cummings, Redwood City, Calif., 1989.

4. R. Ananthanarayanan, M. Ahamad, and R. LeBlanc, "Application Specific Coherence Control for High-performance Distributed Shared Memory," *Proc. 3rd USENIX Symp. Experience with Distributed and Multiprocessor Systems*, ASENIX Assoc., Berkeley, Calif., 1992, pp. 109–128.

5. T. Anderson et al., "Scheduler Activations: Effective Kernel Support for the User-level Management of Parallelism," *ACM Trans. Computer Systems*, Vol. 10, No. 1, Feb. 1992, pp. 53–79.

6. T. Anderson, E.D. Lazowska, and H.M. Levy, "The Performance Implications of Thread Management Alternatives for Shared-memory Multiprocessors," *IEEE Trans. Computers*, Vol. 38, No. 12, Dec. 1989, pp. 1631–1644.

7. A. Appel and K. Li, "Virtual Memory Primitives for User Programs," *Proc. 4th Int'l Conf. Architectural Support for Programming Languages and Operating Systems (SIGPLAN Notices, Vol. 26, No. 4)*, ACM Press, New York, N.Y., 1991, pp. 96–107.

8. R. Atkinson et al., "Experiences Creating a Portable Cedar," *Proc. ACM SIGPLAN '89 Conf. Programming Language Design and Implementation*, ACM Press, New York, N.Y., 1989, pp. 322–328.

9. B. Bershad et al., "Lightweight Remote Procedure call," *ACM Trans. Computer Systems*, Vol. 8, No. 1, Feb 1990, pp. 37–55. Also appeared *Proc. 12th ACM Symp. Operating Systems Principles*, ACM Press, New York, N.Y., Dec. 1989.

10. B. Bershad et al., "User-level Interprocess Communication for Shared Memory Multiprocessors," *ACM Trans. Computer Systems*, Vol. 9, No. 2, May 1991, pp. 175–198.

11. T.E. Bihari and P. Gopinath, "Object-oriented Real-time Systems: Concepts and Examples," *Computer*, Vol. 25, No. 12, Dec. 1992, pp. 25–32.

12. A. Birrell et al., "Synchronization Primitives for a Multiprocessor: A Formal Specification," *Proc. 11th ACM Symp. Operating Systems Principles, (SIGOPS Notices Vol. 21, No. 5)*, ACM Press, New York, N.Y., 1987, pp. 94–102.

13. A. Birrell and B. Nelson, "Implementing Remote Procedure Calls," *ACM Trans. Computer Systems*, Vol. 2, No. 1, Feb. 1984, pp. 39–59.

14. D. Black et al., "Microkernel Operating System Architectures and Mach," *Proc. USENIX Workshop on Micro-Kernels and Other Kernel Architectures*, USENIX Assoc., Berkeley, Calif., 1992, pp. 11–30.

15. D.L. Black, "Scheduling Support for Concurrency and Parallelism in the MACH Operating System," *Computer*, Vol. 23, No. 5, May 1990, pp. 35–43.

16. T. Bloom, *Dynamic Module Replacement in a Distributed Programming System*, doctoral dissertation, Laboratory for Computer Science, Massachusetts Institute of Technology, MIT/LCS/TR-303, Mar. 1983.

17. R. Bryant, H. Y. Chang, and B. Rosenburg, "Experience Developing the RP3 Operating System," *Proc. 2nd USENIX Symp. Experience with Distributed and Multiprocessor Systems*, USENIX Assoc., Berkeley, Calif., 1991, pp. 1–18.

18. R. Campbell, N. Islam, and P. Madany, "Choices, Frameworks and Refinement," *Computing Systems*, Vol. 5, No. 3, Summer 1992, pp. 217–257.

19. R. Campbell, G. Johnston, and V. Russo, "Choices (Class Hierarchical Open Interface for Custom Embedded Systems)," *Operating Systems Review*, Vol. 21, No. 3, July 1987, pp. 9–17.

20. R. Campbell, V. Russo, and G. Johnston, "The Design of a Multiprocessor Operating System," *Proc. USENIX C++ Conf.*, USENIX Assoc., Berkeley, Calif., 1987, pp. 109–125.

21. N. Carriero and D. Gelernter, "The s/net's Linda Kernel," *ACM Trans. Computer Systems*, Vol. 4, No. 2, May 1986, pp. 110–129.

22. J.B. Carter, J.K. Bennett, and W. Zwaenepoel, "Implementation and Performance of Munin," *Proc. 13th ACM Symp. Operating Systems Principles*, ACM Press, New York, N.Y., 1991, pp. 152–164.

23. J. Chase et al., "The Amber System: Parallel Programming on a Network of Multiprocessors," *Proc. 12th ACM Symp. Operating Systems Principles*, ACM Press, New York, N.Y., 1989, pp. 147–158.

24. D. Cheriton, "The V Kernel: A Software Base for Distributed Systems," *IEEE Software*, Vol. 1, No. 2, Apr. 1984, pp. 19–42.

25. D. Clark and D. Tennenhouse, "Architectural Considerations for a New Generation of Protocols," *ACM Computer Comm. Re.*, Vol. 20, Sept. 1990, pp. 200–208.

26. C. Clemencon, B. Mukherjee, and K. Schwan, "Distributed Shared Abstractions (DSA) on Large-scale Multiprocessors," *Proc. 4th USENIX Symp. Experiences with Distributed and Multiprocessor Systems*, USENIX Assoc., Berkeley, Calif., 1993, pp. 227–246.

27. E. Cooper and R. Draves, "C Threads," Tech. Report CMU-CS-88-154, Dept. of Computer Science, Carnegie Mellon University, June 1988.

28. P.C. Corbett, S.J. Baylor, and D.G. Feitelson, "Overview of the Vesta Parallel File System," *Proc. IPPS'93 Workshop Input/Output Parallel Computer Systems*, 1993, pp. 1–16.

29. A. Cox and R. Fowler, "The Implementation of a Coherent Memory Abstraction on a NUMA Multiprocessor: Experiences with Platinum," *Proc. 12th ACM Symp. Operating Systems Principles*, ACM Press, New York, N.Y., 1989, pp. 32–44.

30. W. Crowther et al., "The Butterfly Parallel Processor," Tech. Report, BBN Laboratories Incorporated.

31. S. Curran and M. Stumm, "A Comparison of Basic CPU Scheduling Algorithms for Multiprocessor UNIX," *Computing Systems*, Vol. 3, No. 4, Oct 1990, pp. 551–579.

32. W. Dally et al., "Architecture of a Message Driven Processor," *Proc. 14th Ann. Int'l Symp. Computer Architecture*, Vol. 15, No. 2, IEEE CS Press, Los Alamitos, Calif., 1987, pp. 189–196.

33. P. Dasgupta et al., "The CLOUDS Distributed Operating System," *Computer*, Vol. 24, No. 11, Nov. 1991, pp. 34–44.

34. M.L. Dertouzos and A.K. Mok, "Multiprocessor On-line Scheduling of Hard-real-time Tasks," *IEEE Trans. Software Eng.*, Vol. 15, No. 12, Dec. 1989, pp. 1497–1506.

35. P. Dibble and M. Scott, "Beyond Striping: The Bridge Multiprocessor File System," *Computer Architecture News*, Vol. 17, No. 5, Sept. 1989, pp. 32–39.

36. P. Dibble, M. Scott, and C. Ellis, "Bridge: A High-performance File System for Parallel Processors," *Proc. 8th Int'l Conf. Distributed Computing Systems*, IEEE CS Press, Los Alamitos, Calif., 1988, pp. 154–161.

37. J. Dinger, K. Rothermel, and K. Urbschat, "ECSE: An Efficient Environment for Layered Communication Protocols," *Proc. 2nd IEEE Workshop Future Trends of Distributed Computer Systems*, IEEE CS Press, Los Alamitos, Calif., 1990, pp. 305–314.

38. W.A. Doeringer et al., "A Survey of Lightweight Transport Protocols for High-speed Networks," *IEEE Trans. Comm.*, Vol. 38, No. 1, Nov 1990, pp. 2025–2039.

39. D. Eager, J. Zahorjan, and E.D. Lazowska, "Speedup Versus Efficiency in Parallel Systems," *IEEE Trans. Computers*, Vol. 38, No. 3, Mar. 1989, pp. 408–423.

40. J. Edler, J. Lipkis, and E. Schonberg, "Process Management for Highly Parallel UNIX Systems," *Proc. USENIX Workshop UNIX and Supercomputers*, USENIX Assoc., Berkeley, Calif., 1988, pp. 1–17.

41. E.W. Felten and J. Zahorjan, "Issues in the Implementation of a Remote Memory Paging System," Tech. Report 91-03-09, Dept. of Computer Science & Engineering, University of Washington, Mar. 1991.

42. R. Fitzgerald and R. Rashid, "The Integration of Virtual Memory Management and Interprocess Communication in Accent," *ACM Trans. Computer Systems*, Vol. 4, No. 2, May 1986, pp. 147–177.

43. G.C. Fox et al., *Solving Problems on Concurrent Processors*, Prentice-Hall, Englewood Cliffs, N.J., 1988.

44. J.C. French, T.W. Pratt, and M. Das, "Performance Measurement of the Concurrent File System of the Intel iPSC/2 Hypercube," *J. Parallel and Distributed Computing*, Vol. 17, No. 1, Jan. 1993, pp. 115–121.

45. M. Gamerl, "Maturing Parallel Transfer Disk Technology Finds More Applications," *Hardcopy*, Vol. 7, No. 2, Feb. 1987, pp. 41–48.

46. A. Garg, "Parallel Streams: A Multi-processor Implementation," *Proc. Winter 1990 USENIX Conference*, USENIX Assoc., Berkeley, Calif., 1990, pp. 163–176.

47. E.F. Gehringer, D.P. Siewiorek, and Z. Segall, *Parallel Processing: The Cm* Experience*, Digital Press, Digital Equipment Corporation, 1987.

48. K. Gharachorloo et al., "Memory Consistency and Event Ordering in Scalable Shared Memory Multiprocessors," *Proc. 17th Ann. Int'l Symp. Computer Architecture*, IEEE CS Press, Los Alamitos, Calif., 1990, pp. 15–26.

49. A. Gheith et al., "KTK: Kernel Support for Configurable Objects and Invocations," *Proc. 2nd Int'l Workshop Configurable Distributed Systems*, 1994.

50. A. Gheith and K. Schwan, "CHAOS-arc–Kernel Support for Multi-weight Objects, Invocations, and Atomicity in Real-time Applications," *ACM Trans. Computer Systems*, Vol. 11, No. 1, Apr. 1993, pp. 33–72.

51. M. Gien, "Microkernel Design," *UNIX REVIEW*, Vol. 8, No. 11, Nov. 1990, pp. 58–63.

52. A. Gottlieb et al., "The NYU Ultracomputer," *IEEE Trans. Computers*, Vol. C-32, No. 2, Feb. 1990, pp. 175–189.

53. Y. Gourhant and M. Shapiro, "FOG/C++: A Fragmented-object Generator," *Proc. USENIX C++ Conf.*, USENIX Assoc., Berkeley, Calif., 1990, pp. 63–74.

54. G. Graunke and S. Thakkar, "Synchronization Algorithms for Shared-memory Multiprocessors," *Computer*, Vol. 23, No. 6, June 1990, pp. 60–70.

55. A.S. Grimshaw and E.C. Loyot, "ELFS: Object-oriented Extensible File Systems," Tech. Report No. TR-91-14, School of Computer Science, University of Virginia, July 1991.

56. A.S. Grimshaw and J. Prem, "High Performance Parallel File Objects," *Proc. 6th Distributed Memory Computing Conf.*, IEEE CS Press, Los Alamitos, Calif., 1991, pp. 720–723.

57. A. Gupta, A. Tucker, and S. Urushibara, "The Impact of Operating Systems Scheduling Policies and Synchronization Methods on the Performance of Parallel Applications," *Proc. 1991 ACM SIGMETRICS Conf. Measurement and Modeling of Computer Systems*, ACM Press, New York, N.Y., 1991, pp. 120–132.

58. R.F. Gurwitz, M.A. Dean, and R.E. Schantz, "Programming Support in the CRONUS Distributed Operating System," *Proc. 6th Int'l Conf. Distributed Computing Systems*, IEEE CS Press, Los Alamitos, Calif., 1986, pp. 486–493.

59. Z. Haas, "A Protocol Structure for High-speed Communication over Broadband ISDN," *IEEE Network Magazine*, Jan. 1991, pp. 64–70.

60. G. Hamilton, M. Powell, and J. Mitchell, "Subcontract: A Flexible Base for Distributed Programming," *Proc. 14th ACM Symp. Operating Systems Principles*, ACM Press, New York, N.Y., 1993, pp. 69–79.

61. J.H. Hartman and J.K. Ousterhout, "Performance Measurements of a Multiprocessor Sprite Kernel," *Proc. USENIX Summer Conf.*, USENIX Assoc., Berkeley, Calif., 1990, pp. 279–287.

62. M. Herlihy, "A Methodology for Implementing Highly Concurrent Data Structures," *Proc. 2nd ACM SIGPLAN Symp. Principles and Practice of Parallel Programming (SIGPLAN Notices Vol. 25, No. 3)*, ACM Press, New York, N.Y., 1990, pp. 197–206.

63. R. Hou and Y. Patt, "Trading Disk Capacity for Performance," *Proc. 2nd Int'l Symp. High Performance Distributed Computing*, IEEE CS Press, Los Alamitos, Calif., 1993, pp. 263–270.

64. N. Hutchinson et al., "RPC in the X-kernel: Evaluating New Design Techniques," *Proc. 12th ACM Symp. Operating Systems Principles*, ACM Press, New York, N.Y., 1989, pp. 91–101.

65. N. Hutchinson, S. Mishra, and L. Peterson, "Tools for Implementing Network Protocols," *Software–Practice and Experience*, Sept. 1989, pp. 895–916.

66. N. Hutchinson, L. Peterson, and H. Rao, "The X-kernel: An Open Operating System Design," *Proc. 2nd Workshop Workstation Operating Systems*, 1989, pp. 55–59.

67. K. Hwang and F. Briggs, *Computer Architecture and Parallel Processing*, Computer Science Series, McGraw-Hill, New York, N.Y., 1984.

68. H. Burkhardt III et al., "Overview of the KSR1 Computer System," Tech. Report KSR-TR-9202001, Kendall Square Research, Boston, Mass., Feb. 1992.

69. Intel Corporation, Beaverton, Ore., *Touchstone Delta System User's Guide*, 1991.

70. Intel Corporation, Supercomputer Systems Division, *Paragon User's Guide*, Oct. 1993.

71. A. Jones and K. Schwan, "Task Forces: Distributed Software for Solving Problems of Substantial Size," *Proc. 4th Int'l Conf. Software Eng.*, IEEE CS Press, Los Alamitos, Calif., 1979, pp. 315–330.

72. A.K. Jones et al., "StarOS, A Multiprocessor Operating System," *Proc. 7th ACM Symp. Operating Systems Principles*, ACM Press, New York, N.Y., 1979, pp. 117–127.

73. A.K. Jones and P. Schwarz, "Experience Using Multiprocessor Systems: A Status Report," *Computing Surveys*, Vol. 12, No. 2, June 1980, pp. 121–166.

74. E. Jul et al., "Fine-grained Mobility in the Emerald System," *ACM Trans. Computer Systems*, Vol. 6, No. 1, Feb. 1988, pp. 169–133.

75. A. Karlin et al., "Empirical Studies of Competitive Spinning for a Shared-memory Multiprocessor," *Proc. 13th ACM Symp. Operating Systems Principles*, ACM Press, New York, N.Y., 1991, pp. 41–55.

76. Kendall Square Research, Waltham, Mass., *KSR1 Principles of Operation*, Oct. 1991.

77. Kendall Square Research, Waltham, Mass., *Tech. Summary*, 1992.

78. J. Kepecs, "Lightweight Processes for UNIX Implementation and Application," *Proc. 1985 USENIX Summer Conf.*, USENIX Assoc., Berkeley, Calif., 1985, pp. 299–308.

79. Y. Khalidi and M. Nelson, "An Implementation of UNIX on an Object Oriented Operating System," *Proc. 1993 Winter USENIX Conf.*, USENIX Assoc., Berkeley, Calif., 1993, pp. 469–479.

80. B. Lampson and D. Redell, "Experiences with Processes and Monitors in MESA," *Comm. ACM*, Vol. 23, No. 2, 1980, pp. 105–117.

81. E.D. Lazowska et al., "The Architecture of the Eden System," *Proc. 8th ACM Symp. Operating Systems Principles*, ACM Press, New York, N.Y., 1981, pp. 148–159.

82. E.D. Lazowska and M. Squillante, "Using Processor-cache Affinity in Shared-memory Multiprocessor Scheduling," *IEEE Trans. Parallel and Distributed Systems*, Vol. 4, No. 2, Feb. 1993, pp. 131–143.

83. T. Leblanc, B. Marsh, and M. Scott, "Memory Management for Large-scale NUMA Multiprocessors," Tech. Report TR 311, Department of Computer Science, University of Rochester, Mar. 1989.

84. T. Leblanc, "Shared Memory versus Message-passing in a Tightly-coupled Multiprocessor: A Case Study," *Proc. 1986 Int'l Conf. Parallel Processing*, IEEE CS Press, Los Alamitos, Calif., 1986, pp. 463–466.

85. C.E. Leiserson et al., "The Network Architecture of the Connection Machine CM-5," *Proc. 1992 ACM Symp. Parallel Algorithms and Architectures*, ACM Press, New York, N.Y., 1992.

86. S. Leutenegger and M. Vernon, "The Performance of Multiprogrammed Multiprocessor Scheduling Policies," *Proc. 1990 ACM SIGMETRICS Conf. Measurement and Modeling of Computer Systems*, ACM Press, New York, N.Y., 1990, pp. 226–236.

87. R. Levin et al., "Policy/Mechanism Separation in Hydra," *Proc. 5th ACM Symp. Operating Systems Principles*, ACM Press, New York, N.Y., 1975.

88. B. Lindgren et al., "An Architecture and Toolkit for Parallel and Configurable Protocols," *Proc. Int'l Conf. Network Protocols*, 1993.

89. B. Lindgren et al., "Parallelism and Configurability in High-Performance Protocol Architectures," *Proc. 2nd Workshop High-Performance Communications*, 1993, pp. 1–7.

90. M. Livny and U. Manber, "Distributed Computation via Active Messages," *IEEE Trans. Computers*, Vol. C-34, No. 12, Dec. 1985, pp. 1185–1190.

91. S. Lo and V. Gligor, "A Comparative Analysis of Multiprocessor Scheduling Algorithms," *Proc. 7th Int'l Conf. Distributed Computing Systems*, IEEE CS Press, Los Alamitos, Calif., 1987, pp. 356–363.

92. P. Madany et al., "A Class Hierarchy for Building Stream-oriented File Systems," *Proc. 1989 European Conf. Object-Oriented Programming*, 1989, pp. 311–328.

93. P. Madany et al., "A C++ Class Hierarchy for Building UNIX-like File Systems," *Proc. USENIX C++ Conf.*, USENIX Assoc., Berkeley, Calif., 1988, pp. 65–79.

94. S. Majumdar, D. Eager, and R. Bunt, "Scheduling in Multiprogrammed Parallel Systems," *Proc. 1988 ACM SIGMETRICS Conf. Measurement and Modeling of Computer Systems*, ACM Press, New York, N.Y., 1988, pp. 104–113.

95. S. Majumdar, D. Eager, and R. Bunt, "Characterization of Programs for Scheduling in Multiprogrammed Parallel Systems," *Performance Evaluation*, Vol. 13, No. 2, Oct. 1991, pp. 109–130.

96. B. Marsh et al., "First-class User-level Threads," *Proc. 13th ACM Symp. Operating Systems Principles*, ACM Press, New York, N.Y., 1991, pp. 110–121.

97. D. Masters, "Improve Disk Subsystem Performance with Multiple Serial Drives in Parallel," *Computer Technology Review*, Summer 1987, pp. 76–77.

98. C. McCann, R. Vaswani, and J. Zahorjan, "A Dynamic Processor Scheduling Policy for Multiprogrammed, Shared Memory Multiprocessors," *ACM Trans. Computer Systems*, Vol. 11, No. 2, May 1993, pp. 146–178.

99. J. Mellor-Crummey and M. Scott, "Algorithms for Scalable Synchronization on Shared-memory Multiprocessors," *ACM Trans. Computer Systems*, Vol. 9, No. 1, Feb. 1991, pp. 21–65.

100. J. Mogul and A. Borg, "The Effects of Context Switches on Cache Performance," *Proc. 4th Int'l Conf. Architectural Support for Programming Languages and Operating Systems (SIGPLAN Notices Vol. 26, No. 4)*, ACM Press, New York, N.Y., 1991, pp. 75–84.

101. R. Moore et al., "The Encore Multimax (tm): A Multiprocessor Computing Environment," Tech. Report ETR 86-004, Encore Computer Corporation, 1986.

102. B. Mukherjee, "A Portable and Reconfigurable Threads Package," *Proc. Sun User Group Tech. Conf.*, 1991, pp. 101–112.

103. B. Mukherjee, G. Eisenhauer, and K. Ghosh, "A Machine Independent Interface for Lightweight Threads," *Operating Systems Review*, Vol. 28, No. 1, Jan. 1994, pp. 33–47.

104. B. Mukherjee and K. Schwan, "Experiments with a Configurable Lock for Multiprocessors," *Proc. 22nd Int'l Conf. Parallel Processing*, Vol. 2, CRC Press, Boca Raton, Fla., 1993, pp. 205–208.

105. B. Mukherjee and K. Schwan, "Improving Performance by Use of Adaptive Objects: Experi- mentation with a Configurable Multiprocessor Thread Package," *Proc. 2nd Int'l Symp. High Performance Distributed Computing*, IEEE CS Press, Los Alamitos, Calif., 1993, pp. 59–66.

106. J. Ousterhout, "Scheduling Techniques for Concurrent Systems," *Proc. Distributed Computing Systems Conf.*, IEEE CS Press, Los Alamitos, Calif., 1982, pp. 22–30.

107. J.K. Ousterhout et al., "The Sprite Network Operating System," *Computer*, Vol. 21, No. 2, Feb. 1988, pp. 23–36.

108. IEEE POSIX P1003.4a, *Threads Extension for Portable Operating Systems*.

109. K. Park and L. Dowdy, "Dynamic Partitioning of Multiprocessor Systems," *Int'l J. Parallel Programming*, Vol. 18, No. 2, Apr. 1989, pp. 91–120.

110. D.A. Patterson, G. Gibson, and R.H. Katz, "A Case for Redundant Arrays of Inexpensive Disks (RAID)," *Proc. 1988 ACM SIGMOD Conf.*, ACM Press, New York, N.Y., 1988, pp. 109–116.

111. L. Peterson et al., "The X-kernel: A Platform for Accessing Internet Resources," *Computer*, Vol. 23, No. 5, May 1990, pp. 23–33.

112. T.W. Pratt et al., "A Comparison of the Architecture and Performance of Two Parallel File Systems," *Proc. 4th Conf. Hypercube Concurrent Computers and Applications*, 1989, pp. 161–166.

113. R. Rashid and G. Robertson, "Accent: A Communication Oriented Network Operating System Kernel," *Proc. 8th ACM Symp. Operating Systems Principles*, ACM Press, New York, N.Y., 1981, pp. 64–75.

114. R. Rashid et al., "Machine-independent Virtual Memory Management for Paged Uniprocessor and Multiprocessor Architectures," *IEEE Trans. Computers*, Vol. 37, No. 8, Aug. 1988, pp. 896–908.

115. D. Ritchie and K. Thompson, "The UNIX Time-sharing System," *Comm. ACM*, Vol. 17, No. 7, July 1974.

116. J.M. Rosario, R. Bordawekar, and A. Choudhary, "Improved Parallel I/O via a Two-phase Runtime Access Strategy," *Proc. IPPS'93 Workshop Input/Output Parallel Computer Systems*, 1993, pp. 56–70.

117. M. Rozier et al., "Overview of the CHORUS Operating System," *Proc. USENIX Workshop on Micro-Kernels and Other Kernel Architectures*, USENIX Assoc., Berkeley, Calif., 1992, pp. 39–69.

118. V. Russo, "Object-oriented Operating System Design," *TCOS Newsletter*, Vol. 5, No. 1, 1991, pp. 34–38.

119. V. Russo and R. Campbell, "Virtual Memory and Backing Storage Management in Multiprocessor Operating Systems Using Object-oriented Design Techniques," *OOPSLA'89 Conf. Proc. (SIGPLAN Notices*, Vol. 24, No. 10), ACM Press, New York, N.Y., 1989, pp. 267–278.

120. V. Russo, G. Johnston, and R. Campbell, "Process Management and Exception Handling in Multiprocessor Operating Systems Using Object-oriented Design Techniques," *OOPSLA'88 Conf. Proc. (SIGPLAN Notices*, Vol. 23, No. 11), ACM Press, New York, N.Y., 1988, pp. 248–258.

121. V. Russo, P. Madany, and R. Campbell, "C++ and Operating Systems Performance: A Case Study," *Proc. USENIX C++ Conf.*, USENIX Assoc., Berkeley, Calif., 1990, pp. 103–114.

122. V. Russo and P. Muckelbauer, "Process Scheduling and Synchronization in the Renaissance Object-oriented Multiprocessor Operating System," *Proc. 2nd USENIX Symp. Experiences with Distributed and Multiprocessor Systems*, USENIX Assoc., Berkeley, Calif., 1991, pp. 117–132.

123. V. Russo, *An Object-Oriented Operating System*, PhD Thesis, Department of Computer Science, University of Illinois at Urbana-Champaign, Jan. 1991.

124. P. Sadayappan and F. Ercal, "Nearest-neighbor Mapping of Finite Element Graphs onto Processors Meshes," *IEEE Trans. Computers*, Vol. C-36, No. 12, Dec. 1987, pp. 1408–1420.

125. M. Schroeder and M. Burrows, "Performance of Firefly RPC," *ACM Trans. Computer Systems*, Vol. 8, No. 1, Feb. 1990, pp. 1–17.

126. K. Schwan and W. Bo, "Topologies—Distributed Objects on Multicomputers," *ACM Trans. Computer Systems*, Vol. 8, No. 2, May 1990, pp. 111–157.

127. K. Schwan, P. Gopinath, and W. Bo, "CHAOS—Kernel Support for Objects in the Real-time Domain," *IEEE Trans. Computers*, Vol. C-36, No. 8, Jul 1987, pp. 904–916.

128. K. Schwan and A.K. Jones, "Specifying Resource Allocation for the Cm* Multiprocessor," *IEEE Software*, Vol. 3, No. 3, May 1984, pp. 60–70.

129. "Sequent Computer Systems, Inc.," *Dynix Programmer's Manual*, 1986.

130. K. Sevcik, "Characterizations of Parallelism in Applications and Their Use in Scheduling," *Proc. 1989 ACM SIGMETRICS Conf. Measurement and Modeling of Computer Systems*, ACM Press, New York, N.Y., 1989, pp. 171–180.

131. M. Shapiro, "Object-support Operating Systems," *TCOS Newsletter*, Vol. 5, No. 1, 1991, pp. 39–42.

132. M. Shapiro and M. Makpangou, "Distributed Abstractions, Lightweight References," *Proc. USENIX Workshop Micro-Kernels and Other Kernel Architectures*, USENIX Assoc., Berkeley, Calif., 1992, pp. 263–267.

133. M.H. Solomon and R.A. Finkel, "The Roscoe Distributed Operating System," *Proc. 7th ACM Symp. Operating Systems Principles*, ACM Press, New York, N.Y., 1979, pp. 108–114.

134. M. Stumm and S. Zhou, "Algorithms Implementing Distributed Shared Memory," *Computer*, Vol. 23, No. 5, May 1990, pp. 55–64.

135. A. Tanenbaum, *Modern Operating Systems*, Prentice-Hall, Englewood Cliffs, N.J., 2nd ed., 1992.

136. A. Tanenbaum and R. Van Renesse, "Distributed Operating Systems," *Computing Surveys*, Vol. 17, No. 4, Dec. 1985, pp. 419–470.

137. A. Tevanian et al., "MACH Threads and the UNIX Kernel: The Battle for Control," *Proc.Summer 1987 USENIX Conf.*, USENIX Assoc., Berkeley, Calif., 1987, pp. 185–197.

138. D. Thiebaut and H. Stone, "Footprints in the Cache," *ACM Trans. Computer Systems*, Vol. 5, No. 4, Nov. 1987, pp. 305–329.

139. "Thinking Machines Corporation, Cambridge, Massachusetts," *CM5 Tech. Summary*, Oct. 1991.

140. R. Thomas and W. Crowther, "The Uniform System: An Approach to Runtime Support for Large Scale Shared Memory Parallel Processors," *Proc.1988 Int'l Conf. Parallel Processing*, Vol. 2, The Pennsylvania State University Press, University Park, Penn., 1988.

141. A. Tucker and A. Gupta, "Process Control and Scheduling Issues for Multiprogrammed Shared Memory Multiprocessors," *Proc. 12th ACM Symp. Operating Systems Principles*, ACM Press, New York, N.Y., 1989, pp. 159–166.

142. R. Vaswani and J. Zahorjan, "The Implications of Cache Affinity on Processor Scheduling for Multiprogrammed, Shared Memory Multiprocessors," *Proc. 13th ACM Symp. Operating Systems Principles*, ACM Press, New York, N.Y., 1991, pp. 26–40.

143. R.W. Watson and S.A. Mamrak, "Gaining Efficiency in Transport Services by Appropriate Design and Implementation Choices," *ACM Trans. Computer Systems*, Vol. 5, No. 2, May 1987, pp. 97–120.

144. W. Wulf, R. Levin, and S. Harbison, *Hydra/C.mmp: An Experimental Computer System*, McGraw-Hill Advanced Computer Science Series, New York, N.Y., 1981.

145. W. Wulf, R. Levin, and C. Pierson, "Overview of the Hydra Operating System," *Proc. 5th ACM Symp. Operating Systems Principles*, ACM Press, New York, N.Y., 1975, pp. 122–131.

146. M. Young et al., "The Duality of Memory and Communication in the Implementation of a Multiprocessor Operating System," *Proc. 11th ACM Symp. Operating Systems Principles*, ACM Press, New York, N.Y., 1987, pp. 63–76.

147. J. Zahorjan, E.D. Lazowska, and D. Eager, "The Effect of Scheduling Discipline on Spin Overhead in Shared Memory Parallel Systems," *IEEE Trans. Parallel and Distributed Systems*, Vol. 2, No. 2, Apr. 1991, pp. 180–198.

148. J. Zahorjan and C. McCann, "Processor Scheduling in Shared Memory Multiprocessors," *Proc.1990 ACM SIGMETRICS Conf. Measurement and Modeling of Computer Systems*, ACM Press, New York, N.Y., 1990, pp. 214–225.

149. H. Zhou and K. Schwan, "Dynamic Scheduling for Hard Real-time Systems: Toward Real-time Threads," *Proc. Joint IEEE Workshop Real-Time Operating Systems and Software and IFAC Workshop on Real-Time Programming*, 1991, pp. 13–21.

150. S. Zhou et al., "Heterogeneous Distributed Shared Memory," *IEEE Trans. Parallel and Distributed Systems*, Vol. 3, No. 5, Sept. 1992, pp. 540–554.

151. M. Zitterbart, "High-speed Transport Components," *IEEE Network*, Vol. 5, No. 1, Jan. 1991, pp. 54–63.

PART IV
FORMAL METHODS

CHAPTER 10

FORMAL METHODS TO GENERATE AND UNDERSTAND DISTRIBUTED COMPUTING SYSTEMS

Bruce McMillin,* and Grace Tsai
Department of Computer Science
University of Missouri-Rolla
Rolla, MO 65401 USA

Hanan Lutfiyya,[†]
Department of Computer Science
University of Western Ontario
London, Ontario N6A 5B7 Canada

Abstract. *This chapter explores correctness through cooperative axiomatic reasoning, provides an additional basis for understanding parallel algorithm design and specification, and is used for runtime assurance of distributed computing systems through operational evaluation. This mathematical model allows for the generation of executable assertions which detect faults in the presence of arbitrary failures. The mathematical model of choice consists of two components: CSP and an associated axiomatic verification system. A method is developed that translates a concurrent verification proof outline into an error-detecting concurrent program.*

Keywords. Formal Methods, Operational Evaluation.

---

*Supported in part by the National Science Foundation under Grant Numbers MSS-9216479 and CDA-9222827, and, in part, by the Air Force Office of Scientific Research under contract number F49620-92-J-0546.

†Supported in part by the National Sciences and Engineering Research Council of Canada (NSERC) under contract number OGP0138180-S365A2, and in part, by University of Western Ontario NSERC internal funding under contract number Z001A8-S365A1.

10.1

A MATHEMATICAL MODEL OF DISTRIBUTED SYSTEMS BEHAVIOR

A *formal model* (or mathematical model) is a model of the system using well-understood mathematical entities such as sets and functions. Formal methods used in developing computer systems are mathematically based techniques for describing systems. A formal method consists of a formal model and associated mathematical techniques, which provides the user with a framework for specifying and analyzing the system.

The problem of specifying an abstract system is that of specifying a particular mathematical object for which good mathematical techniques may have already been developed over the years. The existence of a formal model of an abstract system implies that a formal statement of the problem is needed that is in terms of the formal model being used. Separating the problem from its solution is an important contribution of having a theoretical foundation in that it opens the door to alternative solutions [4].

There are numerous examples of the use of mathematical models in computer science literature. One example from the study of network topology is the ability to compute the information-carrying capacity of a network. Graphs can be used as the model of network topology, while the concept of the cut is useful for modeling the carrying capacity of the network. Other examples include queueing models for analyzing the performance of a system, Markov chains for reliability analysis, and axiomatic and denotational specifications for formally describing programming languages.

In general, theoretical foundations can provide (1) criteria for evaluation, (2) means of comparison, (3) theoretical limits and capabilities, (4) means of prediction, and (5) underlying rules, principles, and structure. The power of a mathematical model is that it forces one to think clearly about the problem one is trying to solve. The process of stating the question leads one to identify relevant variables, state explicitly any assumption being made, and so forth. These very factors are often instrumental in leading one to a solution. Models ignore irrelevant details. This focuses attention on the essential feature; a model produces generality, for results that depend on fewer assumptions are more widely applicable.

10.1.1 The Axiomatic Approach to Program Verification

The axiomatic approach to program verification is based on making assertions about program variables before, during, and after program execution. These assertions characterize properties of program variables and relationships between them at various stages of program execution. Program verification requires proofs of theorems of the following type:

$$\langle P \rangle S \langle Q \rangle$$

where P and Q are assertions, and S is a statement of the language. The interpretation of the theorem is as follows: if P is true before the execution of S and if the execution of S terminates, then Q is true after the execution of S. P is said to be the *precondition* and Q the *postcondition* [5]. A statement, S, is *partially correct* with respect to the precondition P and a postcondition Q, if, whenever, P is true of S prior to execution, and if S terminates then Q is true of S after the execution of S terminates. A program, S, is *totally correct* if it is partially correct and it can be shown that this program terminates.

CSP programs are composed of a set of communicating sequential processes. In many programs, it is desirable to save part of the communication sequence between processes. This is done with use of *dummy* or *auxiliary* variables that relate program variables of one process to program variables of another. The need for such variables has been independently recognized by many. The first reference that shows the usefulness of auxiliary variables is found in [2].

Overall Proof Approach   As discussed earlier, a CSP program is made up of component sequential processes executing in parallel. In general, to prove properties about the program, first properties of each component process are derived in isolation. These properties are combined to obtain the properties of the whole program.

Example 1.   Assume that we want to prove the following:

$$\langle true \rangle [\rho_1 \| \rho_2 \| \rho_3] \langle x = u \rangle$$

where

$$\rho_1 :: \rho_2!x$$
$$\rho_2 :: \rho_1?y; \rho_3!y$$
$$\rho_3 :: \rho_2$$

The following properties can be proven about each of the component processes:

$$\langle x = z \rangle \; \rho_1 \langle x = z \rangle$$
$$\langle true \rangle \;\; \rho_2 \langle y = z \rangle$$
$$\langle true \rangle \;\; \rho_3 \langle u = z \rangle$$

We can use the properties that $x = z$ and $u = z$ and transitivity to show that $x = u$.

There are two approaches to proving the correctness of communicating processes. The first approach is to divide the correctness proof into two parts. The first part is the sequential proof of each individual process that makes assumptions about the effects of the communication commands. The second part is to ensure that the assumptions are *legitimate*. This will be discussed later. This approach is taken in [1] and [9]. The second approach allows us to prove properties of the individual processes using the axioms and rules of inference applicable to the statements in the individual processes. The axioms and rules of inference are designed in such a way that it is not necessary in a sequential proof of a process to make assumptions about the behavior of other processes. These properties are then used to prove properties of the entire program. This is the approach of [20].

It has been shown [10] that it is irrelevant as to which axiomatic proof system of program verification is chosen. This was done by showing that the axiomatic systems are equivalent in the sense that they allow us to prove the same properties. No system is more powerful than the others. However, there are very different approaches to thinking about the verification of the program and the applicability in a practical environment. The proof system presented in [9] is presented here for its relative ease of use.

Axioms and Inference Rules Used for Sequential Reasoning   In addition to the axioms and inference rules of predicate logic, there is one axiom or inference rule for each type of statement, as well as some statement-independent inference rules. The following are common to all the axiomatic systems and apply to reasoning about sequential programs. The basis of the axiomatic approach to sequential programming can be found in [5].

The *skip* axiom is simple, since execution of the skip statement has no effect on any program or auxiliary variables.

$$\langle P \rangle skip \langle P \rangle$$

The axiom states that anything about the program and logical variables that holds before executing **skip** also holds after it has terminated.

To understand the *assignment* axiom, consider a multiple assignment statement, $\bar{x} := \bar{e}$, where $\bar{x}$ is a list of $x_1, x_2, \ldots, x_n$ of identifiers, and $\bar{e}$ is a list of $e_1, e_2, \ldots, e_n$ of expressions. If execution of this statement does not terminate, then the axiom is valid for any choice of postcondition P. If execution terminates, then its only effect is to change the value denoted by each target x_i to that of the value denoted by the corresponding expression e_i before execution was begun. Thus, to be able to conclude that P is true when the multiple assignment terminates, execution must begin in a state in which the assertion obtained by replacing each occurrence of x_i in P by e_i holds. This means that if $P_{\bar{e}}^{\bar{x}}$[1] is true before the multiple assignment is executed and execution terminates, then P will be true after the assignment. Thus we have the following:

$$\langle P_{\bar{e}}^{\bar{x}} \rangle \bar{x} := \bar{e} \langle P \rangle$$

It may seem strange at first that the precondition should be derived from the postcondition rather than vice versa, but it turns out that this assignment rule, as well as being simple, is very convenient to apply in constructing proofs about programs.

There are also a number of rules of inference, which enable the truth of certain assertions to be deduced from the truth of certain other assertions.

A proof outline for the composition of two statements can be derived from proofs for each of its components.

$$\frac{\langle P \rangle S_1 \langle Q \rangle, \langle Q \rangle S_2 \langle R \rangle}{\langle P \rangle S_1; S_2 \langle R \rangle}$$

When executing $S_1; S_2$, if Q is true when S_1 terminates it will hold when S_2 starts. From the second hypothesis, if Q is true just before S_2 executes and S_2 terminates, then R will hold. Thus if S_1 and S_2 are executed one after the other and P holds before the execution, then R holds after the execution.

Execution of an alternate command ensures that a statement S_i is executed only if its guard b_i is true. Thus, if an assertion P is true before execution of the alternate command, then $P \wedge b_i$ will hold just before S_i is executed. The second part of the hypothesis assumes that none of the guards are true. If the hypothesis is true and if the alternate statement terminates, then this is sufficient to prove that Q will hold should the alternate statement terminate.

$$\frac{\forall i: \langle P \wedge b_i \rangle c_i; S_i \langle Q \rangle, \langle P \wedge \forall i: \neg b_i \rangle \rightarrow \langle Q \rangle}{\langle P \rangle if \, 2 \, b_i; c_i \rightarrow S_i \, fi \langle Q \rangle}$$

---

[1] This stands for predicate P with each x_i replaced with e_i.

The consequence rule allows the precondition of a program or part of a program to be strengthened and the postcondition to be weakened, based on deductions possible in the predicate logic.

$$\frac{P \rightarrow P', \langle P' \rangle S \langle Q' \rangle, Q' \rightarrow Q}{\langle P \rangle S \langle Q \rangle}$$

The need for auxiliary variables was discussed earlier. Two of the proof systems use auxiliary variables. The auxiliary variables must not affect program control during execution. The following rule allows us to draw conclusions from proof outlines of programs annotated with auxiliary variables.

$$\frac{\langle P \rangle S' \langle Q \rangle}{\langle P \rangle S \langle Q \rangle}$$

where S is obtained from S' by deleting all references to auxiliary variables and P and Q do not contain any free variables that are auxiliary variables.

The inference rule for the repetition command is based on a loop invariant, that is, an assertion that holds both before and after every iteration of a loop.

$$\frac{\forall i: \langle P \wedge b_i \rangle c_i; S_i \langle P \rangle}{\langle P \rangle * [2 \, b_i c_i \rightarrow S_i] \langle P \wedge \forall i: \neg b_i \rangle}$$

The hypotheses of the rule require that if execution of S_i is begun when the assertion P and b_i is true, and if execution terminates, then P will again be true. Hence, if an assertion P is true just before the execution of a repetition command, then P is true at the beginning and end of each iteration. Thus, P will hold if the repetition terminates. The repetition ends when no Boolean guard is true, so $\neg b_1 \wedge \neg b_2 \wedge \cdots \wedge \neg b_n$ will also hold at that time.

Levin and Gries' technique [9] does not have distributed termination, which is contrary to Hoare's original version of CSP [6]. Distributed termination provides the means for automatic termination of a loop in one process because another process has terminated. It is assumed that termination of all loops occurs when all Boolean guards are false.

Example 2.   Let us examine how these rules are applied to the following sample program.

var t, i ,b[0 $\cdots$ n $-$ 1]: integer;
$t := 0$;
$i := 0$;
do $[i \neq n \rightarrow t := t + b[i]; i := i + 1]$ **od**

This program sums up the elements of an array b. The result is put into the variable t. Now to prove the partial correctness of this program, we will prove that if the program is started in a state where $n \geq 0$ holds and execution terminates, then t will contain the sum of the values in $b[0]$ through $b[n-1]$. The composition rule implies that in order to prove the above program correct, it is sufficient to prove that

$$\langle n \geq 0 \rangle t := 0 \langle t = 0 \rangle \tag{10.1}$$

$$\langle t = 0 \rangle i := 0 \langle t = 0 \wedge i = 0 \rangle \tag{10.2}$$

$$\langle t = 0 \wedge i = 0 \rangle do[i \neq n \rightarrow t := t + b[i]; i := i + 1]od \left\langle t = \sum_{j=0}^{i-1} b[j] \right\rangle \tag{10.3}$$

Outline 10.1 and 10.2 are easy to prove using the assignment axiom. Note that using normal predicate logic inference rules, it can be shown

$$t = 0 \land i = 0 \rightarrow t = \sum_{j=0}^{i-1} b[j].$$

Remember that since i is equal to 0, that there are no values of j between 0 and $i - 1$. Hence,

$$t = \sum_{j=0}^{i-1} b[j]$$

is vacuously true. Therefore, by applying the *rule of consequence*, we can prove Outline 10.3 by showing the following:

$$\left\langle t = \sum_{j=0}^{i-1} b[j] \right\rangle do[i \neq n \rightarrow t := t + b[i]; i := i + 1] od \left\langle t = \sum_{j=0}^{i-1} b[j] \right\rangle \quad (10.4)$$

To prove Outline 10.4, it will be sufficient to prove that

$$\left\langle t = \sum_{j=0}^{i-1} b[j] \land i \neq n \right\rangle t := t + b[i]; i := i + 1 \left\langle t = \sum_{j=0}^{i-1} b[j] \right\rangle \quad (10.5)$$

$$\left\langle t = \sum_{j=0}^{i-1} b[j] \land i = n \right\rangle \rightarrow \left\langle t = \sum_{j=0}^{n-1} b[j] \right\rangle \quad (10.6)$$

In order to prove 10.5, it is sufficient to prove

$$\left\langle t = \sum_{j=0}^{i-1} b[j] \land i \neq n \right\rangle t := t + b[i]; \left\langle t = \sum_{j=0}^{i} b[j] \right\rangle \quad (10.7)$$

$$\left\langle t = \sum_{j=0}^{i} b[j] \right\rangle i := i + 1 \left\langle t = \sum_{j=0}^{i-1} b[j] \right\rangle \quad (10.8)$$

Outlines 7 and 8 can each be proven by applying the assignment axiom. Outline 10.6 can be shown by substituting i for n and using the consequence rule.

Communication and Parallel Decomposition Rules   The communication axiom is as follows:

$$\langle P \rangle \beta \langle Q \rangle$$

where β is a communication command.

Remember that $\langle P \rangle S \langle Q \rangle$ means total correctness if S terminates. S terminates in the absence of deadlock. The parallel rule implies that a proof for a parallel program is based on the isolated sequential proofs of the processes it comprises. Take any such program S. A sequential proof for it only proves facts about it running in isolation. With only one process running, communication commands deadlock. Thus, any predicate Q may be assumed to be true upon termination of a communication command because termination never occurs.

The *law of the excluded miracle* [3] states that the statement false should never be derived. This is the requirement to ensure a sound logic. The communication axiom does violate the law of the excluded miracle. This allows us to deduce that the following is true:

$$\langle true \rangle A?x \langle x = 5 \wedge x = 6 \rangle$$

The postcondition, however, is obviously false. Thus, one might come to the conclusion that the proof system is not sound. This is the result of allowing the communication axiom to make assumptions about the behavior of other processes in order to prove properties of an individual process. In order to justify those assumptions a *satisfaction proof* must be done. This ensures that the proof system is sound. Hence, the parallel inference rule is as follows:

$$\frac{(\forall i: \langle P_i \rangle S_i \langle Q_i \rangle) \text{satisfied and interference} - \text{free}}{\langle (\forall i: P_i) \rangle [||_{i=1:n}, \, \rho_i :: S_i] \langle (\forall i: Q_i) \rangle}$$

The parallel rule implies that we can construct the proof of a parallel program from the partial correctness properties of the sequential programs it comprises.

It has been mentioned that a satisfaction proof is needed to ensure soundness of the proof system. Let us examine the proof outline of the matching communication pair:

$$\rho_1 : [\ldots \langle P \rangle \rho_2?x \langle Q \rangle]$$

$$\rho_2 : [\ldots \langle R \rangle \rho_1!y \langle S \rangle]$$

The effect of these two communication commands is to assign y to x. This implies that $Q \wedge S$ is true after communication if and only if

$$(P \wedge R) \rightarrow (Q \wedge S)_y^x$$

A satisfaction proof is such that the above is proven for every matching communication pair. This is called the *rule of satisfaction*.

Earlier we discussed the need for auxiliary variables. An auxiliary variable may affect neither the flow of control nor the value of any nonauxiliary variables. Otherwise, this unrestricted use of auxiliary variables would destroy the soundness of the proof system. Hence, auxiliary variables are not necessary to the computation, but they are necessary for verification. The proof system in [9] (GAA) allows for auxiliary variables to be global, that is, variables that can be shared between distinct processes. Global auxiliary variables (GAVs) are used to record part of the history of the communication sequence. Shared references to auxiliary variables allow for assertions relating the different communication sequences. This necessitates a *proof of noninterference*, which consists of showing that for each assertion T in process ρ_i, it must be shown that T is invariant over any parallel execution. This is the noninterference property of [17].

Asynchronous Message-passing Systems   The proof systems that have been discussed up to this point are designed for synchronous programming primitives. Our work uses an extension of work discussed in [19]. The work of [19] describes how to extend the notion of a *satisfaction proof* and *noninterference proof* for asynchronous message-passing primitives. The extension is based on introducing for each pair of processors ρ_i and ρ_j, two auxiliary variables δ_{ij}, γ_{ij}, where δ_{ij} is the set of all messages sent from process i to process j and γ_{ij} is the set of all messages j actually receives from i. This extension involves assuming that actual sending and receipt of a message implies that δ_{ij} and γ_{ij} are immediately updated. It is also assumed that $\gamma_{ij} \subseteq \delta_{ij}$ is invariantly true throughout program execution.

10.2

OPERATIONAL EVALUATION

It is important for both life-critical and non–life-critical distributed systems to meet their specification at run time [8]. Large, complex, distributed systems are subject to individual component failures that can cause system failure. Fault tolerance is an important technique to improve system reliability. The fault detection aspect identifies individual faulty components (processors) before they can negatively affect overall system reliability.

A failure occurs when the user observes that a resource does not perform as expected. The failure is the result of some part of the resource entering a state contrary to the specification of the part. The cause of the resource entering such a state is referred to as a fault. When a system can recover from a fault without exhibiting a failure, then the system has fault tolerance. Reliability is a measure of the probability that a specific resource will perform a required function for a specified period of time, usually the item's lifetime, even in the presence of faults. The higher the probability, the higher the reliability of the system is considered to be.

Many methodologies for improving system reliability have been developed throughout the years. These different methodologies fall into two basic groups: fault-masking techniques and concurrent techniques. Early attempts at improving system reliability used fault-masking methods; these methods make the hardware tolerant of faults, through the multiplicity of processing resources. In contrast, concurrent fault detection methods attempt to locate component errors that can lead to system failure. Once the faults are identified, reconfiguration and recovery [21] are used to deal with the faults. This paper focuses on detecting the occurrence of errors. Recovery and reconfiguration are different issues. Work in concurrent detection methods includes self-checking software [22] and recovery blocks [18], which instrument the software with assertions on the program's state; watchdog processors [15], which monitor intermediate data of a computation, and algorithm-based fault tolerance [7], which imposes an additional structure on the data to detect errors. These methods define structure for fault tolerance, but generally do not give a methodology for instantiating the structure.

Application-oriented fault tolerance [16], by contrast, provides a heuristic approach, based on the *natural constraints* to choosing executable assertions from the software specification. These executable assertions [22], in the form of source language statements, are inserted into a program for monitoring the runtime execution behavior of the program. The general form is as follows:

if ¬ ASSERTION then ERROR

Executable assertions are used to ensure that the program state, in the actual runtime environment, is consistent with the logical state specified in the assertion; if not, then an error has occurred and a reliable communication of this diagnostic information is provided to the system such that reconfiguration and recovery can take place. The heuristics for selection of the actual executable assertions are based on the three metrics of *progress, feasibility*, and *consistency*.

What our earlier work lacks is a theoretical foundation built upon mathematical models and theories. In general, theoretical foundations can provide (1) criteria for evaluation, (2) means of comparison, (3) theoretical limits and capabilities, (4) means of prediction, and (5) underlying rules, principles, and structure. This paper describes Changeling as a formal method using the mathematical model of axiomatic program verification to construct executable assertions for error checking in distributed systems. Application of the Changeling system is a two-step process. First, from a verification proof outline, Changeling converts a shared-memory proof outline into a distributed-memory proof outline, which closely matches the distributed operational environment. Second, Changeling transforms the assertions from the proof outline into executable assertions.

10.2.1 Changeling and Application-oriented Fault Tolerance

Application-oriented fault tolerance works on the principle of testing at runtime the intermediate logical assertions from the verification proof outline, that is, application-oriented fault tolerance works on the following principle:

> *If we test and ensure that intermediate results of a program's computation meet its specification, the end solution meets its specification if the intermediate results meet their specification. If processor errors occur that do not affect the solution, then they are not errors of interest. Program verification provides these tests.*

The above principle yields a formal statement of application-oriented fault tolerance; we generate the executable assertions from the logical assertions used in the verification proof outline of $\langle P \rangle S \langle Q \rangle$. The executable assertion generated corresponding to any logical assertion Q_i from the verification proof outline is the following:

if ¬ Q_i then ERROR

Formally, this ensures that if P is true before the concurrent program S begins execution, S tests at runtime that S satisfies the specification as defined by P and Q by using the embedded executable assertions generated from the assertions of the verification proof. Conversely, the assertions of the verification proof represent the properties that must be satisfied by the runtime environment; an error that causes the execution of the program not to satisfy the specified assertions will be flagged as an error by the executable assertions.

The reader may be suspicious that some program S may be changed into a program S' by an error that satisfies the specification as defined by P and Q. Consider, as an example, a program S computing some value x with postassertion $\langle Q \rangle \equiv \langle x \geq 0 \rangle$. Suppose that S should compute $x = 3$. A program S' may actually compute $x = 4$. The postcondition is still satisfied, although the value is not what was intended. This is not a problem with the validity of the postassertion, it is a weakness of the specification. If $x = 3$ was really intended, then the proper postassertion should have been $\langle Q \rangle \equiv \langle x = 3 \rangle$. If $\langle Q \rangle \equiv \langle x \geq 0 \rangle$ is a sufficient specification for the application at hand, then there is no problem.

To eliminate confusion between the testing of intermediate results (via logical assertions) for correctness with respect to the algorithm and the evaluation of the executable assertions derived from the verification proof in the runtime environment, we will refer to the former as the *verification environment* and the latter as the *(distributed) operational environment*.

To summarize, the transformation of an algorithm to an error-detecting algorithm involves using the assertions of the verification proof as executable assertions that are to be embedded into the algorithm.

Taking an application from the verification environment to the distributed operational environment is not a straightforward task. It is this difficulty that inspired the development of Changeling. Changeling consists of four distinct components:

1. The GAA proof system described in Section 10.1.
2. An HAA proof system that mimics closely the distributed operational environment.
3. Formal conversion from GAA to HAA.
4. Formal translation of assertions in the HAA proof system to executable assertions and reducing state information to improve runtime efficiency.

These components are described in the following paragraphs.

History of Auxiliary Variable (HAA) Verification System   The logical assertions from the GAA verification environment cannot be directly used as executable assertions in the distributed environment; in the distributed environment, there are no global variables. Thus, to evaluate, at runtime, logical assertions containing global auxiliary variables, an explicit updating mechanism must be created. Here we develop the verification proof system (HAA) in which updates of global auxiliary variables are exchanged at communication time. This matches, more closely, the operational environment. We show that every verification proof outline in the GAA proof system has the same properties in the HAA proof system, that is, satisfaction and noninterference; thus implying that the HAA proof system has the soundness and completeness properties of the original GAA proof system. The existence of the HAA proof system allows for proofs that can be directly transformed to executable assertions in the runtime environment.

Developing the HAA system requires us to keep track of which processes communicate with which other processes. Each process needs to record its global auxiliary variable updates with respect to all other processes. When communication occurs between two processes, they need to exchange the updates and locally apply them. This is formalized in the following definitions.

Definition 1. *For a process ρ_i, h_i denotes the sequence of all communications that process ρ_i has so far participated in as the receiving process. Thus, h_i is a list consisting of tuples (these are different from the [20] tuples; all future reference to tuples will refer to the following tuples) representing matching communication pairs of the form*

$$[\rho, (Var, Val), T, C]$$

where ρ is a process ρ_i receives from, Var is the variable that ρ is transmitting to ρ_i with formal parameter Val, T denotes the time at which the value Val was assigned to variable Var and C denotes the communication path.

Since we have several processes running in parallel and there exists no concept of a global time, the time T is a local time represented by an instantiation counter that is incremented by one after every execution of a statement. This permits an ordering (time stamping) for all updates of the GAVs within each process.

To be able to account for the different operations performed on the auxiliary variables, each process has to keep a history of variable updates with respect to the last communication with the other processes. These variable sets are described using the subscript of the corresponding process.

Definition 2. *Let g_{ij} depict the GAV set in process ρ_i with respect to process ρ_j, that is, g_{ij} contains the changes that were made to the GAVs in ρ_i since the last communication with ρ_j. G_i is the set of sets $g_{i0}, g_{i1}, \ldots, g_{i(N-1)}$ in process ρ_i. Thus, when two processes ρ_i and ρ_j communicate, the values of their respective subsets, $g_{ij} \in G_i$ and $g_{ji} \in G_j$, are exchanged.*

When two processes ρ_i and ρ_j communicate, where ρ_j is the sender, ρ_j will augment the communication by sending the values of global auxiliary variables that ρ_j updated, or received updates of, between the last and current communications between ρ_i and ρ_j. We batch the changes made to the local copies of the global auxiliary variables by ρ_j since the last communication (with any other processor) in g_{jj}. Before a communication, the function ψ applies changes to all g_{jk}s, and g_{jj} is reset to null to collect future changes. Definition 4 formally describes the communication of g_{ji}. Definition 5 formally describes how process ρ_i updates G_i based on the communicated g_{ji} after communication has taken place.

Definition 3. *The actual set of GAVs to be sent during a communication between ρ_i and ρ_j, where ρ_j is the sender, is determined based on the variables in g_{jj}, that is, all the variables that were updated in ρ_j since the last communication with any process. The set g_{jj} is updated every time an assignment to a GAV takes place in ρ_j and reset at communication time to the empty set. The following function $\psi(G_j, g_{jj})$ describes the update of all variable histories before a communication.*

$$\rho_j: \ (\forall k, 0 \leq k \leq N - 1)(\forall g_{jk} \in G_j)$$
$$[if \ k \neq j \ then \ g_{jk} \leftarrow g_{jk} \cup g_{jj} \ else \ if \ k = j \ then \ g_{jj} \leftarrow \emptyset]$$

The following definition formally defines the semantics of global auxiliary variable communication.

Definition 4.   *The* primary *communication is a matching communication pair for the exchange of variables between processes that are not GAVs. It can be described by a tuple* $[\rho_j, (Var, Val), t, j]$ *where* $t = T_j$ *is the current value of the local time. It is easy to see that all communications in the GAA system are primary since GAVs are updated globally. An* augmented *communication permits the exchange of the GAVs after a primary communication occurs. In an augmented communication, the values of* g_{ji} *are marshaled into a message sent to process* ρ_i.

For each process ρ_i, after an augmented exchange with ρ_j, ρ_i updates its set of GAVs in G_i with the new values received. This interchange is described in Figure 10.1 for two processes ρ_i and ρ_j, and one matching communication pair within the execution sequence of the two processes.

Definition 5.   *The updates performed in the different processes are described by a function* $\phi(G_i, g_{ji})$ *on the set of the GAV history and the variables to be updated. The actual update function* ϕ *is now defined on all the subsets within* G_i *on tuples of the form* $[\rho_j, (g_{ji}, gvar_j), T, j]$.

$$\rho_i : \quad (\forall k, 0 \le k \le N - 1)(\forall g_{ik} \in G_i)$$
$$[if \; k \ne j \; then \; g_{ik} \leftarrow g_{ik} \cup gvar_j$$
$$else \; if \; k = j \; then \; apply(gvar_j); \; g_{ij} \leftarrow \emptyset \;]$$

When processes ρ_i and ρ_j communicate, all old values in the set g_{ij} will be replaced by the new variables. Additionally, these new values (from $gvar_j$) are unmarshaled and applied to update the local values of process ρ_i. In this way, communication propagates GAV updates throughout the concurrent program.

It can be seen that the so-called *global auxiliary variables* in the HAA system are not really global in the sense that all processes have the same values of the variables at all times. Indeed, it is likely that at the end of the process execution some processes that ran in parallel will have different values within their set of GAVs. We show that, because of noninterference, this is not a problem with respect to the proof system.

Within a process execution, two communicating processes can have arbitrary interleavings of their statements up to the communication but are conceptually synchronized at the communication point. The assertions will not interfere with each other due to the noninterference property of the GAA system, which provides for arbitrary execution orders. Since two (or more) processes will only change (write onto) the same global auxiliary variable if they have to communicate with each other, they will also exchange other variables/data, and the values of the auxiliary variables will be available for both processes at the critical point: right after a communication takes place. Thus, sending only the history of the global variable updates instead of immediately providing the other process(es) with the latest information will not cause any problems, since the values of the variables will be available at the communication points, where they are in fact provided.

For process P_i:
/* execute arbitrary set of statements excluding communication but
including assignments to auxiliary variables */
S_{i1}; $\langle T_i := 1 \rangle$
S_{i2}; $\langle T_i := T_i + 1 \rangle$
$\ldots$;
S_{ik}; $\langle T_i := T_i + j \rangle$
/* update the auxiliary variables */
$G_i \leftarrow \psi(G_i, g_{ii})$; $\langle T_i := T_i + 1 \rangle$
/* perform communication with process P_j;
the first communication represents the actual communication */
/* the next two communications represent the exchange augment of the auxiliary
variables */
P_j? V; $\langle T_i := k \rangle$
P_j? g_{ji}; $\langle T_i := k + 1 \rangle$
P_j! g_{ij}; $\langle T_i := k + 2 \rangle$
/* update the auxiliary variables */
$G_i \leftarrow \phi(G_i, g_{ji})$; $\langle T_i := k + 3 \rangle$

For process P_j:
/* execute arbitrary set of statements excluding communication
but including assignments to auxiliary variables */
S_{j1}; $\langle T_j := 1 \rangle$
S_{j2}; $\langle T_j := T_j + 1 \rangle$
$\ldots$;
S_{jk}; $\langle T_j := T_j + 1 \rangle$
/* update the auxiliary variables */
$G_j \leftarrow \psi(G_j, g_{jj})$; $\langle T_j := T_j + 1 \rangle$
/* perform communication with process P_i;
the first communication represents the actual communication */
/* the next two communications represent the exchange augment of the auxiliary variables */
P_i ! V ; $\langle T_j := k \rangle$
P_i ! g_{ji} ; $\langle T_j := k + 1 \rangle$
P_i ? g_{ij} ; $\langle T_j := k + 2 \rangle$
/* update the auxiliary variables */
$G_j \leftarrow \phi(G_j, g_{ij})$; $\langle T_j := k + 3 \rangle$

FIGURE 10.1 An HAA proof outline for one matching communication pair.

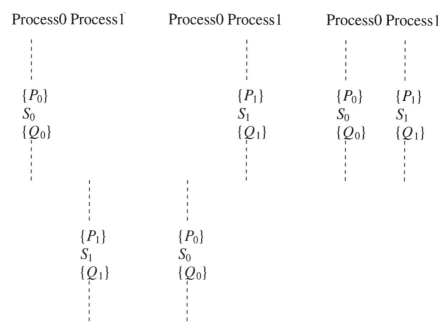

FIGURE 10.2 Some possible process execution sequences before communication takes place.

An example of three possible process execution sequences that are subject to noninterference is shown in Figure 10.2. For any two processes, noninterference will guarantee that the execution order of the two processes or any arbitrary interleaving of them will not invalidate the assertions made on the respective process statements.

Noninterference and the rule of satisfaction can be used to show that the soundness and completeness properties of the original GAA system will hold in the new HAA proof system.

Theorem 1.   *[13] The history of the auxiliary variables approach (HAA) retains the properties of the global auxiliary variables approach (GAA).*

Reliable Communication of State Information   The HAA proof system provides for direct transformation of assertions from the verification environment into executable assertions for the nonfaulty distributed operational environment. However, we are concerned with the distributed faulty environment. Thus, it is necessary to ensure that faulty processors cannot fool executable assertions by incorrect augmented communication of $g's$ through sending inconsistent messages to different processors. It is necessary for this to be detected. This is the purpose of *consistency* executable assertions. Mathematically, this can be described as follows:

Definition 6. *For a nonfaulty process ρ_i, if there exist any two tuples t_1, $t_2 \in h_i$ such that*

$$t_1 = [j, (Var, Val_1), T, C_1]$$

$$t_2 = [j, (Var, Val_2), T, C_2]$$

then if $Val_1 \circ Val_2$ the system is said to be inconsistent; otherwise the system is said to be consistent.

$\circ$ is defined as a set of functions such that each $\circ' \in \circ$ is of functionality $dt \rightarrow T, F$, where dt is an abstract data type. Examples of $\circ'$ are $\neq$, $\subseteq$, $\neg prefix$, or some other operator appropriate to the choice of the data type of Var. Where no ambiguity results, we will refer to a particular $\circ'$ simply as $\circ$.

The strongest motivation for the consistency condition is to supplement the power of the executable assertions derived from the HAA system. When the value of a variable computed in time T is communicated to a set of processors on more than one path, there will be two or more tuples in h_i that satisfy the precondition. Under a bounded number of faults, the consistency of Definition 6 ensures that a nonfaulty processor receives a consistent set of input values for its executable assertions, otherwise, $Val_1 \circ Val_2$, and an inconsistent system can be detected. The degree of fault tolerance is based on standard network flow arguments and is not repeated here. It should be noted that all faults in communication links are mapped to a processor, thus it is enough to assume only faulty processors.

Consistency does not have to be explicit. In other words, an error-detecting program may have to explicitly add code to implement consistency. This can be done in many ways. There are classes of problems that have the property of natural redundancy in the problem variables. This implies that there are types of errors, which, if they occur at stage i, eventually, at some stage j (where $j > i$), stage j satisfies the properties as defined by the intermediate assertions of a verification proof, despite the fact that the error had occurred in stage i. If a program variable is naturally redundant, then this means that this program variable can be constructed from other variables.

Runtime Efficiency Considerations The transformation from the HAA verification environment to the operational environment described above is optimal in the sense that all violations of the program's specification (in terms of the postconditions on each statement and within the limits of consistency) are caught under a bounded number of faults. However, when runtime efficiency is considered, not all of these assertions, nor all of the communicated GAVs, are necessary. These two aspects of reducing complexity are treated as follows:

- Assertions involving *local variables* to a particular process, which are necessary in the verification environment, are useless in the distributed operational environment. Since the unit of failure and reconfiguration is at the processor level, a processor cannot be trusted to diagnose itself as faulty or fault-free. Thus, assertions using only local variables incur a runtime overhead that is not necessary and all such assertions can be deleted.
- The fault coverage of certain assertions using the GAVs may be *subsumed*. Thus, many of the remaining assertions may be removed as well. Likewise, removing some of the

assertions may result in certain GAVs no longer being required. Furthermore, certain assertions may be too expensive to evaluate in the operational environment and may be deleted for that reason.

We applied this transformation to several concurrent applications including concurrent database transactions schedules [11], bitonic sorting [12], and concurrent branch and bound [14], and obtained performance and error coverage data on each.

10.3

SUMMARY

This chapter focused on using CSP and axiomatic program verification as a model for describing the behavior of distributed systems. Using this model, we developed a technique that translates a concurrent verification proof outline of an algorithm for use into an error-detecting concurrent program.

Bibliography

1. R. Apt and W. Roever, "A Proof System for Communicating Sequential Processes,"*ACM Trans. Programming Languages and Systems*, Vol. 2, No. 3, 1981, pp. 359–385.
2. M. Clint, "Program Proving: Coroutines," *Acta Informatica*, Vol. 2, 1973, pp. 50–63.
3. E. Dijkstra, *A Discipline of Programming*, Prentice-Hall, Englewood Cliffs, N.J., 1976.
4. M. Fischer, "A Theoretician's View of Fault Tolerant Distributed Computing," *Fault-Tolerant Distributed Computing, Lecture Notes in Computer Science* Vol. 448, 1990, pp. 1–9.
5. C. Hoare, "An Axiomatic Basis for Computer Programming," *Comm. ACM*, Vol. 12, No. 10, 1969, pp. 576–583.
6. C. Hoare, "Communicating Sequential Processes," *Comm. ACM*, Vol. 21, No. 8, 1978, pp. 666–677.
7. K. Huang and J. Abraham, "Fault-tolerant Algorithms and Their Applications to Solving Laplace Equations," *Proc. 1984 Int'l Conf. Parallel Processing*, IEEE CS Press, Los Alamitos, Calif., 1984, pp. 117–122.
8. J. Laprie and B. Littlewood, "Probabilistic Assessment of Safety-critical Software: Why and How?" *Comm. ACM*, Vol. 35, No. 2, 1992, pp. 13–21.
9. G.M. Levin and D. Gries, "A Proof Technique for Communicating Sequential Processes," *Acta Informatica*, Vol. 15, 1981, pp. 281–302.
10. H. Lutfiyya and B. McMillin, "Comparison of Three Axiomatic Proof Systems," UMR Department of Computer Science, Tech. Report CSC91-13, 1991.
11. H. Lutfiyya, B. McMillin, and A. Su., "Formal Derivation of an Error-detecting Distributed Data Scheduler Using Changeling," in *Formal Methods in Programming*, UMR, Department of Computer Science, Tech. Report CSC 92-14, July 1993.
12. H. Lutfiyya, M. Schollmeyer, and B. McMillin, "Fault-tolerant Distributed Sort Generated from a Verification Proof Outline," in *Responsive Computer Systems—Dependable Computing and Fault-Tolerance*, H. Kopetz and Y. Kakuda, eds., Vol. 7, Springer-Verlag, Berlin, 1992. Also as UMR, Department of Computer Science, Tech. Report C.Sc. 91-12.

13. H. Lutfiyya, M. Schollmeyer, and B. McMillin, "Formal Generation of Executable Assertions for Application-oriented Fault Tolerance," UMR, Department of Computer Science Tech. Report CSC 92-15, 1992.

14. H. Lutfiyya, A. Sun, and B. McMillin, "A Fault Tolerant Branch and Bound Algorithm Derived from Program Verification," *Proc. IEEE Computer Software and Applications Conference (COMPSAC)*, IEEE CS Press, Los Alamitos, Calif., 1992, pp. 182–187.

15. A. Mahmood, E. McCluskey, and D. Lu, "Concurrent Fault Detection Using a Watchdog Processor and Assertions," *IEEE 1983 Int'l Test Conf.*, IEEE CS Press, Los Alamitos, Calif., 1983, pp. 622–628.

16. B. McMillin and L. Ni, "Reliable Distributed Sorting through the Application-oriented Fault Tolerance Paradigm," *IEEE Trans. Parallel and Distributed Computing*, Vol. 3, No. 4, 1992, pp. 411–420.

17. S. Owicki and D. Gries, "An Axiomatic Proof Technique for Parallel Programs I," *Acta Informatica*, Vol. 6, 1976, pp. 319–340.

18. B. Randall, "System Structure for Software Fault Tolerance," *IEEE Trans. Software Engineering*, Vol. SE-1, No. 2, 1975, pp. 220–232.

19. R. Schlichting and F. Schneider, "Using Message Passing for Distributed Programming: Proof Rules and Disciplines," *ACM Trans. Programming Languages and Systems*, Vol. 6, No. 3, July 1984, pp. 402–431.

20. N. Soundararahan, "Axiomatic Semantics of Communicating Sequential Processes," *ACM Trans. Programming Languages and Systems*, Vol. 6, No. 6, 1984, pp. 647–662.

21. R. Yanney and J. Hayes, "Distributed Recovery in Fault Tolerance Multiprocessor Networks," *4th Int'l Conf. Distributed Computing Systems*, IEEE CS Press, Los Alamitos, Calif., 1984, pp. 514–525.

22. S. Yau and R. Cheung, "Design of Self-checking Software," *Proc. Int'l Conf. Software Reliability*, IEEE CS Press, Los Alamitos, Calif., 1975, pp. 450–457.

CHAPTER 11

PROCESS CALCULUS AND PARALLEL OBJECT-ORIENTED PROGRAMMING LANGUAGES*

David Walker
Department of Computer Science
University of Warwick, Coventry CV4 7AL, UK

Abstract. *Techniques for giving simple accounts of the semantics of parallel object-oriented programming languages are illustrated through a study of the language $\pi o\beta\lambda$ (parallel object-based language). A two-level operational semantics is given in which the global transitions of a configuration are derived in a simple way from labeled transitions describing the possible actions of its constituent objects. A second semantics by translation to a fragment of the Higher-order π-calculus is presented. A close correspondence between the semantics is described.*

11.1

INTRODUCTION

The primary concern of this paper is the illustration of techniques that may be used to give simple semantics for parallel object-oriented programming languages. A program of such a language typically describes a highly mobile concurrent system in which new objects are created as computation proceeds and the linkage between components changes as references to objects are passed in communications. Providing adequate models for such systems is challenging. But the challenge is one that must be addressed if parallel object-oriented programs are to be subject to rigorous analysis. Among the most well-developed work on semantics of parallel object-oriented languages is that on the POOL family [3]. For example, in [1] an operational semantics for a member of the family is given while [2] offers a denotational semantics based on metric spaces. The metric space model is complex, as one would expect, given the nature of the kind of language under consideration, and its usefulness for reasoning about programs remains to be investigated.

---

*I am grateful to Cliff Jones and Davide Sangiorgi for discussions about this work.

A goal of the present work is to find models that are as simple and tractable as possible. We illustrate the semantic techniques by applying them to a version of the design language $\pi o\beta\lambda$ (parallel object-based language) introduced in [5]. They are applicable, however, to a wide variety of languages.

The principal technique is to give semantics for a language by a structural translation of it to a general model of concurrent agents. An early example of the semantics-by-translation technique was Landin's interpretation of ALGOL in λ-calculus. Extensive study of the rôle of λ-calculus as foundation for functional languages and sequential object-oriented languages has been undertaken. To model adequately parallel object-oriented languages we need a richer base theory that expresses interaction among agents with independent state. Process calculi, of which the first example was Milner's CCS [8], provide *general* frameworks for the description and analysis of systems of such agents. By giving semantics for a language by translation to a suitable calculus, we are freed from the difficult task of constructing an adequate semantic model: see the discussion of [2] above. But this method of semantic definition offers a second potential benefit, namely that one may use the process calculus theory to derive an *abstract* description of the behavior expressed by a program and to reason about it. Further, one may hope that by attempting to use the calculus in this way, one may be guided in fruitful development of the theory itself. Thus this problem domain, which offers many difficult challenges, seems a natural point at which interaction between theory and practice may be fostered.

Milner [8] gave semantics for a simple parallel imperative language by translation to CCS. This work was extended in [12, 13] to simple parallel object-oriented languages, and in particular to give an account of inheritance; see also [7] in this volume for use of CCS in modeling aspects of object-oriented systems. In this work we use a recent development in process calculus. The π-calculus [10], a descendant of CCS, provides a general framework in which one may naturally describe systems that have evolving structure. Its basic entities are *names*. These may be thought of as names of links via which processes may interact. In the π-calculus, and its extension the polyadic π-calculus [9], the only entities that processes may pass to one another are (tuples of) names. By suitable encodings both data and functions may be represented as processes, an idea of Hewitt [4]. The polyadic π-calculus thus provides an arena for the study, in undiluted form, of a wide range of computational phenomena.

An alternative basis for modeling mobile systems, exemplified in the Calculus of Higher-Order Communicating Systems (CHOCS) of [17], involves taking *process passing* rather than name passing as primitive. An extension of both the π-calculus and CHOCS, in which names and abstractions of processes of arbitrarily high order may be passed in communications, is the Higher-order π-calculus of [16]. The thesis [15] develops the algebraic theory of this calculus and uses it to explore encodings of functions as higher-order processes. It also shows that processes of the Higher-order π-calculus may be compiled to processes of the (first-order, polyadic) π-calculus by a mapping that, in a strong sense, is behavior-respecting.

In [18] the author gave semantics for two small POOL-like languages by encoding them in the (monadic) π-calculus. This work was refined in [19], where a semantics for a minor variant of the POOL of [1] was given by translation to the polyadic π-calculus. Further, the operational semantics of [1] was reformulated as a two-level transitional semantics in which the global transitions of a configuration are derived in a very simple way from labeled transitions describing the possible actions of its constituent objects, and a close correspondence between the semantics was established. In the present chapter ideas from [19] are modified and extended to give a two-level operational semantics for the version of $\pi o\beta\lambda$. This method of semantic definition gives a particularly perspicuous account of the meaning of the language. Then an alternative semantics by translation to a fragment of the Higher-order π-calculus is presented. In this translation, data such as integers are represented as first-order abstractions while operators on data and program constructors are encoded as second-order abstractions. Although by the compilation result of [16] mentioned earlier the higher-order abstractions may be encoded at first-order, the gain in clarity obtained by working in the richer setting is marked. After presenting and illustrating the translational semantics, a close correspondence between it and the operational semantics is described. In both, a program is interpreted as a transition system. The principal difference between the two is that in the translational semantics data are represented as processes that must be "evaluated" by reduction in the calculus. A rough paraphrase of the correspondence is that the transition system determined by the translational semantics simulates in a well-behaved way that given by the operational semantics. One point of establishing this correspondence is to show that the translational semantics, which may at first sight appear unduly concrete, is reasonable. This point is discussed further in Section 11.5, which contains also a detailed description of the correspondence and a brief account of an application of a translational semantics: a proof of the soundness of a program transformation from [5], which introduces concurrency into a design.

The translation given here modifies and extends techniques used in the papers [8, 18, 19] mentioned earlier. In [17] a semantics by translation into a calculus called Plain CHOCS is given for a small object-oriented language with each phrase being encoded as a process and a relabeling operator playing a crucial rôle. In [6], a semantics for $\pi o\beta\lambda$ by translation to the polyadic π-calculus is described and its use as a basis for justifying design steps discussed. The present paper differs from these in using higher-order abstractions to give the translational semantics and in offering a comparison between this semantics and an operational semantics formulated in a quite different way.

11.2

THE PROGRAMMING LANGUAGE

The programming language is very similar to the design notation $\pi o\beta\lambda$ introduced in [5], which in turn is strongly influenced by the POOL family of languages [3]. Its programs describe computational systems as collections of *objects*, each of which is a self-contained entity possessing data and procedures, or *methods*. Communication between objects is via a *rendezvous*, in which an object α may request that another object β execute one of its methods with parameters, which may be simple values or references to objects, supplied by α. The activity of α is suspended until the result of the call, if there is one, is returned to it. A return need not be the last act of an object in the execution of a method and thus objects may enjoy concurrent activity. An interesting language feature is the commit statement (called yield in [5]) via which β above may free itself from the task of returning to α by passing on the responsibility for doing so to another object. Objects may be created as computation proceeds, and with the passing of references, highly mobile concurrent systems may be described. A program comprises a sequence of *class declarations* each of which consists of declarations of variables and methods. Each object is an *instance* of a class. On creation it assumes a quiescent state in which it may receive a message invoking one of the methods in the definition of its class. On completing execution of such an invocation it returns to the quiescent state. Only one method may be active in an object at any one time.

The language has simple types NAT and BOOL and constant symbols 0, 1, ... and nil, the last of which is overloaded and is used to represent a reference to no object and an undefined value of type NAT. In the abstract syntax definitions below we use K, to range over constants, M over methods names, A over class names, T over type names, that is, NAT, BOOL and class names, X, Y, Z over variables of types NAT and A, E over expressions, S over statements and P over programs, and we write $\widetilde{Z}$ for a tuple $Z_1, \ldots, Z_n$ of syntactic entities. Expressions are the well-typed phrases given as follows:

$$E ::= K \mid X \mid \text{new}(A) \mid E!M(\widetilde{E}) \mid \text{op}(\widetilde{E})$$

The value of new(A) is a reference to a newly created object of class A. The evaluation of $E!M(\widetilde{E})$ involves the left-to-right evaluation of E and the expressions in the tuple $\widetilde{E}$, followed by the invocation in the object to which the value of E is a reference of the method M of the class of that object with parameters the values of $\widetilde{E}$. The value of the expression is the simple value or reference returned to the object as the result of the method invocation. We assume that the basic operation symbols op of the simple types are =, <, not, and and. Statements are the well-typed phrases given as follows:

$$S ::= X := E \mid S_1; S_2 \mid \text{if } E \text{ then } S_1 \text{ else } S_2 \mid \text{while } E \text{ do } S$$
$$\mid E!M(\widetilde{E}) \mid \text{return} \mid \text{return } E \mid \text{commit } E!M(\widetilde{E})$$

The assignment, sequence, conditional, and iterative statements are standard. In examples we sometimes use a one-armed conditional derived in a conventional way. The statement $E!M(\widetilde{E})$ is similar to the analogous expression except that the calling object is simply released from the rendezvous on execution by the appropriate object of a return statement, with no value being returned. Execution of return E involves evaluation of E and return of the value to the object ultimately responsible for the invocation of the method in which the statement occurs. When an object α executes a commit statement by invoking a method in an object β, it stipulates that the return be to another object γ thereby freeing itself from the task of returning to that object.

Declarations are given as follows. First, variable declarations are given by

$$Vdec ::= \text{var } X_1 : T_1, \ldots, X_n : T_n$$

Then method declarations are given by

$$Mdec ::= \text{method } M(\widetilde{Y} : \widetilde{T}) : T, Vdec, S$$

where $\widetilde{T}$ are the types of the formal parameters $\widetilde{Y}$, T is the optional result type and S is the body of the method with *Vdec* declaring variables local to it. Sequences of method declarations are given by

$$Mdecs ::= Mdec_1, \ldots, Mdec_q$$

class declarations by

$$Cdec ::= \text{class } A, Vdec, Mdecs$$

and finally program declarations by

$$Pdec ::= \text{program } P, Cdec_1, \ldots, Cdec_r$$

By convention the first class in *Pdec* furnishes the root object, which alone exists at the beginning of a computation of the program. Further, to initiate the computation, the root object spontaneously executes a distinguished method of its class.

In what follows we consider only well-typed programs. To illustrate the language we give a class declaration from [5] for an integer priority queue with methods for adding an integer and removing the smallest integer (returning nil if the queue is empty).

```
class Q
var V:NAT, P:Q
method Add(X:NAT)
    return ;
    if V=nil then (V:=X ; P:=new(Q))
    else if V<X then P!Add(X)
        else (P!Add(V) ; V:=X)
method Rem():NAT
    return V ;
    if not(V=nil) then (V:=P!Rem() ; if V=nil then P:=nil)
```

Each instance of the class represents a single cell that stores an integer and a pointer to another cell. A queue is composed of a chain of cells with new cells being created and appended to the chain as integers are added. Two invariants of the chain are that only its first cell is accessible to other objects and that its last cell has an undefined value and a nil pointer, these being the values of the variables of any object when it is created. The smallest integer held in the queue (or nil if the queue is empty) is returned and removed by the Rem method while the Add method returns no value. Since the return is not the last act in the execution of either of the methods, there may be concurrent activity within a queue. Moreover, a process adding (removing) a value to (from) the queue may proceed in parallel with such activity. Contrast this with the following sequential class definition. In this case a process adding an integer, for example, is blocked until the integer is inserted into the queue and a return ripples back to the first cell.

```
class Q'
var V:NAT, P:Q'
method Add(X:NAT)
```

```
         if V=nil then (V:=X ; P:=new(Q'))
         else if V<X then P!Add(X)
               else (P!Add(V) ; V:=X) ;
         return
   method Rem():NAT
   var T:NAT
         T:=V ;
         if not(V=nil) then (V:=P!Rem() ; if V=nil then P:=nil) ;
         return T
```

It seems that replacing one of these class definitions by the other in any program should not alter its observable behavior. Indeed, [5] describes a design method in which program transformations such as those leading from the simpler sequential class Q′ to the more complex concurrent class Q are central. A brief account of how a translational semantics may be used as a basis for establishing this is given in the final section.

11.3

THE OPERATIONAL SEMANTICS

In this section we define an operational semantics for the language $\pi o \beta \lambda$. The purpose of such a definition is to describe how programs are to be executed. In contrast, a denotational semantics for a language gives a more abstract account of the meaning of programs by interpreting them as mathematical objects in a suitable semantic domain. The two methods are complementary, each serving different purposes. As mentioned in the introduction in relation to the metric space semantics for POOL [2], the nature of parallel object-oriented languages is such that adequate semantic domains for them are inevitably complex. The operational semantics we describe here, while also intricate, is rather easier to grasp. An essential factor in ensuring this is the relative simplicity of the semantic objects. The semantics associates a program with a transition system whose points represent configurations and whose transition relation describes how a step in execution of the program may lead from one configuration to another. A particular execution of the program corresponds to a path through the transition system. A configuration consists of two parts: an environment that records the class definitions of the program and the class of each of the objects present in the system; and a state that records the local store, identity, and state of each object. The initial configuration associated with a program is determined from its text. The transition relation is defined by a family of axioms and rules that form an inference system. The judgments of this system are of the form that one configuration may evolve to another in one execution step. This primary inference system is underpinned by a second system that describes the possible actions of the individual objects comprising the system. A global transition at the level of configurations is inferred from local transitions representing autonomous activity or interaction of objects at the level of individual objects.

Several textbooks on programming language theory contain expositions of operational semantics. The primary source for the modern structural approach to the method is [14]. The most demanding test of its applicability to date is the formal definition of the programming language Standard ML [11].

The operational semantics of $\pi o\beta\lambda$ is based on a transition system whose points represent global configurations of systems of objects. The global transition relation is defined in terms of a family of labeled transition relations that describe the possible actions of individual objects. We assume an infinite set of *object names* ranged over by α, β, γ. We refer to the object names together with the symbols nil, true, false, 0, 1, ... as *values* and use v to range over values. The following kinds of entity are used in the semantics. A *family of method definitions* is a finite partial function μ from method names to pairs $\langle \widetilde{Y} \cup \widetilde{Z}, S \rangle$, with $\widetilde{Y}$ the formal parameters, $\widetilde{Z}$ the local variables, and S the body of the associated method. A *class definition* is a pair $\langle \widetilde{X}, \mu \rangle$, with $\widetilde{X}$ the instance variables and μ the family of method definitions of the associated class. An *environment* is a pair $\Phi = \langle \Phi_1, \Phi_2 \rangle$ with Φ_1 a finite partial function from class names to class definitions, and Φ_2 a finite partial function from object names to class names. A *store* is a finite partial map σ from variables to values. A *state* is a finite set Γ of triples of the form $\langle \alpha, S, \sigma \rangle$. Finally, a *configuration* is a pair $\langle \Phi, \Gamma \rangle$ consisting of an environment and a state. A configuration $\langle \Phi, \Gamma \rangle$ provides an instantaneous description of a computation of a program as follows. Φ_1 records the definitions of the classes of the program and is unchanged throughout the computation. Φ_2 records the name and class of each existing object; it is augmented each time an object is created. Γ records the local store and unexecuted statement of each existing object.

To give the semantics we regard each expression as a statement and augment the classes of expressions and statements as follows:

$$E ::= \dots \mid v \mid \text{wait}_T$$
$$S ::= \dots \mid \text{quiescent}_A \mid \text{wait} \mid \text{return}_\beta E \mid \text{return}_\beta \mid \text{commit}_\beta E!M(\widetilde{E})$$

We write $S \Rightarrow \beta$ for S with each subexpression return E replaced by $\text{return}_\beta E$, each subexpression return replaced by return_β and each subexpression commit $E!M(\widetilde{E})$ replaced by $\text{commit}_\beta E!M(\widetilde{E})$. The rôles of these additional forms are explained below. The global transition relation on configurations

$$\langle \Phi, \Gamma \rangle \rightarrow \langle \Phi', \Gamma' \rangle$$

is defined in terms of a family of local transition relations

$$\langle \alpha, \mu \rangle \vdash \langle S, \sigma \rangle \xrightarrow{\ell} \langle S', \sigma' \rangle$$

where the label ℓ is either empty or of one of the forms $\text{new}(A, \beta)$, $\text{call}(\beta, M, \tilde{v}, \gamma)$, $\text{respond}(\beta, M, \tilde{v}, \gamma)$, $\text{result}(\beta, v)$, $\text{return}(\beta, v)$, $\text{proceed}(\beta)$ or $\text{release}(\beta)$. If the label is empty or of the form $\text{new}(A, \beta)$ the transition represents an autonomous action of α. In the other six cases the label carries information pertinent to the way α may interact with other objects. The local relations are defined by the following axioms and rules. First we have the axioms for expressions.

(VAR) $\langle \alpha, \mu \rangle \vdash \langle X, \sigma \rangle \longmapsto \langle \sigma(X), \sigma \rangle$

(NEW) $\langle \alpha, \mu \rangle \vdash \langle \text{new}(A), \sigma \rangle \overset{\text{new}(A,\beta)}{\longmapsto} \langle \beta, \sigma \rangle$

(CALL1) $\langle \alpha, \mu \rangle \vdash \langle \beta!M(\tilde{v}), \sigma \rangle \overset{\text{call}(\beta,M,\tilde{v},\alpha)}{\longmapsto} \langle \text{wait}_T, \sigma \rangle$ provided $\beta \neq \text{nil}$

(OP1) $\langle \alpha, \mu \rangle \vdash \langle \text{op}(\tilde{v}), \sigma \rangle \longmapsto \langle v, \sigma \rangle$ where $v = \widehat{\text{op}}(\tilde{v})$

(WAIT1) $\langle \alpha, \mu \rangle \vdash \langle \text{wait}_T, \sigma \rangle \overset{\text{result}(\beta,v)}{\longmapsto} \langle v, \sigma \rangle$

The axioms (VAR) and (OP1) are straightforward with $\widehat{\text{op}}$ being the interpretation of op. In (NEW), the name β may be chosen arbitrarily; a side-condition in one of the global rules will ensure that a fresh name is used. (CALL1) may be applied when all subexpressions have been evaluated. The label on the arrow records that the call is to β and that the result should be returned to α, while wait_T records that T is the result type of M. In the global transition system a call action will synchronize with a respond action emanating from the axiom (QUIESCENT) below. The axiom (WAIT1) represents the reactivation of α on receipt of the result of type T of a method call. It may receive any value of type T from any object— this reflects that a call by α may be committed by the object to which it is made—to another object. In the global transition system a result(β, v) action of α will synchronize with a return(α, v) action arising from the return of the result v to α by an object β; such an action will emanate from the axiom (RETURN1) below. The axioms for statements are as follows:

(ASSIGN1) $\langle \alpha, \mu \rangle \vdash \langle X := v, \sigma \rangle \longmapsto \langle \text{nil}, \sigma[X := v] \rangle$

(SEQ1) $\langle \alpha, \mu \rangle \vdash \langle \text{nil}, S, \sigma \rangle \longmapsto \langle S, \sigma \rangle$

(COND1) $\langle \alpha, \mu \rangle \vdash \langle \text{if true then } S_1 \text{ else } S_2, \sigma \rangle \longmapsto \langle S_1, \sigma \rangle$

(COND2) $\langle \alpha, \mu \rangle \vdash \langle \text{if false then } S_1 \text{ else } S_2, \sigma \rangle \longmapsto \langle S_2, \sigma \rangle$

(LOOP) $\langle \alpha, \mu \rangle \vdash \langle \text{while } E \text{ do } S, \sigma \rangle \longmapsto \langle \text{if } E \text{ then } (S; \text{while } E \text{ do } S)$

$\text{else nil}, \sigma \rangle$

(CALL2) $\langle \alpha, \mu \rangle \vdash \langle \beta!M(\tilde{v}), \sigma \rangle \overset{\text{call}(\beta,M,\tilde{v},\alpha)}{\longmapsto} \langle \text{wait}, \sigma \rangle$ provided $\beta \neq \text{nil}$

(RETURN1) $\langle \alpha, \mu \rangle \vdash \langle \text{return}_\beta v, \sigma \rangle \overset{\text{return}(\beta, v)}{\longmapsto} \langle \text{nil}, \sigma \rangle$

(WAIT2) $\langle \alpha, \mu \rangle \vdash \langle \text{wait}, \sigma \rangle \overset{\text{proceed}(\beta)}{\longmapsto} \langle \text{nil}, \sigma \rangle$

(RETURN2) $\langle \alpha, \mu \rangle \vdash \langle \text{return}_\beta, \sigma \rangle \overset{\text{release}(\beta)}{\longmapsto} \langle \text{nil}, \sigma \rangle$

(COMMIT1) $\langle \alpha, \mu \rangle \vdash \langle \text{commit}_\gamma \ \beta!M(\tilde{v}), \sigma \rangle \overset{\text{call}(\beta,M,\tilde{v},\gamma)}{\longmapsto} \langle \text{nil}, \sigma \rangle$

provided $\beta \neq \text{nil}$

(QUIESCENT) $\langle \alpha, \mu \rangle \vdash \langle \text{quiescent}, \sigma \rangle \overset{\text{respond}(\beta,M,\tilde{v},\gamma)}{\longmapsto} \langle (S \Rightarrow \gamma); \text{quiescent}, \sigma' \rangle$

where $\mu(M) = \langle \tilde{Y} \cup \tilde{Z}, S \rangle$ and $\sigma' = s \lceil \tilde{X} \cup \{\tilde{Y} := \tilde{v}\} \cup \{\tilde{Z} := \text{nil}\}$ where $\Phi_1(\Phi_2(\alpha))_1 = \tilde{X}$.

The axioms for assignment, sequence, conditional, and iterative statements are straightforward. The axiom $(\mathtt{RETURN1})$ describes how a result is returned from α to β. $(\mathtt{CALL2})$, $(\mathtt{WAIT2})$, and $(\mathtt{RETURN2})$, concerning valueless method calls, are similar to the corresponding axioms for methods returning results. $(\mathtt{COMMIT1})$ describes how α may delegate to β the task of returning to γ. Note the recording of the information in the label on the arrow. In $(\mathtt{QUIESCENT})$ a request from any object β to execute any appropriate method M with any appropriate parameters $\tilde{v}$ may be accepted, with $S \Rightarrow \gamma$ capturing that the appropriate body should be executed and the return made to γ or the responsibility for returning to γ committed to another object. Note that the store σ' records the values of the instance variables $\tilde{X}$, the parameters $\tilde{Y}$, and the local variables $\tilde{Z}$ of the newly activated method M; parameters and local variables from a previous method call are discarded. On completion of the call the object assumes its quiescent state.

To complete the definition of the local transition relations we have the following eight rules. The first seven share the premise

$$\langle \alpha, \mu \rangle \vdash \langle E, \sigma \rangle \overset{\ell}{\longmapsto} \langle E', \sigma' \rangle$$

The conclusions of the rules are

$(\mathtt{CALL3})$ $\quad \langle \alpha, \mu \rangle \vdash \langle E!M(\tilde{E}), \sigma \rangle \overset{\ell}{\longmapsto} \langle E'!M(\tilde{E}), \sigma' \rangle$

$(\mathtt{CALL4})$ $\quad \langle \alpha, \mu \rangle \vdash \langle \beta!M(\tilde{v}, E, \tilde{E}), \sigma \rangle \overset{\ell}{\longmapsto} \langle \beta!M(\tilde{v}, E', \tilde{E}), \sigma' \rangle$

$(\mathtt{OP2})$ $\quad \langle \alpha, \mu \rangle \vdash \langle op(\tilde{v}, E, \tilde{E}), \sigma \rangle \overset{\ell}{\longmapsto} \langle op(\tilde{v}, E', \tilde{E}), \sigma' \rangle$

$(\mathtt{ASSIGN2})$ $\quad \langle \alpha, \mu \rangle \vdash \langle X := E, \sigma \rangle \overset{\ell}{\longmapsto} \langle X := E', \sigma' \rangle$

$(\mathtt{COND3})$ $\quad \langle \alpha, \mu \rangle \vdash \langle \mathtt{if}\ E\ \mathtt{then}\ S_1\ \mathtt{else}\ S_2, \sigma \rangle \overset{\ell}{\longmapsto} \langle \mathtt{if}\ E'\ \mathtt{then}\ S_1\ \mathtt{else}\ S_2, \sigma' \rangle$

$(\mathtt{RETURN3})$ $\quad \langle \alpha, \mu \rangle \vdash \langle \mathtt{return}_\beta\ E, \sigma \rangle \overset{\ell}{\longmapsto} \langle \mathtt{return}_\beta\ E', \sigma' \rangle$

$(\mathtt{COMMIT2})$ $\quad \langle \alpha, \mu \rangle \vdash \langle \mathtt{commit}_\beta\ E, \sigma \rangle \overset{\ell}{\longmapsto} \langle \mathtt{commit}_\beta\ E', \sigma' \rangle$

These rules are mostly straightforward. Note that parameters and operands are evaluated from left to right. The final standard rule is

$$(\mathtt{SEQ2}) \quad \frac{\langle \alpha, \mu \rangle \vdash \langle S_1, \sigma \rangle \overset{\ell}{\longmapsto} \langle S_1', \sigma' \rangle}{\langle \alpha, \mu \rangle \vdash \langle S_1; S_2, \sigma \rangle \overset{\ell}{\longmapsto} \langle S_1'; S_2, \sigma' \rangle}$$

The global transition relation

$$\langle \Phi, \Gamma \rangle \longrightarrow \langle \Phi', \Gamma' \rangle$$

is defined from the local relations by the following five rules. They describe how the configuration may change as a result of the independent activity of one object $(\mathtt{LOCAL})$, the creation of a new object (NEW), the initiation of a method call (COM1), the return of a result of a method call (COM2), and the return of a valueless method call (COM3). A coherence side condition common to all the rules is that if $\langle \alpha, \mu \rangle$ appears in a premise and Φ in a conclusion then $\mu = \Phi_1(\Phi_2(\alpha))_2$, that is, the family of method definitions referred to is the appropriate one for an object of α's class.

(LOCAL)
$$\frac{\langle \alpha, \mu \rangle \vdash \langle S, \sigma \rangle \longmapsto \langle S', \sigma' \rangle}{\langle \Phi, \Gamma \cup \{\langle \alpha, S, \sigma \rangle\} \rangle \longrightarrow \langle \Phi, \Gamma \cup \{\langle \alpha, S', \sigma' \rangle\} \rangle}$$

(NEW)
$$\frac{\langle \alpha, \mu \rangle \vdash \langle S, \sigma \rangle \overset{\text{new}(A,\beta)}{\longmapsto} \langle S', \sigma' \rangle}{\langle \Phi, \Gamma \cup \{\langle \alpha, S, \sigma \rangle\} \rangle \longrightarrow \langle \Phi', \Gamma \cup \{\langle \alpha, S', \sigma' \rangle, \langle \beta, \text{quiescent}_A, \sigma'' \rangle\} \rangle}$$

provided $\beta \notin$ names $(\Gamma) \cup \{\alpha\}$, $\Phi' = \langle \Phi_1, \Phi_2[\beta := A] \rangle$,

$\Phi_1(A)_1 = \widetilde{X}$, and $\sigma'' = \{\widetilde{X} := \text{nil}\}$

(COM1)
$$\frac{\langle \alpha, \mu_\alpha \rangle \vdash \langle S_\alpha, \sigma_\alpha \rangle \overset{\text{call}(\beta,M,\tilde{v},\gamma)}{\longmapsto} \langle S'_\alpha, \sigma'_\alpha \rangle \quad \langle \beta, \mu_\beta \rangle \vdash \langle S_\beta, \sigma_\beta \rangle \overset{\text{respond}(\alpha,M,\tilde{v},\gamma)}{\longmapsto} \langle S'_\beta, \sigma'_\beta \rangle}{\langle \Phi, \Gamma \cup \{\langle \alpha, S_\alpha, \sigma_\alpha \rangle, \langle \beta, S_\beta, \sigma_\beta \rangle\} \rangle \longrightarrow \langle \Phi, \Gamma \cup \{\langle \alpha, S'_\alpha, \sigma'_\alpha \rangle, \langle \beta, S'_\beta, \sigma'_\beta \rangle\} \rangle}$$

(COM2)
$$\frac{\langle \alpha, \mu_\alpha \rangle \vdash \langle S_\alpha, \sigma_\alpha \rangle \overset{\text{result}(\beta,v)}{\longmapsto} \langle S'_\alpha, \sigma'_\alpha \rangle \quad \langle \beta, \mu_\beta \rangle \vdash \langle S_\beta, \sigma_\beta \rangle \overset{\text{return}(\alpha,v)}{\longmapsto} \langle S'_\beta, \sigma'_\beta \rangle}{\langle \Phi, \Gamma \cup \{\langle \alpha, S_\alpha, \sigma_\alpha \rangle, \langle \beta, S_\beta, \sigma_\beta \rangle\} \rangle \longrightarrow \langle \Phi, \Gamma \cup \{\langle \alpha, S'_\alpha, \sigma'_\alpha \rangle, \langle \beta, S'_\beta, \sigma'_\beta \rangle\} \rangle}$$

(COM3)
$$\frac{\langle \alpha, \mu_\alpha \rangle \vdash \langle S_\alpha, \sigma_\alpha \rangle \overset{\text{proceed}(\beta)}{\longmapsto} \langle S'_\alpha, \sigma'_\alpha \rangle \quad \langle \beta, \mu_\beta \rangle \vdash \langle S_\beta, \sigma_\beta \rangle \overset{\text{release}(\alpha)}{\longmapsto} \langle S'_\beta, \sigma'_\beta \rangle}{\langle \Phi, \Gamma \cup \{\langle \alpha, S_\alpha, \sigma_\alpha \rangle, \langle \beta, S_\beta, \sigma_\beta \rangle\} \rangle \longrightarrow \langle \Phi, \Gamma \cup \{\langle \alpha, S'_\alpha, \sigma'_\alpha \rangle, \langle \beta, S'_\beta, \sigma'_\beta \rangle\} \rangle}$$

The side condition on β in (NEW) ensures that a new object receives a fresh name; $names(\Gamma)$ is the set of first components of the elements of Γ. The harmonization between sender and receiver in the rules (COM1), (COM2), and (COM3) is achieved via the labels on the arrows in the premises. The *initial configuration* associated with a program declaration

$$Pdec \equiv \text{program } P, Cdec_1, \ldots, Cdec_r$$

is $\langle \Phi, \Gamma \rangle$ where Φ_1 is given by the definitions of the classes, $\Phi_2 = \{\langle \alpha, A \rangle\}$ for an arbitrary α where A is the name of the class declared in $Cdec_1$, and $\Gamma = \{\langle \alpha, S; \text{quiescent}, \sigma \rangle\}$ where for some distinguished method name M and values $\tilde{v}$, $\mu(M) = \langle \widetilde{Y} \cup \widetilde{Z}, S \rangle$ and $\sigma = \{\widetilde{X}, \widetilde{Z} := \text{nil}\} \cup \{\widetilde{Y} := \tilde{v}\}$ where $\Phi_1(A) = \langle \widetilde{X}, \mu \rangle$.

11.4

THE PROCESS CALCULUS SEMANTICS

In this section we describe a semantics for $\pi o \beta \lambda$ by a phrase-by-phrase translation to a process calculus called the Higher-order π-calculus. As explained in Section 11.1, a process calculus provides a *general* framework for the description and analysis of systems of interacting agents. A central feature of process calculus theory is its concentration on techniques for giving *abstract* accounts of process behavior. By giving the programming language semantics by translation to an appropriate calculus, we can use the associated techniques to obtain abstract descriptions of the behavior determined by programs and to reason about it. The π-calculus is particularly well suited to the task of describing systems of objects generated by parallel object-oriented programs. It provides a succinct means of describing formally the behavior of systems whose interconnection structure changes as computation proceeds. The Higher-order π-calculus differs from it in that not only may agents pass to one another links that may be used to interact with other agents, but they may pass also abstractions of agents that may be applied to appropriate (link or agent) parameters to yield new behavior. As we will see below this allows a highly structured translation.

Before proceeding to the technical core of this section, which explains the translation in detail, we illustrate with an example the form an abstract process calculus description may take. Consider the priority queue class Q defined in Section 11.2. An object of this class is a cell and a queue is composed of a chain of cells. By applying the translation and then using the techniques of the calculus to simplify the behavior we obtain the following description of the behavior of a cell:

$$E \overset{\text{def}}{=} add(x, ret).\overline{ret}.new(add', rem').\,C(x) + rem(ret).\overline{ret}(\texttt{nil}).E$$

$$C(k) \overset{\text{def}}{=} add(x, ret).\overline{ret}.\text{cond}(k < x : \overline{add'}(x).\,C(k), \overline{add'}(k).\,C(x))$$
$$+ rem(ret).\overline{ret}(k).(\nu\,ret')\overline{rem'}(ret').ret'(x).\text{cond}(x = \texttt{nil} : E, C(x))$$

Here E represents an empty cell. Its *object identifier* is the pair of names (add, rem) via which its methods may be invoked with appropriate parameters. As will be explained below, a taxonomy of names into sorts is used to guarantee the well-formedness of the descriptions. The ability of the cell to react to an invocation of either of its methods is represented by the sum expression on the right-hand side: each summand represents a possible activity. In the first case the Add-method may be invoked with an integer parameter x. The name parameter ret is to be used for return to the caller. It will be a private name generated by the caller. (The π-calculus gives a simple account of private names.) After returning, the cell receives the object identifier of a new instance of the class from the agent that represents the class definition. This agent's sole activity is to furnish private new instances on request. The cell then becomes stable in the $C(x)$ state storing the value it received and with a private link to the next cell in the chain. The behavior in response to a Rem invocation is analogous except in that case no new cell is created. The behavior of $C(x)$ is determined by the second definition in which $\text{cond}(b, P, Q)$ represents the conditional agent that behaves as P if the Boolean expression b is true, and as Q otherwise. Note that E and C are defined by mutual recursion.

A chain of cells storing the integers $k_1 < \cdots < k_n$ is then described by the composition

$$C^*(k_1, \ldots, k_n) \overset{\text{def}}{=} (\nu\tilde{c})(C(k_1) \mid \cdots \mid C(k_n) \mid E)$$

where $\mid$ represents parallel composition of the individual cells and $(\nu\tilde{c})$ that the intercell links are private (restricted) to the cells concerned. Moreover, the behavior of C^* can itself be simplified to a form analogous to the description of E and C above. This simplification forms the basis for a proof that the class Q and the simpler sequential class Q′ in Section 11.2 are interchangeable; see Section 11.5 on this point.

We now give the semantics for $\pi o \beta \lambda$ by translation to a fragment of the Higher-order π-calculus of [16]. Each phrase is represented as an agent of the calculus. In particular each program declaration is encoded as a process that, via the dynamics of the calculus, determines a transition system; this is the interpretation of the program. We examine the relationship between this interpretation and the transition system associated with the program by the operational semantics in Section 11.5.

We first present briefly the fragment of the Higher-order π-calculus we use[1] referring to [16] for a description of the full calculus. Its basic entities are *names*. These may be thought of as names of links via which processes may interact. It is useful to introduce a taxonomy of names. We assume a set S of *subject sorts*. The set $\mathcal{O}$ of *object sorts* is then $(S \cup S^*)^*$, the set of finite tuples each of whose elements is a subject sort or a finite tuple of subject sorts. We write $(\alpha_1, \ldots, \alpha_n)$ for the object sort of length n consisting of $\alpha_1, \ldots, \alpha_n \in S \cup S^*$. A *sorting* is a function $\Sigma : S \to \mathcal{O}$. Each name x is assigned a subject sort s and the sorting determines that only entities with the object sort $\Sigma(s)$ may be communicated using x; these entities are tuples of names and abstractions of processes.

To give the syntax of the calculus we assume an infinite set of names $x, y, \ldots$ of each subject sort and write $x : s$ to indicate that x is of sort s. For each object sort θ we assume infinite sets of variables $X, \ldots$ and constants $K, \ldots$ of sort θ, written $X : \theta$ and $K : \theta$. The set of *processes* P, Q is given by

$$P ::= \Sigma_{j \in J} \pi_j . P_j \mid P \mid Q \mid (\nu x)P \mid K \langle \widetilde{H} \rangle \mid X \langle \widetilde{H} \rangle$$

where: $(\widetilde{H})$ ranges over tuples of names and agents with an *agent* being a process or an *abstraction* of the form $(\widetilde{I})P$ where $(\widetilde{I})$ is a tuple of names and variables; a *prefix* π is of the form $\overline{x}(\widetilde{H})$ or the form $x(\widetilde{I})$; the indexing set J in the summation is finite; and each constant K has a defining equation $K \overset{\text{def}}{=} F$ where F is an abstraction. We write $\mathbf{0}$ for an empty summation and π for $\pi.\mathbf{0}$. The essence of respecting Σ, which is defined formally by a family of rules, is that each well-sorted agent is assigned an object sort, with $P : ()$ for each process P, so that definitions, applications, and prefixes are consistent with Σ. Thus extending ':' componentwise to tuples we have, for example, that if $K \overset{\text{def}}{=} (\widetilde{I})P$ and $K : \theta$ then $(\widetilde{I}) : \theta$ and in $K \langle \widetilde{H} \rangle$ we must have $(\widetilde{H}) : \theta$; and in $\pi = \overline{x}(\widetilde{H})$, if $x : s$ then $(\widetilde{H}) : \Sigma(s)$. Composition is extended to abstractions as follows: if $F = (\widetilde{I})P$ and $F' = (\widetilde{I'})P'$ then $F \mid F' \overset{\text{def}}{=} (\widetilde{I}\widetilde{I'})(P \mid P')$ provided $\widetilde{I}$ (resp. $\widetilde{I'}$) contains no names free in P' (resp. P). If $F : \theta$ and $F' : \theta'$ then $F \mid F' : \theta^\frown \theta'$ where '$^\frown$' is concatenation. Partial application of abstractions is a very convenient abbreviation and we have that if $G : \theta^\frown \theta'$ and $(\widetilde{H}) : \theta$ then $G \langle \widetilde{H} \rangle : \theta'$.

To allow a simple presentation of the dynamics of the calculus, a relation of *structural congruence* on agents, written $\equiv$, is defined. It is generated by a set of equations and identifies agents that differ only by a change of bound names or in the order or grouping of terms in summations, compositions, and restrictions. Further, if $K \overset{\text{def}}{=} F$ then $K \equiv F$, and if the name x is not free in P then $(\nu x)(P \mid Q) \equiv P \mid (\nu x)Q$. In this chapter we strengthen the definition by adding the equation $(\nu x)\Sigma_{j \in J} \pi_j . P_j \equiv (\nu x)\Sigma_{j \in L} \pi_j . P_j$ where on the right-

---

[1] The restriction is effected by limiting objects sorts to be of second order.

hand side $L = \{j \in J \mid \pi_j$ is not of the form $x(\tilde{I})$ or $\overline{x}(\tilde{H})\}$. By doing this we can state more precisely the correspondence between the operational and translational semantics of the programming language. The behavior of processes is given by the *reduction* relation, $\longrightarrow$, defined by the following rules:

(COM) $\qquad (x(\tilde{I}).P + \cdots) \mid (\overline{x}(\tilde{H}).Q + \cdots) \longrightarrow P\{\tilde{H}/\tilde{I}\} \mid Q$

(PAR) $\qquad$ if $P \longrightarrow P'$ then $P \mid Q \longrightarrow P' \mid Q$

(RES) $\qquad$ if $P \longrightarrow P'$ then $(\nu x)P \longrightarrow (\nu x)P'$

(STRUCT) $\quad$ if $P \longrightarrow P'$, $P \equiv Q$ and $P' \equiv Q'$ then $Q \longrightarrow Q'$

where $P\{\tilde{H}/\tilde{I}\}$ represents substitution of the components of $(\tilde{H})$ for the corresponding components of $(\tilde{I})$ in P.

To give the semantics for the programming language we take as subject sorts NIL, NAT, BOOL, LINK $[A]$, METHOD $[\tilde{T}; T]$, and METHOD $[\tilde{T};]$ for A a class name, T a type name, and $\tilde{T}$ a tuple of type names. The sorting Σ has

$$\Sigma(\text{NIL}) = ()$$
$$\Sigma(\text{NAT}) = ((\text{NIL}, \text{NIL}, \text{NIL}))$$
$$\Sigma(\text{BOOL}) = ((\text{NIL}, \text{NIL}))$$

To give the remainder of the sorting it is convenient to introduce some synonyms. We set OBJECT[NAT] $\equiv (\text{NIL}^3)$ and OBJECT[BOOL] $\equiv (\text{NIL}^2)$ where (NIL^3) abbreviates $(\text{NIL}, \text{NIL}, \text{NIL})$, and so on; and we set LINK[NAT] $\equiv$ NAT and LINK[BOOL] $\equiv$ BOOL. If A has methods $M_1, \ldots, M_q$ and M_i has type $U_i = \tilde{T}_i; T_i$ or $\tilde{T}_i;$ (with no result type) then we set OBJECT[A] $\equiv$ METHOD[U_1], $\ldots$, METHOD[U_q]. If $\tilde{T} = T_1, \ldots, T_r$ then we set OBJECTS[$\tilde{T}$] $\equiv$ OBJECT[T_1], $\ldots$, OBJECT[T_r]. Then the remainder of the sorting is

$$\Sigma(\text{LINK}[A]) = (\text{OBJECT}[A])$$
$$\Sigma(\text{METHOD}[\tilde{T}; T]) = (\text{OBJECTS}[\tilde{T}], \text{LINK}[T])$$
$$\Sigma(\text{METHOD}[\tilde{T};]) = (\text{OBJECTS}[\tilde{T}], \text{NIL})$$

As an example, for the priority queue class Q defined in Section 11.2 we have

$$\text{OBJECT}[Q] \equiv \text{METHOD}[\text{NAT};], \text{METHOD}[; \text{NAT}]$$
$$\Sigma(\text{METHOD}[\text{NAT};]) = ((\text{NIL}^3), \text{NIL})$$
$$\Sigma(\text{METHOD}[; \text{NAT}]) = (\text{NAT})$$

Rather than trying to explain the sorting immediately, which would require anticipating the translation in detail, we will do so gradually beginning by encoding natural numbers together with an undefined value. For the natural number k we set

$$Z_k : (\text{NIL}^3) \stackrel{\text{def}}{=} (szu)(\overline{s}.)^k \overline{z}$$

and to represent the undefined value

$$\text{UNDEF} : (\text{NIL}^3) \stackrel{\text{def}}{=} (szu)\overline{u}$$

A natural number register is represented by

$$\text{REG}_{\text{NAT}} : (\text{NAT}^2, (\text{NIL}^3)) \overset{\text{def}}{=} (get\ put\ X)$$
$$\overline{(get}\,(X).\text{REG}_{\text{NAT}}\langle get\ put\ X\rangle$$
$$+ put\,(Y).\text{REG}_{\text{NAT}}\langle get\ put\ Y\rangle)$$

with X representing the value stored and get (put) the name used for reading (writing) the register.

We represent the Boolean values by the abstractions T (true) and F (false) defined by

$$\text{T} : (\text{NIL}^2) \overset{\text{def}}{=} (tf)\overline{t}$$
$$\text{F} : (\text{NIL}^2) \overset{\text{def}}{=} (tf)\overline{f}$$

The total operations $=$ and $<$ on natural numbers with undef, where for the sake of illustration we assume $k <$ undef for each natural number k, are represented as the following abstractions each of which emits at val the abstraction representing the outcome of the comparison of the values represented by X and X':

$$\text{EQ} : ((\text{NAT})^2, \text{BOOL}) \overset{\text{def}}{=} (XX'val)(\nu nn' : \text{NAT}, szus'z'u' : \text{NIL})$$
$$(X\langle n\rangle \mid n(Y).(X'\langle n'\rangle \mid n'(Y').$$
$$(Y\langle szu\rangle \mid Y'\langle s'z'u'\rangle \mid E\langle szus'z'u'val\rangle)))$$

$$E : (\text{NIL}^6, \text{BOOL}) \overset{\text{def}}{=} (szus'z'u'val)(z.(z'.\overline{val}(\text{T}) + s'.\overline{val}(\text{F}) + u'.\overline{val}(\text{F}))$$
$$+ s.(z'.\overline{val}(\text{F}) + s'.E\langle szus'z'u'val\rangle + u'.\overline{val}(\text{F}))$$
$$+ u.(z'.\overline{val}(\text{F}) + s'.\overline{val}(\text{F}) + u'.\overline{val}(\text{T})))$$

$$\text{LESS} : ((\text{NAT})^2, \text{BOOL}) \overset{\text{def}}{=} (XX'val)(\nu nn' : \text{NAT}, szus'z'u' : \text{NIL})$$
$$(X\langle n\rangle \mid n(Y).(X'\langle n'\rangle \mid n'(Y').$$
$$(Y\langle szu\rangle \mid Y'\langle s'z'u'\rangle \mid L\langle szus'z'u'val\rangle)))$$

$$L : (\text{NIL}^6, \text{BOOL}) \overset{\text{def}}{=} (szus'z'u'val)(z.(z'.\overline{val}(\text{F}) + s'.\overline{val}(\text{T}) + u'.\overline{val}(\text{T}))$$
$$+ s.(z'.\overline{val}(\text{F}) + s'.L\langle szus'z'u'val\rangle + u'.\overline{val}(\text{T}))$$
$$+ u.(z'.\overline{val}(\text{F}) + s'.\overline{val}(\text{F}) + u'.\overline{val}(\text{F})))$$

In a similar vein, for the Boolean operations we use

$$\text{NOT} : ((\text{BOOL}), \text{BOOL}) \overset{\text{def}}{=} (Xval)(\nu b : \text{BOOL}, tf : \text{NIL})$$
$$(X\langle b\rangle \mid b(Y).Y\langle tf\rangle \mid (t.\overline{val}(\text{F}) + f.\overline{val}(\text{T})))$$

$$\text{AND} : ((\text{BOOL})^2, \text{BOOL}) \overset{\text{def}}{=} (XX'val)(\nu bb' : \text{BOOL}, tft'f' : \text{NIL})$$
$$(X\langle b\rangle \mid b(Y).(X'\langle b'\rangle \mid b'(Y').$$
$$(Y\langle tf\rangle \mid Y'\langle t'f'\rangle \mid (f.\overline{val}(\text{F}) + t.(f'.\overline{val}(\text{F}) + t'.\overline{val}(\text{T})))))))$$

We now define the translation $[\![\cdot]\!]$ by induction on the structure of phrases beginning with variable declarations. We have $[\![\mathrm{var}X : T]\!] : (\mathrm{LINK}[T]^2)$ where

$$[\![\mathrm{var}X : \mathrm{NAT}]\!] : (\mathrm{NAT}^2) \overset{\mathrm{def}}{=} (get\ put)\mathrm{REG}_{\mathrm{NAT}}\langle get\ put\ \mathrm{UNDEF}\rangle$$

and

$$[\![\mathrm{var}X : A]\!] : (\mathrm{LINK}[A]^2) \overset{\mathrm{def}}{=} (get\ put)((\nu\tilde{a})\overline{get}(\tilde{a}).\mathrm{REG}_A\langle get\ put\ \tilde{a}\rangle \\ + put\ (\tilde{a}').\mathrm{REG}_A\langle get\ put\ \tilde{a}'\rangle)$$

where

$$\mathrm{REG}_A : (\mathrm{LINK}[A]^2, \mathrm{OBJECT}[A]) \overset{\mathrm{def}}{=} (get\ put\ \tilde{a})(\overline{get}(\tilde{a}).\mathrm{REG}_A\langle get\ put\ \tilde{a}\rangle \\ + put\ (\tilde{a}').\mathrm{REG}_A\langle get\ put\ \tilde{a}'\rangle)$$

The definition of $\mathrm{REG}_{\mathrm{NAT}}$ reflects that when it is declared, the value of a variable of type NAT is undefined, while the $(\nu\tilde{a})$ in the definition of $[\![\mathrm{var}X : A]\!]$ captures that a variable of type A initially contains a reference to no object. A sequence of variable declarations is represented as a composition (written Π) of the agents representing the individual variables:

$$[\![\mathrm{var}X_1 : T_1, \ldots, X_n : T_n]\!] \overset{\mathrm{def}}{=} \Pi_{i=1}^n [\![\mathrm{var}X_i : T_i]\!]$$

Now we give the encodings of expressions. We will have $[\![K : T]\!] : (\mathrm{LINK}[T])$, $[\![X : T]\!] : (\mathrm{LINK}[T]^2)$ and $[\![\mathrm{new}(A)]\!] : (\mathrm{LINK}[A]^2)$; recall that $\mathrm{LINK}[\mathrm{NAT}] \equiv \mathrm{NAT}$ and $\mathrm{LINK}[\mathrm{BOOL}] \equiv \mathrm{BOOL}$. We set

$$[\![X : A]\!] : (\mathrm{LINK}[A]^2) \overset{\mathrm{def}}{=} (get\ val)get\ (\tilde{a}).\overline{val}(\tilde{a})$$

which reads the value of X at get and emits it at val; in general an abstraction representing an expression will have a parameter (val in the definitions) at which the representation of the value is emitted as the last act of an instantiation of the abstraction. Next we set

$$[\![\mathrm{new}(A)]\!] : (\mathrm{LINK}[A]^2) \overset{\mathrm{def}}{=} (new\ val)new\ (\tilde{a}).\overline{val}(\tilde{a})$$

Below we will see that the agent representing the declaration of class A will have a parameter (new) at which it may emit a reference to an agent representing a new instance of the class. For the $\mathtt{nil}$ expression representing a reference to no object we set

$$[\![\mathrm{nil} : A]\!] : (\mathrm{LINK}[A]) \overset{\mathrm{def}}{=} (val)(\nu\tilde{a})\overline{val}(\tilde{a})$$

using the same idea as in the definition of $[\![\mathrm{var}X : A]\!]$. For constants and variables of type NAT we set

$$[\![k]\!] : (\mathrm{NAT}) \overset{\mathrm{def}}{=} (val)\overline{val}(Z_k)$$

$$[\![\mathrm{nil}]\!] : (\mathrm{NAT}) \overset{\mathrm{def}}{=} (val)\overline{val}(\mathrm{UNDEF})$$

$$[\![X]\!] : (\mathrm{NAT}^2) \overset{\mathrm{def}}{=} (get\ val)get\ (Y).\overline{val}(Y)$$

For a composite expression $E : T$ we will have $[\![E]\!] : \theta^\frown(\text{LINK}[T])$ where θ consists of sorts corresponding to the distinct variables and new expressions occurring in E and the last parameter is the name used for delivering the value. The abstraction $[\![E]\!]$ is defined by applying the abstraction representing its principal operator (EQ, LESS, and so on) to the representations of its components. Suppose $E_0, E_1 : \text{NAT}$ and assume inductively that $[\![E_0]\!] : \theta_0^\frown(\text{NAT})$ and $[\![E_1]\!] : \theta_1^\frown(\text{NAT})$. Then for a unique θ, with $\tilde{p} : \theta$ there are unique $\tilde{p}_0 : \theta_0$ and $\tilde{p}_1 : \theta_1$ determined by the structure of the expressions so that

$$[\![E_0 = E_1]\!] : \theta^\frown(\text{BOOL}) \stackrel{\text{def}}{=} (\tilde{p})\text{EQ}\langle[\![E_0]\!]\langle\tilde{p}_0\rangle, [\![E_1]\!]\langle\tilde{p}_1\rangle\rangle$$

$$[\![E_0 < E_1]\!] : \theta^\frown(\text{BOOL}) \stackrel{\text{def}}{=} (\tilde{p})\text{LESS}\langle[\![E_0]\!]\langle\tilde{p}_0\rangle, [\![E_1]\!]\langle\tilde{p}_1\rangle\rangle$$

To illustrate how $\tilde{p}_0$ and $\tilde{p}_1$ are determined consider

$$[\![X = X]\!] : (\text{NAT}, \text{BOOL}) \stackrel{\text{def}}{=} (get)\text{EQ}\langle[\![X]\!]\langle get\rangle, [\![X]\!]\langle get\rangle\rangle$$

and

$$[\![X = Y]\!] : (\text{NAT}^2, \text{BOOL}) \stackrel{\text{def}}{=} (get_X\, get_Y)\text{EQ}\langle[\![X]\!]\langle get_X\rangle, [\![Y]\!]\langle get_Y\rangle\rangle$$

Now suppose $E_0, E_1 : \text{BOOL}$ and $[\![E_0]\!] : \theta_0^\frown(\text{BOOL})$ and $[\![E_1]\!] : \theta_1^\frown(\text{BOOL})$. Then with $\tilde{p} : \theta_0$,

$$[\![\text{not } E_0]\!] : \theta_0^\frown(\text{BOOL}) \stackrel{\text{def}}{=} (\tilde{p})\text{NOT}\langle[\![E_0]\!]\langle\tilde{p}\rangle\rangle$$

and for a unique θ, $\tilde{p}_0 : \theta_0$ and $\tilde{p}_1 : \theta_1$ where $\tilde{p} : \theta$,

$$[\![E_0 \text{ and } E_1]\!] : \theta^\frown(\text{BOOL}) \stackrel{\text{def}}{=} (\tilde{p})\text{AND}\langle[\![E_0]\!]\langle\tilde{p}_0\rangle, [\![E_1]\!]\langle\tilde{p}_1\rangle\rangle$$

Finally we illustrate the encoding of the call expression by considering $E \equiv E_0!M(E_1)$ where $E_0 : A$, $E_1 : \text{NAT}$ and in class A, $M : (\text{NAT}; \text{BOOL})$. The abstraction corresponding to a method call of this type is $\text{CALL} \equiv \text{CALL}(M, A, \text{NAT}; \text{BOOL})$ defined by

$$\text{CALL} : ((\text{LINK}[A]), (\text{NAT}), \text{BOOL}) \stackrel{\text{def}}{=} (X_0 X_1 val)(\nu val_0 : \text{LINK}[A], val_1 : \text{NAT}, w : \text{NIL})$$
$$(X_0\langle val_0\rangle \mid w.X_1\langle val_1\rangle$$
$$\mid val_0(\tilde{a}).\overline{w}.val_1(Y).(\nu b)\overline{\tilde{a}_M}(Y, b).b(Z).\overline{val}(Z))$$

Its third component receives a value from X_0 then triggers X_1 and receives a value from it. It then sends the value and a private return link $b : \text{BOOL}$ to the appropriate agent using $\tilde{a}_M : \text{METHOD}[\text{NAT}; \text{BOOL}]$ (the M-component of the object referred to by $\tilde{a}$), and finally receives and then emits the result. Then assuming that $[\![E_0]\!] : \theta_0^\frown(\text{LINK}[A])$ and $[\![E_1]\!] : \theta_1^\frown(\text{NAT})$ we have for a unique θ, $\tilde{p}_0 : \theta_0$ and $\tilde{p}_1 : \theta_1$ where $\tilde{p} : \theta$,

$$[\![E]\!] : \theta^\frown(\text{BOOL}) \stackrel{\text{def}}{=} (\tilde{p})\text{CALL}\langle[\![E_0]\!]\langle\tilde{p}_0\rangle, [\![E_1]\!]\langle\tilde{p}_1\rangle\rangle$$

As a concrete example consider $E \equiv (X!M(Y))$ and $(\text{not } (Y < 3) \text{ and } (Z = Y))$ where $Y, Z : \text{NAT}$, $X : A$ and the method M of class A has type $\text{NAT}; \text{BOOL}$. Then

$$[\![E]\!] : (\text{LINK}[A], \text{NAT}^2, \text{BOOL}) \stackrel{\text{def}}{=} (get_X get_Y get_Z)$$
$$\text{AND}\langle\, \text{CALL}\langle[\![X]\!]\langle get_X\rangle, [\![Y]\!]\langle get_Y\rangle\rangle,$$
$$\text{AND}\langle\, \text{NOT}\langle\text{LESS}\langle[\![Y]\!]\langle get_Y\rangle, [\![3]\!]\rangle\rangle,$$
$$\text{EQ}\langle[\![Z]\!]\langle get_Z\rangle, [\![Y]\!]\langle get_Y\rangle\rangle\rangle\rangle$$

The extension to methods of other types is straightforward.

Each statement S is encoded as an agent $[\![S]\!] : \theta^\frown(\text{NIL})$ where θ consists of sorts corresponding to the distinct variables and new expressions occurring in S together with names associated with method calls, and the final parameter (d in the definitions) is used to signal termination of execution of S. Using abstractions corresponding to program constructors and giving a little less detail than previously, we have the following. For assignment,

$$[\![X := E : T]\!] : \theta^\frown(\text{LINK}[T], \text{NIL}) \stackrel{\text{def}}{=} (\tilde{p})\text{ASSIGN}_T\langle[\![E]\!]\langle\tilde{p}\rangle\rangle$$

where

$$\text{ASSIGN}_T : ((\text{LINK}[T]), \text{LINK}[T], \text{NIL}) \stackrel{\text{def}}{=} (X \; put \; d)(v \; val : \text{LINK}[T])$$
$$(X\langle val\rangle \mid val(Y).\overline{put}\,(Y).\bar{d})$$

For sequence,

$$[\![S_1; S_2]\!] : \theta^\frown(\text{NIL}) \stackrel{\text{def}}{=} (\tilde{p})\text{SEQ}\langle[\![S_1]\!]\langle\tilde{p_1}\rangle, [\![S_2]\!]\langle\tilde{p_2}\rangle\rangle$$

where

$$\text{SEQ} : ((\text{NIL}), (\text{NIL}), \text{NIL}) \stackrel{\text{def}}{=} (XYd)(vd' : \text{NIL})(X\langle d'\rangle \mid d'.Y\langle d\rangle)$$

For the conditional statement,

$$[\![\text{if } E \text{ then } S_1, \text{else } S_2]\!] : \theta^\frown(\text{NIL}) \stackrel{\text{def}}{=} (\tilde{p})\text{COND}\langle[\![E]\!]\langle\tilde{p_0}\rangle, [\![S_1]\!]\langle\tilde{p_1}\rangle, [\![S_2]\!]\langle\tilde{p_2}\rangle\rangle$$

where

$$\text{COND} : ((\text{BOOL}), (\text{NIL}), (\text{NIL}), \text{NIL}) \stackrel{\text{def}}{=} (XYZd)(vval : \text{BOOL}, tf : \text{NIL})$$
$$(X\langle val\rangle \mid val(W).W\langle tf\rangle \mid (t.Y\langle d\rangle + f.Z\langle d\rangle)))$$

For the iterative statement,

$$[\![\text{while } E \text{ do } S]\!] : \theta^\frown(\text{NIL}) \stackrel{\text{def}}{=} (\tilde{p})\text{LOOP}\langle[\![E]\!]\langle\tilde{p_0}\rangle, [\![S]\!]\langle\tilde{p_1}\rangle\rangle$$

where

$$\text{LOOP} : ((\text{BOOL}), (\text{NIL}), \text{NIL}) \stackrel{\text{def}}{=} (XY)\text{COND}\langle X, \text{SEQ}\langle Y, \text{LOOP}\langle X, Y\rangle\rangle, (d)\bar{d}\rangle$$

We illustrate the call statement by considering $S \equiv E_0!M(E_1)$ where $E_0 : A$ and $E_1 : \text{NAT}$. The abstraction corresponding to a method call of this type is $\text{CALL} \equiv \text{CALL}(M, A, \text{NAT};)$ defined by

$$\text{CALL} : ((\text{LINK}[A]), (\text{NAT}), \text{NIL}) \stackrel{\text{def}}{=} (X_0X_1d)(vval_0 : \text{LINK}[A], val_1 : \text{NAT}, w : \text{NIL})$$
$$(X_0\langle val_0\rangle \mid w.X_1\langle val_1\rangle$$
$$\mid val_0(\tilde{a}).\overline{w}.val_1(Y).(vr : \text{NIL})\overline{\tilde{a}_M}(Y, r).r.\bar{d})$$

This abstraction differs only slightly from that for the corresponding expression. Then

$$[\![S]\!] : \theta^\frown(\text{NIL}) \stackrel{\text{def}}{=} (\tilde{p})\text{CALL}\langle[\![E_0]\!]\langle\tilde{p_0}\rangle, [\![E_1]\!]\langle\tilde{p_1}\rangle\rangle$$

For the `return` statements we have

$$[\![\text{return } E : T]\!] : \theta \widehat{\ }(\text{LINK}[T], \text{NIL}) \stackrel{\text{def}}{=} (\widetilde{p})\text{RETURN}_T \langle [\![E]\!]\langle \widetilde{p}\rangle\rangle$$

where

$$\text{RETURN}_T : ((\text{LINK}[T]), \text{LINK}[T], \text{NIL}) \stackrel{\text{def}}{=} (X \ ret \ d)(v \ val : \text{LINK}[T])$$
$$(X\langle val\rangle \mid val(Y).\overline{ret}(Y).\overline{d})$$

and

$$[\![\text{return}]\!] : (\text{NIL}^2) \stackrel{\text{def}}{=} (ret \ d)\overline{ret}.\overline{d}$$

Finally, to illustrate the `commit` statement, consider $S \equiv \text{commit } E$ where $E \equiv E_0!M(E_1)$ with $E_0 : A$, $E_1 : \text{NAT}$ and $E : \text{BOOL}$. Then, with the penultimate parameter being a return link to be passed on to the object to which the commitment is made, the appropriate abstraction is $\text{COMMIT} \equiv \text{COMMIT}(M, A, \text{NAT}; \text{BOOL})$, defined by

$$\text{COMMIT} : ((\text{LINK}[A]), (\text{NAT}), \text{BOOL}, \text{NIL}) \stackrel{\text{def}}{=} (X_0 X_1 ret \ d)$$
$$(v \ val_0 : \text{LINK}[A], val_1 : \text{NAT}, w : \text{NIL})$$
$$(X_0\langle val_0\rangle \mid w.X_1\langle val_1\rangle$$
$$\mid val_0(\widetilde{a}).\overline{w}.val_1(Y).\overline{\widetilde{a}_M}(Y, ret).\overline{d})$$

Then

$$[\![S]\!] : \theta\widehat{\ }(\text{BOOL}, \text{NIL}) \stackrel{\text{def}}{=} (\widetilde{p})\text{COMMIT}\langle[\![E_0]\!]\langle\widetilde{p}_0\rangle, [\![E_1]\!]\langle\widetilde{p}_1\rangle\rangle$$

It remains to give the translations of method, class, and program declarations. We exemplify the encoding of the first by considering $Mdec \equiv \text{method } M(Y : \text{NAT}) : \text{BOOL}, Vdec, S$ where $Vdec \equiv \text{var} X : A$ for some class A. Suppose $[\![S]\!] : \theta\widehat{\ }(\text{NAT}, \text{BOOL}, \text{LINK}[A]^2, \text{NIL})$ where the NAT parameter corresponds to Y which is read but not written in S, the BOOL parameter names a link for the return of the result of a call, and the $\text{LINK}[A]$ parameters correspond to X which is both written and read in S. Then

$$[\![Vdec, S]\!] : \theta\widehat{\ }(\text{NAT}, \text{BOOL}, \text{NIL}) \stackrel{\text{def}}{=} (\widetilde{p})\text{DEC}_A\langle[\![Vdec]\!], [\![S]\!]\langle\widetilde{p}\rangle\rangle$$

where $\widetilde{p} : \theta\widehat{\ }(\text{NAT}, \text{BOOL})$ and

$$\text{DEC}_A : ((\text{LINK}[A]^2), (\text{LINK}[A]^2, \text{NIL}), \text{NIL}) \stackrel{\text{def}}{=} (ZWd)(v \ get, put : \text{LINK}[A])$$
$$(Z\langle get \ put\rangle \mid W\langle get \ put \ d\rangle)$$

Then for $Mdec$ the appropriate abstraction is

$$\text{METH} \equiv \text{METH}(\text{NAT}, \text{BOOL}) : ((\text{NAT}^2), (\text{NAT}, \text{BOOL}, \text{NIL}), \text{METHOD}[\text{NAT}; \text{BOOL}], \text{NIL})$$

defined by

$$\text{METH} \stackrel{\text{def}}{=} (ZWm \ d)(v \ get, put : \text{NAT}(Z\langle get \ put\rangle \mid m(V, ret).\overline{put}(V).W\langle get \ ret \ d\rangle)$$

so that now with $\tilde{p} : \theta$,

$$[\![Mdec]\!] : \theta^\frown(\text{METHOD}[\text{NAT}; \text{BOOL}], \text{NIL}) \stackrel{\text{def}}{=} (\tilde{p})\text{METH}\langle[\![\text{var}Y : \text{NAT}]\!], [\![Vdec, S]\!]\langle\tilde{p}\rangle\rangle$$

To exemplify the encoding of class declarations consider $Cdec \equiv \text{class} B, Vdec_B, Mdecs$ for some $Vdec_B$ and $Mdecs \equiv Mdec_1, Mdec_2$ with $[\![Mdec_1]\!] : \theta_1^\frown(\text{METHOD}[\tilde{T}_1; T_1], \text{NIL})$ and $[\![Mdec_2]\!] : \theta_2^\frown(\text{METHOD}[\tilde{T}_2; T_2], \text{NIL})$. Then for some θ determined by θ_1 and θ_2,

$$[\![Mdecs]\!] : \theta^\frown(\text{METHOD}[\tilde{T}_1; T_1], \text{METHOD}[\tilde{T}_2; T_2]) \stackrel{\text{def}}{=} (\tilde{p})\text{BODY}\langle[\![Mdec_1]\!]\langle\tilde{p}_1\rangle,$$
$$[\![Mdec_2]\!]\langle\tilde{p}_2\rangle\rangle$$

where $\tilde{p} : \theta$, $\tilde{p}_1 : \theta_1$, $\tilde{p}_2 : \theta_2$ and

$$\text{BODY} : ((\text{METHOD}[\tilde{T}_1; T_1], \text{NIL}), (\text{METHOD}[\tilde{T}_2; T_2], \text{NIL}), \text{METHOD}[\tilde{T}_1; T_1],$$
$$\text{METHOD}[\tilde{T}_2; T_2])$$

is defined by

$$\text{BODY} \stackrel{\text{def}}{=} (Z_1 Z_2 m_1 m_2)(\nu d : \text{NIL})((Z_1\langle m_1, d\rangle + Z_2\langle m_2, d\rangle) \mid d.\text{BODY}\langle Z_1, Z_2, m_1, m_2\rangle)$$

Then for the class definition we have for some θ' and θ'' with $\theta = \theta'^\frown\theta''$ and $\tilde{p} : \theta'$,

$$\text{Obj}_B : \theta'^\frown(\text{METHOD}[\tilde{T}_1; T_1], \text{METHOD}[\tilde{T}_2; T_2]) \stackrel{\text{def}}{=} (\tilde{p})\text{DEC}_B\langle[\![Vdec_B]\!], [\![Mdecs]\!]\langle\tilde{p}\rangle\rangle$$

where DEC_B is similar to DEC_A above but of the appropriate sort, and for some p',

$$[\![Cdec]\!] : \theta'^\frown(\text{LINK}[B]) \stackrel{\text{def}}{=} (\tilde{p}\, new)(\nu \tilde{a})\overline{new}(\tilde{a}).(\text{Obj}_B\langle\tilde{p'}, \tilde{a}\rangle \mid [\![Cdec]\!]\langle\tilde{p}, new\rangle)$$

Finally for a program declaration $Pdec \equiv Cdec_1, \ldots, Cdec_r$ where $[\![Cdec_i]\!] : \theta_i^\frown(\text{LINK}[A_i])$, setting $\text{NEW} \equiv \text{LINK}[A_1], \ldots, \text{LINK}[A_r]$ and with $\text{RootObject}: \theta^\frown(\text{OBJECT}[A_1])$ representing the root object, we have for some $\tilde{p}, \tilde{p}_i$,

$$[\![Pdec]\!] : () \stackrel{\text{def}}{=} (\nu \widetilde{new} : \text{NEW}, \tilde{a} : \text{OBJECT}[A_1])$$
$$(\Pi_{i=1}^r [\![Cdec_i]\!]\langle\tilde{p}_i, new_i\rangle \mid \text{RootObject}\langle\tilde{p}, \tilde{a}\rangle)$$

As an illustration consider the priority queue class Q from Section 11.2. Let S be the body of the method Add. Then

$$[\![S]\!] : (\text{LINK}[Q], \text{NAT}^2, \text{LINK}[Q]^2, \text{NAT}, \text{NIL}^2) \stackrel{\text{def}}{=}$$
$$(new, get_V, put_V, get_P, put_P, get_X, ret)$$
$$\text{SEQ}\langle[\![\text{return}]\!]\langle ret\rangle,$$
$$\text{COND}\langle\text{EQ}\langle[\![V]\!]\langle get_V\rangle, [\![\text{nil}]\!]\rangle,$$
$$\text{SEQ}\langle\text{ASSIGN}_{\text{NAT}}\langle[\![X]\!]\langle get_X\rangle, put_V\rangle,$$
$$\text{ASSIGN}_Q\langle[\![\text{new}(Q)]\!]\langle new\rangle, put_P\rangle,$$
$$\text{COND}\langle\text{LESS}\langle[\![V]\!]\langle get_V\rangle, [\![X]\!]\langle get_X\rangle\rangle,$$
$$\text{CALL}\langle[\![P]\!]\langle get_P\rangle, [\![X]\!]\langle get_X\rangle\rangle,$$
$$\text{SEQ}\langle\text{CALL}\langle[\![P]\!]\langle get_P\rangle, [\![V]\!]\langle get_V\rangle\rangle,$$
$$\text{ASSIGN}_{\text{NAT}}\langle[\![X]\!]\langle get_X\rangle, put_V\rangle\rangle\rangle\rangle\rangle\rangle$$

Hence we have

$$[\![\mathrm{method\,Add}(X:\mathrm{NAT}),\,S]\!]:(\mathrm{LINK}[Q],\mathrm{NAT}^2,\mathrm{LINK}[Q]^2,\mathrm{METHOD}\,[\mathrm{NAT};],\mathrm{NIL})$$

defined as follows where $\widetilde{p}=new,get_V,put_V,get_P,put_P$ and METH is similar to the abstraction of the same name above but of the appropriate sort:

$$[\![\mathrm{method\,Add}(X:\mathrm{NAT}),\,S]\!]\stackrel{\mathrm{def}}{=}(\widetilde{p})\mathrm{METH}\langle[\![\mathrm{var}\,X:\mathrm{NAT}]\!],[\![S]\!]\langle\widetilde{p}\rangle\rangle$$

Similarly

$$[\![\mathrm{method\,Rem}():\mathrm{NAT}]\!]:(\mathrm{NAT}^2,\mathrm{LINK}[Q]^2,\mathrm{METHOD}[;\mathrm{NAT}],\mathrm{NIL})$$

and so

$$\mathrm{Obj}_Q:(\mathrm{LINK}[Q],\mathrm{METHOD}[\mathrm{NAT};],\mathrm{METHOD}[;\mathrm{NAT}])$$

11.5

COMPARISON AND APPLICATIONS

Despite the fact that the operational and translational semantics are defined by quite different means, in both a program is interpreted as a transition system. In the operational semantics the possible transitions of a configuration are derived in a natural way from labeled transitions describing the possible actions of its constituent objects. These transitions are in turn defined by inference rules systematized by the structure of program phrases. In the process calculus semantics this structure guides the translation, while transitions are given by the reduction relation of the calculus which is itself defined by structural inference rules. One may hope, therefore, for a close correspondence between the transition systems, and a detailed analysis reveals that such does indeed exist. To state it, consider a program declaration $Pdec$. The transition system determined by the operational semantics is $(\mathcal{P},\longrightarrow,\Omega^0)$ where $\Omega^0=\langle\Phi^0,\Gamma^0\rangle$ is the initial configuration associated with $Pdec$ and $\mathcal{P}$ the set of configurations reachable from it via the global transition relation $\longrightarrow$. The translational semantics associates with $Pdec$ the transition system $(\Pi,\longrightarrow_\pi,[\![Pdec]\!])$ where Π is the set of processes reachable from $[\![Pdec]\!]$ under the reduction relation (here written $\longrightarrow_\pi$ for clarity). The translation $[\![\cdot]\!]$ can be extended in a natural way to associate with each configuration $\Omega=\langle\Phi,\Gamma\rangle$ a process $[\![\Omega]\!]$. In particular we have $[\![\Omega^0]\!]\equiv[\![Pdec]\!]$. Moreover we have the following result.

Theorem 1.   *If $\Omega^0\longrightarrow^*\Omega\longrightarrow\Omega'$ then $[\![\Omega]\!]\longrightarrow_\pi^*\equiv[\![\Omega']\!]$.*

Thus any computation in the operational semantics can be mirrored directly up to structural congruence in the translational semantics, with the proviso that, because in the latter data are represented as processes that must be evaluated by reduction, a sequence of reductions may be required to match a single transition in the operational semantics. A consequence of this is that, in general, many processes reachable from $[\![\Omega^0]\!]$ will not be translations of configurations reachable from Ω^0. Indeed, if there is an infinite computation from Ω^0 there may be infinite reductions from $[\![\Omega^0]\!]$ in which no process but the first is of the form $[\![\Omega]\!]$. However if there are no infinite computations from Ω^0 then there are no infinite reductions from $[\![\Omega^0]\!]$. Moreover, by a detailed analysis it can be shown that any process reachable from $[\![\Omega^0]\!]$ can be reduced by the completion of a number of sequences corresponding to transitions of the encoding of a configuration reachable from Ω^0:

Theorem 2.   *If $[\![\Omega^0]\!] \longrightarrow_\pi^* P$ then for some Ω, $\Omega^0 \longrightarrow^* \Omega$ and $P \longrightarrow_\pi^* \equiv [\![\Omega]\!]$.*

These theorems are proven using techniques described fully in [19].

11.6

CONCLUSION

In conclusion we return briefly to the question of the interchangeability of the priority queue classes described in Section 11.2. A central concern in process calculus has been the study of precisely defined behavioral equivalences of agents and the development of techniques for reasoning about them. Within this framework we can formulate the question as follows: Are the agents encoding two programs containing the respective class definitions behaviorally equivalent? To answer the question we have to consider some further points. First, the observable behavior of a $\pi o\beta\lambda$ program would naturally involve input and output. Although this has been omitted here, it causes no difficulty. Second, the encoding of data as agents illustrated here is not conducive to a simple abstract treatment of the programs' behaviors. Third, account must be taken in any analysis of the possibility of runtime errors. These factors are taken into account in [20] in which a semantics by translation to a calculus in which agents may pass names and simple data values is used as the basis for a proof of the precise statement of the interchangeability result. Moreover, the transition system associated with the translation of a program in this calculus is isomorphic to that arising from a natural operational semantics as in Section 11.3, thus confirming the reasonableness of the translational semantics. One outstanding challenge is to extend the techniques to justify *general* transformation rules.

Bibliography

1. P. America et al., "Operational Semantics of a Parallel Object-oriented Language," *Proc. Conf. Record 13th Ann. Symp. Principles of Programming Languages*, ACM Press, New York, N.Y., 1986, pp. 194–208.
2. P. America et al., "Denotational Semantics of a Parallel Object-oriented Language," *Information and Computation*, Vol. 83, 1989, pp. 152–205.
3. P. America, "Issues in the Design of a Parallel Object-oriented Language," *Formal Aspects of Computing*, Vol. 1, 1989, pp. 366–411.
4. C. Hewitt, "Viewing Control Structures as Patterns of Passing Messages," *J. Artificial Intelligence*, No. 8, 1977, pp. 323–364.

5. C. Jones, "Constraining Interference in an Object-based Design Method," *Proc. TAPSOFT'93*, Springer-Verlag LNCS Vol. 668, Heidelberg, Germany, 1993, pp. 136–150.

6. C. Jones, "A pi-calculus Semantics for an Object-based Design Notation," *Proc. CONCUR'93*, Springer-Verlag LNCS Vol. 715, Heidelberg, Germany, 1993, pp. 158–172.

7. D. Kafura and R.G. Lavender, "Concurrent Object-oriented Languages and the Inheritance Anomaly," this volume.

8. R. Milner, "A Calculus of Communicating Systems," *Lecture Notes in Computer Science 92*, Springer-Verlag, Heidelberg, Germany, 1980.

9. R. Milner, "The Polyadic π-calculus: A Tutorial in Logic and Algebra of Specification," F. Bauer et al., eds., Springer, 1993.

10. R. Milner, J. Parrow, and D. Walker, "A Calculus of Mobile Processes," Vols. I and II, *Information and Computation* 100, 1992, pp. 1–77.

11. R. Milner and M. Tofte, *Commentary on Standard ML*, MIT Press, Cambridge, Mass., 1991.

12. O. Nierstrasz and M. Papathomas, "Towards a Type Theory for Active Objects," in *Object Management*, D. Tsichritzis, ed., University of Geneva, 1990.

13. M. Papathomas, "Language Design Rationale and Semantic Framework for Concurrent Object-oriented Programming," doctoral thesis, University of Geneva, 1992.

14. G. Plotkin, "A Structural Approach to Operational Semantics," Tech. Report DAIMI FN–19, University of Aarhus, 1981.

15. D. Sangiorgi, "Expressing Mobility in Process Algebras: First-order and Higher-order Paradigms," doctoral thesis, University of Edinburgh, 1992.

16. D. Sangiorgi, "From π-calculus to Higher-order π-calculus—and Back," *Proc. TAPSOFT'93*, Springer-Verlag LNCS Vol. 668, Heidelberg, Germany, 1993, pp. 151–166.

17. B. Thomsen, "Calculi for Higher-order Communicating Systems," doctoral thesis, University of London, 1990.

18. D. Walker, "π-Calculus Semantics for Object-oriented Programming Languages," *Proc. TACS'91*, Springer-Verlag LNCS Vol. 526, Heidelberg, Germany, 1991, pp. 532–547.

19. D. Walker, "Objects in the π-calculus, in *Information and Computation*, 1992.

20. D. Walker, "Algebraic Proofs of Properties of Objects," *Proc. European Symp. Programming (ESOP'94)*, Springer-Verlag, Heidelberg, Germany, 1994.

CHAPTER 12

FORMAL DESIGN OF PARALLEL PROGRAMS USING UNITY

Beverly A. Sanders*
Institute für Computersysteme
Swiss Federal Institute of Technology (ETH Zürich)
ETH Zentrum, CH-8092 Zürich, Switzerland

Abstract. *A formal method for program design allows one to construct a proof that a program satisfies its specification. UNITY is a formal method invented by Chandy and Misra, whose hallmark is its simplicity. Since its introduction in 1988, UNITY has been successfully used for a variety of problems, and based on this experience, modifications have been suggested that make it easier to use. This paper gives a brief tutorial on UNITY, emphasizing recent developments.*

12.1

INTRODUCTION

A formal method for program development comprises a mathematically well-defined notation for writing specifications, a mathematically well-defined notation for writing programs, and a proof theory that allows one to prove that the program satisfies the specification. In some methods, for example TLA [11], the same notation is used for both programs and specifications. It is not necessary that the program notation be the same language that one will eventually use to implement the program. What is important, however, is that the specification be at a higher level of abstraction than the program. The term *formal* indicates that proofs are carried out by applying syntactic transformations according to a given set of rules. This means that each step in a proof is easily checked and opens up the possibility of automated support for constructing and checking proofs.

There are limitations to what the use of a formal method can bring. A formal proof cannot provide an ironclad guarantee that a program will behave as desired. First, correctness is relative to the specification and there is no way to prove that the specification accurately describes the desired behavior. Second, the formal method assumes a model, and reality

---

*Supported in part by Swiss National Science Foundation grant 5003-034260.

may not correspond to the model.[1] For example, a power failure will generally cause an assumption that progress is eventually made to be violated. Another source of model errors are bugs in compilers and hardware. Third, it is possible to make mistakes in proofs. Further, formal methods cannot be practically applied to justify every line of code or substitute for creativity and insights into the problem to be solved.

However, important benefits can be derived from the understanding and use of a well-engineered formal method. Although no ironclad guarantee can be given, the use of a formal method can significantly increase confidence in the resulting program. Also, a formal method motivates effective, disciplined ways to think about problems, which often results in more elegant and general solutions—even if a detailed proof is not carried out. Formal methods can be practically applied to verify algorithms and high-level designs.

In this chapter, we will give an introduction to UNITY by Chandy and Misra, originally described in [4]. Since its introduction, a significant amount of experience has been gained using UNITY on a wide variety of problems, and these have resulted in suggestions for modifications of the method from various sources in order to make it easier to use. Since a thorough treatment of the original method is available in [4], this paper will describe some of the more promising (in the opinion of the author) recent proposals.

UNITY can be viewed as a combination of a subset of Hoare logic [8, 9] and Dijkstra's wp calculus [6, 7], which was originally developed for sequential programs and a subset of temporal logic [17]. In Hoare logic, one specifies a program F by a Hoare triple $\{p\}S\{q\}$, where p and q are predicates on the state space of the program, which means that a program starting in a state satisfying p will terminate in a state satisfying q. An equivalent formulation in the wp calculus is $[p \Rightarrow wp.S.q]$, where wp is a predicate transformer[2] giving the weakest precondition. In these methods, one gives a rule for sequential composition and axioms or a definition of wp for every construct in the programming notation. An extremely convenient feature of the wp calculus is that for simple programming language constructs (assignment, if), wp can be calculated in a straightforward way.

Early attempts to generalize these approaches to concurrent programs involved adding new constructs for concurrency and interprocess communication and modifying the proof theory appropriately. One consequence of the generalization was that it was no longer possible to reason about termination—$\{p\}S\{q\}$ acquired the meaning, if S is started in a state satisfying p, then it will terminate in a state satisfying q, or fail to terminate. The corresponding predicate transformer formulation is $[p \Rightarrow wlp.S.q]$, where wlp is the weakest liberal precondition and indicates the weakest predicate so that S, starting in a state satisfying the predicate, will either terminate in a state satisfying q or fail to terminate. This approach is described in [1, 15, 16]. Although useful for some problems, constructing proofs is complicated and what can be specified is less than what we would like.

In UNITY, a different approach is taken. Instead of extending a notation for sequential programming with new constructs, the programming notation is simplified. Instead of giving a specification in terms of first and last states, one gives properties that define, as in temporal logic, the allowed (infinite) sequences of states that a program may generate. In

---

[1] This problem is not unique to formal methods. All program development is based on assumptions of how the hardware and programming language implementation work.

[2] A predicate transformer is a function from predicates to predicates.

the next sections, we will describe the programming notation, specification language, and proof theory in more detail and give a detailed example. The conclusion will give a brief comparison with other formal approaches.

12.1.1 Programming Notation

A program is denoted by a set of variable declarations giving the names of variables and their types; a predicate *init* indicating the allowed initial states (by default, *init* = *true*); and a nonempty set of terminating commands, where the commands are expressed as guarded, multiple, deterministic assignment statements. Assignments are written, for example, as follows:

$$x, y := f(x, y), g(x, y, z) \text{ if } b$$

An assignment is executed by first evaluating the guard b (which may be omitted if equal to *true*). If the guard holds, then expressions f and g are evaluated and the computed results are assigned to x and y. Evaluating the guard and expressions on the right side, and making the assignments, are done in a single atomic action. If the guard does not hold, then the command has no effect.

Commands in a program are separated by a bar "$\Box$" The state of the program is changed by executing a command. The choice of the command to execute at each step is nondeterministic, subject to a fairness constraint that each command must be attempted infinitely often. Since the program is a set of commands (rather than a sequence) the order in which commands are given is irrelevant. This approach helps to make correctness proofs simpler because there is no flow of control determined by hidden program counters: all control information is coded in the guards. The disadvantage is that it is more work to specify programs that are largely sequential than in an extended sequential language. UNITY programs do not terminate—the analogy to termination is reaching a fixed point where no command changes the state.

When convenient, several commands may be denoted using quantification. For example,

$$(\forall \Box \ i : i \leq 0 < n : x[i], x[i+1] := x[i+1], x[i] \text{ if } x[i] > x[i+1]) \tag{12.1}$$

generates n commands separated by a $\Box$. This program nondeterministically sorts the array x and reaches a fixed point when the array is sorted.

The mapping from commands to processors is informal, thus a given program can be implemented in many ways. For example, any UNITY program could be implemented in a sequential way on a single processor by putting all the commands in a loop. Any other way of scheduling commands for execution is allowed, provided the fairness constraint is satisfied. Each command could also be placed on a separate processor. Because of this flexibility, the same notation can be used to represent most interesting computation models. Shared memory is trivial to represent; the shared variables belong to commands mapped to more than one process. Message communication can be modeled by sequence variables to which the sender appends messages. The receiver removes the head of the sequence.

Efficiency concerns are also treated informally. A program with many commands that read and modify the same shared variable will not gain much by executing the commands on different processors, due to the synchronization required to ensure that each command is executed atomically. Thus, depending on the desired architecture, we can impose informal constraints on the structure of the program. For example, for a shared-memory architecture, we might want a program in which each statement accesses at most one variable that is read or modified by commands mapped to a different processor. To allow a straightforward mapping to a message-passing architecture, commands mapped to different processors should only share sequence variables representing communication channels.

12.1.2 Specification

The execution of a program generates a sequence of states. In general, due to the nondeterministic selection of commands, a program is associated with a (possibly infinite) set of such possible sequences. A property is formally a predicate on programs, which indicates constraints on the allowed sequences of states. It is helpful, both intuitively and formally, to consider properties as belonging to one of two classes: safety and progress, which are discussed below.

12.1.3 Preliminaries

In this section, we show how the predicate transformer wp[3], which was originally proposed for reasoning about sequential programs, can be used in the definition of a new predicate transformer awp, which captures useful information about UNITY programs. wp and awp are the basis of the proof rules for properties we will use in reasoning about programs.

For any individual command s in a UNITY program, $wp.s.q$ represents the weakest predicate such that an execution of s in a state where $wp.s.q$ holds is guaranteed to terminate in a state satisfying q. Thus if $[p \Rightarrow wp.s.q]$, then an execution of command s in a state satisfying p will terminate in a state satisfying q. For the commands allowed in the UNITY program notation, wp is easily calculated:

$$wp."x := e".q \equiv [(x := e).q]$$

where $(x := e).q$ indicates q with all occurrences of x textually replaced by e. wp for a conditional, multiple assignment is as follows:

$$wp."x, y := f(x, y), g(x, y, z) \text{ if } b".q(x, y, z)$$
$$\equiv$$
$$[b \Rightarrow q(f(x, y), g(x, y, z), z)] \land [\neg b \Rightarrow q(x, y, z)]$$

For a program F, we define a predicate transformer $awp.F$ as:

$$awp.F.q \stackrel{\Delta}{=} (\forall s : s \text{ is a command of } F : wp.s.q) \qquad (12.2)$$

From the meaning of wp it follows that $awp.F.q$ is the weakest predicate p such that executing any command of F in a state that satisfies p will terminate in a state that satisfies q.

---

[3] Hoare triples also could have been used.

Safety Properties   A safety property expresses constraints on the allowed state changes a program can effect, in other words, it says "nothing bad happens." Typical safety properties would be "mutual exclusion is never violated" or "a hungry philosopher remains hungry until he eats."

The first safety property is *co*, (for constrains)[14] where *p co q* means that if *p* holds at some point in a computation, then *q* will hold on the next step. Further, we require that if *p* holds then *q* also holds. The latter requirement means that a stuttering step that doesn't change the state will never violate a *co* property.

For example, one could formalize the requirement that "a hungry philosopher remains hungry (H) until he eats (E)" with the following *co* property:

$$H \; co \; H \vee E$$

Using awp, we can give a proof rule that allows *co* properties to be verified in a straightforward way.

$$([p \Rightarrow q] \wedge [p \Rightarrow awp.q]) \Rightarrow p \; co \; q \tag{12.3}$$

A property satisfied by the sort program given above (12.1), and easily shown using (12.3), is that once the array is sorted, it will remain sorted. Formally this is expressed with a *co* property with the same predicate on both sides:

$$(\forall i : 0 \leq i < N : x[i] \leq x[i+1]) \; co \; (\forall i : 0 \leq i < N : x[i] \leq x[i+1])$$

The special case where the same predicate appears on the left and right sides is called a stable property.

$$stable \; p \stackrel{\Delta}{=} p \; co \; p$$

While many *co* and *stable* properties can be proved directly from the text of the program using (12.3), it is also useful to be able to deduce new *co* properties from given ones. To this end, there are several useful metatheorems, proven in [14]. These are listed below and include rules that allow taking the disjunction of both sides of two *co* properties, taking the conjunction of both sides of two *co* properties, strengthening the left and weakening the right side, and transitivity.

Theorem 1.   *(co disjunctive)*
For arbitrary set W :

$$[(\forall \, w : w \in W : p_w \; co \; q_w) \Rightarrow ((\exists \, w : w \in W : p_w) \; co \; (\exists \, w : w \in W : q_w))] \tag{12.4}$$

Theorem 2.   *(co conjunctive)*
For arbitrary set W :

$$[(\forall \, w : w \in W : p_w \; co \; q_w) \Rightarrow (\forall \, w : w \in W : p_w) \; co \; (\forall \, w : w \in W : q_w)] \tag{12.5}$$

Theorem 3.   *(strengthen left side, weaken right side of co)*

$$(p \; co \; q \wedge [p\prime \Rightarrow p] \wedge [q \Rightarrow q\prime]) \Rightarrow (p\prime \; co \; q\prime) \tag{12.6}$$

Theorem 4.   *(co is transitive)*

$$(p \; co \; q \wedge q \; co \; r) \Rightarrow p \; co \; r \tag{12.7}$$

In [4], safety properties were primarily specified with *unless* where p unless $q \equiv p \wedge \neg q \; co \; p \vee q$. The advantage of *co* is the ease of manipulation using the above easy-to-remember theorems.

Another safety property defined in [4] is *invariant*, where *invariant* p means that p holds during the entire execution of the program. For example, one could formalize the basic safety requirement of a mutual exclusion algorithm with an invariant property

$$invariant \; MUTEX$$

where
$$MUTEX = (\forall \; i, j : j \neq i : \neg(i.in - cs \wedge j.in - cs))$$

Invariant properties can be verified using the following rule:

$$(stable \; p \wedge [init \Rightarrow p]) \; \Rightarrow \; invariant \; p \tag{12.8}$$

If p is stable and holds initially, then it holds at all times during program execution. Often, determining which invariants are satisfied by a program is the key step in understanding the program. Invariants are especially useful because of the substitution rule.

Substitution Rule   Within a single program, invariants can be substituted for *true* and vice versa in properties and programs.

Progress Properties   Safety properties can be satisfied trivially by programs that never change the state. For example, a mutual exclusion algorithm that never allows any process to enter its critical section satisfies the invariant property given above. Thus we need progress properties to specify that "something good eventually happens." Let us define a program property, $p \hookrightarrow q$, ("to always") where p and q are predicates on program states. This property has the following meaning: If $p \hookrightarrow q$ holds in F, and there is a point in a computation of F at which p holds, then there is a point in the computation after which q continues to hold for ever [3, 5].

Thus the requirement that all requests by processes to enter their critical sections are eventually granted can be formalized as follows:

$$(\forall \; k : \#requests \geq k \hookrightarrow \#entries \geq k) \tag{12.9}$$

The following rule allows $\hookrightarrow$ properties to be proved from the program text:

$$\begin{aligned}
&[([p \wedge \neg q \Rightarrow awp.(p \vee q)] \\
&\quad \wedge \; (\exists s : s \text{ is a command in } F : p \wedge \neg q \Rightarrow wp.s.q) \\
&\quad \wedge \; \text{stable } q) \\
&\Rightarrow \\
&p \hookrightarrow q]
\end{aligned} \tag{12.10}$$

Additionally, we have rules similar to those for *co*. The proofs are given in [5].

Theorem 5. ($\hookrightarrow$ *is transitive*)
$$(p \hookrightarrow q \land q \hookrightarrow r) \Rightarrow p \hookrightarrow r \tag{12.11}$$

Theorem 6. ($\hookrightarrow$ *disjunctive*) *For arbitrary set W:*

$$(\forall\, w : w \in W : p_w \hookrightarrow q_w) \Rightarrow ((\exists\, w : w \in W : p_w) \hookrightarrow (\exists\, w : w \in W : q_w)) \tag{12.12}$$

Theorem 7. (*strengthen left side, weaken right side of* $\hookrightarrow$)
$$(p \hookrightarrow q \land [p\prime \Rightarrow p] \land [q \Rightarrow q\prime]) \Rightarrow (p\prime \hookrightarrow q\prime) \tag{12.13}$$

Theorem 8. ($\hookrightarrow$ *finitely conjunctive*) *For finite set W:*

$$[(\forall\, w : w \in W : p_w \hookrightarrow q_w) \Rightarrow (\forall\, w : w \in W : p_w) \hookrightarrow (\forall\, w : w \in W : q_w)] \tag{12.14}$$

The only difference between the metatheorems for *co* and $\hookrightarrow$, is that the conjunctivity metatheorem for $\hookrightarrow$ is only valid over finite sets while for *co*, it is valid for arbitrary sets.

We also have a theorem relating stable and $\hookrightarrow$ properties.

Theorem 9.
$$\text{stable } p \Rightarrow (p \hookrightarrow p) \tag{12.15}$$

As an example, using (12.10) one can show directly from the text of the sort program that
$$NOO \le k \land k > 0 \hookrightarrow NOO < k$$
where NOO is the number of out-of-order pairs. Then using transitivity with induction on NOO, and disjunction, we obtain the rule that
$$NOO > 0 \hookrightarrow NOO = 0$$

In [4], and most other temporal logic-based methods including TLA, $\mapsto$ ("leads-to") is the primary property for specifying progress properties. $p \mapsto q$ means that if at some point in a computation p holds, then at that or some later point, q will hold. In contrast to $p \hookrightarrow q$, q is not required to remain true. Formally, $\hookrightarrow$ is less expressive than $\mapsto$ since all $\hookrightarrow$ properties are $\mapsto$ properties, but not vice versa. However, $\hookrightarrow$ can be easier to work with since $\mapsto$ does not satisfy the conjunctivity property. Although it seems more natural to specify progress properties with $\mapsto$, for example, *requested* $\mapsto$ *granted* rather than (12.9). The proof of $\mapsto$ properties usually require the definition of a well-founded set. With the $\hookrightarrow$ properties, we express this directly.

12.2

PARALLEL COMPOSITION

Being able to build large programs from smaller pieces is important in order to manage the complexity of large systems. In this section, we give a composition operator for UNITY programs and give a new property *Rely* for expressing compositional properties of programs.

12.2.1 Program Union

The *parallel composition*, or union of programs F and G, is defined if and only if the variable declarations in F and G are compatible, and is denoted by $F \| G$.[4] The set of variables of $F \| G$ is the union of the sets of variables of F and G. Likewise, the set of commands of $F \| G$ is the union of the sets of commands of F and G. The initial condition is the conjunction of the initial conditions of F and G. A variable appearing in both F and G is shared by both programs.

If the parallel composition of F and G is defined, then awp is the conjunction of the individual awp.

$$[awp.F \| G.q \equiv awp.F.q \wedge awp.G.q].$$

From this rule, it is easy to see that

$$([p \Rightarrow awp.F.q] \wedge [p \Rightarrow awp.G.q]) \Rightarrow [p \Rightarrow awp.F \| G.q]$$

Thus *pcoq* in F and $p\ co\ q$ in G imply $p\ co\ q$ in $F \| G$, provided that there have been no appeals to the substitution axiom in the proofs of the individual properties. Unfortunately, the substitution rule doesn't work together with program composition, since the invariant that might have been used with the substitution rule need not hold in the composed program. (See [18] for more detailed discussion on this point.) For this reason, we will not use the substitution rule in later examples.

Ideally, we would like to be able to derive progress properties of a composed program from the properties of the components. Unfortunately, it is easy to find examples in which a progress property holds in both components, but not in the composition of the components. In general, there are two approaches to helping solve the problem. One is to restrict the ways that different components of a composed program can interact. Various proposals have appeared in the literature.[5]

The other approach, which we will explore further in the next subsection, is to weaken the properties that can be specified.

12.2.2 Rely

Chandy [3] proposed the following program property: Define a function R (for *Rely*) that maps a pair of program properties to a program property, where:

$$R\,(U, V).F \;\equiv\; (\forall\,G : U.(F \| G) : V.(F \| G)) \tag{12.16}$$

where U, V are program properties and F and G are programs. Thus $R\,(U, V).F$ means that for any program G composed with F, if property U holds for $(F \| G)$, then property V holds for $(F \| G)$. Intuitively, U is a requirement placed on the environment in which a component program will be embedded. In practice, Rely properties are helpful when U is a weak, easy-to-prove property and V is a stronger, more difficult property.

---

[4] In [4], the symbol ☐ was used to denote parallel composition.

[5] In several proposals for modeling concurrent programs, that is, I/O automata [12], such restrictions were built into the model. The UNITY approach is to define a general, unrestricted type of program composition, leaving open the way for theories applying to special cases.

For example, define the property $E(p, q)$ as:

$$E(p, q) \triangleq (\exists s : s \text{ is a command in } F : [p \wedge \neg q \Rightarrow wp.s.q])$$

Then from (12.10):

$$[E(p, q) \Rightarrow R((p \wedge \neg q \text{ co } p \vee q) \wedge (\text{ stable } q), p \hookrightarrow q)]$$

Rely properties satisfy metatheorems [5] similar to those for co and $\hookrightarrow$:

$$[(\forall i \in S : R(U_i, V_i)) \Rightarrow R((\forall i \in S :: U_i), (\forall i \in S :: V_i))] \tag{12.17}$$

$$[(\forall i \in S :: R(U_i, V_i)) \Rightarrow R((\exists i \in S :: U_i), (\exists i \in S :: V_i))] \tag{12.18}$$

Also,

$$[R(U, V) \wedge R(V, W) \Rightarrow R(U, W)] \tag{12.19}$$

$$[R(V, V)] \tag{12.20}$$

$$[U \Rightarrow V] \Rightarrow [R(U, V)] \tag{12.21}$$

Further, we have the inheritance theorem [3], which states that a program inherits all the Rely properties of its components.

Inheritance Theorem

$$[R(U, V).F \Rightarrow (\forall G : R(U, V).F \| G)] \tag{12.22}$$

12.3

EXAMPLES

In this section, we sketch proofs for two examples. The first is a metatheorem illustrating reasoning about $\hookrightarrow$ and Rely properties. The second example is a proof of correctness of a parallel program, the Sieve of Eratosthenes. The metatheorem is used twice in the proof of Sieve. We will give a few of the proofs in excrutiating detail.

12.3.1   A Theorem about Progress

In this section, we illustrate reasoning with to-always and Rely properties by proving a useful theorem. First, we state and prove two lemmas.

Lemma 1.

$$[R(U, V) \wedge R(U \wedge V, W) \Rightarrow R(U, W)] \tag{12.23}$$

Proof.

$R(U, V)$

$\Rightarrow$ {conjunction (12.17) with $R(U, U)$ (12.20) }

$R(U, U \wedge V)$

$\Rightarrow$ {(12.19) with $R(U \wedge V, W)$ }

$R(U, W)$

Lemma 2.

$$[(\forall k : x \geq k \wedge x \leq N \hookrightarrow x > k) \wedge (\forall k : \text{stable } x > k)$$

$$\Rightarrow \tag{12.24}$$

$$(true \hookrightarrow x > N)]$$

Proof.

$(\forall k : x \geq k \wedge x \leq N \hookrightarrow x > k))$

$\Rightarrow$

$(\forall k : k \leq N : (x \geq k \wedge x \leq N \hookrightarrow x > k))$

$\wedge (\forall k : k > N : (x \geq k \wedge x \leq N \hookrightarrow x > k))$

$\Rightarrow$ {Induction on $j = N - k$}

$(\forall k : k \leq N : (x \geq k \wedge x \leq N \hookrightarrow x > N))$

$\wedge (\forall k : k > N : (x \geq k \wedge x \leq N \hookrightarrow x > k))$

$\Rightarrow$ {weaken right side of to-always property in second conjunct}

$(\forall k : k \leq N : (x \geq k \wedge x \leq N \hookrightarrow x > N))$

$\wedge (\forall k : k > N : (x \geq k \wedge x \leq N \hookrightarrow x > N))$

$\Rightarrow$ {disjunction}

$(\forall k : (x \geq k \wedge x \leq N \hookrightarrow x > N))$

$\Rightarrow$ { $x > N \hookrightarrow x > N$, from $(\forall k : \text{stable } x > k))$, (12.15)}

$(\forall k : (x \geq k \vee x > N \hookrightarrow x > N))$

$\Rightarrow$ {strengthen left side}

$(\forall k : (x \geq k \hookrightarrow x > N))$

$\Rightarrow$ {disjunction over k}

$true \hookrightarrow x > N$

Now, we state the theorem:

Theorem 10.

$$[R((\forall k : \text{stable } x \geq k), (\forall k : x \geq k \wedge x \leq N \hookrightarrow x > k))$$

$$\Rightarrow \tag{12.25}$$

$$R((\forall k : \text{stable } x \geq k), true \hookrightarrow x > N)]$$

Proof.   Let $U := (\forall k : \text{stable } x \geq k))$, $V := (\forall k : (x \geq k \wedge x \leq N \hookrightarrow x > k))$, and $W := (true \hookrightarrow x > N)$. Then $R(U \wedge V, W)$ follows from (12.24), and the theorem itself from (12.23).

12.3.2 Parallel Sieve of Eratosthenes

In this section, we look at an example, a parallel implementation of the Sieve of Eratosthenes [2]. The program contains a Boolean array a, and on reaching a fixed point, an element $a[i]$ should be true if and only if i is prime. Formally,

$$Init \hookrightarrow (\forall i : 0 < i \le N : prime(i) = a[i]) \tag{12.26}$$

Init describes a valid initial state which will yield the desired results. It will be derived as part of the proof.

The idea of the solution is that one master process traverses the array. Variable m: *natural* indicates the next element to examine. On finding an element with $a[i]$, which is potentially prime, a slave process p is started by setting its variable $p.b$: *natural* to i. The process then proceeds to falsify all elements of a that are multiples of i. The next element to falsify is indicated by a variable $p.n$: *natural*. For simplicity, we assume that there are enough processors available.

For convenience, we define the following predicates:

$$[mult(j, k) \equiv (\exists l : 1 < l \le k : j = l * k)] \tag{12.27}$$

$$[prime(i) \equiv \neg(\exists m : 1 < m : mult(i, m))] \tag{12.28}$$

$$[sweep(j, k) \equiv (\forall l : k < l < j : mult(l, k) \Rightarrow \neg a[l])] \tag{12.29}$$

$$[started(k) \equiv \tag{12.30}$$
$$(\forall l : 1 < l < k : \neg a[l] \lor (\exists p : p.b = l \land mult(p.n, p.b)$$
$$\land sweep(p.n, p.b)))]$$

Informally, $mult(j, k)$ means that j is a multiple of k by some factor other than 1; $prime(i)$ is obvious, and $sweep(j, k)$ means that for all multiples of k that are less than j, the corresponding element of a has been falsified. $started(k)$ means that for all potentially prime elements of a less than k, a process to falsify multiples has been started and is in a valid state. *mult, sweep,* and *started* will be used in the proof to define stable properties of the programs. These stable properties are analogous to loop invariants for sequential programs.

Specification of Slave p Slave p becomes active when the variable $p.b$ is made nonzero by the master. At the same time, the master initializes the variable $p.n = 2p.b$. The slave then traverses array a, falsifying elements $a[p.n]$ and incrementing $p.n$ by $p.b$. Eventually, all multiples of $p.b$ less than N will be falsified.

Slave p satisfies the following properties:

- A slave takes no actions before it has been started, or after it has terminated.[6]

$$(\forall x : x \text{ is arbitrary predicate} : stable \ (p.b = 0) \land x) \tag{12.31}$$

$$(\forall \ : x \text{ is arbitrary predicate} : stable \ (p.n > N) \land x) \tag{12.32}$$

---

[6]$(p.b = 0 \lor p.n > N)$ is a fixed point of slave p.

- A slave does not change the value of m $p.b$, or the b or n component of other slaves.

$$(\forall q, k : \text{stable } q.b = k) \tag{12.33}$$

$$(\forall k : \text{stable } m = k) \tag{12.34}$$

$$(\forall q, k : q \neq p : \text{stable } q.n = k) \tag{12.35}$$

- A slave never makes any element of a true.

$$\text{stable } \neg a[i] \tag{12.36}$$

- A slave only falsifies the element of a selected by $p.n$

$$(p.n \neq i \wedge a[i]) \text{ co } a[i] \tag{12.37}$$

- The condition that $p.n$ is a multiple of $p.b$ will never by falsified, for self or other processes

$$(\forall p : \text{stable } mult(p.n, p.b)) \tag{12.38}$$

- All multiples of $p.b$ that are less than $p.n$ are false and $p.n$ is a multiple of $p.b$ is stable.

$$(\forall p : \text{stable } mult(p.n, p.b) \wedge sweep(p.n, p.b)) \tag{12.39}$$

- $p.n$ will eventually increase provided that it is nondecreasing in a composed program

$$R\left((\forall k : \text{stable } p.n > k), (p.n \geq k \wedge p.n \leq N \hookrightarrow p.n > k)\right) \tag{12.40}$$

For example, these properties are easily proved directly from the text of the one command program given below:

Slave p

$$a[p.n], p.n := false, p.n + p.b \text{ if } (p.b > 0 \wedge p.n \leq N)$$

The following properties are derived from those above and will be used together with the specification of the master to show (12.26).

- An element of a corresponding to a prime number won't be falsified

$$\text{stable } (\forall p : mult(p.n, p.b) \wedge p.b \neq 1) \wedge prime(i) \wedge a[i] \tag{12.41}$$

- In a composed program, eventually all multiples of $p.b$ that are at most N will be falsified.

$$\begin{aligned} R\,((\forall k : \text{ stable } m \geq k) \\ \wedge \text{ stable } (mult(p.n, p.b) \wedge sweep(p.n, p.b)), \\ (mult(p.n, p.b) \wedge sweep(p.n, p.b)) \hookrightarrow sweep(N+1, p.b)). \end{aligned} \tag{12.42}$$

Proof.

$\quad$ stable $(mult\ (p.n,\ p.b) \wedge sweep\ (p.n,\ p.b)) \wedge (true \hookrightarrow p.n > N)$
$\Rightarrow \quad\quad \{(12.15),\ \text{conjunction}\ \}$
$(mult\ (p.n,\ p.b) \wedge sweep\ (p.n,\ p.b)) \hookrightarrow$
$(mult\ (p.n,\ p.b) \wedge sweep\ (p.n,\ p.b)) \wedge p.n > N))$
$\Rightarrow \quad\quad \{\text{weaken right side},\ sweep\ (p.n,\ p.b) \wedge p.n > N \Rightarrow sweep\ (N+1,\ p.b)\}$
$mult\ (p.n,\ p.b) \wedge sweep\ (p.n,\ p.b) \hookrightarrow sweep\ (N+1,\ p.b)$
$\Rightarrow \quad\quad \{(12.21)\ \}$
$R\ (\text{stable}\ (mult\ (p.n,\ p.b) \wedge sweep\ (p.n,\ p.b)) \wedge (true \hookrightarrow p.n > N),$
$mult\ (p.n,\ p.b) \wedge sweep\ (p.n,\ p.b) \hookrightarrow sweep\ (N+1,\ p.b))\quad(*)$

$\quad\quad \{\text{let}\ x := p.n,\ (12.25),(12.40)\}$
$R\ ((\forall k :\ \text{stable}\ p.n > k)\ , true \hookrightarrow p.n > N)$
$\Rightarrow \quad\quad \{\text{conjunction},\ (12.20)\}$
$R\ ((\forall k :\ \text{stable}\ p.n > k) \wedge \text{stable}\ (mult\ (p.n,\ p.b) \wedge sweep\ (p.n,\ p.b)),$
$(mult\ (p.n,\ p.b) \wedge sweep\ (p.n,\ p.b)) \wedge (true \hookrightarrow p.n > N)$
$\Rightarrow \quad\quad \{\text{transitivity}\ (12.19)\ \text{with}\ (*)\}$
$R\ ((\forall k :\ \text{stable}\ m \geq k) \wedge \text{stable}\ (mult\ (p.n,\ p.b) \wedge sweep\ (p.n,\ p.b))\ ,$
$(mult\ (p.n,\ p.b) \wedge sweep\ (p.n,\ p.b)) \hookrightarrow sweep\ (N+1,\ p.b))$

12.3.3 Specification of Master

The master satisfies the following properties:

- A master does not change the value of a

$$\text{stable}\ a[i] \tag{12.43}$$

$$\text{stable}\ \neg a[i] \tag{12.44}$$

- The master does not "reuse" processors

$$(\forall k : k > 0 :\ \text{stable}\ p.b = k) \tag{12.45}$$

- The master does not falsify the *mult* $\wedge$ *sweep* properties of the slaves

$$\text{stable}\ mult(p.n,\ p.b) \wedge sweep(p.n,\ p.b) \tag{12.46}$$

- $p.n$ is nondecreasing in master.

$$(\forall k :\ \text{stable}\ p.n \geq k) \tag{12.47}$$

- $p.b$ is never set to 1 by the master

$$\text{stable}\ p.b \neq 1 \tag{12.48}$$

- For all $i : i < m$ where $a[i]$ holds, a processor has been dispatched to eliminate multiples of i.

$$\text{stable } started(m) \qquad\qquad (12.49)$$

- m is nondecreasing

$$(\forall k : \text{ stable } m \geq k) \qquad\qquad (12.50)$$

- m will eventually increase provided it is nondecreasing in a composed program.

$$R\left((\forall k : \text{ stable } m \geq k), (m \geq k \wedge m \leq \sqrt{N} \hookrightarrow m > k)\right) \qquad (12.51)$$

These properties are satisfied by a master which, at each step, finds a p such that $p.b = 0 \wedge p.n = 0$ and performs the following assignment:

$$
\begin{array}{ll}
p.b, p.n, m := m + 1 & \text{if} a[m] \wedge 1 < m < \sqrt{N} \\[2ex]
\quad\;\; m := m + 1 & \text{if} \neg a[m] \wedge 1 < m < \sqrt{N}
\end{array}
$$

From these properties, we can conclude

$$R\,((\forall k : \text{ stable } m \geq k) \wedge \text{ stable } started(m),$$
$$started(m) \hookrightarrow started(\sqrt{N} + 1)\,)$$

The proof uses (12.25) and is similar to the proof of (12.42).

12.3.4   Properties of Composed Program

Let *sieve* be the program obtained by composing the master and all of the slaves. From the inheritance theorem for compositional properties (12.22), and the given specification, the following properties are easily seen to hold for *sieve*:

-

$$started(m) \hookrightarrow started(\sqrt{N} + 1) \qquad\qquad (12.52)$$

-

$$(\forall p : (mult(p.n, p.b) \wedge sweep(p.n, p.b)) \hookrightarrow sweep(N + 1, p.b))) \qquad (12.53)$$

-

$$(\forall i : 1 < i \leq N :$$
$$\text{stable } (\forall p : mult(p.n, p.b) \wedge p.b \neq 1) \wedge prime(i) \wedge a[i]) \qquad (12.54)$$

-

$$(\forall k : k > 1 : \text{ stable } p.b = k) \qquad\qquad (12.55)$$

-

$$\text{stable } \neg a[i] \qquad\qquad (12.56)$$

Now, it remains to show that these properties imply the original specification (12.26).

Proof. *(of 12.26)*:

true
$\Rightarrow$ {from (12.54),(12.15), pred. calc., weaken right side}
$(\forall i : 1 < i \le N \wedge prime(i) : (\forall p : mult\ (p.n, p.b) \wedge p.b \ne 1) \wedge a[i]) \hookrightarrow a[i])$
$\Rightarrow$ {conjunction, interchange quantification}
$(\forall p : mult\ (p.n, p.b) \wedge p.b \ne 1) \wedge (\forall i : 1 < i \le N \wedge prime(i) : a[i]) \hookrightarrow$
$(\forall i : 1 < i \le N \wedge prime(i) : a[i])$ (*)

true
$\Rightarrow$ {from (12.52), strengthen left side, $m = 2 \Rightarrow started(m)$}
$m = 2 \hookrightarrow (\forall i : 1 < i \le \sqrt{N} : \neg a[i] \vee (\exists p : p.b = i \wedge mult\ (p.n, p.b)$
$\wedge sweep(p.n, p.b))$ (**)

true
$\Rightarrow$ {disjunction of (12.53) over p,
conjunction with $p.b = i \wedge p.b > 1 \hookrightarrow p.b = i \wedge p.b > 1$}
$(\exists p : p.b = i \wedge p.b > 1 \wedge mult\ (p.n, p.b) \wedge sweep(p.n, p.b)$
$\hookrightarrow sweep(N + 1, p.b) \wedge p.b = i \wedge p.b > 1$
$\Rightarrow$ {disjunction with $\neg a[i] \hookrightarrow \neg a[i]$, weaken r.s.}
$(\forall i : 1 < i < \sqrt{N} : \neg a[i] \wedge (\exists p : p.b = i \wedge p.b > 1 \wedge mult\ (p.n, p.b)$
$\wedge sweep(p.n, p.b))$
$\hookrightarrow \neg a[i] \wedge sweep(N + 1, i))$
$\Rightarrow$ {conjunction, transitivity with (**)}
$m = 2 \hookrightarrow (\forall i : 1 < i \le \sqrt{N} : \neg a[i] \wedge sweep(N + 1, i))$
$\Rightarrow$ {weaken right side}
$m = 2 \hookrightarrow (\forall i : 1 < i \le \sqrt{N} \wedge prime(i) : \neg a[i] \wedge sweep(N + 1, i))$
$\Rightarrow$ {conjunction with (*)}
$m = 2 \wedge (\forall p : mult\ (p.n, p.b) \wedge p.b \ne 1) \wedge (\forall i : 1 < i \le N \wedge prime(i) : a[i])$
$\hookrightarrow (\forall i : 1 < i \le \sqrt{N} \wedge prime(i) : \neg a[i] \wedge sweep(N + 1, i))$
$\wedge (\forall i : 1 < i \le N \wedge prime(i) : a[i])$
$\Rightarrow$ {pred. calc., Assume $Init \Rightarrow$ left side, see below }
$Init \hookrightarrow (\forall i : 1 < i \le N \wedge prime(i) : a[i]) \wedge (\forall i : 1 < i \le \sqrt{N}$
$\wedge prime(i) : sweep(N + 1, i))$
$\Rightarrow$ {definition of $sweep$}
$Init \hookrightarrow (\forall i : 1 < i \le N \wedge prime(i) : a[i])$
$\wedge (\forall i : 1 < i \le \sqrt{N} \wedge prime(i) : (\forall j : 1 < j \le N : mult\ (j, i) \Rightarrow \neg a[j])$
$\Rightarrow$ {interchange quantification}
$Init \hookrightarrow (\forall i : 1 < i \le N \wedge prime(i) : a[i])$
$\wedge (\forall j : 1 < j \le N : (\forall i : 1 < i \le \sqrt{N} \wedge prime(i) : mult\ (j, i) \Rightarrow \neg a[j])$
$\equiv$ {predicate calculus}

$$Init \hookrightarrow (\forall i : 1 < i \le N \wedge prime(i) : a[i])$$
$$\wedge (\forall j : 1 < j \le N : (\exists i : 1 < i \le \sqrt{N} \wedge prime(i) : mult\,(j, i)) \Rightarrow \neg a[j])$$
$$\equiv \qquad \{\text{definition of } prime\}$$
$$Init \hookrightarrow (\forall i : 1 < i \le N \wedge prime(i) : a[i]) \wedge (\forall j : 1 < j \le N : \neg prime(j)$$
$$\Rightarrow \neg a[j])$$
$$\equiv \qquad \{\text{predicate calculus}\}$$
$$Init \hookrightarrow (\forall i : a[i] \equiv prime(i))$$

The remaining step is to give an appropriate value for *Init*. In the above proof, we assumed

$$Init \Rightarrow \qquad\qquad\qquad\qquad\qquad\qquad\qquad (12.57)$$
$$(m = 2 \wedge (\forall p : mult(p.n, p.b) \wedge p.b \ne 1) \wedge$$
$$(\forall i : 1 < i \le N \wedge prime(i) : a[i]))$$

The following is easily established by a program, and satisfies (12.57):

$$Init \stackrel{\Delta}{=} (m = 2 \wedge (\forall p : p.b = 0 \wedge p.n = 0) \wedge (\forall i : 1 < i \le N : a[i]))$$

12.4

CONCLUSION AND COMPARISON WITH OTHER APPROACHES

We have given a brief introduction to a formal method based on UNITY for parallel programs including several examples using the recently proposed properties co, $\hookrightarrow$, and R (Rely). We have concentrated on a single formal method in order to make the presentation as accessible as possible. UNITY is, however, by no means the only possibility. Very close to UNITY in terms of its basic model of computation (sequences of states) is TLA [11]. TLA (temporal logic of actions) extends temporal logic with a notation for specifying actions, which allows both commands and properties such as invariant and leads-to to be denoted as temporal logic expressions and reasoned about in the same framework. TLA is somewhat more expressive than UNITY, allowing nondeterministic commands and more precise statements of fairness assumptions, but lacks the underlying theory based on predicate transformers. In contrast to temporal logic-based approaches such as UNITY and TLA, one finds algebraic approaches such as Milner's process algebra [13] and Hoare's CSP [10]. These approaches typically associate a program with the sequences of events that occur and a main focus is on finding algebraic laws for composing processes and reasoning about event sequences. CSP has an extremely large number of metatheorems, in contrast to the small set of UNITY and TLA.

Bibliography

1. G.R. Andrews, *Concurrent Programming: Principles and Practice*, Benjamin/Cummings, Redwood City, Calif., 1991.

2. S.H. Bokhari, "Multiprocessing the Sieve of Eratosthenes," *Computer*, Vol. 20, No. 4, Apr. 1987, pp. 50–60.

3. K.M. Chandy, "Using Triples to Reason about Concurrent Programs," Tech. Report Caltech-CS-TR-93-02, California Institute of Technology, 1993.

4. K.M. Chandy and J. Misra, *Parallel Program Design: A Foundation*, Addison-Wesley, Reading, Mass., 1988.

5. ·K.M. Chandy and B.A. Sanders, "Conjugate Predicate Transformers for Reasoning about Concurrent Computation," Tech. Report, Informatik Department, Swiss Federal Institute of Technology, ETH Zurich, 1993.

6. E.W. Dijkstra, *A Discipline of Programming*, Prentice-Hall, New York, N.Y., 1976.

7. E.W. Dijkstra and C.S. Scholten, *Predicate Calculus and Program Semantics*, Springer-Verlag, Berlin, Germany, 1990.

8. C.A.R. Hoare, "An Axiomatic Basis for Computer Programming," *Comm. ACM*, 1969.

9. C.A.R. Hoare, "Parallel Programming: An Axiomatic Approach," *Computer Languages*, 1975.

10. C.A.R. Hoare, *Communicating Sequential Processes*, Prentice-Hall, New York, N.Y., 1986.

11. L. Lamport, "A Temporal Logic of Actions," Tech. Report 79, DEC SRC, 1991.

12. N. Lynch and M. Tuttle, "Hierarchical Correctness Proofs for Distributed Algorithms," *Proc. 6th ACM Symp. Principles of Distributed Systems*, ACM Press, New York, N.Y., 1987.

13. R. Milner, *A Calculus of Communicating Systems, LNCS 92*, Springer-Verlag, Heidelberg, Germany, 1980.

14. J. Misra, "Safety," unpublished manuscript, University of Texas at Austin, July 1992.

15. S.S. Owicki and D. Gries, "An Axiomatic Proof Technique for Parallel Programs," *Acta Informatica*, 1976.

16. S.S. Owicki and D. Gries, "Verifying Properties of Parallel Programs: An Axiomatic Approach," *Comm. ACM*, 1976.

17. A. Pnueli, "The Temporal Logic of Programs," *Proc. 18th Symp. Foundations of Computer Science*, IEEE CS Press, Los Alamitos, Calif., 1977, pp. 46–57.

18. B.A. Sanders, "Eliminating the Substitution Axiom from UNITY Logic," *Formal Aspects of Computing*, Vol. 3, No. 2, 1991.

INDEX

ABOUT THE EDITORS

Thomas Lee Casavant is as an assistant professor specializing in the design and analysis of parallel/distributed computing systems, environments, algorithms, and programs in the School of Electrical Engineering at Purdue University, West Lafayette, Indiana. There, he is director of the Parallel Processing Laboratory. From July 1993 through June 1994, he was on sabbatical as a guest professor with the Department of Informatik (Computer Science) at the Swiss Federal Institute of Technology in Zurich, Switzerland. From June 1987 to June 1988, he was Director of the PASM Parallel Processing Project. From July 1988 to July 1989, he was Director of Purdue University's Parallel Processing Laboratory. He has developed upper-division graduate courses in advanced computer architecture, distributed computing, parallel processing, an undergraduate course in Operating System Engineering, and has been instrumental in the organization of the joint Electrical Engineering/ Computer Science seminar series on Parallel Processing.

He has published over 75 technical papers and written/edited two volumes on parallel and distributed computing. He has presented his work at tutorials, invited lectures, and conferences in the United States, Asia, Europe, and Russia. His work in the area of distributed computing includes the design and implementation of an operating system for a point-to-point network of workstations to behave as a single integrated transparent multiprocessor, contributions to the design of the AT&T 3B4000 distributed multiprocessor system at AT&T Bell Laboratories in 1984, research in parallel computer architecture and systems, the design and analysis of load-balancing-based scheduling algorithms, distributed algorithm modeling, routing and task management in parallel systems, graph theory, and research in theory and implementation of programming tools for parallel/distributed computing. He has been invited to lecture on topics spanning the fields of computer systems and parallel processing in general.

Casavant received the BS degree in computer science with high distinction from the University of Iowa, Iowa City, Iowa. He received the MS and PhD degrees in electrical and computer engineering from the University of Iowa in 1982, 1983 and 1986, respectively. He is a senior member of the IEEE and a member of the ACM. He is serving on the editorial board of *IEEE Transactions on Parallel and Distributed Systems* (TPDS) and is an associate editor for the *Journal of Parallel and Distributed Computing* (JPDC). He served as guest editor for the August 1991 issue of *Computer* on "Distributed Computing Systems," as guest editor for the June 1993 issue of *JPDC* on "Visualization for Parallel Processing," as program vice-chair (1990) and program committee member (1991) for the IEEE International Conference on Distributed Computing Systems, as program co-chair (1991) and program committee member (1989, 1990, and 1992) for IEEE International Computer Software and Applications Conference, and as program committee member for the IEEE Symposium on the Frontiers of Massively Parallel Computation (1992), as well as numerous other conferences.

Pavel Tvrdík has been an assistant professor in the department of computer science at Czech Technical University in Prague, Czechoslovakia since 1989. From March 1988 through March 1989, he was a research fellow with Shinshu University, Nagano City, Japan; from September 1993 through June 1994, he was a visiting researcher with LIP, Ecole Normale Superiéure, Lyon, France; and in February 1995, he was a visiting professor with LRI, Universite Paris Sud, Orsay, France. At Czech Technical University, he has lead upper division seminars in advanced computer architectures and has developed undergraduate and post graduate courses on Parallel Systems and Algorithms. His research interests include architectures of VLSI processors and parallel computers, interconnection networks and communication algorithms, and design and analysis of parallel algorithms.

Tvrdík received the Ing. (MSc) and CSc (PhD) degrees in computer science from the Czech Technical University, Prague, Czechoslovakia in 1980 and 1991, respectively. He has published over 15 technical papers in this area. He is a member of the IEEE Computer Society and Czech Chapter of the Association for Computing Machinery.

František Plášil is an associate professor and vice-chair in the department of software engineering at Charles University in Prague, Czechoslovakia, faculty of mathematics and physics. He is also the partner manager of project TOCOOS (Tools for the Composition of Open Object-Oriented System) under the EC COPERNICUS Program (the project is coordinated by MARY COMPUTER SYSTEMS (UK). His recent work has been on operating systems and languages with concurrency. He has participated in several compiler projects, including an Ada compiler.

From 1989–1991, he was visiting associate professor at the University of Denver, department of math and computer science. From 1993–1995, he was visiting professor (part-time teaching) at the Institute of Microprocessor Techniques at the University of Linz, Austria.

Plášil received the PhD in computer science in 1978 from the CTU Prague. His research interests are in object-oriented paradigm in languages with concurrency and parallelism and in operating systems. He is also the leader of the OBJIX project (a microkernel-based object-oriented operating system). He is the author of many publications and textbooks. His professional activities include that of Chairman to the Czech ACM Chapter.

CONTRIBUTORS

MASSIVELY PARALLEL ARCHITECTURES

Thomas L. Casavant, ECE Department, University of Iowa, Iowa City, IA 52242
tomc@eng.uiowa.edu

Samuel A. Fineberg, Computer Sciences Corporation, Numerical Aerodynamic Simulation, NASA Ames Research Center, M/S 258-6, Moffett Field, CA 94035-1000
fineberg@nas.nasa.gov

Michelle L. Roderick, Adaptec Inc., Boulder Technology Center, 2845 Wilderness Pl., Suite 200, Boulder, CO 80301
michelle@btc.adaptech.com

Brent H. Pease, Apple Computer, Advanced Technology Group/Interactive Media, One Infinite Loop, M/S 301-3k, Cupertino, CA 95014
brent@taurus.apple.com

DATA-DRIVEN AND MULTITHREADED ARCHITECTURES FOR HIGH-PERFORMANCE COMPUTING

Jean-Luc Gaudiot, Electrical Engineering Systems, University of Southern California, Los Angeles, CA 90089
gaudiot@usc.edu

Chinhyun Kim, Electrical Engineering Systems, University of Southern California, Los Angeles, CA 90089

PROPERTIES OF A VARIETY OF INTERCONNECTION NETWORKS FOR LARGE-SCALE PARALLELISM

Wayne G. Nation, IBM Corporation, AS/400 Division, 3605 Highway 52 NW, Rochester, MN 55904

Gene Saghi, Electrical Engineering Department, University of Idaho, Moscow, ID 83844

Howard Jay Siegel, Parallel Processing Laboratory, School of Electrical Engineering, Purdue University, West Lafayette, IN 47907-1285
hj@ecn.purdue.edu

PARALLEL ALGORITHM FUNDAMENTALS AND ANALYSIS

Bruce McMillin, Department of Computer Science, University of Missouri-Rolla, Rolla, MO 65401

Jun-Lin Liu, Department of Computer Science, University of Missouri-Rolla, Rolla, MO 65401

DIRECTIONS IN PARALLEL PROGRAMMING: HPF, SHARED VIRTUAL MEMORY, AND OBJECT PARALLELISM IN PC++

François Bodin, IRISA, University of Rennes, France

Thierry Priol, IRISA, University of Rennes, France

Dennis Gannon, Department of Computer Science & CICA, Indiana University, Bloomington, IN

Piyush Mehrotra, ICASE, NASA Langley, Hampton, VA

CONCURRENT OBJECT-ORIENTED LANGUAGES AND THE INHERITANCE ANOMALY

Dennis G. Kafura, Department of Computer Science, Virginia Tech, Blacksburg, VA 24061

R. Greg Lavender, MCC, 3500 W. Balcones Center Drive, Austin, TX 78759

SCALAPACK: LINEAR ALGEBRA SOFTWARE FOR DISTRIBUTED MEMORY ARCHITECTURES

James Demmel, Computer Science Division and Mathematics Department, University of California, Berkeley, CA 94720

Jack Dongarra, Computer Science Department, The University of Tennesee, Knoxville, TN 37996
Mathematical Sciences Section, Oak Ridge National Laboratory, Oak Ridge, TN 37831

Robert van de Geijn, Mathematical Sciences Section, Oak Ridge National Laboratory, Oak Ridge, TN 37831
Department of Computer Sciences, The University of Texas, Austin, TX 78712

David Walker, Department of Computer Sciences, University of Texas, Austin, TX 78712

TECHNIQUES FOR PERFORMANCE MEASUREMENT OF PARALLEL PROGRAMS

Jeffrey K. Hollingsworth, Computer Sciences Department, University of Wisconsin, Madison, WI 53706

Barton P. Miller, Computer Sciences Department, University of Wisconsin, Madison, WI 53706

James E. Lumpp, Jr., Department of Electrical Engineering, University of Kentucky, Lexington, KY 40506-0046

OPERATING SYSTEMS FOR PARALLEL MACHINES

Bodhisattwa Mukherjee, College of Computing, Georgia Institute of Technology, Atlanta, GA 30332-0280

Karsten Schwan, College of Computing, Georgia Institute of Technology, Atlanta, GA 30332-0280

FORMAL METHODS TO GENERATE AND UNDERSTAND DISTRIBUTED COMPUTING SYSTEMS

Bruce McMillin, Department of Computer Science, University of Missouri-Rolla, Rolla, MO 65401

Grace Tsai, Department of Computer Science, University of Missouri-Rolla, Rolla, MO 65401

Hanan Lutfiyya, Department of Computer Science, University of Western Ontario, London, Ontario N6A 5B7, Canada

PROCESS CALCULUS AND PARALLEL OBJECT-ORIENTED PROGRAMMING LANGUAGES

David Walker, Department of Computer Science, University of Warwick, Coventry CV4 7AL, UK

FORMAL DESIGN OF PARALLEL PROGRAMS USING UNITY

Beverly A. Sanders, Institute für Computersysteme, Swiss Federal Institute of Technology (ETH Zürich), ETH Zentrum, CH-8092 Zürich, Switzerland